BATTLEGROUND
CRIMINAL JUSTICE

BATTLEGROUND

CRIMINAL JUSTICE

VOLUME 1 (A–L)

Edited by Gregg Barak

GREENWOOD PRESS
Westport, Connecticut • London

3/'08

Library of Congress Cataloging-in-Publication Data

Battleground : criminal justice / edited by Gregg Barak.
    p. cm.
    Includes bibliographical references and index.
    ISBN 978–0–313–34040–6 (set : alk. paper) — ISBN 978–0–313–34041–3 (v. 1:
alk. paper) — ISBN 978–0–313–34042–0 (v. 2 : alk. paper)
    1. Criminal justice, Administration of—Encyclopedias.   2. Criminal justice, Administration
of—United States—Encyclopedias.   I. Barak, Gregg.
    HV7411.B38   2007
    364.03—dc22   2007021778

British Library Cataloguing in Publication Data is available.

Library of Congress Catalog Card Number: 2007021778
ISBN-13: 978–0–313–34040–6 (set)
ISBN-13: 978–0–313–34041–3 (vol. 1)
ISBN-13: 978–0–313–34042–0 (vol. 2)

First published in 2007

Greenwood Press, 88 Post Road West, Westport, CT 06881
An imprint of Greenwood Publishing Group, Inc.
www.greenwood.com

Printed in the United States of America

CONTENTS

GUIDE TO RELATED TOPICS

This is a list of the entries in *Battleground: Criminal Justice*, grouped together by broad topic. To find more specific subjects covered in this work, please see the index.

LAW AND SOCIETY
Antiterrorism Laws
Disenfranchisement Laws for Felonies
Espionage Act of 1917
Exclusionary Rule
Foreign Intelligence Surveillance Act
Gang Injunction Laws
Homeland Security
Immigration and Employment Law Enforcement
International Humanitarian Law Enforcement
Patriot Act
Search Warrants
Second Amendment
Sex-Offender Laws
Stalking Laws
State Crime Control
Supremacy of International Law to National Law
Three Strikes
Torture and Enemy Combatants

LAW ENFORCEMENT
Community Police
Driving while Black
Lethal Force
Militarization of Policing
Miranda Warnings
Police and Psychological Screening
Police Brutality
Police Corruption
Police-Minority Relations
Police Use of Force

PROSECUTION, COURTS, AND ADJUDICATION
Adversarial Justice
Alternative Responses to Crime by Society
Bail
Cameras in the Courtroom
Conspiracy and Substantial Assistance
Eyewitness Identifications
Indigent Defendant Representation
International Criminal Court
Problem-Solving Courts
Prosecutorial Discretion
Restorative Justice
Sentencing and Judicial Discretion
Trial Consultation
Tribal Court Criminal Jurisdiction

PUNISHMENT AND CORRECTIONS
Boot Camps
Clemency
Convict Criminology
Corporal Punishment
Corrections Education
Cruel and Unusual Punishment
Dangerous Offenders
Death Penalty in the United States
Executions—Televised
Faith-Based Prison Programs
Guantanamo Detainees
Hawaiians (Ethnic) and Incarceration
Juveniles Treated as Adults
New Penology
Parole
Prison Construction
Prison Privatization

PREFACE

CONTENT

Battleground: Criminal Justice is a comprehensive, two-volume set that discusses the major controversies or issues involving the administration of criminal justice. The 100 entries of this reference work, written by 66 expert contributors, span the criminal justice system of the United States, with a few entries included that deal with instructive foreign criminal justice issues, such as prison problems in the Caribbean and post-apartheid justice in South Africa. They include entries on some of the crimes or criminals caught up in controversies of crime control, such as those involving domestic violence and sexual assault or acts by sexual offenders or perpetrators who have been diagnosed as legally insane. In addition, these entries cut across a full array of institutional arrangements, including social, political, economic, and legal and are inclusive of all sectors of society.

What may be most significant about these so-called controversies in criminal justice are the cultural imprints that these entries represent. That is to say, the controversies hoisted and elucidated upon here reflect a multiplicity of cultural stances, including supposed liberal, moderate, radical, and conservative points of view. The important relevant arguments pertaining to any of these controversies will be found within this two-volume encyclopedia. The leading principle in presenting the information on these controversies is, whenever possible, to locate and to be guided by the empirical (research) realities underlying these debates, controversies, or disagreements.

ARRANGEMENT

The issues of criminal justice profiled here are arranged alphabetically. The table of contents contains a list of all the entries in alphabetical order. As a further guide to the reader, however, a topically arranged list of all the entries, "Guide to Related Topics," follows the alphabetic list in the contents. Here you will discover that I have classified the 100 entries into six areas or clusters: "Law and Society"; "Law Enforcement"; "Prosecution, Courts, and Adjudication"; "Punishment and Corrections"; "Science and Criminal Justice"; and "Social Issues, Crime, and Justice." Although I have classified them into the six clusters, some of these could have been ordered under another heading. For example, "Exclusionary Rule," "Second Amendment," or "Expert Witness Testimony" could each be cataloged under "Prosecution, Courts, and Adjudication." The comprehensive index at the end of the second volume will give the reader more options for subject access to the contents of this work.

ENTRIES

Each entry runs approximately 2,000 to 5,000 words. Although there are some deviations specific to some of the entries, entries present a sequence of the following sections:

- "Introduction," in which the controversy is briefly summarized.
- "Background," in which the controversy is presented historically.
- "Key Events," in which important dealings, ideas, or persons are reviewed.
- "Legal Decisions," in which key court cases are briefly summarized.
- "Future Prospects," in which future issues or possible resolutions are discussed.
- "Further Reading," with approximately five to twelve suggested books, articles, or Web sites.

Sidebars highlight interesting aspects of the controversy, explain certain concepts, or present factual or statistical information.

Battleground: Criminal Justice closes with a bibliography of useful materials on general topics in criminal justice and with a subject index.

CRIMINAL JUSTICE ISSUES IN THIS WORK

At least four common denominators apply to most of the entries in this encyclopedia. First, although fresh controversies emerge from time to time, especially propelled by new technologies, such as the use of DNA testing to convict or extricate an alleged offender of a crime or by the introduction of pioneering laws such as those prohibiting stalking or the expanded prosecution of the pollution of the environment, most controversies in criminal justice or between the rights of the individual versus the rights of the state have a relatively long history, some dating as far back as the signing of the Magna Carta in 1215. In that historic moment, in a small borough outside of London called Runnymede, King John acquiesced to his barons and agreed to document the protected rights of feudal lords, setting the stage for what would eventually evolve into legal procedures—the rule of law—which both subjects and kings alike would have to abide by or suffer the legal consequences.

The second unifying issue of these controversies is that, although the policies and practices surrounding some of the newer contentions in criminal justice have not been reviewed or tested by appellate courts, let alone the U.S. Supreme Court, most of these have an established legal history as well, one that is legislative if not also judicial. For example, the legal definitions of the insanity defense have been changing for more than 150 years. More generally, what is considered as criminal or as criminal violence has been evolving at least since the thirteenth century and continues right up to this day. Similarly, the consequences or punishments for violating the criminal law have also varied considerably. For example, not all states in the United States have the death penalty, and for a brief three-year period, 1973 to 1976, the U.S. Supreme Court outlawed the death penalty across the nation.

Third, although many of the controversies examined here are complex, most come to be viewed dualistically or in terms of one side versus another side. In terms of the public's attitudes toward the death penalty or the Patriot Act, for example, or regarding the views of the efficacy of these practices by professional justicians, sides are usually reduced to those who are either pro or con, in favor of or opposed to. On closer scrutiny, however, there are usually more sides than these simple dichotomies. Although some folks may be opposed to or in favor of the death penalty, there are others who find the death penalty acceptable under certain conditions and unacceptable under other conditions. Similarly, when it comes to the controversial Patriot Act, Homeland Security Act, or the Military Commissions Act (related to unlawful enemy combatants, such as those held at Guantanamo Bay detainment camp), there are also persons who are in favor of some provisions and opposed to other provisions.

Fourth, although a few criminal justice controversies seem to have been put to sleep, such as the right of all persons accused of a felony crime to be represented by an attorney at law, whether they can afford one or not, as was the case in 1963 with *Gideon v. Wainwright*, most of the controversies will continue to be debated well into the future, such as treatment versus punishment, gun control, or the police use of racial profiling. And so-called settled issues often spawn or evolve into related issues of controversy. In the case of post-*Gideon* matters of legal representation, for example, one issue today has to do with whether and when it is acceptable for an indigent criminal defendant to waive his or her right to appointed counsel. Finally, even when the law eliminates or abolishes certain policies or practices, such as the United States did with indeterminate sentencing in the 1970s or federal parole in the 1980s, controversies may persist around the value of resurrecting these. In the 1970s, for example, the death penalty was declared to be unconstitutional by the Supreme Court and executions were stopped for a short period of time, from mid-1972 until the Court subsequently reversed itself a few years later in 1976.

Thus, even when practices and policies seem fixed or permanent in stature, without controversies surrounding them, they may, in fact, be subject to change. For example, the original human right (the "Great Writ") of habeas corpus giving every citizen the right to challenge the legality of his or her detention by the state, first codified by the British Parliament in 1640 and 1679 and one of a handful of common laws explicitly referred to and protected in the U.S. Constitution, seemed to be invincible or beyond reproach. In 2006, however, the Great Writ was substantially weakened by the passage of the Military Commissions Act. This act passed by the Congress and signed by President George W. Bush eliminated habeas corpus for anyone defined as an "unlawful enemy combatant" as well as all aliens, including permanent residents—holders of a green card—in the United States. It appears that federal courts, at least for the time being, have been stripped of their historical role in assessing the legality of detentions, so long as the executive branch claims that these arrests are part of the war on terror. Of course, it will not be too long before a test case of the Military Commissions Act finds itself winding its way to the U.S. Supreme Court for review of its constitutionality.

In sum, when it comes to "law and order" or to "equal [criminal] justice for all," virtually no policies or practices are absolute or constant; all are subject to reform, change, repudiation, or innovation. From time to time, these policies, controversial or not, will be subjected to new laws and new interpretations of those rules, reflecting a much older social and cultural controversy about where we as a civil society draw the lines between the rights of the individual to his or her liberty or freedom versus the rights of the state to maintain the peace, property, and security of all. Hence, as you read these different thought-provoking entries on and sometimes beyond criminal justice, keep in mind that most of these controversies will have a past, a present, and a future.

Gregg Barak
Eastern Michigan University

A

ADVERSARIAL JUSTICE

INTRODUCTION

No subject of legal scholarship has enjoyed greater influence during the last half-century than that of adversarial justice. Yet adversarial justice, the essence of law, remains underexamined and poorly understood. An inquiry into this subject of considerable controversy provides a fruitful and an extremely fertile field for recognizing that contemporary notions of justice reflect conceptual and concrete expressions of the dominant ideologies of liberalism and their attendant institutional practices of adversity.

Typically, contemporary scholarship and administrative policies fail to locate justice within the broader contexts of ideologies, let alone daily institutional practices. Adversarial justice discharges claims and meanings, which reflect contradictory and complementary discourses on the tensions between individual rights and state powers. By studying the wide array of implications and applications of adversarial justice, one gains an understanding of the controversy inherent in the relatively disjunctive relationship between adversity and justice. It is in the nature of adversarial justice that one realizes the challenges and limitations of law, present and past. The appeal to adversity is not just the reach of jurisprudence; it is the most comprehensive and most fundamental guiding principle of contemporary criminal justice.

This entry presents the sources of the adversarial that condition the form and content of justice. For some, various forms of contest, continuous and episodic, trigger balance, harmony, and justice. For others, the connective tissues of conflict allow the control fibers of the state considerable elasticity or range of motion that compromises justice. It is not simply an awareness of the extent to which the articulations of the adversarial influence justice but, rather, an appreciation of how justice is constituted by prevailing ideologies. This viewpoint highlights the manner in which the justice defaults to adversarial processes; that is, adversity reduces justice to technical legal practices, thereby rendering law inaccessible except to the well represented. This view also acknowledges the need to proffer alternatives to adversarial justice.

Adversarial justice is an evolving system of statutory rules and common-law principles that continues to have an impact on all U.S. courts. The concept of adversarial justice, abstracted from English medieval common-law history and eighteenth-century liberal political theories, defies simplistic definitions. Adversarial justice refers to the common-law system of conducting proceedings in which litigants and not the judge have the primary responsibility for defining, investigating, and advancing their respective interests.

The term *adversarial* connotes a competitive battle or contest between contestants, notably between the prosecutor (as representative of the state) and the accused, who typically employs a surrogate (a defense attorney). These partisan parties or adversaries are responsible for presenting their case (evidence) to a judge and/or jury who, in turn, decide which side wins the legal battle in the courtroom. Judges seek to balance the interests of contending parties participating in the disputations, leaving it to the contestants or opponents to square off to uncover truth by examining evidence through the questioning of evidence and by advancing differing propositions of fact and law. The adversarial system assumes that the fairest and most effective method of determining the truth is to permit parties to fight their own battles by putting their best respective cases in their own way. The outcome of adversarial justice, however, as a tool for dispute resolution (litigation), typically depends upon the qualities and resources of the respective parties.

BACKGROUND

The core values and practices of adversarial justice can only be understood by situating its relative advantages and/or disadvantages with its competing archetypal legal model: inquisitorial justice. By contextualizing adversarial justice within common-law traditions and by juxtaposing the merits and/or shortcomings of adversarial justice against inquisitorial justice, one develops the necessary background to fully appreciate current core values and practices of the U.S. legal system. The main alternative to the common-law adversarial justice system is the civil law system, which is used in Continental Europe and most of the rest of the world.

Briefly, the common-law, adversarial system developed in England during the Middle Ages and was exported to countries such as United States and the British Commonwealth countries through colonization. In Europe, civil law inquisitorial justice systems had their basis in Roman law later transformed into the Napoleonic Codes, the German Civil Codes, as well as ecclesiastic laws. Civil law systems in Europe and Asia have generally styled themselves on either the French or German model.

The common-law system of jurisprudence consists of case law, statutes, codes, and equity, which originated in England and was later applied and adapted in the United States and other countries of the English Commonwealth. The term *common law* signifies the law common to the whole jurisdiction as opposed to local or customary law, ecclesiastic law, and merchant law. Originally, this common law was the law administered by the royal courts in England, common to the whole realm. The term *common law* also refers to case law, as opposed to statutory law. The common law is not set down in codes, statutes, and regulations but found in the sum of binding precedents of actual court decisions.

Statutes, which reflect English common law, are interpreted in terms of common-law traditions. The development of precedent contributed to the development of the common law. The legal principle of *stare decisis* binds all courts to the previous decisions of the higher courts. The decisions or the opinions of higher courts must be followed regardless of whether the reasoning and decision appear correct or erroneous to the lower court. Stare decisis and the whole complex of case law developed only gradually in common law. The strict application of stare decisis occurred at the end of the eighteenth century with the introduction of efficient publications of court decisions.

KEY EVENTS

The evolutionary development of adversarial justice has been influenced not only by the uses of the law but also by different concepts about the origins of law and its functions and structure. History demonstrates that whenever the power of the state is deployed against an individual accused, the process is adversarial given that the resources of the state are much greater than those of the individual accused. Historically, the adversary paradigm was based on the search for truth, the protection of rights, and the determination of right or wrong. Evidence-based reason within a competitive setting framed procedural rules that originated 800 years ago. The common law of England evolved over hundreds of years, beginning with Anglo-Saxon tribal customs as well as Norman rationalization and centralization of law, further refined during the Enlightenment and ideologically anchored in English liberal philosophy.

According to many historians,[1] the period between the Norman Conquest (1066) and the Magna Carta (1215) was the most crucial time for the development of English law, administrative institutions, and royal authority. Although the moral authority of common law came from adherence to Anglo-Saxon custom, which had been long established prior to the 1066 Norman Conquest, adversarial justice was developing in theory, uniform in practice, and well respected. Legal changes enforced by King Henry II and his advisors, between 1154 and 1189, represented the pivotal moment in the history of common law.

Despite the 1066 Norman Conquest of England, King William sought to Anglicize Norman law in England rather than form two separate sets of laws—one for the conquerors and another for the conquered. Accordingly, Anglo-Norman law resorted to a stable and formal court (a royal court or a lord's court) rather than to the preexisting feudal Anglo-Saxon unwritten community-based remedies for justice, all of which varied according to local and arbitrary customs. The Normans invented the institution of the eyre, a system of traveling judges who represented the king in local courts. It was the decisions of these judges in eyre that formed the body of legal precedent that became known as the common law. Common law was built case by case (case law).

The legal process served to centralize the political authority of King William and his successors. The legal reforms of Henry I and Henry II systematized legal habits and practices. For instance, King William's son Henry I issued the Leges Henrici (1116), securing royal jurisdiction over certain offenses against the king's peace—arson, robbery, murder, false coinage, and crimes of violence—which were interpreted as offenses against the king, and offenders were thus subject to royal authority.

In 1154, Henry II institutionalized common law by creating a unified system of law common to the country through incorporating and elevating local custom to the national, ending local control and peculiarities, eliminating arbitrary remedies, and reinstating a jury system of citizens sworn on oath to reliably investigate criminal accusations and civil claims. The creation of a powerful and unified court system curbed the power of canonical (church) courts. In 1166, King Henry II by the Royal Decree of Clarendon established separate secular courts. The king's judges and commissioners went out on circuit to hear cases. They used the old laws and ironed out their differences by keeping in touch with one another and following one another's decisions.

To know what the law was, you had to know what the judges had decided—in other words, precedent. The king's judges carried over from the old courts the use of tribal ordeals (grasping a burning-hot piece of iron and walking a defined number of paces or ordeals of water). By a law of Henry II, in 1164, it was directed that the sheriff shall make 12 legal men from the neighborhood to swear that they will make known the truth according to their conscience—a trial by jury or the trial by 12 men sworn to speak the truth.

Another major development occurred in England on June 15, 1215, when a large group of barons confronted a despotic King John and demanded that traditional rights be recognized, written down, confirmed with the royal seal, and sent to each of the counties to be read to all freemen in the form of a Great Charter—the Magna Carta. King John acquiesced to the demands of his rebelling barons and nobles, relinquishing his own and future sovereigns' absolute power over subjects. At Runnymede, King John granted to all freemen of the kingdom the rights and liberties the great charter described. All future sovereigns and magistrates were to be governed by the rule of law. King John was forced to recognize the supremacy of ancient liberties, to limit his ability to raise funds, and to reassert the principle of due process.

The Magna Carta limited the king's power and introduced something new to English law: the principle of majority rule. At King John's urging, Pope Innocent II annulled the "shameful and demeaning agreement, forced upon the king by violence and fear." The civil war that followed ended only with King John's death in October 1216.[2] Enshrined as Article 38 of the Magna Carta was the adversarial principle that a person could not be tried until formally accused. The Great Charter was the essential basis of the whole structure of the British and U.S. constitutions, especially the declarations of the rights of the citizen and the foundations of Anglo-American jurisprudence about the liberty of the citizen. Accordingly, freemen were not to be dealt with except in accordance with law. The Magna Carta adds, "To no one will we sell, to no one will we deny, or delay right or justice."[3]

SIGNIFICANT HISTORICAL MOMENTS

- 1225—King John's son Henry III reissued the Magna Carta; copies of the document were made and sent to the counties so that everyone would know their rights and obligations.
- 1275—Imposition of jury trial in criminal cases by the Statute of Westminster.
- 1297—Statute of Edward I enacted by Parliament, which did not exist in 1215, confirms and enacts the principal provisions of the original Magna Carta.
- 1341—The trial of peers of the realm and the king's ministers contains recognition of the principle of the Magna Carta that the jury is to fix the sentence.
- 1354—The phrase *due process of law* appears in a Liberty of the Subject statute of Edward III.
- 1628—Parliament's Petition of Right referred to the Great Charter and alleged that King Charles had violated its terms; Petition of Right, a parliamentary declaration of the liberties of the people, assented to by King Charles I; the Magna Carta resurrected and reinterpreted by Sir Edward Coke; Coke, attorney general for Elizabeth I, chief justice during the reign of James I, and a leader in Parliament in opposition to Charles I, used the Magna Carta as a weapon against the oppressive tactics of the Stuart kings.
- 1679—Habeas Corpus Act under King Charles II, another outcome of a struggle between a weak king and empowered English nobles; this act established the right of habeas corpus ("have the body") whereby accused have a right to be brought before a judge and charged with a crime in a timely fashion.
- 1689—English Bill of Rights assented to by King William III and Queen Mary II.
- By 1701—The king's power to control what happened in the courts diminished. Judges once appointed were to remain in office so long as they did their job properly; its virtually sacred status came to be encapsulated in a phrase, "the palladium of English/British liberty" (Evans, 1997), which was repeated throughout the eighteenth and nineteenth centuries.

John Evans, "Bad King John and the Australian Constitution Commemorating the 700th Anniversary of the 1297 Issue of Magna Carta," Occasional Lecture Parliament of Australia, http://www.aph.gov.au/senate/pubs/occa_lect/flyers/171097.htm (accessed February 2, 2007).

Before signing the Declaration of Independence—the first of the American Charters of Freedom—in 1776, the Founding Fathers employed the Magna Carta as historical precedent for asserting their rightful liberties and for resisting King George III and the English Parliament. Note the allusion to the Great Charter in the words of the U.S. Constitution: "the Supreme Law of the Land," just as the rights granted by the Magna Carta were not to be arbitrarily canceled by subsequent English laws. The drafters of the Declaration of Independence incorporated liberties guaranteed by the Magna Carta, the writings of Sir Edward Coke, and the 1689 English Bill of Rights directly into their own statutes for justification. For Coke, authority emanated directly from the people, not from any governmental body. The U.S. Constitution, like the Magna Carta, stood as a bulwark against tyranny, protecting individual freedoms of all individuals against arbitrary and capricious rule.[4]

According to the historical developments listed in the sidebar, adversarial justice requires a balance between the resources of the state and the rights of the accused. Adversarial justice continued to be developed and was further refined during the Enlightenment and in the proliferation of liberal thought in the seventeenth and eighteenth centuries. The forces of modernity and liberalism and their respective foci on reason and rights provided further synthetic unity to the foundations of contemporary adversarial justice. The seventeenth century witnessed the elaborate and profound philosophical discussions about scientific reasoning.

The Enlightenment

Modernity, as an ideology with its emphasis on both the rational and the division of labor, has influenced law to such an extent that law was reconstituted as a rational calculation of efficiency measuring social value (contractual considerations and exchanges) by specialized technicians. Modernity contributed to the classification and division of legal concepts, methods of induction and deduction, the analysis and synthesis of rules, and the testing of evidence. Traditional beliefs were replaced by science, argument, and experience. Knowledge and truth were based on empiricist ideas of science and utilitarian reasoning. The framers of the U.S. Constitution staunchly defended the role of reason and science in law. Law as a form of domination is shaped by objectivity, grounded rationalism, and necessity. The immutability or universality of reason, according to law, ensures the constitution of justice. Reason is used to clarify extant antagonisms. From the Enlightenment, ideas developed about (1) hierarchy of authority; (2) impersonality, impersonal rules that explicitly state duties, responsibilities, standardized procedures, and conduct of office holders; (3) written rules of conduct, bounded rules set out specialized tasks, so that everyone knows who has responsibility for what, promotion based on achievement, on the principle of trained competence; (4) specialized division of labor; and (5) efficiency.

Liberalism

Modern jurisprudence is based on liberal notions of the law as a contest between the freedom of the individual and the powers of the state. Law protects human freedom from arbitrary coercion. Complementing the Enlightenment's emphasis on reason was liberalism's focus on individual rights. The roots of liberalism are found in the respect for the sanctity of the individual. The liberal conception of rights and freedom existed only under the law. Early liberal philosophy argued rule of law as rights-based secured freedom. Social contracts enforced rights. The liberal position, indebted as it is to the tradition of contractarian theory, regards the expansion of legally guaranteed liberties as the key point on which law must focus. For example, John Locke's second treatise on law and government[5] influenced a number of concepts incorporated later not only in founding documents but also in subsequent U.S. Supreme Court decisions, especially protection of life, liberty, and property. Truth can only be obtained through legal confrontation. In short, adversarial justice assumes that truth will arise from a free and open competition over who has the correct facts.

RATIONALIZING THE LAW

Modernity:	Ideology of Reason (science)
	Institution of Specialized and Bureaucratic Rules
Liberalism:	Ideology of Rights (freedom)
	Institution of Contract

LEGAL DECISIONS/STATUTES

Laws have advanced adversarial ethics that ensure the delicate balance between discoveries of the facts at any cost, on the one hand, and considerations for basic and fundamental rights of the citizen on the other. Ideally, legal principles and rules of adversarial justice are explicitly based on notions of fair, efficient and free competition that does not disadvantage either prosecution or defense. Logically, both parties in this contest enjoy reasonable opportunities to present their respective arguments and equal opportunities to challenge evidence and question witnesses. Case law and statutes ensure the following: that each side has competent legal counsel, that the trier of fact decides the case based strictly on statutory law and case precedent, that court-appointed legal counsel is provided to indigent accused criminals, that the waiver of the right to counsel by an accused must be knowingly made and understood, to name only a few. American history is replete with statutes and cases that ostensibly protect the rights of the accused. Procedural fairness that minimizes the rights violations of accused by the state seemingly characterizes the core values and practices of adversarial justice. Legal rights are calibrated to balance the authority of the government and protect the inviolability of rights. The U.S. Constitution governs criminal law, specifically the first ten amendments, known as the Bill of Rights catalog of procedural protections, passed in 1791. The Fourteenth Amendment, passed in 1868, incorporates the first ten amendments, making them binding on the states, but they have also been selectively or individually incorporated in landmark U.S. Supreme Court cases.[6]

A SAMPLE OF THE PROTECTIONS/STANDARDS OF PROOF

Fourth Amendment: The Supreme Court has consistently held to a common law doctrine of "reasonableness" regarding police search, seizure, and/or warrants. This exclusionary rule was argued in *Weeks v. U.S.* (1914) and *Mapp v. Ohio* (1961).

Fifth Amendment: The due process of law protects against deprivation of liberty (protection against repressive governmental interference) including protection against double jeopardy (*Benton v. Maryland* 1969), self-incrimination, warning about the rights before custodial interrogation (*Miranda v. Arizona* 1966), the right to "plead the fifth" (*Malloy v. Hogan* 1964), a right to counsel during police interrogations (*Escobedo v. Illinois* 1964), and the right not to take the witness stand (*Griffin v. California* 1965).

Sixth Amendment: In all criminal prosecutions, the accused shall enjoy the right to a speedy and public trial by an impartial jury, to be informed of the nature and cause of the accusation, to confront witnesses, to have compulsory process for obtaining witnesses in his favor, and to have the assistance of Counsel for his defense. In *Barker v. Wingo* (1971), the Supreme Court held that determinations of whether the right has been denied must be made on a case-by-case basis. Factors to be considered are length of delay, the reason for the delay, the time and manner in which the defendant's right was asserted, and the degree of prejudice caused by the delay. The defense, under the Sixth Amendment, must have an opportunity to "confront" and cross-examine witnesses. This Confrontation Clause, a common law principle, prevents the admission of hearsay affording the defendant the opportunity to challenge the credibility of such statements.

The Sixth Amendment also guarantees the right of defendants to procure the assistance of counsel. The Supreme Court expanded the interpretation of *Powell v. Alabama* (1932), which held that in a capital case, where the defendant is unable to employ counsel, and is incapable adequately of making his own defense because of ignorance, feeblemindedness, illiteracy, or the like, it is the duty of the court, whether requested or not, to assign counsel. In *Johnson v. Zerbst* (1938), *Hamilton v. Alabama* (1961), and *Gideon v. Wainwright* (1963) the Supreme Court ruled that courts are required by the Sixth and Fourteenth Amendments to provide lawyers to indigent defendants.

Seventh Amendment: In civil cases, the Seventh Amendment guarantees a defendant a right to a jury trial in federal court.

Eighth Amendment: The Eighth Amendment prohibits excessive bail as well as cruel and unusual punishment. In 1972, the death penalty was declared unconstitutional in *Furman v. Georgia* (1972) but declared constitutional once again in *Gregg v. Georgia* (1976).

Fourteenth Amendment: With the Fourteenth Amendment, the Supreme Court extended the right to a trial by jury to defendants in state courts. The requirement that prosecutors disclose evidence to the defense is an ethical norm patterned after the constitutional duty to disclose exculpatory privilege, that is, the communication would not be disclosed, is one of the oldest, most litigated, and complex, defined and developed rights (*Wigmore* 1979). In *Fisher v. United States* (1976), the Court noted that full disclosure between an attorney and client was necessary for the adversarial justice.

KEY ELEMENTS OF ADVERSARIAL JUSTICE

The rules and procedures of adversarial justice seek to balance conflict with consensus, given that a monopoly of resources in litigation serves to alienate the people from the law. That is, adversarial justice has developed a number of normative practices, which seek to balance the discovery of the facts with basic and fundamental rights of the citizen, notably the presumption of innocence. An adversarial judicial system is intended to protect the rights of all while providing justice to all.

Three crucial components make up such a system: equality, impartiality, and transparency. When a judicial system possesses these characteristics, the system not only inspires confidence in those who do not prevail; more importantly, it conveys to the parties that their autonomy and dignity as persons is respected. For equality to exist, both sides in the case must enter the courtroom as equals. It is crucial that the burden of proof fall properly on one side and that the other side is charged with asserting affirmative defenses. The related principle of equality is impartiality. When adjudication between parties is impartial, even the party that does not prevail can perceive the process as legitimate and obliged to protect her rights, freedom, and interests. The third crucial component of an adversarial adjudicatory system is transparency in court proceedings. Even if the system reaches the proper outcome in most instances, it will still have no credibility with the public if the people cannot understand what is being done and why. These three principles are the cornerstones of adversarial justice. What then are the rules of evidence and the roles of key participants?

Evidence and Cross-Examination

The rules of evidence are based on the procedural decisions of the adversaries who are engaged in preparing the case, presenting facts, and raising a series of objections. Evidence is elicited by direct questioning (examination) of witnesses who may then be cross-examined by the opposing party. This cross-examination is considered the best way of ascertaining the truth in common-law jurisdictions. The techniques of confrontation, including the language, tone, and demeanor of questioning, serve to test the witnesses, discredit evidence, and divert attention. Each counsel is required to advance his or her client's case as strongly as possible and to damage the opponent's case as much as possible. Within adversarial justice, the cross-examination is necessary in order to ensure compliance with standards of rights. In criminal cases, the prosecutor must prove the guilt of an accused beyond a reasonable doubt; whereas in civil cases, the plaintiff must establish its case on a balance of probabilities. The position of the accused is further protected by rules of evidence, which restrict the availability of materials that may be put before a trier of fact. Rules of evidence were developed by judges to prevent juries from misusing materials put before them in court.

In addition, the disclosure of evidence is a fundamental part of the accused's right to a fair trial. This requirement strives to balance the vast inequality of resources between the state (investigation and prosecution) and the defendant. Given the burden of proof and the presumption of innocence, it is therefore the duty of prosecuting authorities to disclose evidence to the defense. Through a discovery process that aids in the review of evidence before it is presented to judge or jury, all parties therefore will have a relatively good idea of the scope of agreement and disagreement of the issues to present at trial. Disclosure, the result of investigations by the state authorities in assembling a case against an accused, includes details of the prosecution's case and any potentially exculpatory information. The common-law principle of seeking the truth is only possible if the defense attorneys can scrutinize the police investigation and its attendant prosecution.

Role of Participants

Common-law jurisprudence maintains that adversarial justice is democratic because it is participatory, allowing the parties to define and control the dispute. Parties pursue those avenues of inquiry perceived to promote their interests. For instance, attorneys are expected to champion their client's best interests, protect their client, and present only favorable evidence. Guided by professional codes of conduct regarding loyalty, confidentiality, and competence, the duty of lawyers to their client is foremost. Clients, in turn, enjoy rights-based legal claims afforded by both case law and constitutional protections. Prosecutors in this contest are governed by codes of professional conduct that maintain that the duty of the prosecutor is to seek justice, not merely to convict. Too often, the prosecutor enjoys a close relationship with the judiciary, governmental agencies that control criminal investigations.

Judges are considered the pillars of the adversarial system. Adversarial justice, however, limits the involvement of judges in both investigatory and adjudicatory functions. Unlike their counterparts in the inquisitorial system, U.S. judges do not control or direct the investigation, collection of evidence, or presentation of evidence. First, judges play a passive and reactive role in dispute resolution, seldom interfering with counsels' development of cases. Accordingly, their powers, duties, and discretions are to ensure that justice is administered fairly. In this system of adjudication, the role of the judge as an umpire or referee is governed by traditional, customary, or common-law rules that maintain the integrity of impartiality. This dispassionate or neutral umpire oversees the rules of the game, decides whether parties are playing by the rules, and which adversary wins. The trial judge rules on disputed points of procedure and evidence and may ask questions to clarify the evidence of a witness but otherwise does not take an active part.[7]

Judicial discretion, as a source of judicial power, ensures that the examination and cross-examination of witnesses occur in a professional manner. The key procedural element of this system is for the judge to regulate the adversarial imbalance between prosecution and defense by protecting the accused's right to fair trial while at the same time not unduly hampering the effectiveness of the state. Ideally, judges balance the rights of the accused person to a fair trial, the state's crime control, and the right of society to retribution for criminal wrongs. Judges are bound by relevant precedents in law and the dictates of tradition structured by written rules of procedure and evidence (Judicature Acts) that require restraint, propriety, and impartiality. The integrity of the adjudicator is advanced by demanding the litigants to shoulder the responsibilities of effective competition. Truth-seeking and decision-making methods are promoted by accountability and independence that are compromised whenever judges fail to ensure the clash of submissions and the competition of evidence. Well-established jurisprudential and public-opinion positions assume that the most efficient means of arriving at approximate truth is to harnesses the power of self-interest to unearth the best evidence. To assess tactics over truth, common-law judges are expected to interpret law in the statutes or in case law. The institutional rules and roles are typically designed to ensure adversarial justice, never to be mistaken for social justice. Clearly, law mediates the relationship between adversity and justice.

FUTURE PROSPECTS

Adversarial justice is embedded within numerous contexts—social, political, economic, and legal. Despite its hyperbolic niceties, the frequently invoked rights-based contexts conceal as much as they reveal. A circumspect appreciation of law demonstrates the limitations of prevailing traditional models. Adversarial justice is a product of orthodox liberalism; that is, classical notions relentlessly dwell on freedoms from government interference. Characteristically, the judiciary was empowered to disallow infringements on individual liberties. An excessive reliance on the judiciary as a forum for the provision of freedom, however, invites difficulties.

By its very nature, the judiciary is an extremely conservative mechanism that seldom assumes an activist stance on issues of universal entitlements—freedom and equality. The judiciary defines inequality as unfair individual practices that will be vindicated on an individual case basis. Procedural equality is not a guarantee of substantive equality, oriented toward the ideal of equality of opportunity. The illusory language, convoluted logic, and ambiguous style of legal procedures succeed in creating confidence only among individuals who know the law and in mystifying notions of equality for the majority of citizens. Even a perfunctory glance at history demonstrates that a wide spectrum of groups have been routinely subordinated, despite the benevolent intentions of those who administer legal procedures.

Benign and often paternalistic provisions are inadequately designed to consider existing distribution of resources. The elderly, youths, disabled, women, the poor, racial and ethnic communities, social activities, natives, gays—to name only a few—are all too familiar with the dubious benefits of legal procedures. Procedures for legal redress simply target individual villains. This pathological orientation directs attention away from the more oppressive structural inequalities.

Critiques are mounted against the adversary system from a variety of perspectives. First, adversarialism as a solution is problematic. The adversarial system promotes beliefs and attitudes that not only obstruct fair and effective dispute resolution but also legitimize socially undesirable behaviors—competitive aggression, hostility, and the pursuit of self-interest. The search for truth cannot be limited to such convenient binaries of winners and losers. Competition in law has created a marketplace of justice and an increasing commercialization of legal practice, profit maximization, and retainer-driven corporatized justice. The ethos of competition rewards resources. Unequal resources tend to subvert justice as in the case of a powerful, wealthy litigant and the underresourced litigant. Often, costs determine the skills among advocates, the time frame of a trial, the prejudices of judges, and so forth, which further exacerbate legal disputes. Interestingly, most legal cases in these systems do not go to trial and are resolved by plea bargain.

Second, adversarial justice is not the only possible form of conflict resolution. Other creative problem-solving opportunities exist that provide for the empowerment of its participants. The mediation of a dispute can be achieved without a right-wrong determination and without a factual finding. The focus in mediation is on the future, specifically what the future may hold for the parties. Resolution can be accomplished without the need to battle and without seeing the others as an opponent. Related to mediation is the concept of alternative dispute resolution (ADR), which has attracted considerable attention. This mediation organizes parties around common interests and encourages the development of restorative processes. These communitarian approaches include informal justice, peacemaking, positive justice, relational justice, family group conferencing, effective cautioning, and community accountability conferencing. Together, these alternative approaches to adversarial justice suggest that there are other pathways to resolving conflicts without the need to do battle with the other party.

See Also: Alternative Responses to Crime by Society; Problem-Solving Courts; Restorative Justice; Social Justice; War on Drugs.

Endnotes

1. See William Blackstone, *Commentaries on the Laws of England,* with introductions by Stanley N. Katz (Chicago: University of Chicago Press, 1979; originally published 1769); Matthew Hale, *The History of the Common Law* (Birmingham, U.K.: Gaunt, 1993); David Hume, *The History of England from the Invasion of Julius Caesar to the Revolution in 1688,* foreword by William B. Todd, 6 vols. (Indianapolis, IN: Liberty Fund, 1983).
2. See J. C. Holt, *Magna Carta* (Cambridge: Cambridge University Press, 2006); John Hudson, *The Formation of the English Common Law: Law and Society in England from the Norman Conquest to Magna Carta,* Medieval World Series (London: Longman, 1996).
3. See Blackstone, *Commentaries.*
4. See Holt, *Magna Carta;* Hudson, *The Formation of the English Common Law;* Robert A. Kagan, *Adversarial Legalism: The American Way of Law* (Cambridge, MA: Harvard University Press, 2001); Constitution of the United States: 2002 Edition and Supplements, U.S. Government Printing Office, http://www.gpoaccess.gov/constitution/browse2002.html#2002A.
5. See John Locke, *Two Treatises of Government* (Cambridge: Cambridge University Press, 1988).

6. See Donald Dworkin, *Freedom's Law: The Moral Reading of the American Constitution* (Cambridge, MA: Harvard University Press, 1997); G. S. Wood, *The Creation of the American Republic, 1776–1787* (New York: Norton, 1972).

7. See L. J. Denning in *Jones v. National Coal Board*, 2 QB 55, 63 (1957).

Further Reading: Abel, Richard, *The Contradictions of Informal Justice, the Politics of Informal Justice* (New York: Academic Press, 1987); Braithwaite, John, *Crime, Shame and Reintegration* (New York: Cambridge University Press, 1989); Ellison, Louise, *The Adversarial Process and the Vulnerable* (Oxford: Oxford University Press, 2001); Fuller, Lon, "The Adversary System," in *Talks on American Law,* ed. H. Berman (New York: Vintage Books, 1961); Kagan, Robert, *Adversarial Justice: The American Way of Law* (Cambridge, MA: Harvard University Press, 2002); Kennedy, Duncan, *A Critique of Adjudication* (Cambridge, MA: Harvard University Press, 1998); Landsman, Stephan, *Readings on Adversarial Justice: The American Approach to Adjudication* (St. Paul, MN: West, 1988); Luban, D., *Lawyers and Justice: An Ethical Study* (Princeton, NJ: Princeton University Press, 1988).

L. A. Visano

AFRICAN AMERICAN CRIMINAL (IN) JUSTICE

INTRODUCTION

Although the U.S. criminal justice system has a long and well-documented history of racism, sexism, and discrimination against the poor and powerless, controversies still exist about whether, for example, institutionalized racial discrimination still exists or how a racist past has shaped the lives and mind-set of modern African Americans. Black Americans, in particular, have felt the collective wrath and injustice of state coercion from colonial times through the nineteenth century and well into the twentieth century. This entry focuses on the evolution of the intentional and systematic repression aimed at fitting African Americans into their so-called proper place in the economic, political, social, cultural, and legal order.

BACKGROUND

Crime was not a serious concern during the colonial period. Early settlements in the New World were, as legal historian Lawrence M. Friedman aptly puts it, "tight little islands." Villages were small and isolated. Their populations were religiously, ethnically, socially, and culturally homogeneous—and largely white. The early settlers knew their neighbors intimately and kept them under close surveillance. Colonial criminal justice systems were small, informal, and aimed at correcting the transgressions of misguided neighbors, friends, and relatives. Punishments were based upon the philosophy of reintegrative shaming: public humiliation followed by reintegration into the community. Put simply, the early colonists were their brother's keepers.

The arrival of the first captive Africans at Jamestown, Virginia, in 1619—possibly as indentured servants, not slaves—was a pivotal event in American history. Africans filled the labor void, providing profits and sparking economic expansion, but they were not willing workers. Resistance was a constant concern. Slaves disobeyed their masters, worked slowly, feigned sickness, destroyed and stole property, poisoned and harmed farm animals, attempted escape, and, in extreme cases, burned buildings, murdered their masters, and plotted revolts. The so-called children of Ham were, quite simply, deviant and dangerous: profitable social dynamite that needed close surveillance and a repressive system of social control.

Laws were the key to combating black resistance. Legislatures passed a variety of colony-specific laws that were aimed at controlling slave behavior and maximizing profits. South Carolina, a slave state, prohibited slaves from traveling without a pass, owning property, selling goods without a master's written permission, carrying weapons, or meeting in groups. Masters were required to thoroughly inspect cabins every two weeks to look for weapons. White citizens were allowed to stop and question blacks, ask for passes, and even seize inappropriate clothing. Freed slaves were required to leave the state. Laws in Dutch New Netherlands were decidedly less strict. Slaves were allowed to marry, attend church, own property, trade goods, seek an education, join the militia, and even carry weapons. But when the British took over New Netherlands in 1664, the new rulers of New York instituted a much more restrictive set of laws. New York became like South Carolina.

Masters were the first line of defense in monitoring slave behavior, enforcing these laws, and maintaining social order. In most colonies, short of murder, masters generally had a free hand in administering justice without trial. Other colonial law enforcement officers—sheriffs, constables, and night watchmen—also kept slaves and free blacks under close surveillance. When serious crimes were committed (e.g., murder, rape, assault, arson, rebellion), slaves were formally charged in court; in many colonies, however, they were denied even minimal legal rights and faced the prospect of harsh punishment. Punishment and deterrence aimed at instilling terror—not benevolent reintegrative shaming—was the aim of slave discipline.

U.S. political, economic, social, and legal institutions were radically transformed during the first half of the nineteenth century. Emancipation from England and the ratification of the Constitution and Bill of Rights laid the foundation for the rise of democracy and new state-specific crime control systems. The publication of Adam Smith's classic work—*The Wealth of Nations* (1776)—and industrialization accompanied the early development and expansion of capitalism in the New World. Exploding immigration produced large cities, especially in the North, and a host of city-related problems, including crime and delinquency. Slavery remained essentially unchanged, however, especially in the South. Repressive laws and crass unyielding social control were needed to maintain order and preserve profits.

The aims, structure, and character of early-nineteenth-century criminal justice systems were, however, region specific. Northern states developed formal criminal justice institutions, largely aimed at the social control of immigrants, particularly the Irish, who were widely perceived as criminally inclined drunkards. Black criminals were a secondary concern. Southern states relied upon informal surveillance and social control. Slaves merited the closest scrutiny, but free blacks, Northern abolitionists, Southern Negro sympathizers, and black and white criminals were all viewed as threats to the Southern way of life. In short, the South was under siege.

Northern states responded to their crisis in crime and social disorder by introducing formal police systems. During the 1840s and 1850s, a number of large cities—such as New York, Boston, and Philadelphia—disbanded their ineffective night watch, restricted sheriffs and constables to court duties, and turned policing over to newly created law enforcement agencies. Although these new police departments were largely ineffective—policemen were unqualified, untrained, and corrupt—arrests increased. Courts were expanded to handle the increased volume of cases. Prisons and reformatories were introduced to hold offenders. The demographic profile of prison populations varied by state, but they were usually lower-class, white, urban immigrants and their children—the Northern criminal classes.

Southern criminal justice was informal, decentralized, and aimed, first and foremost, at one group: slaves. Southern states expanded the content and harshness of slave codes prior to the Civil War. Masters continued to serve as the first line of policing and social defense. Slave patrols were expanded and more slave catchers were hired. Sheriffs, constables, and newly created police forces, located in larger Southern cities, were constantly on the alert for escaped slaves, black and white criminals, and other threatening groups (e.g., abolitionists encouraging escape or revolt). Militias remained on high alert to deal with slave revolts. The laws in many Southern states continued to grant all white citizens the authority to stop, question, and arrest free blacks and slaves. For free blacks and slaves, the South was a repressive police state.

Early-nineteenth-century Southern courts and systems of punishment were also racially driven. In fact, there were at least four court systems and four sets of legal procedures—white male, white female, black male, and black female—which remained devoid of meaningful rights. Free blacks were often afforded an intermediate status. Black slaves accused of insurrection faced special tribunals that handed out harsh and swift punishments—often death—to prevent future transgressions. A number of Southern states opened prisons prior to the Civil War, but they were almost exclusively reserved for white offenders. In the minds of many Southerners, even the lowest white criminal was to be spared the humiliation and moral contagion of incarceration with "darkies" and "niggers."

The end of the Civil War and passage of the Thirteenth, Fourteenth, and Fifteenth Amendments to the U.S. Constitution filled freedmen with optimism and hope for equality and justice. Blacks did, indeed, make considerable progress during Reconstruction, but these gains were short-lived. The triumph of the so-called Redeemers—white conservative racists—summarily ended these political, economic, social, and legal gains. The Redeemers were determined to return free blacks to their slave status. Laws and the criminal justice system, coupled with informal means of terror (e.g., lynching), were keys to putting blacks in their proper place and reviving the Old South.

The Redeemers began their calculated assault on black progress and civil liberties by seizing control of the political system. Newly elected white supremacists passed repressive legislation, including vagrancy laws aimed at fostering the sharecropping system. Sheriffs, constables, and newly formed police departments replaced masters, slave patrols, and slave catchers in intimidating former slaves. Black arrest rates soared, courts were overwhelmed with "colored" defendants, and Southern prisons took on a new function: race control. After 1865, Southern prisons and chain gangs were nearly completely black.

African Americans continued to be regarded as second-class citizens, especially in the South, throughout the first half of the twentieth century. Separate but equal laws—legitimized by the United States Supreme Court's notorious *Plessy v. Ferguson* decision (1896)—kept blacks in a decidedly inferior status: Schools and housing developments were rigidly segregated; blacks were excluded from government jobs and segregated in the military; they were isolated in whites-only businesses, including restaurants and movie theaters; and they were relegated to using colored-only water fountains and restroom facilities. Disenfranchisement was widespread; in some Southern states, fewer than 5 percent of blacks were registered to vote in the 1950s.

Police forces in the South, and sometimes in the North, were exclusively white. Black faces were rarely seen in courts, unless they were defendants. A variety of ruses were employed to exclude blacks from serving on juries. Blacks continued to be disproportionately incarcerated in Southern and Northern prisons. In many institutions, they were rigidly segregated. Black defendants were far more likely to receive the death penalty, especially for rape, and blacks who murdered whites were much more likely to receive the death penalty than whites who murdered blacks. Simply stated, black victims had less value than white victims in the U.S. criminal justice system.

Crass political, economic, and legal discrimination continued relatively unabated into the 1950s. The 1960s was, however, a pivotal period in U.S. racial and legal history. The rise of the black civil rights movement, women's rights movement, protests against the Vietnam War, and dozens of race riots in cities across the United States raised serious doubts about the veracity and legitimacy of the U.S. government. The promise of freedom, equality, and justice was exposed as sheer hypocrisy, especially for African Americans.

Critics also turned their ire on the U.S. criminal justice system. Television cameras provided graphic accounts of police beating black rioters in the North and civil rights marchers, including children, in the South. The rise of criminal justice and criminology as academic disciplines in the 1960s resulted in an explosion of research highlighting disparities between the promise and practice of the justice system: inadequacies in the public defender system, the discriminatory dimensions of bail, abuses in plea bargaining, discrimination in the hiring and training of minority police, the paucity of minority judges and probation and parole officers, inhumane conditions and racial discrimination in prisons, and racial and class discrimination in sentencing and the application of the death penalty.

The United States Supreme Court, particularly under Chief Justice Earl Warren (1953–68), issued a series of landmark rulings that expanded the legal rights of black and white defendants. Attempts were made to rehabilitate offenders, shut down prisons, and move offenders back to the community. Money was appropriated to improve public defender systems, offer bail to more poor offenders, hire more minority police officers, and divert offenders from the criminal justice system to avoid harmful labels. During this period and into the early 1970s, individual states and the federal government did, indeed, make progress in combating racism, sexism, and discrimination in the United States.

These trends and transformations were, however, short lived. The election of Ronald Reagan as president in 1980 marked the birth of a conservative revolution along with the bankruptcy of rehabilitation. Advocates of the new conservative paradigm argued that criminals were free, rational, and hedonistic actors who needed and deserved punishment. Discussions about racism, sexism, and discrimination, as well as questions raised about the fairness of capitalism and democracy, were dismissed as softhearted and soft-minded liberal drawl. A return to the policies of the past—a get-tough approach on crime and criminals—was the new elixir for crime and deviance.

During the 1980s and 1990s, conservative politicians and crime-control experts—joined, on occasion, by politically astute get-tough liberals, like President Bill Clinton—transformed the criminal justice system: a return to fixed sentencing, three-strikes-and-you-are-out laws, preventive detention for suspected criminals, restrictions on the insanity defense, an end to minority hiring and promotion programs in policing, the increased use of transfers to adult courts for juveniles, boot camps for youthful offenders, electronic monitoring for less-serious offenders, the opening of new prisons and reformatories, the introduction of supermax prisons, an expansion in the use of the death penalty, and a get-tough war on drugs.

Many of these policies have, however, had a decidedly detrimental effect on African Americans, and there is considerable evidence that the remnants of racism are still pervasive in the U.S. justice system. Researchers have provided clear and convincing evidence that the death penalty continues to discriminate against the poor and powerless, particularly blacks. Public defender systems remain seriously underfunded, and prosecutors continue to use peremptory challenges to exclude blacks from juries. African Americans are still underrepresented on many police forces, especially in higher ranks. Egregious cases of police abuse—for example, Rodney King (1991), Abner Louima (1997), and Amadous Diallo (1999)—confirm the suspicion that some law enforcement officers are still racially biased. And the discovery of the so-called driving while black (DWB) syndrome in the 1990s provided evidence supporting ongoing African American suspicions and complaints: Police officers discriminate against black drivers.

Mandatory sentencing laws and the war on drugs have, however, had a particularly harmful—if not disastrous—effect on African Americans. Racially biased legislation aimed at crack cocaine has resulted in an explosion in black incarceration. Millions of young African American males are currently incarcerated in state and federal correctional institutions or are under the control of probation and parole officers. Jerome Miller's thought-provoking analysis of modern crime control reaches a sobering conclusion: The U.S. criminal justice system is engaged in a tragically misguided search-and-destroy mission aimed at young urban black males. Young black males—much like their slave ancestors—remain the dangerous-criminal class in the United States.

KEY EVENTS

Many key events have reflected and shaped the course of African American crime, criminal justice, and social control. Two broad classes of events, however, have played a particularly important role in the treatment of African Americans: black revolts and lynchings.

Revolts

Prior to the Civil War, many defenders of slavery, particularly in the South, argued that Africans needed the guidance of white masters and mistresses. The accursed children of Ham were biologically, psychologically, socially, culturally, and spiritually inferior. Indeed, it would be immoral to leave black Africans to their own vices on the Dark Continent. White masters provided slaves with food, clothes, shelter, and Christian moral instruction. Quite simply, slaves were happy to live in captivity.

Black revolts provide clear and convincing evidence that slaves were not, in fact, content to live in bondage. Herbert Aptheker's classic study of slave revolts— *American Negro Slave Revolts*—documents 250 cases of rebellion in the United States.[1] In fact, many slave masters lived in a state of abject terror. Laws and criminal justice systems in colonial and nineteenth-century slave societies were, in large part, structured to detect and deal with black rebels, and the penalties were swift and severe.

The 1741 "great negro plot" in New York City, as one example, resulted in a bloody state response. One hundred and seventy people were put on trial, which was largely devoid of accepted colonial legal procedures. Seventy blacks and 7 whites were banished from British North America, 16 blacks and 4 whites were hanged, and 13 blacks were burned at the stake. Revolts led by Gabriel Prosser in Virginia in 1800, Denmark Vesey in South Carolina in 1822, and Nat Turner in Virginia in 1831 were all thwarted, largely due to black spies. Prosser, Vesey, Turner, and dozens of their black coconspirators were put to death. As in New York City, no efforts were spared in crushing black rebels.

Revolts did not, however, affect only white masters and slave rebels. Whites who did not own slaves also lived in fear, knowing that black revolutionaries would not restrict killing to their masters. Moreover, slave revolts—rumored or real—always had harsh consequences for free blacks and slaves. Masters, slave patrols, sheriffs, and militias invariably launched so-called rebel sweeps to uncover weapons and black revolutionaries. Black revolts also provided abolitionists with a valuable propaganda tool: If slaves were happy living in captivity, why were they revolting?

REVOLTS, RIOTS, AND REBELLIONS

Race riots—much like revolts—were also products of deeply embedded racial friction; however, the aims, structure, and dynamics of race riots varied over time. Eighteenth-, nineteenth-, and early-twentieth-century riots were, almost without exception, started by whites and aimed at blacks. The response of local, state, and federal law enforcement officials was, at best, unpredictable, and these riots—sometimes called clearances, which were aimed at driving all blacks out of an area—often resulted in wholesale and indiscriminate mayhem and murder. Twentieth-century riots were much more balanced affairs. Increasingly, blacks defended themselves against white attacks, and they sometimes initiated riots aimed at white property and symbols of power.

The causes and dynamics of the infamous New York City Draft Riot, which occurred over a five-day period in July 1863, reflect this historical pattern. The passage of a new draft law, which allowed the rich to hire a substitute to fight in the Civil War for $300, as well as growing competition over jobs between lower-class white workers (particularly the Irish) and blacks, sparked the riot. Roving mobs of hundreds, if not thousands, of hostile whites indiscriminately attacked and murdered blacks, shooting, stabbing, beating, and hanging them. Blacks cowered in terror, and thousands abandoned their homes and fled the city. New York City police offered a mixed response, with some officers supporting the rioters. The riot was finally put down by federal troops returning from the battle of Gettysburg.

Early-twentieth-century riots in Atlanta (1906), Springfield, Illinois (1908), East St. Louis (1917), and Chicago (1919) were also initiated by whites and aimed at blacks, and the response of police and other criminal justice officials was, once again, mixed. However, race riots in the second half of the twentieth century were often initiated by blacks and aimed at white institutions and symbols of power. The riots or rebellions of the 1960s—which occurred in New York City, Chicago, Los Angeles, Detroit, Newark, and dozens of other cities across the country—received widespread media coverage. Television coverage of black rioters burning buildings, looting stores, and battling police left little doubt that racial tensions and hostility were, indeed, still serious social concerns.

Lynchings

The liberation of millions of slaves following the Civil War created a panic in the South. Conservative white Southerners could not rely upon Northern carpetbagger governments to prevent crime and maintain order. A new type of informal social control was employed: lynching.

The historical record is far from complete, but more than 5,000 cases of lynching have been documented, with most occurring in the South between 1880 and 1920. Black men, women, and children were hung, shot, stabbed, burned, dismembered, and put on display—sometimes in public places, like courthouses—in an effort to instill terror and remind blacks of their so-called proper place in the U.S. economic, political, social, cultural, and legal order. The rape, or alleged rape, of a white woman was one of the primary rationales for lynching, but thousands of blacks were lynched for other so-called offenses, such as stealing a chicken, uttering an insulting remark, making a sarcastic grin, calling to a white girl, talking big, failing to yield the sidewalk, failing to remove a hat, and refusing to remove a military uniform.

"Nigger hunts" and "coon barbecues" were, by design, savage affairs, often witnessed by thousands of spectators. In 1918, Mary Turner, who was eight months pregnant, was hung for threatening to press charges against mob members who lynched her husband. Before she died, her baby was cut from her stomach and stomped to death. A Texas jury convicted Jesse Washington of raping a white woman after four minutes of deliberation. The mob did not wait for sentencing. Washington was dragged from the courtroom, kicked, stabbed, and pummeled with rocks and shovels. At the execution site, he was suspended from a tree limb and doused with oil. His fingers, toes, ears, and penis were cut off. Then he was burned alive. His body was dragged through town by a man on horseback. The lynching of Will Porter in Livermore, Tennessee, in 1911 for shooting a white man was particularly bizarre. The mob took him to a theater, tied him to a chair on the stage, and sold tickets. Those who purchased orchestra tickets got six shots at Porter, balcony seats only one.

Blacks knew that they could not count on government officials to protect them from lynch mobs. Some law enforcement officers showed extraordinary courage in defending their charges. Several were killed or severely injured in the course of doing their job. The historical record indicates, however, that other law enforcement officers willingly handed alleged black criminals over to mobs and, in some cases, coordinated extralegal executions. Lynch-mob members did not wear masks, and photographs were often taken of the lynched as a trophy to the perpetrator. However, police investigations invariably reported that victims were killed by persons unknown or, in extreme cases, committed suicide. A number of Southern governors, senators, and congressmen openly advocated lynching, particularly for the crime of violating a white woman, and bragged about their participation in lynching mobs.

Lynching was enormously successful. Well into the twentieth century, African Americans lived in fear knowing that they could be murdered for any reason at any time. Walter White and Thurgood Marshall were both, on several occasions, nearly lynched. If the head of the National Association for the Advancement of Colored People (NAACP) and the nation's first African American Supreme Court justice came close to being murdered, who could be safe from the fury of the white mob?

IMPORTANT PERSONS AND LEGAL DECISIONS

Frederick Douglass (1817–95), an escaped slave from Maryland, was the foremost intellectual leader and spokesman for African Americans during the nineteenth century. Douglass was a powerful abolitionist-movement lecturer and achieved national and international fame with the publication of his autobiography, *Narrative of the Life of Frederick Douglass: An American Slave* (1845). This book—along with two other extended autobiographies and his work as editor of black newspapers (*North Star* and *Frederick Douglass' Paper*)—provided him with a forum to attack slavery and call for basic civil liberties for African Americans.

Douglass's pre–Civil War speeches and writings examined a variety of topics: for example, the kidnapping of blacks from Africa, the horrors of the African passage, the hypocrisy of Christian slave masters, the immorality of breaking up black families, and the failures of the U.S. Constitution and Bill of Rights. Douglass served as an advisor to President Abraham Lincoln and played an instrumental role in the formation of black military units during the Civil War. After the Civil War, Douglass worked for broader political, economic, and legal rights, including the enforcement of voting rights laws and an end to Jim Crow laws and lynching. Douglass's work as an abolitionist, orator, writer, newspaper editor, political activist, and statesman provided nineteenth-century African Americans with an articulate voice: the herald for freedom and justice.

Sojourner Truth (1797–1883), an escaped slave from New York, and Harriet Tubman (1820–1913), an escaped slave from Maryland, also made important contributions to the battle for justice. Truth, who was illiterate, made her impact as a charismatic speaker. She moved audiences with calls for an end to slavery and, in particular, distinguished herself from Douglass by calling for women's political and legal rights. Tubman, however, was the most courageous black civil rights leader. After escaping in 1849, she made numerous trips back into the South (between seventeen and twenty, depending upon the source)—knowing that she faced certain execution—and led several hundred slaves to freedom. Harriet Tubman, the legendary symbol of black resistance, was hailed as the Black Moses.

The late-nineteenth- and early-twentieth-century black civil rights movement was dominated by two leaders who were, in fact, mortal enemies: Booker T. Washington (1856–1915) and W.E.B. Du Bois (1868–1963). Washington was, without question, the most powerful, controversial, complex, and divisive black leader. Washington was an educator who achieved national fame—especially among whites—by calling on blacks to accept gradual progress toward civil rights and focus on agricultural endeavors and vocational occupations. Du Bois, a brilliant scholar who was Harvard University's first black graduate, ridiculed Washington, called for immediate rights, and urged blacks to seek higher education. Washington used millions of dollars in contributions from white benefactors to build the Tuskegee Machine. Washington's machine smeared, blacklisted, and spied on Du Bois and other black leaders who opposed his philosophy. While Washington was destroying his opposition, however, he was secretly financing many of their causes, including legal challenges against Jim Crow. Ultimately, Du Bois prevailed. After a lifetime of extraordinary achievement, including playing an instrumental role in the founding of the NAACP, however, he became thoroughly disenchanted, renounced his United States citizenship, and moved to Ghana, where he died in 1963.

Thurgood Marshall (1908–93) was the most important champion for black legal justice. Marshall became intimately familiar with racial repression and Jim Crow laws while growing up in Baltimore, Maryland. After graduating from Howard Law School, he became chief legal counsel to the NAACP. Marshall coordinated the NAACP's legal assault on *Plessy v. Ferguson* and Jim Crow laws and actually presented oral arguments in the landmark *Brown v. Board of Education* (1954) case before the United States Supreme Court. Marshall went on to become the nation's first African American solicitor general, attorney general, and United States Supreme Court justice. He continued to serve as the voice of the poor and powerless, denouncing institutional racism from his seat on the Supreme Court, until declining health forced him to resign in 1991.

Martin Luther King Jr. (1927–1968) has generally been recognized as the father of the modern civil rights movement. King played an instrumental role in the founding of a number of leading civil rights organizations in the 1950s and 1960s. Adopting a Christian-Gandhian model, he coordinated marches and protests and urged his followers to use passive resistance—not violence and riots—to rally world opinion and force an end to racial discrimination. Television coverage of the civil rights movement's most prominent leader and his followers being arrested and handcuffed by police on numerous occasions attracted attention to his cause and shamed the nation. King's brilliant "I have a dream" speech, delivered at the March on Washington rally in 1963, has been widely hailed as one of the most important moments in the history of the civil rights movement. King's assassination in Memphis, Tennessee, in 1968 shook the nation, delivering a clear message: Modern white supremacists, much like lynchers of the past, were willing to kill to keep African Americans in their so-called proper place.

Landmark legal decisions also provide important insights into African American's ongoing battle for political, economic, social, and legal justice. Key nineteenth-century decisions leave little doubt that United States Supreme Court justices, much like the rest of the country, were torn over the issue of racial equality; however, they opted for repression. In the 1856 Dred Scott decision, the Court ruled that slaves who traveled to free states could not sue for freedom because they were chattel and had no legal standing. Chief Justice Roger Taney explained that slaves were "a subordinate and inferior class of beings, who had been subjugated by the dominant race, and, whether emancipated or not, yet remained subject to their authority, and had no rights or privileges but such as those who held the power and the Government might choose to grant them." In *United States v. Cruikshank* (1875), the Court issued a ruling that had the effect of limiting the federal government's power to intervene in cases of black voter disenfranchisement and lynching. In *Plessy v. Ferguson* (1896), the Court legalized the so-called separate but equal doctrine, making blacks inferior citizens well into the 1960s.

Since the late 1960s, the United States Supreme Court has, without question, played an instrumental role in dismantling overt legal repression. The Court has, however, demonstrated ambivalence on a number of important issues, including the death penalty. In the 1972 *Furman v. Georgia* decision, the Court ruled that the death penalty was being applied in an arbitrary, capricious, and racist manner and was, as a result, cruel and unusual punishment. In the 1976 *Gregg v. Georgia* decision, the Court reinstated the death penalty, permitting two-stage death penalty proceedings. *McCleskey v. Kemp* (1987), however, reflected the Court's legal and moral ambivalence. The Court conceded, after examining empirical evidence, that Georgia's court system was, indeed, racist. They ruled against Warren McCleskey, however, who was subsequently executed, on the grounds that the statistical evidence did not prove discrimination in this specific case. In future cases, the Court shifted the burden of proof in death penalty cases back to the defendant: black defendants would have to prove discrimination in their particular case—to be sure, a costly, difficult, and unlikely challenge.

FUTURE PROSPECTS

The history of African American crime, criminal justice, and social control is, indeed, troubling. From colonial times into the 1950s, blacks were subjected to overt and crass political, economic, social, cultural, and legal oppression. The U.S. Constitution and Bill of Rights—along with noble claims of freedom, equality, and justice—clearly did not apply to black Americans.

Much progress has been made. The separate but equal doctrine has been dismantled. Blacks are no longer riding in the back of trains and buses, attending legally segregated schools, and drinking out of colored-only water fountains. African Americans are not excluded from law enforcement positions or other government jobs nor denied admission into colleges and law schools. They have been afforded, at least on paper, all of the legal rights accorded whites. A trip to almost any court reveals black judges, defense attorneys, prosecutors, and probation officers. African Americans are in charge of police departments in many of the largest U.S. cities, and black wardens can be found at the head of local, state, and federal correctional institutions across the country.

For conservatives, this progress provides clear and convincing evidence that the American dream has finally been fulfilled. Blacks have overcome the discrimination of the past and are now fully accepted citizens, enjoying the full protection of the state. But liberals remain unconvinced. African Americans, who have experienced generations of systematic repression, are particularly skeptical. The remnants of racism—particularly the explosion in black incarceration and continued disproportionate execution of poor black offenders—raise serious questions about the hidden dimension of race control, resurrecting the specter of the past. History matters. The color of justice in the United States remains, then, a matter of personal perception—a battleground for future generations.

See Also: Driving while Black; Equal Justice and Human Rights; Police-Minority Relations; Police Use of Force.

Endnote

1. Apthecker's definition includes a number of elements to be counted as rebellion: The act must have included at least ten slaves; freedom was the primary aim; and contemporary accounts labeled it as an insurrection, revolt, or rebellion (162). A modified version—including acts containing five rebels—would result in many more revolts.

Further Reading: Apthecker, Herbert, *American Slave Revolts* (New York: International, 1993; originally published 1943); Barak, Gregg, Paul Leighton, and Jeanne Flavin, *Class, Race, Gender, and Crime: The Social Realities of Justice in America* (Lanham, MD: Rowman and Littlefield, 2007); Friedman, Lawrence, *Crime and Punishment in American History* (New York: Basic Books, 1993); Kennedy, Randall, *Race, Crime and the Law* (New York: Pantheon, 1997); Miller, Jerome G., *Search and Destroy: African-American Males in the Criminal Justice System* (New York: Cambridge University Press, 1996); Tonry, Michael, *Malign Neglect: Race, Crime, and Punishment in America* (New York: Oxford University Press, 1995); Walker, Samuel, Cassia Spohn, and Miriam DeLone, *The Color of Justice: Race, Ethnicity and Crime in America* (Belmont, CA: Wadsworth, 1996).

Alexander W. Pisciotta

ALTERNATIVE RESPONSES TO CRIME BY SOCIETY

INTRODUCTION

The general public, not to mention law and policy makers, seems to believe that, aside from the death penalty, incarceration is the most severe form of punishment the criminal justice system can impose. In fact, the notion of a continuum of criminal justice sanctions typically places probation on the low end and imprisonment on the high end, with a variety of alternative sanctions falling somewhere in the middle.[1] Unfortunately, the development of a continuum of alternative responses in crime control and the ranking of these alternatives have been developed by legislators and policy makers who had no reliable means of rating the severity of the sanctions imposed, had little or no access to experiential data, and depended primarily on individuals with no firsthand knowledge of the actual impact of the alternatives.[2] As such, the common belief that penal-correctional sanctions must be bound by probation on the one end and imprisonment on the other may not only be misleading in many contexts, but it also represents the fundamental controversy underlying the development of alternative responses to crime, namely, that there is anything but a consensus on what constitutes an alternative and on what the alternative is alternative to.

In other words, politicians have their notions of severity and leniency as do criminals, psychologists, penologists, criminologists, and risk-management specialists. There is no agreement between these persons or more generally between those engaged in law enforcement, prosecution, adjudication, and punishment/corrections about which particular alternatives should be used in response to a myriad of offenses. At the same time, over the years, there have been tangible changes in ideologies, theories, and practices associated with society's different responses to crime. As a result, alternatives, or, perhaps more accurately, new emphases—some innovative and others not—emerge and develop and become mainstream, and then other alternatives to those emerge and develop.

BACKGROUND

Traditionally, criminal sanctions had four goals: retribution/punishment,[3] rehabilitation,[4] incapacitation,[5] and deterrence.[6] The concept of restoration[7] was added later on as a fifth goal. The concept of alternatives was developed in an attempt to modify and/or expand the way in which society sanctions criminal acts. Over time, the goals of these sanctions have evolved, which has led to a necessary change in the sanctions themselves.

For example, correctional leaders began to embrace the idea of combining a psychology about personality and human development to probation in the 1940s. They began to emphasize a medical model for probation, and rehabilitation (as opposed to punishment) became the overriding goal. This medical model was popular until the 1960s, when it was replaced by the reintegration model. The main thrust of the reintegration model was to reduce the rate of recidivism by making the prisoner's return to the community easier. The reintegration model assumed that crime was a direct result of poverty, racism, unemployment, unequal opportunities, and other social factors.

The concept of probation underwent yet another change in the late 1970s and remains that way today. The goals of rehabilitation and reintegration have been replaced by what is referred to as *risk management*.[8] The risk-management approach attempts to minimize the probability that any given offender will commit new offenses by applying different degrees of control over the probationer's activity based on the probationer's assessed degree of risk. In essence, the risk-management approach is a combination of the just deserts model[9] of criminal sanction and the idea that the community must be safe.

In the 1960s and early 1970s, legislation was also passed to establish financial and programmatic incentives for community corrections.[10] The incentives were expected to embrace a wide range of alternatives to incarcerations from which judges and other officials could choose. The main goal was to alleviate prison overcrowding and support prisoner reintegration and reduce rates of recidivism.[11]

Today, despite research findings that demonstrate that offenders perceive the pains of punishment in one way, policy makers generally categorize alternatives into two categories: (1) low-control alternatives for the less severe crimes or low-risk offenders (e.g., fines or restitution, community service, drug/alcohol treatment, probation, intensive supervision probation, and home confinement), or (2) high-control alternatives for the more serious crimes or high-risk offenders (e.g., boot camp, shock incarceration, and community supervision). Simple probation lies on one end of the continuum (less severe punishment or low-control alternatives) and traditional incarceration lies at the other end of the continuum (most severe punishment) (see fig. A.1).

High-control alternatives, although not as severe as incarceration, are seen as the last option before incarceration. On the other hand, studies show that offenders ranked seven alternative sanctions more severely than prison: (1) boot camp, (2) jail, (3) day reporting, (4) intermittent incarceration, (5) halfway house, (6) intensive supervision probation, (7) electronic monitoring. They viewed prison as more punitive only compared to community service and regular probation.[12] Regardless of the rank in the punishment continuum, the goal of these alternatives is to successfully reintegrate offenders into the community. These alternatives move away from the medical model and, in fact, suggest that the use of prisons should eventually be avoided altogether. In this approach, probation

Figure 1.
Probation
∇
Intensive Supervision Probation
∇
Restitutions & Fine
∇
Community Service
∇
Substance Abuse Treatment
∇
Day Reporting
∇
House Arrest & Electronic Monitoring
∇
Halfway House
∇
Boot Camp
∇
Prisons and Jails

Figure A.1   Sentencing alternatives.

would be the sentence of choice for nonviolent offenders to allow them to participate in vocational and educational programs and ultimately make the adjustment to the community easier.

LEGAL DEVELOPMENTS

Approximately two-thirds of adults under the supervision of the criminal justice system live in the general community while on either parole or probation. As discussed throughout this entry, probation is a type of community sentence in which the individual is sentenced to some form of community supervision either as punishment for a crime or as a part of a sentence (usually served after spending a portion of the sentence in prison). Notwithstanding the fact that there is no right to parole and despite the fact that these individuals are still under the legal control of the correctional system, they, just as those incarcerated, still have rights. As such, while in the community, probationers and parolees enjoy conditional liberty that is dependent on and regulated by very specific restrictions. These restrictions, by their very nature, may violate the constitutional rights of the probationer/parolee. For example, these individuals are denied the right of free association with prior crime partners or victims. However, because of cases such as *Griffin v. Wisconsin* (1987),[13] parolees are now able to give public speeches and receive publications.

Another legal question arises with respect to probationers and parolees who violate the terms of their probation or parole. The rule of thumb in such cases is that the offender may be sent to prison. Additionally, if the offender commits another crime, their probation or parole will likely be revoked. For minor violations (e.g., missing an AA meeting), the probation/parole officer has the discretion as to how severe the penalty should be. Having said that, the Supreme Court has had to address the issue of due process when revocation is an option.

In the case of *Mempa v. Rhay* (1967),[14] the U.S. Supreme Court determined that a probationer has the right to be represented by counsel in a revocation or sentencing hearing before a deferred prison sentence could be imposed. Additionally, in *Morrissey v. Brewer* (1972),[15] the Court ruled that parolees faced with the possibility of the revocation of parole must be afforded prompt due process before an impartial hearing officer.

CONTROVERSIAL ASPECTS WITHIN THE ALTERNATIVES

In evaluating the benefits of alternatives, some researchers have noted that "An expanded range of sentencing options gives judges greater latitude to exercise discretion in selecting punishments that more closely fit the circumstances of the crime and the offender."[16] They argued that this type of scheme, if administered effectively, would free up prison cells for violent offenders, whereas less restrictive alternatives would be used to punish nonviolent offenders.[17] However, there is a growing body of research that suggests that many offenders actually have a negative perception of alternative sanctions.[18] In fact, some studies suggest that a significant number of offenders actually believe that serving time in prison is easier than many alternatives, and, depending on the alternative, up to one-third of offenders refused to participate even if it meant a shorter prison stay.[19] Some of the reasons given for choosing imprisonment over alternatives include: (1) concerns about abuse of power and antagonism by the personnel who run the program, and (2) the likelihood that the program would fail and revocation to prison after investing time and effort in the program.

Pretrial Diversion

Pretrial diversion is the first and perhaps most important alternative within the criminal justice system. Pretrial diversion allows the defendant to agree to conditions set forth by the prosecutor (e.g., counseling or drug rehabilitation) in exchange for the withdrawal of charges. This concept began because of a belief that the formal processing of people through the criminal justice system was not always the best course of action.[20] There are three main reasons given for the use of pretrial diversion: (1) many of the crimes committed were caused by offenders with special circumstances, such as vagrancy, alcoholism, emotional distress, so forth, examples of which cannot be managed effectively within the criminal justice system; (2) formal criminal justice labeling often has a stigma attached to it that actually hurts or cripples attempts at rehabilitation and in the long run can promote an unnecessarily harsh penalty for a relatively minor offense; and (3) the cost of diversion is cheaper than the cost of criminal justice processing.

The concept of diversion is very controversial because some argue that it allows offenders to get off easy. Yet there are those who argue that the rationale for diversion is sound because incarceration, in effect, does nothing to change the offender's disadvantaged status and the stigma of conviction will ultimately decrease the offender's chances of becoming a productive citizen. Nonetheless, support for diversion seems to wax and wane depending on whether society supports rehabilitation of offenders or incarceration of offenders.

Despite mixed success, critics view pretrial diversion programs negatively as it is applied in expanding the state's authority, or widening the net of social control.

In other words, the reach of this alternative correctional program targets or sanctions individuals charged with less serious offenses more seriously than originally intended.

Intensive Supervision Probation

According to the Bureau of Justice Statistics (BJS) *1997 Special Report* (see fig. A.2),[21] approximately 10 percent of all probationers and parolees who participate in alternative sanction programs are under intensive supervision probation. Intensive supervision probation was designed in the 1980s in response to the issue of prison overcrowding. Specifically geared research was conducted to identify a solution, and it was determined that there were a small number of inmates who could, under the right circumstances, be released into the community with minimal risk to the public.[22] Two hundred inmates were initially selected, but over time the number has risen to well over a thousand participants. Over a four-month period, the inmate must file an application, which must be approved by a three-person screening panel. If approved, a resentence hearing must be held before three judges. If the judges approve the application, the inmate will begin a 90-day trial period in intensive supervision probation. Despite some shortcomings, this program has been extremely helpful in relieving prison overcrowding.

Yet 10 years after its inception, research showed that nearly one-third of nonviolent offenders who were given the option to participate in intensive supervision probation chose prison instead.[23] They felt that the combination of having to work every day, having to submit to random drug tests, and having their privacy invaded was more punitive that serving a prison term. A significant number of them also indicated that intensive supervision probation had so many conditions attached to it that there was a high probability of violating a condition and being revoked back to prison. These offenders view intensive supervision probation as more punitive than imprisonment and equated one year in prison to five years of intensive supervision probation.

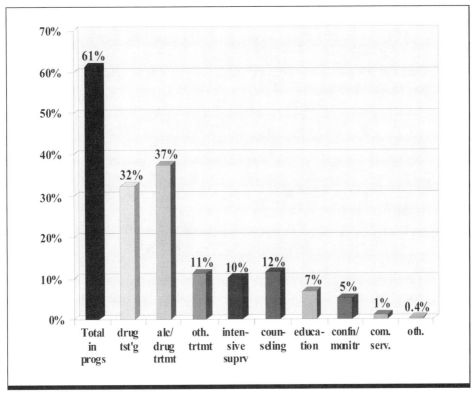

Figure A.2   Percentage breakdowns of program interventions.

Substance Abuse Treatment/Intensive Parole Drug Program (IPDP)

As the title indicates, the Intensive Parole Drug Program (IPDP) is an intensive supervision program for parolees with a history of substance abuse (drugs and alcohol). This program was implemented in certain states as a part of the Department of Corrections' Stop the Revolving Door initiative, which has an antirecidivism focus. The program focuses on relapse prevention, intervention strategies, and counseling referrals. Sanctions may include community-based treatment, residential placement, or return to custody with institutional program treatment. Any parolee[24] identified as having a substance abuse problem can be referred. Candidates come from a range of programs—from therapeutic community programs to mutual agreement programs or from halfway houses. IPDP is a six-month-minimum program with participants having the option to stay an additional three months. The issue with these types of programs is that although some offenders welcome the opportunity for treatment, they feel that the intrusive nature of the program itself outweighs any possible benefit. As is the case in other programs, offenders who are offered the opportunity to participate frequently decline and choose to serve time instead.

Electronic Monitoring and House Arrest

Electronic monitoring and house arrest are typically used together in conjunction with intensive supervision. House arrest restricts the offender to home except when at school, work, or court-assigned treatment, and electronic monitoring becomes the technological means of securing compliance. Electronic monitoring has been described as the most important penal invention of the 1980s.[25] It tries to incorporate some of the goals of criminal justice sanctions, yet it fits into a category all its own. Electronic monitoring is a "supervision tool that provides information about the offender's presence at, or absence from, his or her residence or other location."[26] Although the system does not track offenders' whereabouts like a homing device, it is able to determine if offenders are at home when they should be.

Harvard psychologist Robert Schwitzgebel[27] developed the first electronic monitoring device in the mid-1960s. He felt that his invention could provide a humane and inexpensive alternative to custody for many people involved in the justice process. The goal of an electronic monitoring system is to provide community supervision staff with an additional tool to intensely supervise offenders who are not incarcerated. This form of supervision does not support any form of treatment or assistance, but it is more cost efficient than incarceration, which provides a direct contrast and alternative to incapacitation or imprisonment. Critics of electronic monitoring argue that the concept is self-serving for the manufacturers of the house-arrest equipment. The also argue that there are many rehabilitative-type services and products available but point out that these services are labor intensive and expensive and would no doubt eat into the corporation's profits.

Boot Camp and Shock Incarceration

Boot camps combine basic elements of both rehabilitation and retribution. They provide rigorous physical activity that many believe to be more beneficial than punitive alternatives. "Boot camps are highly popular residential alternatives (intermediate sanctions) typically used for young offenders which provide for very structured and military-like activities such as strict discipline, physical training and labor, drill, and a regimented schedule of daily activities."[28] A sentence of boot camp, also known as shock incarceration, is usually for a relatively short time, approximately three to six months.

The first boot camp programs were implemented in Georgia and Oklahoma in 1983 to help relieve prison and jail crowding. They were first developed in the adult criminal justice system and then expanded to the juvenile justice system.[29] Boot camps were created for several reasons. As mentioned previously, one of the main goals of alternatives is to alleviate the overcrowding of prisons. That is, "certain offenders who would normally be sentenced to a prison term (e.g., two to four years) are diverted to a shorter, yet equally punitive and effective, boot camp sentence (e.g., 90 to 180 days)."[30]

Deterrence (both specific and general) is inherent in the concept of shock incarceration. The hope is that the shock of incarceration will serve both as a deterrent specific to the criminal and the crime as well as a general deterrent to would-be criminals in the immediate community. Boot camp is considered one of the most demanding alternatives, and the findings on its effectiveness as a deterrent to offenders committing further crimes is mixed at best. Moreover, offenders who are offered the opportunity to serve a sentence in boot camp instead of in prison, more often than not, opt to serve prison time because boot camp is seen as being more intrusive than prison.

Day Reporting Centers (DRCs)

The day reporting centers (DRCs) are community-based facilities that provide a strict regimen of supervision and programming for ex-offenders. The 1980s began the era of the use of DRCs in the United States, but this concept actually originated in England as a way to reduce the prison population. The goal of DRCs is to combine high levels of control over offenders so as to meet public safety needs while providing intensive services to address the rehabilitative needs of the offender. Day reporting is an alternative that reduces the cost of jails completely because the offender does not require housing or confinement.

The rationale behind the implementation of this type of alternative is that sometimes the crime committed does not justify a jail sentence. In fact, it has been argued that some offenders are, by nature, more responsive to less severe punishment and that they may actually be harmed, more than their crime may merit, by serving a jail term. The use of DRCs would allow offenders to report to a location in a manner similar to reporting to a probation officer. Offenders in this program would be required to account for their activities during the day, including job-searching activities for those participants who are unemployed. Offenders would also be subjected to daily drug and alcohol testing, as would regular offenders. Failure of either of these mandatory tests would result in disqualification from the program.

Day reporting incorporates three of the sanctions that were discussed earlier, and it is in keeping with these that the goals of this type of alternative are formed. As such, the objectives of DRCs are threefold: (1) punishment through restricting clients' activity and requiring community service; (2) incapacitation through intensive supervision, firm enforcement of attendance agreements, and strict adherence to program structure; and (3) rehabilitation through services aimed at "enabling the unable by developing social and survival skills, remedying deficiencies in education, and increasing employability."[31]

Daily programming includes, but is not limited to, educational/vocational training, drug/alcohol treatment, anger management, and conflict resolution. Many of the alternatives are implemented for the purpose of combating the overcrowding and enormous cost of imprisonment. In order to reduce the cost of prisons, the criminal justice system "requires that sanctions be tailored as carefully as possible to ensure that they provide only the supervision or services necessary to achieve their intended goal(s)."[32] Alternatives, therefore, present more effective methods of reducing society's total spending on the correctional system in general and the prison population specifically.

The work crew is another option that allows qualifying offenders to work off a portion of their sentence and/or their fine by working on public work projects selected and supervised by participating jurisdictions.[33] In the end, the amount of work that the offender does for the time period is assessed and deducted from the total sum of time he or she would have spent incarcerated. It is important to note that the difference between the work crew just discussed and work release is that the latter is an option some jurisdictions use to allow individuals to continue to work at their existing jobs according to their established schedule, but they must reside at the jail overnight.[34] This alternative reduces the cost to correctional institutions for daily services, however, and those work release programs that do not have work release centers still require jails to cover the cost of night services.

Residential Community Correctional Facilities (Halfway Houses)

Halfway houses are residential facilities designed to (1) house adult offenders (with at least 70 percent of its residents placed by federal, state, or local authorities), (2) operate independently of the other corrections institution, and (3) permit clients to leave the premises during the day for work, education, or community programs. Additionally, halfway houses are critical in rehabilitating ex-offenders. In addition to providing high levels of surveillance and treatment, the 24-hour residency makes these facilities the community sanction that is closest to the total institutional setting of a prison or jail (halfway between prison and freedom) because, despite the setting, the movements, behavior, and mood of the residents can be continuously monitored.

Halfway houses also provide a safe haven for offenders who have been confined for long periods of time, allowing a smooth transition back into the community. Some offenders who live in halfway houses can actually work and pay rent. They are allowed to leave only to report to jobs, and they must return promptly at the end of the workday. In essence, halfway-house residents have more freedom and responsibility than people in prison but less freedom than ordinary citizens.

A halfway house is a "rehabilitation center where people who have left an institution, such as a hospital or prison, are helped to readjust to the outside world."[35]

Recidivism was a major concern for the criminal justice system, and this form of alternative was supported as a way to combat it. Another purpose of halfway houses is to monitor those offenders just leaving prison to make sure that they are ready to function in society again. It was implemented to also provide offenders the opportunity to gradually recondition themselves to the world. The offender is leaving a structured environment in prison, and the halfway house provides a transitioning period for the offender to enter a free public. Thus, halfway-house residents have greater freedom and responsibility than people in prison, but less freedom than ordinary citizens.[36] Due to the existence of halfway houses in the community, some safety concerns exist. Such concerns are limited when compared to if the offender were released from prison directly into society without any formal supervision.

Another benefit of halfway houses is that an offender must perform community service in the form of manual labor for the government or private, nonprofit organizations without receiving any payment. The courts, on a discretionary basis, give the number of community service hours to the offender.

Fines

Fines are typically used in conjunction with other sanctions such as probation and incarceration (a typical sentence would be two years' probation and a $500 fine). The biggest complaint about fines as a sanction is the difficulty of collection. A significant number of offenders are poor and simply cannot afford it. On the other hand, judges also complain that well-to-do offenders will be in a better position to meet the financial penalty and less likely to learn the lesson the penalty was intended to teach.

As a result, several states, including Arizona, Connecticut, Iowa, New York, and Washington, have tested an alternate concept referred to as *day fine*—developed in Sweden and Germany—which imposes a fine based on a fixed percentage of the offender's income. The day fine concept will ensure that the financial penalty imposed on the offender will have the same impact regardless of income.

Forfeiture

Forfeiture is the act of seizing personal property (e.g., boats, automobiles, or equipment used to manufacture illegal drugs), real property (e.g., houses), or other assets (e.g., bank accounts) derived from or used in the commission of illegal acts. Forfeiture can take both civil and criminal forms. Under civil law, the property can be seized without an actual finding of guilt. Under criminal law, however, forfeiture is only imposed as part of the sentence for a guilty verdict.

The practice of forfeiture was not actually used after the American Revolution but became more popular with the 1970 passage of the Racketeer Influence and Corrupt Organizations (RICO) Act and the Continuing Criminal Enterprise (CCE) Act. As its popularity grew in usage, congressional amendments were made to streamline implementation in 1984 and 1986.[37]

Community Service and Restitution

The concepts of community service and restitution are relatively new alternatives. "Community service is a compulsory, free, or donated labor performed by an offender as punishment for a crime."[38] "Community service can be arranged for individuals on a case by case basis or organized by correctional agencies as programs."[39] Community service provides a chance for offenders to give back to the community for the wrong that they did to society.

The first documented community service program in the United States was in Alameda County, California, in 1966.[40] Community service sentencing first began in response to indigent women having to go to jail because they could not afford traffic and parking fines. "To avoid the financial costs of incarceration and the individual cost to the offenders [who were often women with families], physical work in the community without compensation was assigned instead."[41] This alternative had such outstanding results that it spread nationwide into the 1970s. It was advocated by the idea of "symbolic restitution," whereby offenders symbolically repay society for the harm they caused through good deeds in the form of free labors benefiting the community.[42]

Restitution is often viewed as financial compensation but can also take the form of community service hours at a community project. Both community service and restitution operate under the assumption that the offender's personal or financial contribution to the victim or to the community will compensate for any loss caused by the offender's illegal behavior.

An offender is given community service usually in conjunction with restitution. "Restitution is the payment by the offender of the costs of the victim's losses or injuries and/or damages to the victim."[43] Restitution provides either direct compensation to the victim by the offender, usually with money although sometimes with services (victim restitution), and unpaid compensation given not to the victim but to the larger community (community service). Restitution, as an alternative, is similar to restoration in that both concepts seek to place the victim and/or the community back into the position they were in (whether financial or emotional) before the crime was committed.

Victim restitution programs were adapted in the United States in 1972 with the Minnesota restitution program. It "gave prisoners convicted of property offenses the opportunity to shorten their jail stay, or avoid it altogether, if they went to work and turned over part of their pay as restitution to their victims."[44]

FUTURE PROSPECTS

According to policy makers, the concept of alternatives to criminal justice is different from the traditional criminal justice sanctions in four significant ways: (1) It is restorative as opposed to retributive, (2) it uses problem-solving rather than adversarial strategies, (3) the community jurisdiction takes on a more important role than the legal jurisdiction, and (4) the ultimate goal is not to punish the offender but to improve the community through collaborative problem solving. Critics and offenders argue, on the other hand, that the alternatives and community corrections strategies are becoming increasingly punitive despite its emphasis on rehabilitation.

The bottom line is that the offenders are the ones who must evaluate the severity and impact of alternative sanctions. If offenders perceive the alternatives as being too severe, they will choose prison, and the entire concept will serve no purpose. Even offenders receiving identical punishments will react differently to perceived degrees of intrusiveness; some may perceive the punishment as more severe than others, depending on age, race, sex, and prior punishment history.[45] According to this research, African American offenders, men, older offenders, unmarried offenders, offenders without children, drug offenders, and repeat offenders rated prison as less punitive than alternatives.

Hence, to ignore these research findings and to disregard the viewpoints of those directly involved—offenders, victims, and community members—is to make policies based on preconceived ideas, biases, and stereotypes.

See Also: Domestic Violence Practices; Peacemaking Criminology; Problem-Solving Courts; Restorative Justice; Social Justice.

Endnotes

1. R.D. Petersen and D.J. Palumbo, "The Social Construction of Intermediate Punishments," *Prison Journal* 77 (1997): 77–92.
2. N. Morris and M. Tonry, *Between Prison and Probation Intermediate Punishment in a Rational Sentencing System* (New York: Oxford University Press, 1990).
3. The term *retribution/punishment* also connotes the dispensing or receiving of reward or punishment according to what the individual deserves. It implies the payment of a debt to society and thus the expiration of the offense and is codified in the biblical injunction "an eye for an eye."
4. Rehabilitation was the major reason for sentencing in the mid-twentieth century. It is a utilitarian philosophy, defined as the process of restoring an individual (a convict) to a useful and constructive place in society through some form of vocational, correctional, or therapeutic retraining or through relief, financial aid, or other reconstruction measure.
5. Incapacitation refers to the deprivation of legal/constitutional freedom and the ability to perform certain civil acts. Its main purpose is to remove offenders from society.
6. Specific and general deterrence is based on a utilitarian philosophy that focuses on an understanding of human behavior. It works best when individuals believe they will get caught and punished and when their punishment is severe enough to represent a threat.
7. Restoration means "reparation," or restoring an individual or a community to a state that existed before the crime was committed.
8. Joan Petersilia, Susan Turner, James Kahan, and Joyce Peterson, *Granting Felons Probation: Public Risks and Alternatives* (Santa Monica, CA: Rand, 1985), 39, 41.
9. Just deserts is the same concept as retribution: The severity of the punishment should equal the seriousness of the crime.
10. In 1965, California passed the Probation Subsidy Act. In 1973, Minnesota passed the first comprehensive Community Corrections Act. In 1976, Colorado passed legislation patterned after Minnesota's. In 1978, Oregon passed similar legislation.
11. In 1971, the incarceration rate was 96 per 100,000. By 2003, the rate was 477 per 10,000. See T. Clear, G. Cole, and M. Reisig, *American Corrections,* 7th ed. (Belmont, CA: Wadsworth, 2006).
12. P.B. Wood and H.G. Grasmick, "Toward the Development of Punishment Equivalencies Male and Female Inmates Rate the Severity of Alternative Sanctions Compared to Prison," *Justice Quarterly* 16 (1999): 19–50.
13. *Griffin v. Wisconsin,* 483 U.S. 868 (1987).
14. *Mempa v. Rhay,* 389 U.S. 128 (1967).
15. *Morrissey v. Brewer,* 408 U.S. 471 (1972).
16. W.M. DiMascio, *Seeking Justice: Crime and Punishment in America* (New York: Edna McConnell Clark Foundation, n.d.), 32–33.
17. Prison overcrowding, the cost of prisons, and the increasing recidivism rates contributed to the creation of alternatives within the criminal justice system. (Recidivism is the recurrence of a criminal behavior by the offender. Rates of recidivism can be assessed in three ways: by the rearrested, reconviction, and reincarceration.) Prisons now account

for approximately 80 percent of every correctional dollar spent, and the nation's prisons cost $2.45 billion in 1996. Increasing rates of recidivism seem to be directly correlated to increasing rates of rearrested, reconviction, and reincarceration, which, in turn, results in the increasing need for prison space. Alternatives to the traditional types of punishment (more specifically imprisonment) within the criminal justice system were the result of a need to change this trend.

18. D. C. May, P. B. Wood, J. L. Mooney, and K. I Minor, "Predicting Offender-Generated Exchange Rates: Implications for a Theory of Sentence Severity," *Crime and Delinquency* 51 (2005): 373–99.

19. Ibid.

20. Michael Geerken and Hennessey D. Hayes, "Probation and Parole: Public Risks and the Future of Incarceration Alternatives," *Criminology* 31, no. 4 (November 1993): 549–64.

21. T. Bonczar and L. Glaze, *BJS Bulletin Probation and Parole in the United States 1998,* 9 (Washington DC: US Department of Justice, Office of Justice Programs, 1999).

22. J. Petersilia and Susan Turner, *Intensive Supervision Probation for High Risk Offenders Findings from Three California Experiments,* R-3936-NIJ/JA (Santa Monica, CA: Rand, 1990).

23. J. Petersilia, "When Probation Becomes More Dreaded than Prison," *Federal Probation* 54 (1990): 23–27.

24. Clear et al., *American Corrections.*

25. "The 2002–2003 Electronic Monitoring Survey," *Journal of Electronic Monitoring* 15, no. 1 (Winter-Spring 2002): 5.

26. State of Michigan, *Electronic Monitoring of Offenders in the Community* (Department of Corrections, 2006), http://www.michigan.gov/corrections/0,1607,7-119-1435-5032--,00.html.

27. I. M. Gomme, "From Big House to Big Brother: Confinement in the Future," in *The Canadian Criminal Justice System,* ed. N. Larsen, 489–516 (Toronto: Canadian Scholars' Press, 1995).

28. George E. Rush, *The Dictionary of Criminal Justice,* 6th ed. (New York: McGraw-Hill, 2004).

29. D. L. MacKenzie, D. B. Wilson, and S. Kider, "Effects of Correctional Boot Camps on Offending," *Annals of the American Academy of Political and Social Science* 578 (2001): 126–43.

30. P. Begin, *Boot Camps: Issues for Consideration* (Ottawa, ON: Research Branch, Library of Parliament, 1996), http://dsp-psd.communication.gc.ca/Pilot/LoPBdP/BP/bp426-e.htm.

31. Ibid.

32. Ibid., 10.

33. T. R. Clear, *Harm in American Penology* (New York: State University of New York Press, 1994).

34. D. R. Gill, *Alternatives to the Present Uses of the Jails* (Chapel Hill: Institute of Government, University of North Carolina, 1967).

35. G. Caputo, *North Texas Crime and Criminal Justice Series 4: Intermediate Sanctions in Corrections* (Denton, TX: University of North Texas Press, 2004), 72.

36. Marta Nelson, Perry Deess, and Charlotte Allen, *The First Month Out: Post-Incarceration Experiences in New York City* (New York: Vera Institute of Justice, 1999).

37. Karla R. Spaulding, "Hit Them Where It Hurts: RICO Criminal Forfeitures and White-Collar Crime," *Journal of Criminal Law and Criminology* 80 (1989): 197–98.

38. James Inciardi, Steven Martin, and Clifford Butzin, "Five-Year Outcomes of Therapeutic Community Treatment of Drug-Involved Offenders after Release from Prison," *Crime and Delinquency* 50, no. 1 (2004): 94, 102–4; Dale Parent and Liz Barnett, *Transition from Prison to Community Initiative* (Washington, DC: National Institute of Corrections, 2002), http://www.nicic.org/pubs/2002/017520.pdf.

39. Ibid.

40. Ibid.

41. Ibid.

42. Ibid.

43. Department of Health and Human Services, *Combining Substance Abuse Treatment with Intermediate Sanctions for Adults in the Criminal Justice System* (Washington, DC: GPO, 2005), 4.

44. Ibid.

45. W. Spelman, "The Severity of Intermediate Sanctions," *Journal of Research in Crime and Delinquency* 32 (1995): 107–35.

Further Reading: Allen, Harry E., ed. *Repairing Communities through Restorative Justice* (Lanham, MD: American Correctional Association, 2002); Anderson, David, *Sensible Justice: Alternative to Prison* (New York: New Press, 1998); Clear, Todd R., and David R. Karp, *The Community Justice Ideal: Promoting Safety and Achieving Justice* (Boulder, CO: Westview, 1999); Tucker, Susan, and Eric Cadora, *Ideas for an Open Society: Justice Reinvestment* (New York: Open Society Institute, 2003); Vass, Anthony A., *Alternatives to Prison: Punishment Custody and the Community* (Newbury Park, CA: Sage, 1990).

Dianne Williams and Jessica Williams

ANTITERRORISM LAWS

INTRODUCTION

Because counterterrorism runs the gamut from surveillance to detention, often it collides with democratic ideals and principles. In many liberal democracies, these two tendencies have given rise to much controversy in terms of how antiterrorism laws affect the civil liberties of citizens and aliens within a state. Because of their political consequences, these laws can be viewed from two different critical frameworks: needs of national security and protection of civil liberty. In most countries that have adopted antiterrorism laws, this tension underlies almost every analysis of antiterrorism laws. Critics of such laws say that they capitalize on the fears generated among common people by acts of terrorism. Taking undue advantage of panic, unscrupulous governments, by misusing these laws, may become authoritarian. Advocates, on the other hand, maintain that antiterrorist laws to a great extent are deemed necessary for various security measures legitimately undertaken. Generally, antiterrorism laws are stopgap measures intended to last during the continuance of a situation of emergency. In reality, however, often they linger much longer after the immediate crisis is over. An example of this is the U.S. Espionage Act of 1917, which was passed to facilitate prevention of espionage in World War I. This law was extended by the Sedition Act of 1918, which made it a crime to speak out against the government. Today, major portions of the Espionage Act are still alive in the United States, although it has been much amended and supplemented by other laws.[1] History is replete with other similar examples.

BACKGROUND

The term *antiterrorism laws* is a broad-spectrum one. It covers legislations, regulations, judicial orders and decisions, and executive orders. In countries with a federal structure such as the United States, it includes laws from various levels of government, such as federal, state, and local governments. In most countries, local legislations, ordinances, and regulations supplement federal- or national-level laws. The universe of antiterrorism laws also includes supranational laws such as international conventions and treaties. Thus, it is an umbrella term that covers different laws that broadly have any of the objectives of preventing, punishing, or fighting terrorism. These laws, despite their wide range and differing modes of operation, have various key features in common with one another. For example, the usual litany of offences these laws seek to criminalize include committing a terrorist act, being a member of a terrorist organization, providing or receiving training concerned with terrorist acts, associating with a terrorist organization, supporting or planning a terrorist act, receiving funds from, or making funds available to a terrorist organization.

Globally, international conventions can be ratified by all states. But some are regional multilateral terrorist conventions (e.g., Council of Europe Convention on the Prevention of Terrorism, 2006). Bilateral treaties are also possible. The first international treaty dealing with terrorism is the Convention for the Prevention and Punishment of Terrorism of 1937 (Geneva Convention of 1937), which defined the obligations of states in international counterterrorism (prosecution, extradition, and providing legal assistance). A number of conventions require the acts causing the harms to be independently unlawful. This unlawfulness is usually determined with reference to domestic laws of the countries involved. Most of the conventions deal with international terrorism perpetrated by individuals. Most conventions also have an intended or calculated requirement in which the acts and consequences are either intended or perhaps calculated. The recent debate in international law is sparked by the term *war on terror*. The laws of war apply to parties on an armed conflict. Does that mean that suspected terrorists could avail themselves of the protection of the Geneva Conventions? Would this not clothe them with the legitimacy accorded to lawful combatants? Arguments flow back and forth, but there is no settled proposition on this issue.

LEGAL DEVELOPMENTS

The various antiterrorist laws share the infamy of civil liberty challenges to their existence. Some of the rights they affect include (but are not limited to) privacy and informational self-determination of citizens, freedom of the person, freedom of expression, private property rights, and freedom of movement (such as through asylum or immigration). The fear generated by antiterrorism laws is that the presumption of innocence could be replaced with general suspicion, arrests and searches could happen without warrants, and much greater suspicion could fall on noncitizens than on citizens. Legal challenges occur in four areas:

1. Racial Profiling

Many think that a consequence of terrorism and antiterrorism laws is an increase in racial profiling because law enforcement officials are more likely to take into account the race of the suspect when deciding whether to investigate a suspect of terrorism. Some cite how the U.S. Supreme Court in *Korematsu v. U.S.*[2] upheld the internment of Japanese Americans after Japan's attack on Pearl Harbor in 1941 as a cautionary tale of the kind of racial profiling that antiterrorism laws can encourage. That decision legitimized U.S. citizens being held in prisoner-of-war-like camps on U.S. soil in a shameful period in U.S. history. Laws such as the Omnibus Crime Control and Safe Streets Act of 1968 facilitate police surveillance. This is the wiretapping law that permits interception of communications without prior judicial order provided there are adequate grounds for a judicial order. Although laws such as these are important tools for legitimate counterterrorism surveillance, they could also be misused in a targeted manner.

2. Surveillance and Criminal Defense

U.S. criminal defense lawyers point out that wiretapping of detainee's conversations with counsel takes place leading to a corrosion of the attorney-client privilege that is central to any defense. Concerns are voiced about whether a presumption of innocence until proved guilty exists in practice anymore. Today, criminal defense lawyers could be potentially charged with providing material support or resources to terrorists. This material support clause has been interpreted to include several activities. One of the controversial cases on this point involves an attorney (Lynne Stewart) who was found guilty in New York on five counts of defrauding the government, conspiracy, and providing support for terrorism. Her alleged support for terrorism was that she aided her client (a suspected foreign terrorist) in contacting the media in his home country (Egypt). The government placed the attorney's communications with the client under surveillance in order to support its case against her. Many perceive this to be in violation of a criminal defendant's right to counsel, a Sixth Amendment guarantee in the U.S. Constitution. It should be kept in mind, however, that in the United States courts have not consistently supported the government in terrorism cases. In the very same issue of surveillance, for example, executive agencies (such as the National Security Agency) proposed a warrantless surveillance program that a federal judge declared unconstitutional.[3]

3. Detention

Alleged secret detention hearings have raised concerns of abuse of process in many parts of the world. In the Guantanamo Bay detainment camp, suspects have limited or no access to defense counsels. Very often detainees have limited access to evidence or charges against them. Whether a detainee can file a habeas corpus petition to end his or her detention depends to a large extent on his or her status as a U.S. citizen. Citizenship plays a pivotal role, as can be gathered from recent Supreme Court cases. For example, although in *Rasul v. Bush*[4] the U.S. Supreme Court said that it could scrutinize whether foreign nationals have been rightfully imprisoned in Guantanamo, the same court in *Hamdi v. Rumsfeld*[5] made a distinction between U.S. citizens and noncitizens. The Court acknowledged that the government can detain unlawful enemy combatants but reserved the right to challenge such detentions for U.S. citizens. The Court narrowly defined who could be designated as enemy combatants and thus could be detained during an ongoing conflict. In another case on the issue of enemy combatants, a U.S. citizen, Jose Padilla, was designated an enemy combatant. Here, the Second Circuit Court of Appeals stated that the president cannot designate a U.S. citizen seized on U.S. soil as an enemy combatant without specific authorization from Congress. Later, the Supreme Court decided this case on a jurisdictional issue, asking the defendant to file it again where he was detained (in New York). Thus, citizenship is a crucial issue in detention cases. Because at present the U.S. government seeks to hold detainees for the duration of the conflict (the war on terror), such detention times could be very long indeed.

THE U.S. SUPREME COURT ON RIGHTS OF TERRORISM SUSPECTS
Hamdi v. Rumsfeld, 542 U.S. 507 (2004)

Justice Sandra Day O'Connor announced the judgment of the Court and delivered an opinion, in which the chief justice, Justice Kennedy, and Justice Breyer join.

At this difficult time in our Nation's history, we are called upon to consider the legality of the Government's detention of a United States citizen on United States soil as an "enemy combatant" and to address the process that is constitutionally owed to one who seeks to challenge his classification as such. The United States Court of Appeals for the Fourth Circuit held that petitioner's detention was legally authorized and that he was entitled to no further opportunity to challenge his enemy-combatant label. We now vacate and remand. We hold that although Congress authorized the detention of combatants in the narrow circumstances alleged here, due process demands that a citizen held in the United States as an enemy combatant be given a meaningful opportunity to contest the factual basis for that detention before a neutral decision maker.

On September 11, 2001, the al Qaeda terrorist network used hijacked commercial airliners to attack prominent targets in the United States. Approximately 3,000 people were killed in those attacks. One week later, in response to these "acts of treacherous violence," Congress passed a resolution authorizing the President to "use all necessary and appropriate force against those nations, organizations, or persons he determines planned, authorized, committed, or aided the terrorist attacks" or "harbored such organizations or persons, in order to prevent any future acts of international terrorism against the United States by such nations, organizations or persons." Authorization for Use of Military Force ("the AUMF"), 115 Stat. 224. Soon thereafter, the President ordered United States Armed Forces to Afghanistan, with a mission to subdue al Qaeda and quell the Taliban regime that was known to support it.

---

http://www.sinc.sunysb.edu/Class/pol325/Hamdi.htm

Hamdan v. Rumsfeld, Secretary of Defense, et al., 126 S.Ct. 2749 (2006).

Argued March 28, 2006; Decided June 29, 2006; No. 05-184. 2006

Justice Stevens delivered the opinion of the Court, except as to Parts V and VI–D–iv, concluding:

> The Government's motion to dismiss, based on the Detainee Treatment Act of 2005 (DTA), is denied. DTA §1005(e)(1) provides that "no court . . . shall have jurisdiction to hear or consider . . . an application for . . . habeas corpus filed by . . . an alien detained . . . at Guantanamo Bay." The military commission at issue is not expressly authorized by any congressional Act. . . . The military commission at issue lacks the power to proceed because its structure and procedures violate both the UCMJ and the four Geneva Conventions signed in 1949. Pp. 49–72. . . . Even assuming that Hamden is a dangerous individual who would cause great harm or death to innocent civilians given the opportunity, the Executive nevertheless must comply with the prevailing rule of law in undertaking to try him and subject him to criminal punishment.

http://www.law.cornell.edu/supct/html/05-184.ZS.html

4. Torture: Interrogation, Rendition, and Deportation

Torture, and its permissibility, in interrogation of suspects is a matter of intense controversy in most of the world. Stripped of nuances, this debate exists because although most nations proscribe torture, most also leave it uncertain which conduct is or is not torture. This is especially true in situations in which national security is at stake. Some countries, like the United States, drawing from Article 3 of the Convention against Torture (CAT), do not deport (from U.S. territory) or participate in rendition (from any country in the world to any other) if an alien can show "a chance greater than 50 percent that he will be tortured if removed." At present the United States strictly prohibits torture in all situations, although allegations abound about the actual treatment of people in custody.[6]

CONTROVERSIES IN DEFINITIONS AND APPLICATIONS

It is important to keep in mind that many of the controversies and debates that surround antiterrorism laws originate from a binary, conflictual matrix that is adopted in these discussions: national security versus civil liberty. Perhaps these two are not really opposing values. Fair trial and intelligence gathering need not always be on a collision course in a democracy. Apart from civil liberty challenges, however, there are other legal bottlenecks in antiterrorism laws. Most of the antiterrorism laws choke over defining what terrorism is. This basic definition is contentious, and umpteen variations exist.[7] Schmid and Jongman studied 109 official and academic definitions of terrorism and found that 83.5 percent mentioned violence, 65 percent mentioned political goals, and

51 percent mentioned inflicting fear or terror.[8] The U.S. government is estimated to have some 150 definitions of the term *terrorism*. Emergency management, public health, surveillance, investigation, creation of new offenses, punishment, and detention are just some of the grounds covered by the laws. Very often the definition of terrorism determines, or at least indicates, which of these areas are given more importance in a certain region. Whether terrorism is primarily a criminal law problem or one guided by the laws of war depends on what is the focus of a law: recovery from acts or prevention of terrorism or criminal sanctions with a combative edge.

Most states define terrorist acts for reasons similar to why they have other criminal laws: to give notice of what is this proscribed criminal conduct, what are its ingredients, and what the consequences on someone who transgresses these standards are. A definition of terrorism, however, has an added importance because of the consequences of terrorism on detention powers and investigative powers. Once a case is determined as that of terrorism, the detention times are usually longer and the investigative powers have more teeth. Thus, domestic laws usually distinguish between terrorism and organized crime or terrorism. An act of homicide resulting from a terror attack could be treated as a more severe offense than other homicides. After the attacks on the Twin Towers of the World Trade Center in New York City and on the Pentagon in Washington, DC, on September 11, 2001, by terrorists, prevention of terror attacks has obtained precedence over other goals. Separating terrorist acts from other criminal ones is thus even more important.

Another contentious debate is whether there should be a special court system for terror attacks. To have a separate judicial system for trying terrorism suspects, U.S. federal bureaucrats devised rules for trying them in military tribunals, but the U.S. Supreme Court did not approve of the proposed rules (Hamdan decision).[9] If not military tribunals, many think that terrorism cases can be tried in a special court system in which they would be handled expeditiously and by expert judges. The Foreign Intelligence Surveillance Act (FISA) court in the United States[10] is an example of a special court system, although its mandate is limited to searches and surveillance. It is anticipated that in a special court system ensuring the rights of defendants is a challenge because such courts may not follow the due process requirements that other criminal courts follow. However, the risks of handling terrorism cases with other garden-variety criminal cases could be that the entire system becomes loaded against suspects and defendants of all kinds as emotions against terrorism make it difficult to see all crimes and suspects in a fair context. Because evidence requirements are sometimes more lax in terrorism cases for the prosecution and punishment meted out is heightened, deciding other criminal cases alongside these cases could turn a court's culture to a disproportionately proprosecution one.

KEY MOMENTS AND EVENTS

The attacks of September 11, 2001, in New York City and Washington, DC, are referred to commonly as the events of 9/11 and are perceived to have changed the way terrorism is understood by world governments and ordinary people. In the United States, swift legal changes were carried out, and the Uniting and Strengthening America by Providing Appropriate Tools Required to Intercept and Obstruct Terrorism Act of 2001 (USA PATRIOT Act; hereafter, Patriot Act) was enacted on October 26, 2001.[11] However, this behavior is not an exception and this legislation is not an aberration. It is common for antiterrorism laws to follow on the heels of momentous destructive events. Because they originate after a terrorist attack or threat, they usually provide means of bypassing or side-stepping some other laws, which are already in place in a country. At these times of emergency, exceptional measures are considered urgent and necessary, and the laws reflect that need. For example, in 1995 when the Oklahoma City bombing took place, new legislation took birth immediately. Following the London bombings of July 7, 2005, the initial drafts of the Terrorism Act of the United Kingdom were drawn up, and it became law on March 30, 2006. Similarly, legislative changes focusing on use and transportation of explosives took place in Spain after the March 11, 2004, terrorist attacks in Madrid.

The legislative histories of the legislations passed after terror attacks reveal another similarity between the laws. Most of them are passed with great speed or at least with greater speed than other ordinary laws are passed. For example, in Britain, the Anti-Terrorism, Crime and Security Emergency Bill of 2001 was passed within a month of its submission to the legislature. Earlier, in Britain, the 1974 Prevention of Terrorism Act was also passed within a day and received the Royal Assent within 48 hours because of the urgency presented by the Birmingham pub bombings of November 1974. After the 9/11 terror attacks, in many countries laws were passed with alacrity. In Germany, the Second Security Package of laws was passed within weeks of 9/11. In France, after only a couple of weeks of deliberation, the parliament passed security amendments as part of the Day-to-Day Security Law. The link between the attacks and subsequent laws bares these laws to the jabs of criticism that these are knee-jerk in nature. The pace at which these laws are passed is usually very rapid, causing human rights watchdogs such as Human Rights Watch, Reporters sans Frontières, and International Federation of Human Rights to prick their ears. In fact, they have rated current terror legislation in the United States, Britain, Canada, Germany, and France (among others) as panicked, restrictive of liberties, authoritarian, and ineffective in antiterrorism functions. From a security perspective, speed is of the essence because terrorist events reveal lapses in security that have to be remedied. For example, after 9/11 the problem of so-called sleeper terrorists and how to neutralize them gained prominence. Sleepers are terrorists who are waiting to act whenever they get an opportunity. Punishing terrorism does not facilitate preventing sleepers.

It is to overcome such problems that terrorism laws gain breadth. The Patriot Act covers 350 subject areas. From surveillance and interception of communications to anti-money-laundering regulations and tighter immigration, it has a wide wingspan. Indeed, there is very little it does not touch. Its proponents say it has several safeguards built into its framework, such as high-level approval requirements for many investigatory procedures, various reporting requirements (to Congress and annual public reports), greater judicial oversight, and audits of justice departments, to name just a few. Its opponents reply that these safeguards are inadequate when a law is broad and invasive.

DID YOU KNOW?

The sole person ever charged in the United States in connection with the 9/11 attacks is Zacarias Moussaoui. He faced a federal jury in Virginia in a death-penalty trial after he pleaded guilty. As a result of his conviction, he is currently serving a life sentence at the administrative maximum security prison facility in Florence, Colorado. For complete coverage of this trial, see http://www.courttv.com/trials/moussaoui/index.html.

Also read the following report on how close Moussaoui was to the death penalty.

Report: Lone Holdout Juror Kept Moussaoui Alive

WASHINGTON (AP)—A single holdout kept the jury from handing a death sentence to Zacarias Moussaoui, the only person charged in this country in the 9/11 attacks. But that juror never explained his vote, said the foreman of the jury that sentenced the confessed al Qaeda conspirator to life in prison last week. The foreman, a math teacher in Northern Virginia, told The Washington Post that jurors voted three times—11–1, 10–2 and 10–2—in favor of the death penalty on the three terrorism charges that each qualified Moussaoui for execution. On April 26, the third day of deliberations, the jury's frustrations reached a critical point because of several 11–1 votes on one charge. But no one could figure out who was casting the dissenting vote, the foreman said, because that person didn't identify himself during any discussion—and each of the votes were done using anonymous ballots. "But there was no yelling," she said in an interview for the Post's Friday editions. "It was as if a heavy cloud of doom had fallen over the deliberation room, and many of us realized that all our beliefs and our conclusions were being vetoed by one person. . . . We tried to discuss the pros and cons. But I would have to say that most of the arguments we heard around the deliberation table were" in favor of the death penalty.

---

http://www.courttv.com/trials/moussaoui/051206_ap.html

FUTURE PROSPECTS

After 9/11, many countries tightened national security agendas by introducing amendments or new legislations. Apart from France, Britain, and Germany, which made immediate changes, in 2002 the Australian government introduced several omnibus terrorism laws. Canada amended its Criminal Code by the Anti Terrorism Act 2001 (ATA).[12] Some countries have created new offences because of 9/11. For example, Greece in 2001 and again in 2004 created new offences and enhanced punishments. Turkey classified new acts as terrorism in June 2006 (e.g., human trafficking, drug smuggling, and pollution of the environment).

Other terror attacks provoked similar reactions. Denmark's parliament adopted two new antiterror measures conceived in the aftermath of the July 2005 London terrorist attacks. Using more technology, such as video monitoring of public places, is the thrust of the Danish laws. Similar amendments were carried out in Norway to its Penal Code in which electronic and technical measures are considered indispensable. Some means to strengthen prosecution of terrorism has been to give greater investigatory powers given to the police (e.g., the Italian Penal Code, which was primed in 2005) and by charging with conspiracy when direct evidence is unavailable (e.g., after the March 11, 2004, Madrid train bombings, the prosecution of the suspected bombers was based on several conspiracy charges).

Today, many pending bills and proposed draft legislations grapple with terrorism. All of these are not criminal laws, although they may have criminal provisions implanted in them. Reforms of other laws are also significant reforms for counterterrorism purposes. In the United States, tort reform took place after 9/11 in terms of the Air Transportation Safety and System Stabilization Act, which offered victims government compensation in exchange for taking away their right to sue the airline companies. Because terrorism also involves funding the terrorist acts, it also includes money being sent across the globe via commercial channels. Thus money-laundering legislations target this activity. The aim of these laws is to freeze assets to block funding and track down terrorists from their money trail. This is also the aim of the International Convention for the Suppression and Financing of Terrorism that was adopted by the General Assembly of the United Nations in December 1999. Other finance-related antiterrorism laws include the Bank Secrecy Act that requires U.S. financial institutions to assist U.S. government agencies in detecting and preventing money laundering. After 9/11, another economic legislation that deals with terrorism is the Terrorism Risk Insurance Act of 2002, which facilitates obtaining terrorism coverage in insurance. The primary purpose is to ensure that the coverage is affordable for businesses.

Legislation is definitely not the only means to tackle terrorism. At least one democracy, India, in recent times repealed its controversial antiterrorism legislation (the Prevention of Terrorism Act, 2002).[13] With such repeals, intelligence gathering becomes even more crucial.[14] In most countries, legal interventions are supplemented by enforcement and investigatory agencies that tackle terrorism. International networks of research groups exist. These groups are counterterrorism think tanks.[15] Finally, because of globalization, terrorism has twisted free, by and large, of the nation-state framework.[16] International networks of terrorists and technological advancements that make geographic location almost insignificant make it difficult to locate terrorists within a purely national framework. Countering terrorism, on the other hand, is not free from the nation-state because a nation where an act takes place will respond most strongly to terrorism. Other nations that perceive a similar threat will follow suit. This is what happened in many Western allies of the United States after 9/11. Thus, national antiterrorism laws will always be crucial even if international conventions multiply in number. National or international, legislative, judicial or executive, a successful antiterrorism law will try and strike the right balance between national security and civil liberties.

See Also: Espionage Act of 1917; Foreign Intelligence Surveillance Act; Homeland Security; Immigration and Employment Law Enforcement; Patriot Act; Torture and Enemy Combatants.

Endnotes

1. 18 U.S. 793, 794 (1917).
2. 319 U.S. 432 (1943).
3. Detroit, U.S. District Court, August 17, 2006.
4. 542 U.S. 466 (2004).
5. 542 U.S. 507 (2004).
6. Human Rights Watch, "Summary of International and U.S. Law Prohibiting Torture and Other Ill-treatment of Persons in Custody" (2004), http://hrw.org/english/docs/2004/05/24/usint8614_txt.htm.
7. H.H.A. Cooper, "Terrorism: The Problem of Definition Revisited," *American Behavioral Scientist* 44, no. 6 (February 2001): 881–93; "One person's terrorist will ever remain another's freedom fighter" (882).
8. P. Schmid and A. J. Jongman, *Political Terrorism: A New Guide to Actors, Authors, Concepts, Data Bases, Theories, and Literature* (Amsterdam: North-Holland Publishing, 1988), 32–38.
9. 126 S.Ct. 2749 (2006).
10. In 1978, the Foreign Intelligence Surveillance Act (FISA) was passed to govern electronic surveillance, searches, pen registers, and trap and trace devices and access to certain business records for foreign intelligence requirements. The Intelligence Reform and Terrorism Prevention Act of 2004 expanded FISA.
11. The Patriot Act was renewed in March 2006.
12. It has tried to balance its international legal obligations with domestic needs. In June 2006, however, after 17 Muslim Canadians were arrested, there was a claim that Canada's antiterror legislation discriminates by focusing on so-called brown Muslim and Arab groups.
13. On December 9, 2004, the Indian Parliament passed the Prevention of Terrorism (Repeal) Bill.
14. Brett Murphy, "India Government Urged to Revive Repealed Anti-Terror Law after Mumbai Bombings," Jurist (July 16, 2006), http://jurist.law.pitt.edu/paperchase/2006_07_16_indexarch.php. The Indian prime minister points out that intelligence gathering is the main pillar of counterterrorism.
15. Ronen Shamir, "Without Borders? Notes on Globalization as a Mobility Regime," *Sociological Theory* 23, no. 2 (June 2005): 197.
16. Austin T. Turk, "Sociology of Terrorism," *Annual Review of Sociology* 30 (2004): 271–86.

Further Reading: Cooper, H.H.A., "Terrorism: The Problem of Definition Revisited," *American Behavioral Scientist* 44, no. 6 (February 2001): 881–93; Galicki, Zdzisllaw, "International Law and Terrorism," *American Behavioral Scientist* 48, no. 6 (February 2005): 743–57, http://hrw.org/english/docs/2004/05/24/usint8614_txt.htm; Haubrich, Dirk, "September 11, Anti-Terror Laws and Civil Liberties: Britain, France and Germany Compared," *Government and Opposition* (Blackwell, 2003), 3–28; Shamir, Ronen, "Without Borders? Notes on Globalization as a Mobility Regime," *Sociological Theory* 23 (June 2005): 2; Turk, Austin T., "Sociology of Terrorism," *Annual Review of Sociology* 30 (2004): 271–86.

Devyani Prabhat

BAIL

INTRODUCTION

Bail is a process whereby an accused individual is released from custody into the community to await later court proceedings. Some people argue that bail is discriminatory against the poor and that the process of arriving at bail can be racially and ethnically biased and, thus, can infringe on a person's due process rights granted by the U.S. Constitution. Other people contend that current bail procedures are a rationally based mechanism for helping ensure the appearance at trial of those accused individuals who may be a threat to the community and that it is too easy for some alleged violent offenders to qualify for bail and the courts should more frequently prohibit these individuals from obtaining bail and instead house them as pretrial detainees.

An initial bail hearing or subsequent rehearing can range from as short as a minute or up to several days in length, depending on the nature of the charges, the notoriety of the case, and the state jurisdiction within which the proceeding occurs. Depending on the discretion of the trial judge, the accused may be permitted to present evidence, cross-examine witnesses, and testify. Judges vary in how much time they will extend to the parties in arguing issues pertaining to bail.

The Eighth Amendment to the U.S. Constitution states, "excessive bail shall not be required."[1] Although excessive bail is prohibited, the amendment does not create a right to bail. The general thinking is that bail is excessive if it is higher than is reasonably calculated to ensure the individual's presence at a future court proceeding.

BACKGROUND

A person's bail is first addressed at the initial appearance stage during which the judge assesses the amount to be set, based generally on the severity of the offense and the accused's prior record. Those charged with violent offenses such as rape, robbery, and aggravated assault tend to have bail set at higher amounts than those charged with property offenses such as auto theft and burglary. Judges are more hesitant to release alleged violent offenders on low bail because the court and the community are concerned with the perceived dangerousness of such offenders. It is not unusual for those persons charged with murder in the first degree to be denied bail outright.

Permitting the accused to be released on bail allows the person to be free in the community while enabling them to better prepare for trial by obtaining easier assess to legal counsel and assisting in the marshaling of witnesses and evidence. Additionally, it prevents the infliction of pretrial punishment on someone who may be innocent of the charges. The consequences of not making bail and thus being subject to pretrial detention may include losing one's job, being unable to pay bills, and having one's family face possible eviction and the necessity of seeking public assistance.

A person's bail, particularly in felony cases, can basically be satisfied in three different ways: (1) cash bail, in which the individual pays the total amount with his own money; (2) real property, in which the individual puts up a piece of his real estate; or (3) bail bond, the most prevalent method in which a professional bail bondsperson posts the amount on behalf of the accused.

The bail bondsperson is a private individual who generally requires a 10 percent fee for his or her services. For example, if the court sets bail at $1,000, the individual must pay the bondsperson $100, which is nonrefundable. Even if the accused makes all future court appearances, the bondsperson retains this fee. When an individual provides the court with his own money for bail, however, the money is returned (minus perhaps a small administrative fee) upon fulfilling his obligation to be present for all court proceedings. Some states, such as Illinois and Oregon, prohibit bail bondspersons in whole or in part from operating within their jurisdictions.

A bail bondsperson's office is generally in close proximity to courthouses, and the role of bail bondspersons is interesting in that they, as the common expression goes, "hold the keys to the jailhouse door." That is, this private entrepreneurial individual, in effect, has a major role to play in whether the accused is released or remains in jail as a pretrial detainee. The accused principally deals with public employees such as police, prosecutors, and judges; therefore, the role of the private bondsperson is, some would suggest, unique. Another responsibility of the bail bondsperson is to arrange for the return of an accused to the jurisdiction of the court should the accused fail to show up for a court appearance. This is generally accomplished through retaining the services of a so-called bounty hunter.

In misdemeanor and ordinance violation cases, the use of so-called police station house bail is sometimes used in selected jurisdictions. After being booked, the police desk sergeant or some other designated police official sets bail through the use of a predetermined bail release schedule that has the approval of the local

HAS JUSTICE BEEN SERVED?

An interesting offshoot to the paying of the court a high cash bail by accused felons, particularly high-level drug dealers, has occurred on a few occasions in the United States. Generally, it fits this scenario: The judge sets extremely high bail, the accused pays the bail amount with his own money, and then the accused skips the country. The concern is that justice has not been served because the accused's exact whereabouts are unknown. And yet the community is left with an unexpected cash windfall that may be used as revenue to provide for other necessary public services.

judiciary. For instance, if the alleged offense is a petty theft less than a certain dollar amount, the bail schedule might indicate that bail shall be set at $250.

A fair number of individuals find it difficult to pay even low amounts of bail money to the court or a bondsperson to secure their release. For some individuals, even obtaining $100 may be impossible. Due to this inability to pay the set amount, the person will be required to be housed in jail until the trial date. An ironic result of this situation is that some individuals will plead guilty early in the judicial process (who otherwise might not be inclined to do so) with the understanding that they will be placed on probation or be able to pay their fine on a monthly installment basis. This process allows them to avoid further pretrial confinement, yet the individual may find it puzzling that they were not permitted to be released due to an inability to post bail yet were permitted to plead guilty and then be immediately released. The prosecutor, under this system, obtains a quick plea to the offense, which allows the case to be easily resolved.

The current system of bail makes it difficult for a poor person to post bail, regardless of the amount set by the court. As a result of this dilemma, certain alternatives to bail have surfaced over the years. In minor criminal cases, the police can, as an alternative to arrest, issue in the field what is generally referred to as a citation, which directs the person to appear in court at a designated time to answer for the alleged offense. This procedure places faith in the individual to voluntarily show up for the court appearance without the necessity of the police formally arresting the person and likewise does not require the person to post any amount of money to assure his or her appearance.

Another alternative to bail is the use of release on recognizance (ROR), which surfaced in the 1960s in New York City. It involves releasing the accused into the community without any money being submitted to the court after a background investigation has been conducted that indicates that the individual appears to be a good candidate to voluntarily return to court. The investigation generally looks at the person's roots within the community as demonstrated by perhaps having steady employment, long-term residence within the area, family support, and no prior criminal record. Research on the effectiveness of ROR has demonstrated that the vast majority of individuals released in this manner have voluntarily returned for later court appearances.[2]

Other alternatives to bail include: (1) conditional supervised release, in which the individual does not have to deposit any money with the court but is subject to some court oversight; (2) third-party release, in which a respected member of the community periodically checks on the accused, who again has been released without depositing any money with the court; and (3) what is sometimes referred to as administrative court release, a rather infrequent practice, in which the court does obtain a monetary sum from the individual, but, unlike the traditional bail bondsperson who generally takes 10 percent as a fee, the court instead returns the entire amount (assuming court appearances are made) to the accused, minus perhaps a very nominal fee for administrative processing purposes.

A somewhat common phrase attributed to victims of a crime or eyewitnesses to a crime is that the arrested person is released on bail prior to the victim or witness statements being reduced to writing by the police. Victims and witnesses are concerned about intimidation and threats made to them by the accused who has been released on bail. Prosecutors sometimes find that charges must be dismissed against individuals when the victim or witnesses fear testifying against the accused. The general public may express displeasure with those released on bail who engage in criminal behavior while in such a release status. A 1982 study found that 16 percent of those released on bail were rearrested, and of that group, 30 percent were arrested more than once.[3] A later study found that serious offenders such as rapists and robbers were rearrested even more frequently.[4]

A UNIQUE ARGUMENT FOR BAIL BY DEFENSE COUNSEL

Two legal factors receive primary consideration during a bail hearing, namely: (1) the seriousness of the current alleged offense and (2) the prior record of the accused. One would normally expect that a significant prior record would generally increase the amount of the bail set by the court, given the thinking that the individual is less likely to return for future court proceedings, as a new conviction would expose him to a seemingly higher sentence. In an interesting twist, however, a few attorneys have been known to argue at the bail hearing that notwithstanding another new charge of violence being lodged against their client, the client can nonetheless be trusted (based on being present at prior-offense court appearances) to reappear for subsequent hearings, and thus low bail ought to be set by the court. In other words, despite the fact that the client may have a propensity toward violent conduct, he is nonetheless an "honest" person "whose word is his bond" and thus he will always appear for court appearances. The argument being that one may have a distinguishing trait toward violence yet not necessarily a trait toward being a dishonest person. Not surprisingly, most judges, in the exercise of their discretion, are not swayed by such an argument.

The bail amount set is based primarily on considerations of the current alleged offense and the prior criminal record. Yet the issue of whether racial and ethnic status plays any role in whether bail is granted and the amount of bail set has been the subject of research. One such study of large urban courts involved a sample of 36,000 individuals. It was found that the extralegal characteristics (attributes) of race and ethnicity of the person, as opposed to strictly legal variables (current alleged offense and prior criminal record), played a role in judicial decisions to deny bail to black and Latino individuals.

This study suggested that this disparity in the pretrial processing of blacks and Latinos was due to judicial stereotyping of individuals when judges were faced with insufficient information about cases and had limited time to make bail-related determinations.[5] Another urban area study of bail found that the legal factors—current alleged offense and prior criminal record—were the strongest determinants of whether an accused was released, yet the study also found differential processing of persons depending on whether they were white, black, or Hispanic. The principal conclusion of the study was that Hispanics were more likely to be detained pending trial than white or black defendants, particularly as it pertained to drug cases.[6] Additionally, Hispanics were subjected to a burden of being "more likely to be denied bail, more likely to have to pay bail to gain release, required to pay higher amounts of bail, and more likely to be held on bail."[7] In contrast, another study looking at racial disparity in bail pretrial proceedings, it was found that blacks who lived in cities with less than a 10 percent black population do not commonly experience differential processing.[8]

Judges may take into consideration the arguments of prosecutors and defense attorneys, among other interested parties, in determining if bail should be permitted and at what monetary amount it should be set. A study conducted in New York City involved observations of almost 2,000 pretrial cases to determine factors influencing release and bail decisions. The researchers found that prosecutors dominated release and bail decisions, hence playing a significant and influential role in bail review proceedings.[9]

KEY STATUTES AND LEGAL DECISIONS

Beginning in the 1970s, a number of states began to enact statutes making the obtaining of bail more restrictive. This shift in policy reflected a general societal perception that too many individuals released on bail were posing a potential danger to the general public. Supporters of this change contended that although the Eighth Amendment to the U.S. Constitution prohibits excessive bail, it does not give all defendants the right to bail. In judicial determinations as to whether bail should be permitted or at what amount it ought to be set, crime control and community safety factors began to be weighed more heavily than in the past. Concerns about those on bail fleeing the jurisdiction, possible witness intimidation, and the potential commission of new offenses (particularly violent acts) by those who were granted bail became important public policy issues.

In 1984, the U.S. Congress, as well, keyed on what they considered the potential future dangerousness posed by those released on bail by passing the Federal Bail Reform Act of 1984.[10] The preventive detention provisions of this 1984 legislation significantly altered the previous 1966 Bail Reform Act by making it more difficult for those charged with federal offenses, particularly violent crimes, to secure release on bail. Since the passage of the 1984 statute, the number of federally charged individuals denied bail outright has increased.[11] In 1987, the U.S. Supreme Court, in the landmark case *U.S. v. Salerno,* held the provisions of the Federal Bail Reform Act of 1984 to be constitutional.[12] The Court, in essence, found that the provisions of the act did not violate the due process clause and that the Eighth Amendment was not violated, as a trial court may consider dangerousness as a valid reason to prohibit pretrial release.

The 1975 U.S. Supreme Court case of *Gerstein v. Pugh* held that the Sixth Amendment to the U.S. Constitution does not require the individual states to provide an indigent defendant an attorney at their initial bail review hearing.[13] This means that accused individuals who are poor will generally not be represented by counsel at the initial appearance bail determination stage. Although states, by way of their own constitutions or by state statute, may choose to mandate such representation at the initial bail review proceeding, most do not do so. A study completed in Baltimore, Maryland, measured the impact of having attorney representation at the initial bail review hearing by tracking 4,000 lower-income defendants accused of nonviolent offenses.[14] The research results indicated that "more than two and one half times as many represented defendants were released on recognizance from pretrial custody as were unrepresented defendants. Additionally, two and one half times as many represented defendants had their bail reduced to an affordable amount."[15]

Another legal issue pertains to whether bail pending appeal is constitutionally permissible. In other words, an individual on bail is subsequently convicted for the alleged offense for which he or she was on bail and is now seeking continued bail status while appealing the conviction. Although technically available to defendants, the enactment of the Federal Bail Reform Act of 1984 has made it extremely difficult to obtain bail while appealing a conviction. According to the statute, to merit such status, a federally convicted individual "must convince the court not only that he is not a flight risk or danger to the community, and that his appeal is not for purposes of delay and raises a substantial question likely to result in reversal, but must also convince the court that 'exceptional reasons' exist that warrant his release."[16]

MATERIAL WITNESS MAY BE REQUIRED TO POST BAIL

An interesting aspect of bail is that it can be applied to material witnesses. In other words, a key witness, who the prosecution believes will be instrumental in securing a conviction, may be required to post bail to ensure his appearance. Take, for example, a major drug case or a murder case in which the material witness indicates to the prosecutor that he will be out of the country at the time of the defendant's trial or the prosecutor has good reason to believe the material witness will flee the area and thus not be available to testify. The prosecutor may believe the case hinges on the witness's testimony, and hence the prosecutor seeks to have bail set for the witness. Bail being set for a material witness is, of course, extremely rare. It is conceivable, however, that under the previous scenario, a material witness could be denied bail or not be able to secure monetary funds to post bail and thus be confined (albeit presumably under rather comfortable conditions) as a jailhouse pretrial detainee. And, yes, although hard to imagine, a situation could arise in which the material witness is detained, whereas the accused has been released on bail.

FUTURE PROSPECTS

The overcrowding in jails and the high costs of housing someone in jail are key public policy issues. Nationwide, about half of those confined in local jails have been unable to post bail and are awaiting trial as pretrial detainees. In the future, it will not be surprising to see more public officials give additional consideration to expanding such alternatives to bail as ROR, supervised (conditional) release, third-party release, and the increased use of police-issued citations to appear in court. Research has shown that those accused individuals awaiting trial in jail are "more likely to be convicted" and more likely to "receive longer sentences" than those released on bail.[17] Given such noteworthy research findings, it would behoove the accused, in the future, to seek out an alternative to bail release mechanisms.

Bail being set at perceived high amounts is a topic of interest to many observers of the judicial process. Money expended by the accused to cover high bail also has an impact on how much money the accused will then have remaining to retain an attorney and pay, if convicted, court costs and fines. Given the financial implications, it would not be surprising to see a future movement on the part of advocates for the accused that seeks to have more sophisticated bail risk assessment instruments (based on current alleged offense and prior record) to better estimate who should be granted bail and at what bail amounts. After all, the criminal justice system currently makes use of such risk assessment instruments for juveniles and adults who are being sentenced or considered for parole. And certainly, such instruments will need to neutralize the influence of extralegal factors such as race and ethnicity.

Technological improvements have had an impact on bail. Increased use of computers and greater access to data have allowed judges to base bail decisions on more informed judgment because information is more readily available. Also, greater opportunities have developed in which initial bail decisions can be made by video arrangements between the judge in the courtroom and the accused in the county jail. This process is becoming more prevalent and saves the court money relative to offender transport and security matters. Other significant advancements are the use of electronic tracking devices such as ankle monitoring bracelets and global positioning satellite capabilities that enable the person released on bail to be under constant electronic surveillance and hence provide the public with a better sense of security. In the future, additional resources will need to be provided to monitor accused individuals released on bail so as to prevent criminal behavior and to ensure the safety of an apprehensive public. The added expenditure of money to monitor those released on bail is minuscule compared to the costs of incarcerating someone awaiting trial.

Another future issue is whether all accused indigent individuals ought to be provided, at no expense, an attorney to represent them at the initial bail review hearing. As mentioned earlier, currently an indigent individual does not have such a constitutional right; however, such a right can be extended by individual state constitutions or by state statutes, and some states have done so. As indicated earlier, research has shown that a failure to provide an attorney to represent the accused at the initial bail review hearing can seriously impact whether an alternative to bail is considered, whether bail is set, and at what amount it is set. Just as important, the preparation of a meaningful later defense may be impeded by the failure to provide counsel at this early court proceeding. In the future, the U.S. Supreme Court may wish to reexamine this issue. Additionally, individual state legislatures that do not presently provide such a statutory right may choose to reassess the matter.

Currently, the sentencing stage of the trial is more legally regulated than the bail hearing stage. In other words, even though trial judges are generally provided some discretion at the sentencing stage (depending on whether one is in a determinate versus indeterminate sentencing state), that discretion is still more likely to be subject to statutory guidelines and detailed appellate court oversight. In contrast, the bail hearing stage extends to the trial judge an extraordinary amount of discretion in setting bail. Appellate courts are extremely hesitant to review a trial court's bail amount decision and, when they do occasionally examine such matters, they are very reluctant to find the amount to be excessive under the Eighth Amendment. In the future, appellate courts will have to decide if they want to provide more judicial oversight of trial court determinations of bail.

Future research and public policy decision making on bail will have to address how to fairly resolve the dilemma between upholding the due process rights of the accused while securing the safety of the general public.

See Also: Cruel and Unusual Punishment; Prosecutorial Discretion.

Endnotes

1. Eighth Amendment, United States Constitution.
2. H. Zeisel, "Bail Revisited," *American Bar Foundation Research Journal* 4 (1979): 769–89.
3. Donald Pryor and Walter F. Smith, "Significant Research Findings Concerning Pretrial Release," *Pretrial Issues* 4, no. 1 (Washington, DC: Pretrial Services Resource Center, February 1982): 1–16.
4. Bureau of Justice Statistics, *Report to the Nation on Crime and Justice,* 2nd ed. (Washington, DC: U.S. Department of Justice, 1988), 77.
5. Traci Schlesinger, "Racial and Ethnic Disparity in Pretrial Criminal Processing," *Justice Quarterly* 22 (2005): 170–93.
6. Stephen Demuth, "Racial and Ethnic Differences in Pretrial Release Decisions and Outcomes: A Comparison of Hispanic, Black, and White Felony Arrestees," *Criminology* 41 (August 2003): 873–908.
7. Ibid., 901.
8. Marvin Free, "Bail and Pretrial Release Decisions: An Assessment of the Racial Threat Perspective," *Journal of Ethnicity in Criminal Justice* 2 (2004): 23–44.
9. M. Phillips, "Factors Influencing Release and Bail Decisions in New York City," *New York Criminal Justice Agency,* ed. M. Phillips (New York, 2004), 39.
10. Federal Bail Reform Act, 18 USC 3141 (1984).
11. Thomas E. Scott, "Pretrial Detention under the Bail Reform Act of 1984—An Empirical Analysis," *American Law* Review, 27 (1989): 1–51.
12. *United States v. Salerno,* 479 U.S. 1026 (1987).
13. *Gerstein v. Pugh,* 420 U.S. 103 (1975).

14. Douglas L. Colbert, Ray Paternoster, and Shawn Bushway, "Do Attorneys Really Matter? The Empirical and Legal Case for the Right of Counsel at Bail," *Cardozo Law Review* 23 (May 2002): 1719–93.

15. Ibid., 1753–55.

16. Barry Tarlow, "Bail Pending Appeal: The Bail Reform Act," *The Champion* 29 (November 2005): 71.

17. Caleb Foote, "The Bail System and Equal Justice," *Federal Probation* 23 (1959): 43–48.

Further Reading: Dhami, M. K., "From Discretion to Disagreement: Explaining Disparities in Judge's Pretrial Decisions," *Behavioral Sciences and the Law* 22 (2005): 367–86; Fagan, Jeffrey, and Martin Guggenheim, "Preventive Detention and the Judicial Prediction of Dangerousness for Juveniles: A Natural Experiment," *Journal of Criminal Law and Criminology* 86 (1996): 415–48; Johnson, Brian R., and Greg L. Warchol, "Bail Agents and Bounty Hunters: Adversaries or Allies of the Justice System?" *American Journal of Criminal Justice* 27 (2003): 145–65; Smith, Brian C. "Is Bail Being Used for Pre-Trial Punishment?" *The Montana Lawyer* 31 (2006): 12–15; Zeglarski, Lorri J. "New Jersey's Assembly Bill Finally Attempted to Regulate Bounty Hunters," *Seton Hall Legislative Journal* 28 (2004): 381–413.

Rick M. Steinmann

BOOT CAMPS

INTRODUCTION

For new recruits, boot camps come as a shocking transition to a new way of life. Discipline is ultrastrict, and a primary emphasis is placed on physical training, hard work, and unquestioning obedience to authority. The recruit is told what to do at all times; that is, when to sleep and get up, when to eat, when to rest, and so on. If orders are not obeyed, the recruit is punished, often severely. Once boot camp is over, the recruit has become a different person if not in reality, then in ideology. The dream of correctional boot camps taking young, nonviolent offenders, subjecting them to a military atmosphere, and diverting them from a life of crime is a controversial one, with boot camp aficionados arguing that the rigid discipline promotes positive behavior, whereas opponents argue that it is a potentially harmful influence.

Correctional boot camps have been part of the penal system of the United States for the since the early 1980s. In most U.S. states, participation in such programs is offered to young, first-time offenders in place of a prison term or probation; likewise, in some states, a youth can also be sentenced to serve time (ranging from 90 to 180 days) in a boot camp to make up for prison sentences of up to 10 years. How serving prison time and boot camp time is equated differs between facilities and states. Offenders not finishing a program must serve the original prison sentence.

During the early 1980s and 1990s, boot camps received great attention as an alternative sentencing option; that is, it was envisaged as punishment that fell between traditional incarceration and probation for both adult and juvenile offenders. The primary goal was the reduction of imprisonment costs by placing lower-risk, nonviolent offenders in abbreviated, highly structured programs outside of crowded mainline institutions. Depending upon the program, the structure usually involved discipline, regimentation and drill, physical conditioning, hygiene and sanitation, work, education, treatment, and counseling.

There was and is no one single definition for boot camps. The military model was its most frequent form, but other approaches existed as well. To recognize the range of methods, the definition expanded to include work-intensive correctional programs that did not technically qualify as boot camps but had related features. This covered all intensive programs that included a full day—up to 16 hours—of work, physical training, study, and counseling. Experiential programs provided camp settings for youthful offenders who underwent physical conditioning, athletic competition, and challenging outdoor experiences instead of military drill and ceremonies. When the public thought about boot camps, however, the concept centered on military discipline to generate respect for authority while emphasizing good support services once an inmate was released—with an overriding purpose of reducing recidivism.

Boot camps were and are commonly referred to as shock incarceration (scaring someone into doing what is right). This involved the use of an abbreviated sentence with a highly intensive daily regimen. Typically, the camps used a military format with drill instructors overseeing offenders dressed in fatigues who were frequently subjected to such punishment as push-ups for minor infractions of rules.[1] The central goal for this program was that it give the young offender a taste of prison life for a short period of confinement followed by release back into the community under supervision.

SECURING OBEDIENCE

The key element in all concepts of boot camps is the highly structured schedule that permits no idle time and creates a sense of stress and urgency in the offender. The military format is typically used to develop that mental state and to secure obedience.

BACKGROUND

The roots of the boot camp concept began with efforts to replace long prison terms with effective ways to deter criminals from repeat offenses; in short, to create inexpensive programs.[2] Boot camps may have originated in 1888 at the New York State Reformatory at Elmira, New York, which operated until 1920 on a military training model emphasizing discipline and regimentation. So-called shock probation (primarily an abbreviated sentence of 30 to 90 days that demonstrated to first-time offenders the harshness of prison before they returned to their community under probation) was initiated in Ohio in the mid-1960s. In the late 1970s, a form of shock education—the *Scared Straight!* indoctrinations—was attempted with at-risk youths. In 1974, Idaho started a short-term (four-month) treatment program for felony offenders (both adults and juveniles who were tried as adults) on an old Air Force base in a remote location. In 1989, the program was expanded to include a military format.

In 1983, Oklahoma opened the nation's first correctional boot camp, and later that year Georgia opened the Dodge Correctional Institution boot camp. In 1985, Mississippi opened the nation's third boot camp. The use of militaristic camps began to achieve popular and political support in the late 1980s, accelerating in the 1990s due to public outrage regarding the perception of rising crime and liberal treatment of offenders.

In 1980, federal and state prisons incarcerated 316,000 people. In 1990, that number had grown to 740,000, not including jail populations. By 2000, the number of prisoners had surpassed 1.3 million; by 2002, the figure had risen to more than 2 million.[3] A tragic result of this explosion has been a return of offenders into their communities before receiving just punishment or rehabilitation. Thus, one reason for boot camp popularity was the fear that the United States was turning into an armed camp—it is us versus them. In essence, the public became fed up with crime and criminals, with the average citizen wanting longer prison sentences, greater penalties, as well as just punishment of offenders.

In 1988, during the U.S. presidential race, then–Vice President George H.W. Bush ran ads about Willie Horton, a black man convicted of murder and sentenced to life without parole, who had been released on a weekend furlough during the term of Massachusetts Governor Michael Dukakis and subsequently committed several crimes. Bush accused Democratic presidential nominee Dukakis of holding liberal views regarding punishment and crime. Many pundits felt that after Dukakis had been branded the "L" word (meaning, liberal), he did not stand a chance against the law and order of Bush.[4] Many Americans felt that the nation's jails were more akin to country clubs and wanted certainty that the inmates were doing hard time. Many liked the idea of boot camp because it reminded them of the military: yelling, screaming, marching, and physical exercise. Blue-collar and white-collar individuals alike enjoyed seeing prisoners sweating and being forced to submit to discipline.

Interestingly, one primary reason for boot camps was that long periods of incarceration led to institutionalization, by which the prisoner learned the survival skills needed while being locked up but were considered dysfunctional at his or her release. This, in turn, often created a vicious circle in which more than two-thirds of ex-inmates recidivated within three years of release, with the return to the community serving as a brief stop on the road back to prison.[5] In order to circumvent this process, boot camps incorporated education and treatment options, especially those concerning drug and alcohol addiction.

KEY EVENTS

Even at the beginning, the success of boot camps was guarded. Evaluation research produced mixed results, suggesting that the boot camp approach was not the answer to all problems as originally hoped. Beginning with evaluations in Louisiana and Georgia, early research found that boot camp graduates did not fare any better in terms of rearrest than inmates released from prison or on probation and were, in fact, more likely to have parole revoked for technical violations.[6]

Dissatisfaction has grown. An overweight, 14-year-old girl named Gina Score died after being put on a forced run in a South Dakota boot camp. She collapsed several times on a 2.7 mile obstacle course, but no one assisted her; rather, the staff felt she was malingering. Score lay in a pool of her own urine, gasping for every breath. She frothed at the mouth and began twitching uncontrollably, crying "Mommy." Finally, after three hours lying prostrate in the sun, an ambulance was called. Unfortunately, it was too late, and she died of heat stroke after reaching the hospital.[7] The case resulted in intensive press coverage and furious questions about why a child who had committed petty theft (she had taken $25) was subjected to such brutal treatment.

A similar story involved a Nicholaus Conteraz, a 16-year-old male who had been convicted for joyriding in a stolen car. He was sentenced to the privately run Arizona Boys Ranch, and while there suffered from bouts of 103-degree fever, muscle spasms, severe chest pains, and impaired breathing. Even so, he was forced to participate in calisthenics and running, though his medical condition worsened. At one point, he defecated on his bed and complained that his body was in severe agony. On the day of his death, he was thrown to ground several times by the staff and was forced to do push-ups because he kept falling down. An autopsy later showed that his abdomen was filled with more than two-and-a-half quarts of pus from an infection.[8]

Many have argued that boot camps were nothing more than fads. By 1996, 27 states were operating 48 juvenile boot camps—all but one opened after 1990. It was felt that boot camps began to thrive because they made a good story and that the truth regarding them was unknown. When evaluations emerged in the mid-1990s, it was found that juvenile boot camps suffered recidivism rates of 64 percent to 75 percent—statistics worse than the recidivism associated with traditional youth corrections institutions. The U.S. Department of Justice, which initially championed the boot camps, reported in 1997 that "the efficacy of these programs is questionable at best."[9]

Critics state that juveniles are only pretending and only perform well while interred at the boot camp; that is, once the juvenile or young person has been set free, he or she will revert to maladaptive behavior. Another key criticism that took several years to appear was that boot camps were no cheaper than prisons—a quantum shift from what was said in the mid-1980s when boot camps were stated to be much less expensive than traditional prisons. Several states have actually shown data indicating that boot camps exceed prison costs.

High rates have also been found in noncompliance, absenteeism, and new arrests. Many graduates of the boot camp programs also fail to complete the aftercare portion of the program. Staff selection is critical to a boot camp's success. The screening, selection, and training of qualified individuals may fall by the wayside at some locations. Power-hungry 20-year-olds are hired at some camps, which, naturally, have resulted in disaster. The brutalizing environment can also negatively affect a juvenile. The harshness of the environment does improve self-esteem, but upon release, they go back home to crime-ridden neighborhoods and fall back in with the wrong crowd.

CRITICISMS OF BOOT CAMPS

1. Costs: Research found that the average daily price to keep a juvenile at a correctional boot camp ranges from as low as $65.00 to as high as $188.00 (depending upon the state in question).
2. Admittance: Some had 1,400 youths, whereas others admitted no more than 25 individuals per facility.
3. Age: Some admitted 10-year-olds, whereas one had a 40-year-old Caucasian male.

FUTURE PROSPECTS

Quite possibly, the most powerful element making boot camps and related programs work is the aftercare, the continued contact with the graduates to ensure that education, training, and job placement occur. When correctional-based boot camps were first created, they were intended for a more violent audience to punish them with the militaristic attitudes of Marine Corps boot camp lifestyle; thus, aftercare services were not accentuated. The in-your-face style, combined with an arduous task-filled day, was used scare the offenders straight. Unfortunately, recidivism rates would stay the same because the audience targeted was repeating offenders who were set in their behavior.[10] Due to these findings, the new audience targeted was changed to the first-time nonviolent offender. The purpose behind the change was due to the notion that the earlier and more intense the contact with these new offenders, the more likely the recruits could relate and accept the disassociation from criminal life. One problem with first-time offenders was whether they had been exposed to physical or sexual abuse. Critics were worried that these types would not be able to respond to the militaristic influence of a correctional boot camp and would become truly antisocial. Hence, recidivism was high.[11] Aftercare is the only method found that works consistently in lowering recidivism, yet it is often the weakest link in the boot camp process. Juveniles graduating from boot camp facilities need to be able to come out being more confident about themselves in order not to reoffend. In addition, incarceration-based treatment simply may not be enough to stop offending, and additional efforts to continue treatment and care in a transitional setting may be necessary to help offenders successfully incorporate the lessons learned institutionally into a real-world setting.

One study found that prison employment in a vocational or apprenticeship training program could have both short- and long-term effects that reduce the likelihood of recidivism, particularly for men. Male probationers had 28 percent longer survival times than the comparison group when recidivism was defined as a new offence. Obviously, aftercare in the form of vocational training and employment should be considered a major component of a program's probation strategy in that it has been shown to cause a reduction in recidivism rates. Researchers must continue to investigate recidivism and its relationship to the trades and spread the word to those institutional programs that are either not or are borderline successful. The criminal justice system, as a whole, must provide more investigative opportunities to enhance and monitor the reintegration of adults and youths back into society following an institutional stay.[12] In essence, boot camp prisons have taught that neither punishment nor treatment will be effective if offenders are not transitioned back into the community. The challenges facing ex-inmates are already formidable, and they will need direct assistance with housing, transportation, alcohol and drug treatment, and personal relationships. Boot camps show forcefully that punishment alone is ineffective and that merely subjecting offenders to harsh environments does little to change offending behavior. When aftercare services are provided, however, recidivism is lowered and the convict is transitioned back into the community with professional help.

See Also: Juvenile Justice; Juveniles and Social Justice; Juveniles Treated as Adults.

Endnotes

1. American Correctional Association, *Standards for Juvenile Correctional Boot Camps Programs* (Laurel, MD: American Correctional Association, 1995).
2. Ibid.
3. P. Cromwell, L. F. Alarid, and R. V. del Carmen, *Community-Based Corrections,* 6th ed. (Florence, KY: Thomas Wadsworth, 2005).
4. T. Newburn and T. Jones, "Symbolic Politics and Penal Populism: The Long Shadow of Willie Horton," *Crime Media Culture* 1, no. 1 (2005): 72–87.
5. B. B. Benda and N. J. Pallone, eds., *Rehabilitation Issues, Problems, and Prospects in Boot Camp* (New York: Haworth Press, 2005).
6. Ibid.
7. Ibid.
8. R. Bodfield and E. Volante, "Death Deserved an Academy Award," *Arizona Daily Star,* April 29, 1998, 1.
9. L. D. Harrison, "The Revolving Prison Door for Drug-Involved Offenders: Challenges and Opportunities," *Crime and Delinquency* 47 (2001): 463.
10. Benda and Pallone, *Rehabilitation Issues.*
11. P. M. Hiller and A. J. Beck, "Prison-Based Substance Treatment, Residential Aftercare and Recidivism," *Addiction* 94 (1999): 833–42.
12. Ibid.

Further Reading: Benda, B. B., and N. J. Pallone, eds., *Rehabilitation Issues, Problems, and Prospects in Boot Camp* (New York: Haworth Press, 2005); Cromwell, P., L. F. Alarid, and R. V. del Carmen, *Community-Based Corrections,* 6th ed. (Florence, KY: Thomas Wadsworth, 2005); Langan, P. A., and D. J. Levine, *Recidivism of Prisoners Released in 1994* (Washington, DC: U.S. Department of Justice, Bureau of Justice Statistics, June 2002); MacKenzie, D. L., and G. S. Armstrong, eds., *Correctional Boot Camps: Military Basic Training or a Model for Corrections?* (Thousand Oaks, CA: Sage, 2004); MacKenzie, D. L., and E. E. Herbert, eds., *Correctional Boot Camps: A Tough Intermediate Sanction* (New York: Diane, 1996).

Li-Ching Hung and Cary Stacy Smith

CAMERAS IN THE COURTROOM

INTRODUCTION

Many commentators, jurists, attorneys, and scholars have argued that television cameras influence courtroom participants and their decision making, transform the courtroom into a theater, and injure the defendant's rights to a fair trial. The very fact that people and corporations are making money from broadcasting such programming is said to be unethical. Proponents counter these arguments by suggesting that the coverage actually keeps the process in check: Judges are less likely to act unjustly or arbitrarily, participants are on their best behavior, and perhaps more information may become available when viewers realize they have important knowledge regarding the participants of a televised case.[1] True gavel-to-gavel coverage may also allow the U.S. public to be educated in the ways of the courts because full coverage will give the average American a better insight into the justice system compared to the popular sound bites featured on the evening news. In turn, these uninhibited views of courtroom proceedings may yield public confidence in the judicial system. Although these issues are being continuously being debated, it seems that television coverage in some form will remain, regardless of sanctions or formal restrictions, because public demand will doubtfully diminish.

BACKGROUND

The U.S. justice process seems to have always captured the attention and imagination of the public. From Aaron Burr to Bill Clinton, Bruno Hauptmann to O. J. Simpson, these classic forms of drama and human-interest stories have

CRITICAL QUESTIONS IN THE CAMERA/COURTROOM DEBATE

- Is a televised trial a fair trial?
- Does a public trial mean a televised trial?
- Does televising trials change the court process?
- If so, what impact do cameras have?

remained contemporary delights for the masses. It should not be surprising, then, that television coverage of trials continues to expand—whether via gavel-to-gavel coverage as with *California v. Orenthal James Simpson* or with external commentary as with *California v. Michael Joe Jackson*. Media coverage, however, namely television coverage from within the courtroom, may bear unintended consequences that are detrimental to the criminal and civil justice process.

Cohn and Dow delve deep into this issue in their comprehensive assessment of televised trials.[2] By their account, the controversy of televised trials dates back to the 1930s with the criminal trial of Bruno Richard Hauptmann, the man accused of the kidnapping and murder of Charles Lindbergh's infant son. The popularity of Colonel Lindbergh and the tragic circumstances of losing his young son sparked a massive media event that culminated during the trial of the accused. At the onset of trial, a handful of cameras were allowed to record the proceedings, including four still photographers and two newsreel cameras. The court would soon tailspin out of control:

> The trial would be widely denounced for its "carnival atmosphere." "The Flemington Circus—This Way to the Big Tent," screamed one newspaper headline. Another blared, "It's a Sideshow, a Jamboree . . ." But careful hindsight indicates that the courtroom cameras contributed relatively little to the offensive spectacle. The court was often packed well beyond its capacity of 260. At one point 275 spectators and witnesses and 135 journalists jammed the room. The case was a magnet for the elite of the writing and broadcast world . . . [and] there were also daily sightings of non-journalistic celebrities as the case assumed a chic role in New York society.[3]

Despite the fact that the cameras truly did not have a role in the mockery of the legal establishment that the Hauptmann trial brought about, the external frenzy had instigated changes in the manner in which court proceedings were publicized. It was years later, as the electronic media were trying to get back into the courtroom, that the courts dealt with the constitutional issues of televised trials. Are televised trials fair trials? Does the public via the surrogate of the press have a constitutional right to a televised trial under our guarantee of a public trial as stated in the First Amendment to the U.S. Constitution?

The argument for a fair trial is truly the core of this debate. The Sixth Amendment to the U.S. Constitution dictates that any citizen accused in criminal prosecutions has "the right to a speedy and public trial, by an impartial jury of the State and district wherein the crime shall have been committed." This right was intended by the founding fathers to be augmented by the First Amendment right to a public trial. In theory, if the courtroom forum was kept open to public scrutiny and accountability, the autocratic justice that occurred in the English Star Chamber would not be possible.[4] A balance must be struck between these two rights—fair and public trial—as they can become conflicting:

> As with all persistently controversial issues, television in the courtroom is a two-edged sword. It is both invasive and informative. Though it brings the trial to the widest possible audience, in doing so it creates pressures and temptations for all participants. Though it reduces community speculations, rumors, and fears about what transpires in the courtroom, it also thrusts the general public (which may possess information the jury may not have) into assessments of specific cases and of the justice system in general. The public as a watchdog is an insurance against autocracy; but as an outside influence on a controlled deliberative process, it may also interfere with justice.[5]

Many times media coverage can become apparently out of hand. The courts do have remedies for such occurrences, however: gag orders, jury sequestering, restraining orders, careful voir dire (the jury selection process), continuances, and changes of venue. If these remedies cannot solve the bias caused by media coverage, then judges have the ability to exclude certain types of media coverage guided by the laws of a jurisdiction. Yet, even if these protections are utilized, there is no guarantee that the participants at trial are not considerably influenced by the presence of cameras—whether in favor of the defense or the prosecution or in favor of justice or miscarriages of this principle. To date, the research on this topic does not give a clear answer to this conundrum.

SENSATIONAL TRIALS

- O. J. Simpson—Criminal trial: January 24, 1995 (opening statements) to October 3, 1995 (verdict). Civil trial: October 23, 1996 (opening statements) to February 5, 1997 (verdict)
- Michael Jackson—January 31, 2005 (jury selection) to June 13, 2005 (verdict)
- William Kennedy Smith—December 2, 1991 (opening statements) to December 23, 1993 (verdict)
- The Menendez Brothers—First trial (tried together): January 20, 1992 to December 8, 1992. Second trial: October 11, 1995 to March 20, 1996 (verdict)
- Dr. Sam Sheppard—First trial: November 4, 1954 to December 21, 1954 (verdict)
- Iran-Contra—May 5, 1987 (beginning of hearings) to May 6, 1988 (indictment)
- Patty Hearst—January 15, 1970 (indictment) to January 25, 1971 (verdict)
- Charles Manson—July 24, 1970 (indictment) to January, 25, 1971 (verdict)

KEY EVENTS

For many years, the courts were making more concessions for televised court-room coverage. This was true until the commencement of the murder trial of football star O. J. Simpson. The Simpson trial and its impact on the legal establishment and the broader social climate have been key in shaping more restrictive laws, rules, and regulations of television in courtrooms across the United States, especially in California. Undoubtedly, the controversies caused by the broadcasting of courtroom and trial images are inextricably linked to carnival-like hearings of Simpson and Michael Jackson. The entertainment properties of such depictions, which include pop-star Jackson's dance on one of the sport-utility vehicles in his entourage and placing the camera on the Goldman and Brown families during key arguments of the Simpson trial, are what often leaves a bad taste in jurists' and legislatures' mouths. To this end, sensationalism has brought tightened restrictions on the media, just as in the Lindbergh/Hauptmann trial.

High-profile events can also empower victim's advocacy groups that have the ability to deeply influence legal reforms. For example, the murder of Polly Klaas in California led to the adoption of the well-known three-strikes laws when the little girl served as the poster child for the advocates of the reform.[6] Similarly, the kidnapping and murder of young Amber Hagerman in Texas helped shape the adoption of a nationwide notification system for missing children known as the Amber Alert System. Alerts can be seen and heard everywhere—electronic highway signage, broadcast radio and television, and tickers on Web sites (see http://codeamber.org). The rape and brutal murder of young Megan Kanka, who was the inspiration of the so-called Megan's laws[7] across the United States, serves as another example of how potent victim's rights movements can be in affecting legal reform. Thus, it seems any sensationalized trial—whether directly televised or not—becomes a key event for the criminal justice system and legislatures.

LEGAL DECISIONS

The stream of influential decisions regarding cameras in the courtroom began just after the Lindbergh/Bruno Hauptmann fiasco. With the legal community up in arms, the American Bar Association House of Delegates formulated and adopted Judicial Canon 35 in 1937. Essentially, this served as guidance for judges and the legal actors in terms of the inappropriate nature of photography and broadcasting of court proceedings. Essentially, this canon banned cameras from the courtroom, which later was expanded to moving pictures, or the television camera. This had no bearing on traditional (print) court reporting because this was viewed as conforming to the dignity and decorum of the courtroom and had constitutional protection.

This judicial canon had no official binding power as would a legal decision or legislative action. It did, however, serve as a compass for many judges and would serve as the guidance for the first legal decision on this matter. This occurred with *Estes v. Texas* in the 1960s. Billie Sol Estes, a powerful Texan financier, had stood trial in 1962 for strong-arming local farmers to purchase fictitious farm goods and to take out mortgages on properties that did not exist. The publicity was intense before and throughout the trial—so intense that a change of venue order was issued. At trial, the judge, following the letter of the law in Texas, had allowed television and still cameras at both the pretrial hearings and the actual trial. At the time, television cameras were large and obtrusive, with long cables needed to power these devises in a room not meant for this purpose. Cohn and Dow report, "Almost everyone conceded it was a disruptive scene."[8] It seemed this case was ripe for a challenge.

Indeed, this challenge has heard by the U.S. Supreme Court during Earl Warren's tenure as chief justice. The defense lawyers argued that the intense camera coverage—photographic and television broadcast—had impeded on their client's right to a fair trial under the due process clause of the Fourteenth Amendment. In a five-to-four decision, the Court agreed that the coverage was prejudicial, and cameras were thus banned from all U.S. courts. There was, however, some wiggle room left in the decision for states to experiment with trial coverage and for procamera enthusiasts to fight back.

This fight occurred in a trial originating in a Florida courtroom. *Chandler v. Florida* was bound to be a well-followed case. It involved two Miami Beach police officers, Noel Chandler and Robert Granger, who were involved in the burglary of a restaurant in the city they policed. Beyond this, which in of itself would be enough to garner intense media coverage, a witness serendipitously tapped into and audio recorded these officers during the commission of their crime as they utilized police walkie-talkies during the burglary.[9] At this time, Florida had a pilot program that allowed television coverage of select parts of the trial, including the prosecutor's witness and closing arguments, and the public was glued to their television sets.

The attorneys for the police officers took this matter to the U.S. Supreme Court after the subsequent conviction of their clients. This time, procamera groups submitted an amicus brief to defend the use of cameras in the courtroom. With time, cameras have become less intrusive and more commonplace when compared to the *Estes* era. Beyond this, research was proffered that suggested that television did not interrupt proceedings. In fact, arguments were made that televising trials, as the pilot program in Florida had done, was educative for the public and therapeutic to those involved in the criminal justice process. The strength of these arguments, supplemented with the fact that "seventeen states and the conference of chief justices supported Florida's position in amicus briefs" helped convince the Court that Florida's pilot program fell within the parameters of due process.[10] As long as a specific bias or prejudice cannot be proven on a case-by-case manner, these practices fall within constitutionality.

Since *Chandler*, states have been expanding their rules on television courtroom coverage. In 1996, 48 states had created concessions for television coverage in some manner, with many states allowing for extensive coverage (including gavel-to-gavel) on a case-by-case basis. The federal court system, on the other hand, has maintained the ban with some experiments of limited coverage. To date, the U.S. Supreme Court has been impervious to anything other than print media coverage and, rarely, audio feeds.

FUTURE PROSPECTS

In July 1991, Court TV began broadcasting courtroom images more so than any other television network in history. Since then, the cable channel has expanded its operation and has become modestly profitable with the help of many controversial and sensational trials. This stigma continues to drive corporate officials and producers to stress that their coverage is fair and balanced and does not cover only salacious trials. In fact, Court TV claims that they refuse to cover some trials due to the potential of sensationalism.

HAVE A LOOK!

See what TVW has to offer at http://www.tvw.org.

Court TV has a very extensive Web site that details trials in progress across the United States as well as information on forensic science, the investigative process, and much more. Visit the site at http://www.courttv.com.

Other models of courtroom coverage do exist. In Washington State, TVW—a public access channel—covers the local legislature, commissions, and appellate court arguments live and gavel-to-gavel. This model mirrors that utilized by C-Span and does not include much of the flash and glamour more likely assigned Court TV. Since TVW's beginnings in 1995, the network has grown with technology and now places many important feeds and programming online. This model has been catching on in other jurisdictions and will expand rapidly in the next decade. Additionally, as more technologically advanced courthouses are being built to suit the needs of the new generations of techno-savvy courtroom work groups, the potential for the expansion of coverage becomes even greater.

It is very unlikely that television courtroom coverage will wane in the future. On the other hand, it is extremely likely that another so-called trial of the century will come along to charge up the debate once again. In fact, it is only a matter of time.

See Also: Crime and Culture Consumption.

Endnotes

1. Television reaches more people than does print media and will continue to do so in the future.
2. Marjorie Cohn and David Dow, *Cameras in the Courtroom: Television and the Pursuit of Justice* (New York: Rowman and Littlefield, 2002).
3. Ibid., 15.
4. The Star Chamber is a name given to the medieval court of the king of England that was closed to the public. The court was notorious for autocratic, Draconian, and erratic rulings.
5. Ronald L. Goldfarb, *TV or Not TV: Television, Justice, and the Courts* (New York: New York University Press, 1998), xxi.

6. Samuel Walker, *Sense and Nonsense about Crime and Drugs: A Policy Guide,* 5th ed. (Belmont, CA: Wadsworth, 2001).

7. The law requires the registration of sex offenders and places this information in searchable databases. The judge in this case placed a total ban on cameras in the courtroom; however, the coverage of this trial outside of the courtroom was nevertheless intense.

8. Cohn and Dow, *Cameras in the Courtroom,* 19.

9. The witness was an amateur radio operator and enthusiast apparently at the right place and at the right time to record the crime in progress.

10. Goldfarb, *TV or Not TV,* 63.

Further Reading: Cohn, Marjorie, and David Dow, *Cameras in the Courtroom: Television and the Pursuit of Justice* (New York: Rowman and Littlefield, 2002); Goldfarb, Ronald L., *TV or Not TV: Television, Justice, and the Courts* (New York: New York University Press, 1998); Kirtley, Jane, "Banned from the Courtroom," *American Journalism Review,* no. 45 (March 2002): 74; Lassiter, Christo, "TV or Not TV. That Is the Question," *Journal of Law and Criminology* 86, no. 3 (1996): 928–1001; Vinson, C. Danielle, and John S. Ertter, "Entertainment or Education: How Do Media Cover the Courts?" *Press/Politics* 7, no. 4 (2002): 80–97.

David N. Khey

CLASS JUSTICE

INTRODUCTION

Karl Marx maintained that the root of most crime and injustice could be found in class conflict. Within and without the academies of crime and justice, this contention is highly controversial. In fact, it is so controversial that here in the United States, the whole idea of class itself is often in a state of political and social denial. Unlike gendered justice and sexism or racial (ethnic) justice and racism, class justice and classism has not been recognized in either the substantive or procedural sides of the law. Opponents of class justice argue that we are not only a so-called classless society but also that we are a democracy in which all individuals are subjects of due process, equal protection, and the rule of law. Although proponents of class justice do not take issue with the fact that no person, more or less, is above the law, they do contend that many actions are beyond incrimination and adjudication, whereas other actions are selectively enforced and differentially punished according to class interests.

BACKGROUND

Throughout most of the nineteenth century and well into the twentieth century, a blatant kind of class justice prevailed in the selective enforcement and differential application of the criminal and civil law to the haves and the have-nots. The laws themselves were heavily influenced by a reverence for private property and laissez-faire social relations. In terms of commercial transactions, the philosophy of the day was caveat emptor, "let the buyer beware." In the area of business, farmers and new merchants alike were allowed the freedom to expand their particular domains and to compete and acquire both property and capital with little legal interference. By contrast, labor was highly regulated. Unions were considered an illegal interference with freedom of contract and an unlawful conspiracy infringing upon the employer's property rights.

The administration of criminal (and civil) justice was chaotic, often corrupt, and subject to the buying of law enforcement and juries. An independent and decentralized criminal justice system designed for a more homogenized, pioneer, and primarily agricultural society was ill adapted for the needs of an increasingly complex, urban, and industrialized society. A social and cultural environment that was experiencing increasing numbers of immigrants from southern and eastern Europe, a changing means of rapid communication and transportation, and an expanding presence of wage-earning working classes called for a coordinated system of criminal justice.

By the end of the nineteenth century, the buying of justice that had prevailed earlier (available to those who could afford representation in the legislatures, in the courts, and in the streets) was threatening the very legitimacy of criminal justice in the United States. The initial laissez-faire emphasis on the right to acquire private property had blossomed into a full-fledged national preoccupation with wealth and power. Political corruption became widespread, and political machines dominated urban areas: "The machines controlled city governments, including the police and the courts. Payrolls were padded and payoffs were collected from contractors."[1] Graft and other forms of bribery contributed not only to the buying of justice by those who could afford it but also to a changing national morality. Rackets, pull, and protection were common antidotes to stubborn legal nuisances. Prevailing values of wealth and success predominated as guiding principles of right and wrong. "The ability to 'make good' and 'get way with it' offsets the questionable means employed in the business as well as professional world. Disrespect for the law and order is the accompanying product of this scheme of success."[2]

Those who were marginalized, especially the poor, unemployed, women, and people of color, were rarely, if ever, in a position to buy justice. As the marginalized groups of immigrants and others grew in urban centers across the United States, and as the miscarriages of justice flourished, the need to reform the institutions of criminal justice grew, because the country was beginning to experience bitter class wars. The working classes aggressively resisted exploitation through on-the-job actions and wide social movements. To combat challenges to the emerging monopoly or corporate order of industrial capitalism, the wealthy ruling classes initially employed illegal violence, such as the hiring of thugs and private armies. Later, they retained the services of private security companies, such as Pinkerton's, to infiltrate and break up worker organizations.

KEY EVENTS

Double Standards of Justice

In 1964, William Rummel received three years in prison after being convicted of a felony for fraudulently using a credit card to obtain $80 worth of goods.

Five years later, he passed a forged check in the amount of $28.36 and received four years. In 1973, Rummel was convicted of a third felony: obtaining $102.75 by false pretenses for accepting payment to fix an air conditioner that he never returned to repair. Rummel received a mandatory life sentence under Texas's recidivist statue. He challenged this sentence on the grounds that it violated the Eighth Amendment's prohibition of cruel and unusual punishment by being grossly disproportionate to the crime.

In *Rummel v. Estelle* (1980), the U.S. Supreme Court affirmed Rummel's life sentence for the theft of less than $230 that never involved force or the threat of force. Justice Louis Powell's dissent noted "it is difficult to imagine felonies that pose less danger to the peace and good order of a civilized society than the three crimes committed by the petitioner" (445 U.S. 263, 295). However, Justice William Rehnquist's majority opinion stated there was an "interest, expressed in all recidivist statues, in dealing in a harsher manner with those who by repeated criminal acts have shown that they are simply incapable of conforming to the norms of society as established by its criminal law" (445 U.S. 263). After "having twice imprisoned him for felonies, Texas was entitled to place upon Rummel the onus of one who is simply unable to bring his conduct within the norms prescribed by the criminal law" (445 U.S. 284).

Now consider the case of General Electric (GE), which is not considered a habitual criminal offender. Nevertheless it has been prosecuted for diverse crimes over many decades. In the 1950s, GE and several companies agreed in advance on the sealed bids they submitted for heavy electrical equipment. This price-fixing defeated the purpose of competitive bidding, costing taxpayers and consumers as much as a billion dollars. GE was fined $437,000—a tax-deductible business expense—the equivalent of a person earning $175,000 a year getting a $3 ticket. Two executives spent only 30 days in jail, even though one defendant had commented that price-fixing "had become so common and gone for so many years that we lost sight of the fact that it was illegal."[3]

In the 1970s, GE made illegal campaign contributions to Richard Nixon's presidential campaign. Widespread illegal discrimination against minorities and women at GE resulted in a $32 million settlement. Also during this time, three former GE nuclear engineers—including one who had worked for the company for 23 years and managed the nuclear complaint department—resigned to draw attention to serious design defects in the plans for the Mark III nuclear reactor because the standard practice was "sell first, test later."[4]

In 1981, GE was convicted of paying a $1.25 million bribe to a Puerto Rican official to obtain a power plant contract. GE has pleaded guilty to felonies involving illegal procurement of highly classified defense documents, and in 1985 it pleaded guilty to 108 counts of felony fraud involving defense contracts related to the Minuteman missile. In spite of a new code of ethics, GE was convicted in three more criminal cases over the next few years, in addition to paying $3.5 million to settle cases involving retaliation against four whistle-blowers who helped reveal the defense fraud. (GE subsequently lobbied Congress to weaken the False Claims Act.) In 1988, the government re-turned another 317 indictments against GE for fraud in a $21 million computer contract.

In 1989, GE's stock brokerage firm paid a $275, 000 civil fine for discriminating against low-income consumers, the largest fine ever under the Equal Credit Opportunity Act. A 1990 jury convicted GE of fraud for cheating on a $254 million contract for battlefield computers, and journalist William Greider reported that the $27.2 million fine included money to "settle government complaints that it had padded bids on two hundred other military and space contracts."[5]

Because of tax changes that GE had lobbied for and the President Ronald Reagan tax cuts generally, GE paid no taxes between 1981 and 1983 when net profits were $6.5 billion. In fact, in a classic example of corporate welfare, GE received a tax rebate of $283 million during a time of high national deficits even though the company eliminated 50,000 jobs in the United States by closing 73 plants and offices. Further, "Citizen GE," whose advertising slogan has been "Brings good things to life," is one of the prime environmental polluters and is identified as responsible for contributing to the damage of 47 sites in need of environmental cleanup in the United States alone.

Even though felons usually lose political rights, GE's political action committee contributes hundreds of thousands to Congress each year, and it now owns NBC television with all of its influence. In spite of having been convicted of defrauding every branch of the military, representatives from GE are frequently invited to testify before Congress. If the corporation's revenues were compared to the gross domestic product of countries, it would be in the top 50 largest economies in the world. With this kind of political, economic, and social power, it is easy to understand why "three strikes and you're out" does not apply to the big hitters like GE.

The pattern outlined in these examples was reinforced in 2003, when the Supreme Court upheld a 50-year sentence for two acts of shoplifting videos from Kmart. Under California's three-strikes law, Leandro Andrade's burglary convictions from the 1980s counted as the first two, and the prosecutor decided to charge the shoplifting incidents as strikes, which carry a mandatory 25 years each. The Supreme Court, citing *Rummel v. Estelle,* held that the sentences were neither disproportionate nor unreasonable (*Lockyer v. Andrade,* 538 U.S. 63).

At the same time, Enron's chief financial officer, Andrew Fastow, negotiated a plea bargain for 10 years in prison. Fastow had been instrumental in fraud, which resulted in the largest bankruptcy in U.S. history at that time. He had worked the deals to launder loans through allegedly independent entities to make them appear as revenue for Enron, and he helped push the accountants to approve the deals and used the massive banking fees Enron paid to silence Wall Street analysts who asked questions about Enron's finances. Fastow was originally charged with 109 felony counts, including conspiracy, wire fraud, securities fraud, falsifying books, as well as obstruction of justice, money laundering, insider trading, and filing false income tax returns. The sentence was negotiated in an environment in which getting tough on corporate crime was seen as a high priority.[6]

Class, Crime, and the Law

The rich and powerful use their influence to keep acts from becoming crimes, even though these acts may be more socially injurious than those labeled criminal. Further, they are also able to use mass-mediated communication to shape the public discourse and moral outrage about crime. In short, the corporate elite's relative monopoly over the airways allows them to act as so-called transmission belts for creating consensus over what is and is not a crime. For example, Jeffrey Reiman in the eighth edition of *The Rich Get Richer and the Poor Get Prison* (2007) notes that multiple deaths that result from unsafe workplaces tend to get reported as accidents and disasters, whereas the term *mass murder* is reserved exclusively for street crime. Although there are differences between the two, especially in the level of intentionality, it is not clear that one should be a regulatory violation and the other should be a crime.

If the point of the criminal law is to protect people's well-being, then why was no crime committed in the 2005 deaths of 12 miners in West Virginia: "Time and again over the past four years, federal mining inspectors documented the same litany of problems at central West Virginia's Sago Mine: mine roofs that tended to collapse without warning. Faulty or inadequate tunnel supports. A dangerous buildup of flammable coal dust."[7] In the two years before this explosion, the mine was cited 273 times for safety violations, one-third of which were classified as "significant and substantial," and "16 violations logged in the past eight months were listed as 'unwarrantable failures,' a designation reserved for serious safety infractions for which the operator had either already been warned, or which showed 'indifference or extreme lack of care.' "[8] This state of affairs seems to fit within the criminal law categories of knowing, reckless, or negligent, but most matters like this stay within the realm of administrative sanctions and the civil law.

Outside of mining, the situation is the same. From 1982 to 2002, the Occupational Safety and Health Administration (OSHA), which has primary responsibility for the nation's workplace safety, identified 1,242 deaths it concluded were related to "willful" safety violations. Only 7 percent of cases were referred for prosecution, however, and "having avoided prosecution once, at least 70 employers willfully violated safety laws again, resulting in scores of additional deaths. Even these repeat violators were rarely prosecuted."[9] One of the many barriers is that causing the death of a worker by willfully violating safety laws is a misdemeanor with a maximum sentence of six months in jail, so such cases are of little interest to prosecutors. This level of punishment was established in 1970 by Congress, which has repeatedly rejected attempts to make it tougher; consequently, harassing a wild burro on federal lands carries twice the maximum sentence of causing a worker's death through willful safety violations. Compare the lack of change in the punishment for a worker's death with the escalating toughness for all types of street crime, in which Congress's "tough on crime" attitude led to three-strikes laws, expansion of the number of strikable offenses, mandatory minimums, increasingly severe sentencing guidelines, and increased offenses eligible for the death penalty. Since the early 1990s, however, Congress has voted down all laws to increase penalties for workplace deaths, even recent modest proposals to increase the maximum penalty to 10 years.[10]

In terms of class justice generally, much of the harmful and illegitimate behavior of the elite members of society has not traditionally been defined as criminal, but nearly all the harmful and deviant behavior perpetrated by the poor and the powerless, the working and middle classes, is defined as violating the criminal law. Thus, basing crime-control theory and practice on a neutral criminal law ignores the fact that the legal order and the administration of justice reflects a structural class bias that concentrates the coercive power of the state on the behaviors of the relatively poor and powerless members of society. These omitted relations of class justice reveal the importance of two systemic operations in the administration of criminal justice: selective enforcement and differential application of the law. Selective enforcement of harms by the law refers to the fact that most harm perpetrated by the affluent is "beyond incrimination."[11] As for the harms committed by the politically and economically powerful that do come within the purview of criminal law, these are typically downplayed, ignored, or marginalized through differential application of leniency and/or compassion.

Similarly, criminologist Stephen Box suggests that one of the most important advantages of corporate criminals lies "in their ability to prevent their actions from becoming subject to criminal sanctions in the first place."[12]

Although certain behaviors may cause widespread harm, criminal law does not forbid abuses of power in the realm of economic domination, governmental control, and denial of human rights. As we saw in the opening narrative of this entry, being a habitual offender is against the law in most areas, where "three strikes and you're out" applies to street criminals. But habitual offender laws do not apply to corporate persons (like GE) that can repeatedly commit serious crimes without being subjected to these statutes or to the legal possibility of a state revoking a corporation's charter to exist.

In some cases, harmful actions will be civil offenses rather than criminal ones, but the difference is significant because civil actions are not punishable by prison and do not carry the same harsh stigma. A plea to civil or administrative charges does not amount to an admission of guilt and thus cannot be used against a business in other related litigation. Other destructive behavior may not be prohibited by civil law or regulations created by administrative agencies. In this respect, the tobacco industry produces a product that kills 400,000 people each year, but its actions are not illegal, not a substantial part of the media campaign of the Office for National Drug Control Policy or Partnership for a Drug Free America, or even subject to federal oversight as a drug.

When corporations are charged, they can use their resources to evade responsibility. Criminologist James Coleman (1985) did an extensive study of the enforcement of the Sherman Antitrust Act in the petroleum industry and identified four major strategies that corporations employ to prevent full application of the law. First is endurance and delay, which includes using expensive legal resources to prolong the litigation and obstruct the discovery of information by raising as many motions and legal technicalities as possible. Second is the use of corporate wealth and political connections to undermine the will of legislators and regulators to enforce the law's provisions. Third is secrecy and deception about ownership and control to prevent detection of violations and make them more difficult to prove. Fourth are threats of economic consequences to communities and the economy if regulations are passed and/or fully enforced.

One of the classic statements on this topic, first referred to by former General and President Dwight Eisenhower as the "military-industrial complex," is a book by C. Wright Mills called *The Power Elite* (1956). He contended that an elite composed of the largest corporations, the military, and the federal government dominates life in the United States. Mills argued that these three spheres of power are highly interrelated, with members of each group coming from similar upper-class social backgrounds, attending the same private and Ivy League universities, even belonging to the same social or political organizations. In addition to their mutual "ruling class interests," corporate elites also make large political donations to both the Republicans and Democrats to ensure their access to the law-making process.

Reiman suggests that the result of these relations is that law is like a carnival mirror. It distorts our understanding of the harms that may befall us by magnifying the threat from street crime because it criminalizes more of the conduct of poor people. At the same time, it distorts our perception about the danger from crime in the office suites by downplaying and not protecting people from the harms perpetrated by those above them in the class system. As a consequence, both the criminal law and the administration of justice do "not simply *reflect* the reality of crime; [they have] a hand in *creating* the reality we see."[13] Thus, to say that the criminal law appropriately focuses on the most dangerous acts is a problematic statement because the criminal law shapes our perceptions about what is a dangerous act.

Reiman also argues that the processing of offenders serves to "weed out the wealthy." Selective enforcement means that many harmful acts will not come within the realm of criminal law, and if they do, it is unlikely they will be prosecuted, "or if prosecuted, not punished, or if punished, only mildly."[14] This observation is consistent with the analysis in Black's highly referenced and acclaimed book, *The Behavior of Law* (1976). Black sought to discover a series of rules to describe the amount of law and its behavior in response to social variables such as stratification, impersonality, culture, social organization, and other forms of social control. When it comes to issues of class, the variables of stratification and social organization are the two most relevant.

Black proposed that the law varies directly with hierarchy and privilege, so that the more inequality in a country, the more law. He also applied his proposition to disputes between two parties of unequal status and wealth. Based on a wide variety of cases, Black concluded there is likely to be more law in a downward direction, such as when a rich person is victimized by a poorer one. This means the use of criminal rather than civil law, for example, and a greater likelihood of a report, investigation, arrest, prosecution, and prison sentence. In contrast, when the wealthier harms the poorer, Black predicted there would be less law, meaning civil law, monetary fines rather than jail, and therapeutic sanctions rather than punitive ones. Further, Black argued that there is likely to be more law in the downward direction when an individual victimizes a group high in social organization such as a corporation or the state. Conversely, less law and a pattern of differential application are likely to be the result of a corporate body or the state victimizing individuals or groups of individuals that have lower levels of social organization, such as poor communities.

FUTURE PROSPECTS

Although attention has been paid to examples from occupational safety, the analysis provided here also applies to financial crimes, including several episodes of massive and widespread fraud. For example, Representative Frank Annunzio, who was chairman of the House Subcommittee on Financial Institutions that investigated the prosecution of criminals involved in the savings and loan (S & L) wrongdoings of the late 1980s, makes the same points that Reiman and Black do in his opening remarks to one congressional hearing:

> Frankly, I don't think the administration has the interest in pursuing Gucci-clad white-collar criminals. These are hard and complicated cases, and the defendants often were rich, successful, prominent members of their upper-class communities. It is far easier putting away a sneaker-clad high school dropout who tried to rob a bank of a thousand dollars with a stick-up note, than a smooth talking S & L executive who steals a million dollars with a fraudulent note.[15]

These comments highlight the difficulty and reluctance in prosecuting upper-class criminals even though the harm done is much greater than street crime. Some S & L executives personally stole tens of millions of dollars, and others were responsible for the collapse of financial institutions that needed government bailouts to the tune of $1 billion. The total cost of the S & L bailout ultimately climbed to about $500 billion, yet few S & L crooks went to prison, and the ones who received a prison sentence were sentence to an average of two years, compared with an average of nine years for a bank robber.[16]

After such expensive and widespread fraud, Congress briefly decided to get tough but soon removed all the regulations put in place to safeguard against similar fraud. According to the authors of *Big Money Crime,* soon after the S & L crisis, Congress went on a wave of "cavalier" financial deregulation, creating the "paradox of increasing financial deregulation coming on the heels of the most catastrophic experiment with deregulation in history."[17] These actions set the stage for the 2002 financial crimes involving Enron, WorldCom, Global Crossing, Tyco, and several other billion-dollar corporations. Although a few of the responsible chief executives found themselves doing time behind bars, most of those involved in these fraudulent crimes found themselves escaping courtesy of class justice. At the same time, the victims of these crimes—workers, consumers, investors, retirees, and more—received little or no compensation, despite the fact that many lost their life savings.

Historically then, based on the past—long-term and short-term—and on the present and given the prevailing political and economic arrangements and barring a major revolution in the organization of multinational or global capitalism, class justice is looking very secure into the foreseeable future.

See Also: Equal Justice and Human Rights; Social Justice.

Endnotes

1. Charles D. Edelstein and Robert J. Wicks, *An Introduction to Criminal Justice* (New York: McGraw-Hill, 1977), 7.
2. Nathaniel E. Cantor, *Crime: Criminals and Criminal Justice* (New York: Henry Holt, 1932), 145.
3. Quoted in Stuart Hills, ed., *Corporate Violence: Injury and Death for Profit* (Savage, MD: Rowman and Littlefield, 1987), 191.
4. Ibid., 170.
5. William Greider, *Who Will Tell the People? The Betrayal of American Democracy* (New York: Simon and Schuster, 1996), 4.
6. Paul Leighton and Jeffrey Reiman, "A Tale of Two Criminals: We're Tougher on Corporate Criminals, but They Still Don't Get What They Deserve," supplement to Jeffrey Reiman, *The Rich Get Richer and the Poor Get Prison,* 7th ed. (Boston: Allyn and Bacon, 2004), http://paulsjusticepage.com/RichGetRicher/fraud2004.htm.
7. Joby Warrick, "Safety Violations Have Piled Up at Coal Mine," *Washington Post,* January 6, 2006, A4.
8. Ibid.
9. David Barstow, "When Workers Die: U.S. Rarely Seeks Charges for Deaths in Workplace, "*The New York Times,* December 22, 2003, http://reclaimdemocracy.org/weekly_2003/when_workers_die.html.
10. Ibid.
11. Mark Kennedy, "Beyond Incrimination: Some Neglected Facets of the Theory of Punishment," *Catalyst* 5 (Summer 1970): 1–30.
12. Quoted in John Braithwaite, "Poverty, Power and White Collar Crime," in *White Collar Crime Reconsidered,* ed. Kip Schlegel and David Weisbord (Boston: Northeastern University Press, 1992), 89.
13. Jeffrey Reiman, *The Rich Get Richer and the Poor Get Prison,* 6th ed. (Boston: Allyn and Bacon, 1998), 57; emphasis in the original.
14. Ibid.
15. Hearings before the Subcommittee on Financial Institutions Supervision, Regulation, and Insurance of the Committee on Banking, Finance, and Urban Affairs, U.S. House of Representatives, 101st Congress, 2nd Session, "When Are the Savings and Loan Crooks Going to Jail?" (Washington, DC: U.S. Government Printing Office, 1990), 23.
16. Ibid.
17. Kitty Calavita, Henry Pontell, and Robert Tillman, *Big Money Crime* (Berkeley and Los Angeles: University of California Press, 1997), 10.

Further Reading: Auerbach, Jerold S., *Unequal Justice: Lawyers and Social Change in Modern America* (New York: Oxford University Press, 1976); Barak, Gregg, *In Defense of Whom? A Critique of Criminal Justice Reform* (Cincinnati, OH: Anderson, 1980); Barak, Gregg, Paul Leighton, and Jeanne Flavin, *Class, Race, Gender, and Crime: The Social Realties of Justice in America,* 2nd ed. (Lanham, MD. Rowman and Littlefield, 2007); Black, Donald, *The Behavior of* Law (New York: Academic Press, 1976); Coleman, James, "Law and Power: The Sherman Antitrust Act and Its Enforcement in the Petroleum Industry," *Social* Problems 32, no. 3 (1985): 264–74; Hartmann,

Thom, *Unequal Protection: The Rise of Corporate Dominance and the Theft of Human Rights* (New York: Rodale, 2002); Mills, C. Wright, *The Power Elite* (New York: Oxford University Press, 1956); Reiman, Jeffrey, *The Rich Get Richer and the Poor Get Prison,* 8th ed. (Boston: Allyn and Bacon, 2007); Simon, David, *Elite Deviance,* 6th ed. (Boston: Allyn and Bacon, 1999).

Gregg Barak and Paul Leighton

CLEMENCY

INTRODUCTION

Clemency has evolved into a highly contested, politicized site of intervention by contemporary movements for gender, race, and class equality that are seeking a last hope for justice, particularly for women who killed their abusers and for all who are sentenced to death.

Proponents of capital punishment believe clemency should be limited or abolished, arguing that it is a relic of the past, a function of mercy without rational justification, or an arbitrary instrument that has been abused. Because many, if not most, clemencies occur in the flurry of administrative actions at the end of a term, they are often inconsistent and controversial. Clemency, it is argued, should be reserved at most for occasional, retributive justice, to remedy only the most blatant judicial errors.

Clemency advocates point to wrongful convictions and executions, the bloated prison industry, and the atrophy of clemency at both federal and state levels. They note the ways that political self-interest and corporate media have traded on public fear, contributing to overincarceration even as violent crime has declined. Their concern is for clemency's critical role as a redress to systemwide injustices such as those involving the arbitrariness of the death penalty and women's unequal access to fair trials due to society's inadequate response to their battering.

BACKGROUND

Clemency has been a power vested in the sovereign as an integral component of the law since the earliest legal codes were recorded. Imprecise in definition and inconsistent in handling, clemency is a discretionary power to remit sentences, after conviction, by means of pardon, commutation, reprieve, or amnesty. Generally, a pardon is the most sweeping remission of the consequences for violating the law: It erases both the punishment and the guilt of the offender after conviction and may be absolute or conditional. Commutation shortens the offender's sentence, generally to time served, or may substitute a term sentence for a death sentence. A reprieve is a temporary suspension to postpone execution of the sentence. Amnesty usually refers to release of persons convicted of political offenses.

In the United States, the power to grant clemency was incorporated into the U.S. Constitution, as well as into state constitutions, as a vital function of the system of checks and balances.[1] It has traditionally been used to correct injustices in individual cases but has also served as a response to systemic problems in application of the law. In the case of courts and laws that have been too harsh or unjust, clemency can send a message that change is needed to ensure justice. The U.S. Supreme Court stated that clemency is a "fail safe";[2] and further, without clemency, our government "would be most imperfect and deficient."[3]

Clemency differs from judicial review in that it is the only mechanism that allows for the full circumstances of a case to be presented without the constraints of court technicalities. As the last remedy to unfair trials, excessive sentences, and the denial of equal rights, it is critical in cases in which inequities resulted from systemic gender, race, or sexual bias, such as those involving capital punishment of primarily black defendants and life or long sentences for women defendants who acted in self-defense against abusers. Although clemencies are often granted for a range of reasons in last-minute terms of presidents and governors, in recent years it has been those involving the death penalty and battered women that have raised important legal questions about the responsible use of clemency and its role in the U.S. system of justice.

Prior to the 1960s, clemencies were granted in approximately 20 percent to 25 percent of capital cases. In 1972, the Supreme Court issued a moratorium on capital punishment, finding all death penalty laws at the time unconstitutional because of their arbitrariness.[4] When the death penalty was reinstated in 1976, the Supreme Court's assumption that clemency is a meaningful fail-safe was undermined by the ascendance of tough-on-crime strategies of politicians and mainstream news media as clemencies dropped drastically. Since 1976, only 229 death row inmates have been granted clemency.[5]

Amid the punitive legal landscape of the late twentieth century, the U.S. Congress and all 50 state legislatures ignored decreasing violent-crime rates and enacted mandatory minimum sentences without allowance for extenuating circumstances. Most states curtailed parole, circumscribed sentencing guidelines, passed mandatory sentencing laws, and all but ignored clemency. Judicial and legislative remedies for addressing postconviction claims and appeals became more and more restricted by law.

Margaret C. Love, the attorney responsible for pardons at the U.S. Justice Department from 1990 to 1997, noted, "clemency has been taken hostage in the war on crime."[6] The rise of the prison industry and executions, particularly of women, proceeded with ever-diminishing threat to politicians' careers and corporate media's profits. During his term as governor of Texas, George W. Bush denied all clemency petitions except one and oversaw the executions of 150 men and 2 women before he was elected president in 2000.[7] Once routine in capital cases, clemency became a rare event even as the number of petitions grew and the struggles over gender and race bias in the courts and the death penalty intensified.

BATTERED WOMEN, INEQUALITY, AND LEGAL REFORM

The end of the twentieth century also saw the beginning of one of the most significant sociopolitical movements in U.S. history. Since the mid-1970s, the battered women's movement, which arose out of the larger feminist movement, has worked in local communities to establish shelters, hotlines, and advocacy for battered women. Groups of battered women brought class-action suits against police departments and prosecutors to compel them to provide equal protection under the law and to arrest and prosecute batterers. They lobbied local, state, and federal legislators to pass laws and allocate funds to combat domestic violence. The effort was unique in that it consisted of crime victims themselves who, denied equal protection by the courts and public institutions, established their own system of protection for themselves and their children. One result of the battered women's movement has been a dramatic decrease in men who are killed by female partners over the past thirty years. However, the number of women murdered by male partners has not decreased significantly during that period.*

The tenacity of public attitudes, laws, and institutions that make allowances for individual batterers while blaming women for their own abuse is grounded in gender and race inequalities. Criminal remedies, such as mandatory and preferred arrest provisions, send a clear social message of support to victims, and civil tort suits and protection orders make a public statement that battering is illegal; however, their arbitrary, often ineffective enforcement has a deleterious effect on women's lives and safety.** The deeply resistant criminal-legal system and socioeconomic barriers to women's independence are interlocking structures that connect domestic violence to women's imprisonment and death.

Courts, laws, and law enforcement have all been unwilling to acknowledge that their failure to protect battered women too often results in their being killed or being forced to kill. In light of self-defense laws that do not recognize reasonable actions in situations involving women's abuse, judges' refusals to admit evidence of domestic violence or give proper instructions to juries, and other institutional failures in women's cases, legal reform for battered women who kill became one of the most significant areas of feminist lawmaking in recent years. The backlash that continues to plague this effort has made the promise of equality inaccessible and clemency the last hope for justice for wrongly convicted battered women.

---

*Callie Marie Rennison, "Intimate Partner Violence, 1993–2001," U.S. Department of Justice, Bureau of Justice Statistics Crime Data Brief (2003), http://www.ojp.usdoj.gov/bjs/pub/pdf/ipv01.pdf.

**Elizabeth Schneider, *Battered Women and Feminist Lawmaking* (New Haven, CT: Yale University Press, 2000), 94, 147.

LEGAL DEVELOPMENTS

Since the U.S. Constitution provides no guidance regarding clemency decisions, both the legislative and judicial branches of the federal government have attempted at various times to interpret or limit the use of clemency. Nevertheless, the Supreme Court has consistently remained deferential to the executive in clemency decisions, refusing to consider certain claims of new evidence and stating that clemency is the constitutional safeguard against error and injustice.

In ex parte *Garland* (1866), the Court upheld the executive's sole power to pardon when it addressed a congressional requirement that persons who wished to practice in federal court must swear a loyalty oath to assure that they had never borne arms against the United States nor given "aid, comfort, counsel or encouragement" to its enemies.[8] Garland, who was granted a pardon for acts he committed as a Confederate sympathizer, wanted to practice law in federal court. The Court declared that a pardon restores all civil rights and erases all punishments and established that Congress could not limit the effect of a pardon through a legislative act.

In *Burdick v. United States* (1915), the Court confronted a pardon that infringed on an individual's constitutional rights.[9] Burdick invoked his Fifth Amendment privilege against self-incrimination and refused to testify before a federal grand jury. The president offered Burdick a pardon if he testified, but Burdick still refused. The Court stated that, because negative consequences could still flow from Burdick's admission of guilt, he should not have to testify because a pardon should not erode an individual's constitutional rights.

In *Herrera v. Collins* (1993), the Supreme Court stated that executive clemency has provided the fail-safe in our criminal justice system.[10] *Hererra* reaffirmed the principle that an executive has the obligation to consider clemency in those cases in which judicial or legislative limitations deny a prisoner's access to post-conviction redress.

In *Ohio Adult Parole Authority v. Woodward* (1998), the U.S. Supreme Court held that the power of clemency is subject to judicial review and that the Fourteenth Amendment requires that minimal due process be accorded capital inmates in clemency proceedings.[11] Although the minimal requirement stated in this case provided for very little in the way of fair and unbiased process, it has given hope that this may open the door to greater fairness in clemency decisions, especially if the Court revisits this decision and requires that clemency be administered following due process principles rather than minimal process.

Because appeals focus on legal and procedural errors and allow virtually no avenue for relief in the face of a conviction based on factual error, clemency petitions often allow the only opportunity to bring new evidence in a case. Ultimately, the language of the Constitution provides for just two limitations on the pardon power. The first is that the power to pardon is vested solely in the president. The second bars pardons in the case of impeachment against a federal official.[12]

KEY EVENTS

In 1989, the first prisoner to be exonerated through DNA identification technology was released in Chicago, Illinois.[13] From 1989 to 2003, at least 440 more exonerations followed across the United States; 244 of them were cleared by DNA evidence, 196 by other means. Disturbingly commonplace, the exonerations gave clear evidence of a seriously flawed criminal justice system. With few exceptions, all of the exonerees were sentenced to death or long prison terms. The most common causes of wrongful convictions were eyewitness misidentification in the case of rape and deliberately false evidence given for some reward by the actual perpetrator, codefendant, or informant in the case of murder. Other causes were police perjury, falsified evidence, or coerced confessions. It is estimated that more than two-thirds of capital cases have resulted in exonerations or reversals of sentences or convictions by state or federal courts. The high rates of false convictions found through DNA evidence and intensive investigations raised serious questions about the errors plaguing the tens of thousands of cases involving life or long-term sentences that are not so thoroughly investigated but, in fact, are forgotten.

At the turn of the millennium, two unprecedented mass clemencies responded in part to the growing grassroots abolition movements to end women's abuse and capital punishment. In December 1990 and January 1991, Governor Richard Celeste of Ohio granted clemency to 25 women who had killed their abusers. Governor Celeste's act was based on the recognition that the criminal justice system was fatally flawed for battered women defendants: The facts about domestic terrorism in the cases had not been presented at trials, and those who accepted plea bargains did so because they were advised that juries would not believe them and judges would be unlikely to give instructions on self-defense.

Media response to the event was largely positive. In the wave of public excitement, a grassroots clemency movement for battered women prisoners emerged in the hope that more governors would follow suit. It has been estimated that between two thousand and five thousand women who killed their abusers are serving life or long terms due to unfair trials that failed to present the facts of their cases. Since the Celeste commutations, governors in 17 states have granted clemencies to at least 56 battered women.[14] In some states, governors have chosen to accelerate the parole process for women who killed their abusers rather than risk their political careers in granting clemencies.

Before leaving office, Governor Celeste made another astonishing act of clemency, commuting eight death sentences to life. His stated reason was the "profound racial bias [that] cast doubt over virtually every death sentence, especially in the case of the four women on death row, all of whom were African American. . . . More than half of the men on death row were African American. But even more disturbing was the evidence that these men were at best marginally able to function in our society; they were men with very low IQs, with evidence of serious mental illness, and with chronic addictions." This time, his mass clemencies produced a firestorm of protest from the media and public. Governor Celeste's willingness to act on injustice based on gender and racial bias and mental illness was groundbreaking.[15]

In 2000, Illinois Governor George Ryan declared a moratorium on the death penalty in response to the exonerations that were revealing persistent errors in the administration of capital punishment. Since the death penalty was reinstated in that state in 1977, 12 death row inmates had been executed and 13 were exonerated. In 2003, he granted clemency to all 167 persons on the state's death row. His actions were fiercely attacked by capital-punishment advocates who accused him of abusing his power but were applauded both by legal scholars across the country and by the growing movement to abolish the death penalty.[16]

Since Governor Ryan's moratorium, the population of inmates on death row nationwide has decreased each year. There were 3,254 prisoners on death row in 2005. In 2002, the U.S. Supreme Court barred the execution of retarded people; in 2006, the Court ended capital punishment for juveniles. Although the death penalty is not yet abolished, executions have also been dropping steadily. In 2005, 60 persons were executed, down from 98 in 1999, and 96 were sentenced to die in 2005, down from 320 in 1996.[17]

REHABILITATION VERSUS RETRIBUTION CLEMENCY DEBATES

Debates about strategies to expand the use of clemency and diverging visions of how clemency should function turn on differences between rehabilitative and retributive notions of justice. Some blame the ascendance of retributive approaches to punishment, such as mandatory sentencing, reinstatement of the death penalty, denials of due process by the courts, and the partial dismantling of parole, for the collapse of clemency and other rehabilitative forms of justice. Because racial and gender bias brought disproportionate sentences to women and people of color as a result of prevailing stereotypes and ignorance about issues of abuse, some have concerns that rates of error in those death cases may also be higher. Rehabilitative approaches to clemency emphasize mercy, forgiveness, and redemptive philosophies of justice that would extend uses of clemency to postconviction transformations or contributions.

Retributive justice advocates of clemency argue that this approach has historically been more successful and less politically explosive. They point out that most clemencies have been granted for justice-enhancing reasons, such as doubts about innocence or fair trials, questions of proportionality of the sentence relative to that received by codefendants, or questions of culpability due to mental capacity. Favoring an expanded definition of retributive justice, this argument is meant to encourage a more unbridled, open-handed discretion on the part of the executive granting clemency.

FUTURE PROSPECTS

Despite the politically explosive nature of the clemency power, it remains a critical component of our system of justice that needs to be exercised in a fair, openhanded, and principled manner throughout an executive's tenure in office. Historically, U.S. jurisprudence has consistently disregarded the rights of women, especially victims of abuse; people of color; lesbians, gays, and transgender people; the poor; and the mentally ill. Because the law has widely permitted, even codified, prejudice and violence, judges and jurors continue to normalize such brutality, especially within the domestic sphere. The racial composition of the prisons, together with the economic status and backgrounds of abuse among the prison population, gives further evidence of injustice.

In the twenty-first century, a new abolition movement has emerged with a vision to repudiate prisons altogether. Emphasizing strategies of decarceration, the movement emphasizes a continuum of alternatives that includes revitalization of education at all levels, free health care, and a system of justice based on restorative and reconciliation practices of justice rather than retribution and vengeance. Effective alternatives involve both redefining crime by recognizing people who have committed acts of harm—as have most of us—as humans whose obligation is to take responsibility for the acts and assume the debt and transforming the social and economic conditions that track so many poor and black children into the juvenile and adult prison systems.

Abolitionists of woman abuse, the death penalty, and the prison industry acknowledge that clemency is an imperfect tool for dealing with people on death row because some are still executed. Feminists add that many women who killed their abusers should never have been prosecuted or sentenced to prison in the first place. Commuting the sentences of persons wrongly convicted does not change the systems that denied equal protection and access to fair and unbiased trials. Since the mid-1980s, battered women have received clemencies in a number of states and people on death row have had their sentences commuted to life by several governors; however, the vast majority continue to serve out long, often excessive, prison terms. Clemency is often the only available tool to rectify the failures of the current criminal justice system. As long as the death penalty stands, and as long as battered women are denied their right to a fair trial and society fails in substantive ways to end the crisis of woman abuse, clemency will continue to be indispensable.

See Also: Cruel and Unusual Punishment; Prisoner Litigation.

Endnotes

1. U.S. Constitution, Article II, Section 2, Clause 1; U.S. Department of Justice, Attorney General's Survey of Release Procedures: Pardons 1–53 (1939).
2. *Herrera v. Collins,* 506 U.S. 390 (1993).
3. Ex parte *Wells,* 59 U.S. 307, 319 (1855).
4. From the Supreme Court's decision in *Furman v. Georgia,* 409 U.S. 902 (1972), striking down all death penalty statutes, to the 1976 decision in *Gregg v. Georgia,* 429 U.S. 875 (1976), reinstating capital punishment, no executions occurred.
5. See Death Penalty Information Center, Facts About Clemency, http://www.deathpenalty info.org/article. php?did=126&scid=13.
6. Margaret Cole Love, "Of Pardons, Politics and Collar Buttons: Reflections on the President's Duty to be Merciful," *Fordham University Law Journal* 27 (2000): 1483, 1493.
7. See Amnesty International, "Death and the President" (AMR 51/158/2003, 2003), http://web.amnesty.org/library/index/engamr511582003.
8. 71 U.S. 333 (1866), outlining the sweeping scope of the president's power to pardon.
9. 236 U.S. 79 (1915).
10. Ibid., n. 2.
11. 523 U.S. 272 (1998).
12. The Federalist No. 74 (Alexander Hamilton).
13. The 1979 rape conviction of Gary Dotson was vacated by the Cook County Circuit Court in Chicago, Illinois.

14. See National Clearinghouse for the Defense of Battered Women, "Battered Women Who Have Received Clemency" (July 17, 2000); National Clearinghouse for the Defense of Battered Women, "Clemency Timeline" (2002); California Habeas Project, "Success" (2005), http://habeasproject.org/success.htm; Free Battered Women, "Freedom Campaigns," http://www.freebatteredwomen.org/news.html2 (2007).

15. Richard F. Celeste, "Executive Clemency: One Executive's Real Life Decisions," *Capital University Law Review* 31 (2003): 139.

16. See Mark Aaronson et al., "An Open Letter to Governor Ryan" (December 30, 2002), http://www.law.northwestern.edu/depts/clinic/wrongful/documents/LawProfLet1.pdf.

17. Death Penalty Information Center, http://www.deathpenaltyinfo.org.

Further Reading: Ammons, Linda L., "Why Do You Do the Things You Do? Clemency for Battered Incarcerated Women: A Decade's Review," *American University Journal of Gender, Social Policy and Law* 11 (2003): 533–65; Davis, Angela Y., *Are Prisons Obsolete?* (Toronto: Hushion House, 2003); Gagne, Patricia, *Battered Women's Justice: The Movement for Clemency and the Politics of Self-Defense* (New York: Twayne, 1998); Kobil, Daniel, "How to Grant Clemency in Unforgiving Times," *Capital University Law Review* 31, no. 2 (2003): 219–41; Liebman, James S., et al., "A Broken System: Error Rates in Capital Cases, 1973–1995" (2001), http://www.law.columbia.edu/media_inquiries/news/_events/2002/broken_system; Rapaport, Elizabeth, "Staying Alive: Executive Clemency, Equal Protection, and the Politics of Gender in Women's Capital Cases," *Buffalo Criminal Law Review* 4 (2001): 967–1007; Schneider, Elizabeth, *Battered Women and Feminist Lawmaking* (New Haven, CT: Yale University Press, 2000).

Carol Jacobsen

COMMUNITY POLICE

INTRODUCTION

One of the most controversial issues in criminal justice today revolves around the meaning and implementation of community policing. Disagreements over the nature, philosophy, and organization of community policing are further complicated because proponents and opponents cannot necessarily be categorized by their politics, left or right, as criticisms come from both sides of the political spectrum, especially with respect to notions of doing too little or too much in the name of crime control. At the same time, many police scholars and police administrators remain skeptical about the effectiveness of community policing despite the popularity and widespread acceptance of community policing programs in many communities. That is to say, these so-called social realists appreciate the contradictions in law and order that prevail in some communities. Hence, they see community policing as an impossibility with respect to those communities where the police are viewed not as their friends but as their enemies, like that of an occupying force serving interests external to the community.

Proponents of community policing argue that in order to adequately address neighborhood crime and disorder, effective policing has to address the social and economic conditions of the community and seek to transform the cultures that produce crime and conflict. In the main, advocates of this kind of community policing argue that both the police and the community need to pull together their resources and capabilities to identify and solve crime and social-disorder problems in the community. They argue that such an approach broadens police attitudes, focus, and mandate from a narrow focus on crime to efforts to reduce the fear of crime, improvement of the quality of life, services, legitimacy, and concern for civil rights. Finally, proponents of community policing argue that the appropriate organizational changes allow for citizen involvement and participation in policy formulation and implementation, ultimately providing for a shared police accountability between the community and the government.

Critics of community policing are not in agreement themselves, offering differing critiques of community policing. Some maintain that community policing is soft on crime or deflective of true crime fighting because of its policies of employing counseling and other community-based social-work methods for dealing with nonconforming behaviors. Other critics contend that community policing may have the unintended consequence of broadening police reach and power into the domain that is better handled by the families and community. A third group of critics argue that because of the lack of consensus over what constitutes community policing, it has been difficult to evaluate community policing programs to determine their effectiveness. In other words, although community policing programs have been adjudged effective in some communities, in others, the results have been disappointing and the programs have been adjudged as failures.

Other arguments against community policing are that the empowerment of communities to police themselves may lead to overvigilance and targeting and oppression of minority groups in the community. At the same time, many police officers view themselves as professionals trained to fight crime and disorder and are reluctant to share this power with ordinary community members who they consider lack the requisite knowledge and know-how of crime fighting. Other opponents argue that crime fighting not only may endanger the lives of community members but also may compromise people's privacy. Other critics assert that community policing more or less enthrones another regime of paternalistic control of the people by the police. Finally, there are criticisms against community policing because it is viewed as a false panacea for all the social problems underlying crime. As such, governments may then neglect to carry out the structural changes or necessary social and economic reforms within and without the community, resulting in a situation in which public expectations are not met and the conflicts and frustrations leading to crime within the community grow.

BACKGROUND

When Sir Robert Peel, the chief architect of modern policing, established the London Metropolitan Police, he envisioned a community policing model. One of the main principles of the Peelian police model is that "the police are the public and the public are the police,"[1] and this statement laid the foundation of community policing.

The recent worldwide interest in community policing is one more acknowledgement that for policing to be effective and perceived as legitimate by the people, it should derive and be enmeshed in the daily life of local communities. From this perspective, policing is viewed as an extension of the civil society from which it derives its authority. Community policing is a policing philosophy that calls for the active and meaningful involvement and partnership of the police and the community in social control and order maintenance. The local residents are recognized as stakeholders in community safety and also as major sources of community values and therefore important in the definition and maintenance of order. Crime is also recognized as a local event and that it mostly derives from the prevailing conditions and culture of the neighborhood.

Community policing is also known as problem-solving policing because of the understanding that many crimes indicate underlying socioeconomic problems. And as such, as a proactive policing approach, it seeks to identify and address the underlying social problems that may lead to crime and disorder problems in the community. In this respect, community policing is geared toward crime prevention, reduction of fear of crime, enhancing police connection and collaboration with the community, as well as police accountability to the community and respect of civil rights and freedoms. Skogan[2] further notes that community policing should be a move toward the police strategically adapting their organization to a changing environment, rather than just carrying out certain activities. The organizational changes of the police include team policing, community outreach programs, community crime prevention programs, and problem-oriented and crime fear reduction awareness campaigns.

Friedman's[3] definition of community policing is one that captures all the key elements: Community policing is a policy and a strategy aimed at achieving more effective and efficient crime control, reduced fear of crime, improved quality of life, improved police services, and police legitimacy through a proactive reliance on community resources that seeks to change crime-causing conditions. It assumes a need for greater accountability of police, greater public share in decision making, and greater concern for civil rights and liberties. Similarly, Trojanowicz and Bucqueroux regard community policing as the first major reform in a half-century of policing that has changed the way the police think and act. This revolutionary movement broadens the police mandate beyond a narrow focus on fighting crime to include efforts that also address fear of crime, social and physical disorder, and neighborhood decay.

UNDERPINNING THEORETICAL ARGUMENTS

Wilson and Kelling's 1982 "broken windows" theory[4] explains the relationship between community decay and apathy by community members and social disorder and even crime. In contrast, they observe, that when community members take steps to preserve their community and actively cooperate with the police in enforcing order in their neighborhoods, it can vastly improve the quality of life of community members and the reduction of crime. In this respect, even minor offenses are viewed as potential threats to community well-being rather than

JAPAN'S MODEL OF COMMUNITY POLICING

The Japanese police are widely recognized as a very effective community policing model. The emphasis of the Japanese police is on the police collaboration with citizens and the provision of services to the people. The policing function is deeply immersed in the people's culture and the daily life of community residents. The police recognize that they need the trust, cooperation, and partnership of the people to be effective. Police departments are located strategically for easy access and interaction of community members with the police. Furthermore, the police are required to live within the neighborhood they police. The Japanese police model has revealed that when the police reside in the community where they police, they tend to be more committed as they also have a stake in the well-being of the community. They also execute their job with responsibility and sensitivity. The police realize that if they employ high-handed and oppressive methods in the execution of their duties, there will be a backlash. The potential of the people taking out their anger against the police's children and spouses is high because they share other social amenities with the residents of the community. Clearly in the Japanese policing system, the police accountability is primarily to the community and secondarily to the government.

merely as nuisances. Ridding the community of drug addicts, prostitutes, youth gangs, and homeless people is one way to preserve the community order. Buildings in state of disrepair are quickly renovated as community preservation and order maintenance is given priority attention in a community concerned with its safety.

Other advocates of community policing such as Trojanowicz and Bucqueroux further note that modern police operate with little or no input from the community. The overcentralization of police organizations and lack of police accountability to the community undermine police effectiveness and legitimacy, which lead to frustrations of community members. The failure of the police to prevent or reduce crime increases the communities' frustration with the police, fueling the demand for change. Furthermore, traditional policing is incident driven, and its efficiency and effectiveness is measured by crime detection and arrest of offenders and response times. Hence, the police do not consider police responses to public calls and police collaboration with the community a priority. Community policing advocates therefore seek to restore community contribution to the definition of order. It is also a challenge to the state's monopoly over the definition of order. Furthermore, it is a recognition of the complex nature of social problems and that a proactive, holistic, and multifaceted approach is more effective than a reactionary, simplistic, and superficial response common with traditional policing.

Christie[5] has strongly argued that police responsibility, accountability, legitimacy, and effectiveness will be greatly enhanced when the police live within the community they police. Bureaucratic control of the police is not very effective, he insists, as the police are selective in their recordings of their activities and witnesses are often not available to testify against the police. The most effective way to keep the police in check and hold them accountable is for the public themselves, who are the objects of control, to have some measure of power over the police. Power, he argues, is more accountable when it is vulnerable. The police feel somewhat vulnerable when they live where they operate because of the fear of backlash against their abuse of power in the community.

Finally, consultation and mobilization according to White[6] citing Bayley is another method of holding police accountable and also building a successful partnership between the police and the community. These consultations can occur through chance encounters between the citizens and the police in the streets and during formal community meetings and forums. The citizens during these meetings are able to convey to the police their problems in the community and concerns with police responses to these problems. The police also use these meetings to educate the community about crime and strategies to prevent and control crime. The police also use these meetings to promote their mission and activities and share with the community their expectations and challenges.

THE COMMUNITY POLICE IDEAL

Community policing is also an attempt to design an efficient and effective crime-control strategy geared toward the reduction of fear of crime. It also seeks to bring about social and economic policies that will bring about improved quality of life in the community. The police collaboration with the community is intended to enhance police effectiveness and legitimacy while enhancing improved police services. With increased community involvement and participation in decision making and policy implementation, the police respect for civil rights and liberties of citizens will be enhanced. Community policing is a negotiated and democratic policing. The interest in community policing is an indication of the people's dissatisfaction with traditional policing. The approach and strategy of traditional policing is antithetical to democratic principles and practice. The states' monopoly over the definition and maintenance of order undermines the police and community's connection and well-being. Traditional policing is undemocratic, lacks legitimacy, and is ineffective in the prevention of crime and, above all, in the reduction of citizens' fear of crime. Traditional policing is anachronistic with a modern, complex, and diverse society's policing needs. Available records show that traditional policing is reactive rather than proactive and that its delivery of services is not tailored to the needs of society.

STRATEGIES OF COMMUNITY POLICING

Following are some of the community policing strategies:

Problem-Oriented Policing

Problem-oriented policing is popularly known by the acronym SARA, in which S stands for scanning, meaning mechanisms put in place to identify the community problems demanding police response. A stands for analysis, in which stakeholders seek to understand the cause, scope, and effect of the problem. R stands for response, in which the police working in collaboration with the community apply well thought-out responses to the identified community problems. The final A stands for an assessment that is an evaluation of the effectiveness of the analysis and responses to the community problems in question.

Foot Patrols

Police foot patrols are a community policing strategy geared toward making more visible police presence in the community. It is believed an increase in police-citizen interaction will lead to building trust and a bond between citizens and the police, leading to the reduction of citizens' fear of crime. This will also enhance the community's sense of personal safety and reduction in citizens' calls for service. Foot patrols also enhance police knowledge of the community and also the problems and needs of the community, necessary for effective policy making.

Crime Prevention Programs

There are many crime prevention programs designed by community policing advocates and practitioners. They include mechanisms put in place to proactively prevent crime from occurring by identifying conditions that create opportunities for crime committal. Such crime prevention programs include Operation Identification, Neighborhood Watch, Citizen Patrols, Crime Prevention through Environmental Design, and media campaigns to raise the citizens' awareness about crime.

FUTURE PROSPECTS

Community policing recognizes that crime and conflict derive from the community's social condition and culture. Tending to these social problems and seeking to positively transform the community's culture are major goals of community policing. To accomplish these objectives, community policing seeks to involve the community in policy formulation and implementation because it understands that the most important asset of the police is the bond and trust of the community it serves. The decentralization of power and policy making is a major strategy of community policing. Some police recognize that their mandate to operate is from the people, and therefore their accountability is to the people primarily and to the government secondarily. On the other hand, other police understand that in some communities, they are no different than occupying forces and that community policing is an oxymoron and that structural changes are all but ignored by the established political and economic order. Moreover, in those communities favorable to and unfavorable to community policing, with live-in or live-out community police forces, there is still resistance from many within the police ranks to many of the ideas associated with community policing.

Dialectically then, community policing is a policing philosophy in which the police and the community allegedly constitute partners in the definition of order, enforcement of laws, and order maintenance. In other words, in some communities police share interests in common with all citizens as common stakeholders in order maintenance; however, in other communities the interests of the powerful, criminal and noncriminal, may not be the same as the interests of the local community of citizens. Within such contradictions, community policing allegedly is more effective when the police live and work in the community.

After all, if the police live in the community, they have a stake in its wellbeing. Similarly, police accountability and sensibility should also be enhanced when they police the community where they live. Because all of the community is allegedly involved in policy decision making, organization, and implementation, community policing therefore is a proactive policing approach that seeks to identify and address the underlying social problems that may lead to crime and disorder in the community. Finally, in the context of such conflicts of interest, the ongoing struggle for community policing in the near and distant future will continue to raise issues with what the ideal state-society relationship or conditions of law and order might look like.

See Also: Militarization of Policing; Police-Minority Relations.

Endnotes

1. P. P. Purpura, *Police and Community: Concepts and Cases* (Boston: Allyn and Bacon, 2001), 23.
2. W. G. Skogan, *Community Policing: (Can It Work?)* (Belmont, CA: Thomson Wadsworth, 2004).
3. R. R. Friedman, *Community Policing: Comparative Perspectives and Prospects* (New York: St. Martin's Press, 1992).
4. J. Q. Wilson and G. L. Kelling, "Broken Windows: Police and Neighborhood Safety," *Atlantic Monthly* 249, no. 3 (1982): 29–38.
5. N. Christie, *Limits to Pain* (Oslo, Norway: Universitetet Forlaget, 1981).
6. M. D. White, *Current Issues and Controversies in Policing* (Boston: Pearson and Allyn and Bacon, 2007).

Further Reading: Bayley, D. H., *Forces of Order: Police Behavior in Japan and the United States* (Berkeley and Los Angeles: University of California Press, 1976); Friedman, R. R., *Community Policing: Comparative Perspectives and Prospects* (New York: St. Martin's Press, 1992); Skogan, W. G., *Community Policing: (Can It Work?)* (Belmont, CA: Thomson Wadsworth, 2004); Trojanowicz, R., and B. Bucqueroux, *Community Policing: A Contemporary Perspective* (Cincinnati, OH: Anderson, 1990); Trojanowicz, R., V. E. Kappeler, and L. K. Gaines, *Community Policing: A Contemporary Perspective,* 3rd ed. (Cincinnati, OH: Anderson, 2002); White, M. D., *Current Issues and Controversies in Policing* (Boston: Pearson and Ally and Bacon, 2007).

O. Oko Elechi

COMPSTAT AND CRIME REDUCTION

INTRODUCTION

A controversial debate that has raged for some time in criminology is whether policing strategies can effectively reduce crime. In the 1990s, innovative policing strategies were believed to be a principal contributor to the unique, unexpected, dramatic decline in crime rates in the United States.[1] One innovative policing strategy adopted by police departments, but begun in New York, is COMPSTAT, short for "computer statistics" or "compare statistics." COMPSTAT gained enormous publicity and was regarded as the primary factor contributing to New York City's unprecedented reduction in crime in the 1990s. Politicians and police executives excitedly acclaimed that COMPSTAT strongly debunked the long-time negation of some criminologists' view that police can do little in respect to crime reduction. In 1996, COMPSTAT won Harvard University's Kennedy School of Government's prestigious Innovations in American Government Award. Some criminal justice scholars touted COMPSTAT as a policing revolution01 and a new policing paradigm.[2]

The emergence of COMPSTAT, a goal-oriented, results-based strategic management process that uses advanced information technology, operational strategies, and managerial accountability to reduce crime and improve quality of life, however, did not end the debate among criminologists, criminal justice scholars, economists, and police practitioners in respect to the effectiveness of COMPSTAT. COMPSTAT's paradigmatic status, its effectiveness in crime reduction, and its aggressive policing and zero-tolerance crime-control strategies are still contentious.

BACKGROUND

COMPSTAT was first adopted by the New York Police Department (NYPD) and was launched as a contingent response to sharply escalating violent-crime rates in New York City during the late 1980s and early 1990s. In 1990, New York registered a record 2,245 homicides, well above the previous record of 1,826 in 1981. The NYPD's failure in reducing crime and ameliorating fear of crime ignited prevailing public distrust toward the NYPD. Private business even had begun to offer corporation-provided security services.[3]

In August 1992, in the Crown Heights neighborhood of Brooklyn, a black kid was run down and killed by a car in a motorcade of Lubavitcher Jews. This car accident later devolved into a riot initiated by blacks. The public fervently criticized the NYPD's slow response and inaction. Because of their hesitance and failure to control the riot, critics link the NYPD's inaction to the social unrest that accompanied this accident. Mayor Rudolph Giuliani responded to the riot by appointing William Bratton as the commissioner of the NYPD. Bratton was the former commissioner of New York Transit Police and the initiator of COMPSTAT in New York. From the beginning, Bratton set the NYPD's mission as controlling crime and social disorder.[4]

Bratton strongly believed that police could effectively reduce crimes with right strategies and tactics. In his mind, an effective anticrime strategy requires accurate and timely intelligence, rapid-focused deployment of personnel and resources, effective tactics, and relentless follow-up and assessment. After closely examining the NYPD's organizational structure and operational strategies, Bratton and his executive team found that the NYPD had become a bureaucratic dinosaur that was suffering dysfunctions of bureaucratic organizational structure, which significantly curtailed the NYPD's capacity to design and implement effective anticrime strategies.[5]

Besides the dysfunctions of the NYPD's bureaucratic structure, Bratton was also dissatisfied with the community policing model adopted by former commissioner Lee P. Brown, which relied on street-level police and parole officers to prevent and control crimes. In Bratton's mind, developing effective tactics to prevent and control crime needs professional expertise, experience, and organizational support, which are what those street-level police, usually novice, do not have. Moreover, community policing distracts police agencies' attention from crime reduction. In the model of community policing, police are treated as social workers rather than crime fighters.[6]

Bratton adopted the broken windows theory as his guiding principle for his war on crime. As a part of its zero-tolerance policy, the NYPD would no longer tolerate misdemeanors and quality-of-life offenses. The NYPD would make arrests for vagrancy, vandalism, littering, minor drug possession, prostitution, public drunkenness and urination, aggressive panhandling, and harassment by "squeegee pests." It was believed that via aggressive policing, the NYPD sent a strong signal to the public that the NYPD began to take serious actions to reduce crime and maintain community order.

Bratton and his executive team started to reorganize the NYPD, adopt new technologies, and establish a series of internal accountability mechanisms to guarantee the success of his war on crime campaign. Sustained and developed by Bratton's successors, these measures have evolved into a results-oriented strategic management model, COMPSTAT.[7]

ORGANIZING COMPSTAT

First, traditional, functional, division-based management was changed to geographic, jurisdiction-based management. Authority, resources, and power were decentralized to the precinct police commanders. Functionally differentiated units and specialists (e.g., parole, detective, narcotics, juvenile, traffic, etc.) were placed under the command of the precinct commander, or arrangements were made to facilitate their responsiveness to the commander's needs. Under this new arrangement, precinct commanders are responsible for crime reduction and community disorder control.

Second, a special unit, called COMPSTAT Unit (CPU), was established. The CPU was designed for collecting and analyzing crime and managerial data and producing intelligence reports to facilitate the decision-making and performance assessment of police commissioners and commanders of the NYPD.

Based on the data collected from precincts, the CPU compiles weekly COMP-STAT reports for police commissioners, chiefs of the department, and precinct commanders for immediate reference. In COMPSTAT reports, statistics like the number and percentage changes of index crimes, misdemeanors, and quality-of-life offences are reported by jurisdictions (precinct, borough, and citywide) on weekly, monthly, and yearly bases. The report also ranks all precinct commands by the number of crimes committed and arrests conducted. This also serves as a bone of contention for many concerned citizens.

Besides the weekly COMPSTAT report, which primarily focuses on crime and enforcement data, the CPU also prepares the Commander Profile Report. The Commander Profile Report aims to present and assess precinct commanders' internal management performance. Data like population and demographics of their jurisdictions, the number and ranks of personnel assigned, the number and type of civilian complaints made against officers, the number of vehicle accidents involving department vehicles, sick rates, the number of line-of-duty injuries suffered by officers, response time to various types of calls for service, and overtime expenditures are reported. With the Commander Profile Report, police executives are able to carefully monitor and assess how well commanders motivate and manage their personnel resources and how well they address important management concerns. Other advantages facilitated by the CPU's database and statistical reports are the commanders' performance reports, which are amenable to being assessed across time and geographic locations.

The CPU significantly improved the pin map technology traditionally used by police organizations with computer mapping technology to track crime. The CPU now uses the more advanced geographic information system (GIS) mapping software to map crime patterns. The computerized pin map produced by the CPU can show where and when crimes occur, and law enforcement actions are taken with real-time data. Interacting with the COMPSTAT database, advanced GIS technology can show the correlations between crimes and geographic clusters vividly and straightforwardly. With the support of the GIS system, hot spots, places where crimes most often are committed, are quickly identified, and its temporal and spatial distributions are indicated, which help police commanders effectively deploy personnel and resources to prevent and control crimes. Moreover, by examining the correlation between arrests made and crime incidences at hot spots across time, the COMPSTAT map tells the effectiveness of the strategies adopted and resources deployed. Not only does it help precinct commanders examine and redesign their tactics and actions, but it also serves as performance indicators for police chiefs to assess the performance of their subordinates.

Third, COMPSTAT meetings, formally known as Crime Control Strategy Meetings, were developed to help reinforce the effectives of COMPSTAT as an effective tool to address crime reduction. The COMPSTAT meetings gradually evolved as the most salient element of COMPSTAT and are now an institutional component of COMPSTAT. COMPSTAT meetings are held twice each week in the Command and Control Center of the NYPD. Practically all the NYPD's top executives attend the meetings with borough commanders, precinct commanders, and the heads of the investigative and enforcement units working within particular geographic areas.

During the meetings, COMPSTAT maps and reports prepared by the CPU are projected on a large screen in front of the conference room. Based on the projected statistics, commanders make presentations on the latest crime occurrences, quality-of-life offenses within their jurisdictions, the effectiveness of strategies and tactics they already used, and actions and measures they are going to take to address unsolved problems. During their presentations, police commissioners and chiefs may interrupt and ask the presenter to explicate particular issues and answer certain questions regarding their crime-control strategies, tactics, and internal management. In the presentation, police commanders are expected to demonstrate that they have firsthand information and detailed knowledge on the crimes and quality-of-life issues within their jurisdictions, they are competent to detect the pattern and roots of these crimes and misdemeanors, they have designed and implemented strategies and tactics to address these problems, and they are going to take innovative measures to further reduce crime and improve quality of life in their communities.

Not only do COMPSTAT meetings serve for performance reporting and evaluation, they also serve as a platform for open and candid communication and experience sharing and brainstorming. COMPSTAT meetings create a communication environment Bratton called a "seamless web."[8] In COMPSTAT meetings, commanders directly and openly tell their supervisors what barriers they encountered and what supports they need for reducing certain crimes and improving community quality of life. Based on COMPSTAT crime map and reports, executives and commanders brainstorm with each other and discuss how to detect crime patterns and identify roots and causes of crimes and quality-of-life offenses. They share their experience and expertise with each other to improve existing efforts and invent new crime-control strategies and tactics. If necessary, cross-functional unit and jurisdiction collaborations are discussed and initiated in the COMPSTAT meetings. This open, horizontal, candid communication environment is rare in police organizations with their military characteristics and hierarchical communication.

COMPSTAT meetings play a central role in establishing a strong internal accountability system within the NYPD. It sends a strong signal to police officers at each level. Crime reduction and quality-of-life improvement become the utmost goals of the NPYD. Middle police managers should be responsible for crime reduction and order maintenance within their jurisdictions. They should demonstrate their competence and effectiveness in crime reduction and quality-of-life improvement; otherwise they will be replaced or fired. In its early days, precinct commanders who failed to answer questions from commissioners and executives and failed to demonstrate their effectiveness in crime reduction in the COMPSTAT meetings were criticized, even humiliated, by commissioners and executives. In Commissioner Bratton's first year of administration, more than two-thirds of the department's 76 precinct commanders were replaced.[9]

COMPSTAT meetings have become the showcase of COMPSTAT, and the meetings are guided by the six key elements of COMPSTAT: mission clarification, internal accountability, geographic organization of operational command, organizational flexibility, data-driven problem identification and assessment, and innovative problem solving. These elements work together to change the NYPD's traditional culture, organizational structure, and operational rules and procedures.[10]

In sum, though short for *computerized statistics* or *compare statistics*, COMPSTAT cannot merely be understood as an automated office system or data-driven performance measurement and reporting system because it is more than that. It is a strategic management process. It is a policing reform initiated by NYPD commissioner Bratton and sustained by his successors. It aims to change the NYPD's culture, organization structure, administrative and operational rules, and procedures in order to effectively address external challenges in a turbulent time. As a police strategic management model, its underlying philosophy, principles, and organizational elements are illustrated in figure C.1.

CONTROVERSIES IN COMPSTAT

Though COMPSTAT is highly touted by politicians, police executives, and some scholars of criminal justice and was granted a prestigious innovation award, skepticism and criticism have hounded COMPSTAT since its inception.

COMPSTAT has been highly touted by some criminal justice scholars as a new policing paradigm—strategic management paradigm—as pointed out previously. It is purported that COMPSTAT offers a practical solution for U.S. police organizations to address the dilemma caused by the traditional legal/rational policing paradigm and community policing paradigm. Advocates argue that COMPSTAT combines the advantages of two paradigms and escalates U.S. policing practice to an unprecedented level. On one hand, COMPSTAT reemphasizes the imperativeness of police professionalism, police organizations'

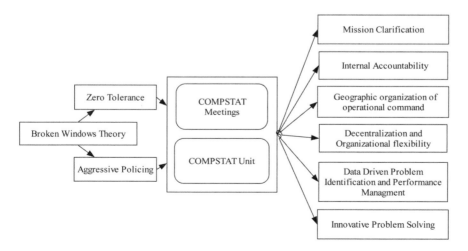

Figure C.1 COMPSTAT model.

responsibility in reducing crime and reducing social disorder, and the importance of strong executive leadership and control; on the other hand, it decentralizes power, resources, and discretion to middle police officers, encouraging them take advantages of advanced information technology to design and implement innovative preventive crime-control strategies and tactics. COMPSTAT, in short, is an excellent blend of some seemingly contradictory management principles that strikes a delicate balance between reform and problem solving, hierarchy and leadership, control and creativity.[11]

Nonetheless, other scholars of criminal justice have questioned the paradigmatic status of COMPSTAT. Although some of them admit that the COMPSTAT model adopted by the NYPD is a significant policing innovation, critics argue that COMPSTAT has not risen to the paradigmatic status as its proponents claim. Some point out that, at best, COMPSTAT is just a combination of technical innovation and administrative innovation. In other words, all these changes just "create the organization-wide conditions under which operations are carried out, guided, and reported on rather than new substantive and operational methods for reducing crime, disorder and fear."[12]

Moreover, it is argued that COMPSTAT is by no means as strategic as its proponents claim because it does not substantively change the mission and goals of the police department. COMPSTAT regresses police departments back to its traditional role as crime fighters; COMPSTAT does not substantively change police departments' principal operation methods. Arrests and direct patrol at hot spots are still primary ways police rely on to deter and control crime, which is by no means a new type of policing.

In addition, COMPSTAT does not significantly alter the basic internal and external working relationships of police departments. Though COMPSTAT decentralizes, empowers precinct commanders, and makes arrangements for coordinating the relationships between specialty units and commands, it does not disband specialty units and redistribute its personnel and resources to precinct commands. The internal working relationship between the police department and its environment has not been changed substantively from traditional policing practices.

In terms of external working relationship, though citizens and public media are invited to attend COMPSTAT meetings, COMPSTAT has not been used as a forum for reshaping the relationships between the police and the communities. COMPSTAT is just used as a so-called public theater to show the efforts police departments have made to control crime in order to improve public awareness and support. COMPSTAT does not substantively change the external working relationships of police departments like the community policing paradigm does.[13]

Some critics also point out that COMPSTAT is not a coherent management framework. Some of its organizational and operational principals and strategies are conflicting and might not work and achieve what its proponents expect. For example, the stringent internal accountability system and data-driven performance measurement system might thwart police managers' willingness to develop innovate problem-solving strategies and tactics. Because the twice-a-week

COMPSTAT meetings strictly hold precinct commanders accountable to their performance measured by narrowly defined objective performance indicators, precinct commanders would tend to focus their efforts on what is subject to be measured, especially those areas that can show their effectiveness visibly and instantly. Fearful of negative evaluations, a precinct commander might develop very conservative operational strategy and tactics. In an environment with very high uncertainty, the best way to protect them might be just resorting to the tradition. Commanders might just copy what other precincts are doing or even try to find out in advance what police executives prefer rather than proactively exploring new opportunities, new strategies, and new tactics to accomplish their missions.[14]

In addition, innovative problem solving requires precinct commanders to collect any possible information within their jurisdiction to find out the most appropriate solution to address specific problems. COMPSTAT standardizes what data should be collected and the way to analyze the data, which might significantly constrain the capacity of operational commanders in innovative problem solving.

Critics also points out that though the geographic organization of command attempts to promote internal accountability, given scarce organizational resources, the stringent internal accountability system might lead to interjurisidictional competition rather than collaboration, which ignites another type of notorious turf battle.[15] A survey of a stratified sample of U.S. police agencies with municipal policing responsibilities found that the predominant reason for the implementation of COMPSTAT programs nationally was to reinforce traditional hierarchical structures of police organizations. It concluded that, "This leads us to question whether the rapid rise of COMPSTAT in American police agencies can be interpreted more as an effort to maintain and reinforce the 'bureaucratic' or 'paramilitary' model of police organization that has been under attack by scholars for most of the last two decades than as an attempt to truly reform models of American policing."[16]

Another controversy in COMPSTAT is about the efficacy of COMPSTAT in reducing crimes. The effect of COMPSTAT on crime reduction seems quick and long lasting. Only after two years of implementation, it was claimed that crime reductions for 1995 in all categories on average was more than 40 percent.[17] From 1993 to 1998, the seven major index offenses showed an overall decline of 50.05 percent, and during this same period, New York City dropped from a position of 114th to 163rd in the ranking of the 200 most dangerous U.S. cities with population greater than 100,000.[18] The total number of reported crimes for the seven major crime categories declined an unprecedented 65.99 percent in 2003 from the levels reported in 1993.[19]

For criminologists, however, the coincidence between COMPSTAT and a drop in crime rate in the 1990s does not mean there is a cause-effect relationship. Whether COMPSTAT was a contributing factor and to what extent it contributed to the dramatic decline in crime rate in New York City is still under debate.

In 2001, George Kelling and William Sousa conducted a comprehensive study, "Do Police Matter? An Analysis of the Impact of New York's Police Reform," on whether the sharp crime declines was the result of COMPSTAT. Their conclusion is that COMPSTAT played a major role in reducing crime. So-called broken windows policing is significantly and consistently linked to declines in violent crime, and it prevented more than 60,000 violent crimes between 1989 and 1998.[20]

Some critics pointed out, however, that Kelling and Sousa's study did not control for some other very important factors like poverty, family structure, and immigration trends that are commonly associated with violent crimes. More important, they argued that Kelling and Sousa overlooked the possibility of reciprocal causation between their policing measure and violent crime: Decreases in violent felonies may enable the police to devote greater attention to less serious offenses, which results in increases in misdemeanor arrests. Contradictorily, their study showed that there was no significant direct impact of COMPSTAT on the incidence of homicide in the 1990s.[21]

Economist Stephan Levitt, professor of economics at the University of Chicago and the author of *The New York Times* best seller *Freakonomics,* found that the five most commonly suggested factors explaining the unique, unexpected, universal, and dramatic crime drop in the United States in 1990s were the strong economy of the 1990s, changing demographics, gun control laws, laws allowing the carrying of concealed weapons, and the increased use of capital punishment, contrary to the belief that better policing strategies played a role in reducing the crime rate. He specifically doubts the claim that New York City's policing strategy is the key to the dramatic crime decline in that city. He found that the drop in crime in New York City began in 1990, four years before the implementation of COMPSTAT, and except for homicide, there was no obvious break in crime after COMPSTAT was implemented.[22]

Besides the endless academic quarrels, probably the most fatal attack against COMPSTAT is from its insiders. The Patrolmen's Benevolent Association and the Sergeant's Benevolent Association of the NYPD claimed that the miraculous crime decline was achieved by fudging crime statistics. They alleged that some police officers are forced to manipulate crime statistics to maintain the appearance of a drastic reduction in crime. Some journalists keep reporting cases that some precinct commanders thwart crime victims reporting crime, downgrade serious crime to misdemeanors, and underreport crime incidences.[23]

Recently, a journalist derided New York City Mayor Michael Bloomberg's campaign advertisement, "The neighborhoods of New York have become safer than ever," by comparing the apparent contradictory discrepancy between the reported number of assaulted residents who visited hospitals reported by the New York City Department of Health and Mental Hygiene and the number of reported serious assaults reported by the NYPD.[24] All these frauds are attributed to the stringent internal accountability mechanism of COMPSTAT. Although these charges are just anecdotal and most of them have been dismissed by the NYPD, the negative impact of these allegations and charges on the credibility and legitimacy of COMPSTAT are harmful.

Moreover, some critics further question that even if COMPSTAT did have a dramatic effect on reducing crime, the costs of enforcing an aggressive policing strategy such as COMPSTAT, which many believed infringed upon liberty, justice, and fairness, would outweigh its value. Some argue that the ultimate goal of policing is to protect the U.S. Constitution, which is a much higher calling for police officers. Controlling crime and maintaining order cannot be pursued at the expense of constitutional rights, liberty, and social justice.

Underlying aggressive policing also breeds distrust of police departments in the public sphere and exacerbates the conflictual relationship between the government and citizens, which is absolutely antidemocratic.[25] A 1997 survey of 1,259 NYPD officers working in all 76 New York City precincts showed that officers who accepted the aggressive policing paradigm are significantly more likely to violate the constitutional rights of citizens by conducting illegal searches and stops.[26] The arrest, beating, and torture of a black Haitian immigrant, Abner Louima, in 1997 and the shots fired by NYPD police officers on unarmed black men such as Patrick Descombe and Amadou Diallo in 1998 and 1999, respectively, unfortunately demonstrate how easy aggressive policing tactics can be abused and what damage it can have on individual families and society. Sadly, the success of COMPSTAT, which brought personal fame to New York City and helped reinvigorate tourism and property values, concealed the darkest side of aggressive policing, especially in the early days of COMPSTAT.[27]

FUTURE PROSPECTS

COMPSTAT has significantly changed the landscape of U.S. policing. A 1999 Police Foundation survey showed that a third of the nation's 515 largest police departments had implemented a COMPSTAT-like program and 20 percent were planning to do so by 2001.[28] In 2000, it is reported that 219 police agency representatives visited NYPD COMPSTAT meetings in 1998, 221 in 1999, and 235 in the first 10 months of 2000.[29]

So far, police departments in Indianapolis, Indiana; Louisville, Kentucky; Boston, Massachusetts; Baltimore City, Maryland; Prince George's County, Maryland; Newark, New Jersey; New Orleans, Louisiana; Broward County, Orange County, and Polk County sheriff's offices in Florida; Seattle, Washington; Los Angeles, California; Philadelphia, Pennsylvania; and the Illinois and Delaware State Police have adopted and implemented COMPSTAT programs in their organizations. Whether COMPSTAT is a new police paradigm or whether it can actually reduce crime is still debatable, and ideas underlying COMPSTAT, results-oriented performance management, utilization of advanced information technology, internal accountability, organizational decentralization, and empowerment reflect the current trend of organizational development and reform currently in policing. Thus, COMPSTAT, despite its critics and skeptics, is still evolving and appears to have a potential and promising future.

Designers and implementers of COMPSTAT should learn lessons from the past because it has been noted that negative behavioral impacts of the results-based, goal-oriented, data-driven performance measurement system should be cautioned. COMPAST should also, it is asserted, develop a more sophisticated data-collection and performance-measurement system. More community-oriented information should be included in the data-collection and performance-measurement process of COMPSTAT. Police officers should not be just narrowly measured by the number of crimes they reduced but more assessed by how they encourage citizens and cooperate and engage in their daily policing, how they work together with citizens to address community problems, and how they serve citizens with due respect and courtesy.

In the past, COMPSTAT reflected more elements of the traditional legal/rational policing paradigm rather than a true synthesis of the traditional policing model and the community policing model. In the future, COMPSTAT should incorporate more elements from the community policing paradigm, further changing its internal and external working relationships, building flexible organizational structures, empowering street-level officers, and becoming a platform for open and sincere communication between citizens and police. COMPSTAT meetings should be moved to local communities rather than held in police headquarters, further enhancing transparency and external accountability. Moreover, COMPSTAT should expand its scope and redefine its mission. It should not be just a crime-control tool. It should be a strategic management process contributing to promote democratic values and the public welfare.

See Also: Surveillance—Technological.

Endnotes

1. S. Levitt, "Understanding Why Crime Fell in the 1990s: Four Factors that Explain the Decline and Six that Do Not," *Journal of Economic Perspective* 18, no. 1 (2004): 163–90.
2. W. Walsh, "Compstat: An Analysis of an Emerging Police Paradigm," *Policing: An International Journal of Police Strategies and Management* 24, no. 3 (2001): 347–63; J. R. Firman, "Deconstructing Compstat to Clarify Its Intent," *Criminology and Public Policy* 2, no. 3 (2003): 457–60; V. E. Henry, *The Compstat Paradigm: Management Accountability in Policing, Business and the Public Sector* (Flushing, NY: Looseleaf Law, 2002); E. B. Silverman, *NYPD Battles Crime: Innovative Strategies in Policing* (Boston: Northeastern University Press, 1999).
3. V. E. Henry, "COMPSTAT Management in the NYPD: Reducing Crime and Improving Quality of Life in New York City," *129th UNAFEI International Senior Seminar* (2006), http://www.unafei.or.jp/english/pdf/PDF_rms/no68/07_Dr.%20Henry-1_p100-116.pdf.
4. P. K. Manning, "Theorizing Policing," *Theoretical Criminology* 5, no. 3 (2001): 315–44.
5. Walsh, "Compstat"; W. F. Walsh and G. F. Vito, "The Meaning of Compstat," *Journal of Contemporary Criminal Justice* 20, no. 1 (2004): 51–69.
6. W. Bratton, *Turnaround: How America's Top Cop Reversed the Crime Epidemic* (New York: Random House, 1998).
7. V. E. Henry, *The Compstat Paradigm: Management Accountability in Policing, Business and the Public Sector* (Flushing, NY: Looseleaf Law, 2002).
8. V. E. Henry, "Interview with William J. Bratton," *Police Practice and Research: An International Journal* 1 (2000): 397–434.
9. Silverman (1999).
10. D. Weisburd, S. D. Mastrofski, A. M. Mcnally, and J. J. Willis, "Reforming to Preserve: COMPSTAT and Strategic Problem Solving in American Policing," *Criminology and Public Policy* 2, no. 3 (2003): 421–56.

11. J. R. Firman, "Deconstructing Compstat to Clarify Its Intent," *Criminology and Public Policy* 2, no. 3 (2003): 457–60.
12. Mark Moore, "Sizing Up Compstat: An Important Administrative Innovation in Policing," *Criminology and Public Policy* 2 (2003): 3.
13. Ibid.
14. Henry, *The Compstat Paradigm.*
15. Walsh and Vito, "The Meaning of Compstat."
16. Weisburd et al., "Reforming to Preserve.", 433.
17. Manning, "Theorizing Policing."
18. Silverman, *NYPD Battles Crime.*
19. Henry, "COMPSTAT Management in the NYPD."
20. G. L. Kelling and W. H. Sousa, "Do Police Matter? An Analysis of the Impact of New York City's Police Reforms," in *Civic Report* (Tech. Rep. No. 22) (New York: Center for Civic Innovation at the Manhattan Institute, 2001).
21. R. Rosenfeld, R. Fornango, and E. Baumer, "Did Ceasefire, Compstat and Exile Reduce Homicide?" *Criminology and Public Policy* 4, no. 3 (2005): 419–50.
22. Levitt, "Understanding Why Crime Fell in the 1990s."
23. N. Stix, "'Disappearing' Urban Crime," *A Different Drummer* (2004), http://www.geocities.com/nstix/urbancrime.html.
24. P. Moses, "These Stats Are a Crime," *The Village Voice,* January 11, 2005, http://www.villagevoice.com/news/0544,moses,69552,5.html.
25. J. A. Eterno, and E. B. Silverman, "The New York City Police Department's Compstat: Dream or Nightmare?" *International Journal of Police Science and Management* 8, no. 3 (2006): 218–31.
26. J. A. Eterno, "Zero Tolerance Policing within Democracies: The Dilemma of Controlling Crime without Increasing Police Abuse of Power," *Police Practice and Research: An International Journal* 2, no. 3 (2001): 189–217.
27. Manning, "Theorizing Policing."
28. Weisburd et al., "Reforming to Preserve."
29. E. Gootman, "A Police Department's Growing Allure: Crime Fighters from around World Visit for Tips," *The New York Times,* October 24, 2000, B1.

Further Reading: Bratton, W., *Turnaround: How America's Top Cop Reversed the Crime Epidemic* (New York: Random House, 1998); Kelling, G., C. M. Coles, and J. Q. Wilson, *Fixing Broken Windows: Restoring Order and Reducing Crimes in Our Communities* (New York: Free Press, 1996); Manning, P. K., "Theorizing Policing," *Theoretical Criminology* 5, no. 3 (2001): 315–44; Peak, K., and R. Glensor, *Community Policing and Problem Solving: Strategies and Practices* (Upper Saddle River, NJ: Prentice-Hall, 1999); Silverman, E. B. *NYPD Battles Crime: Innovative Strategies in Policing* (Boston: Northeastern University Press, 1999).

Wenxuan Yu and Byron E. Price

CONSPIRACY AND SUBSTANTIAL ASSISTANCE

INTRODUCTION

Some people believe that the present system in the United States of charging individuals with conspiracy and rewarding the individuals who substantially assist the government to convict them is evidence that the world depicted in George

Orwell's novel *1984* exists. Criminal conspiracy charges bear many similarities. The defendants who are charged with conspiracy are held responsible for the crimes committed by all of the members of the conspiracy. The other members of the conspiracy cooperate with the government and help convict the defendants. The U.S. Department of Justice lauds the cooperation and substantial assistance of citizens and points out that, as a practical matter, without substantial assistance from cooperating individuals, the federal criminal justice system would come to a screeching halt. Opponents of substantial assistance argue that such deals undermine justice, ethics, and the rule of law.

ORWELL'S *1984*

When George Orwell's *1984* first appeared in print, many people feared that soon Big Brother would be watching us and that the government would turn all the children against their parents.* In *1984,* the children are trained to turn in their parents when their parents do something wrong. The government questions the children and encourages and rewards them when they snitch on their parents. There is no family loyalty. In today's criminal justice system, individuals who commit crimes can substantially assist the government to convict one of their cohorts. The cooperating individuals are rewarded with either a reduced jail sentence or no jail sentence at all.

Others believe that charging someone with conspiracy is akin to the world created by Shirley Jackson in her short story "The Lottery."** In "The Lottery," every year the townspeople get together for the annual lottery. Each family draws a ticket. Every individual in the family with the winning ticket then draws a straw. The member with the shortest straw is stoned to death by the townspeople. The story gives no reason for the stoning, but high school teachers often hypothesize that the stoning represents the town offering a sacrificial lamb to their god. One individual takes responsibility for the sins of all the townspeople and then the rest of the town is cleansed.

*George Orwell, *1984.* (New York: Harcourt, Brace & Company, 1949).

**Shirley Jackson, "*The Lottery and Other Short Stories,*" (New York: Farrar, Straus and Giroux, 2005).

BACKGROUND

Traditionally, federal judges were able to sentence individuals according to their individual discretion. If a judge felt that an individual had made a mistake, was truly remorseful, and deserved a second chance, the judge could give a lenient sentence. If, on the other hand, the judge found someone to be a habitual offender who did not show remorse, the judge could give a longer sentence. In many respects, this made sense. Judges had experience sentencing many people and were in a position to make decisions pertaining to the individuals who appeared in front of them.

Many people felt that judges had too much unrestrained discretion, however. Some judges tended to be harsh; some judges tended to be lenient. It became a luck of the draw for defendants. Additionally, defendants who were likable often received more lenient sentences than defendants who were not as personable, even when the two individuals were similarly situated and had committed similar crimes.

LEGAL DEVELOPMENTS: PRO AND CON

In 1984, Congress established the United States Sentencing Commission.[1] Some of the purposes of the commission were to establish sentencing policies and practices to "provide certainty and fairness" and avoid "unwarranted sentencing disparities."[2] Sentencing guidelines were then formulated and became mandatory.[3] Judges who for years had used their discretion in sentencing defendants were suddenly faced with the job of sentencing someone according to a number grid.

> The Federal Sentencing Guidelines have been well received by the attorneys general who have served this country since the inception of the guidelines. In a memo dated Monday, September 22, 2003, former Attorney General John Ashcroft gave his opinion of the United States Sentencing Guidelines:
>
> The passage of the Sentencing Reform Act of 1984 was a watershed event in the pursuit of fairness and consistency in the federal criminal justice system. With the Sentencing Reform Act's creation of the United States Sentencing Commission and the subsequent promulgation of the Sentencing Guidelines, Congress sought to "provide certainty and fairness in meeting the purposes of sentencing." 28 U.S.C. §991(b)(1)(B).
>
> In contrast to the prior sentencing system—which was characterized by largely unfettered discretion, and by seemingly severe sentences that were often sharply reduced by parole—the Sentencing Reform Act and the Sentencing Guidelines sought to accomplish several important objectives: (1) to ensure honesty and transparency in federal sentencing; (2) to guide sentencing discretion, so as to narrow the disparity between sentences for similar offenses committed by similar offenders; and (3) to provide for the imposition of appropriately different punishments for offenses of differing severity.[4]

Although the U.S. Attorney General's office applauds the Federal Sentencing Guidelines, many have criticized them. One of the more vocal critics is the Honorable Nancy Gertner, a judge from the Federal District Court of Massachusetts in Boston. Judge Gertner wrote an article for the American Bar Association entitled "Federal Sentencing Guidelines: A View from the Bench." Judge Gertner wrote: "While sentencing prior to the Sentencing Reform Act of 1984 (SRA) 18 U.S.C. §§ 3551 *et seq.*, was far from perfect, criticism of the federal sentencing guideline regime has come from all corners of the legal profession, including the judiciary and academia."[5]

Judge Gertner and others claim that the there are many flaws in the Federal Sentencing Guidelines. Although sentences are supposed to be uniform, they are not. There is regional disparity (some prosecutors bring more serious charges than others) and racial disparity. The guidelines are harsh. Some crimes have mandatory minimum sentences. Nonetheless, often the guidelines sentence is harsher than the mandatory minimum. The discretionary power that has been taken away from judges has been given to prosecutors. The prosecutor is the one who decides which charge to bring and which facts to bring to the court's attention. These facts, referred to as "relevant conduct" can increase (enhance) a sentence.[6]

In 2003, Supreme Court Justice Anthony Kennedy expressed his dissatisfaction with the United States Sentencing Guidelines and asked the American Bar Association to form a commission to study certain issues in federal sentencing law, including the Sentencing Guidelines themselves.[7] This commission recommended broad changes to the Sentencing Guidelines.[8]

Under the Federal Sentencing Guidelines, there is not a lot of room for flexibility. When the guidelines were mandatory, a criminal defendant did not have much room to negotiate. Congress and the Sentencing Commission built in a loophole, however. Under 28 U.S.C. §994(n), the commission was directed to promulgate guidelines that allow a defendant to receive a lower sentence regardless of whether there is a statutory minimum if that defendant provides "substantial assistance" to the government in the "investigation or prosecution of another individual."

The Federal Sentencing Guidelines does in fact allow a defendant who has provided substantial assistance to receive what is called a *downward departure,* or a lower sentence than he or she would have received if the sentencing guidelines had been applied. This is often referred to as a "5K1" departure because it is referenced in section 5K1.1 of the Federal Sentencing Guidelines and it states, "Upon motion of the government stating that the defendant has provided substantial assistance in the investigation or prosecution of another person who has committed an offense, the court may depart from the guidelines."

The government relies on defendants who provide substantial assistance. Attorney General Ashcroft directed the U.S. attorneys offices to follow the sentencing guidelines when reaching plea agreements. The U.S. attorneys were also directed to charge the most severe provable offense and to ask for sentences at the top of the guideline range. Except in rare cases, the U.S. attorneys were directed to be lenient only when a defendant or potential defendant had provided substantial assistance to the government in the investigation and prosecution of another individual.[9]

One of the criticisms of a 5K1 departure is that it is controlled by the prosecution. First, the government must be willing to work with a particular defendant. Then the government evaluates the assistance and makes a decision on whether to motion the court to give the defendant a downward departure. A defendant cannot motion the court for the departure. If the government is unwilling to file a motion, the defendant will not receive the downward departure. Thus, a defendant often has incentive to do what the government asks him to do and to say what the government asks him to say. This often raises an issue of credibility during a trial.

A person who provides substantial assistance is often referred to as a *cooperating individual* by the government. In order for a cooperating individual to provide substantial assistance to the government, the defendant must have inside knowledge of the crime and the individual who commits this crime. An individual is more likely to have knowledge of a crime when he or she participated in that crime. For that reason, many times, a cooperating individual is used to provide substantial assistance in prosecuting members of his own conspiracy.

In providing substantial assistance, a cooperating individual (CI) will often assist the government in investigating and obtaining evidence against someone who has conspired with him to commit a crime (often referred to as the *target*). One of the most common scenarios occurs in drug conspiracies. A cooperating individual first meets with the government and provides information. Then he or she does a so-called controlled buy. The CI often calls one of his coconspirators and arranges to pick up some drugs. The government provides the CI with marked bills and the CI meets the target and exchanges the marked money for the drugs. The CI then gives the drugs to the government agent. The evidence obtained from the CI becomes evidence against the target. The target is then charged with conspiracy (for committing a crime with the CI) and becomes a criminal defendant.

Once the target is charged, he either enters into a plea agreement or goes to trial. If he goes to trial, the cooperating individual testifies against him. When the CI testifies, he or she will testify as to the amount of drugs sold or distributed by everyone in the conspiracy, including the amount of drugs sold or distributed by the CI.

The conspiracy statute most often used is the one contained in Title 21, Chapter 13, the Drug Abuse Prevention and Control statute (21 U.S.C.A. §846), which reads, "Any person who attempts or conspires to commit any offense defined in this subchapter shall be subject to the same penalties as those prescribed for the offense, the commission of which was the object of the attempt or conspiracy." By statute, the defendant in a drug conspiracy is held accountable not only for his own crimes but also for those committed by his coconspirators. In a drug charge, a defendant is sentenced largely according to the weight of the drugs distributed by the entire conspiracy. One of the biggest criticisms of the cooperating individual who provides substantial assistance in a drug conspiracy case is that the defendant is held accountable for the wrongdoing of all of his coconspirators, not just for his own wrongdoing.

Another criticism of the substantial assistance/conspiracy relationship is that defendants who choose to exercise their constitutional rights are penalized. A defendant has an absolute right under the Fifth Amendment of the United States Constitution to remain silent; however, that silence comes at a price. By remaining silent, a defendant pays the penalty of his or her coconspirator who did not remain silent. A defendant who chooses to remain silent and does not admit his or her guilt also loses out on a downward departure for "acceptance of responsibility."[10]

Opponents of the frequent use of CIs who provide substantial assistance claim that this has created a system that does not address any of the purposes addressed in the sentencing statutes.[11] Granting a downward departure for substantial assistance does not address the goal of deterrence, rehabilitation, or retribution. Cooperating individuals who provide substantial assistance are common. Unfortunately, many people are aware that they can get out of a crime they committed by turning in someone else.

FUTURE PROSPECTS

Although the sentencing reform movement is gaining momentum, so far no one has challenged the practice of giving downward departures to cooperating individuals who assist the government to convict their coconspirators. The government relies on these individuals. It is unlikely that the government would move to change this. Although defendants who do not provide substantial assistance are often penalized, those who do provide assistance are rewarded. This is a loophole attorneys can use to help their individual clients get a lower sentence. It is unlikely that criminal defense attorneys will lead the movement to change this system. For the foreseeable future, this appears to be a phenomenon that will not go away.

See Also: Prosecutorial Discretion.

Endnotes

1. 28 U.S.C. §991.
2. 28 U.S.C. §991(b)(1).
3. In 2005, the United States Supreme Court decided that the United States Sentencing Guidelines were unconstitutional because they were mandatory. As of that time, the guidelines are no longer mandatory but are instead advisory; *U.S. v. Booker* 543 U.S. 220 (2005).
4. Memo by Attorney General John Ashcroft, September 22, 2003.
5. Nancy Gertner, "Federal Sentencing Guidelines: A View from the Bench," *Human Rights Magazine* 29(2): Spring 2002.
6. Ibid, p 13 *Individual Rights and Responsibilities,* http://www.abanet.org/irr/hr/spring02/gertner.html.
7. An address by Anthony M. Kennedy, Associate Justice, Supreme Court of the United States, at the American Bar Association Annual Meeting, August 9, 2003, San Francisco.
8. American Bar Association, "Kennedy Commission Summary of Recommendations," at ABA Division for Media Relations and Communication Services. http://www.manningmedia.net/Clients/ABA/ABA288.
9. Memo by Attorney General John Ashcroft, September 22, 2003.
10. United States Sentencing Guidelines §3E1.1.
11. See 18 U.S.C. §3553(a)(2).

Further Reading: Demleitner, Nora, Douglas A. Berman, Marc L. Miller, and Ronald F. Wright, *Sentencing Law and Policy, Cases, Statutes & Guidelines 2006–2007 Supplement* (Aspen Publishers, 2006); Ellis, Alan, *Federal Post Conviction Guidebook* (2005); Ellis, Alan, *Federal Sentencing Guidebook* (2005); Ellis, Alan, and J. Michael Henderson, *Federal Prison Guidebook* (2005); Jackson, Shirley, "The Lottery"; Orwell, George, *1984;* United States Sentencing Commission, *United States Sentencing Commission Guidelines Manual* (Washington, D.C.: U.S. Government, 2006).

Dawn E. Worsley

CONVICT CRIMINOLOGY

INTRODUCTION

Convict criminology (CC) is a relatively new and controversial perspective in the practical field of corrections and the academic field of criminology. Its very existence challenges crime and correctional problems as traditionally represented in contemporary society by many mainstream researchers, policy makers, and politicians who have minimal contact with jails, prisons, and convicts. In different words, CC started because of the frustration of ex-convict academics with this state of affairs and an attempt to inject more realism and humanism into the study and writings about crime and corrections. Convict criminologists are especially concerned with how the problem of crime is defined, the solutions proposed, and the devastating impacts of those decisions on the men and women labeled criminals, who are locked in correctional facilities, separated from loved ones, and prevented from successfully reintegrating back into the community upon release from custody.

In many ways, the academic study of crime and corrections is still stuck in the nineteenth century, if not directly then indirectly debating the ideas of Jeremy Bentham and Cesare Beccaria, who founded the Classical School of Criminology in the late eighteenth century, and Cesare Lombroso, founder of the Positivist School of Criminology in the late nineteenth century. Meanwhile, as we have entered the twenty-first century, there are approximately 2.2 million Americans behind bars, and tens of millions of convicted felons reside in the community. Whereas slaves have won emancipation, women the vote, minorities their civil rights, gays and lesbians increased measures of legal protection, people with felony convictions are subject to legal prejudice and exclusion. To counteract this situation, the CC group tends to do research that illustrates the experiences of defendants and prisoners, attempts to combat the misrepresentations of media and government, and proposes new and less costly strategies that are more humane and effective.

BACKGROUND

The so-called convict perspective was first introduced in the "New School of Convict Criminology."[1] "The emerging field of convict criminology consists primarily of essays and empirical research written by convicts or ex-convicts, on their way to completing or already in possession of a PhD, or by enlightened academics who critique existing literature, policies, and practices, thus contributing to a new perspective on criminology, criminal justice, corrections, and community corrections."[2] Ex-convict professors who invite and welcome collaboration with critical scholars lead the group. Some of the most important members are so-called non-con academics who have contributed in many ways to the formation, growth, and activities of the group.

Historically, numerous ex-cons have worked at universities in many different disciplines. Most of them stayed in the closet because their criminal history was not relevant to their studies and/or they were afraid to confront the reactions of their colleagues. One exception was Frank Tannenbaum, sometimes referred to as the "grandfather of labeling theory," a Wobbly organizer, political activist, former federal prisoner, professor at Columbia University in the 1930s, and one of the first to openly identify himself as an ex-convict. Although Tannenbaum served only one year in prison, he had a prolific career as a journalist then scholar.

Intellectually, the modern-day origins of CC began with the published work of John Irwin, especially his books *The Felon* (1970), *Prisons in Turmoil* (1980), and *The Jail* (1985). Irwin served five years in prison for armed robbery in the 1950s. In the late 1960s, he was a student of David Matza and Erving Goffman when he completed his PhD at the University of California–Berkeley. Even as he became a prominent prison ethnographer and many of his colleagues knew his background, his ex-convict history was only apparent to the close reader of his texts. Nevertheless, Irwin was out of the closet, doing inside-prison research, but still nearly alone in his representation of the convict perspective.

On the heels of Irwin's work was Richard McCleary, who wrote *Dangerous Men* (1978), a book that came out of his experience and doctoral research, when he was out on parole (in the state of Minnesota). McCleary has gone on to a well-respected career as a quantitative criminologist at the University of California–Irvine.

Later, in Canada, an influential academic journal began that specialized in publishing convict and ex-convict authors. Robert Gaucher, Howard Davidson, and Liz Elliot started *The Journal of Prisoners on Prisons (JPP)*. As Canadian criminologists, they were disappointed with presentations at the International Conference on Penal Abolition III held in Montreal in 1987, where participants were concerned with the lack of prisoner representation. In 1988, *JPP* brought out its first issue and to date has published more than twenty issues featuring convict authors (and other critical writers).

Nevertheless, through the 1980s there were still too few ex-convict professors to support Irwin, McCleary, or *JPP* in establishing a research agenda based on convict research literature. Although the prison population was growing in the 1970s and 1980s, there were still only a handful of ex-convicts completing PhDs in sociology, criminology, and criminal justice.

KEY MOMENTS IN CONVICT CRIMINOLOGY

1970: Publication of John Irwin's *The Felon*.

1978: Publication of Richard McCleary's *Dangerous Men*.

1997: First time ex-convict professors appear together in session at the American Society of Criminology Conference.

1999: First official Convict Criminology Session at the American Society of Criminology Conference.

2001: "The New School of Convict Criminology" published in *Social Justice*.

2003: *Convict Criminology* published.

The so-called War on Drugs (1980–present) dramatically increased the number of middle-class prisoners, some of whom would exit prison, complete advanced college degrees, and become academics. By the 1990s, a significant number of ex-convict graduate students and professors were studying jails, prisons, and community corrections and beginning to document their own observations and experiences.

The Convict Criminology group was organized at the American Society of Criminology (ASC) annual meetings. In 1997, Chuck Terry (then a PhD student) was complaining to Joan Petersilia (his professor at the University of California–Irvine) about "the failure of criminologists to recognize the dehumanizing conditions of the criminal justice system and the lives of those defined as criminal."[3] Petersilia suggested that Terry put together a session for the 1997 ASC conference. Terry invited ex-convict professors John Irwin, Stephen Richards, Edward Tromanhauser, and PhD student Alan Mobley to participate in a session entitled "Convicts Critique Criminology: The Last Seminar." This was the first time a number of ex-convict academics appeared openly on the same panel at a national conference. The session drew a large audience, including national media. That evening, over dinner, Jim Austin, John Irwin, Steve Richards, and Chuck Terry discussed the importance and possibilities of ex-con professors working together to conduct inside studies of prisons. Irwin said he had always wanted to research and write with other ex-con academics, but unfortunately until the 1990s only a few existed.

In spring 1998, Richards spoke with Jeffrey Ian Ross about the possibility of editing a book using manuscripts produced by ex-con academics. Almost immediately, Ross and Richards sent out formal invitations to individuals, including ex-convict professors and graduate students and well-known critical authors of work on corrections. In short order, a proposal was written that would eventually result in the book *Convict Criminology.*

At the 1998 ASC meeting, Richards, Terry, and another ex-con professor, Rick Jones, appeared on a panel honoring Richard Quinney. Meanwhile, the group used the conference as an opportunity to find and recruit additional ex-convict professors and graduate students. Dan Murphy, Rick Jones, and Greg Newbold joined the informal discussion.

In 1999, at the ASC meeting in Toronto, Stephen Richards organized the first official sessions entitled "Convict Criminology." The two sessions, "Convict Criminology: An Introduction to the Movement, Theory, and Research–Part I and Part II," included ex-convict professors Richards, Irwin, Tromanhauser, and Newbold; ex-convict graduate students Terry, Murphy, Warren Gregory, Susan Dearing, and Nick Mitchell; and, non-con colleagues Jeffrey Ian Ross, Bruce Arrigo, Bud Brown, Randy Shelden, Preston Elrod, Mike Brooks, and Marianne Fisher-Giorlando. A number of the papers presented in these two sessions were early versions of chapters that would be published in *Convict Criminology.*[4] As of 2006, more than two-dozen CC sessions have been held at major criminology and sociology conferences.

Stephen C. Richards and Jeffrey Ian Ross coined the term *convict criminology.* In 2001, they published the article "The New School of Convict Criminology" in the journal *Social Justice,* discussing the birth and definition of CC and out-lining the parameters of the movement and research perspective. In 2003, they published the edited book *Convict Criminology,* which included chapters by the founders of the group. The book included a foreword by Todd Clear, preface by John Irwin, eight autobiographical chapters by ex-convict criminologists, and a number of supporting chapters by non-con colleagues writing about jail and prison issues. This was the first time ex-convict academics appeared in a book together discussing their own criminal convictions, time in prison, and experi-ences in graduate school and as professors at universities. CC was born of the courage it took for these authors to step out of the closet and tell it like it is.

KEY EVENTS

The Intellectual and Official Origins of Convict Criminology

CC builds on the work of previous prison scholars. Except now, ex-convicts who have become academics conduct the research and writing. The writing is first person as well as third person or "royal we." The methodology, data col-lection, and analysis reflect this tension inherent in writing from conflicting standpoints.

Theoretically, CC is also rooted in Goffman's notions of stigma and roles developed in his research during the late 1950s and early 1960s. Symbolically, the ex-convict academic represents two antagonistic master roles: the convict and professor. The former role informs the latter role but cannot be forgotten, especially when the subject of the research is prison.

CC also challenges commonly held beliefs, thus it is coterminous with many of the epistemological approaches found in critical criminology, which tries to deconstruct myths and look for deeper meanings. For example, many people, including criminologists, hold firm assumptions or judgments concerning the moral character or behavior of persons convicted of crimes.

Ex-Convicts Suffer Discrimination at Universities and Establish Collective Response

Felons suffer discrimination nearly everywhere they go in respectable society applying for employment. Many give up and live marginal lives or return to crime. Ex-convicts are felons who have done prison time. Most of them have been incarcerated numerous times or for long periods. You can find them stand-ing on street corners, waiting for meals at soup kitchens, or temporarily residing in homeless shelters. Very few of these men and women have attended college or university.

Ex-convicts suffer discrimination at universities. Academia, for all its liberal pretense, discussions of diversity, and support for affirmative action, is often a hostile environment for ex-convict students and faculty. Many universities ask criminal-history questions on student admission forms, and students are denied financial aid, campus housing assignments, and employment because of past criminal convictions. In a similar fashion, faculty appointments, promotions, and tenure may be subject to criminal background checks. Ex-convict professors may not be hired or granted tenure, promotion, or consideration for administrative positions.

In their chapters written for *Convict Criminology*, a number of the convict criminologists have discussed the discrimination they experienced in graduate school or as professors. They also may have acknowledged the assistance they received from faculty sensitive to the prejudice they perceived. Some members of the group have also discussed this discrimination when interviewed by the media.

Today, numerous ex-convict graduate students and faculty in the social sciences still retain their privacy and hide their criminal convictions. In part, they may decide to conceal their past because they fear professional recriminations, including losing their jobs, being denied research support, or exclusion in their communities. Some of them may even teach criminology or criminal justice courses, publish on jails and prisons, and still feel compelled to continue the charade.

PROMINENT EX-CONVICT CRIMINOLOGY PROFESSORS ARE GRADUATES OF THESE UNIVERSITIES

Auckland University (New Zealand)
University of California–Berkeley
University of California–Irvine
Iowa State University

University of Missouri–Kansas City
Prairie View A&M
State University of New York at Albany
Washington University

The CC group is informally organized as a writing and activist collective. The group includes ex-convict professors, graduate students, undergraduate students, and non-con critical colleagues and friends. There is no formal membership or assignment of leadership roles. Individuals voluntarily decide to associate with the group. Different members of the group lead or take responsibility for assorted functions, such as lead author on an academic article, research proposal, or program assessment; mentoring students or junior faculty; or media contact. The group continues to grow as more prisoners exit prison to attend universities, hear about the group, and decide to contribute to activities. Typically, new members resolve to come out when they are introduced to the academic community at ASC or Academy of Criminal Justice Sciences conferences.

The group is not limited to students and faculty who research or teach in criminology, criminal justice, sociology, and social work. CC may also include ex-cons or non-cons who work outside of academia, including government agencies, private foundations, or community groups. For example, the group includes a number of ex-convicts with PhDs employed by government or private agencies that research or administer criminal justice programs. Although these members may not hold positions at universities, they may teach part-time, write research reports that contribute to academic publications or criminal justice policy, and participate on CC panels at ASC, Academy of Criminal Justice Sciences, or American Correctional Association conferences.

The CC group is composed of active members who are out of the closet as well as inactive ex-con students and professors who prefer to conceal their criminal background history. Some ex-cons have personal and professional reasons or a preference to live their lives less public. Nevertheless, they may still participate on occasion or ask for help when necessary. The group appreciates their support and understands and respects their need or desire for privacy.

Finally, a growing group of men and women behind bars hold advanced degrees and publish academic work about crime and corrections. Some of these authors are better published than many professors. A number of them have coauthored books and academic articles with so-called free-world academics.

At the present time, the CC group includes men and women ex-con academics from the United States, United Kingdom, Canada, Australia, New Zealand, and Finland. The United States, with the largest prison population in the world, continues to contribute the most members.

The Activities of the Convict Criminology Group

The CC group mentors students, organizes sessions at regional and national conferences, collaborates on research projects, coauthors articles and monographs, helps organize and support numerous groups and activities related to criminal justice reform, and provides consulting services and organizes workshops for criminal defense attorneys, correctional organizations, and universities. For example, some members of the group have worked on major prison research projects in Kentucky, California, and Ohio. Collectively, the group has published books, journal articles, and book chapters using autoethnographic, or insider, perspectives. Private foundations, including the Soros Foundation Open Society Institute, have supported some CC activities, including conference presentations and research. Individuals may serve as consultants or leadership for community groups working on prison issues or legislation.

The local and national media are interested in how convicts become professors or their insider expertise. Newspapers, radio, and television frequently interview group members. The media may ask one ex-convict professor to recommend another for interviews. They may use these appearances to inform the public on criminal justice issues. Ex-convict professors may also employ media appearances to promote positive publicity for universities, academic programs, and/or correctional programs. Media stories about the group have appeared in print in many countries.

All of the ex-convict members mentor students with felony records at their respective universities. This is analogous to the way gay and lesbian or minority faculty may serve as mentors for students. This may include academic advising, emotional support, or preparation for employment or admission to graduate programs. Many of the group members serve as role models or advisors for convicts or ex-convicts who might be thinking about attending university.

It is estimated that more than 500,000 men and women get out of prison every year in the United States. Some of them will exit prison and enter or return to college. Most large universities and even small colleges provide special advising services for women, gays and lesbians, persons with disabilities, and military personnel. Each of these groups has unique needs and experiences that may complicate their day-to-day living on campus or success in the classroom. Many universities have completely neglected to even consider the specials needs of felons and ex-convicts. No wonder many ex-convicts do not feel welcome on campus.

Upon arriving on campuses, most ex-convicts find few if any academic staff or faculty prepared to advise them on matters concerning the difficult transition from prison to college, the discrimination they may experience, or how the so-called collateral consequences of their felony convictions may impact or limit their choices in academic majors and future careers. For example, felons may not be allowed to even major in education, medicine, nursing, law, or social work.

It could be argued that the most important activity of the CC group is the service it provides to students. Many ex-convict social science professors informally advise and mentor felony students. Some of these are nontraditional students who are older and may have served prison time. Others are traditional (18- to 22-year-old) students who have been arrested or convicted of a crime while they were students. Regardless of the specific circumstance, the responsibility of the ex-convict professor is to provide academic advising and not legal counseling.

A growing number of non-con academics also actively advise and mentor both undergraduate and graduate students with misdemeanor or felony convictions. Some of these have participated in CC activities. Most have not and may simply be faculty who are well educated in social justice issues and have developed the capacity to aid ex-convicts when asked. The ex-convict professors recognize that without the assistance and support of non-con faculty they would not have completed their own degrees.

CC is now being taught in universities and prisons. The convict perspective may be used as part or all of a course. The collected works of the group may be used to teach an entire course. In Wisconsin (2004–7), free college courses entitled "Convict Criminology" or undergraduate teachers inside a number of prisons are teaching "Inviting Convicts to College." The book *Convict Criminology* is used to inspire prisoners. Prisoners exiting prison to enter college use the courses as a bridge. In the final weeks of the course, the student teachers help prisoners complete admission and financial aid forms.

IMPORTANT CONTRIBUTIONS TO:

The Fields of Criminology and Criminal Justice

CC continues to grow as numerous articles and books are added to the literature and the perspective is discussed in textbooks. The CC group emphasizes the use of direct observation and real-life experience in understanding the different processes, procedures, and institutional settings that make up the criminal justice system. The methodology includes correspondence with prisoners, face-to-face interviews, retrospective interpretation of past experience, and direct observation inside numerous correctional facilities. The group is especially skilled at gaining entry to prisons, writing research questions and composing interview questionnaires, and analyzing prison records and statistics.

The group has also called for a careful review of stigmatizing language commonly used in criminal justice articles and textbooks. Most mainstream academic authors continue to use the terms of law enforcement and prison administrators. This only adds to the adverse power of labels and stigma. *Rehabilitation, corrections, retribution, incarceration, incapacitation, abscond,* and *recidivism* are some of these words. Traditional textbooks are filled with terms used to label people by their criminal offense: for example, *criminal, convict, parolee, jailbird, murderer, rapist, thief, armed robber, burglar, sex offender, child abuser, pedophile, pederast, embezzler, forger, drug abuser, drug dealer, career criminal,* and *recidivist.* Unfortunately, these discrediting labels may be used to generalize about a person's moral character years after he or she has completed the sentences and matured into another person.

For example, it could be argued that the word *inmate* suggests a person serving a short prison sentence or a prisoner not fully integrated into the convict world. From a convict perspective, it is disrespectful to use the term *inmate,* as this is the official language used by prison authorities. *Inmate* is the term used by prison officials to demean prisoners. In contrast, the use of the terms *prisoners* or *convicts* recognizes that men and women in prison endure years of confinement, have their own culture that allows them some dignity, and are not simply numbered inmates in a cage.

Further, the use of the term *offenders* is offensive and detrimental to defendants, convicts, and ex-convicts trying to reenter the community. A convict is a person (man or women) convicted of a crime. They are still a person, with a life history, a man or women who is more than the term *offender* implies. CC suggests that authors in the field change the term *inmate* to *prisoner, convict, man,* or *woman* and the term *offender* to *man, woman,* or *person convicted of a crime.* Change the words and see how the discourse improves.

The Study of Jails, Prisons, and Community Corrections

The CC perspective has contributed to the updating of studies on corrections and community corrections. With nearly 7 million Americans currently in the custody of correctional supervision, it was time to incorporate the voice and concerns of the men and women in jail, prison, and on probation or parole. These concerns begin with the offensive language used by academics, policy makers, and politicians and continue with the demeaning or abusive treatment they may have experienced as defendants or prisoners.

Until now, with rare exception, the academic literature discussed the prison abstractly, with little detail or differentiation between security level, state system, or region of the country. When details were provided, for example, on prison conditions or social groups within the prison, the sources were ancient.[5] Many academic articles did not even identify the prison facility, state, or system. Other articles were written without even interviewing or talking with prisoners.

There has been a dramatic increase in the number of ex-con academics willing to step forward and be part of the group. The group offers mutual support for graduate students or junior faculty who decide to come out and share their firsthand experiences with the criminal justice system. As the group grows and these observations collect, a more complete and relatively current picture of modern prisons begins to emerge.[6] Members of the group can write with authority about what they observed or experienced in prison in different states and countries.

The CC literature is now being cited in textbooks and academic journals. There is a greater appreciation for first person, or autoenthnographic, and retrospective accounts. In and around the same time that *Convict Criminology* first appeared in print, many academic book publishers for the first time took risks of publishing manuscripts written by prisoners and edited by established academics (i.e., Alarid, Bernard, Johnson, Toch).

FUTURE PROSPECTS

Convict criminologists will continue to do what we know best. This includes mentoring prisoners and students, conducting research, publishing real accounts of prison conditions, teaching about how people experience the criminal justice system in our classrooms, and reaching out to the public, media, and our academic colleagues as a means to support the humane treatment of defendants and prisoners. The goal is to present a new understanding of the problems of crime and criminal justice, to identify areas that need to be changed, and to assist those who have suffered from the effects of a prison sentence. Through our research, teaching, and mentoring, we hope to lift the veil of false consciousness and change the social reality of crime and punishment in modern society.

See Also: Corrections Education; Miscarriages of Justice; New Penology; Peacemaking Criminology.

Endnotes

1. Stephen C. Richards and Jeffrey Ian Ross, "The New School of Convict Criminology," *Social Justice* 28, no. 1 (2001): 177–90.
2. Jeffrey Ian Ross and Stephen C. Richards, *Convict Criminology* (Belmont, CA: Wadsworth, 2003), 6.

3. Charles M. Terry, *The Fellas: Overcoming Prison and Addiction* (Belmont, CA: Wadsworth, 2003), 112–13; John Irwin, "Preface," in *Convict Criminology,* ed. Jeffrey Ian Ross and Stephen C. Richards (Belmont, CA: Wadsworth, 2003), iii.

4. Ross and Richards, *Convict Criminology.*

5. See, for example, Donald Clemmer, *The Prison Community* (New York: Holt, Rinehart, and Winston, 1940); Gresham Sykes, *The Society of Captives* (Princeton, NJ: Princeton University Press, 1958); Karl Menninger, *The Crime of Punishment* (New York: Penguin, 1968); James Jacobs, *Stateville* (Chicago: University of Chicago Press, 1977).

6. See Richard S. Jones and Thomas Schmid, *Doing Time: Prison Experience and Identity among First Time Inmates* (Stamford, CT: JAI Press, 2000); Jeffrey Ian Ross and Stephen C. Richards, *Behind Bars: Surviving Prison* (New York: Alpha/Penguin, 2002); Terry, *The Fellas;* John Irwin, *The Warehouse Prison: Disposal of the New Dangerous Class* (Los Angeles: Roxbury, 2005).

Further Reading: Irwin, John, *The Warehouse Prison: Disposal of the New Dangerous Class* (Los Angeles: Roxbury, 2005); Jones, Richard S., and Thomas Schmid, *Doing Time: Prison Experience and Identity among First Time Inmates* (Stamford, CT: JAI Press, 2000); Richards, Stephen C., and Jeffrey Ian Ross, "The New School of Convict Criminology," *Social Justice* 28, no. 1 (2001): 177–90; Ross, Jeffrey Ian, and Stephen C. Richards, *Behind Bars: Surviving Prison* (New York: Alpha/Penguin, 2002); Ross, Jeffrey Ian, and Stephen C. Richards, *Convict Criminology* (Belmont, CA: Wadsworth, 2003); Terry, Charles M., *The Fellas: Overcoming Prison and Addiction* (Belmont, CA: Wadsworth, 2003).

Stephen C. Richards, Jeffrey Ian Ross, and Richard S. Jones

CORPORAL PUNISHMENT

INTRODUCTION

Although most Western countries, including the United States, tend to regard corporal punishment as primitive and old school, there are still serious scholars and others who argue for the use of corporal punishment. These supporters of corporal punishment argue that it is quick, cheap, more uniform in application, and can be better matched to the severity of the crime than incarceration without spillover effects on the offender's family, employer, and/or community. Those opposed to corporal punishment argue that it is crude, inhumane, and degrading.

Corporal punishment refers to physical penalties inflicted on the body in ways that cause acute pain, humiliation, and/or disfigurement. Its root is from the Latin *corpus,* or "body," and refers to sentences making specific reference to punishing the body, in contrast with more familiar contemporary punishments involving deprivation of liberty like imprisonment, probation, or parole. For example, incarceration may cause discomfort to the body and potentially subject it to violence such as rape, but it is not the same as whipping, branding, or amputation in which the judicial sentence directly imposes a specific amount of acute pain as punishment for an offense. Although executions obviously harm the body by putting someone to death, under current U.S. law, they must not involve torture or pain and suffering beyond what is minimally necessary to extinguish life.

BACKGROUND

Corporal punishments were a prominent feature of criminal justice in Western history and are currently practiced mainly by non-Western countries. Because of modernist assumptions (history is progress) and ethnocentrism (Western culture is best), corporal punishments tend to be viewed as primitive and barbaric, so there is little public support for reintroducing them even in times of widespread ideological agreement about getting tough with criminals. A wide variety of scholars, however—mostly writing on topics not related to punishment—have critiqued the imperialist beliefs and Orientalism[1] behind beliefs of Western superiority, and philosopher Michel Foucault's *Discipline and Punish* has directly challenged the idea that movement from corporal punishment to prison indicated progress toward civilization.

FOUCAULT AND THE BIRTH OF THE PRISON

The transition to prison from corporal punishments and the spectacle of execution is the subject of *Discipline and Punish* by French philosopher Michel Foucault.* It starts with a gruesome description of an execution in 1757 involving the offender's flesh being torn with red-hot pincers, burning, and an extended unsuccessful effort at drawing and quartering. The executioner finally had to cut apart the body and then burned the pieces. The second type of punishment that Foucault describes is a "house of young offenders" eighty years later, with the prison structured on a strict timetable or schedule, with drum rolls announcing changing activities. Between 1760 and 1840, Foucault argues, "from being an art of unbearable sensations, punishment has become an economy of suspended rights."** These examples define larger penal styles of the different time periods, and he investigates the process whereby public spectacle disappeared, pain is downplayed, prison replaces corporal punishment, punishment becomes hidden and part of "abstract consciousness."

Foucault argues that spectacles of pain associated with corporal punishment were rooted in the sovereign's power to wage war against his enemies and were intended to terrorize citizens into obedience. As systems of social control, however, such displays could backfire or send mixed messages about justice. They were thus inefficient political economies of power, and with the rise of capitalism the state sought better ways of appropriating bodies for the Industrial Revolution rather than killing them. The new goal is one that Foucault describes as the creation of "docile bodies," people who are trained and willing to do whatever people in authority request. The system to do this was based on mechanisms of surveillance, discipline, and control.

The embodiment of this system was Jeremy Bentham's (co-founder of the Classical School of Criminology in the late eighteenth century) model Panopticon prison, whose architecture allowed easy surveillance of the prisoners by the guards, but in such a way the inmates never knew when they were being observed. In a system in which people know they may be observed at any time, they tend to behave at all times as if they are being watched, and they discipline themselves to do what is expected. Foucault states that the technique of domination through omnipresent surveillance overflowed the prison walls to become a model for many social institutions, so "prisons resemble factories, schools, barracks, hospitals, which all resemble prisons."***

The result is generalized surveillance and the formation of a disciplinary society based on specialization (a place for everything and everything in its place), timetables, normalizing judgments (performance standards), repetitive exercises, and drills.**** The end of corporal punishment is thus not seen as a humanitarian step or the flowering of civilization, but a transformation to more totalizing forms of power and domination. Foucault ominously states: "Historians of ideas usually attribute the dream of a perfect society to the philosophers and jurists of the eighteenth century; but there was also a military dream of society; its fundamental reference was not to the state of nature, but to the meticulously subordinated cogs of a machine, not to the primal social contract, but to permanent coercions, not to fundamental rights, but to indefinitely progressive forms of training, not to general will, but to automatic docility."*****

---

* Michel Foucault, *Discipline and Punish* (New York: Vintage, 1979).

** Ibid., 11.

*** Ibid., 228.

**** Ibid., 208, 141–94; Lydia Alix Fillingham, *Foucault for Beginners* (New York: Writers and Readers, 1993), 120–29.

***** Foucault, *Discipline and Punish*, 169.

Most early punishments were corporal punishments, and the first jails and prisons were designed merely to hold offenders until their corporal punishment could be carried out. Until around 1800, communities typically held an offender in the stocks. Just as every community now has a jail, historically every village had stocks. Offenders placed their arms, legs, and/or head through holes cut in boards, whose hinged parts would be closed and locked. Stocks could be used to hold offenders prior to another penalty or as a form of punishment itself because the offender would be "powerless to escape the jests and jeers of every idler in the community."[2]

Another common punishment of this time was the pillory, which was similar to the stocks in design and ubiquity. The public, who would throw at them "rotten eggs, filth, and dirt from the streets, which was followed by dead cats, rats and ordure from the slaughter-house," further humiliated individuals held in this structure.[3] In addition, offenders might have their ears nailed to either side of the head hole or cut off entirely (cropped) for additional ridicule. Some communities put offenders in the pillory during public market days to increase their exposure.

Whipping posts were similar to the pillory in design, but they also had a minimalist form in which they would be little more than a post to which an individual was secured. Variations included tying an offender to a whipping cart and walking him or her through town "till his body became bloody."[4] This technique was popular until the 1800s and could be done with a variety of implements like reeds, birch rods, and whips; a significant chapter in the history of whipping involves the British Navy maintaining military discipline with the cat-o'-nine-tails (made of a rope that was unraveled and knotted at the ends to inflict maximum discomfort). Some conservative or religious communities might not whip women or try to avoid unseemly public spectacles of topless women being flogged and bloodied.

Branding, maiming, and amputation all have more permanent effects than other punishments. Branding involved burning a symbol into an offender's flesh that forever labeled him or her a criminal. Often the symbol would vary depending on the crime. Maiming could take many forms and was usually aimed symbolically at addressing the crime: A blasphemer would have his tongue cut out or fixed to the side of his cheek, thieves would have a hand cut off, and so on.

Certain techniques of corporal punishment like the dunking stool and scold's bridle were reserved for women for gendered crimes like gossiping or being argumentative with male authority. The dunking stool was used occasionally for men accused of slander or for both parties in an argumentative marriage. The stool usually resembled a seesaw, with the offender placed in a chair on one end that was dunked into cold water "in order to cool her immoderate heat."[5]

The scold's bridle was used for women who were thought to inappropriately reprimand or find fault with men or male authority. It was "a sort of iron cage, often of great weight; when worn, covering the entire head; with a spiked plate or flat tongue of iron to be placed in the mouth over the tongue" so "if the offender spoke she was cruelly hurt."[6] The bridles depicted in Held were ornamented to give the wearer's face a bestial appearance, and the women would either be led around town or attached to a post. Women staked out in the public square could expect "painful beatings, besmearing with feces and urine, and serious, sometimes fatal wounding—especially in the breasts and pubes."[7]

CORPORAL PUNISHMENT AND EXECUTIONS

Contemporary executions are done with a pinprick as part of lethal injection, and the trend in the United States has been to try to minimize the physical suffering involved in taking life because of the Supreme Court's interpretations of the Eighth Amendment's prohibition on cruel and unusual punishment. All other Western democracies have abolished the death penalty, even for war crimes and genocide, although until the 1800s abuse and torture were commonly aspects of the death sentence. For example, an English sentence for treason in 1691 required the offenders to be:

> Hanged by the neck, to be cut down while ye are yet alive, to have your hearts and bowels taken out before your faces, and your members cut off and burnt. Your heads severed from your bodies, your bodies divided into quarters . . . and disposed of according to the king's will and pleasure; and the Lord have mercy upon your souls.*

Among the types of corporal punishment employed as part of executions are burning to death, especially for blasphemy or religious crime, in which the flames of man's punishment were meant as a reminder of the flames of hell. Breaking on the wheel involved using an iron bar to break the major bones of the body while the person was tied to a large circle symbolizing eternity. Offenders could also be impaled on a stake while still alive, disemboweled (as in the sentence for treason) while alive and then killed, or drawn and quartered by tying the offender to four horses that pulled in different directions. Beheading had a long history, starting with a long sword and ending with the guillotine; technological changes increased the calculability and efficiency of the process.

Such punishments were intense, but Newman argues that they need to be seen in the context of a time when life was shorter, hasher, and without many of the comforts of modern-day life.** There was no central heating or air-conditioning and little in the way of medical care; dentistry involved a person who tended to be known as a tooth-puller who practiced the trade with implements that may also have been used by a blacksmith. Punishment had to deliver pain well above what was experienced in everyday life. Comparing punishments of an earlier time with current practices is problematic because the baseline for pain and suffering in everyday life has also changed (even if going to the dentist is still unpleasant).

After executions, the corpse might be gibbeted and displayed hanging in chains, and the corpse would be covered in tar and fitted with metal straps. As medical schools realized that corpses were necessary to teach anatomy so surgeons knew what to expect when cutting open a body, poor offenders were dissected, sometimes in a public hall, as part of their sentences. The previous practice of robbing graves for cadavers for anatomy study provoked hostility in villages, which occasionally burned medical schools in retaliation for digging up the deceased because dissection involved the "deliberate mutilation or destruction of identity, perhaps for eternity."***

---

*Robert Johnson, *Death Work* (Belmont, CA: Wadsworth, 1998), 14.

**Graeme Newman, *The Punishment Response* (Albany, NY: Harrow and Heston, 1985).

***Ruth Richardson, *Death Dissection and the Destitute* (New York: Routledge and Kegan Paul, 1987), 29.

CONTROVERSIAL ARGUMENTS

Corporal punishment has been involved in some of the spectacular excesses of criminal punishment, ones that are more easily comprehended than statistics about the overuse of prison. But it is a type of punishment of interest to people across philosophies of punishment. Retributivists are attracted by the increased ability to create so-called just deserts by matching the crime with a wide range of corporal punishments. Utilitarians, going back to Bentham's vision of a spanking machine, see potential for more uniform and precise punishments than incarceration can offer. Humanists, peacemaking criminologists, and others see corporal punishment as inhumane, degrading, humiliating, and so on and so forth.

Because many non-Western countries practice corporal punishment, Westerners tend to see the practice as primitive or barbaric, but Newman points out the ethnocentrism of that thinking. His book *Just and Painful* makes a case for corporal punishment that also serves as a critique of prison, which he sees as overused, violent, and expensive—a place the public sees as too comfortable to have credibility as punishment even though criminologists see them as deplorable places.[8]

Newman's suggestion is to implement corporal punishment in the form of electric shocks to be used instead of prison for minor offenses; he sees the combination of shock and prison to constitute torture, which is a process and different from a one-time infliction of pain. Newman agrees with criticisms from human rights organization about practices in non-Western countries that combine corporal punishment with incarceration. Thus, he would also agree with Amnesty International in condemning Saudi Arabia for sentencing two defendants charged with drug crimes to "to 1,500 lashes each, in addition to 15 years' imprisonment. The floggings were scheduled to be carried out at a rate of 50 lashes every six months for the whole duration of the 15 years."[9]

Under Newman's system, shocks would be done in a public punishment hall, after which the offender would be released. (Prison is reserved for violent offenders and certain repeat offenders who are a threat to public safety.) For Newman, the pain of punishment can be matched to the severity of the crime by controlling the number of shocks, the voltage, and the duration of the jolts. Acute physical pain, he argues, is experienced more similarly by people than the chronic pain of a prison sentence, which will vary between institutions and even for individuals in the same prison. Newman further argues that minority overrepresentation in punishment is a "silent statistic," but if blacks were punished in public to the differential extent they are now, "it would be *too much*. It would force us to be accountable for the excesses of prison."[10]

Although some see Newman's system as humiliating to the offender, he argues that many forms of punishment like boot camps are built on degrading activities like cleaning toilets with toothbrushes. Likewise, bargaining over the number of shocks is no more perverse than bargaining over the number of years someone will spend in an overcrowded and violent prison, but society has grown accustomed to the latter form of plea-bargaining. He argues that the obviously painful nature of corporal punishment would force society to take responsibility for it, in contrast to prison violence and rape that usually judges and the public feel is not their concern because it is not part of the sentence. Corporal punishment in the form of electric shocks could also be administered more cheaply than prison and would not require a primary wage earner or parent to be imprisoned. It would, therefore, cause less disruption to people's lives.

FUTURE PROSPECTS

Newman noted that his book is "a polemic, intended to inflame and provoke."[11] The point is thus less political advocacy of corporal punishment than an attempt to have people think more deeply about why and how society punishes offenders. He fears that many who say they support his position do so for the wrong reasons, whereas others reject it because of complacency with mass incarceration or cultural arrogance about so-called barbaric Islamic countries that practice corporal punishment.

In spite of widespread tough-on-crime rhetoric, the public has ambivalent feelings about the deliberate infliction of physical pain as the official sentence. Additionally, sentencing women, especially white women, to corporal punishment would present another barrier. Women's demands for equal rights have sometimes resulted in a backlash in the form of harsher sentences, a phenomenon referred to as "equality with a vengeance." Yet executions of women are more troublesome to many than the execution of men. The Alabama prison commissioner was fired by the governor in 1996 when he suggested women join the predominantly black men on the state's chain gangs. Corporal punishment, like the chain gang, will continue to attract interest because there is something about the notion of "punishment for punishment's sake, that appeals to an electorate scared of crime [and] fed up with what it sees as coddling."[12]

See Also: Corporal Punishment; Cruel and Unusual Punishment; Death Penalty in the United States; Guantanamo Detainees.

Endnotes

1. Edward Said, *Orientalism* (New York: Vintage Books, 1979).
2. Alice Morse Earle, *Curious Punishments of Bygone Days* (Bedford, MA: Applewood Books, 1995; Chicago: H. S. Stone, 1896), 37.
3. William Andrews, *Old Time Punishments* (1890; repr., New York: Dorset Press, 1991), 85, 86.
4. Earle, *Curious Punishments,* 70.
5. Andrews, *Old Time Punishments,* 4.
6. Ibid., 96.
7. Robert Held, *Inquisition: A Bilingual Guide to the Exhibition of Torture Instruments* (Florence, Italy: Qua D'Arno, 1985), 150–51.
8. Graeme Newman, *Just and Painful: A Case for the Corporal Punishment of Criminals,* 2nd ed. (Albany, NY: Harrow and Heston, 1995); the full text of the first edition is available online at http://www.albany.edu/˜grn92/jp00.html.
9. Amnesty International, "Saudi Arabia," *Annual Report 2002* (2002), http://web.amnesty.org/web/ar2002.nsf/mde/saudi+arabia!Open.
10. Newman, *Just and Painful,* 62; emphasis in original.
11. Ibid., 2.
12. Tessa Gorman, "Back on the Chain Gang: Why the Eighth Amendment and the History of Slavery Proscribe the Resurgence of Chain Gangs," in *Criminal Justice Ethics,* ed. Paul Leighton and Jeffrey Reiman (Upper Saddle River, NJ: Prentice Hall, 2001), 405–6.

Further Reading: Andrews, William, *Old Time Punishments* (1890; repr., New York: Dorset Press, 1991); Earle, Alice Morse, *Curious Punishments of Bygone Days* (Bedford, MA: Applewood Books, 1995; Chicago: H. S. Stone, 1896); Farrell, Colin, *World Corporal Punishment Research* (2003), http://www.corpun.com/; Foucault, Michel, *Discipline and Punish* (New York: Vintage, 1979); Held, Robert, *Inquisition: A Bilingual Guide to the Exhibition of Torture Instruments* (Florence, Italy: Qua D'Arno, 1985); Newman, Graeme, *Just and Painful: A Case for the Corporal Punishment of Criminals,* 2nd ed. (Albany, NY: Harrow and Heston, 1995), http://www.albany.edu/˜grn92/jp00.html; Newman, Graeme, *The Punishment Response* (Albany, NY: Harrow and Heston, 1985).

Paul Leighton

CORRECTIONS EDUCATION

INTRODUCTION

Although prison populations have grown at unprecedented levels over the last 30 years, legislation has resulted in significant cuts in correctional education funding. The debate over correctional education often focuses on the fairness of providing benefits for prisoners. On one side, opponents ask, "Why should prisoners get a free education? I have to pay for school and I am a law-abiding citizen." The other side of the debate reminds us, "These people are eventually going to get out. Don't you want them to have skills that can help them stay out of trouble?"

Although evidence supports those who argue for the importance of correctional education, crime-related legislation is often influenced by the get-tough-on-crime mentality. Ironically, this perspective has resulted in the elimination of many programs that were effective in reducing crime. Although much of the debate has focused on funding for college programs, funding cuts have harmed all education efforts. A broader examination of contemporary correctional education illustrates the range of programs offered in correctional institutions. The benefits of these programs extend to prisoners, correctional institutions, and society as a whole.

BACKGROUND

Correctional education focuses on changing the behavior of offenders through planned learning experiences and learning environments. The goal is to develop or enhance knowledge, skills, attitudes, and values of incarcerated youths and adults.[1] In addition to the opportunity for inmates to improve their knowledge and skills, correctional education encourages inmates to make constructive use of their time.

Eighty-four percent of all state and federal adult correctional facilities have some form of educational programming.[2] Correctional educators provide courses in subjects including literacy, special education, English as a second language, and basic education courses leading to a general equivalency diploma (GED). Programs also offer access to college courses, often as part of a degree program. Most programs focus on the development of basic academic skills, typically along with the completion of a high school diploma or equivalent.[3] A 2004 survey indicates that 40 states offer adult basic education and GED instruction. Vocational programs were available in 69 percent of state institutions, with all states reporting some vocational programs. Postsecondary education was available in 60 percent of these institutions.[4]

Correctional education may also focus on improving individual skills needed to productively function within correctional facilities. These courses include literacy, special education, and other learner-specific areas. Courses may also include parenting, empathy skills, communication and dispute processing, cultural awareness, and other life skills necessary in and out of correctional facilities. Educational opportunities that center on the effective functioning of the institution include library science, barbering or hairstyling, auto and

UNESCO'S STUDY ON EDUCATION AND PRISONERS

According to a UNESCO study based on data from more than sixty countries, many of the 10 million prisoners worldwide have dropped out of school.* In developing countries, the large majority have never seen the inside of a classroom. Prisoners' educational level is low throughout the world, in most cases below the national average. According to this study, although most countries claim that education is available to all inmates, the reality is quite different. The reasons are multiple: insufficient funding, lack of teachers, security problems, overpopulation, and inmates' lack of interest. The UNESCO study emphasizes that education for all is a universal right and restriction of one's freedom does not suspend that right. The authors call for more investment by governments, international organizations, and nongovernmental organizations so that prisons become places of continuous and informal learning, rather than schools of crime.

*Marc de Maeyer, "Liberation through Education: Prisoners Are among the Most Excluded from Education, According to a UNESCO Study," *Education Today* no. 14 (2005), 1–2

small-engine repair, cooking, laundry and tailoring, carpentry, building maintenance, and other vocational skills that may lead to employment opportunities upon release.

In addition to advantages associated with the effective functioning of correctional institutions, prison education programs are among the best tools for reducing recidivism. Individuals who have taken courses while in prison improve their chances of attaining and keeping employment after release and are less likely to commit additional crimes. Individuals who completed college courses in prison also found, and kept, better jobs. These factors work together to reduce recidivism; those with more education find stable employment, which makes them less likely to commit crime.[5]

The more education an inmate receives, the lower the rate of recidivism. Inmates who earned college degrees were the least likely to reenter prison. For inmates who had some high school, the rate of recidivism was 54.6 percent. For college graduates, the rate dropped to 5.4 percent.[6] A Texas Department of Criminal Justice study found that although the state's overall rate of recidivism was 60 percent, the rate dropped to 13.7 percent for those with associate's degrees. The recidivism rate for those with bachelor's degrees was 5.6 percent.[7] The *Changing Minds* study[8] found that only 7.7 percent of the inmates who took college courses returned to prison after release, whereas 29.9 percent of those who did not participate in the college program were reincarcerated. Research demonstrates that crime prevention is more cost-effective than building prisons and that of all crime prevention methods, education is the most cost-effective.[9] Those who benefited from correctional education recidivated 29 percent less often than those who did not have educational opportunities while in the correctional institution.[10] Even small reductions in recidivism can save millions of dollars in costs associated with keeping the recidivist in prison. Additional costs are apparent when we consider that the law-abiding individual will be working, paying taxes, and making a positive contribution to the economy. When we add the reduction of costs, both financial and emotional, to victims of crime, the benefits are even greater. Finally, stresses on the justice system are lowered when the crime rate is reduced.

KEY EVENTS

Education has always been a part of the correctional system in the United States. Because education is a key element in the focus on corrections, correctional education has made important contributions to the prison reform movement. Our emphasis is on contemporary correctional education, beginning in 1965, when Congress passed Title IV of the Higher Education Act. This act permitted inmates and other low-income students to apply for federal Pell Grants to be used for college courses. Major themes of contemporary correctional education include an increase in postsecondary programs and the expansion of federal influence.[11] In 1965, only 12 postsecondary correctional education programs were operating in the United States. Based in part on the availability of federal funding, there were 350 programs with approximately 27,000 inmates in 1982. This represented almost 9 percent of the total prison population at the time receiving some form of postsecondary education.[12]

Although the cost was relatively low, the idea of providing federal Pell grants to prisoners was somewhat controversial, and many argued for the elimination of these grants. Politicians suggested that grants to inmates were provided at the expense of law-abiding students. This argument was coupled with a belief that prison life was too soft. In response to this debate, Congress placed significant restrictions on corrections-based college programs with the passage of the Violent Crime Control and Law Enforcement Act of 1994.[13] This act eliminated Pell grants for prisoners—with devastating effects. In 1990, there were 350 higher education programs for inmates.[14] By 1997, only eight programs remained.[15] The get-tough-on-crime mentality had eliminated an effective crime-reduction tool.

In the 1993–94 school year, more than 25,000 students in correctional facilities were recipients of Pell grants. Although Pell grants were not the only source of revenue for these programs, the grants provided a predictable flow of money that was relied upon for the continued functioning of these programs. Because correctional education programs offer courses in a variety of areas, institutions often rely on a range of funding sources. In addition to private and state funding, the federal government provides support to state correctional education through the Adult Education and Family Literacy Act.[16] However, funding has not kept pace with need. With no assurances of replacement funds, most correctional education programs have been forced to abandon efforts to provide college courses in prison.

EDUCATIONAL VERSUS CORRECTIONAL DOLLARS

In the 1990s, we also began to see a dollar-for-dollar trade-off between corrections and education spending. New York, for example, steadily increased its Department of Corrections budget by 76 percent to $761 million. During the same period, the state decreased funding to university systems by 28 percent, to $615 million.* Much of the increase in corrections spending was the result of longer prison terms and the need for increased prison construction. The costs of policies that rely on longer periods of incarceration are placing limits on educational opportunities in correctional institutions as well as educational institutions throughout the nation.

*R. Gangi, V. Schiraldi, and J. Ziedenberg, New York State of Mind: Higher Education vs. Prison Funding in the Empire State, 1988–1998 (Washington, DC: Justice Policy Institute, 1998).

FUTURE PROSPECTS

At least 26 states have mandatory correctional education laws that mandate education for a certain amount of time or until a set level of achievement is reached. Enrollment in correctional education is required in many states if the inmate is under a certain age. These educational efforts are often directed toward the completion of a high school diploma or equivalency, and states typically provide funding based on success as measured by the rate of GED completion. The Federal Bureau of Prisons has also implemented a mandatory education policy that requires inmates who do not have a high school diploma or a GED to participate in literacy programs for a minimum of 240 hours or until they obtain their GED. In spite of controversies regarding funding and policy responses associated with these debates, correction policies continue to define education as a core responsibility.

As the result of the imprisonment binge since the early 1980s, we are beginning to see prison releases at unprecedented levels. Due to strict sentencing guidelines, these prisoners have often served long mandatory terms and are released only when their terms have been completely served. Many are released unconditionally, without parole or other postrelease supervision. Each of these individuals will be expected to begin leading a productive, law-abiding life outside prison walls. Access to a quality education can increase their chance of success. The vast majority of incarcerated individuals will eventually be released. Society has the potential to save billions of dollars annually through the funding of prison academic programs that prepare individuals for a productive return to society. Even if an individual does recidivate, for each year he is not in prison or reincarcerated, taxpayers continue to save money by not housing individuals for that time period.[17]

Correctional educators continue to face scrutiny and pessimism from those who question the value of their work and the merits of providing educational opportunities to those who have committed serious crimes. Due to these controversies, many prisoners do not have the opportunity to participate in prison education programs. Given the unprecedented prison population and the equally unprecedented rate of release, correctional education has the potential to save millions of dollars while improving the lives and opportunities of individuals who have served their time and have successfully paid their debt to society.

See Also: Convict Criminology; Faith-Based Prison Programs; Spiritual Care of Inmates.

Endnotes

1. U.S. Department of Education, Office of Correctional Education, *The Impact of Correctional Education on Recidivism 1988–1994* (Washington, DC: U.S. Department of Education, 1994).
2. D. B. Wilson, C. A. Gallagher, and M. B. Coggeshall, "A Quantitative Review and Description of Correctional-Based Education, Vocation, and Work Programs," *Correctional Management Quarterly* 3, no. 1 pp. 8–18 (1999).
3. R. M. Foley and J. Gao, "Correctional Education: Characteristics of Academic Programs Serving Incarcerated Adults," *Journal of Correctional Education* 55, no. 1 pp. 6–21 (2004).
4. Ibid.
5. M. Batiuk, P. Moke, and P. Rountree, "Crime and Rehabilitation: Correctional Education as an Agent of Change—A Research Note," *Justice Quarterly* 14, no. 1 pp. 167–180 (1997).
6. M. Harer, *Recidivism among Federal Prisoners Released in 1987* (Washington, DC: Federal Bureau of Prisons, 1987).
7. J. Gerber and E. Fritsch, *Prison Education and Offender Behavior: A Review of the Scientific Literature* (Huntsville, TX: Texas Department of Criminal Justice, Institutional Division, 1993).
8. M. Fine et al., *Changing Minds: The Impact of College in a Maximum Security Prison*, The Graduate Center of the City University of New York (2001).
9. P. W. Greenwood, K. E. Model, C. P. Rydell, and J. Chiesa, *Diverting Children from a Life of Crime: Measuring Costs and Benefits* (Santa Monica, CA: Rand, 1996).
10. S. Steurer, L. Smith, and A. Tracy, *Three State Recidivism Study*, prepared for the Office of Correctional Education, U.S. Department of Education (Lanham, MD: Correctional Education Association, 2001).
11. T. Gehring, *The History of Correctional Education*, Correctional Education Association (n.d.), http://www.ceanational.org.
12. B. I. Wolford and J. F. Littlefield, "Correctional Post-Secondary Education: The Expanding Role of Community Colleges," *Community/Junior College Quarterly of Research and Practice* 9, no. 3, pp. 257–272 (1985).
13. Violent Crime Control and Law Enforcement Act of 1994, H.R. 3355 (1994), http://thomas.loc.gov/cgi-bin/query/z?c103:H.R.3355.ENR:.
14. Wolford, op cit.
15. Center on Crime, Communities, and Culture, "Education as Crime Prevention: Providing Education to Prisoners," *Research Brief* no. 2 (New York: Occasional Paper Series, 1997).
16. Workforce Investment Act of 1998, Pub. L. No. 105–220, §231.e. Stat. 1071 (1998), http://www.ed.gov/policy/adulted/leg/legis.html.
17. J. M. Taylor, "Post-Secondary Correctional Education: An Evaluation of Effectiveness and Efficiency," *Journal of Correctional Education* 43, no. 3 pp. 132–141 (1992).

Further Reading: Batiuk, M., P. Moke, and P. Rountree, "Crime and Rehabilitation: Correctional Education as an Agent of Change—A Research Note," *Justice Quarterly* 14, no. 1 pp. 167–180 (1997); Fine, M., et al., *Changing Minds: The Impact of College in a Maximum Security Prison,* Graduate Center of the City University of New York (2001); Gerber, J., and E. Fritsch, *Prison Education and Offender Behavior: A Review of the Scientific Literature* (Huntsville, TX: Texas Department of Criminal Justice, Institutional Division, 1993); Page, J., "Eliminating the Enemy: The Import of Denying Prisoners Access to Higher Education in Clinton's America," *Punishment and Society* 6, no. 4 pp. 357–378 (2004); Steurer, S., L. Smith, and A. Tracy, *Three State Recidivism Study,* prepared for the Office of Correctional Education, U.S. Department of Education (Lanham, MD: Correctional Education Association, 2001); Tewksbury, R., and K. M. Stengel, "Assessing Correctional Education Programs: The Students' Perspective," *Journal of Correctional Education* 57, no. 1 (2006); U.S. Department of Education, Office of Correctional Education, *The Impact of Correctional Education on Recidivism 1988–1994* (Washington, DC: U.S. Department of Education, 1994).

Kenneth Mentor

CRIME AND CULTURE CONSUMPTION

INTRODUCTION

The production and consumption of crime and crime control are ever-shifting and contested terrains. They are inextricably linked to issues of governance, social control, order maintenance, and moral regulation and are played out not only on street corners, boardrooms, and courthouses but also in the media. Under the conditions of late modernity, images of crime and crime control are now as real as crime and criminal justice itself.[1] And the corporately owned mass media's production of crime and crime control is designed both to entertain and sell.

In different words, although crime is real, it does not exist outside of the sociopolitical and cultural contexts in which it is presented and re-presented, over and over through the mass media.. And it is through this hyperreal process of creation, display, carnival, and mediation that behaviors, individuals, and communities come to be exalted, celebrated, castigated, demonized, and controlled by co-optation, stigmatization, or sanction. Proponents of mediated crime and crime control contend that the intensification of the monopolistic control of mass media by owners such as Rupert Murdoch has superimposed itself as a regulator of deviance and social control in society. Opponents of the view that there is a fundamental interplay between crime, crime control, the media, and consumption in late modernity may be divided into two camps: those who argue that these mediated images of crime and crime control represent primarily distortions of reality that are competing with an array of other institutional influences as well and those who argue that in an age of *You Tube,* the blogosphere, and digital communication that messages of mass dissemination are diversifying norms of deviance and crime control.

BACKGROUND

As globalization charges into its second decade of economic, political, and cultural dominance, consumption is increasingly becoming *the* strategy with which to demarcate, compartmentalize, and control the general public in the West. To be certain, consumption is a subtle, routinized, and vital part of our lives. Contemporary consumption involves more than simply exchanging money over a counter and for a product or service, however; it is about the embrace of, and investment in, a value system and the ways in which our ritualized consumer exercises daily reify and reproduce that value system.

A meaningful analysis of consumer culture must include an examination of advertising because contemporary consumerism and its concomitant control functions would simply not exist were it not for advertising in its myriad forms. Although it is certainly true that ads have been around for many years (i.e., a placard with a shoe hanging outside a cobbler's shop in the eighteenth century was an early form of advertising), the fundamental difference between historical and contemporary forms of advertising (such as what we are exposed to through television, films, the Internet, billboards, and pixilated signs) is that the former was direct and purely informational, whereas the latter are symbolic, crammed with images designed to exploit cultural metaphors and metonyms.[2] A second difference, one of much importance, is that early advertisements made no pretense; they were unambiguously designed to sell a particular product or service. In contrast, contemporary ads are so imbued with cultural mythologies that the sales pitch is hidden behind a multilayered veil of artifice, multiple *entendres*, and postmodern lifestyle scripts.

Like many other shifts in forms of cultural production, the transmogrification of the ad from its early, simple, and direct form to its current incarnation was a complex process tied to other, broader structural changes in society, changes that occurred primarily in the twentieth century. In the time between the eighteenth century and the early twentieth century, advertisements, at least in content, changed only modestly. Although they became more elaborate and sophisticated, they still focused almost exclusively on extolling the facts about products. The artist's rendering of a shoe evolved into a photograph with accompanying text that detailed the materials used, the workmanship contributed, the product's cost and availability, but little else. Beginning in the early 1920s, advertisements began to undergo a shift that heralded their current incarnation. This shift was tied to broader economic forces, particularly advances in mass industrialization, that made the production of consumer goods easier and more efficient than at any other time in history. Tied to this was the assembly-line Fordism and growing alienation in the workplace. In short, the expedited production process coincided with, indeed was contingent upon, an increasingly disempowered workforce in factories. Faster production meant more work, greater specialization and compartmentalization, and, not surprisingly, more disenfranchisement and dissent within the workplace. On the one hand, as much as the birth of modern advertising was driven by the necessity to create new markets for products, on the other hand, it was driven by the desire to neutralize the potentially incendiary mix of discontented workers at home and militant labor movements abroad.

IDEOLOGY AND CONSUMERISM

Ads began to promote an ideology of consumerism both as a means to create a market for the products being produced and as a way to control those most closely tied with the production process.[3] Advocating a consumerist lifestyle as the gateway to social integration quelled class conflict by diverting people's attention away from the productive process (which was increasingly monotonous and alienating) and toward one filled with promises of pleasure. Transforming people from producers of wealth into consumers, advertising forged a market in which none existed before while simultaneously ensuring the continued subservience of wage laborers. Widespread consumer practices, particularly those couched in the rubric of leisure and release from drudgery, quickly became a painkiller for working-class folks.[4] Beyond serving as a safe and malleable outlet for class tension, consumerism provided a veneer of coherence in the face of rapidly imploding cultural traditions.

The promised pleasure through consumption, although highly effective and very much in keeping with the aesthetics of fetishized leisure that first rose to prominence in the early part of the twentieth century, could not sustain itself alone. To rehabilitate consumerism in response to waning consumer behavior around World War II, ads became more serpentine and began to play upon fears of personal ineptitude and related social insecurities, primarily, though by no means exclusively, those of women. Women were on one level obvious and vulnerable targets of such strategies because of the highly gendered division of labor and because they were responsible for a good deal of consumption work. Working-class and immigrant women in particular were frequently the targets of ad campaigns designed to undermine their sense of domestic competence by questioning their commitment to a clean home, well-fed children, and a contented husband. Products were presented as not only a time-saving convenience but, in fact, the only means by which to ensure that a given domestic chore was accomplished satisfactorily. Furthermore, ads did not only make the case for the product of a particular manufacturer; embedded within them was the implicit assumption that, irrespective of brand, the product was a necessity.

COMMERCIALS, TELEVISIONS, BLACKBERRIES, AND BEYOND

The general shift in advertising strategy coincided with the emergence of another cultural production: television. The growth of television as a medium during the post–World War II boom provided a new outlet of previously unheralded power for advertisers. This new visual medium was extremely expensive to produce and almost from the outset relied upon outside funding sources to underwrite it. In the early days of television, much of the outside money came in the form of sponsorship. Companies paid to sponsor a program and in exchange had the program named after them (e.g. *Texaco Star Theater* or *General Electric Theater*).

Ads became an ever more vital place of cultural and economic brokerage as the spot commercial became an increasingly normalized and substantial part of TV culture. Lifestyle advertising, specifically the presentation of characters that advertisers thought the audience should aspire to be, quickly became the staple. Television provided advertisers with considerable opportunities to dynamically link the everyday worlds of the audience with consumption practices. Living thirty-second lives, the upper-middle-class characters in commercials are not only acutely other-directed but also lead their gratified existences and resolve their problems (fleeting as they may be, at least until the next commercial break!) through the unreflexive acquisition and use of consumer products.

As marketplace competition increased and the testimonials of hegemony's organizing agents (i.e., actors cast as meddling neighbors, physicians, professional chefs, mechanics, dry cleaners, and other scripted authorities) became increasingly commonplace, advertisers searched for ways to augment their product push. As competition for consumers' dollars continued to intensify and the marketplace became glutted with parity products, advertisers relied ever more on imagery and suggestive symbolism to maximize the audience's emotional investment and solidify product allegiances.

Contemporary advertisers have considerably refined the strategies developed during the mid-twentieth century and expanded their arsenal into the twenty-first century to include infomercials, advertainment, product placement (both traditional, in films or television programs, and real-life), branding, culture spying, cool-hunting, and a variety of Internet and wireless communications techniques ranging from the ubiquitous pop-up ads (to say nothing of the consumption-glutted appearance of Internet service providers' home pages) through data mining, the global positioning satellite–guided instant anonymous commercial messaging of cell phones and personal digital assistants in designated high-end urban shopping areas and corporate-bricoleur *You Tube* postings.

In a world where work is increasingly deskilled and jobs in the bottom-tier service sectors and the criminal justice–industrial complex are among the few available, we are frenetically assailed by consumerist messages endlessly touting vicarious pleasure and symbolic representations of social worth. Under such conditions, it is little wonder that we watch celebrity chefs' how-to programs on the Food Network in record numbers but cook at home less, eat more fast food than ever before, sit in gridlock in overpriced, gas-guzzling sport-utility vehicles rather than use public transport, feel the need to protect ourselves and our possessions from strangers with home alarm systems, and otherwise engage unreflexive hyperconsumerism to the detriment of our health, the environment, and our communities.

CONSUMING CRIME AND CRIME CONTROL

Arguably one of the most significant and illustrative areas of consumer culture and control is the analysis of crime and the media. As residents of a highly technological society undergoing rapid transformations in the conduits for information, we are subject to an increasing array of choices in forming our ideas about crime and criminal justice. Crime is central to the production of not only news but also of entertainment in late modernity, gripping the collective imagination of television viewers, theatergoers, Internet users, and true-crime book readers. Moreover, the boundary between crime information and crime entertainment has been largely blurred in recent years, most notably but by no means exclusively through reality crime shows.[5]

The intersections of legitimate and illicit consumer practices in the twenty-first century interweave along a multiplicity intersecting axis: pain and pleasure, accommodation and resistance, privacy and public display, approved and fugitive meanings, intertextuality and reification. Only by focusing upon image, style, meaning, and representation in the complex interplay of crime and its control can we make sense of these shifting terrains. Specifically, an examination of the stylized frameworks and experiential dynamics of youth tribes; so-called deviant subcultures; the symbolic criminalization of popular cultural artifacts, practices, and actors; and the mediated construction and marketing of crime and crime control issues reveals the class and racial/ethnic underpinnings of crime's mediated reality.

Crime stories about drugs, sex ,and street violence, particularly those involving youths, immigrants, or other socially disenfranchised groups (irrespective of whether the guise is news or entertainment), always make for compelling narratives and hence disproportionately make up the negotiated accomplishment that is the crime product. The discourse, which increasingly mirrors that of the police and other hegemonic agenda setters within the criminal justice system, privileges conventional strictures through the expert analysis of academic authorities and state technobureaucrats. Media coverage of crime is not about the reality of crime; rather, it constitutes crime as a reality through narrative contextualization in keeping with the economic and cultural hegemony of late capitalism.

Such salable crime products are not simply lucrative packages of "what society tells itself about crime" but are a buffer of social reality that omits, suppresses, and homogenizes inequality and human suffering.[6] Under such conditions, crime, like oligopoly capitalism, is dehistoricized, whitewashed, and transmogrified into mass-marketed pleasure.[7]

FUTURE PROSPECTS

The control that is the center of consumerism's edifice is neither unavoidable nor insurmountable. Many of the same implements utilized by the political, cultural, and economic power brokers to ensnare us in the seamless web of visceral pleasure and empty distraction that veil the destructive values of consumer capitalism can be used to circumnavigate the consumer-capitalism-control nexus. Although it is true that the corporate-owned mainstream media undermine the democratic public sphere by disseminating an ideology that, although serving the hegemonic imperatives of consumer capitalism, devalues human dignity, marginalizes difference, and reduces personal worth to commodity fetishism by pedaling unreflexive hyperconsumption and encouraging unquestioning deference

500+ CHANNELS, BUT NOTHING IS ON

The myth of choice is by far one of the most insidious forms of control exercised under twenty-first-century consumer capitalism. As a shrinking number of corporate oligopolies increase their control over the cultural industries, true choice drops precipitously while the illusion of variety grows. Although afflicting all major economic sectors from retail sales through biomedical research and manifesting itself in the banality of Coke-only university campuses through Kafkaesque surrealism of a branded towns like Disney's Celebration, Florida, this process is perhaps most acute in the media industries.

Whereas on the surface it appears as though consumers have more selection (more television channels, newspapers, etc.) than in the recent past, in reality we are faced with fewer real choices and a narrower perspective because of increasingly oligopolistic ownership patterns and the concomitant horizontal and vertical integration across media. As of this writing, eight media conglomerates (Bertelsmann, CBS, Disney, General Electric, News Corporation, Time Warner, Viacom, and Vivendi) together own more than 90 percent of the U.S. domestic market in all major media, including television and radio, newspapers, book and magazine publishing, Internet access, film studios, and music labels, and in 2006 recorded revenues in excess of $320 billion.* The consolidation of ownership in these cultural industries has, as Mark Crispin Miller contends, "shrunk the media cosmos and created a national entertainment state,"** resulting in few noncorporate, nonconsumerist messages. Such continuous and sustained exposure to messages from the corporate-owned mass media exacts a homogenizing effect on the population and not only mystifies and whitewashes consumerism but has as well moved the nation politically and ideologically to the right since the mid-1980s.

---

*See First Amendment Center, "Who Owns the Media," http://www.freepress.net/content/ownership (accessed January 10, 2006).

**Mark Crispin Miller, "Saddam and Osama in the Entertainment State," in *Popping Culture*, 4th ed., ed. Murray Pomerance and John Sakeris (Boston, MA: Pearson Education, 2006), 200.

---

to authority, there are critical spaces for resistance and social justice that should be observed and explored.

For example, nuanced films and novels such as *Fight Club* and *The Store* offer complex yet highly engaging and accessible narratives documenting the interplay between cultural innovation and institutional intolerance and case studies in fugitive art, recreation, resistance, marginality, and the politics of consumption and control framed by anarchist sensibilities. So, too, a host of recent documentary films such as *The Merchants of Cool*, *The Corporation*, *The Persuaders*, and *Class Dismissed* offers us a toolbox with which to deconstruct and demystify consumerism and social control but and the acumen to promulgate alternative, more social justice–oriented readings of life under late modernity. Finally, there are a plethora of Web sites (some operated by individuals, others parts of grassroots organizations) devoted to fighting for fundamental human and labor rights and environmental justice, such as CorpWatch (http://www.corpwatch.org), behindthelabel.org (http://www.behindthelabel.org), and Fairtrade (http://

www.fairtrade.net), and offering inspiring and entertaining examples of resistance to giant corporations, like Adbusters (http://www.adbusters.org).

Still others focus more explicitly on challenging the interrelated moral entrepreneurship of interest groups, politicians, criminal justice agencies, and the media in the creation and dissemination of the crime product and drawing visitors' attention to the much-neglected areas of state crime and crimes of globalization such as critcrim.org (http://www.critcrim.org), Gregg Barak's Home Page (http://www.greggbarak.com), and Paul's Justice Page (http://www.paulsjusticepage.com).

See Also: Cameras in the Courtroom; Defining Criminal Violence; Executions—Televised; Prison Privatization; Prisoner Experimentation; Provoking Assaults and High-Profile Crimes.

Endnotes

1. Jeff Ferrell, Keith Hayward, Wayne Morrison, and Mike Presdee, eds., *Cultural Criminology Unleashed* (London: GlassHouse Press, 2004).
2. John Fiske and John Hartley, *Reading Television* (London: Routledge, 1989).
3. Stuart Ewen, *Captains of Consciousness: Advertising and the Social Roots of Consumer Culture* (Toronto: McGraw-Hill, 1977).
4. Ibid.
5. Ken Dowler, Thomas Fleming, and Stephen L. Muzzatti, "Constructing Crime: Media, Crime and Popular Culture," *Canadian Journal of Criminology and Criminal Justice* 48, no. 6 (2006): 837–50.
6. Gregg Barak, ed., *Media, Process, and the Social Construction of Crime* (New York: Garland, 1994).
7. Mike Presdee, *Cultural Criminology and the Carnival of Crime* (London: Routledge, 2000).

Further Reading: Barak, G., ed., *Media, Process, and the Social Construction of Crime* (New York: Garland, 1994); Ewen, S., *Captains of Consciousness: Advertising and the Social Roots of Consumer Culture* (Toronto, ON: McGraw-Hill, 1977); Ferrell, Jeff, Keith Hayward, Wayne Morrison, and Mike Presdee, eds., *Cultural Criminology Unleashed* (London: GlassHouse Press, 2004); Hayward, K. J., *City Limits: Crime, Consumer Culture and the Urban Experience* (London: GlassHouse Press, 2004); Marx, K., *Capital: A Critical Analysis of Capitalist Production*, vol. 1 (Moscow: Progress, 1965; originally published 1867); Presdee, Mike, *Cultural Criminology and the Carnival of Crime* (London: Routledge, 2000); Surette, R., *Media, Crime and Criminal Justice: Images and Realities,* 3rd ed. (Belmont, CA: Thomson-Wadsworth, 2007).

Stephen L. Muzzatti

CRIME-CONTROL INDUSTRY

INTRODUCTION

Like the privatization of the administration of criminal justice in general or the contracting out of, for example, health care services in prison specifically, the crime-control industry (CCI) in the United States and the associated criminal justice–industrial complex are highly contested issues. Advocates or proponents, usually consisting of representatives of private enterprise, business lobbyists, and various political-economic interests, argue that the CCI makes the criminal justice system more efficient and saves the taxpayer from spending more money on crime control. Opponents of CCI or the commodification of crime control, mostly academics, policy wonks, and not-for-profit groups, argue that the CCI has not resulted in a reduction in the overall rate of crime. Recent reductions in crime generally, from 1991 to 2006, have had more to do with the economy and the Gulf wars than with the marketization of crime control, these opponents claim. Finally, those who resist the power and influence of the crime-control industry argue that such interests as making money off of crime not only undermine the desire to reduce crime but also undercut the quality of justice and equal protection for all.

For example, a writer of an article appearing in the *Washington Post* observed, "If crime doesn't pay, punishment certainly does."[1] The town supervisor of Chesterfield, New York (too small to be located on the *Rand McNally Road Atlas*), noted one reason for his support of a new prison in his rural community, stating, "A business comes in and a year or two it can't support itself. . . . [A prison] is something you know is going to be there for a long time."[2] Similarly, the city manager in Sayre, Oklahoma (population 4,220), which had just opened a prized new maximum-security prison, stated, "In my mind there's no more recession-proof form of economic development. Nothing's going to stop crime."[3]

The CCI consists of more than the three components of the criminal justice system. In other words, besides the more than 50,000 different governmental agencies employing more than 2.3 million people in this system that share more than a $5 billion per month payroll,[4] the CCI includes the businesses that profit from the existence of crime and/or attempts to control crime. The so-called war on crime (and the War on Drugs) has become a booming business, with literally thousands of companies, ranging from small businesses to Fortune 500 corporations, profiting in some way. Examples include private security firms, companies providing security devices, architectural firms that help design prisons, drug testing firms, gun manufacturers, and media outlets that depend on stories about crime and criminals. Think of it this way: When differentiating between the multitude of occupations in the United States, the Department of Labor often places each of them into several different industries, such as manufacturing, mining, service, retail trade, and so forth. To this list we might legitimately add the crime-control industry.[5] Even higher education profits from crime, as there are more than 3,000 colleges and universities offering degrees in criminal justice.

BACKGROUND

Richard Quinney was among the first to describe this concept of a crime-control industry. In his book *Class, State and Crime,* he wrote that the criminal justice–industrial complex is a part of the social-industrial complex. He described this larger complex as "an involvement of industry in the planning, production,

THE COMMODIFICATION OF CRIMINAL JUSTICE EDUCATION

An advertising brochure for the University of Phoenix concerning a degree in criminal justice states, "The opportunities and options in the field are endless." It also claims that you can "earn your degree in 2 to 3 years, in most cases." It offers courses in many different locations, with classes starting almost every month. On the brochure it is noted, "According to the Bureau of Labor Statistics, the field of criminal justice will expand faster than most other occupations through 2008." Courses are taught by "experienced lieutenants, police chiefs, and captains" and cover "the latest theories, techniques, and technologies being used in criminal justice today." A business reply card is included in this brochure. One can earn a degree by attending part-time through the University of Phoenix (with campuses throughout the western United States) or through distance-learning companies. A company called Distance Learning Systems represents an example of the latter in an ad in the July 2005 issue of *Corrections Today*. Their ad reads as follows: "Crime doesn't pay, but a degree in Criminal Justice does!" Through this program, the ad continues, you can "Combine home study, credit by examination and upper level online course work to earn YOUR bachelor's Degree in Criminal Justice!" This issue also contains ads for Excelsior College, Bellevue University, California University of Pennsylvania, and Mountain Empire Community College, all of which offer degrees, certificates, workshops, and other assorted programs.*

---

*These ads are found on pp. 27, 90, and 100. This issue of *Corrections Today* includes the annual "Buyers Guide," containing about 100 pages of ads for abut 150 different companies.

---

and operation of state programs. These state-financed programs like education, welfare, and criminal justice are social expenses necessary for maintaining social order and are furnished by monopolistic industries." Large corporations, Quinney suggested, have found a new source of profits in this industry, with the criminal justice industry leading the way. Private industry, in short, has found that there is much profit to be made as a result of the existence of crime.[6]

Part of the reason for the growth of the crime-control industry is that policy makers decided that a technocratic approach to the crime problem is the best course to take. This perspective suggests that the solution to crime requires a combination of science and technology. Such a position was stated well by the President's Crime Commission in 1967. The commission wrote:

> More than 200,000 scientists and engineers have applied themselves to solving military problems and hundreds of thousands more to innovation in other areas of modern life, but only a handful are working to control the crimes that injure or frighten millions of Americans each year. Yet the two communities have much to offer each other: Science and technology is a valuable source of knowledge and techniques for combating crime; the criminal justice system represents a vast area of challenging problems.[7]

It is obvious that the government took up the challenge, for since this time the crime-control industry has become enormous. It is so huge that it is almost impossible to estimate the amount of money spent and the profits made. If we include just the annual expenditures of the three main components of the formal criminal justice system, however, we can begin to understand how huge this industry is. Table C.1 shows these expenditures covering the years 1982 and 2004 (the latest figures available from the Department of Justice). As shown here, in 2004 total expenditures increased 430 percent since 1982. The largest increase went toward the correctional system, going up a whopping 589 percent.

CORPORATE INTERESTS, THE PRISON-INDUSTRIAL COMPLEX, AND THE ROLE OF THE AMERICAN LEGISLATIVE EXCHANGE COUNCIL

A little-known fact about the prison-industrial complex is an organization known as the American Legislative Exchange Council (ALEC). The mere existence of this organization demonstrates the classic connections between politics, economics, and the criminal justice system. The membership consists of state legislators, private corporation executives, and criminal justice officials. More than one-third of state lawmakers in the country (2,400) belong, and they are, not surprisingly, mostly Republicans and conservative Democrats. In 1973, Paul Weyrich formed ALEC (who also cofounded the Heritage Foundation and now is the head of a group called the Free Congress Foundation, a far-right conservative group). Their mission is to promote free markets, small governments, states' rights, and, of course, privatization. Corporate membership dues range from $5,000 to $50,000 annually. Corrections Corporation of America is a member of this group, which is not surprising. Other members include a veritable who's who of the Fortune 500, such as Ameritech, AT&T, Bayer, Bell Atlantic, Bell South, DuPont, GlaxcoSmithKline, Merck & Co., Sprint, and Pfizer, to name just a few. Among the companies that have supported ALEC through various grants include Ameritech, Exxon Mobil, Chevron, and several corporate foundations, including the Proctor and Gamble Fund, Exxon Educational Foundation, Bell Atlantic Foundation, Ford Motor Company Fund, among many others.[8]

Table C.1 Criminal Justice Expenditures, Fiscal Years 1982 and 2004 (in billions)

	1982	**1996**	**2004**	**% Increase**
Total	$36	$120	$194	430
Police	$19	$53	$89	368
Judicial	$8	$26	$43	438
Corrections	$9	$41	$62	589

Sources: E. F. McGarrell and T. J. Flanagan, eds., *Sourcebook of Criminal Justice Statistics—1985* (Washington, DC: U.S. Department of Justice, 1986), 2; K. Maguire and A. L. Pastore, eds., *Sourcebook of Criminal Justice Statistics—1998* (Washington, DC: U.S. Department of Justice, 1999), table 1.2; U.S. Bureau of the Census, Criminal Justice Expenditure and Employment Extracts Program (CJEE), "Justice Expenditure and Employment Extracts 2004," NCJ 215648, November 15, 2006.

ALEC's Web site is an educational experience in itself. It proudly lists some of the bills it has been involved in getting passed and indicates some very important keynote speakers at the past three annual meetings. Among the notables giving speeches include Attorney General John Ashcroft, Secretary of Health and Human Services Tommy Thompson, Secretary of Housing and Urban Development Mel Martinez, President and CEO of American Home Products Robert Essner, Chairman and CEO of Pfizer Hank McKinnell, Florida Governor Jeb Bush, Secretary of Labor Elane Chao, and ultraconservative syndicated columnist Cal Thomas.[9]

This organization also puts together papers and policy statements on a wide variety of issues reflecting conservative ideas, including one about the so-called myth of global warming. Bill Berkowitz, who carefully follows conservative trends, has noted that ALEC sponsored more than 3,100 pieces of legislation between 1999 and 2000, with more than 400 of these bills passing.[10] Within ALEC there is a Criminal Justice Task Force. Among the duties of this group is to write model bills on crime and punishment. Among such model bills they helped draft include mandatory minimum sentences, three-strikes laws, truth in sentencing, and the like. One member boasted that in 1995 alone they introduced 199 bills, including truth-in-sentencing bills, which passed in 25 states.

Tommy Thompson, former Wisconsin governor and former head of Health and Human Services in the George W. Bush administration, was once a member of ALEC. He was recently quoted as saying, "I always loved going to these meetings because I always found new ideas. Then I'd take them back to Wisconsin, disguise them a little bit, and declare that 'It's mine.'" Edwin Bender of the National Institute on Money in State Politics says, "Bayer Corporation or Bell South or GTE or Merck pharmaceutical company sitting at a table with elected representatives, actually hammering out a piece of legislation—behind closed doors, I mean, this isn't open to the public. And that then becomes the basis on which representatives are going to their state legislatures and debating issues."[11] As everyone knows by now, these kinds of laws were a big reason for the swelling of the prison population, which in turn added new markets for capitalist profits.

PRISONS AS A MARKET FOR CAPITALISM

Within a capitalist society, there tends to be an insatiable desire to continue "converting money into commodities and commodities into money." Everything, it seems, is turned into a commodity—from the simplest products (e.g., paper and pencils) to human beings (e.g., women's bodies, slaves). Indeed, within a capitalist society, "daily life is scanned for possibilities that can be brought within the circuit of accumulation," because any aspect of society that can produce a profit will be exploited. Life itself has been commodified.[12]

Part of this drive for profits stems from the ideology of the free market, a system of beliefs that undergirds the entire capitalist economic system. According to this ideology, every individual pursues his or her own personal interests, and the result is a collective good for the entire society. It is Adam Smith's "invisible hand" at work. Corporations are free to do whatever they want.

This free market includes the prison system. The amount of money that flows into the coffers of the prison-industrial complex from tax dollars alone is quite substantial. The budget for both state and federal correctional institutions came to $62 billion in fiscal year 2004. The budgets for probation and parole have also been increasing. In fiscal year 1992, the average budgets for both systems came to $23 million; in 2000 (the latest year available as of this writing), the average was $71 million, an increase of 209 percent. What is most interesting about the budgets for probation and parole is that the largest increases went to the parole system, with their average budgets increasing from $25.5 million in 1992 to $43.1 million in 2000, compared to a very modest increase for probation budgets from $55.7 million to $56.3 million. The total budgets for both probation and parole came to just more than $1.7 billion in fiscal year 2000. The costs per prisoner per day steadily increased during the 1990s, going from about $49 in 1991 to about $58 in 1999, which amounts to about $21,170 per prisoner per year.[13] The most recent figures for the Federal Bureau of Prisons reveal that the budget in fiscal 2002 was $4.6 billion, up from $330 million in 1980. In 1980, there were only 44 prisons; in 2002 there were 102, with 11 more under construction.[14]

A good illustration of how companies are cashing in on the boom in corrections is found in the amount of advertising done in journals related to this industry. One example comes from two major journals serving the prison-industrial complex, *Corrections Today* and *The American Jail,* plus the American Correctional Association's (ACS's) annual *Directory.* (*Corrections Today* is the leading prison trade magazine, and the amount of advertising in this magazine tripled in the 1980s.) I have sampled a few issues of these journals and the ACS *Directory* and found advertisements everywhere. In one issue of *Corrections Today,* advertisers at the annual meeting of the American Jail Association used lines such as "Tap into the Sixty-Five Billion Local Jails Market" and "Jails are BIG BUSINESS" to attract customers.[15] Additionally, trade journals that serve the correction industry have seen their advertisements triple since the 1980s. See the sidebar for more examples of advertisements.

ADVERTISEMENTS DIRECTED AT THE CORRECTIONAL INDUSTRY

- Prison Health Services, Inc., a company that has since 1978 "delivered complete, customized healthcare programs to correctional facilities only. The first company in the United States to specialize in this area, we can deliver your program the fastest, and back it up with services that are simply the best."
- Southwest Microwave, Inc., manufactures fence security, with their latest invention known as Micronet 750, which is "more than a sensor improvement"; it is "a whole new paradigm in fence detection technology."
- Rotondo Precast, Inc. boasts "over 21,000 cells . . . and growing."
- Nicholson's BesTea, with "tea for two or . . . two thousand. . . . Now mass-feeding takes a giant stride forward."

- Northwest Woolen Mills, manufactures blankets with the slogan "We've got you covered."
- Motor Coach Industries produces a "Prison on Wheels" with their "Inmate Security Transportation Vehicle."
- A company called Control Screening advertises its special Model 6040-M security parcel X-ray scanner with an ad that reads, "Don't allow suspicious packages into your facility."
- An example of a popular company that has entered the prison market is Western Union, which offers "an automated solution" for all sorts of payments, from court-ordered payments to commissary needs.
- One of the largest food-service companies is Aramark, which says it will "trim the fat from your food service." While "your correctional officers are watching the food line, Aramark will be watching your budget."
- Then there is General Marine Leasing, a company that builds "portable, temporary and modular facilities." Their ad reads, "Overcrowded? Don't let overflow put them back on the street."[16]

A recent story on CNN noted that the increase in prison populations has been "good for business," according to Martha Roenigk, CEO of CompuDyne, a security software and hardware provider to the corrections and homeland security markets. State prison systems spend more than $30 billion annually, and the Bureau of Prisons budgeted $5 billion for just 182,000 federal inmates this year. That translates into plenty of work for companies looking to crack the prison market. According to Irving Lingo, the CEO of Corrections Corporation of America: "Our core business touches so many things—security, medicine, education, food service, maintenance, technology—that it presents a unique opportunity for any number of vendors to do business with us."[17]

The American Correctional Association (ACA) is one of the largest national organizations in the country. Their annual meetings draw hundreds of vendors, usually taking up an entire floor of a hotel or convention center. On the ACA Web site, it mentions the $50 billion or so spent each year on prisons and jails and says to companies, "Don't miss out on this prime revenue-generating opportunity."

The trade journal of the ACA, *Corrections Today,* has a special issue every July in anticipation of the upcoming annual conference in August. There are more than two hundred pages in this special issue. I have a copy of the July 1999 issue, which includes descriptions from more than two hundred different companies that sell everything imaginable. The list includes locks and other security devices, food service, hygiene kits, bedding, blankets, ceiling systems, communications equipment, clothing, weapons, and a wide assortment of architects, engineers, and consultants to build and maintain prisons and jails.

Not surprisingly, prison construction itself has become a booming business. During the 1990s, a total of 371 new prisons opened. (About 92,000 new beds were added each year.) In 1999 alone, 24 new prisons were opened, at a total cost of just over $1 billion. The average cost of building a new prison came to $105 million (about $57,000 per bed; more than the starting salary of public school teachers and newly hired assistant professors and even some full professors). Also in 1999, a total of 146 prisons were adding or renovating beds at a cost of $470 million (about $30,000 per bed). As of January 2000, a total of 29 new institutions were under construction and another 137 institutions were being renovated or adding new beds. Most of the new beds were in either maximum- or medium-security institutions, where the costs are the highest. The total estimated costs of these new building projects came to more than $2.2 billion.[18]

The construction of new prisons has become such a big business that there is a special newsletter called *Construction Report* just to keep vendors up to date on new prison projects.[19] A Google search on the Internet turns up dozens of companies advertising prison construction. One example, among many, is Kitchell (http://www.kitchell.com/criminal.shtml), which, according to their Web site, "has successfully delivered over 110,000 correctional beds, including over 130 criminal justice projects in 17 states." These projects include 42 state prisons, 29 adult jails, and 30 juvenile facilities. They also build police stations, courts facilities, and camps.

Also found on this search was the web site for the North Carolina Department of Corrections (http://www.doc.state.nc.us/) and here I found a chart showing the prisons recently opened or about to open in that state. Between 1989 and May 2006, a total of 25 correctional facilities (including a youth center and two work farms) were opened. Currently there is one under construction, housing potentially 1,500 prisoners, due to be completed in May, 2008. As of July 14, 2007 North Carolina had 38,536 prisoners. Ad of June, 2006 they had an incarceration rate of 362, a rate considerably below the national average of 497.[20] It appears as if this state is hoping to catch up with the rest of the country.

THE PRIVATE SECURITY INDUSTRY

The private security industry is another major component of the crime-control industry. It includes private security police, gated communities, and security devices such as locks, burglar alarms, auto alarms, and electrified fences.[21] Other components of the industry include:

1. The profits made by hospitals and insurance companies from hospital emergency room visits, doctor's fees, insurance premiums on autos, and other insurance covering crime and the salaries of those who deal with victims, such as doctors, nurses, paramedics, and insurance adjusters.
2. The profits from the sale of books, such as college textbooks, trade books, magazine and journal articles, newspapers, the advertisers who profit from

crime stories, television crime shows and their advertisers, and movies about crime, with the enormous salaries paid to actors and actresses who star in them.

3. The money collected by courts through various fines and special courses defendants can enroll in as a condition of or in lieu of their sentence.
4. The money collected by bail bondsmen.
5. The money to be made in urine testing.
6. The gun industry.

PEEING FOR PROFIT: THE CASE OF
THE DRUG TESTING INDUSTRY

Consistent with what seems to be a national obsession over drugs, a report called "Drug Monitoring and Abuse Testing Business," released in January 1997 (produced by Business Communications Company, Norwalk, Connecticut), noted that revenues for drug testing businesses grew as much as 15 percent annually during the first half of the 1990s. In 1996, the drug testing market took in around $628 million in revenues, increasing to about $737 million in 2001.[22]

It has been estimated that about 61 percent of all major businesses test their employees, and more than five hundred school districts test their students. An estimated 20 million to 25 million Americans are tested for drugs each year, compared to around 7 million in 1996.[23] One method of drug testing is the Drug Alert tester, by SherTest Corporation, which targets family members. This device, the company claims, can be used to increase love and care between parents and children by "breaking down the barriers of denial between parent and child." Another company, Barringer Technologies, Inc., makes "particle detection devices" for the police, claiming it has sold "thousands" of $35 testing kits. Psychometrics Corporation introduced a new kit, selling for $75, and the day after it hit the market, the value of the company's stock tripled.[24]

A cursory examination through the Internet of various companies in the drug testing business is quite revealing. To begin with, drug testing is part of a much larger market. A company that does market research, Market Research.com (http://www.marketresearch.com), reports that there is a "point-of-care (POC) diagnostic test market" that is "expected to reach revenues over $900 million in 2008." A fact sheet from a company called Beckman Coulter says that there is a $35 billion marked in biomedical testing alone. This market includes research and development, clinical research testing, and patient care testing. Presumably, testing for illegal drugs falls within the latter category (patient care testing), which totals around $21 billion. According to the publication *Cannabis News* (http://www.cannabisnews.com), home drug testing has become a cottage industry with ads all over the Internet that meet the needs of parents who fear that their teens are using drugs—and also of teens that are afraid of getting caught. Home drug test kits, along with sometimes wacky methods of circumventing them, are available online, and many sites sell both. Searching the Internet myself, I found some interesting examples:

- Mrs. Test (http://www.mrstest.com) features home drug testing kits (e.g., 10 Panel Multi Drug Urine Test Kit, 1 Step THC Marijuana Urine Drug Test Cassette, Cocaine Cassette Drug Urine Test, plus about thirty more similar kits).
- Drug Test Systems (http://www.drugtestsystems.com) is "The Professional Choice for affordable drug and alcohol testing supplies," which includes the DrugCheck Test Cups.
- Test Country (http://www.testcountry.com) is the "Home Test Kit Super-store" and offers such products as the PDT-90 Confidential Hair Testing Kit.
- Meth Test Source (http://www.lowvoltsource.com/drugtest/meth) asks, "Are you an employer who needs to conduct random or comprehensive drug testing on a regular basis? Checkout our 10-packs for great value on quantity purchases."

Thousands of parolees, most of whom have trouble kicking their drug habit (due in large part to the dearth of treatment available, both inside and outside of prison), fail their drug test (a test that has become an important part of the parole and probation system and an important method of controlling them. Those on parole are constantly being tested, so naturally some companies have sough this unique market in order to make a buck. One recently noted that "Beating a drug test has become a major industry," The report further notes that "the prevalence of screening and the reach of the Internet has fostered a thriving cottage industry of entrepreneurs who promise to help workers beat the tests."[25] Many have found a way to use "fake penises and laboratory-cleansed urine" in order to cheat on their urine tests. There are kits people can purchase that often include a "prosthetic penis" connected to a "pouch of battery-warmed reconstituted urine concentrate." One of the most popular kits is called the "Whizzinator" and is made by a company called Puck Technologies of Signal Hill, California (near Long Beach). It sells for $150. A testimonial on their web site boasted that a man passed the tests "over 100 times" (www.thewhizzinator.com). A Canadian company called Clear Test distributes a product called "The Urinator." Their web site claims that the product can be used "hundreds of times" and that clients even "rent it out to their friends."

Another company, known as Clear Choice of New York (http://www.clearchoiceofny.com) claims, "We are positive you will test negative." (This is another example of the beauty of capitalism: If there is a demand for a product, someone willing to take the risks—including aiding in some illegal activity—will provide it.)

FUTURE PROSPECTS

At this juncture in our history, there does not seem to be an end to the continuous buildup of the crime-control industry. If there is one positive in a bleak future, it is that more and more people are becoming aware of the failure of our repressive policies. A cursory look at the Internet finds literally hundreds of Web sites challenging the status quo in a number of areas, including crime.

Some of the general public disenchantment stems no doubt from the war in Iraq and the reports of corporate greed in the rebuilding efforts. Many people have extended the critique of this greed to a more general critique of corporate capitalism in general. The growth of the crime-control industry has corresponded with huge cuts for social programs, which are being felt throughout society. Growing numbers of citizens have felt the effects and seen their tax dollars funneled into corporate coffers and the criminal justice system.

See Also: Class Justice; Prison Construction; Prison Privatization.

Endnotes

1. L. Duke, "Prison Construction Boom Transforms Small Towns," *Washington Post,* September 8, 2000, p. A1.
2. Town supervisor of Chesterfield, New York, quoted in M. Welch, *Punishment in America: Social Control and the Ironies of Imprisonment* (Thousand Oaks, CA: Sage, 1999), 24.
3. P. T. Kilborn, "Rural Towns Turn to Prisons to Reignite Their Economies," *The New York Times,* August 1, 2001, p. A1–2; P. Street, "Race, Place, and the Perils of Prisonomics," *Z Magazine,* July/August 2005, http://zmagsite.zmag.org/JulAug2005/street0705.html.
4. The latest figures can be found in *Sourcebook on Criminal Justice Statistics Online,* http://www.albany.edu/sourcebook/toc_1.html.
5. "The Crime Control Industry and the Management of the Surplus Population," *Critical Criminology* 8 (Autumn, 2000); C. Parenti, *Lockdown America: Police and Prisons in the Age of Crisis* (New York: Verso, 1999), pp. 39–62.
6. R. Quinney, *Class, State and Crime,* 2nd ed. (New York: Longman, 1980), 133.
7. President's Commission on Law Enforcement and Administration of Justice, *The Challenge of Crime in a Free Society* (Washington, DC: U.S. Government Printing Office, 1967), 1.
8. Capital Research Center, http://www.capitalresearch.org.
9. American Legislative Exchange Council, http://www.alec.org.
10. B. Berkowitz, "Smart ALEC's," *Working for Change* (2002), http://www.google.com/search?q=Berkowitz+Smart+ALEC's&sourceid=navclient-ff6ie=UTF-86rlz=1B2RNFA_en__US207.
11. American RadioWorks, http://americanradioworks/publicradio.org/features/corrections/full.html, accessed April, 2002.
12. R. L. Heilbroner, *The Nature and Logical of Capitalism* (New York: W. W. Norton, 1985), 60.
13. C. G. Camp and G. M. Camp, *The Corrections Yearbook 2000: Adult Corrections* (Middletown, CT: Criminal Justice Institute, 2000), 84, 88, 186.
14. K. Johnson, "Federal Prisons Packed with Almost 165,000," *USA Today,* January 22, 2003.
15. S. Donziger, *The Real War on Crime* (New York: Harper/Collins, 1996), 93.
16. These ads were selected from several issues of *Corrections Today,* spanning the past 10 years (1995–2005).

17. Myser, M. "The Hard Sell." CNNMoney.com March 15, 2007. http://money.cnn.com/magazines/business2/business2_archive/2006/12/01/8394995/index.htm.

18. Camp and Camp, *The Corrections Yearbook 2000*, 76.

19. J. Dyer, *The Perpetual Prisoner Machine: How America Profits from Crime* (Boulder, CO: Westview Press, 2000), 13.

20. Sabol, W. J., T. D. Minton and P. M. Harrison. "Prison and Jail Inmates at Mid Year 2006." U.S. Department of Justice, Bureau of Justice Statistics. http://www.ojp.usdoj.gov/bjs/pub/pdf/pjim06.pdf.

21. P. M. Harrison and A. Beck, "Prisoners in 2002" (Washington, DC: Bureau of Justice Statistics, July 2003).

22. For a more complete listing, see Shelden and Brown, "The Crime Control Industry. and the Management of the Surplus Population" *Critical Criminology* 8 (Autumn, 2000): 39–62.

23. D. Hawkins, "Tests on Trial" (2002), *US News and World Report*, http://highbeam.com/doc/1G1-90156934.html.

24. W. G. Staples, *The Culture of Surveillance: Discipline and Social Control in the United States* (New York: St. Martin's Press, 1997), 97.

25. Geller, A. (2004). "Cheating on drug tests fast becoming a growth industry." *USA Today* April 4, http://www.usatoday.com/tech/news/2004-03-29-drug-testing_x.htm. This is one of hundreds of entries on the subject of cheating on drug tests found on the Internet.

Further Reading: Christie, N., *Crime Control as Industry: Towards Gulags, Western Style?* 3rd ed. (London: Routledge, 2000); Donziger, S., *The Real War on Crime* (New York: Harper/Collins, 1996); Dyer, J., *The Perpetual Prisoner Machine: How America Profits from Crime* (Boulder, CO: Westview Press, 2000); Mauer, M., and M. Chesney-Lind, eds., *Invisible Punishment: The Collateral Consequences of Mass Imprisonment* (New York: New Press, 2002); Parenti, C., *Lockdown America: Police and Prisons in the Age of Crisis* (New York: Verso, 1999); Quinney, R., *Class, State and Crime,* 2nd ed. (New York: Longman, 1980); Shelden, R., *Controlling the Dangerous Classes: A Critical Introduction to the History of Criminal Justice* (Boston: Allyn and Bacon, 2001).

Randall G. Shelden

CRUEL AND UNUSUAL PUNISHMENT

INTRODUCTION

The Eighth Amendment to the U.S. Constitution, in one of its major pronouncements, prohibits the imposition of cruel and unusual punishments. Although most of the issues addressed by the U.S. Supreme Court regarding the interpretation of this clause center on applications of capital punishment, the true battleground has concerned something different. The question as to whether the Eighth Amendment requires the Court to strike down sentences of any type as being "disproportionate"—that is, sentences that seem to be greater than the crime warrants—has been a contentious and confusing one in which the Court has struggled to define its role generally and to articulate a test or standard when it has chosen to rule on the proportionality of sentences.

BACKGROUND

In the Court's own words, what law it has established in the proportionality area is a "thicket of Eighth Amendment jurisprudence" and has not been "a model of clarity."[1] Although the Court has found death sentences to be disproportionate in crimes other than murder[2] and disproportionate where the defendant is either mentally retarded[3] or a juvenile,[4] it has struggled to define its involvement in noncapital sentences.

For a long period extending through the twentieth century, it appeared that the Court was prepared to intervene only in a non-death sentence if that sentence involved something harsh and unusual in addition to incarceration. In *Weems v. U.S.*[5] for example, the defendant received a 12-year sentence to be served in hard and painful labor with the defendant chained at the wrists and ankles for the crime of falsifying a public document. In addition, the punishment included the loss of civil rights such as parental authority and permanent surveillance by the government. The Court in striking down the sentence as a violation of the Eighth Amendment noted that other more serious crimes in the jurisdiction were punished less severely and suggested that the punishment was not just but was of "tormenting" severity.[6]

Weems notwithstanding, the cases of *Rummel v. Estelle*[7] and *Hutto v. Davis*[8] appeared to represent the norm of the Court's approach to this issue. William James Rummel was charged under Texas law with obtaining $125 under false pretenses, a felony in Texas. Moreover, because Rummel had previously been convicted of fraudulent use of a credit card to obtain $80 worth of goods and with passing a forged check in the amount of $28.36, he qualified under Texas law as being a habitual criminal. Rummel was prosecuted and convicted under that recidivist statute and given the mandatory life sentence the statute provided. The life sentence under Texas law involved the possibility that the defendant could be paroled in as early as 12 years, a factor the Court thought important in assessing the true nature of the punishment.

The Court, in reviewing and denying Rummel's Eighth Amendment challenge, stated that to the extent proportionality claims had been successful, they had been raised in the context of capital cases and had been a function of the Court's long-standing view of the unique nature of death as a punishment. The Court further stated that non-death sentence challenges had been successful only exceedingly rarely and involved an unusual corporal type of punishment like that found in *Weems*. The *Rummel* Court could not have been clearer when it stated, "Given the unique nature of the punishments considered in *Weems* and in the death penalty cases, one could argue without fear of contradiction by any decision of this Court that for crimes concededly classified and classifiable as felonies, that is, as punishable by significant terms of imprisonment in a state penitentiary, the length of the sentence actually imposed is purely a matter of legislative prerogative."[9]

Two years after *Rummel,* the Court decided in *Hutto* that a prison term of 40 years and a fine of $20,000 for possession and distribution of approximately nine ounces of marijuana was not disproportionately in violation of the Eighth Amendment and was a matter of legislative prerogative. The fact that the opinion was per curiam (signed by the Court as a whole and not authored by any one justice) seemed to underscore the strength of the Court's hands-off approach.

KEY EVENTS

The key event occurring just a year after *Hutto* was the Supreme Court case *Solem v. Helm,*[10] a 1983 case in which the Court seemingly broke with, if not clear precedent, then at least with the strong tenor of its prior proportionality cases. *Solem,* which dealt with a similar situation to *Rummel,* announced what is clearly a proportionality test to assess the constitutionality of noncapital sentences under the Eighth Amendment.

The *Solem* test contained three objective factors a court should consider in determining if the sentence imposed is consistent with the Eighth Amendment. First, a court should look to the gravity of the offense and the harshness of the penalty. Second, a court should compare the sentences imposed on other criminals in the same jurisdiction. Finally, courts should compare the sentences imposed for commission of the same crime in other jurisdictions.

When the Court applied this three-pronged test to the facts of *Solem,* it held the sentence of life without parole to be disproportionate to the crime involved and cruel and unusual in violation of the Eighth Amendment. First, the defendant, Helm, was convicted of the offense of uttering a "no account" check for $100. This, in turn, triggered the application of South Dakota's recidivist statute due to his prior record of six nonviolent felonies. Under the statute, a defendant would receive a mandatory life sentence without the possibility of parole (unlike *Rummel,* in which parole was a possibility). In assessing the gravity of the offense with the harshness of the penalty, the Court clearly came down on the defendant's side.

In terms of the application of the second part, the Court noted that in South Dakota, Helms was sentenced to the same punishment reserved for much more serious crimes such as murder, kidnapping, first-degree rape, and other violent crimes. Finally, in assessing how the defendant would have been treated in other jurisdictions, the Court noted that in 48 of the 50 states, he would have received a less severe sentence.

The significance of this case was its remarkable departure from the Court's long years of hands off on this issue. What had clearly been a position of deferring to state legislatures and their assessments of the proper punishments for crimes, *Solem* seemed to open up the possibility that the courts had entered the fray. The question the case presented was whether the Supreme Court was truly committed to this new activist approach or viewed the case as an aberration dealing with a particularly unusual set of facts and circumstances.

FURTHER LEGAL DEVELOPMENTS

Of course, the cases discussed in the background section make up a significant portion of the Court's legal decisions in this area. It has been the Court's work since *Solem,* however, that has either, depending upon your perspective, fixed the aberration of *Solem* or further muddied the waters with another un-workable standard.

The case of *Harmelin v. Michigan*[11] was the first important proportionality case after *Solem*. It involved the application of a Michigan mandatory life sentence law for certain drug offenses. The defendant, Harmelin, was convicted of possessing 672 grams of cocaine and sentenced to a mandatory life sentence without the possibility of parole. Early in the opinion, it was clear how the Court was going to deal with *Solem's* insistence on performing the three-part proportionality test when it characterized the *Solem* decision as "scarcely the expression of clear and well established constitutional law."[12] Justice Antonin Scalia's lengthy and scholarly discussion of the history of the Eighth Amendment and its historical precedent in the English Declaration of Rights of 1689 supported his interpretation that the amendment prohibited only cruel and unusual punishments (in other words, the manner, not the length, of the punishment) and did not support a proportionality requirement. Important to his interpretation was the notion that proportionality as a legal concept goes back to the Magna Carta and that numerous states at the time of the Constitution had specific provisions requiring proportionality in their sentencing laws and that had the framers intended to graft that notion to the Eighth Amendment, they were well acquainted with the idea and could easily have done so. Scalia concluded his analysis by stating that the cruel and unusual language of the Eighth Amendment relates to the method of punishment only and not to the length of the punishment.

The final pronouncement of the Court on this matter came in *Ewing v. California*,[13] a 2003 case that dealt with the application of California's three-strikes law to a defendant with a lengthy history of criminal convictions but whose only triggering crime was the theft of three golf clubs. Ewing was sentenced under the statute to 25 years to life in prison.

Although the opinion did not garner a majority of the Court, the reasoning of Justice Sandra Day O'Connor's lead opinion relied on the framework set out by Justice Anthony Kennedy in his earlier concurrence in *Harmelin*. Kennedy found that the Eighth Amendment recognizes a limited proportionality principle in noncapital cases, which forbids the imposition of extreme sentences that are "grossly disproportionate" to the crime.[14]

Justice Kennedy identified four principles to consult before making the final determination under the Eighth Amendment. The Court was to look at the primacy of the legislature, the variety of legitimate penological schemes, the nature of the federal system, and the requirement that proportionality review be guided by objective factors. When applying these factors to the specifics of *Ewing*, the Court focused primarily on California's legitimate interests of deterring and incapacitating offenders with long and serious records. These legitimate penological interests, when combined with the primacy of (deference to) the legislature, shaped the Court's affirmation of the sentence.

FUTURE PROSPECTS

The future prospects, in a word, are confusing. Although the concept of proportionality of punishment has a long and rich history in England going back

MAYBE WE WERE WRONG: THE REFORM MOVEMENT IN SENTENCING

It is no coincidence that *Rummel, Solem,* and *Harmelin* occurred during the decade of the 1980s, a decade ushered in by the so-called War on Drugs and the movement to mandatory long-term sentences. States followed the call from the federal government that what was needed to stem the drug and violence epidemic in this country was a tougher lock-'em-up correctional policy. What followed was the increase of arrests, longer sentences, often triggered by recidivist or three-strikes laws, and the construction of new prisons.

Lawmakers and policy makers have begun to look at the wisdom of that movement that has resulted in several disturbing facts. The policies of locking up offenders for longer times and denying them parole opportunities have resulted in an increasingly elderly and infirm prison population at great expense to the public and have driven an inmate population being denied any incentive for early release to be unmanageable.

Reform efforts have come on both state and federal levels. On the federal level, the Second Chance Act addresses the issue of prisoner reentry and would authorize funding for model community programs to assist inmates who are reentering society. On the state level, 18 states have either eliminated some mandatory sentencing laws, eliminated recidivist or three-strikes laws, or reinstituted discretionary parole for certain offenses.*

---

* "The Right Has a Jailhouse Conversion," *New York Times Magazine*, December 24, 2006, 47.

---

to the Magna Carta, and although it has been recognized and applied in capital and noncapital cases in the United States for almost a century, it appears to have gone the way of the Edsel and the dial phone.[15] The future of the Supreme Court's Eighth Amendment jurisprudence, in other words, does not appear to include general proportionality as a working doctrine.

Instead, there appear to be three vastly different approaches on the table, none of which appears to garner a majority of the Court's votes. There is the more extreme position of Justices John Paul Stevens, David Souter, Ruth Bader Ginsburg, and Stephen Breyer, which suggests that a return to the *Solem* three-part test is appropriate. On the other extreme, Justices Scalia and Clarence Thomas adhere to the position that the Eight Amendment contains no proportionality requirement. Finally, and perhaps the most likely ground to be taken, is Justice Kennedy's concurring opinion in *Harmelin*, which recognizes a "narrow proportionality principle" in the Eighth Amendment. It is too early to determine where the new appointees, Chief Justice John Roberts and Associate Justice Samuel Alito, will fall on this issue.

It is also possible to envision a case in which all nine justices would agree on reversing a particular sentence under the Eighth Amendment if it were so extreme as to be unacceptable to any rational person at any time at any place. The idea that legislatures could make overtime parking a felony punishable by life is theoretically possible without a proportionality principle. This notion particularly irked Justice Byron White in his *Harmelin* dissent,[16] but it may take more than chiding from fellow justices about frightening scenarios to gain unanimity in an area in which most justices have seemed content to go their own way.

See Also: Corporal Punishment; Prisons—Supermax; Three Strikes; Torture and Enemy Combatants.

Endnotes

1. *Lockyer v. Andrade,* 538 U.S. 63, 66 (2003).
2. *Coker v. Georgia,* 433 U.S. 584 (1977).
3. *Atkins v. Virginia,* 536 U.S. 304 (2002).
4. *Roper v. Simmons,* 125 S.Ct. 1183 (2005).
5. 217 U.S. 349 (1910).
6. 217 U.S. at 381.
7. 445 U.S. 263 (1980).
8. 454 U.S. 370 (1982).
9. 445 U.S. at 274.
10. 463 U.S. 277 (1983).
11. 501 U.S. 957 (1991).
12. 501 U.S. at 965.
13. 538 U.S. 11 (2003).
14. 501 U.S. at 997.
15. Joy M. Donham, "Note: Third Strike or Merely a Foul Tip?: The Gross Disproportionality of Lockyer v. Andrade," *Akron Law Review* 38 (2005): 369; see Sec. IV for an excellent summary of historical evidence.
16. 501 U.S. at 1018.

Further Reading: Branham, Lynne S, and Michael S. Hamden, *Cases and Materials on the Law and Policy of Sentencing and Corrections,* 7th ed. (St. Paul, MN: Thompson/West, 2005); Donham, Joy M., "Note: Third Strike or Merely a Foul Tip?: The Gross Disproportionality of Lockyer v. Andrade," *Akron Law Review* 38 (2005): 369; Haddad, James B., Linda R. Meyer, James B. Zagel, Gary L. Starkman, and William J. Bauer, *Criminal Procedure, Cases and Comments,* 5th ed. (St. Paul, MN: Foundation Press, 1998), 4; Pater, Joshua, "Struck Out Looking: Continued Confusion in Eighth Amendment Proportionality Review after Ewing v. California," *Harvard Journal of Law and Public Policy* 27 (2003): 399.

William L. Shulman

CSI EFFECT

INTRODUCTION

Within criminal adjudicative circles, a debate has recently emerged about whether a so-called CSI effect exists during criminal trials, and if it does, whether this effect is raising or lowering the threshold of jurors for rendering a guilty or innocent verdict. Many prosecutors and judges have weighed in that the effect exists and that it has raised the bar or burden of proof. Labeling it the

CSI effect, the complainants argue that *CSI* and similar television programs have led jurors to believe that almost every crime can be solved by modern scientific investigative techniques and that all law enforcement agencies have such techniques available to them. The argument contends that when the prosecutor does not produce such forensic scientific evidence at a trial, jurors acquit defendants without understanding that such evidence is irrelevant or unnecessary in the face of other evidence, such as the testimony of witnesses. On the other hand, the legal-social scientific community has expressed doubts about such an effect and about the impact that it might have on acquittals versus convictions or on different types of crime scenarios.

BACKGROUND

Although film and television have long utilized courtroom dramas as their raw material, in recent years it has not only proliferated, it has also changed its focus. Much courtroom media is based on actual cases in a seeming fascination with our criminal justice process. Court TV now makes live gavel-to-gavel Internet coverage of ordinary trials available on a subscription basis.[1] Adding dramatic elements to the often-boring routine of courtroom reality, however, is regarded as essential for popular media success.

This dramatic enhancement of the court process begins with the crime magazine television shows, such as *48 Hours Mystery* or *American Justice* or even *Dateline* on occasion. In those shows, an actual case is used, but only after it has been edited and narrated for dramatic effect. From there it is a short media step to fiction. To attract viewers, some of these fictional shows use plotlines so similar to actual cases that have made the headlines that some viewers may believe them to be true. The ubiquitous *Law and Order* promotes its plots as "ripped from the headlines," and indeed it and other shows seem to immediately replicate some issue in an actual case that was widely disseminated in the rest of the media just a short time before.

The most popular television courtroom portrayals, whether actual or edited or purely fictional, have been about the use of new science and technology to solve crimes. *CSI* first aired in October 2000, and more than six years later it was still called the most popular television show in the world. It is so popular that it has spawned spin-offs that also dominate the broadcast television ratings. Its success has also produced a plethora of similar forensic dramas, like *Cold Case, Bones, Numb3rs,* and many others (see Table C.2).

The fictional plots of these programs often involve the most serious crimes, such as murder or rape, and the heroes are technician investigators. They inevitably solve the crime using some piece of scientific evidence they uncover, such as prints of some kind (finger, foot, teeth, shoe, etc.), blood, fibers, hair, semen, gunshot evidence, and of course DNA.[2]

Prosecutors and judges began to complain of a CSI effect. They complained that watching *CSI* and similar programs created expectations in jurors that they would be presented with scientific evidence in every case and that when it was

Table C.2 The Popularity of CSI: Top 10 Prime-Time Broadcast TV Programs, November 7, 2005–November 13, 2005

Rank	Program	Network	Household Rating	Total Viewers
1	CSI	CBS	18.2	29,546,000
2	Desperate Housewives	ABC	15.8	25,934,000
3	NFL Monday Night Football	ABC	14.3	21,860,000
4	Without a Trace	CBS	13.8	20,784,000
5	Grey's Anatomy	ABC	12.5	19,737,000
6	CSI: Miami	CBS	12.3	18,393,000
6	CSI: NY	CBS	12.3	19,225,000
8	Lost	ABC	12.0	20,012,000
9	Cold Case	CBS	11.1	17,424,000
10	NCIS	CBS	11.0	17,792,000
10	Survivor: Guatemala	CBS	11.0	18,981,000

not forthcoming they would "wrongfully" acquit defendants. The popular media picked up on these complaints and came to regard them as a proved phenomenon.[3]

The existence of any such a CSI effect is disputed, however, and has been the subject of considerable debate. Many of the early studies on the subject were simply compilations of opinion interviews with prosecutors or secondhand accounts of jury deliberations. Serious commentators question whether such a pattern of acquittals in which there is no scientific evidence exists or, even if it does, whether it is the result of other legitimate jury influences.[4] Fitting to their subject, anecdotal reports have generated more light than heat. Until recently, there had been no credible empirical studies to determine if juror expectations or demands for scientific evidence have been heightened as the result of the forensic drama media.

KEY EMPIRICAL STUDIES

Kimberlianne Podlas, in her 2006 study " 'The CSI Effect': Exposing the Media Myth," reviewed and analyzed claims of the alleged CSI effect and attempted to test whether such a phenomenon exists. She surveyed the television-watching habits of 306 college students and then presented them with a rape case scenario in which the sole issue was consent and there was no dispute about the identification of the defendant. After reading the scenario, the students were given a choice of finding the defendant guilty or not guilty and were asked to choose from a list of reasons for their verdict. Podlas examined whether there was a relationship between watching *CSI* regularly and the reasons given for not guilty verdicts. On the basis that the only legally correct verdict was not guilty and that scientific evidence was irrelevant to the verdict, she analyzed the not guilty verdicts that were based on a lack of scientific evidence, such as fingerprints or DNA. She found no difference in those results between students who frequently watched *CSI* and those who did not. She concluded:

> Although the media warns that a "CSI Effect" is seducing jurors into legally unjustifiable "not guilty" verdicts and unwarranted demands for proof of guilt beyond any and all doubt, the empirical results here suggest otherwise. Indeed, the data strongly denies the existence of any negative effect of *CSI* on "not guilty" verdicts, provided that "negative" is defined as improper. If anything, the data hints that, if there is any effect of *CSI,* it is to exalt the infallibility of forensic evidence, favor the prosecution, or pre-dispose jurors toward findings of guilt.[5]

The Podlas study left unanswered concerns and questions. Initially, there are concerns of whether a survey group of college students is representative of a typical jury venire.[6] Second, the respondents in the Podlas study were not given a verdict choice of "not sure" to indicate that they needed to see the witnesses or have more information, and Podlas did not include any guilty verdicts in the analysis. Although Podlas may be technically correct about the legal application of the presumption of innocence, jurors clearly do not apply the reasonable doubt and burden of proof instruction in such a legally literal sense. Finally, as Podlas noted:

> It is not clear whether *CSI* viewers are not influenced by CSI-marked reasons or whether they are not influenced by them any more than non-viewers. Whereas the former suggests either no "CSI Effect" at all or no "CSI Effect" based on frequency of viewing, the latter leaves open the possibility that there still might be a "CSI Effect" across the population. Thus, it might impact frequent viewers and non-viewers alike.[7]

Thus, the question remained: Does a CSI effect of some sort exist?

The first empirical study of the existence of a CSI effect in actual jurors was conducted by Shelton, Kim, and Barak (2006).[8] They surveyed 1,027 persons who had been summoned for jury duty in a state court. The jurors were surveyed before they had been selected, or even interviewed, for selection as jurors in a trial. The survey sought to determine the level of their expectation that the prosecutor would produce scientific evidence in various types of cases and to determine whether those expectations would likely be converted into demands as conditions for a guilty verdict. The survey measured the television watching experiences of the jurors related to various categories of crime-related shows and then sought to determine if juror expectations or demands were specifically related to watching any of those types of programs.

The Shelton, Kim, and Barak study did find significant juror expectations and demands for scientific evidence in many types of criminal cases. However, there

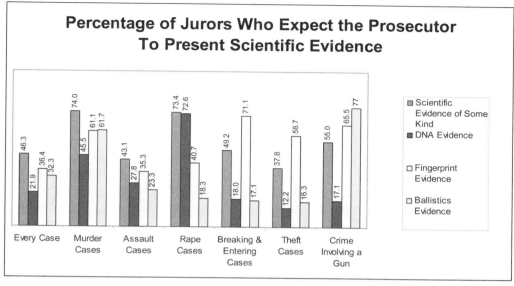

Figure C.2 Percentage of jurors who expect the prosecutor to present scientific evidence.

was little or no indication of a link between those preconceptions and watching particular television shows.

As to juror expectations, the Shelton, Kim, and Barak study confirmed anecdotal claims that jurors now expect the prosecution to present some scientific evidence (see fig. C.2). Almost half of the surveyed jurors expected the prosecutor to present scientific evidence of some kind in every criminal case. They found that as the seriousness of the charge increases, so does the expectation for scientific evidence. Almost three-quarters of the jurors expected scientific evidence of some kind in cases of murder, attempted murder, or rape. Even in the less serious cases of breaking and entering or theft, a significant number of jurors expected some scientific evidence. Specifically as to DNA evidence, the jurors in the Shelton, Kim, and Barak study had high expectations in the more serious cases, with almost half expecting DNA evidence in murder or attempted murder cases and almost three-quarters expecting DNA evidence in cases charging rape or other criminal sexual conduct.

Does watching *CSI* influence these expectations?

First, the Shelton, Kim, and Barak study found that, in general, frequent *CSI* watchers did have higher expectations for all kinds of evidence than did non-*CSI* watchers. In all categories of evidence, both scientific and nonscientific, the evidentiary expectations of *CSI* watchers were consistently higher than those of non-*CSI* watchers. *CSI* watchers also have higher expectations about scientific evidence that is more likely to be relevant to a particular crime than non-*CSI* watchers, and they have lower expectations about evidence that is less likely to be relevant to a particular crime than do non-*CSI* watchers.

Shelton, Kim, and Barak found that watching *CSI* and related programs might marginally increase the expectation of scientific evidence in certain types of cases. *CSI* watchers were slightly more likely to expect scientific evidence of some kind in cases charging murder or attempted murder, rape or other criminal sexual conduct, breaking and entering, and cases involving a gun. They were also slightly more likely to expect DNA evidence in cases charging physical assault or rape or other criminal sexual conduct. They were also slightly more likely to expect fingerprint evidence in cases charging breaking and entering, theft, or cases involving a gun. Finally, *CSI* watchers were slightly more likely to expect ballistics evidence in gun cases.

Regardless of their expectations, the real test of the CSI effect, however, is whether jurors are more likely to acquit if scientific evidence is not forthcoming from the prosecution. The Shelton, Kim, and Barak study did not find that jurors necessarily translated their high expectations into demands for scientific evidence as a condition for a guilty verdict.

Jurors were more likely to find the defendant guilty than not guilty even without scientific evidence if there were testimony from a victim or other witnesses. The only exception to that pattern was in rape cases. In a rape case, only 14.1 percent of the respondent jurors would find the defendant guilty if the victim's testimony is presented without any scientific evidence, whereas 26 percent would find the defendant not guilty without scientific evidence.

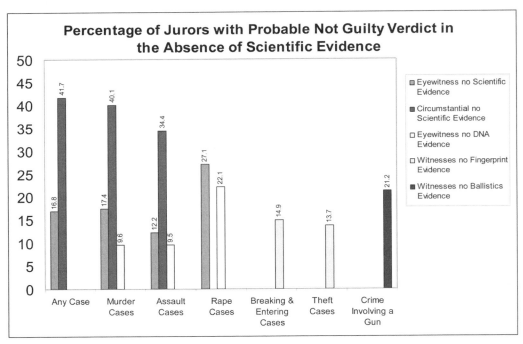

Figure C.3 Percentage of jurors with probable not guilty verdict in the absence of scientific evidence.

As to particular types of scientific evidence, the Shelton, Kim, and Barak study jurors were more likely to find the defendant guilty than not guilty if there was testimony from the victim or an eyewitness even without DNA evidence in either a murder case (33.2% vs. 9.4%) or a physical assault case (39% vs. 9.3%). They were more likely find the defendant guilty in specific types of relevant cases even without any fingerprint evidence The ratios were 31.8 percent versus 14.7 percent in a breaking and entering case, and 31.2 percent versus 13.4 percent in any theft case.

Shelton, Kim, and Barak found that, with two exceptions, the absence of scientific evidence did not appear to make jurors any less likely to convict (see fig. C.3). The two exceptions may be significant in certain prosecutions.

First, in every case in which the prosecutor relies on circumstantial evidence and presents no scientific evidence, the jury is much more likely to acquit. For example, in "any criminal case" in which the prosecution relied on circumstantial evidence without scientific evidence, 41.7 percent of jurors said they would probably acquit. A similar result was obtained for murder (40.1%) and assault cases (34.4%) in which the prosecutor relied on circumstantial evidence without scientific evidence. In scenarios in which there was eyewitness testimony, the absence of scientific evidence was not outcome determinative. This may be simply a reflection of the well-documented misplaced reliance on the reliability of eyewitness identification.[9] Although the judge will later instruct jurors that circumstantial evidence can be used to prove the elements of a crime, jurors apparently want more evidence, and especially scientific evidence, of some kind.

Second, in rape cases, a significant number of jurors (26.5%) would probably find the defendant not guilty if there is no scientific evidence even when the alleged victim testifies to the rape. Further, in rape cases, a significant number of jurors (21.5%) said they would acquit the defendant if the prosecutor does not present DNA evidence. Even though the issue in most rape or sexual misconduct cases is not the identification of the perpetrator when scientific evidence and especially DNA evidence could be important, jurors still indicated they would demand such evidence. This finding may be peculiar to rape cases. A number of studies have found that jurors often ignore the evidence in rape cases and make their decision on the basis of extraneous factors.[10]

But even when jurors are likely to acquit without scientific evidence, is it related to watching *CSI*?

The Shelton, Kim, and Barak study found that when jurors demanded scientific evidence as a condition for a guilty verdict, those demands were not statistically related to watching *CSI* or similar programs. That survey did not find that the demand for scientific evidence as proof of guilt was related to watching crime-related television programs, and there was no statistical relationship between the jurors who specifically watched the *CSI* program and the jurors who insisted upon some scientific evidence for conviction.

Based on the Shelton, Kim, and Barak study, if *CSI effect* means simply the influence that watching the television show *CSI* has on jurors, there is no evidence of such an effect on the likelihood of acquittal. Similarly, if the term

CSI effect means the influence that watching crime-related television shows in general has on jurors, there is no evidence of such an effect on the likelihood of acquittal.

Specifically, the Shelton, Kim, and Barak study found significant statistical differences between *CSI* and non-*CSI* watchers in only 4 of the 13 case scenarios. And three of those were only marginally significant. Ironically, when tested for probable verdicts in "every criminal case," *CSI* watchers were actually more likely than non-*CSI* watchers to find a defendant guilty without any scientific evidence if eyewitness testimony is presented. And *CSI* watchers were more likely than non-*CSI* watchers to find the defendant guilty in breaking and entering theft case without any fingerprint evidence.

IMPORTANCE OF POPULAR CULTURE AND TECHNOLOGY

There are now significant numbers of jurors who expect scientific evidence in every criminal prosecution and significant numbers of jurors who will acquit defendants in cases of circumstantial evidence and in rape cases unless the prosecution presents scientific evidence. If it is not watching *CSI* and similar crime shows on television, what other factors may be causing or influencing that phenomenon?

Shelton, Kim, and Barak suggest that increased expectations and demands for scientific evidence are more likely the result of broader cultural influences related to modern technological advances and that it should be more properly characterized as a so-called tech effect rather than a CSI effect. They suggested "the origins of those expectations lie in the broader permeation of the changes in our popular culture brought about by the confluence of rapid advances in science and information technology and the increased use of crime stories as a vehicle to dramatize those advances."[11]

Scholars have recognized the impact of popular culture on the judicial system, and in particular the criminal justice system, for some time.[12] The impact of technology on popular culture has been enormous since the mid-1970s. The application of computer technology has not only been a major force in new scientific discoveries, it also has changed even the most mundane activities of daily life. Among those changes are basic alterations in the availability and transmission of information. As little as thirty years ago, the public was primarily dependent on newspapers and three or four television networks for information. The information technology revolution, powered by the miniaturization of computers, now makes information available through more cable television outlets than you can count, an Internet that is truly global, and handheld cell phones and personal digital assistants that make the delivery of that information constant and almost immediate. The information with which we are now deluged includes information about the scientific developments themselves.

These developments in science and information are interdependent. Scientists can share information among themselves to speed more discoveries. And because of the mass availability of the information network, those scientific developments almost immediately become available to the entire world. The media latches onto scientific discoveries and almost immediately integrates them into popular culture. It is a short step from those news sources to television and cinematic nonfiction and fiction. Many people have learned more about science and technology from these media than from their formal education.

The application of that new knowledge to the criminal justice system, as portrayed in the media, is the means by which many ordinary citizens learn about crime and punishment. Barak has described the process:

> Mass news representations in the "information age" have become the most significant communication by which the average person comes to know the world outside his or her immediate experience. As for cultural visions of crime projected by the mass media, or the selections and presentations by the news media on criminal justice, these representations are viewed as the principal vehicle by which the average person comes to know crime and justice in America.[13]

Those same "average persons" form the composition of today's criminal jury.

The available research does indicate that these jurors have increased expectations, and perhaps demands, that the scientific advancements they have seen and read about will be used to solve real crimes in real cases. It seems likely, however, that these expectations are the result of significant changes in popular culture related to science and technology and the application of those changes to portrayals of the criminal justice system. Television crime dramas like *CSI* are likely just a single input into agenda setting that jurors experience from the variety of information that is presented to them before they are summoned to jury duty.

FUTURE PROSPECTS

It is not reasonable to expect that juror perceptions of the importance of the role of scientific evidence in the criminal justice system will decrease. Indeed, the rapid pace of new technological developments and of new developments in information delivery continues unabated. At the same time, the number and availability of crime-related television dramas continues to increase. In addition to its regular CBS editions, *CSI* reruns have been syndicated to channels servicing 75 percent of the United States so that viewers, and potential jurors, will be exposed to the show all year.[14] Although perhaps the flow of information about modern crime investigation techniques may be replaced with news and television dramas about the plight of ordinary police investigators who do not have such techniques available, it is doubtful. If anything, it would be reasonable to expect that juror expectations that they will be presented with scientific evidence in criminal trials will increase.

The challenge, and indeed the only relevant question, is whether and how the criminal justice system will respond to these increased juror expectations. As news reports indicate, many prosecutors, police, and judges have simply complained and tried to find ways to convince jurors that they should ignore the knowledge they have received about forensic evidence from popular culture. Clearly, jurors cannot do so, and such an approach is not succeeding.

Rather, it is more likely that the criminal justice system will need to try to keep pace with the dramatic technological changes in our society. That may take a major commitment of additional law enforcement resources. Police and other investigating agencies may need to be equipped with the modern forensic science equipment that jurors know is available. Equally important, those agencies may need to be provided with the significant increases in forensic science personnel that will enable the results of forensic testing to be available to prosecutors in a timely manner.

When scientific evidence is not relevant, prosecutors will need to be better advocates and find better ways of explaining the lack of relevance to jurors. In doing so, they should not assume that jurors come into court with empty minds waiting to be filled only with the case information that the lawyers choose to dole out to them. Rather, they need to understand, and address, the fact that jurors are representatives of popular culture and come into the courtroom filled with a great deal of knowledge about the criminal justice system and the availability of scientific evidence, much of which is correct.

See Also: Adversarial Justice; DNA Usage in Criminal Justice; Prosecutorial Discretion.

Endnotes

1. Court TV Extra provides "an unprecedented opportunity to watch trials online" for $5.95 per month, https://secure.courttv.com/extra/signup/benefits.html.
2. For a review of the forensic content of *CSI* episodes, see Kimberlianne Podlas, " 'The CSI Effect': Exposing the Media Myth," *Fordham Intellectual Property, Media and Entertainment Law Journal* 16 (2006): 429, 453.
3. See, for example, Kit Roane, "The CSI Effect," *U.S. News and World Report,* April 25, 2005, 48, http://www.usnews.com/usnews/culture/articles/050425/25csi.htm; " 'CSI Effect' Making Cases Hard to Prove: Lawyers," *ABC News Online,* September 24, 2005, http://www.abc.net.au/news/newsitems/200509/s1467632.htm; "Justice under the Microscope," *The New York Times,* May 16, 2005, A20; Richard Willing, " 'CSI Effect' Has Juries Wanting More Evidence," *USA Today,* August 5, 2004, http://www.usatoday.com/news/nation/2004-08-05-csi-effect_x.htm; Vince Gonzales, "Prosecutors Feel the 'CSI Effect,'" *CBS Evening News,* February 10, 2005, http://www.cbsnews.com/stories/2005/02/10/eveningnews/main673060.shtml; " 'The CSI Effect': Does the Crime TV Drama Influence How Jurors Think?," *The Early Show,* CBS News, March 21, 2005, http://www.cbsnews.com/stories/2005/02/10/eveningnews/main673060.shtml, http://www.cbsnews.com/stories/2005/03/21/earlyshow/main681949.shtml; Linda Deutsch, "TV Distorting Jurors Expectations?," *Seattle Times,* January 15, 2006; Max Houck, "CSI: The Reality," *Scientific American,* July 2006, http://www.sciam.com/article.cfm?chanID=sa006&articleID=000394C8-1227-1493-906183414B7F0162.
4. Tom R. Tyler, "Viewing CSI and the Threshold of Guilt: Managing Truth and Justice in Reality and Fiction," *Yale Law Journal* 115 (2006): 1050.
5. Podlas, " 'The CSI Effect,'" 465.
6. The use of college students to predict juror behavior has some inherent problems. See H. Feild and N. Barnett, "Simulated Jury Trials: Students vs. Real People as Jurors," *Journal of Social Psychology* 104 (1978): 287.

7. Podlas, " 'The CSI Effect,' " 464.

8. D. Shelton, Y. Kim, and G. Barak, "A Study of Juror Expectations and Demands Concerning Scientific Evidence: Does the 'CSI Effect' Exist?" (2006), unpublished manuscript.

9. See Gary L. Wells and Elizabeth F. Loftus, eds., *Eyewitness Testimony* (Cambridge: Cambridge University Press, 1984); John C. Brigham and Robert K. Bothwell, "The Ability of Prospective Jurors to Estimate the Accuracy of Eyewitness Identifications," *Law and Human Behavior* 7 (1983): 19; Tyler, "Viewing CSI and the Threshold of Guilt," 1069–70.

10. See H. Feild, "Rape Trials and Jurors' Decisions: A Psycholegal Analysis of the Effects of Victim, Defendant, and Case Characteristics," *Law and Human Behavior* 3 (1979): 261; V. Berger, "Man's Trial, Woman's Tribulation: Rape Cases in the Courtroom," *Columbia Law Review* 77 (1977): 1.

11. Shelton et al., "A Study of Juror Expectations and Demands."

12. See R. Sherwin, *When Law Goes Pop: The Vanishing Line between Law and Popular Culture* (Chicago: University of Chicago Press, 2000); R. Sherwin, *Popular Culture and Law* (London: Ashgate, 2006).

13. G. Barak, ed., *Media, Process, and the Social Construction of Crime: Studies in Newsmaking Criminology* (New York: Garland, 1994), 3.

14. King World, "*CSI: NY* Sold in 75% of the Country by King World for Weekend Broadcast Syndication Beginning Fall 2008," press release, January 11, 2005, http://www.kingworld.com/PressRelease.aspx?pressReleaseID=28.

Further Reading: Asimow, M., and S. Mader, *Law and Popular Culture* (New York: Lang, 2004); Shelton, D., Y. Kim, and G. Barak, "A Study of Juror Expectations and Demands Concerning Scientific Evidence: Does the 'CSI Effect' Exist?" (2006), unpublished manuscript; Sherwin, R., *When Law Goes Pop: The Vanishing Line between Law and Popular Culture* (Chicago: University of Chicago Press, 2000); Slack, J., and J. Macgregor, *Culture Technology: A Primer* (New York: Lang, 2005); Tyler, T., "Viewing CSI and the Threshold of Guilt: Managing Truth and Justice in Reality and Fiction," *Yale Law Journal* 115 (2006): 1050.

Donald E. Shelton

DANGEROUS OFFENDERS

INTRODUCTION

Although classifying dangerous offenders has always been a controversial issue among social and behavioral scientists, Ysabel Rennie's history of criminal dangerousness reminds us that this abstract notion is inherent in literally all discussions of criminology. In fact, we judge criminals by how dangerous we think they are: gradations of dangerousness. In his brief discussion, Rennie sets the stage by asking us to consider that the notion of a dangerous offender is a "protean concept, changing its color and shape to suit the fears, interests, needs, and prejudices of a society."[1]

Dating back to ancient Roman times, the poor were historically regarded as more dangerous than the rich and, hence, more criminal. For nearly four hundred years, the criminal law in England was obsessed with vagrants and beggars, who were regarded as a great threat to society. This so-called threat to the noblemen was largely induced by the demise of feudalism, and in its place, the rise of capitalism and the concept of private property resulted in thousands of serfs losing their means of livelihood. By 1820, the number of capital crimes in England had increased to nearly two hundred, most of which were directed at protecting newly emerging forms of private capital. Thus, England's prisons became filled with that so-called dangerous and depraved class.

Were these offenders classified as dangerous really a threat to civil society, however? That depends on one's point of view or ideology regarding crime and punishment. For example, those who are concerned only with private property will define dangerousness differently than those who are concerned only with the well-being of persons, and those who are concerned with both private property and the general citizenry will define it a third way. On one side of this controversy in labeling are those who advocate or defend the usage of such labels as necessary to separating from society the truly dangerous and nonrehabilitative from those who are not dangerous and capable of reform. On the other side of the dangerous offender controversy are those who contend that the label *dangerous offender* is not only highly contested in the first place, but that it is also used in a very arbitrary, capricious, and yet discriminatory fashion against those marginal members of society.

BACKGROUND

The introduction of classical theory in criminology eliminated witches and religion as being dangerous, but political and economic heretics still represented a so-called danger to the state. Thus, among "those who have been seen as dangerous or potentially dangerous have been Christians, slaves, vagabonds, strangers, gypsies, beggars, students, Catholics, Protestants, atheists, nationalists, demobilized soldiers and sailors, witches, Freemasons, labor leaders, and social revolutionaries."[2]

The popular origin of the dangerous classes originated in France by H. A. Frégier, who authored *On the Misery of the Working Classes in England and France.* It did not go without notice that in eighteenth-century France, the price of bread was a good indicator of revolutionary chaos in the streets of Paris. This made the poor twice dangerous: dangerous as thieves and cutthroats and dangerous to the ruling classes as instigators of revolution (uprisings of 1789, 1830, and 1848).[3]

In a similar vein, the early eugenics movement in the eighteenth century carried with it the notion of heredity transmission, the evolution of the species and, of course, the devolution of mankind characterized by atavistic, biological genealogy. Hence, Herbert Spencer wrote about the survival of the fittest, which naturally led to Cesare Lombroso's now famous work on the so-called born criminal.[4]

As early as 1806, French physician Philippe Pinel distinguished between the mentally disordered offender suffering from an illness affecting mood and reasons *(manie avec délire)* and those without such a deficiency *(manie sans délire)*.[5] The latter, of course, was the precursor description to our now well-known sociopath or psychopath. So, too, Raffaele Garofalo and Enrico Ferri developed the notion of dangerousness, or *temibilità,* as part of their notion of positivism. It meant, of course, that so-called dangerous offenders could be removed from society on the basis of a future prediction of serious harm, even if there was no offense at all. This represented a marked break from classical theory, the notion of social defense based not on criminal acts but on the dangerousness of the offender.

What is frequently missing from the literature on dangerousness is a historical or materialist context. Much of this legislation originated with a concern about habitual property offenders in England circa the early nineteenth century, referring again to "thieves and criminals of all kinds, living on the crumbs of society, people without a definite trade, vagabonds, people without a hearth or home."[6] Across the Atlantic Ocean and during the last quarter of the nineteenth century, the eugenics movement in the United States was in full swing. R. L. Dugdale had published his *The "Jukes": A Study in Crime, Pauperism, Disease and Heredity* and Henry Goddard his *The Kallikak Family: A Study in the Heredity of Feeble-Mindedness.*[7] This orientation lasted well into the early twentieth century and was typified by the U.S. Supreme Court's decision in *Buck v. Bell* (1927), which upheld the right of Virginia to sterilize the developmentally delayed. More recent variations on this theme define the dangerous as part of the surplus population or underclass.

Of course, this notion has changed with particular historical circumstances. The dangerous classes have recently been referred to as young black males, gangs, or especially sex offenders. Previously, we had the concept of the "defective delinquent," which was applied to female prostitutes and property offenders. All of this is merely to illustrate that the definition of dangerous offender is a political construct highly dependent upon historical context and state formation.[8] To quote Ezzat Fattah:

> Our insistence on using the concept of dangerousness to protect the physical integrity of the general public is in sharp contrast to our indifference or ambivalence vis-à-vis the hazardous conditions in the workplace, the real dangers in the traffic and other daily risks to our health and safety. And how about the white-collar or corporate violence which results in serious physical harm to employees, consumers or members of the general public?[9]

Indeed, we can even consider this notion in a much wider vein: the concept of dangerous states or elites.[10] The Schwendingers have suggested, in one of their famous articles, that reliance on the legal definition of crime restricts the validity of theoretical explanation. Thus, those considered at high risk of perpetuating white-collar crime, political crime, human rights violations, and degradation of the environment can also be considered extremely dangerous.[11] However, we do not see these perpetrators being adjudicated as dangerous offenders.

Moreover, the language that we use to describe the so-called dangerous offender has varied by epoch, profession, and ideology:

> The "sociopath," is broadly speaking, the same individual whom the nineteenth century called the "moral imbecile," the early twentieth called the "psychopath" and the American Psychiatric Association calls the "antisocial personality." The difference in nomenclature appears to be related to whether one looks at his malefactions from the moral, psychological, or social point of view.[12]

Criminal law forms part of this dominant ideology and is constantly in flux and often contested. Frank Pearce makes the point that there are ideological reasons why street crime and not state or white collar crime is dramatized as the "crime problem":

> If the criminals are also the social failures . . . then their criminality is caused by their *inadequacies* . . . and the major social institutions

are not exposed to critical assessment. . . . [B]y defining them as non-citizens, with no *rights* to employment, education, etc., the system's failure to provide these for them . . . is obscured. . . . The American class society would be threatened if an ideologically sophisticated "lower-class" political movement was to develop.[13]

CONVICT TRANSPORTATION AS A RESPONSE TO THE RISE OF THE DANGEROUS CLASS

As Robert Hughes explains in his book *The Fatal Shore*, convict transportation to Australia was largely devised to protect the propertied classes in greater England (chiefly London) from the "marauding" criminal classes, who tended to be almost exclusively lacking in property. For Hughes, it was not hard to understand the fears of the ruling class and their need to address what they considered a swelling crime wave:

> From 1700 to 1740, the population of England and Wales remained almost constant at about 6 million people. Then it started rising fast—so fast that between 1750 and 1770 the population of London doubled—and by 1851 it stood at 18 million. This meant that the median age of Englishmen kept dropping and the labor market was saturated with the young.
>
> Around 1800, the "mob" was seen, with every reason, as dangerous. It was fuel for the same revolutionary fire that had destroyed the monarchy on the other side of the Channel. . . . Their [propertied Englishmen] fear of the political threat translated itself into repeated exaggerations of criminal nature. Thus, it was all too easy to assign criminal propensities to the marginal, the outcast, the rag-the-boner—in short, to those who might be seen as English *sans culottes*.[14]

The first convict settlements took place in Botany Bay, Australia, with conditions harsh and starvation being the rule, not the exception. Indeed, in the early years of transportation, the death rate on board the often privately chartered vessels was exceedingly high (1 in 85) from tuberculosis, typhus, and simple starvation. The convict assignment system did permit inmates to earn their tickets of leave (parole of sorts) after serving more than half their formal sentences, however, and inmates did have access to magistrates with respect to complaints against their masters and working conditions. This system also had benefits for the Crown as it shifted the costs of subsistence from the state to private entrepreneurs, thus encouraging further free settlement with the promise of free convict labor as part of the bargain. Between 1787 and 1868, the Crown sent 825 shiploads of prisoners with an average of about 200 convicts per ship. The actual total came to about 162,000, the vast majority of whom apparently went on to lead relatively productive, working-class lives, contrary to assumptions of their dangerousness.

DANGEROUS OFFENDER LEGISLATION IN CANADA

A brief look at Canada's dangerous offender legislation underscores the prevailing assumptions from both the liberal and conservative perspectives that these offenders are the worst of the worst. It is assumed that most of them are so-called psychopaths, who manifest an inherent, psychological predisposition to assault women and children. Following the positivist tradition, this so-called dangerousness is individualized in the enduring properties of dangerous offenders to commit future violent and sexual offenses. In Canada this is, literally, an exclusive male phenomenon as there are no current female dangerous offenders in the penitentiary system.[15] Last, is the assumption that Dangerous Offender legislation is needed primarily to deal with nonpsychotic, recidivist sex offenders who offend against women and children. Albeit these offenders have not murdered anyone, they must still be subject to an indeterminate life sentence. Only a small handful can hope for any type of conditional release (parole).

We get some notion of these phenomena through the origins of the dangerous offender legislation as a form of social defense. It originated largely during the eugenics movement, criminal anthropology, and the borrowing of early statutes from England and Massachusetts. White males who were privileged members of elite professions, largely psychiatry and law, dominated this exercise in criminalization. According to Joy Irving, the English statutes were largely influenced by the demise of capital sentencing as a means to regulate the urban poor in London.[16] In a similar way, we can see that the 1977 recodification of the Dangerous Offender statute in Canada was influenced by elite political considerations: the demise of capital punishment in 1976, a widely publicized incident of wanton murder, and the ever-present lobbying of forensic and correctional mental health experts. Nor does this deny the role of outraged interest groups among the public sector.

In Canada, rumblings in support of habitual offender sentencing started as early as 1938 with the publication of the Archambault Royal Commission on the penal system in Canada. In that report, the Royal Commission made note of England's Prevention of Crime Act of 1908 and endorsed similar provisions for Canada. Indeed, the commission members doubted that dangerous convicts would ever be habilitated and suggested that a special prison should be built on an isolated island in the St. Lawrence River south of Quebec City.[17]

Section 752 of the Canadian Criminal Code—the Dangerous Offender provisions—has its origins in legislation adopted in the United Kingdom for persistent offenders circa 1908. This law was the model for Canadian legislation that was codified in 1947 and 1948 as the Habitual Offender and Criminal Sexual Psychopath Acts. Later in 1960, the Criminal Sexual Psychopath Act was amended and renamed the Dangerous Sexual Offender law. In 1977, both of these acts were replaced with the current Dangerous Offender provisions of the Criminal Code.

Of the 383 offenders declared dangerous under Section 752 since 1977 and sentenced to an indeterminate prison term, only 17, or 4.4 percent, are currently on parole. Fifty-one dangerous offenders (13.3%) have either committed suicide, been murdered, or died of natural causes while imprisoned. Of those paroled, 16 remain on supervision and 1 has been deported, as of September 2004.[18]

We can add to our observations by making reference to a basic finding that the Dangerous Offender statute has been generally used to detain recidivist sex offenders who offend against women and children. Thus, the notion of moral regulation of sex offenders permeates this legislation in Canada and the interests who gave rise to its inclusion in the Criminal Code.[19]

Thus, these powerful moral and elite interests have been able to legislate policy against the dangerous few. These interests include elite penal reformers, psychiatrists and psychologists (especially those working in the courts or prisons), members of the legal profession, and various constituencies outraged by the recidivist sex offender. In this regard, the emerging notion of "penal populism" has become salient—interest groups that coalesce around a heinous crime (like a child's murder and rape) and proceed to lobby the state for dangerous offender legislation.[20]

To this extent, Susanna Steinitz is on point when she concludes that the court process is specifically designed to focus on individual pathology, not the more inclusive historical and socioeconomic contexts that gave rise to the defendant's criminal history. In Canada, their working-class histories, sometimes-extreme poverty, educational failure, under- or unemployment, and victimization histories often at the hands of Crown institutions can characterize dangerous offenders.[21] Nevertheless, in the modern courtroom, these factors are either minimized or reinterpreted as high-risk factors deserving of a life sentence.

THE DANGEROUS OFFENDER LABEL AS IN THE EYE OF THE BEHOLDER

In October 2003, an inmate residing at Kingston Penitentiary, a notorious maximum-security institution in the federal prison system, pleaded guilty to eight charges of sexually assaulting other confined inmates while acting as the chairman of the inmate affairs committee. The Crown prosecutor characterized this inmate in this following manner:

> His reign of terror in Joyceville Institution and Kingston Penitentiary was nasty, vicious, and pervasive. He ruled his ranges with an iron fist. He commanded respect, not because of his character, but because of fear and intimidation. Vulnerable people became his sexual playthings. He played out his bizarre sexual fantasies without regard to the harm that he was causing. Human beings and human lives became fodder for him—fodder to his nasty sexual impulses.

Notwithstanding that this convict was already serving a life sentence for second degree murder, the Crown allowed a plea to an additional 15 years of imprisonment. Here is why the court declined to impose a dangerous offender designation:

> But, given the evidence a dangerous-offender designation need not be sought, and fifteen years is a sufficient sentence to recognize the seriousness of the crimes that Mr. Huneault committed, in his position as chair of the Inmate Committee . . . [t]his sentence gives a chance to Mr. Huneault to return, some day, to the general population, and, I believe, serves the interests of justice.

What is important to observe is that the application of a "dangerous" label is often quite arbitrary and subject to a host of interconnecting factors, often local to the court process.*

*Regina v. Michel Huneault, Superior Court of Ontario, East Region in Kingston, Ontario, October 6, 2003.

We can thus observe certain ecology with respect to those persons most at risk for being tagged and prosecuted as the truly dangerous. Class position rooted in poverty and severe social disorganization is clearly salient. Both gender and age composition become relevant—as it relates almost exclusively to males in their late thirties and forties—after they have had time to compile a lengthy criminal record that brings them to the attention of Crown prosecutors. Finally, data collected by the Correctional Service of Canada indicate that aboriginal status is disproportionately affected in dangerous offender prosecutions—21 percent of the cases nationally are aboriginal.[22] Across Canada, aboriginals represent about 3 percent of the nonincarcerated population.

Nevertheless, the dangerous offender statute and its administration helps promote a dominant ideology that these are the worst criminals in Canada, infused with psycho-biological defects that are immune to intervention. The solution does not lie with social development or programs to address education, inequality, child abuse, or drug addiction but with selective incapacitation for life. Statistically, this can be construed as a de facto capital sentence without the hangman's noose, cyanide gas, or needle in the arm. As Richard Quinney noted almost forty years ago:

> Each conception provides a perspective as to what is regarded as crime, how crime should be controlled, how criminals should be punished and treated, and how the population is to conduct itself in an environment of crime and criminals. All these issues are resolved in actions. As thoughts become deeds, a social reality is constructed.[23]

THE DANGEROUS OFFENDER LABEL AS TRUMPING OTHER SOCIAL ILLS

Those who question the dangerous offender label argue for a political function of dangerous offender legislation in the larger context of class inequality and moral panics generated over sex offenders. At the same time, they argue that the state is not giving its highest priority to reduce unemployment, attenuate child poverty, or aggressively intervene on early child abuse. Yet all these issues are implicated in the social histories of many who are labeled as dangerous offenders.

At the heart of this ideological, if not psychological, labeling are notions about the personification of evil and of being subhuman. Such explanations are particularly well adapted to market formation. Thus, individual demonology flourishes in the context of neoliberalism and the security state.[24] This is not to argue that such institutions *cause* the phenomenon of dangerous offenders; merely, that the concept of the severe, atavistic, demonic violent offender provides a rationale that legitimizes the prevailing market economy and further acts as a form of cultural diversion.[25] To quote Katherine Beckett and Theordore Sasson:

> Rather, the wars on crime and drugs are best viewed as political maneuvers by conservative politicians and the economic elites they represent

to defend prevailing social practices and arrangements against various counter-hegemonic threats.[26]

Criminal dangerousness in market societies reinforces ideological notions about criminals that justify the repression of the lower classes and thereby re-affirms the class structure of capital markets.[27] The reason is quite plain: "[I]t is easier [less costly to ruling interests] to change laws than to change our culture, family structures, economic relationships, and ways of doing things."[28]

This is not to argue for a unitary or historical concept of dangerousness. With the deposed Taliban in Afghanistan, we have seen this kind of analysis applied to cultural artifacts (Buddhist statutes), Christian infidels, and women. In China, which is presently undergoing a third wave of executions, the so-called danger-ous consist of poor, common street criminals, the student activists who par-ticipated in the Tiananmen Square protest, and the religious group Falun Gong. In the United States, the so-called dangerous most recently consisted of almost 1,000 Muslim immigrants, largely men, held without criminal charges for sus-pected links to international terrorism. In Canada, those who were dangerous consisted of the foreign born, the unemployed, labor agitators, and alleged com-munists.[29] Thus, dangerousness is a "socially constructed reality . . . subject to social, political, and ideological influences."[30] As Steven Box observed more than two decades ago:

> Definitions of serious crime are essentially ideological constructs. They do not refer to those behaviors which objectively and *avoidably* cause the most harm, injury, and suffering. Instead, they refer only to a sub-section of these behaviors, a sub-section which is more likely to be com-mitted by young, poor educated males who are often unemployed, live in working-class impoverished neighborhoods, and frequently belong to an ethnic minority.[31]

FUTURE PROSPECTS

One might presume that someday the body politic will come to its senses and start questioning these notions of überdangerousness and the lengthy sentences that often accompany them. That dangerous offender statutes seem to prolifer-ate in market societies characterized by significant class and racial stratification could suggest the opposite. The notion of the psychopathic dangerous offender has an important political function to state elites because it detracts attention from state-corporate crime. This is not to suggest that dangerous acts by indi-vidual convicts are not salient in any society, merely that our notions of what constitutes dangerousness ought to be expanded beyond the confines of tradi-tional criminal law statutes. Using the notion of social harm might be a useful approach as a means of critiquing the current application of dangerous offender statutes.[32]

See Also: Prison Rape; Prison Sexual Assault; Prison Violence in the Carib-bean; Prisons—Supermax; Sex-Offender Registries.

Endnotes

1. Ysabel Rennie, *The Search for Criminal Man* (Lexington, MA: Lexington Books, 1978), xvii.

2. Ibid., 31.

3. Honoré A. Frégier, *Des classes dangereuses de la population dans les grande villes et des moyens de les rendre meilleures* (Paris: Chez J.-B. Baillière, 1840).

4. Herbert Spencer, *First Principles* (New York: Appleton, 1864); Cesare Lombroso, *L'Uomo delinquente* (Milan, Italy: Hoepli, 1876).

5. Philippe Pinel, *A Treatise on Insanity,* trans. D. D. Davis (New York: Hafner, 1962; originally published 1806).

6. Anthony Giddens, *Capitalism and Modern Social Theory* (New York: Cambridge University Press, 1971), 38; Steven Spitzer, "Toward a Marxian Theory of Deviance," *Social Problems* 22 (1975): 638–51.

7. R. L. Dugdale, *The "Jukes": A Study in Crime, Pauperism, Disease and Heredity* (New York: G. P. Putnam, 1884); Henry H. Goddard, *The Kallikak Family: A Study in the Heredity of Feeble-Mindedness* (New York: Macmillan, 1919).

8. Nicole Hahn Rafter, *Creating Born Criminals* (Chicago: University of Illinois Press, 1997), 149–66; Dennis Chapman, *Sociology and the Stereotype of the Criminal* (London: Tavistock, 1968).

9. Ezzat A. Fattah, "How Useful Is the Concept of Dangerousness?" *Crimcare Journal* 2, no. 2 (1986): 203–4.

10. Nils Christie, "Dangerous States," in *Dangerous Offenders,* ed. Mark Brown and John Pratt (New York: Routledge, 2000), 181–93; Noam Chomsky, *Keeping the Rabble in Line* (Monroe, ME: Common Courage Press, 1994).

11. Herman Schwendinger and Julia Schwendinger, "Defenders of Order or Guardians of Human Rights?" *Issues in Criminology* 5 (1970): 123–57; William J. Chambliss, "State-Organized Crime," *Criminology* 27, no. 2 (1989): 183–208; David O. Friedrichs, ed., *State Crime,* 2 vols. (Aldershot, U.K.: Ashgate, 1998).

12. Rennie, *The Search for Criminal Man,* 245.

13. Frank Pearce, "Crime, Corporations, and the American Social Order," in *Politics and Deviance,* ed. Ian Taylor and Laurie Taylor (London: Penguin Books, 1973), 15, 17.

14. Robert Hughes, *The Fatal Shore: A History of the Transportation of Convicts to Australia, 1878–1868* (London: Collins Harvill, 1987), 25–26, 166.

15. Matthew G. Yeager, "Ideology and Dangerousness: The Case of Lisa Colleen Neve," *Critical Criminology* 9, nos. 1–2 (Autumn 2000): 1–13; Matthew G. Yeager, "Constructing the Dangerous Offender: A Test of Quinney's Social Reality of Crime" (PhD dissertation, Carleton University, 2006).

16. Joy Irving, "Designating 'Dangerousness': Implications of Indeterminacy in Canada's Dangerous Offender Provisions" (master's thesis, Carleton University, 2001).

17. Joseph Archambault, *Report of the Royal Commission to Investigate the Penal System of Canada* (Ottawa: Queen's Printer, 1938), 218–24.

18. Yeager, "Constructing the Dangerous Offender," 3.

19. Michel Foucault, "About the Concept of the 'Dangerous Individual' in 19th Century Legal Psychiatry," *International Journal of Law and Psychiatry* 1 (1978): 1–18; Alan Hunt, *Governing Morals: A Social History of Moral Regulation* (New York: Cambridge University Press, 1999); Philip Jenkins, *Moral Panic: Changing Concepts of the Child Molester in Modern America* (New Haven, CT: Yale University Press, 1998); Carolyn Strange and Tina Loo, *Making Good: Law and Moral Regulation in Canada, 1867–1939* (Toronto: University of Toronto Press, 1997).

20. Michael Petrunik, "The Hare and the Tortoise: Dangerousness and Sex Offender Policy in the United States and Canada," *Canadian Journal of Criminology and Criminal Justice* 45, no. 4 (2003): 43–73; David Garland, *The Culture of Control: Crime and Social Order in Contemporary Society* (Chicago: University of Chicago Press, 2001); Dawn Walton and Katherine Harding, "What Have the Mounties Learned from a Tragedy?" *Globe and Mail*, February 25, 2006, A4–5.

21. Susanna E. Steinitz, "The Mask of Science: Expert Constructions of Psychopathy in British Columbia Dangerous Offender Hearings, 1978–2000" (master's thesis, Simon Fraser University, 2001); Jacqueline Faubert, "The Emergence and Consequences of Risk Thinking in British Columbia Dangerous Offender Hearings, 1978–2000" (PhD dissertation, Simon Fraser University, 2003); Yeager, "Constructing the Dangerous Offender."

22. Linda T. Roy, "Dangerous Offenders as of August 13, 2006" (printout, Correctional Service of Canada, Ministry of Public Safety and Emergency Preparedness, November 17, 2006).

23. Richard Quinney, *The Social Reality of Crime* (New Brunswick, NJ: Transaction, 1970; republished 2001), 302.

24. Dario Melossi, "Changing Representations of the Criminal," *British Journal of Criminology* 40 (Spring 2000): 296–320; Jonathan Simon, "Managing the Monstrous: Sex Offenders and the New Penology," *Psychology, Public Policy, and Law* 4, nos. 1–2 (1998): 452–67; Katherine Becket and Theodore Sasson, "The War on Crime as Hegemonic Strategy," in *Of Crime and Criminality: The Use of Theory in Everyday Life*, ed. S. Simpson (Boston: Pine Forge Press, 2000), 61–84; Katherine Beckett and Theodore Sasson, *The Politics of Injustice*, 2nd ed. (Thousand Oaks, CA: Sage, 2004); Gary Teeple, *Globalization and the Decline of Social Reform*, 2nd ed. (Amherst, NY: Humanity Books, 2000), 122–26.

25. Herbert I. Schiller, *Mass Communications and American Empire* (New York: Kelley, 1969); Chomsky, *Keeping the Rabble in Line*.

26. Becket and Sasson, "The War on Crime as Hegemonic Strategy," 79.

27. Michael J. Lynch, Raymond Michalowski, and W. Byron Groves, *The New Primer in Radical Criminology: Critical Perspectives on Crime, Power, and Identity* (Monsey, NY: Criminal Justice Press, 2000).

28. Rennie, *The Search for Criminal Man*, 274.

29. Paul Koring, "Detentions Cloaked in Secrecy," *Globe and Mail*, November 5, 2001, A6; Neil A. Lewis and David Johnson, "Jubilant Calls on Sept. 11 Led to F.B.I. Arrests," *The New York Times*, October 28, 2001, A1, B9; Craig S. Smith, "Chinese Fight Crime with Torture and Executions," *The New York Times*, September 9, 2001, 1, sec. A; Geoffrey York, "Under the Hammer: No Pity, No Remorse," *Globe and Mail*, November 1, 2001, A17; Strange and Loo, *Making Good*.

30. Jenkins, *Moral Panic*, 4.

31. Steven Box, *Crime, Power and Mystification* (London: Routledge, 1983), 13.

32. Paddy Hillyard, C. Pantazis, Steve Tombs, and D. Gordon, eds., *Beyond Criminology: Taking Harm Seriously* (Black Point, NS: Fernwood, 2004), 30–54.

Further Reading: Christie, Nils, "Dangerous States," in *Dangerous Offenders*, ed. Mark Brown and John Pratt (New York: Routledge, 2000), 181–93; Foucault, Michel, "About the Concept of the 'Dangerous Individual' in 19th Century Legal Psychiatry," *International Journal of Law and Psychiatry* 1 (1978): 1–18; Pratt, John, *Governing the Dangerous* (Leichhardt, New Zealand: Federation Press, 1997); Rennie, Ysabel, *The Search for Criminal Man* (Lexington, MA: Lexington Books, 1978); Shelden, Randall G., *Controlling the Dangerous Classes* (Boston: Allyn and Bacon, 2001).

Matthew G. Yeager

DEATH PENALTY IN THE UNITED STATES

INTRODUCTION

Few issues in criminal justice are as controversial as the death penalty. For most people who support the death penalty, the execution of killers (and people who commit other horrible acts) makes sense. Death penalty supporters frequently state that executions do prevent those executed from committing heinous crimes again and that the example of executions probably prevents most people who might contemplate committing appalling crimes from doing so. In addition, many death penalty supporters simply believe that people who commit such crimes deserve to die, that they have earned their ignominious fate.

For opponents, the death penalty issue is about something else entirely. For many opponents, the level of death penalty support in the United States is a rough estimate of the level of maturity of the American people. The not-so-subtle implication is that a mature, civilized society would not employ the death penalty. Opponents maintain that perpetrators of horrible crimes can be dealt with effectively by other means and that it makes little sense to kill some people, however blameworthy they are, to teach other people not to kill. These opponents argue that although the perpetrators of terrible crimes may deserve severe punishment, that punishment need not be execution. This entry provides a brief history of the penalty's development in the United States.[1]

BACKGROUND

The first person executed in what is now the United States was Capt. George Kendall, a councilor for the Virginia colony. He was executed in 1608 for being a spy for Spain. The fact that he was executed was not particularly unusual because the death penalty was just another one of the punishments brought to the New World by the early European settlers.

Since Kendall's execution in 1608, more than 19,000 executions have been performed in what is now the United States under civil (as opposed to military) authority. This estimate does not include the approximately 10,000 people lynched in the nineteenth century. Nearly all of the people executed during the past four centuries in what is now the United States have been adult men; only about 3 percent have been women. Ninety percent of the women were executed under local, as opposed to state, authority, and the majority (87%) were executed prior to 1866. About 2 percent of the people executed have been juveniles; that is, individuals who committed their capital crimes prior to their 18th birthdays. Most of them (69%) were black, and nearly 90 percent of their victims were white.

KEY EVENTS

It is important to understand that all of the significant changes in the practice of capital punishment in the United States—culminating in its complete abolition in some jurisdictions—are the result of abolitionist efforts. Those efforts created: (1) degrees of murder, which distinguish between murders heinous enough to warrant death and those murders that do not; (2) a reduction in the number of offenses warranting the death penalty (except for the federal government and some states since 1994); (3) the hiding of executions from public view; and (4) a decreased number of annual executions. Although abolition of the death penalty has been their unremitting goal, abolitionists have been far more successful reforming its practice.

Degrees of Murder

Because of the efforts of early death penalty abolitionists Pennsylvania Attorney General and later U.S. Attorney General William Bradford and Philadelphia physician and signer of the Declaration of Independence Benjamin Rush, Pennsylvania became the first state in legal proceedings to consider degrees of murder based on culpability. Before this change, the death penalty was mandated for anyone convicted of murder (and many other crimes), regardless of circumstance. Neither Bradford nor Rush believed that capital punishment deterred crime, citing the example of horse stealing, which at the time was a capital offense in Virginia and the most frequently committed crime in the state. Because of the severity of the penalty, convictions for the crime were hard to obtain.

Limiting Death-Eligible Crimes

Pressure from abolitionists also caused Pennsylvania in 1794 to repeal the death penalty for all crimes except first-degree murder. Between 1794 and 1798, Virginia and Kentucky joined Pennsylvania in abolishing the death penalty for all crimes except first-degree murder; New York and New Jersey abolished the penalty for all crimes except murder and treason. Virginia and Kentucky, both slave states, confined the reforms to free people; slaves in those states were still subject to a long list of capital crimes. When New Jersey, Virginia, and Kentucky severely restricted the scope of capital punishment, they also appropriated funds for the construction of their first prisons; Pennsylvania and New York had established prisons earlier. Still, a half-century would pass before the first state abandoned capital punishment entirely.

Hiding Executions from the Public

Between 1800 and 1850, U.S. death penalty abolitionists helped change public sentiment about public executions, especially among many Northern social elites. Whereas in 1800 public hangings were mostly solemn events regularly attended by members of all social classes and touted as having important educational value, by midcentury, members of the upper classes were staying away from them because in their minds they had become tasteless, shocking, rowdy, sometimes dangerous, carnival-like spectacles. This view, however, may have been more a matter of perception than reality, as eyewitness accounts suggested that decorum at public executions had not changed that much. In any event, the elite began to view those who attended executions as contemptible rabble out for a good time and concluded that any educational value public hangings once had was being lost on the less-respectable crowd.

Another problem with public hangings during this period was that attendees were increasingly sympathizing with the condemned prisoners, weakening the position of the state. Indeed, some of those who met their fate on the gallows became folk heroes. Increasing acceptance of the belief that public executions were counterproductive because of the violence they caused was yet another change. Stories were circulated about the violent crimes being committed just before or just after a pubic hanging by attendees of the event.

For these reasons, Connecticut, in 1830, became the first state to ban public executions. Pennsylvania became the second state to do so in 1834. In both states, only a few authorized officials and the relatives of the condemned were allowed to attend. By 1836, New York, New Jersey, Massachusetts, Rhode Island, and New Hampshire had enacted similar policies. By 1860, all Northern states and Delaware and Georgia in the South had shifted the site of executions from the public square to an enclosed jail yard controlled by the sheriff and deputies. By 1890, some states had moved executions to inside the jail or a prison building. The last public execution was held in Galena, Missouri, in 1937.

From Mandatory to Discretionary Capital Punishment Statutes

In 1837, Tennessee became the first state to enact a discretionary death penalty statute for murder; Alabama did the same four years later, followed by Louisiana five years after that. All states before then employed mandatory death penalty statutes that required anyone convicted of a designated capital crime to be sentenced to death. The reason for the change, at least at first and in the South, undoubtedly was to allow all-white juries to take race into account when deciding whether death was the appropriate penalty in a particular case. Between the Civil War and the end of the nineteenth century, at least twenty additional jurisdictions changed their death penalty laws from mandatory to discretionary ones. Illinois was the first Northern state to do so in 1867; New York was the last state to make the change in 1963. The reason most Northern states switched from mandatory to discretionary death penalty statutes, and another reason for Southern states to do so, was to prevent jury nullification, which was becoming an increasing problem. Jury nullification refers to a jury's knowing and deliberate refusal to apply the law because, in this case, a mandatory death sentence was considered contrary to the jury's sense of justice, morality, or fairness.

From Local to State-Authorized Executions

A major change took place in the legal jurisdiction of executions during the time of the Civil War. Before the war, all executions were conducted locally—generally in the jurisdiction in which the crime was committed—but on January 20, 1864, Sandy Kavanagh was executed at the Vermont State Prison. He was the first person executed under state, as opposed to local, authority. This shift in jurisdiction was not immediately adopted by other states. After Kavanagh, there were only about two state- or federally authorized executions per year well into the 1890s; the rest were locally authorized. That pattern would shift dramatically during the next 30 years. In the 1890s, about 90 percent of executions were imposed under local authority, but by the 1920s, about 90 percent were imposed under state authority. Today, all executions are imposed under state authority, except those conducted in Delaware and Montana and by the federal government and the military.

States Abolish the Death Penalty

In 1846, the state of Michigan abolished the death penalty for all crimes, except treason, and replaced the penalty with life imprisonment. The law took effect the next year, making Michigan, for all intents and purposes, the first English-speaking jurisdiction in the world to abolish capital punishment. The first state to outlaw the death penalty for all crimes, including treason, was Rhode Island, in 1852; Wisconsin was the second state to do so a year later. Not until well after the Civil War did Iowa, in 1872, and Maine, in 1876, become the next states to abolish the death penalty. Legislatures in both states reversed themselves, however, and reinstated the death penalty in 1878, in Iowa, and in 1883, in Maine. Maine reversed itself again in 1887 and abolished capital punishment and, to date, has not reinstated it. Colorado abandoned capital punishment in 1897 but restored it in 1901.

During the first two decades of the twentieth century, six states outlawed capital punishment entirely (Kansas, 1907; Minnesota, 1911; Washington, 1913; Oregon, 1914; South Dakota, 1915; Missouri, 1917), and three states (Tennessee, 1915; North Dakota, 1915; Arizona, 1916) limited the death penalty to only a few rarely committed crimes, such as treason or the first-degree murder of a law enforcement official or prison employee. Tennessee also retained capital punishment for rape. In addition, 17 other states nearly abolished the death penalty or at least seriously considered abolition, some of them several times. The momentum, however, failed to last. By 1920, five of the states that had abolished the death penalty earlier had reinstated it (Arizona, 1918; Missouri, 1919; Tennessee, 1919; Washington, 1919; Oregon, 1920). No state abolished the death penalty between 1918 and 1957. In contrast, after World War II, most of the advanced Western European countries abolished the death penalty or severely restricted its use.

CHALLENGING THE LEGALITY OF CAPITAL PUNISHMENT

Although specific methods of execution had been legally challenged as early as 1890, and procedural issues before that, the fundamental legality of capital punishment itself was not subject to challenge until the 1960s. It had long been argued that the U.S. Constitution, or, more specifically, the Fifth Amendment, authorized capital punishment and that a majority of the framers of the Constitution did not object to it. Given such evidence, it made little sense to argue that capital punishment violated the Constitution. That conventional wisdom was challenged in 1961. In an article published in the *University of Southern California Law Review,* Los Angeles lawyer Gerald Gottlieb, an affiliate with his local American Civil Liberties Union (ACLU) branch, suggested that "the death penalty was unconstitutional under the Eighth Amendment because it violated contemporary moral standards, what the U.S. Supreme Court in *Trop v. Dulles* (1958) referred to as 'the evolving standards of decency that mark the progress of a maturing society.'" The key question raised by Gottlieb's interpretation, of course, was whether the United States, in fact, had evolved or progressed to the point at which standards of decency no longer permitted capital punishment. For a small group of abolitionist lawyers with the NAACP Legal Defense and Educational Fund (LDF), the answer was yes.

LDF lawyers turned their attention to the death penalty in the 1960s primarily because of the racially discriminatory way it was being administered. Later, however, when they began accepting clients actually facing execution, they realized that they needed to raise issues having nothing to do with race. With this change in focus, there was no longer any reason not to take on the cases of white death row inmates, too, so they did. In attempting to achieve judicial abolition of the penalty, LDF lawyers plotted a general strategy to convince the Supreme Court that the death penalty was employed in a discriminatory way against minorities and to otherwise block all executions by challenging the legal procedures employed in capital cases (the so-called moratorium strategy). If successful, their plan would accomplish three goals. First, it would make those who were still executed appear to be unlucky losers in a death penalty lottery. Second, if the death penalty were used only rarely, it would show that the penalty was not really needed for society's protection. Third, if all executions were blocked, the resulting logjam of death row inmates would lead to an inevitable bloodbath if states ever began emptying their death rows by executing en masse. The LDF lawyers did not believe the country could stomach the gore and would demand abolition of the penalty.

The LDF's moratorium strategy worked. In 1968, executions in the United States were unofficially suspended until some of the more problematic issues with the death penalty could be resolved. The moratorium on executions would last 10 years until 1977, when Gary Gilmore requested to be executed by the state of Utah.

LEGAL DECISIONS BY THE U.S. SUPREME COURT

Furman v. Georgia

On January 17, 1972, Furman's lawyers argued to the Supreme Court that unfettered jury discretion in imposing death for murder resulted in arbitrary or capricious sentencing in violation of their client's Fourteenth Amendment right to due process and his Eighth Amendment right not to be subjected to cruel and unusual punishment. Furman's challenge proved successful, and, on June 29, 1972, the U.S. Supreme Court set aside death sentences for the first time in its history. In its decision in *Furman v. Georgia, Jackson v. Georgia,* and *Branch v. Texas* (all three cases were consolidated and are referred to here as the *Furman* decision), the Court held that the capital punishment statutes in the three cases were unconstitutional because they gave the jury complete discretion to decide whether to impose the death penalty or a lesser punishment in capital cases. The majority of five justices pointed out that the death penalty had been imposed arbitrarily, infrequently, and often selectively against minorities. A practical effect of *Furman* was the Supreme Court's voiding of 40 death penalty statutes and the sentences of more than six hundred death row inmates in 32 states. Depending on the state, the death row inmates received new sentences of life imprisonment, a term of years, or, in a few cases, new trials.

It is important to note that the Court did not declare the death penalty itself unconstitutional. It held as unconstitutional only the statutes under which the death penalty was then being administered. The Court implied that if the process of applying the death penalty could be changed to eliminate the problems cited in *Furman,* then it would pass constitutional muster.

The backlash against *Furman* was immediate and widespread. Many people, including those who had never given the death penalty issue much thought, were incensed at what they perceived as the Supreme Court's arrogance in ignoring the will of the majority and its elected representatives. They clamored to have the penalty restored. Obliging their constituents, the elected representatives of 36 states proceeded to adopt new death penalty statutes designed to meet the Court's objections. The new death penalty laws took two forms. Twenty-two states removed all discretion from the process by mandating capital punishment upon conviction for certain crimes (mandatory death penalty statutes). Other states provided specific guidelines that judges and juries were to use in deciding if death were the appropriate sentence in a particular case (guided discretion death penalty statutes).

Woodson v. North Carolina *and* Gregg v. Georgia

The constitutionality of the new death penalty statutes was quickly challenged, and on July 2, 1976, the Supreme Court announced its rulings in five test cases. In *Woodson v. North Carolina* and *Roberts v. Louisiana,* the Court voted five to four to reject mandatory statutes that automatically imposed death sentences for defined capital crimes. Justice Potter Stewart provided the Court's rationale. First, Stewart admitted that "it is capricious to treat similar things differently" and that mandatory death penalty statutes eliminated that problem. He added, however, that it also "is capricious to treat two different things the same way." Therefore, to impose the same penalty on all convicted murderers, even though all defendants are different, is just as capricious as imposing a penalty randomly. To alleviate the problem, then, some sentencing guidelines were necessary. Thus, in *Gregg v. Georgia, Jurek v. Texas,* and *Proffitt v. Florida* (hereafter referred to as the *Gregg* decision), the Court voted seven to two to approve guided discretion statutes that set standards for juries and judges to use when deciding whether to impose the death penalty. The Court's majority concluded that the guided discretion statutes struck a reasonable balance between giving the jury some direction and allowing it to consider the defendant's background and character and the circumstances of the crime.

It is noteworthy that the Court approved the guided discretion statutes on faith, assuming that the new statutes and their procedural reforms would rid the death penalty's administration of the problems cited in *Furman*. Because guided discretion statutes, automatic appellate review, and proportionality review had never been required or employed before in death penalty cases, the Court could not have known whether they would make a difference. Now, more than thirty years later, it is possible to evaluate the results. A large body of evidence indicates that the reforms have had negligible effects.

Coker v. Georgia *and* Eberheart v. Georgia

The Supreme Court has repeatedly emphasized that the death penalty should be reserved for the most heinous crimes. In two cases decided in 1977, the Court, for all intents and purposes, limited the death penalty to only aggravated or capital murders. Aggravated or capital murders are murders committed with an aggravating circumstance or circumstances. Aggravating circumstances (or factors) or special circumstances, as they are called in some jurisdictions, refer "to the particularly serious features of a case, for example, evidence of extensive premeditation and planning by the defendant, or torture of the victim by the defendant." At least one aggravating circumstance must be proven beyond a reasonable doubt before a death sentence can be imposed. (To date, all post-*Furman* executions have been for aggravated murder.) The Court ruled in *Coker v. Georgia* that the death penalty is not warranted for the crime of rape of an adult woman in cases in which the victim is not killed. Likewise, in *Eberheart v. Georgia,* the Court held that the death penalty is not warranted for the crime of kidnapping in cases in which the victim is not killed. Traditionally, both rape and kidnapping have been capital crimes, regardless of whether the victim died.

Lockett v. Ohio *and* Bell v. Ohio

One of the changes to death penalty statutes approved by the Court in *Gregg* was the requirement that sentencing authorities (either juries or judges) consider mitigating circumstances before determining the sentence. Mitigating circumstances (or factors), or extenuating circumstances, refer "to features of a case that explain or particularly justify the defendant's behavior, even though they do not provide a defense to the crime of murder" (e.g., youth, immaturity, or being under the influence of another person). The requirement that mitigating circumstances must be considered has been the subject of several challenges. The first test was in 1978 in the cases of *Lockett v. Ohio* and *Bell v. Ohio*. In those cases, one of the issues was whether defense attorneys could present only mitigating circumstances that were listed in the death penalty statute. The Court held that trial courts must consider any mitigating circumstances that a defense attorney presents, not just those listed in the statute. The only qualification to this requirement is that the mitigating circumstance must be supported by evidence.

Pulley v. Harris

In *Pulley v. Harris* (1984), the Court decided that there was no constitutional obligation for state appellate courts to provide, upon request, proportionality review of death sentences. Since *Pulley*, many states have eliminated the proportionality review requirement from their statutes, whereas other states simply no longer conduct the reviews.

Lockhart v. McCree

In *Lockhart v. McCree* (1986), the Court ruled that prospective jurors whose opposition to the death penalty is so strong that it would prevent or substantially impair the performance of their duties as jurors at the sentencing phase of the trial may be removed for cause. Stated differently, as long as jurors can perform their duties as required by law, they may not be removed for cause because they are generally opposed to the death penalty. To date, *Lockhart v. McCree* is the latest modification to the Court's earlier *Witherspoon* decision. In *Witherspoon v. Illinois* (1968), the Court rejected the common practice of excusing prospective jurors simply because they were opposed to capital punishment. The Court held that prospective jurors could be excused only for cause. That is, jurors could be excused only if they would automatically vote against imposition of the death penalty, regardless of the evidence presented at trial, or if their attitudes toward capital punishment prevented them from making an impartial decision on the defendant's guilt.

McCleskey v. Kemp

The most sweeping challenge to the constitutionality of the new death penalty statutes was *McCleskey v. Kemp* (1987), wherein the Court considered evidence of racial discrimination in the application of Georgia's death penalty statute. Recall that in the *Furman* decision, racial discrimination was cited as one of the problems with the pre-*Furman* statutes. The most compelling evidence was the results of an elaborate statistical analysis of post-*Furman* death penalty cases in Georgia. That analysis showed that Georgia's new statute produced a pattern of racial discrimination based on both the race of the offender and the race of the victim. In *McCleskey*, the Court opined that evidence such as the statistical analysis—which showed a pattern of racial discrimination—is not enough to render the death penalty unconstitutional. By a vote of five to four, it held that state death penalty statutes are constitutional even when statistics indicate they have been applied in racially biased ways. The Court ruled that racial discrimination must be shown in individual cases—something McCleskey did not show in his case. For death penalty opponents, the *McCleskey* case represented the best, and perhaps last, chance of having the Supreme Court again declare the death penalty unconstitutional.

Atkins v. Virginia

In *Atkins v. Virginia* (2002), the Court ruled that it is cruel and unusual punishment to execute the mentally retarded. A problem with the *Atkins* decision is that the Court did not set a standard for what constitutes mental retardation. That issue was left to the states to decide.

Roper v. Simmons

In *Roper v. Simmons* (2005), the Court held that the Eighth and Fourteenth Amendments forbid the imposition of the death penalty on offenders who were under the age of 18 at the time their crimes were committed.

FUTURE PROSPECTS

Globally, the death penalty is trending toward abolition. As of this writing, more than half of the countries in the world—125 of them—have abolished the death penalty in law or practice. All of the major U.S. allies except Japan have abolished the death penalty. On the other hand, only 71 countries and territories have retained the death penalty; however, the number of countries that actually execute anyone in a given year is much smaller.

During 2005, at least 2,148 prisoners were executed in 22 countries. China, Iran, Saudi Arabia, and the United States accounted for 94 percent of the known executions in 2005, with China estimated to have executed about 82 percent of the total.

In the United States, 14 jurisdictions do not have a death penalty, and among the 39 jurisdictions that do have one, only a handful of them use it more than occasionally, and almost all of them are located geographically in the South. More than 70 percent of all post-*Furman* executions have occurred in the South. Still, executions are more concentrated than the 70 percent figure suggests. Five states—Texas, Virginia, Oklahoma, Missouri, and Florida—account for 65 percent of all post-*Furman* executions; three states—Texas, Virginia, and Oklahoma—account for 53 percent of them; Texas and Virginia account for 45 percent of them; and Texas, alone, accounts for 36 percent of them. Thus, the death penalty today is a criminal sanction that is used more than occasionally in only a few non-Western countries, a few states in the U.S. South, and two U.S. border states. This is an important point because it raises the question of why those death penalty—or more precisely, executing—jurisdictions in the world need the death penalty, whereas all other jurisdictions in the world—the vast majority—do not.

In the states noted previously, the death penalty has proved stubbornly resilient and will probably remain a legal sanction for the foreseeable future. One reason is that death penalty support among the U.S. public, at least according to the major opinion polls, remains relatively strong. According to a 2006 Gallup poll, for example, 65 percent of adult Americans favored the death penalty for persons convicted of murder, 28 percent opposed it, and 7 percent did not know or refused to respond. It is unlikely that the practice of capital punishment could be sustained if a majority of U.S. citizens were to oppose it. However, in no year for which polls are available has a majority of Americans opposed the death penalty (the first national death penalty opinion poll was conducted in December 1936).

The abiding faith of death penalty proponents in the ability of legislatures and courts to fix any problems with the administration of capital punishment is another reason for its continued use in some places. However, the three-decade record of fine-tuning the death penalty process remains ongoing. Legislatures and courts are having a difficult time "getting it right," despite spending inordinate amounts of their resources trying.

Many people support capital punishment even though they are ignorant about the subject. It is assumed by abolitionists that if people were educated about capital punishment, most of them would oppose it. Unfortunately, research suggests that educating the public about the death penalty may not have the effect abolitionists' desire. Although information about the death penalty can reduce support for the sanction—sometimes significantly—rarely is the support reduced to less than a majority, and the reduction in support may be only temporary.

Two major factors seem to sustain death penalty support in the United States: (1) the desire for vindictive revenge and (2) the symbolic value it has for politicians and law enforcement officials. In a recent Gallup poll, 50 percent of all respondents who favored the death penalty provided retributive reasons for their support: 37 percent replied "An eye for an eye/They took a life/Fits the crime," and another 13 percent volunteered "They deserve it." The reasons offered by the next largest group of death penalty proponents (by only 11% each) were "Save taxpayers money/Cost associated with prison" and "Deterrent for potential crimes/Set an example." No other reasons were given by more than 10 percent of the death penalty proponents.

The choice of "An eye for an eye" has been called *vindictive revenge* because of its strong emotional component. Research shows that the public supports the death penalty primarily for vindictive revenge. Those who responded "An eye for any eye" want to repay the offender in kind for what he or she has done. Research also shows that people who support the death penalty for vindictive revenge are generally resistant to reasoned persuasion. That is, they are less likely to change their position on the death penalty when confronted with compelling evidence that contradicts their beliefs.

Politicians continue to use support for the death penalty as a symbol of their toughness on crime. Politicians who oppose capital punishment are invariably considered soft on crime. Criminal justice officials and much of the public often equate support for capital punishment with support for law enforcement in general. It is ironic that although capital punishment has virtually no effect on crime, the death penalty continues to be a favored political silver bullet—a simplistic solution to the crime problem used by aspiring politicians and law enforcement officials. In sum, although the global trend is toward abolishing the death penalty, pockets of resistance in the United States remain and will be difficult to change.

See Also: Cruel and Unusual Punishment; Executions—Televised.

Endnote

1. Sources for all material in this entry may be found in Robert M. Bohm, *Deathquest III: An Introduction to the Theory and Practice of Capital Punishment in the United States,* 3rd ed. (Cincinnati, OH: Anderson, 2007).

Further Reading: Acker, James R., Robert M. Bohm, and Charles S. Lanier, eds., *America's Experiment with Capital Punishment: Reflections on the Past, Present and Future of the Ultimate Penal Sanction,* 2nd ed. (Durham, NC: Carolina Academic Press, 2003); Banner, Stuart, *The Death Penalty: An American History* (Cambridge, MA: Harvard University Press, 2002); Bedau, Hugo, and Paul Cassell, eds., *Debating the Death Penalty: Should America Have Capital Punishment?* (New York: Oxford University Press, 2004); Bohm, Robert M., *Deathquest III: An Introduction to the Theory and Practice of Capital Punishment in the United States,* 3rd ed. (Cincinnati, OH: Anderson, 2007); Haney, Craig, *Death by Design: Capital Punishment as a Social Psychological System* (New York: Oxford University Press, 2005).

Robert M. Bohm

DEFINING CRIMINAL VIOLENCE

INTRODUCTION

One fundamental and yet quiet controversy in the study of crime and justice revolves around the definition of violence in general and of what constitutes criminal violence in particular. Why are some acts of violence defined as illegal, criminal, or otherwise, whereas other acts of violence, even more harmful or injurious, are sanctioned as legitimate, ethical, or moral? Stated differently, people disagree about what acts should or should not be covered as criminal violence by the fields of criminology and criminal justice. This entry explores the different ways in which violence is defined as criminal as well as the different ways in which violence is defined as noncriminal.

BACKGROUND

The study of criminal violence or violent crime, whether in the social and behavioral sciences or in the academic arenas of legal jurisprudence, typically defines the subject matter according to the dictates of the criminal law. So as a starting point for our discussion and in order to contextualize the legal from the social definitions of violence, we turn to the narrow or restrictive definition of criminal violence as defined by the *Uniform Crime Reports.*

UNIFORM CRIME REPORT DEFINITIONS OF VIOLENT CRIME[1]

Murder and nonnegligent manslaughter is the willful (nonnegligent) killing of one human being by another.

The Uniform Crime Report Program does not include the following situations in this offense classification: deaths caused by negligence, suicide, or accident; justifiable homicides; and attempts to murder or assaults to murder, which are scored as aggravated assaults.

Aggravated assault is an unlawful attack by one person upon another for the purpose of inflicting severe or aggravated bodily injury. The Program further specifies that this type of assault is usually accompanied by the use of a weapon or by other means likely to produce death or great bodily harm. Attempted aggravated assault that involves the display of—or threat to use—a gun, knife, or other weapon is included in this crime category because serious personal injury would likely result if the assault were completed. When aggravated assault and larceny-theft occur together, the offense falls under the category of robbery.

Forcible rape is the carnal knowledge of a female forcibly and against her will. Assaults and attempts to commit rape by force or threat of force are also included; however, statutory rape (without force) and other sex offenses are excluded.

Robbery is the taking or attempting to take anything of value from the care, custody, or control of a person or persons by force or threat of force or violence and/or by putting the victim in fear.

DEFINING VIOLENCE

Violence is often viewed as a matter of common sense. In many respects, its definition is not unlike the definition that we use in defining pornography. It is often defined, as you know it when you see it. But the commonsense understandings are time and culture bounded. Certainly, what we define as pornography today is much more graphic than what was considered pornography during the nineteenth century antivice crusades in the United States. Similarly, our definitions of violence have changed over time. At the same time, there are definitions that support the status quo and definitions that challenge the status quo.

Take the example of violence that is committed by governments. The 1934 version of the *Encyclopedia of the Social Sciences* defined violence as "the illegal employment of methods of physical coercion for personal or group ends."[2] By this definition, the state or government could not be violent. The violence of genocide in Nazi Germany would not be defined as violence by this definition of the time. Today, the International Criminal Court and other courts in other countries are trying states and the leaders for the violence of genocide. The United States has been most resistant to allow this court as well as the previous world court to define the violence of states and their leaders as criminal violence. Nevertheless, there are increasing cases taking place between these courts that are redefining our conceptualization of violence.

Nevertheless, in most places, both laws and texts primarily recognize as violence only those forms that come under some type of legal jurisdiction. As a result, the focus, discussion, and policy of these traditional, classical, or culturally bound definitions of violence are directed at those forms of violence that represent the smallest amount of violence that occurs throughout the world. Additionally, most treatments of violence are typically conceived of in sociopsychological or interpersonal terms, with individuals the primary perpetrators.[3] At the same time, these forms of violence are divorced from their institutional and structural roots. In other words, violence is reduced to the actions of individuals or small groups; state (i.e., governmental), corporate-based actions, or violence that is an outcome of the distribution of scarcities within a society are precluded from examination.

Others with a more critical or inclusive definition of violence such as S. J. Ball-Rokeach have defined violence as a product of the hierarchical arrangements of society. She defined violence as "a struggle to maintain, change, or protest asymmetric social relations governing the distribution of scarce resources, by the threat or exertion of physical force."[4] Peter Iadicola and Anson Shupe broadened the scope of what we define as violence beyond this interpersonal basis in defining violence "as any action or structural arrangement that results in physical or nonphysical harm to one or more persons."[5] They further elaborated the definition by describing six additional qualifiers.

First, actions or social relationships based on structural arrangements that result in harmful outcomes must be willfully or deliberately committed or condoned by an actor or agent of the actor. This precludes the accidental death or injury that is by definition not willfully committed. Second, as a corollary to the first point, violence can be intended or not intended by the actor. In this case the action is willed; however, violence is not the intention of the action. This includes the category of action that is legally defined as manslaughter. Here the action that causes the harm is willful but the harm is not intended. Much of what is considered to be corporate violence would fall under this category. An example is the disaster at Bhopal, India, in 1987 in which thousands died as a result of lack of safety and training of maintenance staff at the Union Carbide plant there. Certainly the owners and management who willfully neglected the safety conditions of the plant did not intend to kill the residents in the neighborhoods surrounding the plant; nevertheless, the action of the owners and management that allowed the unsafe conditions to persist would be considered violence under this definition.

Third, the violence may be justified or unjustified. Judgments that actions are unjustifiably or justifiably violent depend on whose interests are at stake or who stands to lose or gain by the violence. Justifiability is the most negotiable of meanings for violent actions. Thus, violence by police officers to thwart a criminal who endangers the lives of themselves or others is defined to be justifiable. Even in this area, however, the rules regarding police use of violence have undergone changes over time. One example of changes in the categorization of violence as justifiable or not is the case of the fleeing felon laws that allow police and civilians in many jurisdictions to use violence to prevent escape of those who are suspected of committing a felony. In recent years, increasing restrictions have been placed on the application of fleeing felon laws. The U.S. Supreme Court ruling in *Tennessee v. Garner* limited the law by restricting it to nonlethal force in most cases. The justices held that deadly force "may not be used unless necessary to prevent the escape and the officer has probable cause to believe that the suspect poses a significant threat of death or serious physical injury to the officer or others."[6]

War violence is often justified to defend the nation. In some cases, however, like the most recent case of the war to overthrow the Iraqi government, the justification can come into question. Was the violence to overthrow the Saddam

Hussein regime justifiable? Is it a violation of law? Will the United States and the leaders of the country be tried as war criminals? Given the power of the regime in control in United States government, it is unlikely that this violence will be defined to be unjustified and illegal. However, would that be the case with other governments that commit such action in self-defense? Saddam Hussein also used the claims of self-defense in the invasion of Kuwait that sparked the first Persian Gulf War and 10 years of economic sanctions and U.S. and British control over two-thirds of the nation. Certainly, the most recent invasion of Iraq that toppled its government raised questions of legality by current and previous secretaries-general of the United Nations. Both Kofi Annan, the then secretary-general of the United Nations (UN), and former Secretary-General Boutros Boutros-Ghali, publicly stated that the attack violated international law as a war of aggression because it lacked the necessary UN Security Council resolution to authorize military force and was not an act of defense and violated the UN charter. The George W. Bush administration argues that the UN Security Council resolutions authorizing the 1991 invasion to liberate Kuwait from Iraqi forces, in addition to Resolution 1441, gave legal authority to use "all necessary means," which is diplomatic code for going to war. But the definitions of this violence, which mounts into the hundreds of thousands of lost lives, could be redefined.

Furthermore, whether it is justified is often determined in part as a result of who is the victor in the conflict. Would the violence used by Saddam Hussein against the Kurdish minority be deemed justifiable if he were not overthrown in the attack of the United States on Iraq in 2003? During the time of Saddam's violent response to the Kurdish minority who were engaged in rebellious activity against the Iraqi government, there was little public outcry from the United States government during the Ronald Reagan presidency.

Fourth, violence and its harmful effects address both physical and psychological well-being. Most definitions of violence recognize that violence does not involve only physical harm. What unites these two forms of well-being is that the safety and security of the person is damaged or threatened to the point of impairing the individual from action that is beneficial to their well-being. One area of controversy as it relates to the nature of harm is that of rape. Most criminal law requires that violence or a threat of violence must be present for forcible rape to occur. But how much of a threat and how much force is necessary for it to be criminal violence?

Fifth, there is the issue of perception or awareness. For violence to exist, must it be recognized as violence by either the recipient of the action, the actor, or both? Iadicola and Shupe note that certain forms of violence may be so integral to the structure of society and the functioning of its institutions that they may not be recognized as violence per se. For example, in the antebellum South, slavery itself was not considered violence, yet by today's standards as defined by national and international law it is violence and it is criminal.

Sixth, the proposed definition of violence is universal as opposed to a relative definition of violence. Whether an act is considered violent in one society or another is certainly relevant as it relates to criminal definitions; however, it is violent nevertheless. Again, take the example of spouse abuse or marital rape.

In most countries in the world today, these acts are not considered to be acts of violence or crime. Nevertheless, harm is done and therefore it is violence.

SPHERES OF VIOLENCE

Where does violence occur? Under what social contexts does violence occur? These contexts can be understood as representing different interactional spheres. We can talk about the interpersonal context or sphere, the institutional context or sphere, and the structural context or sphere. By the context or sphere of violence we are not specifically addressing the cause of the violence. In the sense that the context describes the rules of behavior of actors, however, it is accordingly part of an explanation of the cause of violence. So the institutional context of a soldier or law enforcement officer committing an act of violence against a defined enemy or criminal may in part explain the cause of the action. Similarly, in the institutional context of a corporate officer who decides to authorize a product that he or she knows to be unsafe, the context describes the expectations of behavior of actors that are part of an explanation of the cause of violence. All violence takes place in social contexts.

Interpersonal violence is violence that occurs between people acting outside the role of agent or representative of a social institution. The violence between gangs, violence between strangers as a result of road rage, violence resulting from an altercation between bar patrons, and a mugging or robbery are all examples of interpersonal violence. Neither the offender nor victim is acting in a violent manner to fulfill the expectations or role of a position within an organization or institution.

Institutional violence, on the other hand, is violence that occurs by the action of societal institutions and their agents. Institutional violence is violence by individuals whose actions are governed by the roles that they are playing in an institutional context. For sociologists, institutions represent a collective response to common problems in the society. They are organizational mechanisms to solve problems that all members of the society confront. Sociologists recognize five important institutions in society: economy, polity, family, education, and religion. The violence that occurs within a family between parents and children and husbands and wives are examples of institutional violence. In all cases, the actors are responding to their position and the expectations of their position in the context of the family organization and institution. The violence of police and military is another example of institutional violence. The actors are acting in the context of their institutional role within these organizations. Officers of corporations who neglect the safety hazards of the workplaces they are responsible for managing, hide the defects of products their organization is producing, or overlook the dumping of hazardous wastes into a community's environment are also examples of institutional violence.

Structural violence is violence that occurs in the context of establishing, maintaining, extending, or reducing the hierarchical ordering of categories of people in a society. The violence of slavery, the violence of discrimination that results in the denial of resources needed for a healthy existence, or the violence that serves to displace a population from needed resources for their survival are all examples of structural violence. In all cases, the violence is occurring in the context of hierarchical relations, in class, gender, ethnic, or age systems of stratification.

Although we can think of each of the spheres of violence as conceptually distinct, in reality there is a great deal of overlap between them. For example structural violence can also be institutional, as in the case of the violence of empires in which warfare and state terrorism may be used to establish or maintain hierarchical relations between an imperial center and its colonial and neo-colonial possessions. The violence sponsored by the United States government to overthrow the governments of Nicaragua and Afghanistan in the 1980s and violence of the U.S.-trained and funded Guatemalan military in the 1980s that killed and displaced large numbers of the indigenous population in Guatemala are examples of the overlap of state (institutional) and structural violence. Much of the corporate violence that occurs in the world today is also structural in that the victims of the violence are most likely the poorest populations, and therefore the violence serves to maintain their structural position. There are also overlaps between interpersonal and structural violence as in the case of the violence of what are referred to as hate crimes.

VIOLENCE THAT IS CRIMINAL

The scope of violence is very large in a given society or the world as a whole. Those who study violence recognize, however, that only a small portion of these acts is defined as criminal. So what qualities of the acts of violence define their criminality?

The first qualification that determines whether an act is considered to be criminal violence is that there must be a law that defines the acts as illegal. Furthermore, the law has to exist prior to the occurrence of the act for it to be defined as criminal; however, this is not always the case. The action of the United States government in the passage of the Military Commission Act of 2006 (S. 3930) allows for acts of torture that would be defined as illegal by U.S. and international law that occurred prior to this law to be exempt from prosecution. Section 8 of this law exempts from prosecution acts that would be prosecutable nationally and internationally back to 1997, nine years prior to the passage of the law.[7]

Furthermore, in accordance with the International Criminal Court, violation of international law, such as the law against genocide, can take precedence to national law. If a state does not prohibit the actions of government to commit acts of violence, it still may be defined as crime and be prosecuted by this international body. This may also be the case for economic violence. The United Nations Convention against Transnational Organized Crime opens the door to prosecution of corporations who participate in harmful actions internationally. The U.S. government has yet to ratify this convention. Furthermore, whether violence is recognized to be criminal violence may vary from legal jurisdiction to jurisdiction and over time. The violence in the Darfur region of Sudan is hardly recognized to be criminal by the actions of the Sudanese government. Yet the international community through the United Nations has sought to take action to investigate the criminal nature of these acts of violence through the International Criminal Court. Unfortunately, the U.S. government has vetoed such proposals. Is the violence occurring there criminal if the government that has jurisdiction does not act to define the violence as criminal and act to stop it? Is it criminal violence if the international courts do not try offenders. The case of the violence in Sudan is in many ways reminiscent of the genocidal violence that occurred in Rwanda that was later defined to be criminal internationally after the carnage had taken place.

So which acts of violence are defined as the most deserving of the label *criminal* by criminal justice agencies in the United States? The United States Department of Justice lists the violent crimes that the federal government claims pose the greatest threat in its annual statistics as murder and nonnegligent manslaughter, aggravated assault, forcible rape, and robbery. Furthermore, the determination as to whether the acts of violence have occurred according to the government's statistics is determined by the police in the various jurisdictions that report this information in the annual survey conducted by the Department of Justice. It is important to note that not all jurisdictions report; it is estimated that approximately 2 percent to 3 percent do not. Furthermore, in recent years for jurisdictions in the state of Illinois, valid statistics for the most serious crimes were available only for agencies in cities of 100,000 or more people. The smaller jurisdictions with less than 100,000 population had to be statistically estimated. For these smaller agencies, the only available counts generated by the Illinois State Program were totals based upon an incident level without indication of multiple offenses recorded within single incidents.

This raises another important point to note regarding the federal government's statistics on violent crime. The Department of Justice's Uniform Crime Report uses a hierarchical rule when there are multiple offenses. What this means is that if an offender commits multiple crimes during the same period of criminal behavior under investigation, only the most serious is counted. For example, if a person rapes his victim and then subsequently kills her, only the murder will be recorded. This rule systematically creates an underestimation of the actual occurrence of violence. Nevertheless, in the case of the 2005 statistics and the state of Illinois, the number of reported violent crimes was adjusted by reducing the number of offenses in the jurisdictions with less than 100,000 population by the proportion of multiple offenses reported within single incidents in the National Incident-Based Reporting System database.

Another important qualification of the Uniform Crime Report statistics is that it is based only on police reporting of violent crime. Given that the majority of crime in general and a large portion, up to half in some types of violent crime, are never reported to the police or if police discretion determined that the act was not criminal or a formal response was not warranted, this also compromises the accuracy of the government statistics as a measure of violent crime.

In addition to the discretion of the police in law enforcement, how the act is then recorded by the local policing jurisdiction is another factor that may influence whether the act is recognized. A last step in the process of defining whether criminal violence has occurred is determined by the prosecuting attorney and the courts. This information is not found in the Uniform Crime Report's estimate of the amount of violent crime in the nation. Thus, when violent crime has been reported, registered under the arrest statistics, and reported by the jurisdiction to the Department of Justice in its annual survey, it is recorded as a violent crime even when there is no conviction. So, if a person is arrested for forcible rape but is later found to be innocent, the act would still be listed as part of that jurisdiction's rape statistics. Even in the case of murder, there are convictions when there is no dead body, which raises questions about the certainty of the occurrence of the act. So what is criminal violence and how much is occurring in the nation is not as clear-cut as simple acts that are defined as a violation of criminal law.

VIOLENCE THAT IS NOT CRIMINAL

The forms of violence that are institutional or structural are least likely to be defined as violent. The violence of priests who sexually abuse minors, the corporate officials who are responsible for neglecting safety conditions of a mine that leads to the death of mine workers after having been repeatedly fined for previous violations, government officials who authorize and those who carry out assassinations, torture, and illegal wars are examples of the forms of violence that are least likely to be criminalized in the present as well as in the past. With few exceptions (changes in the law and law enforcement in the areas of family violence are exceptions), the violence of institutional actors are least likely to be defined as violent. The violence that results from structural relations within the world that condones slavery; child labor; extremes in inequality in the distribution of food, clean water, and sanitation; and health resources that lead to gross differences in mortality rates and life expectancies throughout the world are also least likely to be defined as criminal violence. Why? Is it an issue of less harm? The estimate of the carnage of the violence that is institutional and structural far exceeds any estimate of the forms of violence that are defined as criminal.

Or is it an issue of who is more likely to be harmed? The overwhelming dominant pattern as to who is the offender and who is the victim in the case of these excluded forms of violence is that those who are the least powerful are most likely to be the victim, and the offender is more likely to be in positions of power. Is this the same with the forms of violence that are criminalized? It is not as clear-cut. Although the violence that is criminalized and prosecuted is certainly, as in the previous cases, more likely to be directed at those who are least powerful, the offender is also least likely to have much power beyond the power over the victim in committing the act of violence. Thus, when the offender has little power, these actions are most likely to be defined as criminal violence.

Furthermore, which acts of criminal violence would be defined as the most serious and with the more serious penal response? It is when the victim is in a position of power or relatively powerless. The vast majority of states and the federal government have laws that reserve the most severe punishment to those who kill officials of the state or commit acts of treason that threaten the power of the state. In other institutional spheres, is violence more likely to be identified and punished if those who are in positions of power within the organizations are the victims? Would a crime of homicide be more likely pursued if the victim was a powerful member of the community than if the victim was a more powerless member of the community? Thus, the story of criminal violence is one in which those who are least powerful are more likely to be the offender and one in which those who are least powerful are, for the most part, also the victim. However, those violent acts that are most serious are those in which the victim is in a position of power.

What determines whether violence is criminal is not the harm nor even the law; it is how those with the power to define it as violence and the power to act upon that definition define it. Thus, the controversy as to what is crime or, more specifically, what acts of violence are defined as criminal ultimately is a question of power. Those criminologists or criminal justice professionals who limit their definitions of crime and violence to only those acts that are recognized by those with power to define these acts as criminal violence act to support the organization and distribution of power or status quo that is responsible for ultimately defining the law and criminal violence and the nature of law enforcement and prosecution. Ultimately, the question of what is violence and crime is a political question that cannot be avoided.

FUTURE PROSPECTS

Certainly, the trend driven in part by social movements (such as the environmental movement, the antiglobalization movement, the women's movement, and so on) and by the efforts of the United Nations to establish international law to control the incidence of institutional violence and the means to prosecute elites through a court system is that additional types of violence will be criminalized. What we consider violence today will be expanded dramatically. There have been efforts to slow this movement. For example, the United States has failed to ratify and has actively resisted participation of allied states in the International Criminal Court. The record of the United States since the Reagan administration has not been in the forefront of ratifying human rights conventions developed by the United Nations. The United States has failed to ratify such conventions as the International Covenant on Economic, Social and Cultural Rights; the Convention on the Elimination of All Forms of Discrimination against Women; and the Convention on the Rights of the Child. Furthermore, the United States government has failed to ratify most of the major International Labor Organization conventions protecting workers rights. Nevertheless, given this trend in increasing the numbers of international laws, criminal justice professionals and criminologists will increasingly be investigating patterns of violence that are presently not defined as crime.

See Also: Crime and Culture Consumption; Domestic Violence Practices; Prison Violence in the Caribbean.

Endnotes

1. Federal Bureau of Investigation, *Crime in the United States 2005,* U.S. Department of Justice (September 2006), http://www.fbi.gov/ucr/05cius/.
2. Sidney Hook, "Violence," in *Encyclopedia of Social Sciences,* ed. R. A. Seligman and Alvin Johnson (New York: Macmillan, 1934), 15: 264–67.
3. See Albert J. Reiss and Jeffrey A. Roth, eds., *Panel on the Understanding and Control of Violent Behavior* (Washington, DC: National Academies Press, National Research Council, 1993); M. Riedel and W. Welsh, *Criminal Violence: Patterns, Causes, and Prevention* (Los Angeles: Roxbury, 2001); Neil Alan Weiner, Margaret A. Zahn, and Rita J. Sagi, *Violence: Patterns, Causes, and Public Policy* (New York: Harcourt Brace Jovanovich, 1990), xiii.
4. S. J. Ball-Rokeach, "Normative and Deviant Violence from a Conflict Perspective," *Social Problems* 28 (1980): 51.
5. Peter Iadicola and Anson Shupe, *Violence, Inequality, and Human Freedom* (Lanham, MD: Rowman and Littlefield, 2003), 12.
6. *Tennessee v. Garner,* 471 U.S. I (1985).
7. Edward S. Herman, "Torture, Moral Values, and Leadership of the Free World," *Z Magazine,* November 2006, 27–30.

Further Reading: Arendt, Hannah, *On Violence* (New York: Harcourt, Brace, and World, 1969); Barak, Gregg, *Violence and Nonviolence: Pathways to Understanding* (Thousand Oaks, CA: Sage, 2003); Iadicola, Peter, and Anson Shupe, *Violence, Inequality, and Human Freedom* (Lanham, MD: Rowman and Littlefield, 2003); Riedel, Marc, and Wayne Welsh, *Criminal Violence: Patterns, Causes, and Prevention,* 2nd ed. (Los Angeles: Roxbury, 2006); Zahn, Margaret A., Henry H. Brownstein, and Shelly L. Jackson, *Violence: From Theory to Research* (Dayton, OH: LexisNexis, 2004).

Peter Iadicola

DISENFRANCHISEMENT LAWS FOR FELONIES

INTRODUCTION

At the center of the controversy surrounding felony disenfranchisement laws is the debate between the desire to punish and deter crime versus a desire to promote and protect civil liberties. Currently, nearly all incarcerated felons, and many with criminal records, are barred from voting. Forty-eight states disenfranchise incarcerated felons, 37 disenfranchise felony probationers and/or parolees, and 14 disenfranchise ex-felons who have completed their sentences.[1] The disenfranchised population has grown along with the criminal justice system. As the result of a reliance on incarceration and the impact of felony disenfranchisement on recent elections, disenfranchisement has become an important issue. For example, in the 2000 presidential election, an estimated 4.7 million people were disenfranchised as the result of a felony conviction.[2]

BACKGROUND

Many of those disenfranchised for a felony conviction have completed their criminal sentence. Another 1.4 million are on probation or parole. Familiar patterns of racism are apparent, with 13 percent of the black adult male population, approximately 1.4 million African American men, unable to vote. This reflects a rate of disenfranchisement seven times the national average.[3] Given current laws, 30 percent to 40 percent of black males will lose the right to vote at some point in their lives.[4]

STATE DISENFRANCHISEMENT LAWS

1. Forty-eight states and the District of Columbia prohibit inmates from voting while incarcerated for a felony offense.
2. Only two states—Maine and Vermont—permit inmates to vote.
3. Thirty-five states prohibit felons from voting while they are on parole; 30 of these states also exclude felony probationers.
4. Three states deny the right to vote to all ex-offenders who have completed their sentences. Nine others disenfranchise certain categories of ex-offenders and/or permit application for restoration of rights for specified offenses after a waiting period.[5]

LEGAL DEVELOPMENTS

Although the right to vote seemed to have been settled by the Voting Rights Act of 1965,[6] reliance on incarceration as a primary tool in the war on crime and the demographics of those who have been disenfranchised are bringing issues of felony disenfranchisement back to the forefront. Debate over disenfranchisement focuses on whether the practice is a relic of the past or justified by modern conceptions of democratic citizenship. Taking away the right to vote is similar to the medieval practice of civil death, in which violations of the social contract resulted in loss of citizenship rights.[7] In contrast to the practice of exclusion, the U.S. Supreme Court held in *Reynolds v. Sims* (1965) that "the right to vote freely for the candidate of one's choice is of the essence of a democratic society, and any restrictions on that right strike at the heart of representative government."[8]

The Fourteenth Amendment, ratified in1868, recognizes African Americans as citizens with the right to vote. Section 2 of the Fourteenth Amendment reads:

> Representatives shall be apportioned among the several States according to their respective numbers, counting the whole number of persons in each State, excluding Indians not taxed. But when the right to vote at any election for the choice of electors for President and Vice President of the United States, Representatives in Congress, the Executive and Judicial officers of a State, or the members of the Legislature thereof, is denied to any of the male inhabitants of such State, being twenty-one years of age, and citizens of the United States, or in any way abridged, *except for participation in rebellion, or other crime,* the basis of representation therein shall be reduced in the proportion which the number of such male citizens shall bear to the whole number of male citizens twenty-one years of age in such State.[9]

The "participation in rebellion, or other crime" caveat served as an opening for Jim Crow legislatures intent on denying blacks the right to vote. Southern states began to develop felony disenfranchisement laws specifically crafted to result in the disenfranchisement of newly freed African American males.[10] Although the right to vote was specifically granted to African Americans with the 1870 ratification of the Fifteenth Amendment, the adoption of disenfranchisement laws continued with relatively few challenges until the 1970s and 1980s, when these laws were challenged as violations of equal protection and voters' rights.

CONSEQUENCES OF STATE FELONY DISENFRANCHISEMENT LAWS

1. An estimated 5.3 million Americans, or 1 in 41 adults, have currently or permanently lost their voting rights as a result of a felony conviction.
2. Among those disenfranchised, 74 percent are currently living in the community.
3. In 11 states, a conviction can result in lifetime disenfranchisement.
4. Twelve states disenfranchise more than 10 percent of their African American population.
5. Thirteen percent of African American men, or 1.4 million, are disenfranchised, a rate seven times the national average. In some states, one in four black men are prohibited from voting.[11]

In *Richardson v. Ramirez*, the U.S. Supreme Court denied an equal protection challenge by ruling that Section 2 of the Fourteenth Amendment permits the removal of criminals from voter roles.[12] Challenges based on the Voter's Rights Act were similarly unsuccessful as courts refused to strike down felon disenfranchisement statutes because of an absence of causality between the statutes and historical patterns of discrimination.[13]

After a period of calm resulting from the failure of challenges based on equal protection and voter's rights, federal courts of appeals reinstated two challenges to such laws.[14] *Johnson v. Bush* revived a challenge to Florida's disenfranchisement laws. In granting summary judgment, the district court held that the disenfranchisement provision in Florida's 1868 constitution was enacted "with the particular discriminatory purpose of keeping blacks from voting."[15] In *Farrakhan v. Washington*, the court described the "disproportionate impact on minority voting power" and "minority under representation in Washington's political process" that resulted from disenfranchisement.[16] The *Johnson* court similarly asked "whether felon status 'interacts with social and historical conditions to cause an inequality in the opportunities enjoyed by black and white voters to elect their preferred representatives.'"[17] Each of these cases has resulted in optimism among critics of felony disenfranchisement laws.

FUTURE PROSPECTS

Felony disenfranchisement laws are under increased scrutiny. Since 1997, 16 states have taken steps to reform disenfranchisement laws, resulting in more than 600,000 people regaining the right to vote.[18] Following the 2000

IMPACTING ELECTIONS

"Felony disenfranchisement laws, combined with high rates of criminal punishment, may have altered the outcome of as many as seven recent U.S. Senate elections and at least one presidential election."* Research examining the impact of felony disenfranchisement suggests that the Democratic Party would have gained control of the U.S. Senate in 1986 and held control until the present. Results of the 2000 election "would have been reversed had just ex-felons been allowed to vote."** If disenfranchised felons in Florida had been permitted to vote, "Democrat Gore would certainly have carried the state, and the election."*** Adding to the problems in Florida, where an estimated 600,000 former offenders were ineligible to vote, a flawed list of more than 57,000 names was included in the list of felons denied the right to vote.****

*C. Uggen and J. Manza, "Democratic Contradiction? Political Consequences of Felon Disenfranchisement in the United States," *American Sociological Review* 67, no. 6 (2004): 794.

**Ibid., 794.

***Ibid., 792.

****Gregory Palast, "Florida's Flawed 'Voter-Cleansing' Program," *Salon.com*, December 4, 2000, http://dir.salon.com/story/politics/feature/2000/12/04/voter_file/index.html?pn=1.

presidential election, the National Commission on Federal Election Reform unanimously recommended that states not prohibit voting by people who have completed their sentences.[19] As pressures to eliminate overly broad disenfranchisement laws continue, change is likely at legislative and judicial levels.

The public opinion tide may also have turned, with research indicating that 80 percent of Americans believe persons who have completed their sentence should have their right to vote restored.[20] Support for voting rights even extends to violent felons, with 66 percent supporting voting rights for those who have served their entire sentence.[21] In the debate between "a desire to punish and deter crime versus a desire to promote and protect civil liberties, the latter appears to have greater public support."[22] If this perspective dominates future debate, further erosion on felony disenfranchisement laws can be expected.

See Also: Clemency; Convict Criminology.

Endnotes

1. J. Fellner and M. Mauer, "Losing the Vote: The Impact of Felony Disenfranchisement Laws in the United States," Human Rights Watch and The Sentencing Project (1998), http://www.soros.org/initiatives/justice/articles_publications/publications/losingthevote_19981001/losingthevote.pdf.
2. J. Manza and C. Uggen, *Locked Out: Felon Disenfranchisement and American Democracy* (New York: Oxford University Press, 2006).
3. Fellner and Mauer, "Losing the Vote," 1.
4. Marc Mauer, *Felon Voting Disenfranchisement*, 12 Fed. Sent. R. 248 (2002).
5. The Sentencing Project, *Felony Disenfranchisement Laws in The United States* (Washington, DC: The Sentencing Project, 2006), http://www.sentencingproject.org/PublicationDetails.aspx?PublicationID=335.

6. The National Voting Rights Act of 1965, 42 U.S.C. §1973–1973aa-6.
7. A. C. Ewald, "Civil Death: The Ideological Paradox of Criminal Disenfranchisement Law in the United States," *Wisconsin Law Review* 1045 (2002): 1060.
8. *Reynolds v. Sims,* 377 U.S. 533 (1965).
9. U.S. Constitution, Fourteenth Amendment, section 2; emphasis added.
10. J. Schall, "The Consistency of Felon Disenfranchisement with Citizenship Theory," *Harvard Blackletter Law Journal* 22 (2006): 53.
11. The Sentencing Project, *Federal Voting Rights for People with Convictions* (Washington, DC: The Sentencing Project, 2007), http://www.sentencingproject.org/PublicationDetails.aspx?PublicationID=574.
12. *Richardson v. Ramirez,* 418 U.S. 24, 56 (1974).
13. *Wesley v. Collins,* 791 F.2d 1255, 1261 (6th Cir. 1986).
14. P. Karlan, "Convictions and Doubts: Retribution, Representation, and the Debate over Felon Disenfranchisement," *Stanford Law Review* 56 (2004): 5.
15. *Johnson v. Bush,* 214 F. Supp. 2d 1333, 1339 (2002).
16. *Farrakhan v. Washington,* 338 F.3d at 1011, 1017 n.14 (2004).
17. *Johnson v. Bush.*
18. Ryan S. King, *A Decade of Reform: Felony Disenfranchisement Policy in the United States* (Washington, DC: The Sentencing Project, 2006), http://www.sentencingproject.org/Admin/Documents/publications/fd_decade_reform.pdf.
19. National Commission on Federal Election Reform (2001), http://www.reformelections.org/ncfer.asp.
20. J. Manza, C. Brooks, and C. Uggen, *Public Attitudes towards Felon Disenfranchisement in the United States* (Washington, DC: The Sentencing Project, 2003), http://www.sentencingproject.org/Admin/Documents/publications/fd_bs_publicattitudes.pdf.
21. F. Manza, C. Brooks, and C. Uggen, "Civil Death or Civil Rights? Public Attitudes towards Felon Disfranchisement in the United States," *Institute for Policy Research Working Papers,* WP-02-39 (2002): 27, http://www.northwestern.edu/ipr/publications/workingpapers/wpabstracts02/wp0239.html.
22. Ibid., 28.

Further Reading: Hull, E., *The Disenfranchisement of Ex-Felons* (Philadelphia: Temple University Press, 2006); Karlan, P., "Convictions and Doubts: Retribution, Representation, and the Debate over Felon Disenfranchisement," *Stanford Law Review* 56 (2004): 5; Manza, J., and C. Uggen, *Locked Out: Felon Disenfranchisement and American Democracy* (New York: Oxford University Press, 2006); Mauer, M., "Mass Imprisonment and the Disenfranchised Voter," in *Invisible Punishment: The Collateral Consequences of Mass Imprisonment,* ed. Marc Mauer and Meda Chesney-Lind (New York: New Press, 2002); Uggen, C. and J. Manza, "Democratic Contradiction? Political Consequences of Felon Disenfranchisement in the United States," *American Sociological Review* 67, no. 6 (2004): 794.

Kenneth Mentor

DNA USAGE IN CRIMINAL JUSTICE

INTRODUCTION

Deoxyribonucleic acid (DNA) is one of the most valuable discoveries of the twentieth century. Imported from the medical and scientific fields, the application of DNA technology in the criminal justice system has revolutionized the way crimes are investigated and prosecuted. Once considered an irrelevant and "stupid molecule,"[1] DNA is now frequently considered a reliable and powerful silent witness able to identify or eliminate suspects as well as clinch convictions. However, its use in the criminal justice system is not without controversy. Indeed, its use raises quite a number of ethical concerns, and its ability to incriminate the innocent, while less known, is well documented. This has occurred through administrative and technical errors and disturbingly through deliberate distortion of forensic analysis and findings as well as evidence planting. This entry is by no means a comprehensive treatise on DNA; it is meant simply to introduce the reader to some of the contentious issues surrounding the use of DNA in the criminal justice system.

BACKGROUND

DNA is a molecule located in the nucleus of all cells (other than red blood cells), and, with the exception of monozygotic (identical) twins, it is unique to individuals. "Surprisingly, unlike the unwavering excitement that now surrounds DNA, the discovery of its structure was accompanied by much less fanfare."[2] The molecule's rise to prominence only followed the realization that it carried vital genetic information, including disease, from parent to offspring—essentially a "blueprint of life." Since its discovery, DNA technology has been used in a variety of settings, from gene therapy in clinical medicine to genetic engineering in plants and animals for improved agricultural productivity. It has also been applied in a number of other disciplines, such as anthropology, theology, philosophy, law, and, of more relevance to this entry, criminal justice systems the world over.

The use of DNA in police investigations was the result of significant scientific advances made primarily by Sir Alec Jeffreys, professor of genetics at the University of Leicester in England. Jeffreys coined the term *DNA fingerprinting* after discovering that certain regions (loci) of DNA have a high degree of variability that makes them virtually unique to individuals.[3]

This simple scientific fact was first used in a criminal context in a rather complicated double rape and murder case well known as the Pitchfork Case.

THE PITCHFORK CASE

In November 1983, in the small town of Narborough, England, Lynda Mann was raped and strangled to death. The search for her killer proved futile. In 1986, another teenage girl, Dawn Ashworth, was also found dead in Narborough after having been raped. Semen samples revealed that the killer of both girls had the same blood type. Police later arrested a local teenage boy, who falsely confessed to killing Ashworth but denied involvement in the death of Mann.

Aware of Professor Jeffreys work with DNA fingerprinting, police submitted semen samples from both murder cases along with a sample of the suspect to Jeffreys for DNA testing. Forensic analysis concluded that the rapist in either case was not the local boy. It did, however, point to the fact that the killer was the same person in both crimes. Leicester police then conducted the world's first mass screening by asking just fewer than 5,000 men in the area to provide blood or saliva samples to absolve themselves of the offence. After six months of processing all the samples, there was still no match.

In 1987, it emerged that a man had given a blood sample to the police, pretending to be his colleague, Colin Pitchfork. Pitchfork was subsequently arrested. DNA analysis confirmed that he raped both girls. Pitchfork confessed to the murders and was sentenced to life in prison.

The original method created by Jeffreys was initially used by British police forces; however, due to the expense and extensive length of time it took to generate a DNA fingerprint, both the British and U.S. criminal justice systems now use what is accurately referred to as *DNA profiling*. The difference between the two DNA identification methods is an important one, as Jeffreys states:

> Unfortunately—and particularly in the United States—the term "DNA fingerprinting," which we specifically apply to the original multi-locus system in which we look at scores of markers, has been corrupted to be used in almost any DNA typing system. That has created a problem in court, because DNA profiling does not produce DNA fingerprints. . . . So this is a semantic problem, but a serious one.[4]

DNA profiling involves extracting DNA from biological samples taken from hair, body tissue, or fluids such as saliva, semen, or blood. Forensic analysis of loci on the DNA then produces a DNA profile. DNA profiling is less conclusive than DNA fingerprinting, as it examines considerably less loci or markers of a person's DNA. At the current time, DNA profiling cannot examine all the differences between people's DNA; thus, although they will not have the same entire DNA sequence or genome, there is a remote chance that two unrelated people could have the same DNA profile. Hence, the discriminatory power of any DNA profile increases with the number of loci tested. When DNA typing first started being used to facilitate police investigations in England and Wales, the standard analysis involved examination of six loci. Now they examine 10 (plus one that indicates sex). The United States currently examines 13 sites. Given the number of loci that are now examined, unrelated people are extremely unlikely to have the same DNA profile, and, if they are collected and analyzed correctly, DNA profiles are accepted by scientists as well as the courts as being conclusive enough to establish identification irrefutably.

It is this consensus that has greatly contributed to the establishment and expansion of DNA databases. The use of DNA databases enables new profiles to be compared against those already stored on the system. Matches may be found on examining evidence from two (or more) crime scenes, which may mean that a particular suspect was involved in both crimes, and, as is often the case, a match can be made between an individual and a crime scene. Although a match alone does not prove involvement in a crime, it can provide unquestionable proof that a person was present at the scene of a crime. This, together with other evidence, may illustrate beyond a reasonable doubt that an individual is the offender.

KEY EVENTS

The first official forensic database, the National DNA Database (NDNAD) was established in the United Kingdom in 1995. Having previously operated local and state databases, the United States followed suit in 1998 when its national DNA database, the National DNA Index System (NDIS), was launched under the authority of the DNA Identification Act of 1994.[5] The NDIS together with local and state databases make up the Combined DNA Index System (CODIS). CODIS stores profiles on two indexes. The Forensic Index contains profiles recovered from crime scenes, whereas profiles of convicted offenders or certain categories of arrestees are held under the Offender Index.[6] The U.S. national DNA database currently contains profiles of approximately 0.5 percent of the population. In comparison, the British national database is estimated to have profiles of 5 percent of the population and is predicted to increase to 7 percent, or 4.25 million profiles, by 2008.[7]

The potential of DNA technology was pushed further with the introduction of DNA dragnets or sweeps (or mass screenings as they are called in the United Kingdom). Dragnets involve requesting a group of individuals who fit a general description of the suspect to voluntarily provide a DNA sample for profile analysis in order to exclude themselves as suspects. The first dragnet was used in the United Kingdom in the Colin Pitchfork case. Since then, they have become increasingly common in Europe, including one in Germany in 1998 that sampled DNA from 16,000 men in an attempt to find the perpetrator of the murder of a young girl.[8] Although there have been at least 19 DNA dragnets in the United States,[9] they have utilized this method of "elimination by numbers" less frequently than their British counterparts due to potential conflicts with the Fourth Amendment, which provides, among other things, the right against unreasonable searches and seizures.

Familial searching is another milestone in DNA applications in the criminal justice system. It is predominantly used in cases in which a crime-scene profile has failed to match a suspect profile on the national DNA database. Familial searching involves probing the database to find profiles that are similar to the one taken from the crime scene in the hopes of being led to the suspect. The profiles that are found to be similar to the one from the crime scene would be from individuals who have a high probability of being relatives of the perpetrator. This is viable because people inherit 50 percent of their DNA from each parent. Thus, close family members such as parents, children, siblings, and even aunts and uncles are likely to share some genetic markers. First used in the United Kingdom in 2002[10] and in the United States in 2003, familial searching is still relatively new. At the present time, familial searches are not likely to become a regular occurrence in criminal investigations primarily due to the cost of running such a search (in 2004, estimated at $9,000 per search).[11] As forensic DNA technology continues to develop and costs decrease, however, law enforcement may want to make familiar searches common practice.

Both these applications of DNA forensic technology raise important issues regarding ethics, confidentiality, civil liberties, and human rights.[12] Clearly, it is important that all issues of concern are brought to the public forefront for debate and that the government and relevant bodies implement appropriate legislation, policies, and procedures to ensure that innocent individuals and families are not adversely affected. This may require laws, which have been recently passed without adequate public discussion to be amended.

DNA AND THE CRIMINAL JUSTICE SYSTEM SINCE 1987

1987: The first DNA exoneration and mass screening took place in the double murder investigation of Lynda Mann and Dawn Ashworth in England. In Florida, rapist Tommy Lee Andrews became the first ever to be convicted due to DNA evidence.

1988: Colin Pitchfork, the first man apprehended on the basis of DNA profiling, was sentenced to life in prison for the murders of Mann and Ashworth.

1989: Gary Dotson became the first person in the United States to be exonerated and released from prison due to DNA results.

1993: Kirk Bloodsworth was released from prison on June 28, 1993, making him the first person on death row to be exonerated by DNA evidence in the United States. Also, Dr. Kary B. Mullis won the Nobel Prize in Chemistry for the invention of the polymerase chain reaction (PCR) method. Prior to the PCR method, DNA analysis was slow, required large quantities of the sample, and had difficulty analyzing mixed or contaminated samples. PCR enabled profiles to be produced from minute and degraded samples of DNA. In addition to its applications in other fields, PCR enabled DNA profiling to be used in more cases.

1994: For the very first time, analysis of nonhuman DNA led to the identification and apprehension of a criminal. Royal Canadian Mounted Police officers had hairs from a man's pet cat analyzed, which pointed to him being the murderer of his wife.

2001: In May, the Criminal Justice and Police Act (CJPA) of 2001 came into force in England and Wales. This law authorizes the retention of DNA samples and profiles of anyone charged with any offence that carries a penalty of imprisonment or charged with a few specified noncustodial offences.

2004: In England, Craig Harman became the first person in the world to be prosecuted and convicted due to DNA database familial searching.

2006: The DNA Fingerprinting Act of 2005 became law in the United States. This legislation permits the DNA sampling of foreign citizens detained on federal grounds and reduces the stage at which a DNA profile can be uploaded onto the federal database from charge to arrest. It also authorizes government funds to support the analysis and retention of all DNA samples and profiles on the national database. Furthermore this act now requires that individuals who would like their profile removed from the database to file a certified document stating that they have been acquitted or have had charges dismissed before their request will be processed.

LEGAL DECISIONS

During early uses of DNA as evidence, the main assistance with admissibility the courts had was the standard as laid out in *Frye v. United States*. Under the *Frye* test, scientific evidence could only be admitted if it had "gained general acceptance in the particular field in which it belongs."[13] In 1993, however, with the use of DNA profiles becoming more prevalent, the Supreme Court set a new standard in *Daubert v. Merrell Dow Pharmaceuticals, Inc.* This standard expanded the *Frye* test by recognizing the need to highlight issues that might bias or mislead the jury. In particular, it permitted for the first time the admission of new factors, such as publications and probabilities of error, to assist with evaluating the degree of reliability.[14] One of the most significant cases regarding the use of DNA typing in criminal trials was *People v. Castro*.[15] This case fervently contested the admissibility of DNA evidence in court. In its opinion, the Court issued recommendations that would encourage fair and just use of DNA evidence. The Court held that it should be provided with chain of custody of documents and details of any defects or errors. It also held that laboratory results should be provided both to the defense counsel and the court.

Although a number of state and federal cases have created a gateway into the courtroom for forensic DNA evidence, courts have also declined to admit DNA evidence. Some of these cases involved laboratories that had unreliable or dubious practices.[16]

In addition to being used as evidence to convict suspects, DNA technology is increasingly being used to exonerate previously convicted individuals. On June 12, 2006, for the very first time, the U.S. Supreme Court considered the standards necessary to reopen a postconviction death penalty case involving DNA evidence. After serving more than nineteen years on death row, the Supreme Court held that Paul House was entitled to a new trial.[17] House was originally convicted of murder, but recent DNA analysis showed that the body fluids found on the victim's clothes were not his. This new evidence was sufficient to meet the precedent for postconviction claims of innocence as set out in *Schlup v. Delo*.[18]

In addition to case law, DNA has also impacted legislation. The Innocence Protection Act was tabled to the U.S. Senate in February 2000. On October 30, 2004, the Justice for All Act of 2004, which includes the Innocence Protection Act of 2004, became law. This act seeks to do a number of things, the most significant of which are to: (1) enhance and protect the rights of crime victims; (2) reduce the backlog of untested DNA samples; (3) expand forensic laboratories; (4) intensify research into new DNA testing technologies; (5) develop training programs on the proper collection, preservation, and analysis of DNA evidence; and (6) facilitate the exoneration of innocent individuals through postconviction testing of DNA evidence.

In December 2003, a private citizen submitted to the attorney general's office in California a proposed initiative titled DNA Fingerprint, Unsolved Crime and Innocence Protection Act.[19] This proposal sought to widen the category of instances in which DNA samples could be taken and profiles stored on the state's database. Proposition 69, as the proposal became known, was approved by voters in California on November 2, 2004. The effect of this enactment was that as of November 3, 2004, the following categories of people will have a DNA sample taken and uploaded onto the state and national DNA database: (1) any person, adult or juvenile, convicted of any felony (including any person in prison, on probation, or on parole for any felony committed prior to November 3, 2004, or any person on probation or any other supervised release for any offence and who has a prior felony); (2) any person convicted of any sex or arson offence or attempt; and (3) adults arrested for murder, voluntary manslaughter, or felony sex offences (which includes rape) or attempt to commit one of these crimes.[20]

Furthermore, commencing January 2, 2009, all adults arrested for any felony will also be subject to DNA collection and retention. Prior to the passing of Proposition 69, only those convicted of a serious felony such as rape and murder had to submit DNA samples.[21] Thus, Proposition 69 has effectively resulted in the massive expansion of California's DNA database. It is worth noting that Louisiana, Minnesota, Texas, and Virginia already have legislation that authorizes taking DNA samples from adults arrested for a felony. There is, therefore, a clear trend toward a so-called DNA-based criminal justice system.

FUTURE PROSPECTS

As a result of ongoing advances by scientists, extensive legislation, support from police and prosecutors, and substantial funding from the government, the drive to expand the application of DNA technology in the criminal justice system continues. Currently, scientists at the University of Southampton in the United Kingdom are in the process of developing a method of forensic analysis that could enable DNA samples to be transformed into profiles at the scene of the crime.[22] Furthermore, DNA profiling involving testing for race and other physical characteristics has slowly begun. Scientists now have the ability to decipher from DNA analysis the sex and age of an individual, and research is currently being conducted toward identifying eye, hair, and skin color. This can obviously assist the police with composing more accurate descriptions of a suspect. Although this could significantly facilitate criminal investigations, it also raises a number of sociological and ethical issues: What defines race? Is it what the public see, or is it what the individual knows or believes he is? How do we deal with a situation in which racial genetic testing reveals information the individual did not know and may not have wanted to know about himself? Could racial DNA profiling lead to eugenics? These are just some of the issues.[23] Perhaps appropriately, testing for racial characteristics has not yet become common practice. Before further steps are taken to increase its utilization, serious consultation with sociologists, criminologists, ethicists, psychologists, geneticists, and lawyers needs to be conducted.

Given the benefits of the use of DNA technology in the criminal justice system and the perceived breaches of rights it begets, particularly for those who are acquitted or never charged, there have been calls by some to collect DNA samples and store DNA profiles of all citizens on forensic databases. Proponents of a forensic database holding DNA profiles of the entire citizenry argue that it will reduce racial discrimination in the disproportionate storage of profiles of ethnic minorities and simultaneously increase fairness, as everyone would be incurring the same degree of threat to privacy. Furthermore, because everyone would know their DNA was on the database, proponents also hold that such a database would act as a deterrent.[24]

Arguments against this proposal include issues relating to the presumption of innocence and the right to avoid self-incrimination (embodied in the Fifth Amendment in the United States), not to mention the potential misuses of genetic information by government agencies as well as others, such as insurance companies and employers who might benefit from such information. Given the immense financial cost and practical difficulties alone, the prospect of implementing such an idea is fraught with numerous obstacles. Given the speed at which DNA legislation has expanded, however, many believe implementation of these ideas is a real possibility and perhaps inevitable. The key question is whether this will happen explicitly with public debate or by stealth.

DNA, DNA profiles, databases, and related applications have irreversibly changed the way humans think about life, disease, and the resolution of crime. However, it is its use in the criminal justice system that continues to attract the most controversy.[25] The use of DNA in the criminal justice system provides numerous benefits resulting in more convictions of the guilty and more exonerations of the innocent. It also raises serious questions, including but not limited to privacy, probable cause, coercion, consent, confidentiality, civil liberties, subjective identity, and other ethical considerations. Many of these concerns are legitimate, particularly because the introduction of legislation often occurs devoid of public scrutiny. The recent vote on Proposition 69 illustrates that public consultation has been initiated. It is necessary that future consultations be complemented with a discussion of the relevant concerns so that the public can form an educated opinion. Much more public debate is essential to avoid the introduction of unfair legislation and practices and to prevent miscarriages of justice that would ultimately affect us all.

See Also: CSI Effect.

Endnotes

1. James D. Watson, *The Double Helix: A Personal Account of the Discovery of the Structure of DNA* (London: Weidenfeld and Nicolson, 1997), 2.
2. Julia Selman, "From Human Cell to Prison Cell: A Critique of the Use of DNA Profiling in the British Criminal Justice System" (master's thesis, University of Cambridge, 2003), 10.
3. Alec J. Jeffreys, Victoria Wilson, and Swee Lay Thien, "Hyper Variable 'Minisatellite' Regions in Human DNA," *Nature* 314 (1985): 67–73.
4. Alec Jeffreys, "DNA Profiling and Minisatellites," *Science Watch* (1995), http://www.sciencewatch.com/interviews/sir_alec_jeffreys.htm.
5. Federal Bureau of Investigation, *CODIS* (n.d.), http://www.fbi.gov/hq/lab/codis/program.htm.
6. Federal Bureau of Investigation, *CODIS* (2007), http://www.fbi.gov/hq/lab/codis/national.htm.
7. Home Office, "DNA Expansion Programme 2000–2005: Reporting Achievement," Forensic Science and Pathology Unit (2005).

8. See Lauren Dundes, "Is the American Public Ready to Embrace DNA as a Crime-Fighting Tool? A Survey Assessing Support for DNA Databases," *Bulletin of Science, Technology and Society* 21, no. 5 (2001): 369–75.

9. See Tania Simoncelli and Barry Steinhardt, "California's Proposition 69: A Dangerous Precedent for Criminal DNA Databases," *Journal of Law, Medicine and Ethics* 34, no. 2 (2006): 199–213.

10. In 2002, a DNA familial search led to the identification of an offender who was deceased. In 2003, familial searches led to the identification of two other offenders in the United Kingdom, one of whom was Craig Harman, who was convicted of manslaughter in 2004.

11. "The Sins of the Fathers," *The Economist* 371, no. 8372 (April 24, 2004): 60.

12. See Robin Williams and Paul Johnson, "Inclusiveness, Effectiveness and Intrusiveness: Issues in the Developing Uses of DNA Profiling in Support of Criminal Investigations," *Journal of Law, Medicine and Ethics* 34, no. 2 (2006): 234–47; Erica Haimes, "Social and Ethical Issues in the Use of Familial Searching in Forensic Investigations: Insights from Family and Kinship Studies," *Journal of Law, Medicine and Ethics* 34, no. 2 (2006): 263–76.

13. *Frye v. United States,* 293 F. 1013 (D.C. Cir., 1923).

14. *Daubert v. Merrell Dow Pharmaceuticals, Inc.,* 113 S.Ct. 2786 (1993).

15. *People v. Castro,* 545 N.Y.S. 2d. 985 (NY Sup. Ct., 1989).

16. See *Schwartz v. State,* 447 N.W. 2d 422 (1989).

17. See *House v Bell, Warden,* 547 U.S. ____ (2006).

18. See *Schlup v. Delo,* 513 U.S. 298 (1995).

19. Subsequent to his brother and sister-in-law having been murdered some years earlier, Bruce Harrington submitted the proposal; see note 10.

20. Office of the Attorney General, State of California, Department of Justice, Bureau of Forensic Services, "Proposition 69: FAQs" (2007), http://ag.ca.gov/bfs/content/faq.htm.

21. California Legislative Analyst's Office, "Proposition 69: DNA Samples, Collection, Database, Funding, Initiative Statute" (2004), http://www.lao.ca.gov/ballot/2004/69_11_2004.htm.

22. Celeste Biever, "DNA Profiling Moves to the Scene of the Crime," *New Scientist* 189, no. 2534 (January 14, 2006): 28.

23. For a more detailed discussion, see Pilar N. Ossorio, "About Face: Forensic Genetic Testing for Race and Visible Traits," *Journal of Law, Medicine and Ethics* 34, no. 2 (2006): 277–92.

24. Robert Williamson and Rony Duncan, "DNA Testing For All," *Nature* 418 (2002): 585–86. For other issues related to a DNA database of the entire population, see D. H. Kaye and Michael E. Smith, "DNA Databases for Law Enforcement: The Coverage Question and the Case for a Population-Wide Database," in *DNA and the Criminal Justice System: The Technology of Justice,* ed. David Lazer (Cambridge, MA: MIT Press, 2004); Michael E. Smith, David H. Kaye, and Edward J. Imwinkelried, "DNA Data from Everyone Would Combat Crime, Racism," *USA Today,* July 26, 2001, http://www.usatoday.com/news/opinion/2001-07-26-ncguest2.htm; Paul E. Tracy and Vincent Morgan, "Big Brother and His Science Kit: DNA Databases for 21st Century Crime Control?" *Journal of Criminal Law and Criminology* 90, no. 2 (2000): 635–90.

25. For arguments in support of and against the use of DNA profiling, databases, and evidence, see Rockne P. Harmon, "Legal Criticisms of DNA Typing: Where's the Beef?" *The Journal of Criminal Law and Criminology* 84, no. 1 (1993): 175–88; Peter Neufeld, "Have You No Sense of Decency?" *Journal of Criminal Law and Criminology* 84, no. 1 (1993):

189–202. For issues related to DNA profiling in Britain, see Carole McCartney, "The DNA Expansion Programme and Criminal Investigation," *British Journal of Criminology* 46 (2006): 175–92.

Further Reading: Connors, Edward, et al., *Convicted by Juries, Exonerated by Science: Case Studies in the Use of DNA Evidence to Establish Innocence after Trial* (Washington, DC: U.S. Department of Justice, National Institute of Justice, 1996); Gans, J., "Something to Hide: DNA Databases, Surveillance and Self-Incrimination," *Current Issues in Criminal Justice* 13 (2001): 168–84; Gross, Samuel R., et al., "Exonerations in the United States 1989 through 2003," *The Journal of Criminal Law and Criminology* 95, no. 2 (2005): 524–60; Lazer, David, ed., *DNA and the Criminal Justice System: The Technology of Justice* (Cambridge, MA: MIT Press, 2004); National Commission on the Future of DAN Evidence, *The Future of Forensic DNA Testing: Predictions of the Research and Development Working Group* (Washington, DC: U.S. Department of Justice, National Institute of Justice, 2000); Selman, Julia, "A Bioethical Controversy?" *Cambridge Medicine* 17, no. 3 (Spring 2003), 21–23.

Julia Selman-Ayetey

DOMESTIC VIOLENCE PRACTICES

INTRODUCTION

Domestic violence and the question of whether to intervene into the family dwelling affected by physical or psychological abuse has, until recently, been controversial because of the different viewpoints regarding the issue as one of privacy versus one of public accountability. Once domestic violence was viewed as a social problem, the controversies shifted to what was the appropriate form of intervention or who should be responsible for carrying out domestic violence practices, namely law enforcement and criminal justice agencies or social and human service agencies. Another set of controversies surrounding domestic violence practices stems from the often competing or contradictory goals of punishment versus rehabilitation.

BACKGROUND

Historically, domestic violence was seen as a private trouble. It occurred within the privacy of a man's own home. He was in charge of all affairs and persons residing in his home, and he had the right to chastise his wife. According to the Old Testament, women were the source of all evil. Under English common law, the husband was allowed to chastise his wife with restraint. Based on religious beliefs, the law limited the husband's violence. With the secularization of society, however, this violence became problematic. Nevertheless, in the colonies a new liberal Lockean philosophy focusing on public order became the foundation for the establishment of domestic violence laws that remained under the umbrella of private order for centuries.[1]

It was not until the 1970s that feminists adopted the concern for violence against women. Domestic violence came to be understood as the domination of men over women in all spheres of a patriarchal society. In opposition to past liberal philosophy, feminists argued that the power and domination that was at the root of domestic violence required that society redefine this violence as a social problem instead of a private family affair. This argument followed C. Wright Mills's sociological imagination that personal troubles are in fact public issues[2] and would eventually come to change domestic violence practices.

Although the 1970s Battered Women's Movement worked to change domestic violence laws, practices of the 1980s still reflected the definition of domestic violence as a private issue. According to the Uniform Crime Report, in 1989 women were six times more likely than men to be victimized by a spouse, ex-spouse, boyfriend, or girlfriend. Within a nine-year period, intimates committed 5.6 million violent acts against women, an annual average of almost 626,000. One-quarter of these assaults were reported to the police. It was reported that half of the complaints were an effort to prevent the abuse from reoccurring, whereas one-quarter were attempts to punish the abuser. Half of the victims who reported domestic violence to the National Crime Victimization Survey claimed to have had no response from the police because, as they were informed, it was a private matter.[3]

Today, women in the United States are victims of domestic violence every 15 seconds. Research has found that battering is the single largest cause of injury to women. Annually, roughly 1 million women seek medical attention as a result of domestic violence, and their husbands or boyfriends commit 30 percent of all homicides against women.[4] These statistics hardly account for a private matter. Yet research has found that 75 percent of all stranger assaults result in arrest and court adjudication, whereas only 16 percent of all family assaults, usually charged as misdemeanors and not felonies, result in arrest and court adjudication.[5]

KEY LEGAL AND SOCIAL MOMENTS

Examining legal responses to domestic violence, it is commonly believed that under English common law, Judge Sir Francis Buller in the 1780s stated that a husband can physically chastise his wife as long as he did not use a stick thicker than his thumb (see Table D.1). This became known as the *rule of thumb*. Others claim, however, that there is no reference to this statement in English common law. It is known that as early as 1655, Massachusetts Bay Colony prohibited domestic violence. In 1824, however, a husband's right to assault his wife became codified under state law. The Mississippi State Supreme Court ruled that the husband had a right to physically chastise his wife, though in moderation.[6] Although the rule of thumb was referenced in this case, it was not used to justify the decision. In 1871, however, Alabama became the first state to recognize a wife's right to legal protection against her husband's physical abuse.[7] Unfortunately, this ruling soon became a paper promise when victims found that the criminal justice system still held strongly to the belief that domestic violence was a private trouble. In 1879, the court ruled that a man cannot be criminally prosecuted for assaulting his wife unless the violence was cruel or created permanent injury.[8] Even as recently as 1962, a husband's right to physically chastise his wife was legalized in *Joyner v. Joyner.*

It was not until the 1970s with the Battered Women's Movement that domestic violence began to be recognized as a social problem. Specifically, in 1977, Oregon became the first state to legislate mandatory arrest, and in 1979 President Jimmy Carter established the Office of Domestic Violence; however, the landmark case to truly take hold of domestic violence practices was *Thurman v. City of Torrington* (1984).[9] *Thurman* was a civil case in which it was recognized that police had a legal responsibility to respond to and protect victims of domestic violence. The $2.3 million awarded to Tracy Thurman was the key moment that changed police practice in their responses. Although, by 1983, every state had made legal remedies in response to the demands of the Battered Women's Movement, many were still reluctant to intervene in so-called family matters. The *Thurman* case changed this practice.

Another key moment in domestic violence practices was the Minneapolis Experiment.[10] The Minneapolis Experiment, conducted in 1984, found that unlike previous practices, arrest was a greater deterrent to domestic violence. As a result of this experiment, as well as the *Thurman* decision, many states implemented mandatory arrest laws. Since 1984, however, replication of the Minneapolis Experiment has found that arrest only works as a deterrent for the six months immediately following the arrest and not more. Thus, the debate still continues, what is the most effective way to address domestic violence? Nonetheless, by 1986, 46 percent of police departments in cities with populations greater than 100,000 had a proarrest policy based on probable cause. In 1984, it was only 10 percent.[11]

Table D.1 Legal Changes in Domestic Violence Practices

Rule of thumb. It is commonly believed that under English common law, Judge Sir Francis Buller in the 1780s stated that a husband can physically chastise his wife as long as he does not use a stick thicker than his thumb (rule of thumb). Others claim no reference to this statement in English common law, however.

Bradley v. State (1824). A husband had a right to physically chastise his wife, though in moderation.

State v. Oliver (1879). The criminal law did not apply to a husband's assault unless the violence was cruel or created permanent injury to his wife.

Joyner v. Joyner (1962). A husband had a right to use force to compel his wife to "behave" and "know her place."

Thurman v. City of Torrington (1984). In this civil case, police were found to be negligent in responding to and protecting victims of domestic violence.

State v. Ciskie (1988)* and ***State v. Baker*** (1980).** These were the first cases to uphold the use of battered woman syndrome evidence via expert testimony.

---

* *State v. Ciskie*, 110 Wash. 2d 263 (1988).
** *State v. Baker*, 424 A.2d 171 (NH S.Ct., 1980).

DOMESTIC VIOLENCE THEORIES

Three major theories have influenced domestic violence practices. Individually oriented theories examine the character of both the batterer and the battered. These theories have brought about many negative myths and stereotypes about domestic violence and especially about the abused woman. Most people saw battered women as pathological. Recidivists were seen as masochistic, weak, sick, or women who sought out batterers. For this reason, women were referred to psychologists and various social-service agencies. In responding to domestic violence calls, many police officers believed that the man's violence was justified because the woman constantly nagged him; for a man to use physical force, the woman must be at fault. In these cases, the police almost always sided with the man.

The big question with domestic violence was why did the woman remain in an abusive relationship? Many people believed that she was getting a meal ticket, and after so long why did she complain now? Many concluded that she wanted to get revenge after a recent fight with her abuser. The assumption here was that she purposely provoked him until he was angry enough to strike her, and when he did, she called the police. Another myth that the criminal justice and judicial systems utilized was that these women never pressed charges; they were weak-willed women who could not follow through. Therefore, the police did not waste valuable police time, as well as taxpayers' money, arresting the man, especially if he and the abused woman were married. Unfortunately, there is still evidence of these victim-blaming practices within the criminal justice arrest and prosecution decision making.

Family-oriented and subcultural theories focus on characteristics within the family and the socialization patterns. According to these theories, the characteristics of the family predict future violence; that is, violence begets violence. In other words, adults who experience or witness violence during childhood are more prone to becoming violent adults or battered adults. Children are often socialized that women are the property of men or that violence against one's spouse is acceptable. Unfortunately, some of these children grow up to be police officers. Within these theories, however, people believe that violence occurs in families with alcohol or substance abusers, minority families, and low-income families. Police responding to domestic violence calls, who follow these myths, generally do not consider the situation serious, because it is believed that violence is accepted within the cultures of these people.

Feminist theories erased many of these myths from the minds of many people, although not all. These theories utilize a macrolevel analysis. They pointed out the structural violence in Western society. The privatized family structure makes domestic violence an individual problem, not a societal one. Accordingly, our male-dominated society keeps women economically and emotionally dependent on the man, giving her little or no options for a violent-free life. Feminists argue that the male-dominated criminal justice and judicial systems allow, even encourage, this to happen. It was the fight of feminists that forced the police to change their policies toward domestic violence. The change was not the result of the acceptance of the feminist theories, however; instead, it was a result of feminist grassroots movements to sue police departments for failing to protect female victims.

DOMESTIC VIOLENCE PRACTICES

Police Responses

In the early 1980s and prior to that time, police, as well as the courts, felt that domestic violence was a private matter in which they did not want to interfere. According to police, it was not real police work; therefore, the police should not be dragged into it. Domestic violence was given very low priority and avoided if possible. In fact, during the mid-1960s, police departments in urban areas with high crime rates, such as Detroit, were actually screening out domestic violence calls.

Police domestic violence policies are evident in their training manuals. According to the Police Training Academy in Michigan, until recent changes in domestic violence policies, police officers were instructed to avoid arrest whenever possible and to appeal to the vanity of the individuals involved.[12] In responding to a call, the police were to tell the woman to consider time lost and court costs. The officer was to inform the couple that his only interest was to prevent a breach of the peace. He would recommend a postponement due to the unavailability of a judge or court session, even if untrue. This statement was premised on the belief in the myth that battered women often changed their minds about pressing charges before the case came to court. He explained that she would probably reconcile with her abuser before the hearing. Police even went as far as scaring the woman, making her realize that pressing charges would infuriate her abuser, and he would probably retaliate worse than ever. In addition, she had to realize that the police could not babysit her.

In California, the Training Bulletin on Techniques of Dispute Interventions also advised officers to avoid arrest, except to protect life and property and to preserve the peace. In addition, it instructed the officer to encourage the victim to reason with her attacker. In Detroit, Michigan, as in many other cities, police precincts received more domestic violence calls than any other serious crime. Detroit's training consisted of 240 hours, yet only 3 to 5 hours were dedicated to this most frequent and reoccurring crime. Officers were trained to avoid action as well as injury to themselves. Domestic violence was not a crime unless there was severe injury, and many times, even then, no action was taken. The International Association of Police Chiefs stated that it was unnecessary to create a police matter when only a family matter existed.

The role police played in domestic violence was as preservers of the family. This meant no police action was taken, even if this meant persuading the woman not to press charges or denying that they could help her in any way. They played mediator roles in an attempt to reunite the couple. Arrest was made only when there was a disruption of the peace or a chance that the police would have to be called back to the scene.

All studies have shown that police were reluctant to intervene in domestic violence. They were even more reluctant if the couple was married, moving the incident farther into the private realm. A husband had more right over his wife than a boyfriend did because an unmarried couple did not constitute a family. Police were also reluctant to intervene with the domestic affairs of recidivists. Over time, officers became detached from a woman who constantly cried for help but did not leave her abuser. In response to these calls, police often arrived with the intention of keeping the peace but with no intention of intervening.

As mentioned previously, police officials practiced a no-arrest policy. Yet when police did arrest, there were strict guidelines. To begin, there had to be a witness present other than the abused woman and her children. This was something that rarely occurred because domestic violence is a crime that usually occurs in the privacy of one's own home. If an arrest was made, no matter how serious, it was charged as a misdemeanor, which had to be witnessed by an officer. This also almost never happened. To assault another person in front of a police officer is to challenge and show disrespect for the authority of the police. Nonaction protected the officer from personal danger and liability of false arrest. When a woman had a man arrested for domestic violence, many times she would drop the charges. This allowed the man to sue the police department for false arrest. In order to release themselves of this liability, either no arrest was made or the woman was forced to make a citizen's arrest.

A study conducted by the FBI found that domestic disturbances caused the greatest number of officer deaths and injuries. This study created a panic as well as an antipathy toward responding to domestic violence calls. When responding to these crimes, oftentimes officers responded in an aggressive manner in order to protect themselves from any unforeseeable dangers. Their response often made the woman feel that she was a criminal as well. When the FBI released its statistics to the police departments, it created a panic among officers, and police precincts started screening domestic violence calls. However, it was later found and reported that the FBI report overstated the number of officer deaths by three times its actual number. What the FBI did was combine bar fights, gang activities, and restraining deranged people into one disturbance category. In actuality, between 1973 and 1982, only 62 out of 1,085 deaths occurred due to domestic violence. This is a very small number considering that police spend much more time at a domestic violence call than at any other call.

Court Procedures

In a 1975 New York conference on abused wives, Justice Yorka Linakis stated, "There is nothing more pathetic than to see a husband going to his home—usually in the company of a policeman—to collect his meager belongings."[13] A Michigan circuit court judge argued that violence is provoked; therefore, the wife should be cited for contempt on this basis and both should be sentenced to jail. Prior to changes caused by the Battered Women's Movement, these were the kind of attitudes a battered woman would encounter in court. Courts were very insensitive to the distress of a woman. This insensitivity was caused by the ignorance of the problem, inadequate laws, and a heavy backlog of other, more important cases.

When a woman decided to bring charges against her assailant, she had a choice of using the criminal court or family court. The purpose of criminal court is to punish the criminal and deter the crime. If taken to criminal court, domestic violence is considered a crime. Within this broad category is physical injury, sexual abuse, rape, attempted rape, harassment, threat of physical abuse, death, destruction of another's property, kidnapping or involuntary confinement, or violation of a protection order. The state filed a criminal charge when an arrest was made or when a victim filed a private criminal complaint. A private criminal complaint was filed when the victim did not call the police or did call but the police failed to show or did not make an arrest when they arrived. Penalties in a criminal court consist of a jail sentence, a fine, or a term of probation. Although normally there is not enough evidence in a domestic violence case for a conviction, a case must be proved beyond a reasonable doubt. The result is usually a warning to the abuser stating that further violence will be prosecuted. If there is enough evidence for a conviction, the prosecutor will usually plea-bargain, bringing the charges down to a misdemeanor or, more often, a violation resulting in probation or, less seriously, a warning.

Although, by 1983, every state had made new legal remedies in response to the demands of the women's movement, many were still reluctant to intervene in family matters. For this reason, most domestic violence cases have been thrown out of criminal court and sent to family court. In family court, a woman could file for a divorce, custody of children, and alimony from her husband. Major problems with family court, though, are that only spouses and couples with children are allowed to file for remedies. This bars cohabitants and other intimates, who would not receive help and support otherwise, from seeking remedies. Although family court would be more help to an economically dependent woman with no occupational training, it is designed to protect the family assailant rather than the family victim. It has been recognized that family court is inappropriate for handling felony cases. It provides the assailant with counsel and leaves the woman to fend for herself.

There were various civil remedies for which a battered woman could file. An order of protection or restraining order requires the abuser to restrain from violence and to stay away from the victim. It could last up to one year. Violation of this order is contempt of court and punishable by a jail sentence of up to six months, a fine, both, or a term of probation. Major problems with obtaining an order of protection is that it takes several days to receive, and often police do not enforce it, claiming that they have no record of the order or that it is a civil not a criminal matter and, therefore, out of their hands. In order to be protected while she waits for the order of protection, a woman can file for a temporary order of protection. This order can be obtained at night and on weekends. A victim of domestic violence can also file for damages or a peace bond. The problem with these remedies is that it requires the abuser to give money to the court that could otherwise be used to support the victim and her children.

FUTURE PROSPECTS

Although much of the domestic violence research, legislative changes, and court decisions have focused on police practices, much has also been done to change prosecutorial and judicial practices. Specifically, prosecutors tend to oversee victim/witness units that tend to deal predominantly with victims of domestic violence. These units inform the victims of the processing of their cases and aid them in understanding the justice process as well as obtaining victim compensation. Within the courts, domestic violence courts have been implemented. These courts are organized so as to give a substantial amount of focus to these sensitive and complex cases; however, research is still needed to assess the effectiveness of these practices. For example, although most police agencies have implemented proarrest policies, researchers have found that the discretion has been taken from the police and given to the prosecutor. Specifically, the prosecutors tend to screen out many of these domestic violence cases before they can reach the courts. Furthermore, domestic violence courts are not usually a fully structured court. Instead, they operate as early U.S. circuit courts did, in which the domestic violence court convenes one or two days a week, overseen by one judge or, sometimes, a commissioner.

Questions of domestic violence practices have been present since the codification of the law; however, these practices did not truly become controversial until the 1970s, and although these interventions or lack thereof may have peaked in their controversial nature, their legacies die hard. For example, although most police departments have mandatory arrest policies, many police officers still hesitate to make arrests, and when an arrest is made, the offender is usually charged with a misdemeanor, even when serious injuries occur. Furthermore, officer attitudes during arrest often reveal the prevalence of the private-trouble ideology within society. Finally, the fact that many of the domestic violence crimes go unreported reveals further problems in improving domestic violence practices. Victims do not report the crimes for many reasons. Sometimes victims do not believe that the police can or will do anything to help them, and sometimes victims themselves define the problem as a private trouble. As with many other controversies in criminal justice, the cultural roots at the heart of the problem will keep domestic violence practices controversial for some time to come.

See Also: Defining Criminal Violence; Gendered Justice; Peacemaking Criminology; Sexual Assault in Colleges and Universities.

Endnotes

1. For a detailed discussion, see Eve S. Buzawa and Carl G. Buzawa, *Domestic Violence: The Criminal Justice Response* (Newbury Park, CA: Sage, 1990).
2. For a detailed discussion, see C. Wright Mills, *The Sociological Imagination* (New York: Oxford University Press, 1976; originally published 1959).
3. Caroline W. Harlow, *Female Victims of Violent Crime* (Washington, DC: U.S. Department of Justice, 1991).
4. For a detailed discussion, see Joanne Belknap, *The Invisible Woman: Gender, Crime, and Justice,* 2nd ed. (Belmont, CA: Wadsworth, 2001).
5. R. Emerson Dobash and Russell P. Dobash, "With Friends Like These Who Needs Enemies: Institutional Supports for the Patriarchy and Violence against Women" (paper presented at the 9th World Congress of Sociology, Uppsala, Sweden, July, 1978).
6. *Bradley v. State,* 1 Miss. 156 (1824).

7. *Fulgham v. State,* 46 Ala. 146–147 (1871).

8. *State v. Oliver,* 70 N.C. 60, 61–62 (1879).

9. *Thurman v. City of Torrington,* 595 F. Supp 1521 (D. Conn., 1984).

10. Lawrence W. Sherman and R. A. Berk, "The Specific Deterrent Effects of Arrest for Domestic Assault," *American Sociological Review* 49 (1984): 261–72.

11. Michael Steinman, "Lowering Recidivism among Men Who Batter Women," *Journal of Police Science and Administration* 17 (1990): 2.

12. Del Martin, *Battered Wives* (New York: Pocket Books, 1983).

13. For a detailed discussion, see ibid.

Further Reading: Belknap, Joanne, *The Invisible Woman: Gender, Crime, and Justice,* 2nd ed. (Belmont, CA: Wadsworth, 2001); Buzawa, Eve S., and Carl G. Buzawa, *Domestic Violence: The Criminal Justice Response* (Newbury Park, CA: Sage, 1990); Mills, C. Wright, *The Sociological Imagination* (New York: Oxford University Press, 1976; originally published 1959); Pagelow, Mildred D., *Woman-Battering: Victims and Their Experiences* (Beverly Hills, CA: Sage, 1981).

Venessa Garcia

DRIVING WHILE BLACK

INTRODUCTION

Driving while black is a controversial term used to describe traffic stops made by police officers in which race is the primary factor influencing officers' decision to stop. Like racial profiling, driving while black is a form of discrimination in which skin color is used as evidence of the likelihood to commit a crime and serves as the basis upon which law enforcement decisions are made. Studies have proved that black drivers are more likely to be stopped than whites, yet this does not make the concept any less contentious.[1] Opponents of this practice claim that racial profiling disproportionately targets law-abiding minorities and negatively affect minorities' behaviors and attitudes toward law enforcement.[2] However, those supporting law enforcement practices that employ various forms of profiling dispute the role of race in police decision making and believe that traffic stops of blacks and other minorities appropriately reflect offending rates. The term, supposedly coined by minority communities, is a parody of the criminal offense driving while intoxicated (DWI).

BACKGROUND

Racial profiling is driven by policies reflecting racial prejudices and stereotypes toward particular social groups. At various stages in U.S. history, laws were premised on prejudices against blacks. Laws such as those implemented as part of the Slave Codes, the Black Codes, and Jim Crow targeted black populations and maintained a discriminatory system of race-based law enforcement. Groups like slave patrols and the Ku Klux Klan in the Southern United States also operated as informal law enforcement so as to ensure the adherence to these codes.

Although the formal propagation of racially discriminatory law has been abolished, racial groups in the United States claim differential treatment by law enforcement officials. The Kerner Commission reported this disparity in treatment by police in their 1967 report following race riots. President Lyndon B. Johnson charged the Kerner Commission with examining the status of racial relations in the United States. The commission reported that racial uprisings were the result of inequality between blacks and whites. They also found that blacks were reporting high rates of police harassment. This report was significant because it illustrated how, although many battles for racial equality had apparently been won in the civil rights movement, discrimination still existed and was experienced by blacks in the United States.

KEY EVENTS

Events during the 1980s War on Drugs gave rise to the coinage of the term *driving while black*. In an attempt to crack down on drug use and selling, President Ronald Reagan established the Task Force on Crime in South Florida to directly address drug smuggling along Florida highways.[3] The goals of the task force made their way to the Florida Department of Highway Safety and Motor Vehicles, which also sought to more accurately target drug couriers. As part of measures to improve profiling techniques, this department created a drug courier profile that warned state troopers of the characteristics common to this population of offenders. In addition to looking for individuals driving rental cars or not obeying traffic laws, this profile also included a warning that these drug couriers would also exhibit characteristics associated with particular ethnic groups. By attaching criminal behaviors to specific racial or ethnic groups, the drug courier profile gave way to what has now come to be known as driving while black.

Driving while black came to national attention in the 1990s with complaints of racial profiling of black drivers on the New Jersey Turnpike. Many profiling cases go unreported nationwide, and those working within police departments have faced difficulty in exposing discriminatory practices.[4] Nonetheless, an incident in 1998 changed the stakes of this law enforcement practice. In 1998, three unarmed minority males were shot and killed in their vehicle during a traffic stop on the New Jersey Turnpike. The outrage over this incident and subsequent campaigns by the American Civil Liberties Union brought publicity to cases of driving while black. New Jersey Turnpike state troopers eventually faced various lawsuits by victims of profiling.

KEY CASES

The War on Drugs and the subsequent drug courier profile is often cited to have led the way for the U.S. Supreme Court's decision in *Whren v. United States* (1996), allowing for pretextual stops. This ruling made it possible for the police to stop and search vehicles for minor traffic violations. By legally sanctioning vehicle stops for small infractions, this ruling and others extended police discretionary power, giving them more latitude in deciding who is subject to law enforcement.[5] These rulings also constricted the Court's interpretation of Fourth

Amendment rights. The Court's decision that a police stop, pretextual or not, did not violate Fourth Amendment rights opened the door for increased police discretion over vehicles.

Public outrage over racial profiling on U.S. highways brought many cases to both state and federal courts. Since the negative press surrounding the New Jersey State Police's practices, millions of dollars have been awarded in cases brought against the organization. In 2002, three black men were awarded $250,000 in their case against the New Jersey State Police—the largest settlement paid out to plaintiffs in these types of racial profiling cases.[6] The American Civil Liberties Union has led the charge in the courtroom against racial profiling practices and thus successfully represented minority groups in driving-while-black cases. These settlements and others have been paid out with the hopes of reestablishing faith in law enforcement and to restore the idea of fairness in their practices. In addition, many police departments have come under the watchful eye of social scientist and government agencies alike, monitoring their practices and reporting if profiling appears to be driving decision making. In 1999, the New Jersey State Police was put under the supervision of federal monitors by a U.S. Justice Department consent decree requiring that troopers collect data about the race of the drivers they stop.

FOURTH AMENDMENT RIGHTS

The Fourth Amendment of the United States Constitution protects individuals from illegal search or seizures. It also requires the proper issue of warrants given probable cause. Under the Fourth Amendment, law enforcement officials must use their judgment to determine whether there is sufficient evidence to warrant a search. The somewhat ambiguous definition of probable cause gives police officers a great degree of discretionary power. Many believe that this power afforded by the Fourth Amendment allows for a phenomenon like driving while black to occur.

FUTURE PROSPECTS

Racially biased policing practices that allow a phenomenon like driving while black to persist are highly debated. Those against profiling claim the practice undermines the legitimacy of the criminal justice system through using stereotypes to apprehend criminals. They believe it reinforces and legitimizes stereotypes and results in the oversurveillance of certain communities, ultimately alienating them. As a result, the majority of drug arrestees are minorities, and these numbers pale in comparison to the number of the country's minority drug users. In addition to breeding mistrust in the police, profiling practices also develop a shooting bias with black suspects. Studies have claimed that police officers are more likely to shoot at black suspects than white suspects because of a presumption of guilt.[7]

Those in favor of profiling, however, argue that the practice gives law enforcement agents a jump on crime and leads to effective policing (i.e., higher rates of success as measured by apprehension of offenders). Nonetheless, those promoting this perspective typically do not acknowledge race as a significantly influential factor in police decision making and highlight other legal and situational factors in explaining when police decide to stop.

The question remains, however, what would law enforcement look like without various forms of profiling such as driving while black? Is it possible for law enforcement officials to be trained to make pretextual stops without profiling based upon race? In a post-9/11 society, it has been argued that profiling techniques are necessary in order to maintain public safety. The public response to law enforcement techniques that use racial profiling will determine the fate of not only the driving-while-black phenomenon but also other post-9/11 profiling practices.

See Also: African American Criminal (In) Justice; Community Police; Racial Profiling; War on Drugs.

Endnotes

1. See also Samuel Walter, *Searching for the Denominator: Problems with Police Traffic Stop Data and an Early Warning System Solution* (Washington, DC: National Institute of Justice, 2002).
2. See also David A. Harris, "Driving while Black: Racial Profiling on Our Nation's Highways," *American Civil Liberties Union* (1999), http://www.aclu.org/racialjustice/racialprofiling/15912pub19990607.html.
3. Ibid.
4. See also Kelvin R. Davis, *Driving while Black: Cover-up* (Cincinnati, OH: Interstate International Publishing, 2001).
5. See also John C. Hall, *Pretext Traffic Stops: Whren v. United States* (Washington, DC: Federal Bureau of Investigation, 1996); *Ohio v. Robinette* (1996), *Maryland v. Wilson* (1997), and *Wyoming v. Houghton* (1999).
6. This settlement is the largest amount in cases that do not involve arrest, physical injuries, or detention.
7. Harris, "Driving while Black."

Further Reading: Engel, R., J. Calnon, and T. Bernard, "Theory and Racial Profiling: Shortcomings and Future Directions in Research," *Justice Quarterly* 19 (2001): 249–73; Harris, David A., *Profiles in Injustice: Why Police Profiling Cannot Work* (New York: New Press, 2002); Meeks, Kenneth, *Driving while Black* (New York: Broadway Books, 2000); Weitzer, R., and S. Tuch, *Race and Policing in America: Conflict and Reform* (New York: Cambridge University Press, 2006).

Nandi E. Dill

DWI AND DRUG TESTING

INTRODUCTION

Policies that target driving while intoxicated (DWI) or that permit so-called suspicionless[1] drug testing of specified groups (employees, students) demonstrate the conflict between promoting public health and safety and constricting individual liberty and privacy. Anti-DWI laws are programs designed to reduce the damage caused by the mix of alcohol and driving, which kills and injures thousands of Americans each year. Mass drug-testing policies, whether by employers or in schools, are viewed by advocates as means of ensuring well-being and integrity in workplace and academic settings, with the added bonus of discouraging drug use generally.

Opponents of these mass testing polices, for example, are concerned about the affects on certain constitutional rights. One scholar has noted that changes in judicial conceptions of the proper scope of government power have occurred in the wake of attempts to regulate traffic.[2] This is nowhere more evident than in the case of anti-DWI policies and is echoed in the case of drug-testing policies. In a series of court decisions addressing these policies, constitutional safeguards, particularly those related to due process and protection against unwarranted search and seizure, have been narrowed. Widespread public outcry about these practices has largely been muted; citizens appear to be willing to trade freedom for safety, or perceived safety, because it is unclear that these policies are the most effective means of mitigating the damages of drug and alcohol use. The full implications of these losses for situations beyond the narrow issues of DWI and drug use have yet to be seen.

BACKGROUND

DWI policies were enacted against the backdrop of certain facts about use of alcohol and drugs in the United States. It is undeniable that alcohol increases the chances of driving mishaps. In fact, a 0.04 percent blood alcohol concentration (BAC), an amount much less than the current limit of 0.08 percent, can lead to driving errors.[3] Data from 2005 show that close to 40 percent of U.S. traffic fatalities, or some 16,885 deaths, are linked to alcohol use.[4] Nevertheless, substantive numbers of individuals report driving after having used alcohol, approximately some 31.7 million people in 2005, or 13 percent of the population over the age of 12.[5] Further, only a fraction of those who report DWI are ever arrested for it; recent figures demonstrate an arrest prevalence of approximately 1 percent.[6] Drunk driving is more common among males and in those between 21 and 34 years old. It is more likely to occur at night and on weekends, generally the times when leisure activities take place.[7] Whites, persons of mixed race, and Native Americans most often report driving under the influence, whereas blacks, Hispanics, and mixed-race individuals report most often being arrested.[8]

Drug-testing polices are part of the arm of drug policy that focuses on prevention, specifically by lowering the prevalence of use in order to decrease its consequences, including addiction, and other negative aspects of use, like accidents, illness, productivity, and so forth. Employer-based drug testing is a common procedure. Most recent data show that 46 percent of workers report that their employer tests for drugs.[9] This figure is down from 49 percent in 1997.[10] Drug tests, generally using urine as the biological matrix, are done for a number of reasons, most often for preemployment screening, during postaccident investigations, or in cases of suspected on-the-job use. Random drug testing is done largely in settings where safety-related testing occurs.

DID YOU KNOW?

In 2005, of 3.6 million employee drug tests, approximately 4.3 percent were positive for one or more drugs. The most common drugs picked up on positive tests are, in order, marijuana, cocaine, amphetamines, and opiates.

Source: Quest Diagnostics, *Drug Testing Index* (Lyndhurst, NJ: Quest Diagnostics International, 2005), http://www.questdiagnostics.com/employersolutions/DTI_11_2005/dti_index.html.

Drug testing expanded from the workplace into schools following concerns over drug use by youth. According to one study, 18 percent of schools engaged in testing, mostly of students in high school.[11] This number, valid in 2001, has likely changed in the wake of the 2002 *Board of Education v. Earls* decision, which expanded categories of students who could be tested. Mass drug testing also takes place in the criminal justice system, from pretrial to probation or parole supervision. Such testing has not generated the controversy that other forms have created. This is likely due to the reduction in rights of those subject to criminal penalties.

KEY EVENTS

A major review of alcohol and driving, published in 1968, was the first government document to officially link alcohol driving and accidents.[12] Even so, DUI was seen as basically a traffic problem or a by-product problem of alcohol use.[13] This changed in 1980 with the rise of an organization called Mothers against Drunk Driving (MADD), started by Candy Lightner, who lost her 13-year-old to a drunk driver. MADD and similar organizations pushed to make penalties and criminal justice enforcement against drunk drivers more stringent. Drunk driving came to be viewed as a moral problem, with campaigns portraying drunk drivers as villains of the road, thus increasing the public ire directed toward those offenders.[14]

The movement was very successful in obtaining changes in DUI and alcohol policies, among them: (1) lowering the limit of acceptable blood alcohol for drivers; (2) sobriety checkpoints, which are defined areas where police will check vehicles to see if passengers are intoxicated or have some other alcohol-related violation; (3) administrative suspensions; (4) getting the drinking age raised from 18 to 21; and (5) increased penalties for offenders, mostly for recidivists but also for first-timers.[15]

These efforts were facilitated by the ability of the federal government to use its power over state funding of transportation projects to push states into drafting various laws designed to reduce driving under the influence. States were threatened with loss of highway construction funds unless they altered their laws according to federal dictates. Recent efforts in this regard include pushing for a reduction of the acceptable blood alcohol limit to 0.08 percent from 0.10 percent and mandating certain penalties for repeat offenders, including compelling the use of ignition interlocks. These last are devices designed to prevent a car from being turned on unless the driver registers a blood alcohol level below a given amount.

These changes met with some opposition, some of which centered on use of the Breathalyzer, and to the training of officers in discerning driver impairment. This likely reflects the overwhelming influence of per se laws, which penalize having a breath alcohol level above a given amount. A casual Internet survey reveals a cottage industry of defense attorneys advertising methods of fighting the test and DWI charges in general. Other challenges came from concern over the penalties, in particular administrative license suspensions and sobriety checkpoints. These wound up in the courts.

How have these policies worked in reducing DUI? The percentage of drunk-driving deaths has gone down in recent years. Some research has linked the change to various drunk-driving penalties, most specifically the ones directed at youth, such as raising the drinking age.[16] However, it is likely that other factors, for instance, a decline in the use of alcohol, are important as well.

Drug use exploded as a societal concern during the 1980s. This altered focus was linked to a variety of factors, including general concern over crime combined with the heightened use of crime as an issue in elections; the rising cocaine and, later, crack epidemic; and highly publicized incidents (such as the Len Bias cocaine overdose). These factors all contributed to an environment of increased public worry about drug use. Meanwhile, advances in the science and technology of drug-testing devices made the process quicker and more efficient and thus more feasible to carry out on a mass scale. Arguably, workplace drug testing had its inaugural in 1986, when President Ronald Reagan ordered that government agencies drug-test employees who worked in jobs featuring a high risk of injury. This proclamation ushered in the age of employee drug testing, with drug testing in other arenas to follow.[17]

As with DWI policies, the use of such tests was questioned, largely by civil libertarians and some drug-policy experts. They portrayed the tests as inaccurate and decried their intrusion into personal privacy, noting that the bodily fluids used could provide additional information about the person, from disease status to pregnancy. They also disputed the stated reasons for testing—ensuring safety—arguing that policies that addressed impairment of all kinds (from illicit to licit drugs to fatigue) would be more fruitful.[18]

How has workplace testing affected drug use? Data from one drug-testing laboratory shows a decline in the number of workers testing positive for drugs, from 13.8 percent in 1988 to 4.5 percent in 2004.[19] A recent study argues that workplace tests do impact on drug use generally, although the effect is weaker than is generally presumed.[20]

KEY LEGAL DECISIONS

Court challenges to DWI and drug-testing policies have resulted in a gradual redrawing of the line between individual freedom and government intrusion. Take, for instance, administrative suspensions, seen by some as a violation of due process, because one's license is taken away at the point of the DUI arrest. The Supreme Court in *Mackey v. Montrym* upheld these with the caveat that the person obtains a hearing shortly after the suspension.[21]

This opened the door to a more severe application of these laws; today, almost all states have laws using administrative suspension to punish the mere refusal to take a breath test.[22] The Supreme Court in *Michigan Department of State Police v. Sitz* upheld sobriety checkpoints, which are effectively suspicion-less searches.[23] They reasoned that rather than being a police action, checkpoints feature the state acting in its capacity to regulate public safety and thus are more akin to housing or restaurant inspections than crime fighting.

Regarding drug testing, the Supreme Court in *Skinner v. Railway Labor Executives' Association* ruled in 1989 that monitoring employees involved in "safety-sensitive" positions was a state interest overriding the right of individuals not to have their persons (bodily fluids) seized (via drug test) without probable cause.[24] The Court broadened its interpretation of the government's interest in the case of *National Treasury Employees Union v. Von Raab* to include concerns about customs workers facing promotion into positions that placed them at great risk, not for safety violations but for personal corruption due to increased contact with drugs in large quantities.[25] These two cases were cited as precedent in upholding drug testing of students, first in *Vernonia School District v. Acton,*[26] in which random drug testing of student athletes was approved, and then in *Board of Education v. Earls,*[27] which gave the nod to a program in Oklahoma that randomly tested all students involved in extracurricular activities.

What is notable about these court decisions is the basis on which they were decided. Specifically, these policies were upheld as promoters of health and safety and on the basis of administrative, rather than criminal justice, considerations.[28] This is important, as it demonstrates a potential limit to the Court's reach regarding such policies. Evidence for this can be seen by the types of testing plans overturned by the Court, among them a hospital-based program that tested pregnant women, with positive results immediately provided to law enforcement for purposes of prosecution,[29] and a Georgia law that used drug testing as a condition for candidacy for local office.[30]

FUTURE PROSPECTS

One topic that could loom large in future discussions of both DWI and drug-testing policy concerns the issue of drugged driving, or driving under the influence of drugs (DUID). Although it has a low prevalence rate (approximately 5% of those from a 2003 Substance Abuse and Mental Health Services Administration survey admit to drugged driving, versus roughly 16% who admit to DUI),[31] it has emerged as the next step in the evolution of concern over the negative effects of substance use. Recent attention speaks to a push to make drugged driving the next arena in the fight over automobile safety.[32]

Compared to the situation with alcohol, there is little science linking specific levels of drug use to impairment or to car accidents, making solutions to the drugged driving problem more difficult to enact. Most states have laws prohibiting DUID. Most define the offense based on actual impairment; however, several states define the offense based on per se grounds, which refers to using a zero-tolerance measure. There is potential for fresh court challenges based on enforcement of those laws, particularly, as in some cases, if authorities criminalize the presence of substances (marijuana metabolites, for instance) with no psychoactive impact whatsoever.

DID YOU KNOW?

At the end of 2006, 14 states had so-called zero-tolerance laws on drugs and driving: Arizona, Georgia, Illinois, Indiana, Iowa, Michigan, Minnesota, Nevada, Ohio, Pennsylvania, Rhode Island, Utah, Virginia, and Wisconsin. These laws prohibit the presence of illicit drugs in one's system either totally or greater than a certain amount.

Drugged driving is also important because it provides a friendly setting for the use of alternative—that is, non-urine-based—drug-testing technologies, in particular those using saliva. Saliva tests have the potential to capture current intoxication and, thus, to indicate current impairment.[33] Some European countries have conducted evaluation studies of saliva tests for roadside testing of drugged drivers, with mixed success.[34] As they are less intrusive than urine, such tests are very attractive for most drug-testing goals. Additionally, the technology can easily be converted for use in testing surfaces for the presence of drugs. Such devices are being evaluated for use in schools.[35]

The increasing prominence of alternative testing comes in the context of a reduction in employer drug testing, possibly due to concerns over cost. Some view the push for roadside testing as a cynical attempt to improve the flagging fortunes of the drug-testing industry. Others have seen it as a possible boon to public safety. One thing does remain evident: Conflicts over testing policies and the challenges they pose to individual freedom are far from over.

See Also: Problem-Solving Courts

Endnotes

1. *Skinner v. Railway Labor Executives' Association,* 489 U.S. 602 (1989).
2. Michael D. Laurence, "The Legal Context in the United States," in *Social Control of the Drinking Driver,* ed. Michael D. Laurence, John R. Snortum, and Franklin E. Zimring (Chicago: University of Chicago Press, 1988), 136–66.
3. H. Laurence Ross, *Confronting Drunk Driving: Social Policy for Saving Lives* (New Haven, CT: Yale University Press, 1992), 19.
4. National Center for Injury Prevention and Control, "Impaired Driving Facts" (Atlanta, GA: Centers for Disease Control and Prevention, 2006), http://www.cdc.gov/ncipc/factsheets/drving.htm.
5. Robert B. Voas, JoAnn Wells, Diane Lestina, Allan Williams, and Michael Greene, "Drinking and Driving in the United States: The 1996 National Roadside Survey," *Accident Analysis and Prevention* 30 (1998): 267–75.
6. Ibid.

7. Ibid.

8. Raul Caetano and Christine McGrath, "Driving while Intoxicated (DUI) among U.S. Ethnic Groups," *Accident Analysis and Prevention* 37 (2005): 217–24.

9. Christopher S. Carpenter, "Workplace Drug Testing and Worker Drug Use," *Health Services Research* 42, no. 2 (2006): 795–810, http://web.gsm.uci.edu/˜kittc/CarpenterHSRDrug-TestingArticle2006.pdf.

10. U.S. Department of Health and Human Services, Office of Applied Studies, "Worker Drug Use and Workplace Policies and Programs: Results from the 1994 and 1997 National Household Survey on Drug Abuse" (2007), http://www.oas.samhsa.gov/NHSDA/A-11/WrkplcPlcy2-06.htm#P136_7936.

11. Ryoko Yamaguchi, Lloyd D. Johnston, and Patrick M. O'Malley, "Relationship between Student Illicit Drug Use and School Drug-Testing Policies," *Journal of School Health* 73 (2003): 159–64.

12. Ross, *Confronting Drunk Driving,* 175.

13. Joseph, R. Gusfield, "The Control of Drinking and Driving in the United States: A Period in Transition," in *Social Control of the Drinking Driver,* ed. Michael D. Laurence, John R. Snortum, Franklin E. Zimring (Chicago: University of Chicago Press, 1988), 109–35.

14. Ibid.

15. Ibid.

16. Laurence, "The Legal Context in the United States."

17. Donald. W. Crowley, "Drug Testing in the Rehnquist Era," in *Images of Issues: Typifying of Contemporary Social Problems,* ed. Joel Best (New York: Walter de Gruyter, 1990), 123–39.

18. Ibid.

19. Carpenter, "Workplace Drug Testing and Worker Drug Use."

20. Yamaguchi et al., "Relationship between Student Illicit Drug Use and School Drug-Testing Policies."

21. *Mackey v. Montrym,* 443 U.S. 1. (1979).

22. Insurance Institute for Highway Safety, "DUI/DWI Laws," Insurance Institute for Highway Safety, Highway Loss Data Institute (2007), http://www.iihs.org/laws/state_laws/dui.html.

23. *Michigan Department of State Police v. Sitz,* 496 U.S. 444 (1990).

24. *Skinner v. Railway Labor Executives' Association.*

25. *National Treasury Employees Union v. Von Raab,* 489 U.S. 656 (1989).

26. *Vernonia School District v. Acton,* 515 U.S. 646 (1995).

27. *Board of Education v. Earls,* 122 S.Ct. 2559 (2002).

28. Crowley, "Drug Testing in the Rehnquist Era."

29. *Ferguson v. City of Charleston,* 532 U.S. 67 (2000).

30. *Chandler v. Miller,* 520 U.S. 305 (1997).

31. Substance Abuse and Mental Health Services Administration, *Driving under the Influence among Adult Drivers* (Rockville, MD: Center for Mental Health Services, Substance Abuse and Mental Health Services Administration, 2003), http://www.oas.samhsa.gov/2k5/DUI/DUI.pdf.

32. Donna Leinwand, "Growing Danger: Drugged Driving," *USA Today,* October 21, 2004, http://www.usatoday.com/news/nation/2004-10-21-cover-drugged-driving_x.htm; Paul Armentano, "Drug Test Nation," *Reason Online,* February 12, 2005, http://www.reason.com/news/show/32881.html.

33. E. J. Cone, "New Developments in Biological Measures of Drug Prevalence," in *The Validity of Self-Reported Drug Use: Improving the Accuracy of Survey Estimates,* NIDA Research Monograph 167, ed. Lana Harrison and Arthur Hughes (Washington, DC: U.S.

Department of Health and Human Services, 1997), 108–30, http://www.nida.nih.gov/pdf/monographs/monograph167/108-129_Cone.pdf.

34. See Roadside Testing and Assessment, http://www.rosita.org/.

35. Art McFarland, "A New Weapon to Detect Drugs in Schools," 7Online.com, *WABC-TV News*, November 13, 2006, http://abclocal.go.com/wabc/story?section=our_schools&id=4757591.

Further Reading: Cone, Edward. J., "New Developments in Biological Measures of Drug Prevalence," in *The Validity of Self-Reported Drug Use: Improving the Accuracy of Survey Estimates,* NIDA Research Monograph 167, ed. Lana Harrison and Arthur Hughes (Washington, DC: U.S. Department of Health and Human Services), http://www.nida.nih.gov/pdf/monographs/monograph167/108-129_Cone.pdf; Gilliom, John, *Surveillance, Privacy and the Law: Employee Drug Testing and the Politics of Social Control* (Ann Arbor: University of Michigan Press, 1994); Reinarman, Craig, "The Social Construction of an Alcohol Problem: The Case of Mothers against Drunk Driving and Social Control in the 1980s," *Theory and Society* 17 (1988): 91–120; Ross, H. Laurence, *Confronting Drunk Driving: Social Policy for Saving Lives* (New Haven, CT: Yale University Press, 1992); Scott, Michael S., *Drunk Driving,* with Nina J. Emerson, Louis B. Antonacci, and Joel B. Plant, Problem-Oriented Guides for Police, Problem-Specific Guide Series, No. 36 (Washington, DC: U.S. Department of Justice, Office of Community Oriented Policing Services, 2006), http://www.cops.usdoj.gov/mime/open.pdf?Item=1665.

Angela Taylor

ENVIRONMENTAL CRIME CONTROL

INTRODUCTION

The United States implemented numerous environmental laws in the 1970s that aimed to protect and conserve the county's natural resources. Although the introduction of the new legislation was regarded as an essential first step in addressing environmental concerns, many controversial issues began to surround the topic of environmental crime. Controversy arose over the importance placed upon environmental crime, the issue of intent with environmental crime perpetrators, and the production of international environmental crime. The following will include a description of the nature of environmental crime, a review of several environmental legislative decisions, and an exploration of the controversial issues.

BACKGROUND

Environmental crime is a broad and, seemingly, all-encompassing term for any violation of environmental law.[1] This definition includes crimes committed by individuals, groups, and corporate and business offenders that range in severity from mild to severe violations. Examples of environmental crimes include illegal dumping of toxins, illegal disposal of construction and demolition materials, and the contamination of water, soil, or air. Corporations and business entities perpetrate a large portion of environmental crimes,[2] although individuals also commit environmental crime (often in the less-severe form of littering). Nevertheless, in comparison with the types of environmental violations by corporations and businesses, individual cases tend to be minor, infrequent, and generally overlooked by society and law enforcement.

The Environmental Protection Agency (EPA) is a branch of the United States federal government that creates, controls, and enforces environmental laws. Although local law enforcement officials and state attorney general offices have begun the colossal task of investigating and prosecuting environmental crimes, the EPA remains as the principal enforcer of environmental crime. Not all environmental degradation is considered unlawful; transportation, product production, and waste disposal damage the environment; however, these services are necessary for society to function. The EPA has established the specific points at which the levels of environmental degradation reach the state at which they become harmful. Therefore, if levels of toxicity exceed these particular levels designated by the EPA, an environmental crime has occurred. After the initial investigation as to if a site has been illegally damaged, the EPA will arrange for the removal of the hazardous materials. Those persons responsible for the environmental crime, if located, will assume the financial burden of site cleanup. Under the circumstances in which the perpetrator cannot be located, the EPA will finance the cleanup with funds from the Superfund Trust Fund, which is a financial reserve of taxes from chemical and oil companies specifically designed to restore the environment.

CASE STUDY: *EXXON VALDEZ*

An oil tanker called *Exxon Valdez*, owned by the former Exxon Corporation, crashed into Prince William Sound's Bligh Reef in Alaska in 1989. The resulting catastrophic oil spill of between 11 million and 30 million gallons killed thousands of animals, including sea birds, sea otters, harbor seals, bald eagles, orcas, and billions of salmon and herring eggs.

Joseph Hazelwood, the captain of the *Exxon Valdez*, was accused of being drunk at the time of the accident, although he was later cleared of this charge. Hazelwood was convicted of negligence, fined $50,000, and sentenced to 1,000 hours of community service cleaning the Alaskan beaches.

Environmental crime has many negative consequences for the environment, animals, and humans. The victims of environmental crime are often elements in the natural environment that cannot inform law enforcement of the violation. Many times, the environment in a specific area will suffer silently from toxicity that goes undetected.[3] Environmental degradation is the most common negative consequence of environmental crime and is often a result of water pollution, air pollution, and land pollution.

Victims of environmental crime also include people who have suffered due to the negligence of business and corporate wrongdoing. Humans and animals may experience harmful side effects from exposure to noxious toxins, which may result in the development of health defects, such as respiratory problems, birth defects, cancer, or even death. Although these victims are able to inform the proper authorities of the crime, they are often unaware the cause of their suffering is directly related to corporate criminal behavior. Furthermore, if the victims of environmental crimes are aware of the injustice, it is also likely they still will not act or inform authorities. The victims may not fully understand the gravity of the crime and/or may believe informing authorities will not result in punishment of the criminals. Individuals may also perceive the police negatively and might be hesitant to call the attention of police to their neighborhood for fear of exposing their community to further scrutiny for other misconducts. This may be especially true in socially disadvantaged communities that are more likely to be victims of environmental injustice.

BUSINESSES MOST LIKELY TO COMMIT ENVIRONMENTAL CRIME

Gas stations	Hospitals
Photo shops	Furniture builders
Funeral homes	Automotive repair shops
Dry cleaners	

Environmental crime is unique in many ways. It is extremely difficult to detect environmental crimes in comparison with conventional crimes. Conventional crimes frequently come to the attention of the victims, law enforcement personnel, and society quite easily, as it is often simple to determine when an individual has been robbed, assaulted, and so on. Victims of conventional crimes are usually aware of being victimized and, therefore, have the opportunity to inform law enforcement personnel of the criminal behaviors. Furthermore, the evidence in conventional crime cases often visibly shows the occurrence of criminal acts (such as a missing purse or a visible wound). On the other hand, environmental crimes tend to be more elusive and are often undiscovered by victims, law enforcement, and society.[4] Because environmental violations are often undetected by authorities and unsuspecting victims of the crime, it is especially difficult for police to control environmental crime. Countless environmental crimes go unnoticed for years by the authorities and victims, and many are overlooked indefinitely.

Although it is generally recognized that environmental crimes have serious detrimental consequences, debate exists as to the seriousness of the crime and, subsequently, the importance placed upon the control of environmental crime. The U.S. presidential cabinet determines the annual budget for the EPA. The budget allotted to the EPA is based on a number of factors, including the social importance of funding the control of environmental crime in comparison with all other types of governmental spending. Some argue the budget given to the EPA is sufficient to satisfactorily protect society and the environment from environmental infractions. Others contend that the EPA's budget is insufficient to support the development and regulation of environmental crime, to provide financial assistance for programs and grants, and to perform environmental research. Interestingly, research exists that supports the notion that the U.S. public views environmental crime as serious, whereas other research shows citizens are becoming increasingly skeptical of the cost-effectiveness of enforcing environmental regulations, indicating that enforcing environmental laws may be costing society more than its worth.[5]

CRUISE CRIMINALS CAUGHT!

A couple aboard a Princess Cruise ship during summer 1993 videotaped crew members tossing plastic bags filled with trash into the ocean just five miles from the Florida Keys.

The whistle-blowing couple received $250,000 as a reward for turning in the evidence used to prosecute this case of environmental crime.

Other controversial issues within the topic of environmental crime relate to sanctioning the environmental criminal. Because some environmental infractions occur accidentally, and not intentionally, scholars have debated punishing environmental criminals without first considering their criminal intent. To date, there is no known research that reveals the percentage of environmental crimes that are committed intentionally versus those that are unintended mistakes. Some argue that accidental environmental disasters (such as oil spills) are an inevitable part of many businesses, and punishing business owners for mistakes that result in environmental law violations may deter some businesses from offering certain types of services. Business owners may feel the risk of being labeled and punished, as an environmental criminal is not worth offering the services. These scholars further argue that punishing the perpetrators of environmental crime who have committed the crime by accident would be a misdirection of the scarce resources the criminal justice system possesses. Others have maintained that punishing violators of environmental laws based on their criminal intentions (or lack of intentions) would be an unnecessary burden for the EPA and criminal justice system to bear. Furthermore, it is argued that because most environmental crimes go undetected and unpunished, allowing environmental criminals to claim their breach of environmental law was an accident would provide an even easier method for individuals or businesses that intentionally committed the crime to escape punishment. This practice would send the erroneous message to society that environmental crimes are tolerated and accepted by our criminal justice system.[6]

Environmental degradation is a problem for all countries and has produced many controversial issues. International environmental concerns include the destruction of the ozone layer, global warming, marine pollution, and the preservation of biological diversity. International environmental crime, also called transboundary pollution, can occur from pollution generated in one country and sent to another country (e.g., smoke stacks erected to disperse air pollutants in one country eventually settle in another country). Businesses or corporations based in one country can establish a division in another country where environmental laws are less stringent and where the company will be allowed to produce pollution at higher levels (e.g., a shoe company in one country establishes a branch in a foreign country that enables it to dispose of toxic material without violating the environmental laws as it would have in the home country).

CASE STUDY: TIMES BEACH

Times Beach, Missouri, was a small town of 2,240 lower-middle-class residents. The town was faced with a dust problem in the early 1970s due to its insufficient funds to pave roads. Russell Bliss was hired to fix the dust problem by oiling the roads. Between 1972 and 1976, Bliss mixed a toxic substance, dioxin, into the waste oil he poured on the roads. Bliss had used the mixture earlier in 1971 to control dust in horse stables, which resulted in the death of 62 horses.

In 1979, after several investigations of Bliss's actions, a fellow employee of Bliss's confessed that he was using dioxin to treat dust. Tests of soil from Times Beach showed levels of dioxin were 100 times the level believed to be safe. The town flooded in 1982, resulting in evacuation of its residents, and a few weeks later the EPA announced the finding of dangerous dioxin levels in the town soil. The effects of dioxin on Times Beach residents remain unknown; however, residents attribute cases of illnesses, miscarriages, and animal deaths to the dioxin exposure. Russell Bliss was never charged for any wrongdoing.

International environmental degradation raises many controversial issues for debate. Some environmentally concerned individuals and organizations believe transboundary pollution is unethical, arguing that to benefit one country to the detriment of another is only a temporary relief of an inevitably catastrophic consequence of seismic proportions (e.g., global warming, destruction of the ozone layer, etc.). Others argue that the political assumptions and economic systems of entire countries (such as capitalism) are based upon the idea of competition in a free market that considers land and natural resources to be factors of production that are considered a commodity, which would legitimate the use of environmental resources.

Another point of contention concerns the control and regulation of international environmental laws. The Security Council of the United Nations (UN) is the key source for enforcing international laws. The goal of the Security Council is to maintain peace and security among nations, and it has the power to render legal decisions by which nations must abide. However, the Security Council is limited in power in that all members must unanimously agree on a particular action before it may render a formal decision. The UN also established an International Court of Justice to hear cases. The court is limited to hearing cases in which the parties agree to attend; therefore, those cases that need it most are least likely to use it. In some cases, the court can issue only advisory opinions, which are often ignored. The court has four basic principles for nations to abide by, including: (1) to be good neighbor states, (2) to protect the rights of other states, (3) to reasonably use shared resources, and (4) to inform and cooperate with other nations.[7]

Of those that control and regulate international environmental laws, the United Nations is most influential. The World Bank is a primary source of funding for developing countries and, therefore, is very influential in guiding international environment policies. The European Union (EU) is also very influential in creating and controlling environmental laws in Europe. The EU is a coalition of 25 European nations that has instituted hundreds of environmental laws by which each member state must abide.

KEY EVENTS

Environmental crime was of little consequence to public policy or social concern worldwide before the 1970s. During the unique time period surrounding 1970, widespread concern for environmental issues became popular for several reasons. In 1970, U.S. President Richard Nixon activated the first federal organization designed to work toward a cleaner and healthier United States: the EPA. The birth of this federal regulatory agency was an exceptionally significant governmental reaction to increasing public concern over environmental violations. In comparison with the relatively small size of the agency (fewer than 20,000 employees), the EPA is responsible for a long list of duties ranging from the development, implementation, and enforcement of environmental regulations to the sponsorship of partnerships and programs. The EPA also performs environmental research, promotes environmental education, publishes information, and funds projects, research, grants, and educational fellowships. The EPA serves to inform the public of environmental violations and also gives a voice to the many concerned Americans advocating the preservation and conservation of natural resources.

In addition to the establishment of the EPA, several other remarkable social movements began to emerge and flourish in the face of an alarming and depreciating environment. April 22, 1970, marks the first Earth Day in which millions of Americans participated in ecologically friendly events and celebrations. Earth Day is still practiced and celebrated today. Similarly, the EPA has annually dedicated the second week in April as National Environmental Crime Prevention

CASE STUDY: THE LOVE CANAL

The Love Canal is one of the most famous and catastrophic cases of environmental violation and began with William T. Love envisioning a dream community in which, by digging a canal, residents on the eastern edge of Niagara Falls, New York, could have access to inexpensively generated power. When other means of generating electricity ran Love out of business, the canal became a toxic waste dump site in the 1920s. The owners of the property, Hooker Chemical Company, filled and covered the dump site in 1953 and sold it to the city of Niagara Falls for $1.

By the late 1950s, approximately one hundred homes and an elementary school were built on the land. In 1978, the Love Canal exploded, and the dangerous and deadly exposure to the noxious toxins became public. Due to the exposure to the harmful substances, residents experienced nervous system disorders, exceptionally high miscarriage rates, disfiguring birth defects, and cancer. This extreme environmental violation is one example that directly impacted social change, which led to the implementation of environmental legislation.

Week in an effort to continually generate public interest in and concern for a healthy environment.

Internationally, several key events launched the establishment of environmental laws. The UN hosted a two-week meeting in Stockholm, Sweden, in 1972 called the Conference on the Human Environment. The Stockholm Declaration was drafted at this meeting, which introduced the expectation of nations to cooperate with one another, to respect the environmental laws of other countries, and to continue to develop international law regarding liability and compensation for the victims. In 1982, the UN adopted an agreement titled the World Charter for Nature, which further detailed the obligations, planning, and management necessary for members of the international community to abide by when dealing with the natural environment on international grounds.[8]

LEGAL DECISIONS

The United States EPA has enacted a wide variety of laws to protect the environment and the public from hazardous levels of toxicity. The best-known environmental laws include the National Environmental Policy Act (NEPA; 1969), the Clean Air Act (1970), the Clean Water Act (1977), and the Comprehensive Environmental Response, Compensation, and Liability Act (CERCLA or Superfund; 1980). The purpose of NEPA is to find a harmonious balance between the environment and humanity in ways that protect the environment from unnecessary damage and to promote education regarding the positive effects of preserving environmental resources. NEPA also mandates that prior to beginning any activities, federal agencies must consult with the Council for Environmental Quality (CEQ), which will ensure that the proposal will consider the welfare of the human environment. The Clean Air Act prohibits polluting the air in order to safeguard against dangerous toxins, which promotes the health of the environment and its citizens. The Clean Water Act resulted from a growing concern about the water quality, and this legislation regulates the pollutants that may be deposited in all bodies of water in an effort to protect the public, marine life, and environment from exposure to harmful contaminants. CERCLA created regulations for hazardous waste sites, required that violators be held responsible for damages, and initiated a tax on the chemical and petroleum industries that provides a cleanup trust fund for hazardous waste sites. The EPA has instituted dozens of environmental laws to protect the environment and citizens' health by combating the environmental degradation of land, air, and water.

Legal decisions have also been made on international fronts. In 1997, an international treaty was negotiated in Kyoto, Japan, called the Kyoto Protocol. The Kyoto Protocol aimed to reduce the concentration of greenhouse gases in the atmosphere to a level that would prevent dangerous global climate system consequences. As of July 2006, 164 countries have agreed to the Kyoto Protocol. Noteworthy exclusions include the United States and Australia. Some countries that have agreed to the Kyoto Protocol (such as India and China) are not required to lower carbon emissions. The Kyoto Protocol remains a current topic of international debate, especially due to the absence of support from the United States. Supporters of the Kyoto Protocol believe the United States should adopt the Kyoto Protocol, especially because the country is the largest energy-consuming country. Support from the United States would ultimately result in global levels of greenhouse gases reducing significantly. Those in opposition to the Kyoto Protocol view the treaty as detrimental to the country's economic sustainability of production levels and a direct threat to the nation. Opponents also contend that the Kyoto Protocol would result in a loss of U.S. governmental power and control and would, in turn, provide a significant advantage for other competing countries, such as European countries and China.

FUTURE PROSPECTS

Many communities burdened with hazardous waste facilities unknowingly and silently endure daily exposure to noxious toxins, an increased risk for contracting harmful and often deadly diseases, and the stigmatization of living in a polluted community. Equally disturbing, corporations and business entities are continually held unaccountable for such heinous acts. In the wake of these atrocious events, much opportunity exists for groundbreaking work among researchers, including investigating the prevalence of environmental crime, public opinion of environmental crime and environmental criminals, and the extent to which the crimes occur in specific locations (rural versus urban, high or low socioeconomic neighborhoods, etc.).

Environmental law and the enforcement of such laws are relatively recent developments in the United States, which may partially account for the difficulties experienced by the EPA and other regulatory agencies. The nature of environmental crimes, the criminals, and the degree of culpability all play a factor in the subsequent sanctioning and sentencing of environmental offenders. The future of environmental crime control will depend greatly on its perceived importance by presidential cabinets, international nations, policy makers, law enforcement officers, researchers, and society. As environmental violations become more frequent and publicized more regularly, it is likely that the control of environmental crime will continue to change and adapt to meet the ever-growing demands of society.

See Also: Defining Criminal Violence.

Endnotes

1. M. Clifford, *Environmental Crime: Enforcement, Policy, and Social Responsibility* (Gaithersburg, MD: Aspen, 1998).
2. D. O. Friedrichs, *Trusted Criminals: White Collar Crime in Contemporary Society,* 2nd ed. (Belmont, CA: Wadsworth, 2004).
3. L. E. Korsell, "Big Stick, Little Stick: Strategies for Controlling and Combating Environmental Crime," *Journal of Scandinavian Studies in Criminology and Crime Prevention* 2 (2001): 127–48.
4. M. M. O'Hear, "Sentencing the Green Collar Offender: Punishment, Culpability, and Environmental Crime," *Journal of Criminal Law and Criminology* 95 (2004): 133–276.
5. Clifford, *Environmental Crime.*
6. O'Hear, "Sentencing the Green Collar Offender."

7. N. K. Kubasek and G. S. Silverman, *Environmental Law*, 3rd ed. (Upper Saddle River: NJ: Prentice-Hall, 2000).

8. Ibid.

Further Reading: Burns, R. G., and M. J. Lynch, *Environmental Crime: A Sourcebook* (New York: LFB Scholarly, 2004); Epstein, S. S., L. O. Brown, and C. Pope, *Hazardous Waste in America* (San Francisco: Sierra Club Books, 1982); Rebovich, D., *Dangerous Ground: The World of Hazardous Waste Crime* (New Brunswick, NJ: Transaction, 1992); U.S. Environmental Protection Agency, *Compliance and Enforcement Annual Results: FY 2005 Numbers at a Glance* (n.d.), http://www.epa.gov/compliance; Watson, M., "Environmental Offenses: The Reality of Environmental Crime," *Environmental Law Review* 7 (2005): 190–200.

Kathleen A. Fox

EQUAL JUSTICE AND HUMAN RIGHTS

INTRODUCTION

Within the development of alternative responses to the more traditional forms of crime control and criminal justice management and propelled by the practices and ideologies of restorative and social justice and the movement for human rights more generally, on the one hand, and grounded within the solidification and expansion of systems of punishment and surveillance, on the other hand, controversies have stirred over the past half century over the viability or efficacy of equal justice for all.

On one side are those criminologists, justicians, and other advocates of human rights who argue equal justice is neither equal nor just, and that what is called for are systems of criminal justice that recognize the various inequalities operating throughout society. These critics argue policies of equal justice that do not take into account the so-called equal treatment of nonequal offenders or victims by class, race, gender, sexual orientation, and so on or the unequal treatment of analogous social injuries or harms by the powerful and the powerless, respectively, serve to reproduce the status quo of crime, injustice, and victimization.

On another side are those criminologists, justicians, and other strict legal constructionists who argue that equal justice is realized when one's due process and the rule of law have not been violated by the state during its intervention into criminal wrongdoing. At the same time, these proponents of equal justice recognizing patterns of discriminatory discretion call for procedural reforms and better practices to help actualize equal justice for all. These advocates maintain that the problem is not with the equal justice system but with the procedural irregularities in the application of due process and equal protection.

Obviously, the criteria or standards used to judge what is equal and what is justice vary widely. Hence, disagreements ensue around which system or systems of justice are more or less fair, are more or less punitive, are more or less reformative, are more or less individualistic, are more or less social, and so on and so forth.

BACKGROUND

Models of crime control and systems of justice assume different things about crime, criminals, and society. Accordingly, they respond with their respective practices, arrangements, and scenarios for achieving the application of justice. In the everyday practices of crime and social control, there are essentially three systems or approaches to justice: equal, restorative, and social. Inside and outside the United States, the ideals and realities of equal justice are older than the ideals and realities of restorative or social justice. The ideas and practices of equal justice compared to those of restorative and social justice are more individually and less socially oriented approaches to justice.

Historically, the rights of the state versus the rights of the individual or the struggle between the rights of the monarchy and the rights of the commoners have a relatively long trajectory, dating as far back as the signing of the Magna Carta in 1215. In that moment, it was in a small borough outside of London called Runnymede where King John acquiesced to his barons documenting the protected rights of feudal lords, setting the stage for what would eventually evolve into legal procedures or rules of law that both subjects and kings alike would have to abide by or suffer the authorized consequences. Initially through common and eventually international law, notions of what were originally individualistic equal rights for some have evolved into collective equal human rights for all.

During the modern evolution of justice, as history has moved from individual to collective notions of justice, there has been a widening of both the meanings of and the entitlements to fundamental rights. These expanding ideas initially found expression in small philosophical or political circles, gradually finding acceptance, if not consensus, in a significant portion of the body politic and, ultimately, finding articulation and incorporation in the substantive as well as the procedural sides of the law. In terms of the contemporary period, or at least since the end of World War II, a transition away from the relative limits or constraints of legal rights and toward the blossoming or escalating possibilities of human rights has occurred. This escalation includes, for example, the formation of an international court of criminal law whose purposes include the trial of those heads of state who have or could be charged with violating the fundamental human rights of people in such different geographic locales as Rwanda, Bosnia, Iraq, Afghanistan, or Guantanamo Bay.

EQUAL JUSTICE

In the United States, equal justice takes as a given or assumes as unproblematic the rationality of the prevailing political, economic, and social arrangements in general and of the administration of justice in particular. Equal justice refers to equal protection or due process under the rule of law rather than the rule of people. It assumes reasonable fairness in the substantive and procedural ingredients of the law. It also assumes a proper balancing of the rights of the individual and the rights of the state vis-à-vis the legislative and judicial branches of government. In these scenarios of equal justice, crimes are those exceptional harms deemed worthy of the criminal law, and the administration of criminal law is the delivery of the appropriate sanction for those criminals who have acted preferably immorally and rationally rather than irrationally and amorally and who have not had their legal rights violated by agents of the state.

Within this system, whether criminals are bad or mad, they are disconnected from their socioeconomic conditions as well as their class, racial, and gendered experiences and identities, and they are held equally accountable for the harm they inflict regardless of context or situation. Viewed as threatening outcasts who are marked by moral deprivation and a lack of empathy and impulse control, these so-called dangerous members of the criminal classes are socially and culturally constructed as evil people in need of retributive or eye-for-an-eye justice. Also referred to, since the late 1970s and early 1980s, as *just deserts,* this model of punishment, whether justified in terms of deterrence, rehabilitation, or incapacitation, sanctions equally with limited discretion those acts repressed to an escalation of pain and suffering regardless of motive.

The current model of equal justice practiced in the United States has its roots in the mid-eighteenth century, when the European age of reason or enlightenment was busy reforming the more arbitrary and barbaric justice practices dating back to the medieval period. These repressive, but not excessive (e.g., revenge, vengeance), models of equal justice today downplay flexible sentencing, community alternatives, and restitution. They also ignore the social structures, environmental milieus, and ecologies of crime. In addition, these models of justice have traditionally not considered the interests of either the injured parties or their communities, nor of the perpetrators themselves. In short, the adjudicative practices of equal justice serve to reinforce a repressive system of individualized justice that helps sustain as well as institutionalize a permanent underclass of marginally dangerous offenders.

UNEQUAL JUSTICE

Persons who come before the various tribunals of justice have never been, nor are they now, equal. Legalistic fairness, due process, and equal protection in actual practice do not equate with equal justice in a court of law or in the larger courts of public opinion. Class, race, and gender do matter at law and in society. When evaluators of justice, criminal or civil, falsely consider unequal persons by socioeconomic status, gender, or sexual orientation, for example, as equal based on some kind of formal legal equality for all people, they ignore, deny, or dismiss very concrete inequalities that cut across crime, justice, and society, reflecting very real differences in political, economic, and social power.

The limits of the administration of criminal justice, if not as a means of controlling some crimes but as a means of preventing those same crimes in the future, can be attributable not only to the overemphasis on notions of individual or equal justice but also to an overreliance on claims of criminal justice impartiality. As a result, many discussions of injustice focus on the procedural irregularities in the application of due process rather than with the selective and differential applications of the law, not to mention the substantive irregularities in the unequal definitions of analogous harms and injuries in the first place. The point is that there is a long list of harms or injuries that could be legally prohibited but have not been. These social pains emanate mostly from the invested structures of the political economy. Thus, they have not been labeled as constituting crimes worth pursuing because they benefit powerful interests that may or may not trickle down to others in society. Even when such acts as price-fixing, consumer or investor deception, antitrust violations, environmental destruction, racial discrimination, sexual harassment, and the like have been authorized as worth pursing, for a variety of reasons, this pursuit is short lived as we soon return to crime-control business as usual.

The consequences of these omissions of equality are that crime control is stacked against the marginally culpable rather than the affluently culpable. For example, the so-called War on Drugs and its double standards of enforcement have had unintended consequences that extend well beyond the confines of the criminal justice system and into the community and beyond. As particular drugs and marginalized persons (users) were targeted for criminalization, minority communities of African and Latin backgrounds were unequally repressed compared to the majority white populations.

The large-scale removal of young black males from their communities helped deplete the supply of potential marriage partners for young black females, especially during the 1990s. Some commentators have argued that these social relations of punishment encouraged or legitimated young female-headed households, creating precisely the types of family formations that have been linked with higher rates of street crime and domestic abuse. More accurately, these trends in racial and gender punishment reinforced and exacerbated the impoverishment and community inefficacy in which many of these households reside.

Similarly, the increased processing of less serious marginal offenders throughout the criminal justice system has not only created a state of megawarehouses of nonviolent offenders, but it has also undermined the capacity of formal systems of crime control to deliver on their promises of due process and equal protection for all, during a period in U.S. history when the rates of crimes against the person such as murders and crimes against property such as burglary are at fifty-year lows. Nevertheless, assembly-line, plea-bargained equal justice pertains not only to defendants but to the convicted as well, as each of these groups becomes subject to the practices of actuarial justice or to the forecasting of the costs and risks associated with managing so-called dangerous populations. In the end, this type of bureaucratized equal justice for all helps secure and reinforce stereotypical images of both crime and criminals through sophisticated systems of profiling and classification.

HUMAN RIGHTS AND THE EXPANSION OF EQUAL JUSTICE

Human rights and the systems of justice—equal, restorative, and social—cannot be separated from the modern evolution in justice or from a history of the struggle for justice. Each of these systems or models of justice represents an era or generation in the three-tier evolution of the rights of human beings to, ultimately, share exactly the same rights in common as everybody else, regardless of class, race/ethnicity, gender, religion, nationality, or sexual orientation, simply because we are all part of the human species. Stated differently, each of these epochs in the evolution of justice has reflected very different cultural and socioeconomic stratifications: preindustrial, industrial, and postindustrial. Historically, conflicting political traditions have built different visions of what constitutes human rights and over which of its elements has priority. Historically, the evolution of human rights has referred to the expanding notions of rights associated with three generations of rights.

The first generation of rights represented the struggle for equal justice, or the struggle for negative rights in that they called for restraint from the state and/or monarchy. These rights were derived from the American and French revolutions and the struggle to gain liberty or freedom from arbitrary rule. These rights are articulated in the Civil and Political Rights of the International Bill of Rights. Collectively, these rights have helped shape what we usually refer to as governmental control by rule of law rather than by rule of man. A product of this struggle has been an emphasis on the impartial and fair enforcement of the substantive and procedural criminal law.

The second generation of rights represented the struggle for restorative justice, or the struggle for positive rights in that they called for affirmative actions on the part of the state. The rights were derived from the experiences of the Soviet Union, and they have also resonated in the welfare state policies of the West. These rights are articulated in the Economic, Social, and Cultural Rights of the International Bill of Rights. Collectively, these rights have helped shape what we refer to as the minimal duties or social obligations of the state to facilitate the self-realization of the individual. A product of this struggle has been an emphasis on community social welfare, penitence and redemption, and victim-offender reconciliation.

The third generation of rights represents the contemporary struggle for social justice, or the struggle for universal human rights. Evolving out of the emerging conditions of global interdependence, these rights call for international cooperation between all nation-states, such as the establishment of the first international criminal court in 1999. Collectively, these rights recognize that the delivery of human rights for all cannot be satisfied within the body of individual states acting alone. Products of this international struggle are the emphases on ending world hunger, forgiving the debt to underdeveloped Third World nations, and treating all the global victims of AIDS/HIV.

The point is not to dismiss equal justice but to expand its meaning and usages, so as to embrace the fuller rights of political, economic, social, religious, and cultural justice for all as found within the meaning of human rights. In other words, equal justice is a fine place to begin, but it should not be the place where one ends. Hence, all agents or workers of the criminal justice system should aspire to act impartially and objectively, according to both the letter and the spirit of due process and equal protection under the law. In addition, however, equal justice needs assistance from the goals and objectives of both restorative and social justice.

HUMAN TRAFFICKING AND THE LACK OF EQUAL JUSTICE

One concrete illustration of the struggle against social injustice is the emphasis on the effects of a globalizing political economy and the intensification of poverty and hunger and a lowering of living standards for hundreds of millions of people worldwide, on the one hand, and the more than a million people globally who are victims of human trafficking and enslavement, mostly for the purposes of forced labor and sex, on the other hand. In the United States alone, a State Department study estimated that in 2001 there were between 45,000 and 50,000 women and children brought to the United States for illicit purposes. For the same year, there were 104 prosecutions for human trafficking in the United States, involving some 400 to 500 victims, not to mention "approximately 1,000 more victims that [had been] identified but never brought to the attention of law enforcement (for reasons such as fear of deportation)."*

Until the policies of a neoliberal global economy based on fair rather than free social relations are established, the underlying conditions of social injustice and capitalist exploitation will remain a source for human trafficking. Doubling the prosecution of those persons victimizing these women and children through mechanisms of equal criminal justice will have very little impact on the genesis or structural nature of the problem. Only by setting up living conditions that meet the minimum standards of human rights for all will the prerequisite for eliminating the lack of equal justice for all become a reality.

---

*Kevin Bales, "Tracking Modern Day Slavery," *National Institute of Justice Journal* no. 252 (July 2005): 29–30.

These alternative scenarios to equal justice—restorative and social justice—offer substantial ways to improve the quality of justice inside and outside the criminal justice system, serving better to curb and reduce all forms of criminality—personal, institutional, and structural. The models of justice engage in more humanistic and inclusive models of crime control and in more holistic or integrative approaches to crime and justice than do the models of equal justice. Both restorative and social justice models encourage and actively support the participation of offenders, victims, and communities of interest in the processes of democratic social control or in managing local crime and justice. Social justice models, in addition, adopt the perspectives of the struggle for human rights and the resistance of exploitation in all its forms, criminal and noncriminal.

From the joint vantage point of policy development, restorative and social justice aspire toward an evolution in justice based on healing, recovery, reconciliation, and the struggle for diversity, equality, and inclusiveness throughout society. Once again, these approaches do not abandon the legalistic models of the rule of law. Rather, these models play down the struggle for law and order and the need to inflict more pain as they play up the struggle for peace and justice and the need to develop social avenues of socialization, habilitation, and integration.

FUTURE PROSPECTS

Historically, the evolution of justice and the struggle for universal human rights has not followed a linear pathway. On the contrary, every generation of rights—equal, restorative, and social—has not only met with resistance, but also each major stride forward on the pathway to human rights has been trailed by severe setbacks:

> The universalism of human rights brandished during the French Revolution was slowly superseded by a nationalist reaction incubated during Napoleon's conquests, just as the internationalist hopes of socialist human rights advocates were drowned in a tidal wave of nationalism at the approach of World War I. The human rights aspirations of the Bolshevik Revolution and of two liberal sister institutions, the League of Nations and the International Labor Organization (ILO), were crushed by the rise of Stalinism and fascism during the interwar period; the establishment of the United Nations (UN) and adoption of the Universal Declaration of Human Rights were eclipsed by intensifying nationalism in the emerging Third World and global competition between two nuclear-armed superpowers. Finally, the triumphant claims made after 1989 that human rights would blossom in an unfettered global market economy were soon drowned out by rising nationalism in the former Soviet Union, Africa, the Balkans, and beyond.[1]

At the same time, this is not to infer that reactionary forces totally checked or nullified each chapter of progress in human rights. The record informs us otherwise: "[H]istory preserves the human rights record as each generation builds on the hopes and achievements of its predecessors while struggling to free itself from authoritarianism and improve its social conditions."[2] Over time, the evolution of human rights has reflected the historical continuity and change that helped form the Universal Declaration of Human Rights (UDHR) adopted by the General Assembly of the United Nations in 1948. Drawing on the battle cry of the French Revolution, "dignity, liberty, equality, and brotherhood," on the demands of the Industrial Revolution for political, social, and economic equity, and on the communal and national solidarity movements associated with the postcolonial era, the articles of the UDHR brought together in one document the universal meanings of human rights.

In 2007, both domestically and internationally, struggles to obtain human rights for all and controversies surrounding who should be endowed with equal justice for all still remain.

See Also: Class Justice; Gendered Justice; Social Justice; Supremacy of International Law to National Law.

Endnotes

1. Micheline Ishay, *The History of Human Rights: From Ancient Times to the Globalization Era* (Berkeley and Los Angeles: University of California Press, 2004), 4.
2. Ibid.

Further Reading: Barak, Gregg, Paul Leighton, and Jeanne Flavin, *Class, Race, Gender, and Crime: The Social Realities of Justice in America,* 2nd ed. (Lanham, MD: Rowman and Littlefield, 2007); Crawford, James, *The Rights of People* (Oxford: Oxford University Press, 1988); Douglas, William O., *An Almanac of Liberty* (Garden City, NY: Double-day, 1954); Kraska, Peter B., ed., *Theorizing Criminal Justice: Eight Essential Orienta-tions* (Long Grove, IL: Waveland Press, 2004); Leighton, Paul, and Jeffrey Reiman, eds., *Criminal Justice Ethics* (Upper Saddle River, NJ: Prentice-Hall, 2004).

Gregg Barak

ESPIONAGE ACT OF 1917

INTRODUCTION

When the Espionage Act was passed on June 15, 1917, it was heralded as a much-needed tool to protect military information following the U.S. declaration of war on Germany during World War I. With the passing of time, critics of the Espionage Act have voiced concerns that the ambiguities of the legislation have led to the act being used in ways that violate basic constitutional rights. Concerns include violations of the First Amendment and censorship of the press that could diminish the media's ability to report on national security issues of public interest and act as a constraint against unwarranted government secrecy and/or illegal activities.

The Espionage Act made it a crime to convey military information with the intent to injure the United States or advantage a foreign state. The relevant espionage statutes have been codified into United States Code (USC) Title 18 Sections 793 to 798 and have remained almost unchanged since the Espionage Act was enacted.

Section 793 defines six offenses involving activities prior to a foreigner's acquisition of information. Subsections (a) and (b) make it a crime to enter any military installation, to obtain or copy documents connected with national defense during a war with the intent or reason to believe the information would be used to injure the United States or to aid a foreign government. Subsections (c), (d), and (e) make it a crime to have receipt of national defense material that the possessor has reason to believe could be used to the injury of the United States or to the advantage of any foreign nation, to willfully communicate na-tional defense materials, or to pass (or attempt to pass) on information to any person not authorized to receive it. The latter subsections are central to several controversies surrounding the use of the Espionage Act to charge individuals and newspapers for publishing classified information (e.g., the 2005–6 leak to *The New York Times* exposing the U.S. National Security Agency's secret eaves-dropping program).

Section 794 includes several provisions on "Gathering or delivering defense information to aid foreign government." Subsection (a) makes it criminal to attempt to or communicate to a foreign agent any document or information relating to national defense with intent or reason to believe it will be used to injure the United States or advantage a foreign government. Section (b) applies in times of declared war and criminalizes the transfer of information and/or collecting, publishing, recording, or communicating information on troop movements or military plans.

Section 798 deals with the category of communications intelligence. Subsection (1) deals with communicating or publishing information to unauthorized individuals regarding any code, cipher, or cryptographic system and/or (2) the design, use, or constructions of communication devices used by the United States or any foreign government. Section 798 may also become significant to the controversies surrounding the 2005–6 leaks to the media exposing the U.S. National Security Agency's secret eavesdropping program.

BACKGROUND

Restrictions on the dissemination of military information or its operations have existed since the inception of the United States. During the American Revolution, the 1775 Articles of War prohibited unauthorized correspondence by soldiers with an enemy. Furthermore, the Articles of Confederation explicitly recognized the need to keep particular information concerning military and diplomatic activities secret.

The first peacetime governmental directive concerning the protection of information was issued in 1869. The U.S. Army issued an order restricting certain information regarding military sites. The regulation prohibited unauthorized photographs or other views of the military forts. An additional Army order was issued in March 1897 that included restrictions on who could visit defense facilities and dissemination of information regarding the facilities.

It was not until 1911 that any congressional efforts were made to protect military information: the Defense Secrets Act of 1911. The act imposed penalties on individuals that are not lawfully entitled to obtain information regarding national defense. This included the taking of photographs or making sketches of ships or facilities connected with the national defense without proper authority. Penalties were also imposed for communicating such information to unauthorized individuals or to a foreign government.

After the U.S. entry into World War I in April 1917, the Espionage Act of 1917 replaced the Defense Secrets Act of 1911. The Espionage Act was introduced to the 64th Congress two days after President Woodrow Wilson announced to a joint session of Congress that diplomatic relations had been severed with Germany. Heated debates over the content of the Espionage Act took place over two subsequent sessions that produced three bills and two conference reports. The sessions were focused on the debate between freedom of speech and the press and the protection of information that could interfere with national defense. Supporters held the belief that harm could befall military interests without such legislation, whereas others feared that the statute would impede or suppress criticism of the Wilson administration's war efforts. Additionally, critics also feared controlling publications not intended to harm the United States would lead to censorship.

The information-gathering techniques described in the 1911 act were subsequently made criminal in the 1917 act; however, governmental control of publications not intended to harm the United States or advantage a foreign government failed. The exception to this is USC Section 794 (b). This section remains controversial due to the potential of its use against governmental whistle-blowers and the press to communicate material intended to inform the public, spark public debate, and/or monitor governmental activities.

In 1950, Subsection 793 (e) was added to the statute. The history of Subsection 793 (e) takes into account three former statutes and is nearly identical to Subsection 794 (d). Each of these provide two offenses: having unauthorized possession of, access to, or control over any document, writing, photograph relating to national defense and the willful communication of defense information to anyone not entitled to receive it. The retention of information was thus made dependent on the possession of the material being unauthorized. The controversial issue with this subsection is its scope. If taken literally, it would mean that anyone who leaks information to the press, a reporter who holds onto or possesses defense material, or a retired official who uses such information in his memoirs could all be committing a crime. This would mean that public speech, governmental monitoring by the media, and whistle-blowing could all potentially be treated as a serious criminal offense. Additionally, it is these two subsections that could be viewed as unconstitutional under the First Amendment.

BILL OF RIGHTS, FIRST AMENDMENT

Congress shall make no law respecting an establishment of religion, or prohibiting the free exercise thereof; or abridging the freedom of speech, or of the press; or the right of the people peaceably to assemble, and to petition the government for a redress of grievances.

During 1950, Section 798 was also added to United States Code. This section covers cryptographic information or material related to national defense. It makes it criminal to willfully communicate, furnish, or publish classified information dealing with codes or cryptographic systems as well as the communication of intelligence activities of the United States. Based on classification, this section could potentially close the opportunity for defense on the grounds that the information was improperly classified. This contradicts the 1917 act, which states that the government must prove the issue of defense relatedness in its case.

LEGAL DECISIONS

Legal and definitional ambiguities of the Espionage Act have resulted in several judicial cases. One of the earliest cases occurred in 1940 in *Gorin v. United States,* Ninth Circuit Court. At issue was the term *related to national defense.* Gorin had been convicted of violating the precursors of 793 (b), 794 (a, c). The argument presented to the Supreme Court was that without the limitations of national defense (as specified in 793 (a) as protected places and things),

Sections 793 (b) and 794 (a) were too vague. Subsequently, everything could be considered as relating to national defense if broadly constructed. The Court unanimously rejected the defense's position. Additionally, Justice Stanley Reed opined, "National Defense is a generic concept of broad connotations, referring to the military and naval establishments and the related activities of national preparedness . . . the words national defense in the espionage act carry that meaning."[1]

The Court's ruling left unclear the extent of information that could be viewed as respecting national defense and if the phrase *related to national defense* included information that made its way into the public domain despite government control efforts. Additionally, the Court left open a doubt that the breadth of the standard of national defense, as defined, could withstand constitutional challenges when an individual does not intend to harm the United States or advantage a foreign government. Nonetheless, the Court did resolve that statutory culpability was to be held to the standard of injury to the United States or to advantage a foreign government. All other information would not be susceptible to prosecution even with intent without one of these preconditions (see also *Gros v. United States of America,* Ninth Circuit Court, 1943).

The issue of whether classified information is probative to national defense was addressed in *United States v. Soblen* (Second Circuit Court, 1962). This case asserted that juries should directly consider when information was classified as it pertained to the information being related to national defense. A controversial theme with this charge is that courts do not instruct juries on the complexities of government classifications or its use to protect state interests not related to national defense.

An additional landmark case, *New York Times Company v. United States* (1971), addressed the publication of governmental documents. This was the first effort by the federal government to control the publication of a newspaper. *The New York Times* received and published articles from a leaked copy of what is known as the Pentagon Papers. The government brought a suit against *The New York Times* requiring the paper to cease further publications. The core issue was the concept of prior restraint. The appellate court's indecisiveness brought the ultimate decision to the Supreme Court. The landmark decision by the Court set a precedent for the issue of governmental use of prior restraint. The Court ruled that a prior control of publication would be allowed only in the most extraordinary cases that threatened grave and immediate danger to the security of the United States.

At face value, the decision of the Supreme Court suggests that the 1950 act ought not to be construed wherein it could impose censorship or violate the First Amendment of the Constitution. Additionally, the Court held that there was a heavy burden on the government in that prior restraint on publication would be unconstitutional under the First Amendment. Issues left undefined by the Court include who would decide and/or what would constitute what a grave and immediate danger to U.S. security is. This issue is central to the controversy in March 2006 surrounding *The New York Times* publication of leaked information exposing the National Security Agency's secret surveillance program.

KEY EVENTS

During 2001, Attorney General John Ashcroft commissioned a group of top intelligence professionals to examine the legal authority to charge government agents that leak unauthorized classified information under the Espionage Act. The committee concluded the statute was adequate for prosecution. In a letter to Congress, Ashcroft stated the government needed to "entertain new approaches to deter, identify, and punish those who engage in the practice of unauthorized disclosure of classified information."[2] Subsequently, several investigations ensued, including inquiries into the leaked secret war plans given to *The New York Times* and the *Washington Post* and the leak of a letter by Secretary of State Colin Powell to the Pentagon objecting to the Syria Accountability Act.

The indictment of Stephen Rosen and Keith Weissman by the federal government has brought additional attention to the Espionage Act.[3] Although they have been charged under the Espionage Act, this is not an espionage case. The two have been charged for receiving and communicating classified information without authorization. This case poses several legal issues. According to presiding Judge T. S. Ellis III at a March 24, 2006, hearing, the legal issues that have been raised involve "uncharted waters." This is the first case in which the government has sought to criminalize the unauthorized receipt of classified information by nongovernmental agents who did not have security clearances. Defense attorneys' arguments included suggesting the statutes being used were overly broad and ambiguous, thus unconstitutionally vague, and the Espionage Act and subsequent codes apply to the unauthorized transfer of classified documents, not speech. The government's position was that the case was not a First Amendment issue involving protected speech. The final charges by the government included conspiracy to gather, disseminate, and communicate national defense information to persons not entitled to receive it. At the time of this writing, the case remains ongoing.

On December 30, 2005, an additional criminal investigation into the circumstances surrounding the disclosed information exposing the National Security Agency's secret eavesdropping program was undertaken. The investigations into the leaked information is said to be laying the groundwork for a grand jury indictment under the Espionage Act, using Section 798. One of the extraordinary features of this section is that it was drawn with the specific intent to protect national defense information from vigorous public discussion after the attack on Pearl Harbor in 1941. This case is highly controversial as it tests the contradiction between the media's ability to report on national security issues of public interest, improperly classified material, and as a constraint against unwarranted government secrecy and/or illegal activities against governmental claims of national defense and issues of security. If the government's unbounded interpretation of the espionage statutes prevails through these notable cases, research and publication activity that receives communication from internal state sources could arguably be considered illegal. Additionally, conversations revealing unauthorized information could also be considered illegal, significantly reducing the rights historically granted under the First Amendment.

FUTURE PROSPECTS

At the time of this writing, the scope and future utility of the Espionage Act remain uncertain. The two most recent cases, Rosen and Weissman and the *New York Times,* are sure to set precedent for future use of the statute. Subsequent rulings of these two particular cases may lead to additional revisions of the statute in an attempt to clarify some of the ambiguous terminology (e.g., willful, relating to national defense, danger to national security, improper classification of defense materials, and the communication of classified information to unauthorized individuals). Additionally, the cases could lead to a strengthening of governmental security and expanded classifications. On the other hand, the outcome of the Court's decision could favor individuals' and/or media's right to disseminate classified information for public debate when such exposures outweigh any adverse effect on national security. Historically, leaks have served a vital function in democracy and issues of government transparency; as such, these cases could potentially prove to be landmark decisions.

See Also: Foreign Intelligence Surveillance Act; Homeland Security; Patriot Act.

Endnotes

1. *Gorin v. United States,* 312 U.S. (1941), 26, 27–28.
2. John Ashcroft, "Report to Congress on the Unauthorized Disclosure of Classified Information," (Office of the Attorney General, October 15, 2002), http://www.fas.org/sgp/othergov/dojleaks.html (accessed June 13, 2007).
3. This was the first case in which the federal government charged two private citizens for conveying national security information orally, with no classified documents involved.

Further Reading: Edgar, Harold, and Benno Schmidt Jr., "The Espionage Statutes and Publication of Defense Information," *Columbia Law Review* 73, no. 5 (1973): 930–1076; "Espionage Act of 1917," *First World War* (2002), http://www.firstworldwar.com/source/espionageact.htm; 18 U.S.C. 793–798, *Case Law,* http://caselaw.lp.findlaw.com/casecode/uscodes/18/parts/i/chapters/37/toc.html (accessed June 13, 2007); *New York Times Company v. United States,* 403 U.S. 713 (2nd Cir. 1971), *Electric Law Library,* http://www.lectlaw.com.files.case25.htm (accessed May 13, 2007); Sedition Act of 1918 *U.S. Statutes at Large,* 40 (Washington, DC: GPO, 1919), 553, http://www.gwpda.org/1918/usspy.html (accessed June 13, 2007).

Dawn L. Rothe

EXCLUSIONARY RULE

INTRODUCTION

The Exclusionary Rule (Rule) presents one of the most intense battlegrounds in the criminal justice field. In the starkest of terms, the Rule begs to address this question: If the police obtain evidence against a lawbreaker but do so by violating constitutional rules, should the lawbreaker benefit by having that evidence excluded from use in court. This entry will attempt to present the history of the

Rule, the key Supreme Court cases developing and subsequently limiting the Rule, and the major arguments for and against the Rule's existence.

Almost immediately from the beginning of the Rule's legal development in the early 1900s and moving through current events, the Rule has had strong advocates and equally zealous detractors. The Rule presents clearly, like few other battlegrounds in the criminal justice field, the tension between the crime-control models of criminal justice that focus on the efficient processing of guilty lawbreakers and the due process models that have as their focus individual rights and the integrity of the prosecution of citizens.[1]

BACKGROUND

The Fourth Amendment to the United States Constitution protects citizens' homes, property, and affects from unreasonable searches and seizures by the government. The amendment, however, does not provide for what will or even what should happen when evidence of criminal activity is uncovered by virtue of a government actor's violating this constitutional provision. Should the offending party, typically a law enforcement officer, be reprimanded for transgressions? Should he lose his job? Should the aggrieved citizen be entitled to sue the official? Should there be administrative sanctions to deal with the wrongdoing? Or should the government be prohibited from benefiting from their illegal conduct by having discovered evidence excluded from use in prosecuting the lawbreaker?

From this array of possible remedies for a Fourth Amendment violation, the United States Supreme Court determined that the remedy best able to deter improper police conduct and preserve the integrity of the judicial process was to implement a rule that excluded the evidence from use at a criminal trial. The Rule, almost from its inception, has been controversial. To many, the exclusion of arguably reliable evidence of a criminal act is too high a price for the public to pay for the mistakes or transgressions of one or a few law enforcement officials.[2] To others, it represents a windfall only to the lawbreaker and to no one else. The Rule, it is suggested, would be applied to exclude evidence of criminal activity in which the police commit an improper search or seizure, but to the innocent citizen who is likewise subject to improper Fourth Amendment activity, there is nothing to exclude and no benefit of the Rule to access.[3]

One of the issues that continues to fuel the fire of this debate is that estimates of the numbers and types of cases that are impacted by the Rule are widely varied and seemingly reflect more the speakers' attitudes toward the crime-control and due process models than any objectively measurable standard. For example, Edwin Meese III, Ronald Reagan's attorney general, relied on federal government statistics in 1983 to suggest that the Rule was responsible for the release of as many as 55,000 accused criminals per year.[4] Other scholars contend that the Rule has not had a major impact, an impact that is marginal at most on the numbers of criminal defendants who are avoiding prosecution and conviction because of the Rule's application.[5]

Statistics in this area are particularly unreliable. If some evidence is excluded as a result of the Rule but other valid evidence remains to prosecute the defendant, has the defendant benefited from the Rule? If the Rule is invoked to exclude evidence in one case against a defendant but is inapplicable in the defendant's other cases, has there been a windfall? Finally, what of the defendant who convinces an appellate court that the Fourth Amendment had been violated and the evidence should have been suppressed but does not get relief because of the application of the harmless error doctrine holding that the improperly gathered evidence did not interfere with the reliability of the verdict? Arguably the Rule has been applied to the defendant's benefit in all, some, or none of these cases.

In 1994, Congress entered the fray by attempting to legislatively repeal the Rule. In spite of the fact that the Republican Party had recently taken control of both the House and Senate and despite the fact that many crime-control measures were passed as part of an omnibus crime bill, the effort to repeal the Rule failed. Most of the development and subsequent diminishment of the Rule has centered on the activity of the United States Supreme Court. It is there that the tensions have played out and in all likelihood will continue to do so.

KEY EVENTS

The key event, the United States Supreme Court case of *Weeks v. United States,* occurred in 1914 and involved the search of a house belonging to defendant, Weeks, as part of an investigation and ultimate prosecution for using the mails to transport lottery tickets in violation of federal law. The search conducted without a warrant and without consent of the homeowner was determined to violate the Fourth Amendment.

The Court in excluding the evidence derived from the search stated clearly its reason for creating this new rule:

> If letters and private documents can be seized and held and used in evidence against a citizen accused of an offense, the protection of the Fourth Amendment declaring the right to be secure against such searches and seizures is of no value, and, so far as those thus placed are concerned, might as well be stricken from the Constitution. The efforts of the courts and officials to bring the guilty to punishment, praiseworthy as they are, are not to be aided by the sacrifice of those great principles established by years of endeavor and suffering which have resulted in their embodiment in the fundamental law of the land.[6]

LEGAL DECISIONS

In 1961, the Supreme Court in *Mapp v. Ohio* extended the Rule to apply to all state criminal proceedings by making the Rule a part of state due process under both the Fourth and Fourteenth Amendments to the U.S. Constitution. Because the vast majority of criminal prosecutions in the United States arise and are prosecuted in state courts, *Mapp* had a significant impact on the practical application of the Court's Rule.

STATE RIGHTS VERSUS FEDERAL RIGHTS

The notion of which protections of the Bill of Rights that apply to the federal courts should be incorporated into the state due process clause and apply to the state courts has been another controversial topic. Generally speaking, when the Supreme Court believed that a right or protection was a long-standing component of the U.S. concept of liberty and was fundamentally necessary to ensure the defendant a fair trial, that right or protection was made applicable to the states. We have seen that the Exclusionary Rule was so incorporated to the states in the *Mapp* case.

Actually, the Court had an occasion 12 years earlier in *Wolf v. Colorado* to apply the Rule to the states and on that occasion refused to do so. The *Wolf* Court in canvassing the jurisdictions that did not follow the *Weeks* dictates determined that the Exclusionary Rule did not appear to be an ingrained part of the U.S. concept of liberty. When *Mapp* finally overturned *Wolf*, it did so in part based on the notion that times had changed and the various states had determined that remedies other than the Rule had simply been ineffective in punishing noncompliance with the Fourth Amendment.

The fight over which federal rights should apply to state proceedings extended well beyond the Exclusionary Rule. The Sixth Amendment right to counsel and the Fifth Amendment protection against double jeopardy were two others that had a similar rocky history.

Since *Mapp*, the developments in the Supreme Court and to a lesser extent in state courts have been directed toward the narrowing and restricting the application of the Rule. The Supreme Court has carved out two very important exceptions to the Rule. In 1984, in *United States v. Leon*, the court established the so-called good faith exception to the Rule, which allows the government to keep the evidence discovered by an officer who unintentionally violated the Fourth Amendment while acting in good faith and in reliance upon the instructions of a judicial officer.

Leon dealt with an officer who, believing he had a valid search warrant signed by a judge, executed the warrant and uncovered incriminating evidence used to prosecute the defendant. Ultimately, after the defendant's conviction, an appellate court determined that the warrant was insufficient under the Fourth Amendment. The Supreme Court in allowing the use of the evidence anyway determined that the officer was acting reasonably and in good faith. The Court posited that this situation undercut the need for the Rule because there was no misconduct to punish and no future deterrent value to officers like the officer in *Leon*.

Also in 1984, the Court adopted in *Nix v. Williams* what has been known as the inevitable discovery doctrine. Another limitation on the Rule, this doctrine would allow for the introduction of evidence, even if obtained through an unlawful search or seizure, if the government could show that it was highly probable that the evidence would have been discovered through normal police investigation.

FUTURE PROSPECTS

It is unlikely, given the experience of the 1995 Congress, that any changes in the Rule will be the result of federal legislation. And states cannot legislatively or judicially repeal the law because of the supremacy of the federal government in the area of federal constitutional interpretation. It is much more probable that continued modifications and limitations on the Rule will arise from an increasingly conservative federal Supreme Court. Illustrative of this is the recent case *Hudson v. Michigan,* in which the Court speaking through Justice Antonin Scalia refused to apply the Rule to a case in which police unlawfully entered the defendant's home by violating the Fourth Amendment's "knock and announce" requirement and found drugs and weapons.

Justice Scalia's understanding of the Rule would not involve automatically excluding evidence unlawfully obtained; rather, he would have the Court implement a balancing test before courts apply the Rule in the future. Courts would balance the deterrent benefit gained by applying the Rule against the social costs involved in enforcing the Rule. The major cost will generally be the same in any criminal case: the exclusion of relevant incriminating evidence and the possibility that a lawbreaker might go free (or, more pointedly, in Justice Scalia's terms, the risk of releasing a dangerous criminal into society). However, Justice Scalia mentions another social cost to the Rule's application. Defendants, he felt, would generate a constant flood of alleged failures to observe a particular constitutional rule (the knock and announce rule, for example, the issue in *Hudson*), recognizing that the "cost of entering this lottery would be small, but the jackpot enormous: suppression of all evidence, amounting in many cases to a get-out-of-jail-free card."[7]

Regarding the deterrent value of applying the Rule in a knock and announce violation, the *Hudson* Court found that it was related to the strength of the incentive for police officers to violate the knock and announce rule, which generally requires the police with a warrant to knock and announce their presence and wait a reasonable period of time before entering a home. The Court posited that officers had no incentive to act inappropriately because all they would gain from this type of unlawful entry would be to prevent the destruction of evidence and the avoidance of life-threatening resistance by occupants—dangers that if they were present would allow the officers to avoid the application of the knock and announce rule in the first place.

Finally, the Court suggested that the opportunity of an aggrieved citizen to file a civil suit against the offending officers would be a satisfactory and reasonable deterrent with fewer societal costs. The *Hudson* Court specifically mentioned a number of lower federal court civil suits that had gone forward on claims of knock and announce violations. The significance of *Hudson* is that most of the factors to be weighed in the balance will be identical in any criminal case. The so-called floodgate factor will certainly be a factor as defense attorneys are ethically bound to raise on behalf of their clients issues of unlawful state conduct. On the other hand, it can always be argued that the availability of civil actions is the only deterrent that a rogue police officer needs.

The game, as it were, will be played, and the Rule's continued viability will be based on the Supreme Court's assessment of the strength of the police incentive to flout the Fourth Amendment in a given case: the greater the gain by circumventing the amendment's dictates, the stronger the incentive to engage in misconduct and the greater the need for the Rule's application. This reference in *Hudson* seems to recognize that there will be occasions that the Court will consider in the future when the application of the Rule will be warranted and its underlying value recognized.

At the end of the day, then, the battle over this doctrine continues, but despite significant judicial inroads into the Rule's application, it seems that the Rule will continue to be a part of our criminal justice system.

See Also: Miranda Warnings; Search Warrants.

Endnotes

1. See Herbert L. Packer, *The Limits of the Criminal Sanction* (Palo Alto, CA: Stanford University Press, 1968), 149–73.
2. See discussion of *Hudson* case infra, notes 14, 15, and 16 *Hudson v. Michigan,* 547 U.S. ___ (2006) (slip opinion No. 04-1360, pp.1–16); also cited as 2006 U.S. Lexis 8154.
3. See Akhil Reed Amar, *The Constitution and Criminal Procedure: First Principles* (New Haven, CT: Yale University Press, 1998).
4. Edwin Meese III, "A Rule Excluding Justice," *The New York Times,* April 15, 1983, 31.
5. Thomas Y. Davies, "A Hard Look at What We Know (and Still Need to Learn) about the 'Costs' of the Exclusionary Rule: The NIJ Study and Other Studies of 'Lost' Arrests," *American Bar Foundation Research Journal* 3 (1983): 611.
6. *Weeks v. United States*, 232 U.S. 383 (1914). http://tourlaw.edu/patch/weeks.
7. *Hudson v. Michigan.*

Further Reading: Amar, Akhil Reed, *The Constitution and Criminal Procedure: First Principles* (New Haven, CT: Yale University Press, 1998); Davies, Thomas Y., "A Hard Look at What We Know (and Still Need to Learn) about the 'Costs' of the Exclusionary Rule: The NIJ Study and Other Studies of 'Lost' Arrests," *American Bar Foundation Research Journal* 3 (1983): 611–89; Kamisar, Yale, "Essay: The Writings of John Barker Waite and Thomas Davies on the Search and Seizure Exclusionary Rule," *Michigan Law Review* 100 (June 2002): 1821; Kamisar, Yale, Wayne R. LaFave, Jerold H. Israel, and Nancy J. King, *Basic Criminal Procedure,* 10th ed. (St. Paul, MN: West, 2002); Orfeld, Myron W., "The Exclusionary Rule and Deterrence: An Empirical Study of Chicago Narcotics Officers," *University of Chicago Law Review* 54 (1987): 1016–69.

William L. Shulman

EXECUTIONS—TELEVISED

INTRODUCTION

The death penalty is a controversial legal, moral, and political- and public-policy issue, so the idea of televising executions—or making them more available to the public through the Internet—creates controversies on many levels. Advocates of televising executions include people who are both for the death penalty and against it. Some of those who are for capital punishment believe that televising executions would achieve deterrence and/or be part of a beneficial tough-on-crime campaign. Some of those opposed to executions believe that televising them would reduce public support because the reality of state killing would appear inconsistent with other values held by people claiming to be enlightened, civilized, and humane. Others on both sides of the death penalty debate oppose televised executions because they would desensitize people to violence or even have a brutalizing effect on the public.

Another controversy involves the private execution laws, which limit access to official witnesses and a media representative. Although a reporter can witness the execution and take notes, laws forbid making a photographic recording of the execution, which can be seen as a prior restraint on the press or discrimination against visual media. Prisons forbid such access out of concerns for security, privacy, and the possibility of a prison riot as inmates watch the execution.

Additionally, democratic societies value transparency and information for people to make informed policy choices, but others argue that propriety and taste are the more important values here and images do not add important knowledge for death penalty debate. Finally, there is a debate within media ethics about what would be appropriate to show on networks, cable, and Web sites if and when execution footage became available.[1]

BACKGROUND

Throughout much of European history, executions were not only public but also held in public squares with pageantry and spectacle. At times, tens of thousands of people would attend an execution, and they had such a good time that one of the terms for celebration—*gala*—comes from the word *gallows*.[2] The tradition of public executions came to the United States and persisted into the twentieth century, and extralegal executions like lynchings attracted crowds and families even as states curtailed legal executions by portable electric chairs set up so the local community could watch offenders be punished.

States started the slow process of restricting public access in the 1830s through private execution statutes aimed at reducing unsightly public spectacles and in some cases helped preserve the death penalty.[3] Courts accepted paternalistic justifications about the detrimental effects on the public from witnessing executions. One court, in upholding a fine for publishing details of a hanging that took almost fifteen minutes to complete, stated that the execution needed to be surrounded "with as much secrecy as possible, in order to avoid exciting an unwholesome effect on the public mind. For that reason it must take place before dawn, while the masses are at rest, and within an enclosure, so as to debar the morbidly curious."[4] Even denied direct access to the execution, people in places like Mississippi during the 1940s gathered "late at night on the courthouse square with chairs, crackers and children, waiting for the current to be turned on and the street lights to dim."[5]

Media representatives are no longer prohibited from publishing detailed accounts of executions, although lawsuits and other attempts to get photographs or video coverage of an execution have not been successful. The cases usually pit various arguments about the First Amendment against an array of concerns about prison security and the privacy of individuals involved in the process. So far, the courts have given deference to wardens and prison officials, based not only on a string of cases involving suits to televise executions but also on related suits in which courts have upheld restrictions about media access to prisons in general.

LEGAL DECISIONS

The first lawsuit over a televised execution was *Garrett v. Estelle* in 1977, when a station wanted to televise the first execution in Texas since 1964. Although official witnesses to an execution include media representatives, the media policies prohibited cameras, so the issue was less of a pure First Amendment concern than one of equal protection based on reporting tools: If a print reporter with a notebook is allowed, then photojournalists with cameras should also be allowed. The lower court in this case noted: "If government officials can prevent the public from witnessing films of governmental proceedings solely because the government subjectively decides that it is not fit for public viewing, then news cameras might be barred from other public facilities where public officials are involved in illegal, immoral, or other improper activities that may be 'offensive,' 'shocking,' 'distasteful' or otherwise disturbing to viewers of television news." But the appeals court disagreed and noted: "Garret is free to make his report by means of anchor desk or stand-up delivery on the TV screen, or even by simulation."[6]

KQED v. Vasquez is a 1992 case that arose when a public television station sued San Quentin's warden to tape the execution of Robert Alton Harris, California's first execution since 1967. Although the warden had prohibited the press from bringing pencils, notepads, and sketchbooks, part of KQED's suit was based on the reporting tools argument in *Garrett*. Warden Daniel Vasquez then expanded the ban to include all media representatives, with KQED responding that the role of the media is as a watchdog—the eyes and ears of the public—so they should be allowed to attend.

The television station based its claim on a series of Supreme Court rulings that allowed cameras into courtrooms. These rulings allowed cameras access to Harris's trial and "were being used to argue that such coverage should be extended, albeit for the first time in history, to the execution itself."[7] The state argued the prohibitions were grounded in various concerns about security, especially because the case had already inflamed public opinion: Inmates may riot of they saw the execution, guards may be identified and be in jeopardy, and bulky camera equipment could break the glass on the gas chamber causing the release of poisonous gas.[8]

Ultimately, the judge decided that the media should be able to witness the execution and report on it, but without cameras. In an ironic twist, Harris's "execution *was* videotaped by the state of California by order of a Federal District Court judge for use in any future cases involving the constitutionality of a gas chamber execution."[9]

The 1994 case of *Lawson v. Dixon* involved a death row inmate suing the prison to allow then talk show host Phil Donahue to tape his execution. The footage was to air in a documentary about Dixon's life, which the inmate said he hoped could:

> serve as an example to others of the effects of child abuse, anxiety disorder, depression and the pitfalls of a life of crime; and that it be used as an educational medium to aid in the prevention of and hopefully as a deterrent to others who might fall into the same lifestyles and patterns of conduct which I followed. I also feel and am equally committed to do all within my power to inform the public of the true significance of the death penalty and thereby to make a meaningful contribution to the significant public debate over the use of the death penalty.[10]

The courts ultimately found that Dixon did not have a right to have Donahue as a witness with a camera and that Donahue could attend as a witness but did not have a right to attend with a camera. Nothing was preventing him from talking about what he witnessed, but access to the event with a camera was not part of the First Amendment right or one that was outweighed by security concerns and the weight of precedent restricting media access to prison.

DETERRENCE ARGUMENTS

General deterrence is the idea that punishment of one person prevents others from committing crime because of the example. Although many people believe the death penalty deters homicide, researchers have not been able to find a deterrent effect when studying the question through a variety of methods. Indeed, between 1972 and 1976, the United States had no executions because of a Supreme Court decision, thus providing a real-world experiment. Researchers looked at homicide levels in states that were forced by the Supreme Court decision to stop their executions, and then started again after 1976. Additionally, researchers study neighboring states where one has the death penalty and the other does not or similar states that are perhaps not neighboring but that have different positions on the death penalty. In all cases, researchers find no deterrent effect, even when they control for the presence of actual executions as opposed to having the death penalty on the books.

Pro-death penalty supporters of televised executions argue that greater publicity will achieve deterrence. As the father of one victim put it: "[W]hat we should do is fry the bastards on prime-time" to "see if that doesn't give second thoughts to anybody thinking of murder."[11] (Some politicians have also advocated this position, although most have backed away from it recently as exonerations of wrongfully convicted people have made headlines and softened support for the death penalty.) The argument here is that the death penalty does not currently deter because it is done in secret, so it has an abstract quality that gets discounted in calculations about the costs and benefits of crime. Televising executions makes them real, because part of deterrence theory is communications. Punishment needs to be certain, swift, and severe, and these attributes need to be made salient to a potential lawbreaker.

Anecdotal evidence suggests that intense, direct exposure to capital punishment does not produce a deterrent effect, however. European pickpockets frequently plied their trade at the hanging of other pickpockets; both inmates and law enforcement officers who have been around executions have gone on to commit capital murders. The deterrent effect is weak because the rational choice model does not always apply to homicidal situations. Rationality can be short term and not include punishments many years down the road, especially by those who do not believe they are likely to be caught and convicted. Decisions also involve irrational elements and situational seduction because people kill in the heat of passion; they get drunk and/or drugged up. Some may be violent due to brain damage, including from abuse as a child.

The argument about deterrence further assumes that execution footage would stand out in a medium in which violence is more rampant than in the real world. The methods of execution, especially lethal injection, seem tame by comparison to thousands of other televised deaths and gruesome mutilations many people have performed in video games. A more far-reaching critique would be that at some point deterrence becomes an exercise in intimidating citizens into obedience, and increasing deterrence through a "state-sponsored snuff film" will not bring about a just and peaceful society.

BRUTALIZATION AND BACKFIRE EFFECTS

If more publicity creates greater deterrence, then logic would suggest maximum effect would come from grisly executions that are frequently replayed. The rather obvious flaw is that at some point people may well become desensitized to violence or even brutalized. Thus, televised executions might result in decreased concern about killing or even increased homicides.

Further, deterrence rests on the notion that executions convey the message "crime doesn't pay," but it may instead tell the audience that "a man's life ceases to be sacred when it is thought useful to kill him."[12] People may also identify with the state, the stronger party doing the killing, rather than the victim of an execution. The issue is not simply about devaluing life, but about modeling and imitation, which are most likely when the violence is "presented as (1) rewarded, (2) exciting, (3) real, and (4) justified; when the perpetrator of violence is (5) not criticized for his behavior and is presented as (6) intending to injure his victim."[13]

The potential infamy and attention from a televised execution may have an impact on those whose violence comes out of a sense of powerlessness and need for attention. For severely neglected people, negative attention in the form of mass hatred is better than continued neglect. If a televised execution involves nationwide media exposure, it may motivate selected individuals to kill because of the publicity and infamy that would accompany an execution broadcast to the world.

TELEVISION AND THE EVOLVING STANDARD OF DECENCY

Another possibility is that televised executions will be such an unsettling spectacle that they will add support for the movement to abolish the death penalty.

Executions are not the hallmarks of civilization, so exposure has the potential to spread the idea that capital punishment is a regrettable lapse of civility and inconsistent with the "evolving standard of decency" that the Supreme Court uses to interpret the Eighth Amendment's general prohibition on cruel and unusual punishment. Publicity could fuel the abolitionist movement by increasing the salience of premeditated killing being done in our name, especially when the condemned is young, female, has a compelling claim of innocence, or if there are mistakes in the execution.

The argument here is that the limited number of official witnesses without cameras effectively hides executions and suppresses their horror. Death penalty opponents have used this logic to suggest that judges and juries be required to witness the executions they impose as sentences, because support for the death penalty drops if people are required to be an active participant, such as juror or executioner.[14] Increased awareness of executions thus could undermine support, especially of people who want to "preserve the symbolism of capital punishment without having to witness a bloodbath."[15]

This argument about television highlighting the reality of the death penalty is not about the method used but is based on an assumption that executions are ultimately ugly because people representing the state cooperate in the premeditated killing of a helpless person.[16] If the focus is on the actual method of execution causing revulsion, however, then a televised lethal injection is unlikely to undercut support for the same reason it is unlikely to deter: It assumes the state killing would stand out given what one media critic describes as "the tube's day and night splattering of brutality, grossness, commercialism, exploitation and inanity."[17]

An underlying assumption that information about the death penalty will change attitudes harkens back to the Marshall hypothesis, so named after a remark by Justice Thurgood Marshall in *Gregg v. Georgia* (1976), suggesting that the opinion of an informed citizenry would oppose the death penalty. Justice Marshall had in mind certain facts about the arbitrary and unjust administration of the death penalty, and no matter what facts researchers use to measure informed opinion, "most people care a great deal about the death penalty but know little about it, and have no particular desire to know." In fact, "a large proportion of the American public already believes the death penalty is unfair, but supports it nonetheless." Although this conclusion should be qualified a bit based on the declining support for the death penalty in light of recent evidence of numerous wrongful convictions, the larger point is that a televised execution is not likely to be a significant source of opinion change because they are "symbolic attitudes, based on emotions and ideological self-image."[18]

A final critique of this position would question the importance of the information provided by a picture of final moments and execution method, when the most serious critiques of death penalty practices deal with the effect of decades on death row. Indeed, the stress of life on death row is the reason the European Court of Human Rights refused to extradite a person to the United States for execution on the ground it was "inhuman and degrading punishment" and violated article 3 of the European Convention on Human Rights.[19] In contrast, the picture focuses on the method, which may make the public more comfortable with executions. For example, Ted Koppel, the host of *Nightline,* supported the idea of taping and playing an execution on his show before he saw one in person. In spite of his professed "obligation to look it square in the eye," he felt that an execution should not be shown because they appeared hygienic, antiseptic, and quick; he felt that people would ultimately be more complacent with the death penalty after viewing one.[20]

EXECUTION VIDEO ON THE INTERNET—MCVEIGH AND HUSSEIN

Timothy McVeigh was convicted for the 1995 bombing of the Alfred P. Murrah Federal Building in Oklahoma City, Oklahoma, which killed 168, including children in the day care center directly above the blast and was the "deadliest terrorist attack in United States history" up to that point.* McVeigh's motivations appear to be rooted in an antigovernment ideology fueled by the government's killing of Randy Weaver's wife and child at Ruby Ridge, Idaho, and 76 Branch Dividians (including children) at Waco, Texas—an event occurring exactly two years prior to Oklahoma City.

He was convicted and believed the media would edit his comments before sentencing to distort his point, so McVeigh uttered only four sentences, including a quote from former Supreme Court Justice Louis D. Brandeis: "Our government is the potent, the omnipresent teacher. For good or ill, it teaches the whole people by its example."**

McVeigh's trial had been shown via closed-circuit TV to an overflow crowd of survivors of the bombing and victims' relatives, and the government planned to do the same with the execution, presumably without recording it on video because federal law prohibits a photographic recording of an execution. The Internet Entertainment Group, best know for tititlating Webcam footage of dorm rooms, sued the Bureau of Prisons (BOP) for access to the video feed. They proposed to use video provided by the BOP based on cameras controlled by the federal government and make it accessible through the Internet. To help ensure minors did not access the footage, they proposed charging a small fee to be paid for by credit card, which they would donate to a charity to help victims of McVeigh's bombing. McVeigh supported the arrangement, noting that he favored public scrutiny of government actions.

The district court opinion in Entertainment Network v. Lappin is a hodgepodge of cases in which the media in general, and television in particular, have been denied access to prison and military events. Ultimately, Judge John D. Tinder deferred to the prison administrators, who argued that the regulation against recording an execution served penological interests, including "(i) the prevention of the sensationalizing of executions, (ii) the preservation of the solemnity of executions, (iii) the maintenance of security and good order in the Federal Prison System, and (iv) protection of the privacy rights of a condemned individual, the victims, their families and those who participate in carrying out the execution."

The execution happened before there was an appeal, but the opinion raises some important questions and critiques. The solemnity or decorum of executions is less valid than security concerns as a penological interest. Further, is it the act of televising the execution that causes the problem, or is it that television shows the final moments of a process that involves dehumanization and the planned killing of a helpless individual by a group? (Are the bad effects the result of televising a solemn spectacle, or do the consequences flow from TV showing an ugly reality?) The concerns about sensationalism and privacy seem weak given that the federal officials have control over the camera and that McVeigh wanted the execution televised.***

The closed-circuit broadcast was the first time an execution had been televised, even to a limited audience. Unscientific polls from the time indicate that the public does not support televised executions but would watch if one were available. In spite of the potential audience, television executives felt that showing execution footage would be inappropriate—a stance they continued to hold even when footage of Iraqi dictator Saddam Hussein's hanging became available. Both the traditional networks and cable news producers felt footage of the actual execution should not be shown but felt footage up to the point of the noose going around Hussein's neck would suffice.

All the television news producers also felt the same standard should apply to their Web sites, so the crude cell phone video of Hussein's hanging proliferated through Internet sites that let users upload video (YouTube, Google video, and dozens, perhaps hundreds, of smaller sites as well). In some cases, Web sites attach a notice to the video that it is explicit or its graphic nature may not be suitable for some viewers.

---

*Nicholas Kittrie and Eldon Wedlock, eds., *The Tree of Liberty: A Documentary History of Rebellion and Political Crime in America,* vol. 2, rev. ed. (Baltimore: Johns Hopkins University Press, 1998), 776.

** *Olmstead v. U.S.,* 277 U.S. 438 (1928). This case involves government wiretaps, and Brandeis is in dissent because he finds that the government has gone too far; that the ends did not justify the means. Brandeis wrote about the importance of the "right of personal security, personal liberty and private property" and penned his classic phrase about how the Bill of Rights conferred "the right to be let alone."

***Paul Leighton, "Why Is a Photographer at an Execution a Criminal?" *Critical Criminologist* 11, no. 3 (2001), http://paulsjusticepage.com/cjethics/6-emergingissues/lappin-critique.htm.

DO TELEVISED EXECUTIONS REPRESENT A GREAT DAY FOR DEMOCRACY?

The effects listed in the previous sections are not mutually exclusive and may all happen if there is a televised U.S. execution: Some may be deterred, others brutalized; some feel less support for executions, whereas others become more complacent with lethal injection. But recognizing contradictory effects does not resolve the larger tension between being an advanced democratic country and performing executions.

In a scene from the movie *South Park—Bigger, Longer & Uncut,* the United States is executing two Canadians on television, and a character announces, "This is a great day for democracy." Although the humor has a few layers, part of it results from juxtaposing executions with the democratic value of openness and advanced telecommunications being used to achieve the openness. Substituting McVeigh or Hussein removes the humor but reveals the same tension in values.

McVeigh's act of terrorism killed 168, and many argued the death penalty exists exactly for crimes like his. Unlike so many other current cases, there were no lingering questions of McVeigh's guilt and no questions about racial bias. Because this act of terrorism had effects throughout the United States, pro-death penalty President George W. Bush could have ordered the execution be made more available. Using lethal injection on a mass murderer would seem to be an ideal opportunity to make a statement that the United States is not out of step with the civilized world by being the only Western industrial democracy to retain the death penalty. McVeigh's embrace of public scrutiny certainly adds to the impression that the government has something to hide, especially given Camus's argument that "one must kill publicly or confess that one does not feel authorized to kill."[21]

Video of Hussein's hanging did not involve U.S. laws about photographing executions, although it involved some of the same themes, but the execution was an event President Bush described as "an important milestone on Iraq's course to becoming a democracy that can govern, sustain and defend itself, and be an ally in the War on Terror." Yet television executives said that using the footage would be inappropriate, even tasteless. Although there was no discussion about the importance of the method, it is unlikely that footage of a lethal injection would have been substantially more acceptable; a firing squad might have made the footage less acceptable for television while increasing the incongruity of the event as a milestone of democratic progress. Meanwhile, images of combat and bombings are part of standard reporting on Iraq by television media that have also used images of the victims of Hussein's chemical weapons attacks and war crimes.

FUTURE PROSPECTS

The accumulated legal precedent in support of private execution laws makes future challenges more difficult. At the same time, the closed-circuit broadcast of McVeigh's execution and the video of Hussein's hanging seem to increase the likelihood of a televised execution, especially when set against the larger backdrop of a proliferation of video recording devices that bring an increasing number of events to the attention of the world. Indeed, some have argued that a televised (U.S.) execution is likely to occur, with the main question being whether it will be illegally taped by a miniature recording device smuggled in or as the result of a lawsuit decided by a maverick judge.[22]

Although courts can resolve legal issues and social scientists can try to measure the effects of a televised execution, the appropriateness of the public's interest in death will continue as a matter of debate. As one media executive notes:

> If we buy a newspaper to experience the execution through a reporter's eyes, we call that a "health" interest in our penal system. As long as we translate descriptive words on a page into graphic pictures in our head, the fascination is not morbid. However, if we wish to turn on the TV and see our tax dollars at work, we are branded to be little better than the person we are killing. Don't you find it strange that photos of dead victims are all over the media, but their killers' dying images are too provocative for you to endure?[23]

See Also: Cameras in the Courtroom; Crime and Culture Consumption; Cruel and Unusual Punishment; Death Penalty in the United States; Media Portrayals of Criminal Justice; Prisoner Litigation; Spiritual Care of Inmates.

Endnotes

1. Portions of this work first appeared as Paul Leighton, "Fear and Loathing in an Age of Show Business," in *Criminal Justice Ethics,* ed. Paul Leighton and Jeffrey Reiman (Upper Saddle River, NJ: Prentice Hall, 2001), http://paulsjusticepage.com/cjethics/6-emergingissues/tvexecutions.htm.
2. Robert Johnson, *Death Work: A Study of the Modern Execution Process,* 2nd ed. (Pacific Grove, CA: Brooks/Cole, 1998).
3. J. D. Bessler, "Televised Executions and the Constitution: Recognizing a First Amendment Right of Access to State Executions," *Federal Communications Law Journal* 45, no. 3 (1993): 355.
4. Ibid., 365.
5. David Oshinsky, *"Worse than Slavery": Parchman Farm and the Ordeal of Jim Crow Justice* (New York: Simon and Schuster, 1996), 207.
6. Bessler, "Televised Executions," 375.
7. Wendy Lesser, *Pictures at an Execution* (Cambridge, MA: Harvard University Press, 1993), 29.
8. Ibid. Another source notes: "Prison Warden Daniel Vasquez even expressed concern that a television camera operator might become upset during an execution and throw the equipment against the glass to stop the execution"; Marlin Shipman, "Ethical Guidelines for Televising or Photographing Executions," *Journal of Mass Media Ethics* 10, no. 2 (1995): 100.
9. Danielo Yanich, "Making the Movies Real: The Death Penalty and Local TV News," *Crime, Law and Social Change* 26, no. 4 (1996): 306.
10. Quoted in *Lawson v. Dixon,* 25 F.3d 1040 (C.A.4, N.C., 1994).
11. Helen Prejean, *Dead Man Walking* (New York: Vintage/Random House, 1993), 235.
12. Albert Camus, *Resistance, Rebellion, and Death,* trans. Justin O'Brien (NY: Knopf, 1960), 229.
13. David Phillips, "The Impact of Mass Media Violence on Homicides," *American Sociological Review* 48 (1983): 561.
14. Nat Hentoff, "'This Dismal Spectacle,'" *Washington Post,* December 30, 1995, A19; Gary Howells, Kelly Flanagan, and Vivian Hagan, "Does Viewing a Televised Execution Affect Attitudes toward Capital Punishment?" *Criminal Justice and Behavior* 2, no. 4 (1995): 413.
15. Mark Costanzo and Lawrence White, "An Overview of the Death Penalty and Capital Trials: History, Current Status, Legal Procedures and Cost," *Journal of Social Issues* 50, no. 2 (1994): 7.
16. Prejean, *Dead Man Walking,* 216.
17. Walter Goodman, "Executions on TV: Defining the Issues," *The New York Times,* May 30, 1991, C18.
18. Phoebe Ellsworth and Samuel Gross, "Hardening of the Attitudes: Americans' Views on the Death Penalty," *Journal of Social Issues* 50, no. 2 (1994): 19–52, 48. See also Robert Bohm, Louise Clark, and Adrian Aveni, "Knowledge and Death Penalty Opinion: A Test of the Marshall Hypothesis," *Journal of Research in Crime and Delinquency* 28 (1991): 360–87.

19. Johnson, *Death Work*, 222. See also Stephanie Grant, "A Dialogue of the Deaf? New International Attitudes and the Death Penalty in America," *Criminal Justice Ethics* 17, no. 2 (1998): 19.

20. This information came from an interview Kopel gave on National Public Radio's *Diane Rehm Show*, August 6, 1998.

21. Camus, *Resistance, Rebellion, and Death*.

22. Leighton, "Fear and Loathing in an Age of Show Business," 513.

23. Stan Statham, "Dead Man Watching," *Vital Speeches of the Day*, July 1, 2001, 563.

Further Reading: Bessler, J. D. "Televised Executions and the Constitution: Recognizing a First Amendment Right of Access to State Executions," *Federal Communications Law Journal* 45, no. 3 (1993): 355; Howells, Gary, Kelly Flanagan, and Vivian Hagan, "Does Viewing a Televised Execution Affect Attitudes toward Capital Punishment?" *Criminal Justice and Behavior* 22, no. 4 (1995): 411–24; Leighton, Paul, "Fear and Loathing in an Age of Show Business," in *Criminal Justice Ethics*, ed. Paul Leighton and Jeffrey Reiman (Upper Saddle River, NJ: Prentice Hall, 2001); Leighton, Paul, *Televised Execution Resources Web Page* (2007), http://paulsjusticepage.com/cjethics/6-emergingissues/tvexecutions.htm; Lesser, Wendy, *Pictures at an Execution* (Cambridge, MA: Harvard University Press, 1993).

Paul Leighton

EXPERT WITNESS TESTIMONY

INTRODUCTION

The purpose of expert witness testimony is to provide findings of facts for the decision-making process of semijudicial or judicial bodies or to provide the various courts of law with factual information on which to base a resolution, a ruling, or a verdict.[1] The controversies surrounding the use of expert witnesses and expert testimony may revolve around, but are not limited to, such issues as whether experts may be abusing their power to influence the outcomes of adjudication, providing better evidence than lay persons, or speaking on matters relevant to cases that are outside of their expertise. Before an individual may be allowed to offer opinion testimony as an expert, however, it must be established not only that the subject of the opinion is proper for expert testimony, but also that the individual offering the opinion is "a person skilled at touching the matter of inquiry."[2]

> Expert testimony today is very much like a corrida, the traditional bullfight. It has definitely prescribed rituals. The beginning, which is the bailiff's opening statement to the public to rise upon the entrance of the judge, is like the music of the bullfight. The ending, like the dragging out of the bull by the mules, is the moment when the gavel is slammed down. In between, the expert witness is the bull in the arena. The various attorneys entitled to cross-examine will treat him exactly as a bull is being treated—with the pics, the lance, and the sword. Just as the traditional bullfight has established stages, so does the proper expert testimony. Stage #1 is the swearing in and identification of the witness

followed by Stage #2, the statement and presentation of his professional qualifications. If they are not accepted, that is the end of the testimony. The bull is dead; bring in the next bull.[3]

BACKGROUND

The first documented forensic expert was Antistius, who was asked to examine Julius Caesar's corpse to determine the cause of his death.[4] In his opinion, Antistius declared that only one of the 24 sword wounds he suffered actually caused Caesar's death and that it was the sword wound that perforated his thorax.[5] In the beginning, then, only medical experts were allowed to provide expert testimony and then only related to their specific field of practice such as chemistry, biology, or psychiatry. In fact, experts, specifically medical experts, have been used in English courts since the fourteenth century and in the common law courts of North America for more than two hundred years.[6] Since the mid-1980s, social workers have been recognized by courts as having sufficient expertise in several fields of practice and, subsequently, have been qualified as experts in courts of law.[7]

PARTIAL INSANITY

James Hadfield or Hatfield (1771/1772–January 23, 1841) attempted to assassinate George III of the United Kingdom in 1800 but was acquitted of attempted murder by reason of insanity. Hadfield's early years are unknown, but he was severely injured at the Battle of Roubaix in 1794. Before being captured by the French, he was struck eight times on the head with a saber, the wounds being prominent for the rest of his life. After his return to England, he became involved in a millennialist movement and came to believe that the Second Coming of Jesus Christ would be advanced if he himself were killed by the British government. He therefore resolved, in conspiracy with Bannister Truelock, to attempt the assassination of the king and bring about his own judicial execution.

On the evening of May 15, 1800, at the Theatre Royal, Drury Lane, during the playing of the national anthem, Hadfield fired a pistol at the king standing in the royal box. Hadfield missed his target, though it is unclear whether he simply intended to signal an attempt, then addressed the king, announcing "God bless your royal highness; I like you very well; you are a good fellow."

Hadfield was tried for high treason and was defended by Thomas Erskine, the leading barrister of that era. Hadfield pleaded insanity, but the standard of the day for a successful plea was that the defendant must be "lost to all sense . . . incapable of forming a judgment upon the consequences of the act which he is about to do." Hadfield's planning of the shooting appeared to contradict such a claim. Erskine chose to challenge the insanity test, instead contending that delusion "unaccompanied by frenzy or raving madness [was] the true character of insanity." Two surgeons and a physician testified that the delusions were the consequence of his earlier head injuries.* During his opening remarks at the Hadfield trial, Erskine described a person incarcerated at a mental hospital who was suing for his release. Erskine interviewed this person "for the greater part of the day" in the very court-room where Hadfield was now being tried but was unable to "expose his infirmity." The inmate appeared normal to the court and was on his way toward release when Dr. John Sims, a noted physician, chanced into the courtroom to inform Erskine that the prisoner considered himself to be the Lord and Savior of mankind. A single question on this subject and the inmate revealed himself to be quite insane. This anecdote reveals how those with a partial insanity could appear normal to an inexpert examination and how a medical expert could bring out the obvious mental derangement for all to see.

*Richard Moran, "The Modern Foundation for the Insanity Defense: The Cases of James Hadfield (1800) and Daniel McNaughtan (1843)" *The ANNALS of the American Academy of Political and Social Science* 477, no. 1 (1985): 31–42.

LEGAL DEVELOPMENTS

The Federal Rules of Evidence (FRE), the Frye test, and the *Daubert* guidelines form the basis for determining the admissibility of expert medical or scientific testimony.[8] Although the FRE are meant to be applied to federal court proceedings, many state courts have adopted them as a guide for dealing with expert witness testimony. Various sections of the FRE outline the "knowledge, skill, experience, training or education" levels required of experts and allow for judicial discretion in determining who constitutes an expert witness and whether the testimony is relevant to jury deliberations.[9]

FEDERAL RULES OF EVIDENCE*

FRE 702: Authorizes judges to allow the admission of expert testimony when it "will assist the trier of fact to understand the evidence or determine a fact in issue." Under this rule, a witness may be classified as an expert on the basis of knowledge, skill, experience, training, or education.

FRE 703: Permits an expert to base his or her opinion on information "perceived or made known to him or her at or before the hearing" and establishes that a qualified expert's testimony should be based upon information or data reasonably relied upon by experts in the particular field forming opinions or references on the subject.

FRE 704: Provides the basis for allowing an expert to offer an opinion on ultimate factual issues, namely, causality.

FRE 705: Permits an expert witness to offer an opinion "without prior disclosure of the underlying facts or data (on which the opinion is based) unless the court requires otherwise." This rule establishes that the expert witness "may in any event be required to disclose underlying facts or data on cross examination."

FRE 706: Gives judges the authority to appoint their own independent expert witness to ensure that the expert testimony is relevant and scientifically valid.

*Christopher R. McHenry, Walter L. Biffl, William C. Chapman, and David A. Spain, "Expert Witness Testimony: The Problem and Recommendations for Oversight and Reform," *Surgery* 137, no. 3 (2005): 275.

Besides, expert testimony must be based on information that is generally accepted in the scientific community, according to *Frye v. United States* (1923), in which the court decided that a technique used for performing a lie detector test must be "generally accepted within the scientific community before expert opinion about data gained from use of the technique is admissible into evidence."[10] The Frye test, then, is used as the legal basis for judges to exclude expert testimony that is based on information, principles, or opinion not falling within those parameters.

In 1993, the U.S. Supreme Court provided guidelines for expert witnesses in the federal court case of *Daubert v. Merrell Dow Pharmaceuticals, Inc.* when it ruled that expert testimony should be based on information that has been subjected to the scientific method rather than on unsupported speculation.[11] The court also directed trial judges to determine whether expert testimony is relevant and based on valid scientific evidence.[12] Further, the Court gave its support to the FRE guidelines that permit judges to appoint their own independent expert witnesses. In so doing, the Court proclaimed that an expert witness must be able to determine the relevant facts of a case, define the standard of care for management of a specific problem, determine whether a physician's action conformed or deviated from the standard of care, and assess the relationship between the alleged substandard care and the patient's outcome.[13] The problem with this standard of application, according to Christopher McHenry, is that "very little constraint is applied to the testimony of an expert, often giving him or her inordinate latitude to comment on things that are outside his or her area of expertise."[14] Once the expert has been qualified as such, then, the person on the stand, under oath, is allowed to expound upon various topics and issues relevant to the trial, oftentimes without having any brakes applied to his or her utterances, in part because the expert testimony becomes a performance that is not unlike a regular stage performance. What the expert has to convey in the course of the performance is that he is indeed an expert and that his opinion should be taken seriously.[15]

CONTROVERSIES IN EXPERT WITNESS TESTIMONY

Problems with expert witnesses and expert witness testimony have included the fact that some experts have not only been allowed to testify about medical facts but also to offer opinions about material issues of the criminal trial. Their opinions may influence decisions involving criminal sentencing or involuntary commitment, for example.[16] The issue here becomes whether some experts have abused the power to be able to influence the outcome of trials and have turned the criminal trial into a kind of "legalized gamble,"[17] particularly because when judgments have rested on common sense or stereotypes rather than empirical knowledge, professionals have not been shown to outperform lay persons in terms of accuracy; that is, studies show that professional clinicians do not in fact make more accurate clinical judgments than laypersons.[18]

Another issue that complicates the use of expert testimony is the interrelated specialties that have arisen in the medical field such that experts can defer endlessly to colleagues who possess more specialized knowledge of the issue at bar:

> While fifty years ago, medicine was still primarily an art rather than a science, medicine is now interlinked with a plethora of technical and scientific occupations. The proliferation of information and specialties has become such that large health care providers now employ specialists in primary care, and farm out patients for further specialized treatment. In fact, some specialties have become so compartmentalized that surgeons, chemotherapists and radiation specialists no longer feel comfortable weighing the advantages of competing treatment modalities for certain types of diseases, such as cancer of the uterus or prostate gland.[19]

Additionally, there is some concern over the rather subjective nature of expert testimony not only because testimony by a so-called expert is often allowed by judges even though other physicians or scientists do not regard the individual's credentials as those of an expert in a particular field,[20] but also because the perception exists that an expert can be found to support any point of view as long as the financial compensation is right.[21] Moreover, there is no peer review of expert witness testimony to ensure its merit or validity.[22] These and other problems not mentioned here contribute to an increasing skepticism about the veracity and reliability of expert witness testimony.

Moreover, judges and juries are not bound by expert witness testimony; the jury members (and the trial judge) are free to accept or reject the expert's testimony in whole or in part.[23] Attorneys, therefore, must base the decision of whether to offer expert testimony on the likelihood of that expert being able to connect with the jury; that is, to leave an impression that is favorable to winning the verdict. Jury instructions do not require members to heed the advice of experts; in fact, some jury instructions encourage jurors to exercise their own judgment as to whether to believe or include the opinions of experts in their deliberations.

There is also some evidence to suggest that jurors use intuition, credentials, and mannerisms to determine the veracity of expert witness testimony. Put another way, there is nothing to prevent jurors from using their gut feelings about an expert, the prestige of the institutions from which the expert graduated, or the appearance of the expert on the stand to determine the veracity of the expert's testimony even though these supposed markers of accuracy are potentially prejudicial.[24] In fact, some evidence suggests that jurors completely ignore the expert testimony presented on the stand during the trial and, instead, choose to use their own life experiences or common sense to determine guilt or innocence. In such cases, the expert's persuasive effort may well succeed if it aligns more closely with common belief.[25]

When asked about the defense's case, one juror said:

> "I think they tried to prove that he was mentally incapable of understanding what he was doing and brain damaged . . . which didn't have

any effect on me because I know that you can get psychiatrists to argue anything because it's not an exact science." And another juror concluded: "[T]he defense had to show much and they did a good job. We just didn't buy it."[26]

FUTURE PROSPECTS

Several efforts to reform the expert witness process have been undertaken in recent decades (between 1987 and 1998) by respected medical organizations; specifically, the American Academy of Pediatrics, the American Academy of Neurologic Surgeons, the American Academy of Orthopedic Surgeons, and the American Medical Association have published guidelines and/or passed resolutions that subject expert witnessing to peer review and disciplinary sanctions.[27] In 2004, the American College of Surgeons issued a statement on the physician acting as an expert witness that includes recommended qualifications and guidelines for behavior of the physician who acts as an expert witness.[28] In support of the effort to maintain the integrity of expert witnessing, the Collaborative Defense Network for Expert Witness Research, founded in 1984, collects information on and researches the background of expert witnesses (http://www.idex.com). The company offers a wide range of expert witness services, such as testimonial history searches, trial depositions and transcripts, state license discipline searches, and articles by the expert, among others.

In the final analysis, there is much to be said about the need for expert witness testimony in this complicated age of medicine and science. If the jury cannot tell sanity from insanity from their own experience, for example, then persons must guide them with special expertise in the recognition of this hidden condition.[29] Only trained experts can separate the individual who is insane in a partial way, or only with regard to certain subjects, from the normal person.[30] Nevertheless, it is expected that the same types of controversial issues surrounding the use of expert witness testimony will persist into the future.

See Also: Eyewitness Identifications; Forensic Psychology; Mental Health and Insanity.

Endnotes

1. Peter B. Dorram, *The Expert Witness* (Chicago: American Planning Association, 1982).
2. Sol Gothard, "Power in the Court: The Social Worker as an Expert Witness," *Social Work* 34, no. 1 (1989): 65–67.
3. Dorram, *The Expert Witness,* 4.
4. Carl Meyer, *Expert Witnessing: Explaining and Understanding Science* (New York: CRC Press, 1999).
5. Ibid., 2.
6. Ibid., 2.
7. Gothard, "Power in the Court," 65.
8. Christopher R. McHenry, Walter L. Biffl, William C. Chapman, and David A. Spain, "Expert Witness Testimony: The Problem and Recommendations for Oversight and Reform," *Surgery* 137, no. 3 (2005): 274–78.

9. Ibid., 275.

10. *Frye v. United States,* 293 F. 1013 (D.C. Cir., 1923).

11. *Daubert v. Merrell Dow Pharmaceuticals Inc,* 509 U.S. 579, 593–7 (1993).

12. Ibid.

13. McHenry et al., "Expert Witness Testimony," 275.

14. Ibid., 276.

15. Dorram, *The Expert Witness,* 51.

16. David Faust and Jay Ziskin, "The Expert Witness in Psychology and Psychiatry," *Science* 241, no. 4861 (1988): 34.

17. Meyer, *Expert Witnessing,* 3.

18. Faust and Ziskin, "The Expert Witness," 34.

19. Meyer, *Expert Witnessing,* 3.

20. McHenry et al., "Expert Witness Testimony," 276.

21. Ibid.

22. Ibid.

23. Thomas G. Gutheil, *The Psychiatrist as Expert Witness* (Washington, DC: American Psychiatric Press, 1998).

24. Faust and Ziskin, "The Expert Witness."

25. Ibid., 35.

26. Allison Cotton, "Who Is This Defendant? A Study of Capital Punishment and the Effort to Attribute Personality" (PhD dissertation, University of Colorado at Boulder, 2002), 234.

27. McHenry et al., "Expert Witness Testimony," 276.

28. American College of Surgeons, "Statement on the Physician Activity as an Expert Witness," *Bulletin of the American College of Surgeons* 89, no. 3 (2004): 22–23, http://www.facs.org/fellows_info/statements/st-8.html.

29. Frank R. Freemon, "The Origin of the Medical Expert Witness," *Journal of Legal Medicine* 22 (2001): 349–73.

30. Ibid., 361.

Further Reading: Faust, David, and Jay Ziskin, "The Expert Witness in Psychology and Psychiatry," *Science* 241, no. 4861 (1988): 31–35; Freemon, Frank R., "The Origin of the Medical Expert Witness," *Journal of Legal Medicine* 22 (2001): 349–73; Gothard, Sol, "Power in the Court: The Social Worker as an Expert Witness," *Social Work* 34, no. 1 (1989): 65–67; McHenry, Christopher R., Walter L. Biffl, William C. Chapman, and David A. Spain, "Expert Witness Testimony: The Problem and Recommendations for Oversight and Reform," *Surgery* 137, no. 3 (2005): 274–78; Meyer, Carl, *Expert Witnessing: Explaining and Understanding Science* (New York: CRC Press, 1999).

Allison M. Cotton

EYEWITNESS IDENTIFICATIONS

INTRODUCTION

Eyewitness identifications are an important component of U.S. criminal investigation, particularly in those phases of the trial process regarding evidence, prosecution, and plea negotiation.[1] In fact, evidence provided by eyewitnesses is sometimes the only evidence linking a suspect to a crime.[2] For that reason, eyewitness identifications are controversial because, although some witnesses may be confident about their description of a suspect, there are inherent witness-based problems in face-recall techniques, which may limit the ultimate effectiveness of most systems in current use.[3] Moreover, from the point of view of criminal investigation, accurate face recall is of considerable importance, not only because the penalties for crime in the United States range from probation to death, but also because show ups, lineups, and photo arrays rely solely on the accuracy of face recall to build a case.

Issues involving the reliability of eyewitness testimony, specifically the reliability of eyewitness testimony, can be divided into two categories: (1) errors describing the actual event and (2) errors describing the persons involved.[4] Problems with the latter category focus primarily on eyewitness identification of suspects that necessitates a reliance on face-recall data to connect the specific characteristics of suspects' faces with the events of a crime.

Face Recall

Generally speaking, people usually process faces holistically. This means that the faces we encounter form an impression in our mind that incorporates the major details of the faces as well as where the specific features on a face are configured to make the person look the way that he or she appears to us in our recollection. The width of a person's face, the length of the nose, as well as the distance between a person's eyes, for example, are processed together as a combination of features that is then recorded as an image that takes into account the relationship of the features to one another. In a recognition task, witnesses are presented with a target and search their store of faces until a response of familiarity is evoked. Such familiarity can easily be confused with recall from the actual features of the person who was viewed at the crime scene:

> The task of face recall is generally much more difficult than that of recognizing faces, and this difficulty may well be exacerbated by techniques that require the witness to select items from a set of pictorial illustrations and assemble them into a picture of a whole face. The two aspects of the task, decomposition of a holistic image into elements, and visual scrutinizing of pictorial elements, may each interfere with the witness' ability to maintain a visual image of the face she or he is trying to recall.[5]

Therefore, eyewitness identifications must be viewed cautiously.[6]

A CASE STUDY

Jennifer Thompson,[7] the first victim in the court's narrative, is blonde and tiny, five feet tall and 100 pounds. She speaks quietly, and she ends her sentences on the rising, interrogative lilt characteristic of girls raised in the South. It is easy to see the traces of her upbringing as the adored daughter of suburban North Carolina business executives.

But it is easy to see something else in Jennifer's interview, too: the iron resolve with which she survived the attack and pursued her attacker and the

FALSE EYEWITNESS IDENTIFICATIONS

In July 1984, a light-skinned African American man raped Jennifer Thompson, then a 22-year-old student with a 4.0 grade average at Elom College in North Carolina, in her apartment. Two hours later and half a mile away, the same man raped a second woman. Even the North Carolina Appeals Court's austere summary of these attacks conveys a sense of brutality:

> [T]he first victim was awakened by an intruder in her bedroom. The intruder jumped on her, put his hand over her mouth and held a knife to her throat. The intruder pulled the first victim's underwear off, held her legs down and performed . . . sex on her. . . . The intruder stayed in the first victim's apartment for about 30 minutes. She was able to escape by running out the back door and running to a nearby apartment. . . .
>
> The second victim . . . looked up and saw a man in her house. When she sat up, the man fondled her breasts. The man went out the back door and around the house. The second victim went over to close a window, but the man reached through the window and pulled down the top of the garment she was wearing. She tried to use the phone, but it went dead. The man crashed through the front door and grabbed the second victim. The man pushed her down the hall to a bedroom, pulled off her clothes, threw her on the bed and sucked on her breasts. He crawled on top of her, putting his penis in her vagina. The man then left through the front door, after having been in the second victim's house for 20–30 minutes.

Based on the up close and personal eyewitness identifications of the two North Carolina rape victims, Ronald Cotton* was falsely convicted and spent 14 years in the state penitentiary until DNA evidence proved that he was innocent.**

---

*No relation to the author Allison M. Cotton.

**Excerpted from James M. Doyle, *True Witness: Cops, Courts, Science, and the Battle against Misidentification* (New York: Palgrave Macmillan, 2005), 2–5.

---

unflinching honesty with which she is determined to tell the story of the assault and its aftermath. During the rape, her mind was racing:

> At that point, I realized that I was going to be raped and I didn't know if this was going to be the end, if he was going to kill me, if he was going to hurt me and I decided that what I needed to do was outsmart him. Throughout the evening, I would turn on lights, even if it was just for a second, and he would tell me, "Turn the lights off." And at one point, he bent down and turned on my stereo and a blue light came off of the stereo and it shone right up to his face and . . . and I was able to look at that. When I went into the bath room, I shut the light on and he immediately told me to shut it off, but it was just long enough for me to think, "Okay, his nose looks this way" or "His shirt is navy blue, not black," little, brief pieces of light that I could piece together as much as I could piece together.

Jennifer escaped to a neighbor's house and was taken to a local hospital emergency room, where a rape kit was prepared. There, she was interviewed for the first time by Burlington police captain Mike Gauldin. The qualities that strike a viewer watching Jennifer's interview struck Detective Gauldin during their initial encounter: "She was so determined during the course of the sexual assault to look at her assailant well, to study him well enough so that, if given an opportunity later, she would be able to identify her assailant," Gauldin remembered. "A lot of victims are so traumatized, so overcome with fear during the course of the sexual assault itself, that it's unusual to find somebody that's capable of having that presence of mind."

Gauldin asked Jennifer to help a police artist prepare a composite drawing of the rapist. That drawing was widely circulated, and it generated an anonymous tip. An informant provided Gauldin with the name of a man with a criminal record, a man who worked at Somer's Seafood restaurant in the neighborhood of Jennifer's apartment, a black man with a habit of touching white waitresses and teasing them about sex. The caller said the man owned a blue shirt similar to the shirt Jennifer had seen on the night of the rape. Gauldin placed that man's photograph in an array of six individual mug shots of black men and asked Jennifer whether she recognized anyone. The composition of the array was fair, and no one stood out unduly. Gauldin played it straight: He made no effort to prompt Jennifer or tip her off to his suspect. Jennifer remembers her photo identification this way:

> It didn't take me very long. It took me minutes to come to my conclusion. And then I chose the photo of Ronald Cotton. After I picked it out, they looked at me and they said, "We thought this might be the one," because he had a prior conviction of the same . . . same type of circumstances sort of.

Armed with Jennifer's identification, Gauldin obtained a search warrant and set out to arrest Ronald Cotton. Cotton was not at home, but Gauldin did find two pieces of evidence in Cotton's room: a red flashlight like one described by the second rape victim and a shoe with a foam insert consistent with foam found on the floor at Jennifer's apartment. When Cotton heard about Gauldin's search, he turned himself in at the police station, "to clear things up." Cotton gave Gauldin an alibi, but his alibi did not check out. Gauldin arranged to have Cotton stand in a live lineup.

Jennifer methodically examined the line of six black men arrayed across the front of a room in the police headquarters. "They had to do the steps to the right, to the left, and then turn around," she recalled. "And then they were instructed to do a voice presentation to me. They had to say some of the lines that the rapist had said to me that night so I could hear the voice, because the voice was a very distinct voice."

Jennifer narrowed her choices to the man wearing number 4 and Ronald Cotton, who was wearing number 5. She had the police put the lineup members through their routine again. Then she was sure: "It's number 5," she said. Later,

Gauldin explained what had happened: "That's the same guy. I mean, that's the one you picked out in the photo."

"For me," Jennifer remembered "that was a huge amount of relief, not that I had picked the photo, but that I was sure when I looked at the photo that [it] was him and when I looked at the physical line-up I was sure it was him." She was still sure when she testified in court and identified Ronald Cotton.

She was just as sure when she faced Cotton again, in a second trial ordered by the North Carolina Supreme Court. There was a new challenge this time. Cotton's lawyers had pursued inmate rumors that the Burlington rapes actually had been committed by a convict named Bobby Poole. At Cotton's second trial, Poole was brought into court and shown to Jennifer. Jennifer did not flinch then either. "I thought," she told *Frontline*, "Oh, this is just a game. This is a game they're playing." It was not Poole, Jennifer told the jurors, "I have never seen him in my life." She told them it was Cotton. At the second trial, the other Burlington victim testified for the first time, and she also positively identified Cotton. Cotton was convicted again, and Jennifer was elated. "It was one of the happiest days of my life," she recalled. Now she knew for certain that Cotton was never going to get out. She had forced herself to go through two trials; she had picked the right man; she had her justice. "I was sure as I can be," she remembers.

But Jennifer Thompson was wrong. The second Burlington victim was wrong. Mike Gauldin and the Burlington police, despite their conscientious, by-the-book investigation, were wrong. The 24 jurors who in two separate trials had convicted Ronald Cotton were wrong.

Procedural Issues Between Cops and Prosecutors

Mistaken identifications are not uncommon in our system of justice. The police actually see lots of misidentification during criminal investigations. In fact, witnesses—20 percent to 25 percent in one survey—routinely identify fillers in photo arrays or lineups. These confident but mistaken witnesses never make it to the prosecutors because their cases are screened out, but they are a regular feature of an investigator's life. The prosecutors, by contrast, seldom see a case unless the police have a solid identification and something to corroborate it.[8] For that reason, it can be said that the police are primarily responsible for the outcome of eyewitness identifications and, consequently, take great care to make sure that the procedures for conducting show ups, photo arrays, and lineups are closely followed. Contrarily, anything resembling standardized procedures represents a potential danger for prosecutors because defense lawyers are viewed as being eager to pounce on any deviation from the new standard procedures.[9] Although following routine procedures may be a fundamental part of police culture, it may sometimes place an extra burden on prosecutors who want to be able to exercise their judgment in preparing a case for trial. It has, therefore, been argued that the science of memory must count in police stations and courtrooms,[10] not only to alleviate the perils of mistaken identifications based on poor processes but also to ensure the accuracy of prosecution.

The Science of Memory

In 1975, Lavrakas and Bickman found that in a study of 54 prosecuting attorneys in a large metropolitan community, "an eyewitness identification and the victim's memory of the incident (which is also an eyewitness account) are far more important than any other characteristics a witness possesses, such as age, race, or level of income."[11] Lavrakas and Bickman interpreted the prosecutors' responses to mean that having a witness who could recall events accurately was absolutely crucial to the just resolution of criminal cases. The likeableness of the witness as well as his or her appearance and presentation on the stand during the trial were also shown to influence the perception of credibility. Most important, however, was the ability of the witness to portray confidence on the stand as well as give an accurate description of events that could not be easily influenced when the added pressure of cross-examination was applied by the defense. Indeed, this is a difficult task, because defense lawyers are sometimes very well trained in cross-examination techniques that can lead to inconsistent results, particularly when small details of events are challenged over long periods of time:

> When we experience an important event, we do not simply record that event in memory as a videotape recorder would. The situation is much more complex. Nearly all of the theoretical analyses of the process divide it into three stages. First, there is the *acquisition* stage—the perception of the original event—in which information is encoded, laid down, or entered into a person's memory system. Second, there is the *retention* stage, the period of time that passes between the event and the eventual recollection of a particular piece of information. Third, there is the *retrieval* stage during which a person recalls stored information. This three-stage analysis is so central to the concept of the human memory that it is virtually universally accepted among psychologists.[12]

In sum, once the information associated with an event has been encoded or stored in memory, some of it may remain there unchanged, whereas some may not.

BACKGROUND

The three most common types of eyewitness identifications, all of which offer their own relative advantages and disadvantages to criminal investigations occurring in the United States, are among several techniques for identifying suspects that law enforcement officials use to buttress their case for arrest. First, lineups of the sort that appear in popular movies and television shows depicting a suspect who is escorted into a room with three to five supposedly similar-looking people to stand before a witness to a crime have routinely been scrutinized due to the questionable similarity of the participants' physical characteristics. In *Martin v. Indiana* (1977), for example, in which the description of the suspect was that of a tall, 32-year-old African American, only 2 out of 12 people in the lineup were African American, and one of them was only five feet three inches tall.[13]

Second, photo lineups in which eyewitnesses attempt to identify suspects from an array of photographs are not generally considered to be as reliable as live lineups due to the variable quality of the photos. Photo arrays continue to be used due to the diversity of treatments that are available to the administrators of the photo lineups, such as adding additional photos to the lineup so the witness has to choose from an array of numerous photos as opposed to the numeric limitations of a live lineup. Also, additional photos of the actual suspect can be added to the photo array in varying poses and with various ornamentation, such as with or without a beard or glasses. Still, issues arise with the fairness of such techniques where justice is concerned because, for example, when a suspect appeared in 14 of 38 photos, a New Jersey court ruled, in *State v. Madison* (1988), that the photo array was impermissibly suggestive.[14]

Finally, police usually arranges show ups when they present a single suspect to a witness and ask, "Is he the one who raped you?" Show ups have been criticized for inherent prejudice due to the nature of the show up because they usually happen immediately after the crime and some witnesses may view the fact that the police have apprehended the person as a sign that the person is guilty of the crime. The Supreme Court, however, has not ruled that it constitutes a constitutional due process violation if there is additional reason to believe that the suspect is, in fact, the assailant. Some state courts, however, such as in the case of *People v. Guerea* (1974), have routinely ruled that show ups violate due process.[15]

In short, mistaken identification was observed to be the major source of error contributing to wrongful convictions in recent years.[16]

A KEY MOMENT

Hugo Muensterberg is credited with having performed one of the earliest experimental demonstrations of eyewitness misidentification in Berlin in 1902 when, as a college professor, he staged a fight between students during a lecture that resulted in one of the actors pretending to shoot another with a pistol. Students attending the lecture were asked to write down their account of the fight immediately following the event, but only 26 percent of the students were able to give somewhat accurate details, and even those had a small number of erroneous facts such as nonattributed and misattributed language and actions.[17]

IMPORTANT PERSONS AND LEGAL DECISIONS

Three landmark cases that first established constitutional parameters regarding eyewitness identification in criminal trials established procedural standards: In *United States v. Wade* (1967), the Supreme Court held that because a postindictment lineup is a "critical stage" of prosecution, the defendant had a right to have an attorney present.[18] *Gilbert v. California* (1967) augmented the ruling set forth in *Wade* by holding that "a per se exclusionary rule as to such testimony can be an effective sanction to assure that law enforcement authorities will respect the accused person's constitutional right to the presence of his counsel at the critical lineup,"[19] while *Stovall v. Denno* (1967) created a standard whereby the identification procedure may not be "so unnecessarily suggestive and conductive to irreparable mistaken identification that [the suspect is] denied due process of law."[20]

Additional challenges to the procedures set forth by the Supreme Court standards have questioned the constitutionality of eyewitness identifications based primarily on the Sixth Amendment right to counsel. Arguments for Sixth Amendment protection, for example, suggest that suspects are due an attorney if identification occurs at a preliminary hearing even before the indictment but not if the identification is conducted as a part of an on-the-scene show up. Besides, it is well known that although states have the right to increase rights provided by the Constitution (including the Sixth Amendment), states cannot decrease its protections. Pennsylvania, for example, requires an attorney at all postarrest lineups, and Tennessee provides the right to counsel as soon as an arrest warrant is issued. New York even requires the presence of an attorney if a suspect wants to waive his or her right to counsel as an added protection for the validity of the waiver.[21] To that end, "The vast majority of eyewitness identification cases have been decided on due process grounds."[22]

It should also be noted that *Neil v. Biggers* (1972) outlined the following five witness factors to be used in considering whether the defendant's due process rights have been violated: (1) opportunity of the witness to view at the time of the crime, (2) the witness's degree of attention, (3) the accuracy of the witness's prior descriptions, (4) the witness's level of certainty, and (5) the time lapse from the crime to the identification.[23] Opportunity to view can involve factors such as whether the crime and the identification occur in daylight as well as the distance and time duration within which the crime occurred. The case of *Gilliard v. LaVallee* (1974) provided the foundation for considering time duration in eyewitness identifications because, in that case, the kidnap victims were able to view their captors for a period of up to six hours.[24] Similarly, the degree of attention that was paid by eyewitnesses to the crime at the time that it occurred can be said to influence the credibility of eyewitness identifications. Attention is high when undercover officers are making a drug deal (*State v. Denny*, 1984),[25] for example, but low when the assailant awakened a victim during the incident (*People v. Leonard*, 1978).[26] Prior descriptions may cause inconsistency and may not be allowed in trial proceedings in the case in which a witness provides a physical description of a suspect at the scene of a crime by height and weight, for example, but it is later determined that the height and weight of the suspect are significantly different from what the witness first reported.

Although it is commonly agreed that certainty is ascertained with the traditional standard set forth in *Neil v. Biggers* "that a confident witness is an accurate witness,"[27] there is some evidence to suggest that the relative certainty with which a witness identifies a suspect cannot, in fact, be correlated to the degree of accuracy. For example, time lapse can greatly influence the degree of accuracy regardless of the degree of confidence displayed by witnesses. Generally, there is no due process violation based on the length of time lapse between the event and the identification, but the accuracy of identifications has not been shown to increase with time; for example, two years did not present a problem to the New Hampshire court in *State v. Cross* (1986).[28]

Still, other factors may also influence eyewitness identification, such as unconscious transference, which usually occurs when a person actually seen in an unrelated place or context is mistakenly identified as the offender in an eyewitness identification procedure. Also, identifications made by people in some occupations, such as college professors (*Plummer v. State*, 1980),[29] lawyers (*Robinson v. State*, 1985),[30] and security guards (*Royce v. Moore*, 1972),[31] are sometimes viewed more credibly by trial participants.

FUTURE PROSPECTS

In 2001, New Jersey became the first state with guidelines strongly recommending that police use a sequential method of photo identification rather than displaying an array of photos of suspects.[32] Studies have shown that the new method, which does not allow witnesses to compare mug shots side by side, drastically cuts the number of mistaken identifications. Based primarily on a U.S. Justice Department study commissioned in 1999, the results of which showed that many cases overturned with DNA evidence relied heavily on witness identifications of suspects, the push for the sequential method came from law enforcement officials rather than persons who had been wrongly convicted or their advocates.[33] Further, there has been opposition to the variability with which many police departments around the country process eyewitness identifications, and, for that reason, it has been argued that the problem of misidentification can be avoided by scripting data collection with police departments.[34] In addition, conditions are being found in which eyewitness certainty might be more closely related to eyewitness identification accuracy than once thought, especially when external influences on eyewitness certainty are minimized, but the difficulty of exploring that relationship remains due to a perceived disconnect between social science and policing. Police records, for example, do not distinguish between eyewitnesses who make identifications of a filler and those who make no identifications, which can result in a serious underestimation of the rate of filler identifications.[35]

Finally, in a law review article published in 2002, Dori Lynn Yob suggested that the problems with a state-by-state approach point to a broader solution: the adoption of mandatory, uniform, nationwide standards.[36] She goes on to argue that such a broad set of standards would be most effectively implemented through a U.S. Supreme Court decision and proposes that the following changes be made: (1) The witness should be instructed prior to the lineup that the perpetrator may or may not be present and that he or she should not feel pressured to make an identification. (2) The composition of the lineup should not cause a suspect to unduly stand out. (3) Fillers in the lineup should be chosen to fit the eyewitness's initial description of the culprit, rather than to resemble the suspect. (4) When there is more than one witness, a different lineup should be created for each witness, with only the suspect remaining the same. (5) Lineups should always be conducted by someone unconnected to the case who does not know the identity of the suspect. (6) Mock witnesses should be used to test the neutrality of each lineup, and blank lineups should always be used. (7) Sequential lineups should always be used. (8) And lineups should always be videotaped.

In Yob's view, "uniform nationwide guidelines would likely have an impact on the amount of erroneous eyewitness evidence because the guidelines would help attorneys identify and object to faulty identification procedures," and "a critical look at the problems with eyewitness identification evidence should be included in the curriculum of certain high school and college classes,"[37] not only because students at the high school level are more likely to incorporate the education into civic duties they learn to fulfill as they develop, but also because most people do not attend college. For that reason, we are more likely to capture the hearts and minds of the young people in high school today before they become the jurors, judges, and police of tomorrow.

See Also: Expert Witness Testimony.

Endnotes

1. Siegfried Ludwig Sporer, Roy S. Malpass, and Guenter Koehnken, eds., *Psychological Issues in Eyewitness Identification* (Mahwah, NJ: Erlbaum, 1996).
2. Ibid.
3. Ibid., 89.
4. D. Aronstam and G. A. Tyson, "Racial Bias in Eye-Witness Perception," *Journal of Social Psychology* 110 (1980): 177–82.
5. Ibid.
6. Roger L. Terry, "Effects of Facial Transformations on Accuracy of Recognition," *Journal of Social Psychology* 134, no. 4 (1994): 483–89.
7. Excerpted from James M. Doyle, *True Witness: Cops, Courts, Science, and the Battle against Misidentification* (New York: Palgrave Macmillan, 2005), 2–5.
8. Ibid., 175.
9. Ibid., 176.
10. Ibid., 7.
11. Elizabeth R. Loftus, *Eyewitness Testimony* (Cambridge, MA: Harvard University Press, 1996), 12.
12. Ibid., 21.
13. 438 F. Supp. 234 (N.D. Ind., 1977).
14. 109 N.J. 223, 536 A.2d 254 (1988).
15. 78 Misc. 2d 907, 358 N.Y.S. 2d 925.
16. Sporer et al., *Psychological Issues in Eyewitness Identification*, 3.
17. H. Muensterberg, *On the Witness Stand: Essays on Psychology and Crime* (New York: Doubleday, 1908); quoted in Doyle, *True Witness*, 10–34.
18. *United States v. Wade*, 388 U.S. 218; 87 S. Ct. (1967).
19. *Gilbert v. California*, 388 U.S. 263; 87 S. Ct. (1967).
20. *Stovall v. Denno*, 388 U.S. 293; 87 S. Ct. (1967).
21. Sporer et al., *Psychological Issues in Eyewitness Identification*, 10.
22. Ibid., quoting from N. R. Sobel, *Eyewitness Identification: Legal and Practical Problems* (New York: Clark Boardman, 1988), 110.

23. *Neil v. Biggers,* 409 U.S. 188 (1972).

24. *Gilliard v. LaVallee,* 376 F. Supp. 205 (S.D. N.Y., 1974).

25. *State v. Denny,* 350 N.W.2d 25 (N.D., 1984).

26. *People v. Leonard,* 66 A.D.2d 805, 410 N.Y.S. 2d 885 (1978).

27. Sporer et al., *Psychological Issues in Eyewitness Identification,* 13.

28. *State v. Cross,* 128 N.H. 732, 519A.2d 272 (1986).

29. *Plummer v. State,* 270 Ark. 11, 603 S.W.2d 402 (1980).

30. *Robinson v. State,* 473 So.2d 957 Miss. (1985).

31. *Royce v. Moore,* 469 F.2d 808 (1st Cir., 1972).

32. Jennifer L. Harry, "DNA Evidence Changes Identification Methods," *Corrections Today* 63, no. 6 (2001): 3–5.

33. Ibid.

34. Gary L. Wells and Elizabeth A. Olson, "Eyewitness Testimony," *Annual Review of Psychology* 19 (2003): 277–96.

35. Ibid.

36. Dori Lynn Yob, "Mistaken Identifications Cause Wrongful Convictions: New Jersey's Lineup Guidelines Restore Hope, but Are They Enough?" *Santa Clara Law Review* 43 (2002): 213.

37. Ibid.

Further Reading: Doyle, James M., *True Witness: Cops, Courts, Science, and the Battle against Misidentification* (New York: Palgrave Macmillan, 2005); Loftus, Elizabeth F., *Eyewitness Testimony* (Cambridge, MA: Harvard University Press, 1996); Sporer, Siegfried Ludwig, Roy S. Malpass, and Guenter Koehnken, eds., *Psychological Issues in Eyewitness Identification* (Mahwah, NJ: Erlbaum, 1996); Wells, Gary L., and Elizabeth A. Olson, "Eyewitness Testimony," *Annual Review of Psychology* 19 (2003): 277–96; Yob, Dori Lynn, "Mistaken Identifications Cause Wrongful Convictions: New Jersey's Lineup Guidelines Restore Hope, but Are They Enough?" *Santa Clara Law Review* 43 (2002): 213.

Allison M. Cotton

F

FAITH-BASED PRISON PROGRAMS

INTRODUCTION

Two major controversies merge in the issue of faith-based prison programs. The first, whether taxpayers should pay for any prisoners' leisure programming, reflects an ideology that sees punishment as the primary goal of corrections. Programs, if they exist at all, should be minimal. The second issue raises the thorny problem of the constitutional separation of church and state. Civil libertarians and others argue that religion has no place in any state activity, including prisons. Taken individually, each issue generates considerable heat and inflames ideological passions. Together, they pose a complex paradox for which there is no simple resolution.

Working against the ideology of punishment, prison programs are broadly defined as any nonwork assignment that occupies a prisoner's time and is conventionally earned as a privilege. The adage that "prison security begins with programming" reminds us that keeping prisoners busy with productive activities is not simply "hug a thug," soft on crime, or criminal coddling. Whatever the humanitarian benefits of programs for prisoners in easing the pains of imprisonment, programs also serve staff and broader societal interests by contributing to rehabilitation, facilitating reentry back into the community, and providing social interaction that helps reduce prisoners' physical and mental health problems. Above all, programs provide an incentive to prisoners for good behavior. Because programs constitute a valuable privilege within the prison environment, they give prisoners a strong motivation to not jeopardize them with bad behavior. Programs thus become a control mechanism for prison staff: The more prisoners are given, the more that can be taken away. But programs cost money and require staff. Faith-based programs are seen as a way to resolve some of these problems.

WHAT DOES THE SEPARATION OF CHURCH AND STATE MEAN?

In 1947, the U.S. Supreme Court provided one of the clearest boundaries in the separation of church and state. The Court reviewed the constitutionality of a New Jersey school district that used taxpayer money to subsidize the parents of Roman Catholic students to bus their children to faith-based parochial schools. It ruled:

> The "establishment of religion" clause of the First Amendment means at least this: Neither a state nor the Federal Government can set up a church. Neither can pass laws which aid one religion, aid all religions, or prefer one religion over another. Neither can force nor influence a person to go to or to remain away from church against his will or force him to profess a belief or disbelief in any religion. No person can be punished for entertaining or professing religious beliefs or disbeliefs, for church attendance or non-attendance. No tax in any amount, large or small, can be levied to support any religious activities or institutions, whatever they may be called, or whatever form they may adopt to teach or practice religion. Neither a state nor the Federal Government can, openly or secretly, participate in the affairs of any religious organizations or groups and vice versa. In the words of Jefferson, the clause against establishment of religion by law was intended to erect "a wall of separation between church and State."

Everson v. Board of Education of Ewing Tp., 330 U.S. 1 (1947).

Concerning the separation of church and state, critics of faith-based programs, whether funded by taxpayers' money or not, see them as an intrusion of religion into state-run prisons. Battles over the separation of church and state, a cornerstone of the Constitution's First Amendment, have been one of the most controversial issues in the United States for more than two centuries. Especially since the 1980s, the controversies have increased dramatically with the growth of faith-based initiatives, especially evangelicals. This has lead to resistance by non-Christians, civil libertarians, and others who view the First Amendment as establishing a clear barrier between government and religion.

The language of the First Amendment seems broad: "Congress shall make no law respecting an establishment of religion, or prohibiting the free exercise thereof; or abridging the freedom of speech, or of the press; or the right of the people peaceably to assemble, and to petition the government for a redress of grievances." However, courts have historically interpreted this to mean that there should be a rigid wall between religion and state affairs. Although this does not necessarily exclude religious activities in government venues, it does limit their scope and nature. It is within this constitutional background that critics oppose faith-based programs.

BACKGROUND

The first U.S. prisons were based on the Christian doctrine of redemption and transformation of prisoners through religious training, solitude, reflection, or disciplined labor. In the belief that human nature was malleable and that even the worst offenders could be transformed into useful citizens, late eighteenth-century prison reformers began implementing their ideals.[1] Although most corrections texts focus on Auburn Prison in New York and Eastern State Penitentiary (ESP) in Pennsylvania as the earliest U.S. prisons, Newgate Prison, built in 1796 in what is now New York City's Greenwich Village, is arguably the first. The religious foundations of Newgate derived from the philosophy and intents of Thomas Eddy, who laid its philosophical framework.

Like reformers who later established ESP, Eddy was a Quaker, although the prison policy doctrines of the New York Quakers differed from the Quakers in Pennsylvania. Eddy believed that "industrious habits" should be instilled through religious training, and religious instruction should be an integral part of the prison regime. However, his vision was relatively short lived.[2] Overcrowding and other structural and political obstacles led to the building of a larger prison at Auburn in 1816. Auburn shifted to the labor-discipline model, in large part because of the inability of Auburn's original Quaker-influenced board of directors to implement their original ideas, of which Christian redemption formed the cornerstone.

When New York's Sing Sing prison was built in the mid-1820s, the spiritual focus of New York prisons ended. Elam Lynds, the warden, did not believe that prisoners could be rehabilitated. Instead, he advocated hiring out prisoner labor so that prisoners could make money for the prison (and, according to contemporary reports, for himself).[3] Although this did not end religious influences in the subsequent transformation of prison ideology, it did appear to shift the emphasis from moral transformation to hard labor, often for private-sector profit. Religious instruction was secondary.

ESP opened in 1829 in Philadelphia and is often considered the first contemporary prison in the United States. ESP was built on the twin philosophies of spiritual redemption through Bible reading and reflection on one's crimes in solitude; however, the ESP isolation model was not original. In 1818, Allegany County Penitentiary, located in what is now Pittsburgh, admitted its first prisoners. Also called Western State Prison, it was influenced by the Quaker belief that spiritual reformation could result in solicitude and Christian rejuvenation. Western State Prison was torn down barely seven years after it opened, labeled a "complete failure" because of poor ventilation, poor heating, and unsanitary conditions.[4] It was the architecture and conditions that were perceived to have failed, however, not the underlying premise of religion and isolation, which were largely reproduced in ESP. However, the ESP isolation model did not long survive. Isolation took a toll on the mental health of prisoners, it was expensive, and the rehabilitation rate was judged to be lower than at other prisons.

Auburn's shift to allowing prisoners to work together at hard labor as the primary goal of prison, with secondary importance placed on religious instruction, was judged to be both an effective and efficient way of organizing prisons. The ethic of hard work also was consistent with the emerging Calvinist ideology of capitalist industrialization. Although not dead, the emphasis on religious instruction waned. It was not until the growth of the reformatory movement after the American Civil War that programming and religion became more systematically integrated.

Systematic rehabilitative prisoner programming was ad hoc until after the Civil War. In 1876, New York State's Elmira Reformatory marked an important shift in the history of rehabilitative programming. Built as the first rehabilitation-oriented institution in the country, the reformist ideals of the Pennsylvania and Auburn systems, which had withered with the discipline and control practices that characterized most nineteenth-century prisons, were resurrected.[5] Inmates adhered to rigorous programming that required both good behavior and successful demonstration of progress, and religion was the cornerstone of the system. The Elmira model established programming, vocational training, and industry as the core of most twentieth-century prisons.

Religion continued to play a part in prison activity into the twentieth century, as prisons began including chapels in their design. By the mid-twentieth century, religion was recognized as an accepted program in virtually all U.S. prisons, and most prisons employed prison chaplains and allowed volunteer laypersons to attend to prisoners' religious needs. With limited exceptions, however, religious rights were limited primarily to the two Christian doctrines of Roman Catholicism and Protestantism.

It was not until the 1960s that the U.S. Supreme Court expanded religious rights to mandate constitutional recognition of other non-Christian groups.[6]

Although the emphasis on prison and prisoner management underwent dramatic transformations, and although religion remained an important feature of prison life, faith-based initiatives as we have come to known them did not reemerge until the middle of the twentieth century when Black Muslims and the Nation of Islam (NOI) were arguably the first contemporary faith-based prison movements, appearing in the 1950s. Shaped primarily by resistance to racism and inspired by the writings of Elijah Muhammad and later Malcolm X, Black Muslim leaders used religion as a means of attempting to instill moral redemption, racial and self-pride, and strict adherence to behavior codes among young black prisoners, who especially were drawn to the movement.[7] In addition to religious instruction, Black Muslims provided material resources to poor prisoners unable to obtain them on their own, provided protection from prison predators, and emphasized abstaining from normal prison vices, such as smoking, drinking, and gambling. Although Muslims were generally tolerated by suspicious prison staff members who saw them as a potential security threat group, they did not receive recognition as a legitimate religion until 1964, when they successfully litigated allegations of religious and racial discrimination.[8]

CHARLES COLSON AND PRISON MINISTRIES

The roots of the contemporary trend in faith-based programs are often viewed as beginning with Charles Colson's prison ministries. Known as an unethical political operative responsible for the "dirty tricks" practices of President Richard Nixon, Colson experienced a religious conversion in 1973 and was indicted in the wake of the Watergate scandal. In 1974, Colson began serving seven months in federal prison. On release, he became an advocate for prisoners and their families and in 1976 founded Prison Fellowship, a multidenominational Christian organization. The goals of the organization, although doctrinal in nature, emphasized personal transformation for prisoners, reentry programs on release, and reconciliation of prisoners with family and community. Although there have been no systematic studies to date, the organization has been credited with reducing behavioral problems among some prisoners and reducing recidivism on release. The organization has been criticized, however, for aggressively seeking conversions and excluding prisoners whose beliefs are not consistent with those of the organization.

Sources: See Charles W. Colson, *Life Sentence* (Lincoln, VA: Chosen Books, 1979); Prison Fellowship, http://www.prisonfellowship.org/default_pf_org.asp; Inside Prison Fellowship, "Inside Prison Fellowship" (2006), http://www.prisonfellowship.org/default_pf_org.asp. For discussion of benefits and criticisms, see especially Religion Newswriters, "As Budgets Shrink, Evangelicals Expand State Prison Ministries," January 5, 2004, http://www.religionlink.org/tip_040105c.php.

In the final quarter of the twentieth century, religious programming was hindered, in part because of administrators' fears that prisoners were using religion to subvert security by engaging in gang activity or gaining normally unauthorized privileges in the guise of religious rites. Some prisoners attempted to establish idiosyncratic religions with esoteric needs as a means of acquiring resources, such as so-called ritualistic wine, steak, and access to sex. Although litigation on such trivial grounds was often dramatized by the media and prison officials hostile both to prisoners and to their litigation, frivolous cases were relatively infrequent and quickly dismissed by the courts. Litigation to expand the religious rights and privileges of prisoners led some critics to argue that the judiciary, not prison administrators, had gone too far and that prisoners could easily circumvent prison rules simply by invoking a religious premise. Case law applied the reasonableness test to inmates' exercise of religion, however, and courts attempted to balance legitimate religious needs with the security and punitive mission of prisons.[9]

In the 1990s, the religious rights of institutionalized persons were driven by a series of federal and state legislative acts intended to protect religious expression. The first significant law, the Religious Freedom Restoration Act (RFRA; 1993) explicitly affirmed that the exercise of religion is an inalienable right and that "governments should not substantially burden religious exercise without compelling justification." Governments should, the act dictated, strike "sensible balances between religious liberty and competing prior governmental interests.

Even when restrictions are required, the compelling governmental interests should be attained with the least restrictive means." The act provided the right to claim judicial relief to any person who could demonstrate an excessive restrictive burden upon the expression of religion imposed by a state, the federal government, or any official acting under color of law. This dramatically expanded religious expression beyond previous U.S. Supreme Court decisions.[10]

THE SKEPTICAL CRITIC AND THE AVOWED ADVOCATE: A DEBATE

In this scenario of a debate between the representative critic and representative advocate of faith-based programs, we see how both feel passionately and how their points of view strongly differ.

Moderator

Okay, you each have 10 minutes to debate today's issue, giving the three best reasons for your views: Resolved: Faith-based prison programming is unacceptable.

The Critic

Only three reasons, eh? I could give you twenty! OK, here they are. First, they are unethical. Faith-based programming, for example, attempts to impose a Christian view of the world on powerless prisoners. The programs give special privileges to prisoners who participate that aren't available to other prisoners. Look at that Christian Innerchange program in Iowa.

According to court testimony:

> Inmates who participate in the InnerChange program receive numerous privileges denied to non-participating inmates. InnerChange participants live in an honor unit where they are given keys to their own cells and access to private bathrooms, while non-participating inmates live in a lock-up unit where correctional officers have sole control over locks to cell doors and where the toilet stools are located in the middle of cells. InnerChange participants receive a broad range of other benefits denied to non-participating inmates, such as additional visits with family members, free telephone calls to family members, access to computers and word-processing equipment, and access to a large, projection-screen television.[11]

If those privileges aren't available to other prisoners, then prisoners can relieve the pains of imprisonment only by "becoming Christian." It's unethical to use the power of control and the promise of rewards to coerce conversion.

Second, they are ineffective. There is no evidence that the programs work. Recent studies have shown that accounts of success are largely anecdotal, and some of these so-called studies even cook the books and fudge the data.[12] There is no solid scholarly research to show that the faith-based programs differ from other programs or from the behavior of prisoners who don't participate at all. Positive results for participants are probably because prisoners who self-select to be in the programs are already those who are trying to better themselves.[13] Besides, prisoners will do anything to get parole, so participating in prison programs is just another way of manipulating the system.

Third, they are unconstitutional. Faith-based programming is the attempt of Christian evangelicals to convert a captive population to their own view of the world. The InnerChange program in Iowa restricted participation only to those prisoners willing to "convert" to their own view of Christianity. Others need not apply. This barred even other Christians from the program whose view of Christianity might differ from InnerChange's. Prison Fellowship has prisoner conversion as its stated goal: "Our goal is for prisoners to become born again and grow as fruitful disciples of Jesus Christ."[14] This is a clear violation of church and state and proselytizing converts at taxpayer expense. Even the American Civil Liberties Union has stepped in to stop state funding of prison conversion programs.[15]

The Advocate

Your three reasons are passionate, but they fail to persuade, namely because they are wrong. Those who argue against faith-based prison programming neither understand its implementation nor appreciate the outcomes. I reject your reasons on the following grounds.

First, the claim that faith-based programming is unethical rests on the assumption that prisoners are forced into programs because they are relatively powerless to attain resources by other alternatives. Granted, when this is the case, then they may be unethical. However, to assume all programs operate this way is wrong. You cite the Iowa case to support your view. A closer reading would suggest that the Iowa case had two premises: First, if taxpayer funds were not used to support the InnerChange programs, they might be less objectionable. Second, if other prisoners had equal voluntary access to similar programs, then the prison administrators might be in compliance with the Constitution. You are attacking the implementation of a specific faith-based program and not the broader issue of faith-based programs. If faith-based programs provide solace and a haven for prisoners from the predations of the general population, is it not unethical for outsiders, who are immune from the pains of imprisonment, to prevent those who daily experience the travails of prison the opportunity to find stability and seek self-transformation?

Second, to say that there is no evidence that they are effective does not mean that they are ineffective. Researchers are only beginning to assess the impact, and there is consensus that this is a complex issue with many hypotheses and theories to test. Existing evidence, including some you cite, does, in fact, suggest that faith-based programs contribute to prisoner well-being and provide services otherwise unavailable.[16] However, we are in partial agreement: We need more research to find out what works and how it works. If one goal of prisons is rehabilitation, then why shouldn't we use whatever means we can to contribute to the inner transformation of prisoners? Even if you can't "measure" inner transformation, you can measure behavior, and if participation in faith-based programs alters behavior, then what's the problem? Also, it's well established that programming is a necessary component of prison administration. In a time of fiscal constraints and reduction of programming, faith-based programming fills a void. A final point: Your argument that "jail-house conversions" are attempts to manipulate parole boards holds no water for two reasons. First, there is no evidence that parole boards are influenced by religious programs any more than other types of programs. Second, according to the Department of Justice, 90 percent of state and federal inmates already know their time of release because of determinate sentencing that eliminates considerable parole board discretion. This eliminates the manipulative motivation for parole.

The crux of your argument, as it does for many critics, rests on your third premise of unconstitutionality. However, you forget that faith-based prison programming has been part of the correctional enterprise for more than two centuries. It is nothing new; it is simply a return to the original goal of rehabilitation. We should also distinguish between faith-based organizations (Salvation Army, Catholic Charities) and other nonprofit organizations that run faith-based programming and faith-based congregations, such as Prison Fellowship. In the former, faith is secondary; providing services is primary. In the latter, it's the opposite. But even faith-based congregations need not run afoul of the Constitution if they assure voluntary participation, do not use taxpayer money, and prison administrators assure parity of privileges for nonparticipants.

Moderator

Thank you both, but I fear that you each have left us with more questions than answers. But what does this all hold for the future?

FUTURE PROSPECTS

Two factors seem certain about the future of faith-based prison programming: Its advocates will continue to pursue it, and critics will actively oppose it. Recent litigation challenging the constitutionality especially of Christian-based programming is unlikely to slow faith-based prisoner initiatives, because the variety of groups espousing spirituality have become more diverse, even though Evangelicalism remains dominant.[17] Virtually every state utilizes faith-based volunteers to implement some form of programming. Some programs are modest, limited to secular-focused programming, such as book-of-the-month reading groups or substance-abuse intervention. Others are far more ambitious and include entire state prisons or even private faith-based prisons.[18]

The challenge facing all faith-based groups lies in creating voluntary inclusive programming that does not run afoul of the constitutional separation of church and state. One program that appears to balance many of the competing issues is Louisiana State Penitentiary at Angola, a maximum-security prison

THE ANGOLA MODEL

Louisiana State Penitentiary at Angola is considered by many observers to be a model of faith-based prison programming that satisfies the constitutional safeguards of separation of church and state. In a typical month, about 22 percent of the prisoners participate. At least 16 Christian, Jewish, Muslim, and other religions and denominations offer faith-based programs staffed by outside volunteers, including:

- Assembly of God
- Baptist
- Roman Catholic
- Church of Christ
- Church of God in Christ Divine
- Metaphysics Episcopal
- Full Gospel
- Jehovah Witness
- Jewish
- Kairos Ministry
- Methodist
- Muslims
- Nondenominational
- Pentecostal
- Seventh-day Adventist
- United Pentecostal Apostolic

Preliminary evidence suggests that the programs are cost-effective because of the diversity of religious groups, the voluntary nature of the programming, and the relative parity of privileges for prisoners who chose not to participate in faith-based programming. The Angola model is judged by many to comply with constitutional standards.

Sources: Dennis Shere, *Cain's Redemption. A Story of Hope and Transformation in America's Bloodiest Prison* (Chicago: Northfield, 2005); Office of the Warden, Louisiana State Penitentiary, personal communications (January 12, 2007; April 21–22, 2006); *Louisiana State Penitentiary* (2006), http://www.corrections.state.la.us/LSP/.

nearly entirely programmed by faith-based organizations and volunteers. Of the prisoner population of 5,108, 52 percent are serving a life sentence. Because of the length of the sentences, however, an estimated 90 percent to 95 percent of the inmates will die in Angola. Yet prison administrators recognize that, even for lifers, prison programming is essential to prison security and prisoner well-being. Countering critics who argue that there is little need for extensive prison programming for lifers, because they will likely never return to the streets, Angola personnel argue that prison programs enhance security by providing prisoners with an incentive to buy into the program.

Although heavily evangelical, Angola's programs are open to any recognized religious faith, and prisoners participate voluntarily. Because the programs are led by prisoners and staffed by hundreds of outside volunteers, prisoners are able to suggest and develop programs in which they must first earn the privilege to participate. Although to date there have been no systematic studies of the impact of Angola's faith-based initiatives, prison documents indicate a dramatic reduction in violence, serious disciplinary infractions, and other measures of a dysfunctional prison culture since their inception.[19]

Whether Angola will survive constitutional challenges remains to be seen, but it nonetheless provides a possible model of how successful faith-based programming can work. So where to from here?

Ninety-five percent of U.S. prisoners eventually will return to the streets, roughly 75 percent of them within three years. Correctional professionals overwhelmingly agree that prison programming is essential for prison security, inmate well-being, and postadjustment release. Because prisons are increasingly constrained by tight budgets, hostile politicians, and an unsympathetic public, high-level security programs tend to receive fewer resources for programming than lower-security institutions housing shorter-term populations with fewer serious offenses. Programs, some argue, will benefit short-term inmates who will soon return to the street more so than lifers and long-term inmates. One value of faith-based programming is that, when properly administered, program delivery costs are borne by volunteers, not taxpayers. This makes such programming appealing, especially for maximum-security prisons.

Perhaps there can be no resolution to the controversies surrounding faith-based programming. This is not necessarily undesirable, because a healthy tension between two or more opposing sides can be beneficial. Ongoing debates and continued clarification of the issues require all sides to be aware of and sensitive to the legitimate and honest intellectual disagreements of those with differing views. Similar to the controversies underlying right to life and handgun control, the debate over faith-based initiatives in prison has been dominated by the extremes on both sides.

Recent calls to "promote a dialogue that respects the unique contributions of criminology and religion"[20] reflect attempts to bridge the gap and find common ground despite ideological or doctrinal disagreements. Why should we care? Because the public, prison staff, and prisoners share one overriding goal: Positive change, even redemptive change, within the individual inmate, whether brought about by traditional rehabilitative treatment techniques or a religious conversion experienced by a seeker participating in a faith-based prison program, is obviously a desired outcome for those we incarcerate.[21]

See Also: Guantanamo Detainees; Spiritual Care of Inmates.

Endnotes

1. There is some dispute whether the early Auburn model of the penitentiary, which emphasized discipline and prisoner labor, was based on religious principles or on a more pragmatic philosophy of using prison labor to generate profits for the prison. However,

overwhelming evidence indicates that Christian principles shaped Auburn at its inception, although labor for profit replaced it in the mid-1820s. See especially Joshua Stone and Jim Thomas, "The Roots of Faith-Based Prison Programming: A Revisionist View" (paper presented at the American Society of Criminology, Los Angeles, November 2006), http://jthomasniu.org/Papers/relhist.html.

2. See Stone and Thomas, "The Roots of Faith-Based Prison Programming."

3. Gustave de Beaumont and Alexis de Tocqueville, "Conversation with Mr. Elam Lynds," July 6, 1830, http://www.tocqueville.org/ny3.thm#0706b (accessed October 11, 2006); Samuel L. Knapp, *The Life of Thomas Eddy: Comprising an Extensive Correspondence with Many of the Most Distinguished Philosophers and Philanthropists of This and Other Countries* (Whitefish, MT: Kessinger, 2006; originally published 1836).

4. Norman Johnston, *Eastern State Penitentiary: Crucible of Good Intentions* (Philadelphia: Philadelphia Museum of Art, 2000), 29.

5. Joshua Stone, "Elmira," in *Sage Encyclopedia of Prisons,* ed. M. Bosworth (Thousand Oaks, CA: Sage, 2005).

6. The first major U.S. Supreme Court case recognizing a non-Christian occurred when the Black Muslims sued for recognition in Stateville Penitentiary in Illinois (*Cooper v. Pate,* 378 U.S. 546 [1964]). A few years later, in *Cruz v. Beto* (405 U.S. 319, 322 [1971]), the Supreme Court ruled that a Buddhist prisoner must be given a "reasonable opportunity of pursuing his faith comparable to the opportunity afforded fellow prisoners who adhere to conventional religious precepts."

    Since the mid-1980s, Muslims, Orthodox Jews, Native Americans, Sikhs, Rastafarians, and other groups have gained some of the rights considered necessary for the practice of their religions and have broken new legal ground in First Amendment issues. For further discussion, see Jim Thomas and Barbara H. Zaitzow, "Conning or Conversion? The Role of Religion in Prison Coping," *Prison Journal* 86, no. 2 (2006): 242–59.

7. See "Comment: Black Muslims in Prison: Of Muslim Rites and Constitutional Rights," *Columbia Law Review* 62, no. 8 (December 1962): 1488–1504; Christopher E. Smith, "Black Muslims and the Development of Prisoners' Rights," *Journal of Black Studies* 24, no. 2 (1993): 131–46.

8. *Cooper v. Pate,* 378 U.S. 546 (1964); Smith, "Black Muslims and the Development of Prisoners' Rights."

9. For example, see *O'Lone v. Shabazz,* 107 S.Ct. 2400 (1987), which challenged a corrections department regulation that prevented a Muslim inmate from returning early to the institution from a work detail in order to attend religious services held only on Fridays. Inmate Shabazz argued that the regulation violated his right to the free exercise clause of the First Amendment to the U.S. Constitution. The Supreme Court rejected Shabazz's appeal, finding that to require the institution to bring this inmate back in order to attend services would pose a security risk. See also *Turner v. Safley,* 482 U.S. 78 (1987).

10. Josiah N. Opata, *Spiritual and Religious Diversity in Prisons: Focusing on How Chaplaincy Assists in Prison Management* (Springfield, IL: Charles C. Thomas, 2001).

11. *Americans United for Separation of Church and State v. Prison Fellowship Ministries,* No. 4:03-cv-90074, Southern District of Iowa 2004, http://www.au.org/site/DocServer/Mapes.pdf?docID=162.

12. Mark A. R. Kleiman, "Faith-Based Fudging: How a Bush-Promoted Christian Prison Program Fakes Success by Massaging Data," *Slate,* August 5, 2003, http://www.slate.com/id/2086617.

13. Scott D. Camp, Jody Klein-Saffran, Okyun (Karl) Kwon, Dawn M. Daggett, and Victoria Joseph, "An Exploration into Participation in a Faith-Based Prison Program," *Criminology and Public Policy* 5, no. 3 (2006): 529–50; Thomas P. O'Connor, Jeff Duncan,

and Frank Quillard, "Criminology and Religion: The Shape of an Authentic Dialogue," *Criminology and Public Policy* 5, no. 3 (2006): 559–70.

14. Prison Fellowship, "In-Prison Ministry" (2006), http://www.prisonfellowship.org/contentindex.asp?ID=25.

15. American Civil Liberties Union, "ACLU of Virginia Wants Written Assurances from Hampton Roads Jails that Funding for Sectarian Groups Will Stop," American Civil Liberties Union of Virginia, news release, April 7, 2006, http://www.acluva.org/news releases2006/Apr7.html.

16. Byron R. Johnson, David B. Larson, and Timothy C. Pitts, "Religious Programs, Institutional Adjustment, and Recidivism among Former Inmates in Prison Fellowship Programs," *Justice Quarterly* 14, no. 1 (March 1997): 145–66; Jim Thomas and Barbara H. Zaitzow, "Conning or Conversion? The Role of Religion in Prison Coping," *Prison Journal* 86, no. 2 (2006): 242–59; Melvina T. Sumpter, "Editorial Introduction: Faith-Based Prison Programs," *Criminology and Public Policy* 5, no. 3 (2006): 523–28; Camp et al., "An Exploration into Participation in a Faith-Based Prison Program."

17. For example, Operation Starting Line, a national program with nearly 700,000 participating inmates in 883 correctional facilities, is a well-organized, well-funded coalition of Christian evangelists and prison ministry organizations that offers Bible studies and prepares inmates for release. See Prison Fellowship, *Operation Starting Line* (2006), http://www.operationstartingline.net/site_hmpg.asp; *Prison Fellowship*, http://www.prisonfellowship.org/default_pf_org.asp; *Prison Fellowship*, http://prisonministry.net/pfm.

18. For a brief summary of state faith-based prisons in Texas, Iowa, Florida, and elsewhere, see especially Jew on First!, "Government-Funded Right-Wing Christian Evangelical Prison Programs" (2006), http://www.jewsonfirst.org/sep_prisons.php#states. For a summary of how separate faith-based tiers sponsored by the Salvation Army successfully operate in Cook County Jail (Chicago, Illinois), see Jeff Cohen, "Inmates Find 'Christian Tier' a Haven from Troubles of Jail," *Chicago Tribune*, October 10, 2005, Metro 1. For an evaluation of the Life Connections Program in the Federal Bureau of Prisons, see Camp et al., "An Exploration into Participation in a Faith-Based Prison Program."

19. Eric Westphal and Frank Cecchinelli, "Cain and Angola: Louisiana State Penitentiary" (paper presented at the American Correctional Association Poster Conference, Charlotte, NC, August, 2006) http://venus.soci.niu.edu/˜niu-aca/ACA06/ericfrank.doc. See also Eric Westphal and Frank Cecchinelli, "Cain and Angola: Louisiana State Penitentiary" (paper presented at Northern Illinois University Criminal Justice Colloquium, DeKalb, IL, May 3, 2006, http://venus.soci.niu.edu/˜niu-aca/ACA06/ericang.ppt (accessed December 27, 2006); Dennis Shere, *Cain's Redemption. A Story of Hope and Transformation in America's Bloodiest Prison* (Chicago: Northfield, 2005); Office of the Warden, Louisiana State Penitentiary, personal communication (January 12, 2007); Louisiana State Penitentiary (2006), http://www.corrections.state.la.us/LSP/.

20. O'Connor et al., "Criminology and Religion."

21. John D. Hewitt, "Having Faith in Faith-Based Prison Programs," *Criminology and Public Policy* 5, no. 3 (2006): 551–58.

Further Reading: Johnson, Byron R., David B. Larson, and Timothy C. Pitts, "Religious Programs, Institutional Adjustment, and Recidivism among Former Inmates in Prison Fellowship Programs," *Justice Quarterly* 14, no. 1 (1997): 145–66; Knepper, Paul, "Faith, Public Policy, and the Limits of Social Science," *Criminology and Public Policy* 2, no. 2 (2003): 331–52; O'Connor, Thomas P., Jeff Duncan, and Frank Quillard, "Criminology and Religion: The Shape of an Authentic Dialogue," *Criminology and Public Policy* 5,

no. 3 (2006): 559–70; Shere, Dennis, *Cain's Redemption. A Story of Hope and Trans-
formation in America's Bloodiest Prison* (Chicago: Northfield, 2005); Thomas, Jim, and
Barbara H. Zaitzow, "Conning or Conversion? The Role of Religion in Prison Coping,"
Prison Journal 86, no. 2 (2006): 242–59.

Jim Thomas and Joshua Stone

FOREIGN INTELLIGENCE SURVEILLANCE ACT

INTRODUCTION

The terrorist attacks of September 11, 2001 (9/11), helped change the war
on terrorism from a local battle of law enforcement to a global war of counterterrorism. These acts also changed the way the United States has traditionally gathered intelligence on its citizens and on the citizens of other nations.
The new intelligence apparatus created by the Patriot Act of 2001 and the secret
electronic surveillance initiatives by the National Security Agency (NSA) have
become highly controversial issues post-9/11, revolving around the rights of individual liberty and to homeland security. Critics of both the Patriot Act and
the NSA's secret surveillances are concerned that such behavior violates the First
and Fourth Amendments and that these so-called invasions of privacy do not
comply with the Foreign Intelligence Surveillance Act.

The Foreign Intelligence Surveillance Act of 1978 (Public Law 95–511, 92
Stat. 1783), as amended, commonly known as FISA, is the law that established
the policies and procedures the government is required to follow when conducting electronic surveillance for foreign intelligence purposes in the United States.
When the act was passed, it initially involved electronic surveillances, but, as
codified, it has come to apply to the interception of wire, telephone, and computer communications, the searching of businesses and residences, the seizing
of business and library records, or other similar items of evidence.[1]

To provide a mechanism for authorizing these surveillances, the act established the Foreign Intelligence Surveillance Court (FISC) system. The FISC has
the power to issue orders that authorize searches and seizures, and the Foreign
Intelligence Surveillance Court of Review (FISCR) is responsible for reviewing
FISC decisions. The law resulting from the passage of the original FISA and its
amendments is codified in United States Code, Title 50, Sections 1801 to 1862,
Foreign Intelligence Surveillance. FISA was most recently revised on March 9,
2006, with the passage of the USA PATRIOT Act Improvement and Reauthorization Act of 2005.

When determining what actions the government may take or what laws it
may pass in search of national security information, it is important to look to
the U.S. Constitution, Article II, with regard to the powers of the president and
the executive branch. The article vests executive power in the president, who
takes an oath to "preserve, protect and defend the Constitution of the United
States." The president is also designated as, and with the authority of, the commander in chief of the military. The amendments to the Constitution are known

for the limits that are placed on the power of the government. In particular, the Fourth Amendment to the Constitution states:

> The right of the people to be secure in their persons, houses, papers, and effects, against unreasonable searches and seizures, shall not be violated, and no Warrants shall issue, but upon probable cause, supported by Oath or affirmation, and particularly describing the place to be searched, and the persons or things to be seized.

BACKGROUND

It has long been established in criminal cases that federal agents could be authorized, pursuant to a lawfully issued search warrant based upon probable cause, to search and seize anything that could later be used as evidence in a criminal prosecution. As noted previously, criteria for the issuances of warrants are set forth in the Constitution's Bill of Rights,[2] and the Supreme Court has upheld those requirements in numerous decisions. The most notable case involving electronic surveillance is *Katz v. United States,* 389 U.S. 347 (1967). Congress passed FISA in an effort to ensure that Fourth Amendment rights and civil liberties were not abridged by the use of electronic surveillances, especially during the conduct of national security investigations (*United States v. United States District Court,* 407 U.S. 297 [1972]).

In the 1960s, the U.S. public was becoming aware of domestic spying on U.S. citizens by several federal agencies and the military. The Freedom of Information Act was passed in 1966. The U.S. public became more aware of extensive intrusions into their lives, especially those who protested such things as the Vietnam War. There were also investigations by the Federal Bureau of Investigation (FBI) regarding civil rights activists, including the Reverend Martin Luther King Jr. Congress then passed the Privacy Act in 1974 in an effort to give U.S. citizens access to government records that had been kept on them and to limit the distribution to others of personally identifiable information. The public was also very concerned that there could be government records that were not accurate or had unfairly tainted their reputations.

In January 1975, Senator Frank Church held hearings to determine the extent of domestic spying and just how invasive the government had been into the affairs of U.S. citizens. The Church Committee, formally known as the Senate Select Committee to Study Government Operations with Respect to Intelligence Activities, heard testimony regarding the FBI's COINTELPRO, the Central Intelligence Agency's (CIA's) Operation CHAOS, and the NSA's Operations MINARET and SHAMROCK. The committee examined the depth to which government agencies were actively involved in electronic surveillance of Americans. The Church Committee issued numerous reports by 1976. On May 19, 1976, the Senate created the permanent Select Committee on Intelligence to oversee the actions of intelligence agencies.

President Gerald Ford signed Executive Order 11828 on January 4, 1975, creating the U.S. President's Commission on CIA Activities in the United States.

Vice President Nelson Rockefeller chaired the investigation, and it became known as the Rockefeller Commission. In June 1975, it issued a "Report to the President by the Commission on CIA Activities within the United States"; the critical issue addressed by the committee was how the government can maintain the fundamental liberties of Americans at the same time it protects their security.

A remedy was sought as Americans became more and more aware of what had been done on U.S. soil in the name of national security and the extent of the government records that existed. It became apparent that additional legislation was needed. To ensure that there was not going to be any further capricious surveillances of Americans, Congress passed FISA in 1978. Congress set a standard for the electronic surveillances and searches that was similar to the same high level as those followed for criminal investigations. With the exception of certain exigent circumstances, the law would require a court order for electronic eavesdropping. Although the actual procedures are different, government agents are required to present their requests to federal judges sitting in a FISC.

Unique to FISA, however, the court reviews applications for searches and issues orders, not warrants. The respective sections of the act, as amended and included in the code, relate to:

- Electronic Surveillance.
- Physical Searches.
- Pen Registers and Trap and Trace Devices[3] for Foreign Intelligence Purposes.
- Access to Certain Business Records for Foreign Intelligence Purposes.

National security investigations, also referred to as intelligence investigations, routinely involve the seizure of electronic information. This is legally accomplished pursuant to orders issued by the FISC. These investigations collect data that is provided to the members of the intelligence community, and it is used in national policy determinations and the defense against terrorism. Information gathered pursuant to a FISC order may also be used in a criminal prosecution, as long as the criminal investigation was not the real purpose of the issuance of the FISC order.

Although the act sets forth criteria for the use of the FISC system and the issuance of orders, Section 102 of FISA notes that "notwithstanding any other law, the President, through the Attorney General, may authorize electronic surveillance without a court order under this title to acquire foreign intelligence information for periods of up to one year." The act limits these actions to communications exclusively between foreign powers, the acquisition of technical intelligence, and communications in which there is "no substantial likelihood that the surveillance will acquire the contents of any communication to which a United States person is a party."

Structure

Section 103 of FISA created the secret Foreign Intelligence Surveillance Court, which has two tiers. Today, the first tier of the FISC consists of 11 federal judges, and the second tier, the FISCR, is composed of 3 federal judges; each judge is appointed by the chief justice of the Supreme Court and serves a term of seven years. Court records are maintained pursuant to "security measures established by the Chief Justice in consultation with the Attorney General and the Director of Central Intelligence" (Title 50 United States Code Section 1803).

FISA is very specific regarding the type of information over which it has jurisdiction. The court hears requests from federal agencies for orders to seize foreign intelligence information. The act defines[4] this information as:

1. Information that relates to the ability of the United States to protect against:

    a. Actual or potential attack or other grave hostile acts of a foreign power or an agent of a foreign power;
    b. Sabotage or international terrorism by a foreign power or agent of a foreign power; or
    c. Clandestine intelligence activities by an intelligence service or network or a foreign power.

2. Information with respect to a foreign power or foreign territory that relates to, and if concerning a United States person is necessary to:

    a. The national defense or the security of the United States; or
    b. The conduct of the foreign affairs of the United States.

In federal criminal investigations, requests for electronic information and other seizures are taken to the U.S. District Court, where federal agents will request the issuance of a search warrant. However, the activities of a FISC are closed to the public and the press. Participants in FISA court proceedings are required to have security clearances. The individuals who are the subjects of the orders are generally not advised of the searches or seizures, especially when it involves electronic surveillance.

Before an application for an order is presented to the court, the attorney general must approve it. To ensure the integrity of the process and protect civil rights, FISA sets forth specific requirements that each application for an order must meet. Pursuant to Section 104 of the act, codified in Title 50 United States Code Section 1804, the application for an electronic surveillance order must contain the following information:

1. The identity of the federal officer making the application;
2. The authority conferred on the attorney general by the president . . . ;
3. The identity, if known, or a description of the target of the electronic surveillance;
4. A statement of the facts and circumstances relied upon by the applicant to justify his belief that:

    a. The target of the electronic surveillance is a foreign power or an agent of a foreign government; and
    b. Each of the facilities or places at which the electronic surveillance is being directed is being used, or is about to be used, by a foreign power or an agent of a foreign power;

5. A statement of the proposed minimization[5] procedures;
6. A detailed description of the nature of the information sought and the type of communications or activities to be subjected to the surveillance;
7. A certification . . . by the assistant to the president for National Security Affairs or an executive branch official or officials designated by the president from among those executive officers employed in the areas of national security or defense and appointed by the president with the advice and consent of the Senate:

   a. That the certifying official deems the information sought to be foreign intelligence information;
   b. That a significant purpose of the surveillance is to obtain foreign intelligence information;
   c. That such information cannot reasonably be obtained by normal investigative techniques;
   d. That designates the type of foreign intelligence information being sought according to the categories described in section 1801(e) of this title; and
   e. Including a statement of the basis for the certification that:

      i. the information sought is the type of foreign intelligence information designated; and
      ii. such information cannot reasonably be obtained by normal investigative techniques;

8. A statement of the means by which the surveillance will be effected and a statement whether any physical entry is required to effect the surveillance;
9. A statement of the facts concerning all previous applications that have been made to any judge under this subchapter involving any of the persons, facilities, or places specified in the application and the action taken on each previous application;
10. A statement of the period of time for which the electronic surveillance is required to be maintained and, if the nature of the intelligence gathering is such that the approval of the use of electronic surveillance under this subchapter should not automatically terminate when the described type of information has first been obtained, a description of facts supporting the belief that additional information of the same type will be obtained thereafter; and
11. Whenever more than one electronic, mechanical, or other surveillance device is to be used with respect to a particular proposed electronic surveillance, the coverage of the devices involved and what minimization procedures apply to information acquired by each device.

In addition, the judge responsible for reviewing the application may require more information. There may be further reviews and subsequent information that is deemed appropriate before an order is issued. With all of this, it is obvious that FISA was intended to ensure that the focus of the surveillance is agents of a foreign power and not U.S. citizens. It is also obvious that the FISA language did not include any references to criminal search warrants. FISA was intended to be distinct from requests for criminal search warrants yet provide safeguards to individual rights that had been abused in the past. The FISA language clearly requires that the application provided a reasonable basis, probable cause for the request, and a justification for that belief, not unlike similar information that must be contained in an application for a criminal search warrant (Title 50 United States Code Section 1805 (b)).

If the judge determines that the requirements for the order have been met and that probable cause exists, an order approving the surveillance will be issued. The electronic surveillance is for up to a 90-day period, but extensions may be granted for up to one year. If an application for a surveillance order is denied, the judge makes a record and sends it forward to the FISCR.

Emergency orders may also be issued based on a determination by the attorney general in consultation with a FISC judge. Within 72 hours, however, the surveillance must terminate if the information has not been collected or a formal order has not been obtained.

REPORTING OF THE ACTIVITIES OF THE FOREIGN INTELLIGENCE SURVEILLANCE COURTS

In April of each year, the attorney general reports to Congress and the Administrative Office of the Courts on the activities of the Foreign Intelligence Surveillance Courts for the prior year. This information includes:

- The total number of applications made for orders and extensions of orders approving electronic surveillance; and
- The total number of orders and extensions granted, modified or denied (Title 50 United States Code Section 1807).

A review of the Department of Justice (DOJ) submissions to Congress indicates important statistics regarding electronic surveillance and physical searches for the years 2000 to 2005 (see table F.1)

Table F.1 Electronic Surveillance/Physical Search Statistics Reported by the DOJ

Year	Applications Submitted	Applications Approved	Applications Denied or Withdrawn	Court-Modified Proposed Orders	Notes
2005	2,074	2,072	2	61	
2004	1,758*	1,754	3	94	1 filed in 2003
2003	1,727	1,724	4	79	
2002	1,228	1,228		2	
2001	932	934*		2	2 filed in 2000
2000	1,005	1,012*		1	9 filed in 1999

The attorney general is also required to report on a semiannual basis to the House Permanent Select Committee on Intelligence and the Senate Select Committee on Intelligence. The report should include, in particular, the following information:

- Each criminal case in which information acquired has been provided to law enforcement; and
- Each criminal case in which information has been authorized for use at a trial.

There are similar reporting requirements if the surveillance involves pen registers, traps, physical searches, or business records (Title 50 United States Code Sections 1826, 1846, and 1862).

Prohibitions and Remedies

In an effort to discourage the gathering of foreign intelligence information using electronic surveillances that are not authorized by an order of the FISC, the law provides for criminal sanctions for individuals who conduct unauthorized surveillances under color or law or disclose or use electronic information obtained under color of law. Punishments can result in fines of up to $10,000 and/or imprisonment of up to five years. The act also provides for a civil remedy for these violations. The remedies include actual damages, punitive damages, and reasonable attorney and other fees (Title 50 United States Code Section 1810).

Physical Searches

The code also provides for the FISC to issue orders authorizing physical searches for the "purpose of obtaining foreign intelligence information anywhere within the United States" (Title 50 United States Code Sections 1822 (c) and 1823). Section (a) authorizes the president, acting through the attorney general, to conduct physical searches without a court order to acquire foreign intelligence information. This is also enumerated in Executive Order 12949, dated February 9, 1995. The attorney general's certification authorizing the search must meet the criteria set forth in the code. One key criterion is that the certification must note that "there is no substantial likelihood that the physical search will involve the premises, information, material, or property of a United States person" (Title 50 United States Code Section (a)(1)(A)(ii)). The results of these searches are sent to the court with a copy of the attorney general's certification (Title 50 United States Code Section (a)(2)).

The other sections and criteria of the code are similar to those contained in the sections listed previously regarding electronic surveillance. One unique aspect of the section on physical searches is related to congressional oversight. The attorney general must report the "number of physical searches which involved searches of the residences, offices, or personal property of United States persons, and the number of occasions, if any where the Attorney General provided notice" of the search of the residence of a United States person and there was a subsequent determination that there was not a continuing national security interest (Title 50 United States Code Section 1825 (b)). The prohibitions and remedies are similar to those mentioned previously.

Pen Registers and Trap Devices

Pen registers and trap and trace devices used for foreign intelligence and international terrorism investigations are addressed in Title 50 United States Code Sections 1841–1846. The attorney general or a designated attorney for the government can make the application for their use. The subject may not be a United States person or to "protect against international terrorism or clandestine intelligence activities" and that such activities are not protected by the First Amendment to the Constitution. Unlike other prior sections of Title 50, the application can be either to a FISC or an appropriate United States magistrate. Like other sections, there are provisions for emergency authorizations and congressional oversight.

Business Record Access

This section permits the director of the FBI or a designee to apply for a court order requiring the production of any tangible evidence (including books, records, papers, documents, and other items) pursuant to a foreign intelligence investigation not relating to a United States person or to "protect against international terrorism or clandestine intelligence activities" and that such activities are not activities that are protected by the First Amendment to the Constitution. The application for the order can be made either to a FISC or an appropriate United States magistrate (Title 50 United States Code Section 1861 (b)). This section also contains a provision for congressional oversight (Title 50 United States Code Section 1862).

PRESIDENTIAL AUTHORITY AND THE NSA TERRORIST SURVEILLANCE PROGRAM

One very controversial section of FISA refers to the authority of the president, through the attorney general, to authorize electronic surveillance for foreign intelligence information, without a court order, for up to 15 days following a declaration of war by Congress (Title 50 United States Code Section 1811). Because the Constitution is silent on the exact format of a formal declaration of war, this raises the question of when the United States is at war.

REQUESTS TO THE FOREIGN INTELLIGENCE SURVEILLANCE COURT

The DOJ reported that in 2005 there were 155 applications for business records to the FISC and all were approved.

As is noted in the following discussion by the attorney general, it is his opinion that a joint resolution passed by Congress is tantamount to a declaration of war under FISA, and it empowers the president to bypass the procedural requirements of FISA. The joint resolution is more formally known as the "Authorization for the Use of Military Force" and was passed by both the Senate and the House of Representatives on September 18, 2001. It became Public Law 107–40, 115 Stat. 224 (2001) and provided:

> That the President is authorized to use all necessary and appropriate force against those nations, organizations, or persons he determines planned, authorized, committed, or aided the terrorist attacks that occurred on September 11, 2001, or harbored such organizations or persons, in order to prevent any future acts of international terrorism against the United States by such nations, organizations or persons.

In spite of the many reasons behind the passage of FISA, a significant controversy has arisen regarding the NSA's Terrorist Surveillance Program, an electronic eavesdropping program that is operating outside of the FISC. After an unauthorized public disclosure of the program in December 2005, the president acknowledged the existence of this classified NSA program that was being used to protect the national security of the United States. The issue is whether these activities by the NSA, as authorized by the president, may be illegal.

Earlier, in a speech to the United States Senate on April 27, 2005, before the Select Committee on Intelligence, Attorney General Alberto Gonzales discussed the amendments to FISA made by the Patriot Act. He extolled the use of FISA for electronic surveillances and how the controls within FISA "protect against unwarranted government intrusions into the privacy of Americans." His comments also discussed the need for roving warrants, similar to those used in criminal investigations. This was all stated before the U.S. public became aware of the NSA program.

On December 19, 2005, in a press briefing at the White House, Attorney General Gonzales and Gen. Michael Hayden, who was the NSA director at the time and is now the CIA director, advised that the NSA program is still "very" classified and that they could not discuss details of the program and that the unauthorized leak of information regarding the NSA program has "compromised national security." The attorney general confirmed that "the President has authorized a program to engage in electronic surveillance . . . [to intercept the] contents of communications where one . . . party to the communication is outside the United States." He also indicated that there was a "reasonable basis to conclude that one party to the communication is a member of al Qaeda, affiliated with al Qaeda, or a member of an organization affiliated with al Qaeda, or working in support of al Qaeda." The attorney general indicated that it was their intention to "learn of communications, back and forth, from within the United States to overseas with members of al Qaeda."

The attorney general stated that FISA "requires a court order before engaging in this kind of surveillance . . . unless otherwise authorized by statute or by Congress." He indicated that it is the administration's position "that the authorization to use force, which was passed by the Congress in the days following September 11, constitutes that other authorization, that other statute by Congress, to engage in this kind of signals intelligence . . . . [W]e believe signals intelligence is even more a fundamental incident of war, and we believe has been authorized by the Congress. And even though signals intelligence is not mentioned in the authorization to use force, we believe that the Court would apply the same reasoning to recognize the authorization by Congress to engage in this kind of electronic surveillance."

The attorney general also added that, "the President has the inherent authority under the Constitution, as Commander-in-Chief, to engage in this kind of activity. Signals intelligence has been a fundamental aspect of waging war since the Civil War, where we intercepted telegraphs, obviously, during the world wars, as we intercepted telegrams in and out of the United States. Signals intelligence is very important for the United States government to know what the enemy is doing, to know what the enemy is about to do." He noted that, "these two authorities exist to allow, permit the United States government to engage in this kind of surveillance."

When the attorney general was specifically asked why the NSA did not use the FISC, he stated that, "we are not legally required to do, in this particular case, because the law requires that we—FISA requires that we get a court order, unless authorized by a statute, and we believe that authorization has occurred." He also indicated that in order to adequately deal with the kind of program that is in place at the NSA, FISA would likely have to be amended.

At the same time, General Hayden stated that he did not believe that "FISA was envisaged as a tool to cover armed enemy combatants in preparation for attacks inside the United States. And that's what this authorization under the President is designed to help us do." The attorney general also stated that the NSA surveillance "is consistent with requirements of the Fourth Amendment. The touchstone of the Fourth Amendment is reasonableness, and the Supreme Court has long held that there are exceptions to the warrant requirement in—when special needs outside the law enforcement arena. And we think that that standard has been met here."

In a speech at the Georgetown University Law Center on January 24, 2006, Attorney General Gonzales emphasized that the NSA program is "a wartime foreign intelligence program . . . an 'early warning system' with only one purpose: to detect and prevent the next attack on the United States by foreign agents hiding in our midst." The use of FISA would "introduce a significant factor of *delay*."

In a March 24, 2006, letter to Congressman James Sensenbrenner Jr., chairman of the House Committee on the Judiciary, William Moschella, assistant attorney general, stated that the "Terrorist Surveillance Program is consistent with FISA." He relied on *Hamdi v. Rumsfeld*, 542 U.S. 507, 518 (2004), to indicate that the Force Resolution "must be understood to have authorized fundamental and accepted incidents of waging war." He stated that:

> FISA itself contemplates that a later enactment, such as the Force Resolution, could authorize electronic surveillance because it provides that

electronic surveillance is not prohibited if it is authorized by statute [50 United States Code Section 1809(a)]. . . . [S]ubstantial authority indicates that the President has inherent constitutional authority over the gathering of foreign intelligence . . . inherent constitutional authority that FISA could not limit.

In drawing this conclusion, Moschella also relied on the plurality decision, *In re Sealed Case*, 310 F.3d 717, 742 (2002); he noted the record indicated: "We take for granted that the President does have the authority and, assuming that is so, FISA could not encroach on the President's constitutional power . . . . The Force Resolution confirm[s] the President's inherent authority in this area by expressly recognizing that the September 11th attacks render it both necessary and appropriate that the United States exercise its right to self-defense and to protect the United States citizens both home and abroad." He went on to say that, "interpreting the Force Resolution and FISA to permit the Terrorist Surveillance Program is . . . the *correct* reading."

FUTURE PROSPECTS

Congress has questioned the president's authority regarding the Terrorism Surveillance Program and other surveillance activities without requesting authorizations pursuant to FISA. In an effort to clarify the authority of the president and the authority of FISA, Senators Arlen Specter and Dianne Feinstein have introduced a bill in the Senate: "To ensure that all electronic surveillance of United States persons for foreign intelligence purposes is conducted pursuant to individualized court-issued orders, to streamline the procedures of the Foreign Intelligence Act of 1978, and for other purposes." The question is whether the proposed legislation, any other legislation, or even a court review will resolve the issue of whether the administration's classified and secret surveillances, which have not been FISC approved, are legal.

See Also: Antiterrorism Laws; Espionage Act of 1917; Homeland Security; Patriot Act.

Endnotes

1. The act and all of its subsequent amendments incorporated in Title 50 contain an extensive list of definitions to ensure that the terms as referred to in the act and other sections of the code are understood in the context in which they are used.
2. Under British rule, American colonists were subject to the abuses of general warrants and bills of attainder. The Fourth Amendment to the U.S. Constitution is just one response to what the colonists found to be unjust treatment.
3. Pen registers are electronic devices that record outgoing telephone numbers, whereas trap and trace devices record incoming call information. Complete definitions for pen registers and trap devices are found in Title 18, United States Code Section 3127.
4. Section 101 of the act, Title 50, United States Code Section 1801, lists numerous definitions of the terms that are used in FISA and this part of the code as well as definitions found in other titles.

5. By "minimization," the court looks for an assurance that the proposed action is the least intrusive into an individual's right to privacy.

Further Reading: Daalder, I. H., J. M. Lindsay, and J. B. Steinberg, *The Bush National Security Strategy: An Evaluation* (Washington, DC: Brookings Institution, 2002); Howard, Russell D., James J. F. Forest, and Joanne C. Moore, eds., *Homeland Security and Terrorism: Reading and Interpretations* (New York: McGraw-Hill, 2006); Pious, Richard M., *The War on Terrorism and the Rule of Law* (Los Angeles: Roxbury, 2006); Sauter, Mark A., and James Jay Carafano, *Homeland Security: A Complete Guide to Understanding, Preventing, and Surviving Terrorism* (New York: McGraw-Hill, 2005); White, Richard, and Kevin Collins, eds., *The United States Department of Homeland Security: An Overview* (Boston, MA: Pearson, 2005).

Keith G. Logan

FORENSIC PSYCHOLOGY

INTRODUCTION

Recent movies and television shows paint the forensic psychologist as the profiler who predicts criminal behavior to solve crimes and make arrests. Although such fictional portrayals of someone hunting down a serial killer, for example, may appeal to the general public, in reality, the field of forensic psychology is much more than profiling. Forensic psychology is the application of psychology to criminal and civil justice or, more specifically, as the merging of clinical psychology with law.[1] This area of expertise and practice is controversial because there are no formal requirements, regulating agencies, or so-called rites of passage. Forensic psychology is not a licensed field nor are forensic psychologists certified by some kind of examination such as the bar examination for attorneys in which candidates must pass a series of specific tests or evaluations before beginning to practice. In fact, the majority of forensic psychologists are clinical psychologists[2] by training or those who diagnose, assess, and treat cases of serious mental illness as an occupation. Despite this, forensic psychologists are actively exploring the areas of eyewitness memory and jury selection.

BACKGROUND

Forensic psychologists generally have four roles: researcher, court expert, policy evaluator, and advocate.[3] Although these roles are not well publicized outside of the field, a good forensic psychologist is fluent in each area.

First, the forensic psychologist is a scientist or researcher. He or she may conduct experiments investigating the reliability of eyewitness memory, for example, or perhaps design methods for determining the effectiveness of boot camps at rehabilitating young offenders.

Second, forensic psychologists testify as experts during court cases. The expert witness is different from the fact witness, though the forensic psychologist can fulfill the role of either one. Expert witnesses have a special or unique

DID YOU KNOW?

Television, movies, and the news media often sensationalize the role of the forensic psychologist. Although some forensic psychologists do engage in criminal profiling, movies such as *Silence of the Lambs* and *Mindhunters* and television shows such as *Criminal Minds* and the like provide a limited, often distorted view of the nature of forensic psychology. In reality, forensic psychologists are scientists who provide a variety of services to the criminal and civil justice system.

understanding of a certain topic and are hired by attorneys to give testimony concerning this topic, such as the mental competency of a defendant to stand trial. The forensic psychologist as a fact witness, in contrast, is when the psychologist has encountered the defendant during therapy and provides information to the court regarding the defendant's response to therapy.[4]

The third role of the forensic psychologist is that of a policy evaluator. As such, the forensic psychologist assists in evaluating the policies adopted by the legal system; for example, offering a view as to whether mentally retarded individuals should be eligible for capital punishment.

Finally, the forensic psychologist may serve as an issue advocate. This, in particular, may be considered the most disputed role of the forensic psychologist. Here, the forensic psychologist provides his or her knowledge of psychology to one side of an issue. In essence, the forensic psychologist is no longer considered a member of the legal system but instead an employee of a private individual or company.

LEGAL DEVELOPMENTS

As a fixture of both psychology and the legal system, the forensic psychologist works with diverse clientele, including convicted criminals, defendants awaiting trial, children of divorce, crime victims, personal injury complainants, or senior citizens undergoing competency hearings.[5] Recent Supreme Court decisions have caused some state legislatures to require forensic psychologists to use stricter scientific criteria when assessing clients. Several questions must now be answered during the client's assessment.[6] First, is there a hypothesis or idea for the client's condition? Second, have other forensic psychologists reviewed the method of evaluation? Third, does the method of evaluation have a documented error rate? Fourth, does the field of forensic psychology generally see the method of evaluation as acceptable? This new criteria is intended to reduce personal bias from showing up in client assessments.

Forensic psychologists must be ethical. All collected data (e.g., diagnoses, psychological test results, reports) are confidential, unless the client gives permission for others not related to the court proceedings to receive the information. Forensic psychologists are obligated to report all data collected, such as the results of psychological assessments and interviews with relatives. Bias, particularly confirmatory bias, can result when the forensic psychologist includes only information that supports his or her conclusions. In order to reduce such bias, forensic psychologists are encouraged to adopt only one role with their clients—therapist or advocate—and avoid using computer-generated reports in place of true evaluations.

CONTROVERSIAL ISSUES

One controversial issue facing the court system is the reliability of eyewitness memory. Although a forensic psychologist may be called to testify in a court as an eyewitness (e.g., the circumstances surrounding a client who threatened another person), most of the people who testify as eyewitnesses are, indeed, average citizens. Research in this area has established several general and well-supported trends.[7]

The first trend is weapon focus. Witnesses often focus more attention on stimuli associated with high levels of arousal (e.g., the features of the gun used during a robbery), rather than other information like the suspect's face or other identifiable features.

Second, memory errors are likely to occur if information that is feasible but incorrect is given to the eyewitness after the event. For example, the eyewitness before testifying may incorrectly overhear that the traffic light was green instead of red when the cars collided.

Third, older children are preferred as eyewitnesses over younger children. Children may make mistakes if they are asked questions with sophisticated language and are reluctant to say they "don't know" to an adult they perceive as a stranger (e.g., a police officer or attorney). Research suggests that eyewitness memory in both adults and children can be easily molded.

Forensic psychologists have found the cognitive interview to be a useful tool for improving the memory of eyewitnesses.[8] This procedure increases the memory recall of eyewitnesses by asking the witnesses to do four things: mentally go through the incident once again (e.g., contextual reinstatement), describe the event in several time orders (e.g., beginning to ending and ending to beginning), describe the incident from the various visual perspectives of the involved parties, and list as many details about the event as possible.

The goal of the cognitive interview is to elicit new information that may have been unintentionally overlooked during previous police and attorney interviews. It is different from the police standard interview because it asks more questions and uses more mnemonic devices. The cognitive interview may gain more accurate information than the standard interview, but it also results in a high amount of recalled inaccurate information. Furthermore, the cognitive interview appears useful for gaining new information regarding a person's appearance, whereas the standard interview is more suited for improving the recall of an object's features. Research suggests that the contextual reinstatement procedure seems to be the only section of the cognitive interview that is beneficial for memory improvement, thereby leading some forensic psychologists to propose that the three remaining sections of the cognitive interview are unnecessary.

Another controversial issue, again related to the courtroom, involves the use of psychologists in jury selection. During the 1970s, a new field emerged, called scientific jury selection. Prior to such, white men who were educated and middle-aged overly represented most juries.[9] In time, a series of Supreme Court decisions and congressional laws made it easier for members of minority groups and women to be eligible as jurors. With scientific jury selection, forensic psychologists are hired primarily by defense attorneys to act as consultants during jury selection in order to increase the defendant's chances of an acquittal, hung jury, or conviction on a lesser charge.

An attorney selecting jurors based on the likelihood they will or will not acquit the defendant is nothing new. During jury selection, both the prosecuting and defending attorneys question prospective jurors (called a *voir dire hearing*) regarding any prejudices they may have for or against the defendant. Attorneys may also use peremptory challenges, dismissing a prospective juror for any reason except race. The main objective of voir dire is to dismiss jurors who may be biased toward a particular conclusion, but, in essence, attorneys look for as many jurors as possible who will both support their position and convince other jurors to cast similar votes.[10]

Jurors typically have no real problems following or remembering witness testimony, but they find it difficult to apply the various state and federal laws during deliberation. Forensic psychologists have recommended giving jurors notebooks that list the order of testifying witnesses as well as definitions of legal terms. Judges have been encouraged to use simple terminology when instructing the jury before deliberating and to provide a written copy of these instructions.[11]

Forensic psychologists have made several interesting findings. First, the jurors who typically support convicting the defendant tend to have higher levels of education and income than those jurors who vote for acquittal. Second, jurors with a strict adherence to authoritative and conventional values tend to favor conviction, as well as stricter sentences, more frequently than jury members who share less authoritative views. Further, all-white juries are more likely to convict a defendant than are juries with minority members, especially if the defendant is of a different ethnic background. Juries with both white and minority members tend to take longer to deliberate and seem to contemplate a wider range of possible scenarios than do juries that are all white or all minority. In fact, white members of a mixed jury report paying more attention to the testimony and attorney arguments during a trial. One explanation suggests that white jurors think their views on the trial are more likely to be challenged by minority jurors during deliberation; therefore, they better prepare to defend their views.[12]

FUTURE PROSPECTS

The forensic psychologist has a number of roles in the legal system. One may argue, however, the most important role is that of a scientist. Forensic psychologists diagnose patients, provide expert testimony, and investigate controversial topics such as the reliability of eyewitness memory or the validity of methods to improve jury deliberation.

The field of forensic psychology is relatively young (roughly thirty years), but many have long realized its influence on the legal system. Some view forensic psychology as an appropriate avenue to introduce more methodology and scientific thinking to the courts. Others, however, view forensic psychology as possibly having too much influence on the legal process.

Regardless of one's view of forensic psychology, it does represent a new movement or change in our legal system. Science is becoming a prominent fixture in the courts. The science of forensic psychology is now available, and it is up to our legal system to find more ways to benefit from its presence.

See Also: Expert Witness Testimony; Mental Health and Insanity; Police and Psychological Screening.

Endnotes

1. See Society for Police and Criminal Psychology, *What Is Forensic Psychology?* http://faculty.css.edu/dswenson/web/FORENSIC.HTM
2. R. L. Hays-Thomas, "The Silent Conversation: Talking about the Master's Degree," *Professional Psychology: Research and Practice* 31 (2000): 339–45.
3. B. Arrigo and S. Shipley, *Introduction to Forensic Psychology: Issues and Controversies in Crime and Justice,* 2nd ed. (Burlington, MA: Elsevier, 2005).
4. L. S. Wrightsman, E. Greene, M. T. Nietzel, and W. H. Fortune, *Psychology and the Legal System,* 5th ed. (Belmont, CA: Wadsworth, 2002).
5. Ibid.
6. See Wrightsman et al., *Psychology and the Legal System.*
7. See, for example, Arrigo and Shipley, *Introduction to Forensic Psychology.*
8. R. P. Fisher, K. H. Brennan, and M. R. McCauley, "The Cognitive Interview Method to Enhance Eyewitness Recall," in *Memory and Suggestibility in the Forensic Interview,* ed. M. Eisen, G. Goodman, and J. Quas (Mahwah, NJ: Erlbaum, 2002), 265–86.
9. See Wrightsman et al., *Psychology and the Legal System.*
10. Ibid.
11. Ibid.
12. Ibid.

Further Reading: Bartol, C. R., and A. M. Bartol, *Psychology and Law: Theory, Research, and Application,* 3rd ed. (Belmont, CA: Wadsworth, 2003); Bartol, C. R., and A. M. Bartol, *Introduction to Forensic Psychology* (Thousand Oaks, CA: Sage, 2004); Ogloff, J.R.P., *Psychology and Law: The State of the Discipline* (New York: Kluwer, 1999); Walker, L. E., *Introduction to Forensic Psychology: Clinical and Social Psychological Perspectives* (New York: Kluwer, 2003); Weiner, I. B., and A. K. Hess, eds., *Handbook of Forensic Psychology,* 3rd ed. (New York: Wiley, 2005).

Kevin Krug and Stephen W. Verrill

G

GANG INJUNCTION LAWS

INTRODUCTION

Throughout U.S. cities, in both urban and rural regions, the concern over juvenile crime and gang violence shapes how people perceive the latter and former as a menace to society. Although recent statistics show a relative decline in crime rates, gang crime remains the center of attention. Although youth increasingly join street organizations for social status and respect among their peers, the media alleges that these gang members disrupt the quality of life of communities. Tracey L. Meares and Dan M. Kahan argue that the high rates of crime that continue to plague inner-city communities divest residents of their security, weaken legitimate economic life, and spawn pathological cultures of violence that ruin the lives of victims and victimizers alike.[1] Several community residents, gang experts, and prosecutors allege that these so-called superpredators[2] intimidate citizens to submit to their authority so they can sell drugs, party in public, stash weapons, and commit crimes with impunity.

Chris Swecker, assistant director of the Criminal Investigative Division of the Federal Bureau Investigation, said before a subcommittee of the Western Hemisphere House Relations Committee, "Gangs are more violent, more organized, and more widespread than ever before. They pose one of the greatest threats to the safety and security of all Americans. The Department of Justice estimates that 30,000 gangs with 800,000 members impact 2,500 communities across the U.S."[3] Swecker highlights the mainstream discourse and ideology on gang violence, which promotes a moral panic for communities across the United States by describing gangs as disrupting the moral fabric of U.S. society. Accordingly, advocates of gang injunction laws maintain that these civil codes provide law enforcement with more tools to fight gangs and reduce crime. On the other hand, critics and opponents of gang injunction laws maintain that they are ineffective and a waste of taxpayers' dollars that could be better spent on community development and crime prevention.

BACKGROUND

To date, there are no accurate figures on the number of gangs, gang crime, and gang members in the United States. Sociologist Malcolm Klein, one of the leading gang experts in the United States, estimates there are between 800 and 1,000 cities with gang crime problems with more than 9,000 gangs and 400,000 gang members.[4] In 2002, the National Youth Gang Survey found that cities with gang problems more than doubled Klein's figures with a total of 2,300. To calculate gang membership and crime, the U.S. Department of Justice administered the 1998 National Youth Gang Survey to law enforcement agencies. They found a total of 28,700 gangs with an estimated 780,200 gang members in the United States, with 46 percent Latino or Latina and 34 percent African American.[5] Most data on gang members collected by law enforcement derive from self-identification, monikers, tattoo insignia, community input (gang members, community workers, neighbors, teachers, and family members), and their style of dress and demeanor. These are some of the many characteristics that law enforcement officials use to determine gang membership.

GANG INJUNCTION LAWS IN CALIFORNIA

California Civil Code § 3479: Nuisance Defined

A nuisance is anything which is injurious to health, including, but not limited to, the illegal sale of a controlled substances, or is indecent or offensive to the senses, or an obstruction to the free use of property, or unlawfully obstructs the free passage or use, in the customary manner of any navigable lake, or river, bay, stream, canal, or basin, or any public park, square, street, or highway, is a nuisance.*

California Civil Code § 3480 Public Nuisance Defined

A public nuisance is defined as one which affects at the same time an entire community or neighborhood, or any considerable number of persons, although the extent of the annoyance or damage inflicted upon individuals may be unequal.**

---

*California Law Search, "California Civil Code Section 3479" (2006), http://california-law-search.com/civ/3479-3484.html.

**California Law Search, "California Civil Code Section 3480" (2006), http://california-law-search.com/civ/3479-3484.html.

DID YOU KNOW?

In order to determine if you have a case and an effective gang injunction, you must accomplish the following:

- Survey crime in the area to identify problem areas, individuals, and activities.
- Gather quality-of-life information to prove neighborhood damaged by gang nuisance.
- Identify community stakeholders and determine what the community believes are so-called fear factors.
- Examine law enforcement local expertise; identify necessary declarants for court documents.
- Search for nexus of:

  (a) Criminal activity.
  (b) Nuisance activity.
  (c) Individual gang members.*

---

*Julie Bishop, *Gang Injunctions: A Primer* (Los Angeles: City Attorney's Office, 1998).

Nevertheless, law enforcement agencies claim they lack the funding and resources to combat gang activity and to protect communities. In addition, law enforcement and politicians pump fear into the public in order to acquire resources and consent to mount an all-out attack on gangs. The climate of fear nurtured by law enforcement officials has paved the way for the rise of gang injunctions and restraining orders on street organizations. California became the first state to develop a hard-hitting gang injunction procedure by applying public nuisance laws to enforce civil injunctions that prohibit suspected gang members from engaging in both legal and criminal activities in public spaces known as *free zones* or *safety zones*.[6] Free zones and safety zones map out the parameters in a community, usually consisting of a few square blocks, where gang members may not associate with one another.

Gang injunction laws provide prosecutors with discretion to use public nuisance doctrines that prohibit lawful and unlawful behavior. Civil procedures do not require jury trials, defense counsel, and the burden of proving guilt beyond a reasonable doubt.

OPERATIONALIZING THESE LAWS

For a gang injunction petition to be honored in civil court, the prosecutors must establish two sources who identify defendants. Prosecutors often rely upon the community residents, law enforcement intelligence, and informants to establish a person's gang activity. Once this is accomplished, the prosecution must serve gang members with paperwork adjudicating them to the lawsuit, and once served, the injunction becomes effective. During the injunction hearings, the defendant's preexisting gang activity is exposed, even if he or she has not been arrested or convicted for a crime. This represents a disturbing trend in criminal justice in which crimes are punished before they actually happen. Most requests for gang injunctions are granted; however, the judge holds the discretionary power to change the terms of the injunction. In addition, the judge may exclude named individuals from the complaint due to poor evidence implicating an individual to gang affiliation or for failure to serve an individual with a copy of the complaint.

In an effort to expel gang members from a target area, on October 26, 1987, the Los Angeles city attorney and former Mayor James Hahn became the first to use a public nuisance abatement lawsuit in *People v. Playboy Gangster Crips*. This injunction barred 23 individually identified gang members from breaking 6 of 23 injunction terms, which under California law were already illegal. Although this injunction was not completely successful, it established a legal precedent in the use of the public nuisance doctrine to combat an entire urban street organization instead of individuals.[7]

Jeffrey Grogger, urban policy professor at Harvard University, dispels the myth that all gang injunctions operate in the same way. He argues that prohibited activities vary somewhat, but they typically include a mix of activities already forbidden by law, such as selling drugs or committing vandalism, and otherwise legal activities, such as carrying a cell phone or associating in public view with other gang members named in the suit. Once the injunction is imposed, prosecutors can pursue violations of the injunction in either civil or criminal court. The maximum penalty for civil contempt is a $1,000 fine and five days in jail. The maximum penalty under criminal prosecution is a $1,000 fine and six months in jail. Although civil procedures result in less stringent penalties, they have the advantage that their penalties can be imposed without criminal due process.[8]

In 1993, the most complete gang injunction issued thus far took place in the community of Rocksprings in San Jose, California, where gang members from Varrio Sureño Trece, Varrio Sureño Town, or Varrio Sureño Locos (VSL) claimed this area as their turf.[9] Silicon Valley residents felt unsafe and threatened because gang members congregated on sidewalks and lawns, where it was alleged that VST and VSL gang members engaged in a plethora of drug sales, violent activities, loitering, and lewd conduct. The residential condition made people afraid of having their children play outside and deterred residents from having visitors due to the fear of gang reprisal in the four-square-block neighborhood.

As a result, the city of San Jose issued a gang injunction against 38 members of the Varrio Sureño Trece, Varrio Sureño Town, or Varrio Sureño Locos (VSL) gang. The gang injunction enjoined and restrained individuals from engaging in the following activities: intimidating witnesses, which meant confronting, annoying, harassing, challenging, provoking, assaulting, or battering any person known to be a witness to or victim of a crime; making it illegal for gang members to group together (driving, gathering, sitting, and standing) with other known Trece/VSL associates in public or anyplace accessible to public; barring Trece/VSL gang members from carrying any firearms (imitation or real) and dangerous weapons on their persons or in the public view or any space accessible to the public; restraining from fighting anywhere in public view (street, alleys, private and public property); deterring the use of any gang gestures (hand signs, physical gestures, and discourses) that describe or refer to Varrio Sureño Trece, Varrio Sureño Town, or Varrio Sureño Locos; wearing clothing that bears the name or letters that spell out the name of the gang; selling, possessing, or using illegal drugs or controlled substances without a prescription (prohibiting anyone to knowingly remaining in the presence of them as well); no public consumption of alcohol anywhere in public view or anyplace accessible to the public; making it illegal for anyone to spray paint or apply graffiti on any public (alleys, block walls, streets) or private property (residences or cars); banning the possession of any graffiti paraphernalia (spray cans, paint markers, etching tools, whiteout pens, acrylic paint tubes, various paint cap tips, razor blades, or other known graffiti tools) unless going to or from art class; no trespassing on private property; honoring a daily curfew of 10:00 p.m. to sunrise unless going to a legitimate meeting or entertainment activity, engaged in a business trade, profession, or occupation, or involved in an emergency situation; no looking out for another person to warn anyone that a law enforcement officer is approaching by whistling, yelling, or signaling; and violating the law (prohibit violence and threat of violence, including assault and battery, murder, rape, robbery by force or fear).

Defendants from Varrio Sureño Trece, Varrio Sureño Town, and Varrio Sureño Locos challenged the unconstitutional vagueness of this court order in *People ex rel. Gallo v. Acuña*. An appeals court threw out 15 of the 25 original provisions. As a result, the San Jose city attorney appealed two provisions to the California Supreme Court: the terms that prohibited gang members from congregating in safe zones and one barring them from harassing or threatening inhabitants who complained about gang activities. The California Supreme Court approved the use of civil antigang injunctions by rejecting the constitutional challenge to the use of public nuisance abatement injunction against street gangs. This decision took into consideration the interest of the community while restricting the First Amendment rights of free speech and association of gang members.

According to Justice Janice Brown, "To hold the liberty of the peaceful, industrious residents of Rocksprings must be forfeited to preserve the illusion of freedom for those whose ill conduct is deleterious to the community as a whole is to ignore half the political promise of the Constitution and whole of its sense. . . . Preserving peace is the first duty of government, and it is for the protection of the community from the predations of the idle, the contentious, and the brutal that government was invented."[10] The *People ex rel. Gallo v. Acuña* landmark California Supreme Court decision paved the way for municipal government across the state to use similar gang suppression tactics to curtail gang activities.

For example, in 2006 the San Francisco city attorney, Dennis Herrera, sought an injunction against the Oakdale Mob Gang due to their reputation for distributing drugs and for contributing to an increasing violent crime rate, including harming and killing rival gang members and witnesses. To protect residents, Herrera pushed for punishing any gang member who violates a curfew order of 10:00 P.M. or for congregating in a four-block radius safety zone and a plethora of other restrictions.[11] Similarly, in 2005, San Diego County District Attorney Terri Perez filed a court order prohibiting known gang members from grouping together with other associates, displaying gang signs, wearing gang attire, carrying weapons, selling illegal narcotics in public, or fighting in areas of downtown Vista.[12] The widespread use of injunction laws to combat neighborhood gang problems now appear in Austin, Los Angeles, Phoenix, Sacramento, San Antonio, San Diego, San Francisco, San Jose, and Stockton.

Many law practitioners believe that the relative reduction of crime in communities derives from law agencies holding an entire group of gang members accountable for the actions of individuals. From a law enforcement standpoint, gang injunction laws address status offences and nuisance activities before they

INEFFECTIVENESS OF GANG INJUNCTION LAWS

In 1995, the city of Pasadena, California, instituted two separate gang injunction laws. The city later discarded the gang injunction after the Pasadena Police Department and other governing bodies found it difficult to control gang activity as crime spilled over to other regions, making their efforts a complete failure. The failure of gang injunction laws stem from its inadequate ability to address the complex structure of gangs and the emerging crime issues in neighboring areas.*

In 1997, the Southern California division of the American Civil Liberties Union (ACLU) conducted a 10-year longitudinal study on the effectiveness of the gang injunction laws. The ACLU focused on the efficacy of the 1993 injunction law against the predominantly Latino Blythe Street Gang. The ACLU found that gang injunction laws do not meet their objectives in reducing the long-term crime incidences in the Blythe Street's safety zone.**

Opponents of gang injunction laws argue that they are expensive and deplete resources from cities. The constitutional cost of embarking on a gang injunction campaign ranges from $400,000 to $500,000. Several civil libertarians, social justice organizations (e.g., Books not Bars), and law enforcement practitioners argue in favor of investing funds in educational programs geared at preventing crime. Take, for example, Father Gregory Boyle, a Jesuit priest who founded Homeboy Industries in the community of Boyle Heights in East Los Angeles. Although many organizations quickly condemn gang members, Homeboy Industries offers an alternative to punitive approaches by offering gang members their first chance by helping them become gainfully employed. Boyle believes that the best way to effectively deal with gangs requires a major shift in moving away from the symptoms of gangs to addressing the social disease leading to gang formation. Boyle believes that gang injunctions fail to address the structure of poverty and law enforcement's misdiagnosis of the problem.***

---

*Matthew Mickle Werdegar, "Enjoining the Constitution: The Use of Public Nuisance Abatement Injunctions against Urban Street Gangs," *Stanford Law Journal* 51 (1999): 404–45.

**American Civil Liberties Union, "False Premise, False Promise: The Blythe Street Gang Injunction and Its Aftermath" (1997), http://www.streetgangs.com/injunctions/topics/blythereport.pdf.

***Gregory Boyle (guest lecturer, University of California–Santa Barbara, Sociology 144, Chicana/o Communities, February 26, 2004).

become felonious. Julie Bishop, the leading project attorney on gang injunctions for the Los Angeles city attorney office, argues that communities benefit from gang injunction laws:

> [T]hey have an amazing, immediate deterrent effect on the entire [gang] group's activity, not just the few who are "sued" by the City Attorney. They complement Neighborhood Recovery Efforts and address the gang problem from a group perspective. They save traditional law enforcement response for the chronic serious offenders. They have a preventive aspect in that they repeatedly warn defendants of the consequences of continuing their behavior. Julie Bishop, *Gang Injunctions: A Primer* (Los Angeles, CA: City Attorney's Office, October 1998, p. 2)

FUTURE PROSPECTS

As local and federal agencies attempt to ameliorate the gang problem, recent trends reveal a drop in the overall crime rate. At the core, these Draconian gang injunction laws attempt to deter individuals from committing future crimes at the expense of their constitutional rights while exacerbating police repression and extending the prison system in communities of color. As noted in the 1998 National Youth Gang Survey, approximately 80 percent of gang members are African American and Latino or Latina. Gang injunction laws disproportionately affect youth and adult gang members of color.

Victor M. Rios, sociology professor at the University of California–Santa Barbara, argues that the ever-expanding power and punitiveness of criminal justice policies and practices affect every member of poor racialized communities in multiple ways, especially urban youth of color. For example, law enforcement often applies gang injunctions to minorities because of their race, not because they have demonstrated substantial evidence of gang activity or crime. This process has increased the probability of harassment of many law-abiding people of color. Rios notes that this so-called hypercriminalization of communities of color is derived from surveillance, security, and punitive penal practices centered on controlling black and brown populations preemptively—before they have even committed a criminal act.[13]

Lawrence Rosenthal argues that the enforcement of conventional laws, accordingly, allows the police enormous freedom to undertake a variety of quite heavy-handed measures against the residents of the inner-city minority communities, authority that officers who may harbor racial biases are frequently accused of misusing.[14] The taking away of constitutional rights of expression and assembly, like forbidding gang members from interacting with lifelong friends, brothers, and sisters in the same family or banning street attire, does not address the systemic conditions that create gangs. Gang injunction laws exacerbate institutional racism when youths of color—blacks, Latinas, Latinos, and Southeast Asians, for example—will be deemed suspicious and criminal, even if they do not belong to a gang. This means that anyone who fits a gang member profile within the confines of a safe zone may be detained, searched, and arrested without probable cause.

See Also: Juvenile Justice; Juveniles and Social Justice.

Endnotes

1. Tracey L. Meares, Dan M. Kahan, "Law and (Norms of) Order in the Inner City," *Law and Society Review* 32, no. 4 (1998): 183–209.
2. Barry Krisberg, *Juvenile Justice: Redeeming Our Children* (Thousand Oaks, CA: Sage, 2005).
3. Chris Swecker, "Statement of Chris Swecker, Assistant Director, Criminal Investigative Division, Federal Bureau of Investigation, Before the Subcommittee on the Western Hemisphere, House International Relations Committee, April 20, 2005" (2005), http://www.fbi.gov/congress/congress05/swecker042005.htm.
4. Malcolm W. Klein, *The American Street Gang* (New York: Oxford University Press, 2002).
5. National Criminal Justice Reference Service, http://www.fbi.gov/congress05/swecker042005.htm2.
6. Jerome Burdi, "City Safe Zones Would Ban Gangs," *Topix,* January 27, 2007, http://www.topix.net/content/trb/2458370624183364534840215139892182419688.
7. L.A. City Attorney Gang Prosecution Section, "Civil Gang Abatement: A Community Based Policing Tool of the Office of the Los Angeles City Attorney," in *The Modern Gang Reader,* ed. Malcolm W. Klein, Cheryl L. Maxon, and Jody Miller (Los Angeles, CA: Roxbury, 1995), 325–31.
8. Jeffrey Grogger, "The Effects of Civil Gang Injunctions on Reported Violent Crime: Evidence from Los Angeles County," *Journal of Law and Economics* 45 (2002): 69–90.
9. Deanne Castorena, *The History of the Gang Injunctions in California* (Los Angeles: Sage, 1998).
10. Quoted in *People ex rel. Gallo v. Acuña,* 929 P.2d 596, 623 (Cal., 1997) (J. Mosk, dissenting) cert. denied, 117 S. Ct. 2513.
11. Adam Martin, "City Attorney Seeks Injunction against S.F. Gang," *The Examiner,* October 23, 2006, http://www.examiner.com/printa-357777ˉCity_attorney_seeks_injunction_against_S.F._gang.html.
12. Adam Klawonn, "Injunction Sought for 89 in Vista Gang," *San Diego Tribune,* June 8, 2005, http://www.signonsandiego.com/news/northcounty/20050608-9999-1mi8vgang.html.
13. Victor M. Rios, "The Hyper-criminalization of Black and Latino Male Youth in the Era of Mass Incarceration," *Souls* 8, no. 2 (2006): 40–54.
14. Lawrence Rosenthal, "Gang Loitering and Race," *Journal of Criminal Law and Criminology* 91, no. 1 (2002): 99–160.

Further Reading: Fremon, Celeste, *G-dog and the Homeboys: Father Gregory Boyle and the Gangs of East Los Angeles* (Santa Fe, NM: University of New Mexico Press, 2004); Grogger, Jeffrey, "The Effects of Civil Gang Injunctions on Reported Violent Crime: Evidence from Los Angeles County," *Journal of Law and Economics* 45 (2002): 69–90; Klein, Malcolm W., *The American Street Gang* (New York: Oxford University Press, 1995); Rios, Victor M., "The Hyper-criminalization of Black and Latino Male Youth in the Era of Mass Incarceration," *Souls* 8, no. 2 (2006): 40–54; Rodríguez, Luis, *Hearts and Hands: Creating Community in Violent Times* (New York: Seven Stories Press, 2001).

Rebecca Romo and Xuan Santos

GENDERED JUSTICE

INTRODUCTION

Gendered justice is a concept that refers to the differential treatment of males and females by the justice system. One would be hard pressed to find instances of equal treatment of males and females by the criminal justice system with regard to criminality, victimization, and professionals. Throughout the history of U.S. justice, many laws and legal practices have required differential treatment of men and women. With the wave of various women's rights movements, much of the language of the law has been changed to prescribe equal treatment; however, critics argue that the laws, their interpretation, and their enforcement remain unequal. Although some maintain that men and women should be treated equally and that the laws should not differentiate between men and women, others contend that to treat men and women the same when they are not is to treat them unequally.

Gender-specific laws refer to laws applicable to only one sex or that require differential treatment of the sexes based on the argument of necessity. Historically, among these laws were assault laws, which did not include domestic violence as a form of assault; rape laws, which did not include most forms of sexual assault, including marital rape or the rape of a male; sentencing laws, which required indeterminate sentencing for women but not men; jury laws, which did not allow women to serve as jurors; and various laws excluding women from the workforce. On the other hand, gender-neutral laws are written so that no sex receives preferential or discriminatory treatment. Today, most laws are written in a gender-neutral manner; however, many argue that the implementation of many laws has remained gender specific.[1]

That justice is gendered is often undisputed when examining history and when examining some current justice practices, such as women in law enforcement and the death penalty; however, there is controversy as to whether gender inequality still exists. Many claim that although most gender-specific laws have been corrected to reflect gender-neutral laws, the practice of justice as gendered is still very much alive, and that although we tend to focus more on the criminality of males, females are still discriminated against as criminals, victims, and justice officials. Others have argued that when considering most instances of justice, the gendered nature has virtually disappeared. Furthermore, they argue that where there is unequal treatment, it is reflected in the chivalry hypothesis in which females are given leniency on the grounds of protection. Feminist scholars, however, have largely examined this controversy and have found practices that support and do not support the notion. Another controversy in examining gendered justice has been the examination of the root of gender inequality. Many feminist scholars and activists argue that patriarchy is at the root of gendered justice, whereas other nonfeminist scholars and justice practitioners have often argued that gendered justice must be understood in light of the protection historically given women.

BACKGROUND

Gendered Profession

As examined by various scholars, the development of justice with regard to gender is premised in society's ideals of manhood and womanhood.[2] Thus, gendered justice has reflected cultural views of the roles that men and women play in society. Society defines males as rational, objective, analytical, strong, aggressive, and protectors and breadwinners of the family. On the other hand, the law has always defined women through their capacity within the family, either as daughter or as wife and mother. She did not have a separate legal identity. Within society, women were viewed as emotional, passive, irrational, weak, in need of protection, and as nurturers of the family. The social definition of women as irrational is reflected in their omission in the workforce in such positions as lawyers and judges as well as in the laws that forbade women to enter into contracts. Society's view of women as weak and as nurturers is reflected in the case of *Muller v. Oregon* (1908).[3] In this case, the court ruled that women's physical and maternal limitations precluded them from paid labor as well as required maximum work hours. Additionally, many states had laws restricting women from certain jobs. In *Goesaert v. Cleary* (1948),[4] women were prohibited from tending bars, unless they were the daughters or wives of the owner, in order to protect them from unsavory patrons. In the case of *Bradwell v. Illinois* (1873),[5] the law forbidding married women from practicing law was upheld based on the argument that women had the God-given duty to the home and family, not to the workforce. The controversy presents itself with various questions that examine gendered justice. Did the laws reflect the natural order of the sexes? Did the laws represent protection or oppression of women? Was the status of women, as defined by society, the norm or the exception, and did that justify the legislation of gender-specific laws?

Gendered Processing of Offenders and Victims

Examining the justice system's treatment of women as criminals and as victims, we can find many laws and practices that present gendered justice. The idea that men are aggressive has lead to society's conclusion, including practitioners and social scientists, that men are much more inclined to commit crimes, acts that are viewed to be aggressive. As a result, social control of criminals has focused on males. Males are much more likely to be scrutinized, suspected, and arrested for crimes, especially violent crimes. Historically, females were not viewed as capable of such aggressive behaviors as assault and murder. Legally, in fact, women did not have mens rea, criminal intent, in most crimes. Women legally did not possess the mental capability to commit a crime due to the perception that they had a childlike mentality. As a result, women were often given chivalrous treatment. The controversy that males are treated more harshly by the criminal justice system has been supported by this chivalry hypothesis. That is, the idea that protection requires that police, prosecutors, and judges protect the female offender in a chivalrous manner the way a man would protect a woman or a father his daughter.

This angle of the controversy becomes more complex when examining the age, race, and income of the female offender as well as the crime type. Today, social science research has found that the typical adult female offender is less than 30 years old, a racial minority, a single mother, poor, with little formal education, and receives social service assistance. Our main understanding of the criminal comes from official data; that is, data regarding offenders who were arrested. Uniform Crime Reports (UCR) released by the Federal Bureau of Investigations (FBI) reveal that the three most common offenses for which females are most likely to be arrested are running away, which is not a crime, fraud, and larceny-theft. On the other hand, the three most common offenses that males are most likely to be arrested for are burglary, drunkenness, and vandalism. Research, based on self-reports, also reveals that females represent less than 15 percent of all violent offenders, and three-quarters of these violent offenders commit simple assaults. Examining race, some researchers have found that women of color are more likely to be arrested for aggravated and other assaults, burglary, forgery, theft, drug violations, and prostitution. Other research has found that Hispanic women are most likely to be arrested for public order crimes, property offenses, and violent crimes. On the other hand, white women are more likely to be arrested for fraud, liquor law violations, drunkenness, and DUI offenses.

The data, self-reports, and official reports reveal that males commit more serious violent and nonviolent crimes. Furthermore, arrests do not necessarily reflect the extent of the crime committed in society. However, do these data prove the innate nature of males and females? Do these data reflect the socialization of people into gender roles? Or do these data reflect assumptions that lead to differential treatment of groups of people? Although we see patterns of gendered offending, research has also revealed that justice engages in chivalrous treatment of female offenders only when the offense is less serious and more fitting with the passive female role expectation and when the female is white, wealthy, and heterosexual. Females who engage in more serious, especially violent, crimes are treated with the harshness given to males, and in many cases with more harshness, because these females are viewed as stepping out of the gender roles that society has demanded. Examining prostitution laws and enforcement of such laws, the criminal justice system has always focused on the female prostitute alone as the criminal. Although these female offenders were in violation of the law, sex work, though illegal, has always been viewed as so-called women's work. Furthermore, it was viewed that the immoral woman who spreads disease and destroys families was at the very root of the social degradation of society. To date, the enforcement of prostitution laws remains the same.

Despite the fact that males commit more crime and more serious crime than do females, the increased rate of incarceration for males has doubled in since the 1970s, whereas it has quadrupled for females. Although women represent less than 10 percent of the prison population, when comparing these increases in incarceration, this presents gendered justice in the area of sentencing. Furthermore, Hispanic women are three times more likely to be incarcerated than white women, and African American women are seven times more likely to be incarcerated than white women.[6]

Data also prove that criminal victimization is gendered. For example, males are much more likely to be murdered than are females. Furthermore, males and females are more like to be murdered by males. Males are more likely to be murdered by males who are strangers, however, whereas females are more likely to be murdered by males they know, especially as intimate partners or family members. Considering the processing of murderers, males who murder strangers are more likely to receive harsher sentences than are males who murder the women and children in their lives. Similarly, males are more likely to be victims of most violent crimes, except domestic violence and sexual assault. Although these latter crimes tend to be male-on-female crimes, the offenders are rarely arrested, tried, convicted, and incarcerated. In the case of domestic violence, many police officers still do not consider these acts to be criminal assaults under the law and so do not enforce the law. When police enforce the law, many prosecutors do not prosecute or, if they do, judges often dismiss these cases. When an abuser is convicted of a domestic violence offense, incarceration is a rare occurrence.

The most gendered victimizations to occur are sexual assault and domestic violence. The controversies rest within society's victim-blaming ideologies and the lack of criminal justice attention to the problems of these often intertwined crimes. Sexual assault and domestic violence typically involve male-on-female violence. Furthermore, sexual assault usually involves an offender known to the victim. So common are these crimes that social definitions have come to recognize date rape and marital rape. Historically, when the female victim knew the offender before the sexual assault, she was blamed for somehow precipitating, if not facilitating, the rape. As a result, date rapes or other acquaintance rapes were often not defined as real rapes and were not prosecuted. In the case of marital rape, in the past, women had a conjugal duty to her husband, so if he forced himself upon her, the act would not legally be defined as a rape.

Today, marital rape is considered a rape under the law; however, different states use varying definitions as to what constitutes a marital rape, such as the requirement of legal separation. Many have argued that the various exceptions to marital rape laws reproduce gendered justice; what may be considered a rape when strangers are involved may not be considered a rape in certain states if the husband and wife were not legally separated. In cases of date or other forms of acquaintance rape, historically, the female was blamed for her actions or inactions, which resulted in a lack of law enforcement, prosecution, or conviction. As a result, many states implemented rape shield laws that prohibit the courts from using a victim's sexual history as a means of culpability on the part of the victim. Complicating the controversy of whether the criminal justice system is still gendered in these cases, many have found that rape shield laws apply only to stranger rapes, though the more common case is marital, date, or acquaintance rape. Those in support of the current implementation of rape shield laws, however, argue that the exceptions to the laws prove the accusers credibility and are not intentionally used to blame her actions or inactions to the crime.

Victims of domestic violence, like victims of sexual assault, have been forced by the criminal justice system and society alike to explain why the crime occurred. Although, on the one hand, the defendant is innocent until proved guilty, thus requiring the prosecution to prove that a crime was committed and that the defendant committed the crime, domestic violence and sexual assault victims have been found to be placed under stricter rules of scrutiny. As with sexual assault, society's ideologies tend to blame the victim. Historically, criminal justice officials have determined that the spouse either had the right to chastise his wife or to force conjugal relations.

There are several controversies that exist surrounding the social problem of domestic violence. First, does financial and emotional abuse constitute domestic violence? Although social service providers and social scientists have defined such actions as domestic violence, the law does not. Second, should the criminal justice system be involved in domestic violence cases? In many cases, when there is a child in common, the case is diverted to family court. This diminishes the criminality of the offense. Furthermore, contrary to the law, many still claim that domestic violence is a private family affair and should not be placed in the hands of a punitive system. Others claim that although the criminal justice system must be involved in the crime, victims should be empowered to decide the outcome. Still others claim that, although social services should be involved, the offender and victim require counseling and not criminal punishment. Judges are left to decide if mandatory counseling and punitive sentencing would be effective sentencing options. Additionally, many critique the use of the criminal justice system in cases involving repeat calls for help when the victim does not leave the situation or refuses to aid in prosecution.

Gendered Laws

Examining the enforcement of various laws reveals gendered justice. A historical analysis of sentencing laws, for example, reveals that laws and practice reflected the idea that women should not be given the same harsh sentence, as were men, due to their delicate nature. Therefore, prison conditions were not as harsh, and, when women were incarcerated, sentences were not as long. This ideology was applied to female offenders who did not step too far out of their gender role expectations. If the offense was too serious or the female was poor or a woman of color, however, then treatment was harsher. For example, under the Muncy Act of Pennsylvania (1913), women were sentenced under an indeterminate sentencing model that increased their sentence comparable to men. Furthermore, the act was justified on the belief that men and women possessed an inherently different physical and psychological makeup. Several states had similar sentencing laws into the 1970s.

Death penalty laws are written in a gender-neutral language; however, enforcement of these laws by prosecutors and juries still results in a greater likelihood of male offenders receiving the death penalty. Statutory rape laws, on the surface, were designed to protect the innocence of young girls from male sexual predators. In the practice of statutory rape laws, however, the sexual, though not the criminal, behavior of young girls was the focus. Instead of protecting the young girls with these laws, they were often arrested, especially economically marginal and racial minority girls. Similarly, running away, which is a status offense, has more frequently been applied to girls and has centered on promiscuous behavior.

Domestic violence and rape laws tend to result in gendered justice that benefits the male offender. As discussed earlier, historically, domestic violence was not considered a crime. In fact, early English common law allowed for a man to physically chastise his wife and children because they were his property and he was responsible for their actions. Considering rape laws, historically, rape only constituted penile-vaginal penetration if the victim was a female. These laws excluded uncompleted rapes and all other forms of sexual assault. Furthermore, a husband could not be charged with the rape of his wife because she had conjugal responsibilities to him. Today, domestic violence is considered a crime, and all states have legislated sexual assault laws to include all forms of sexual assault. Controversies still exist, however, in how to handle domestic violence cases, with the criminal justice or social service systems, as well as how best to deter these crimes. Controversies also exist in rape and sexual assault cases. These include problems of proof and credibility of the witness—that is, the victim. These controversies have resulted in the continued neglect by the criminal justice system in blaming the victim and have resulted in a lack of reporting by victims. It has been estimated that 80 percent of all sexual assaults go unreported.

KEY MOMENTS

The 1970s and 1980s were times of drastic social reform, which included the antirape, the battered women's, and the women's rights movements. Although much of the justice system's focus remained on the criminal activity of males, activists fought to require that the law and law enforcers recognize the criminality of violence against women. Where once women were defined as the property of their husbands or fathers, activists fought for the legal system to recognize a woman's right to work, a woman's right to refuse the sexual advances of any man, including her husband, and a woman's right to be free from violence at the hands of her intimate or former intimate partner.

Rape law reform in the United States primarily addressed the redefinition of the offense, evidentiary rules, statutory age offenses, and penalty structures.[7] A key moment in the antirape movement occurred in the early 1970s when Judge Victor Baum of Michigan led reform in declaring that a woman could be raped by her husband and that she had the right to defend herself. Following this landmark case, the state of Michigan leads U.S. rape law reform in the fight against sexual assault.

Following Michigan's lead, most states revised their rape laws, now referred to as sexual assault laws, to include all forms of unwelcome sexual activities against females and males. A victim is no longer required to provide a witness to corroborate her testimony or to prove that she resisted. Marital rape is recognized as a crime and the defense is not permitted to use a victim's sexual history in court. Rape law reform has progressed in leaps and bounds; however, there is still

LEGISLATIVE REFORM OF RAPE LAWS

In 1974, Michigan passed Public Act 266, leading the reform of legislation in rape cases. The law did the following:

1. Identified victims as males or females
2. Recognized marital rape as a crime
3. Eliminated requirements to prove victim resistance
4. Eliminated corroboration requirements
5. Identified degrees of sexual assaults

evidence that victim-blaming ideologies are still in practice. First, more than half of the states include exceptions to marital rape laws, usually that the married couple must be legally separated. Second, rape shield laws also have exceptions; that is, a victim's sexual history cannot be used in the trial unless the victim was previously convicted of prostitution, had previous consensual sex with the accused, or had an obvious incentive to lie. Critics argue that these exceptions eliminate the most common sexual assaults, support an ideology that women, especially married women, have a duty to provide sex to their partners, and that women lie. On the other hand, supporters of these exceptions argue that, in fact, women do lie and that if a defendant has a constitutional right to confront his or her accusers and cross-examine the evidence, then this must include the credibility of the witness.

Until the 1970s, the criminal justice system tended to overlook domestic violence. Specifically, police nonresponse was the norm. A key moment in the domestic violence movement was the landmark case of *Thurman v. City of Torrington* (1984)[8] and the Minneapolis Experiment (1984).[9] *Thurman* signified the need for police to respond to and protect victims of domestic violence. Additionally, the case emphasized the fact that police departments would be held liable for failure to enforce the law. The Minneapolis Experiment conducted in 1984 determined that arrest was a greater deterrent to domestic violence than nonarrest. As a result of these two events, many states implemented mandatory arrest laws. Since 1984, the Minneapolis Experiment has undergone scrutiny and has been replicated. Some suggest that arrest only works as a deterrent for the six months

PRECURSOR TO DOMESTIC VIOLENCE MANDATORY ARREST LAWS

Thurman v. City of Torrington

The 1984 civil case Thurman v. City of Torrington emphasized police accountability in protecting victims of domestic violence. Tracy Thurman was a victim of repeated attacks by her husband. One day, Tracy received a telephone call from her estranged husband informing her that he was coming to her home to kill her. In fear of her life, Thurman called the police and was told that the police would respond quickly. The prolonged response time resulted in the brutal attack and near death of Tracy Thurman. The jury in the case awarded Tracy Thurman $2.3 million. As a result of this case and the landmark Minneapolis Experiment, many states implemented mandatory arrest laws.

LEGAL CHANGES AND WOMEN'S INROADS TO CRIMINAL JUSTICE PROFESSIONS

Title VII (1972) of the Civil Rights Act of 1964 prohibited discrimination in any terms of employment in the private sector on the basis of race, religion, creed, color, sex, or national origin.

Equal Employment Opportunity Act of 1972 extended Title VII to state and local governments.

Bona fide occupational qualifications (BFOQ) allowed exceptions to these laws if it was rational to prefer employment of one sex to the other. Lawsuits have eliminated the use of BFOQs for many occupations, including those in criminal justice (KU1).

Crime Control Act of 1974 required the termination of federal funding to criminal justice agencies that were in violation of equal opportunity guidelines.

immediately following the arrest and not more. Thus, the debate still continues: What is the most effective way to address domestic violence?

Women saw significant inroads in the legal profession during the 1970s and 1980s. Although women have been involved in some capacity in the criminal justice professions since the mid-1800s, they did not have equal access or influence in the profession. By the 1970s, it was accepted that women would be part of the profession; however, in large part, women represented token hires. In the early 1970s, however, the federal government implemented several laws requiring equal treatment of the sexes with regard to hiring and firing, compensation, and privileges.

These laws included Title VII of 1972, an amendment to the Civil Rights Act of 1964, the Equal Employment Opportunity Act of 1972, and the Crime Control Act of 1974. By the 1980s, sexual harassment was also defined as a form of sexual discrimination prohibited by Title VII. Although women gained recognition as qualified applicants of criminal justice professions, bona fide occupational qualifications (BFOQ) acted as a backlash allowing employers to exclude from hiring one sex over another based upon necessity. Within criminal justice, it was argued that women's presence in male prisons would be disruptive, dangerous, and a violation of male inmates' right to privacy. Within law enforcement, it was argued that the presence of female officers would place male officers in danger because, it was argued, they were not strong enough to handle violent offenders. Although BFOQs have been successfully challenged in most occupations, many argue that current assignments of most female criminal justice officials represent an unofficial acceptance of BFOQs.

FUTURE PROSPECTS

Controversies surrounding the notion of gendered justice have been present since the formation of the system itself. Are males more violent than females? Should females receive lighter, indeterminate sentences? Is male violence against females exaggerated? Do females precipitate their victimization? Are women as qualified as men to hold criminal justice occupations? The root of these controversies is seeded in the dilemma of difference. Controversies have consistently centered on the question: Are men and women different?

Reproductive differences of the sexes require that we examine the needs of women during pregnancy. The Pregnancy Discrimination Act (a 1964 amendment to Title VII of the Civil Rights Act of 1964) prohibits the hiring and firing of a pregnant woman. However, dangers of certain occupations to the pregnant woman and the unborn child cannot be ignored. Within corrections, gynecologic and dietary needs of women, as opposed to men, have led many to demand for different treatment. The increased likelihood of female inmates to be victims of male violence has also led critics to demand a limitation of male correctional guards within female prisons. However, many argue that the dilemma of difference has opened the gates to treatment of women as different but unequal. Instead, many argue that the equal treatment approach will ensure that women receive equal rights. This does not fit neatly with the fact that there are differences between the sexes. But are most of the socially recognized differences due to socialization? Can there be a way to recognize the differences between the sexes and still treat them equally in all areas of criminal justice? The question seems to be easily answered in the affirmative, however, which would mean breaking with strongly held social norms of maleness and femaleness. Hence, because the law is rooted in culture, the controversies continue.

See Also: African American Criminal (In) Justice; Class Justice; Crime and Culture Consumption; Defining Criminal Violence; Domestic-Violence Practices; Equal Justice and Human Rights; Sexual Assault in Colleges and Universities; Social Justice; War on Drugs.

Endnotes

1. For a detailed discussion, see Joanne Belknap, *The Invisible Woman: Gender, Crime, and Justice,* 2nd ed. (Belmont, CA: Wadsworth, 2001).
2. For a detailed discussion, see Sheryl J. Grana, *Women and (In) Justice: The Criminal and Civil Effects of the Common Law on Women's Lives* (Boston: Allyn and Bacon, 2001).
3. *Muller v. Oregon,* 208 U.S. 412 (1908).
4. *Goesaert v. Cleary,* 335 U.S. 464 (1948).
5. *Bradwell v. Illinois,* 83 U.S. 130 (1873).
6. Lawrence A. Greenfeld and Tracy L. Snell, *Women Offenders: Bureau of Justice Statistics, Special Report* (Washington, DC: U.S. Department of Justice, December 1999), 4.
7. Ronald J. Berger, Patricia Searles, and W. Lawrence Neuman, "The Dimensions of Rape Reform Legislation," *Law and Society Review* 22 (1988): 329–58.
8. *Thurman v. City of Torrington,* 595 F.Supp. 1521 (D.Conn., 1984).
9. Lawrence W. Sherman and R. A. Berk, "The Specific Deterrent Effects of Arrest for Domestic Assault," *American Sociological Review* 49 (1984): 261–72.

Further Reading: Belknap, Joanne, *The Invisible Woman: Gender, Crime, and Justice,* 2nd ed. (Belmont, CA: Wadsworth, 2001); Daly, Kathleen, *Gender, Crime, and Punishment* (New Haven, CT: Yale University Press, 1994); Grana, Sheryl J., *Women and (In) Justice: The Criminal and Civil Effects of the Common Law on Women's Lives* (Boston: Allyn and Bacon, 2001); Merlo, Alida V., and Joycelyn M. Pollock, *Women, Law, and Social Control,* 2nd ed. (Boston: Pearson Education, 2006); Morash, Merry, *Understanding Gender, Crime, and Justice* (Thousand Oaks, CA: Sage, 2006).

Venessa Garcia

GUANTANAMO DETAINEES

INTRODUCTION

The controversies involving the Guantanamo detainees are numerous, especially with respect to the ways in which the United States has ignored the standards and precedents of international law, has more likely than not violated the Geneva Convention, and has treated these detainees as neither criminal defendants nor prisoners of war but rather as so-called enemy combatants.

Shortly after terrorists attacked the United States on September 11, 2001, and before the United States bombed Afghanistan in October 2005, the U.S. government formulated plans to detain captured members of the Taliban and al Qaeda terrorist organizations. Officials considered housing prisoners on prison ships, at the military facility at Fort Leavenworth, Kansas, in the Pacific Islands, on the island of Diego Garcia, or on Alcatraz Island in San Francisco Bay, but the George W. Bush administration determined that Guantanamo would serve as the ideal destination for these prisoners.[1] More fundamentally, U.S. officials had decided not to treat the suspected terrorists either as criminal defendants or as prisoners of war, "Because either option could preclude interrogation to learn of impending attacks. One consequence has been to land detainees in a legal netherworld with no obvious exit."[2]

BACKGROUND

At the far southeastern end of Cuba is a naval base owned and operated by the United States government. This installation, which sits on Guantánamo Bay, consists of a number of camps and is now generally referred to as Guantanamo (or Gitmo, for short). In 1903, based on the Platt Amendment (a treaty between Cuba and the United States), the U.S. government obtained what they claimed was a perpetual lease on the 45 square miles that make up the base. Although the communist regime of Fidel Castro, which came to power in 1959, cashed one of the checks, the Cuban government was virulently opposed to the U.S. presence on the island.

The Guantanamo base has historically been used as a listening post and as a hub for U.S. military and naval activities in the Caribbean. In the 1990s, Guantanamo also housed fleeing Cuban and Haitian refugees, many of whom were suffering from AIDS. In 1993, largely through the work of the New York City–based Center for Constitutional Rights, U.S. Judge Sterling Johnson Jr. declared the camp unconstitutional, and the refugees were relocated.

Gitmo offered several benefits, however: It was technically "outside the jurisdiction of the U.S. legal system, safe from attack, [and] quiet enough for focused interrogations," plus it was relatively close to the United States.[3]

Prisoners detained on U.S. soil would pose a great threat to national security. The military also did not want to move the detainees to U.S. soil because any escaped prisoners would be closer to potential targets. Most important, keeping the detainees in military prisons qualified the prisoners as enemy combatants, a term that falls under a gray area of the law. Even so, this designation has not prevented the United States from detaining suspected al Qaeda and Taliban members in Navy brigs in the United States (e.g., Yaser Esam Hamdi and Jose Padilla), at the now-infamous Abu Ghraib prison in Iraq, and in detention facilities in Eastern European countries.

The first prisoners to arrive at Gitmo did so on January 11, 2002. "The prisoners included some people picked up outside of the so-called war zone of Afghanistan and Pakistan, in places like Bosnia, Zambia, and Gambia."[4] The detainees are of different citizenships or origins, including Saudi Arabia, Yemen, Pakistan, and Afghanistan.

Meanwhile, approximately 9,500 U.S. troops are stationed on Gitmo. The camp is almost totally self-sufficient, producing its own water and electricity. What makes this situation all the more anomalous is the fact that Guantanamo is the only U.S. base on communist soil.

Much of what we know about the conditions at Guantanamo and the treatment of the detainees has been obtained through visits by U.S. politicians, monitoring by delegations from international nongovernmental and human rights organizations, reports from individuals who have been released, statements by lawyers defending those who have been detained, and information from reporters representing selected newspapers (e.g., *The New York Times* and *Washington Post*). One written account of Guantanamo was written by a former guard;[5] another was written by the U.S. Muslim chaplain who was detained for 76 days on charges of espionage that were subsequently dismissed.[6] In addition, a number of Web sites have been developed to inform the public about Gitmo's history and the current state of affairs with the detentions.

The base contains a number of smaller camps that are given alphabetic military names. Detainees were originally housed at Camp X-Ray, but this location was closed in April 2002. Prisoners were relocated to Camps Delta, Echo, and Iguana, each of which contained a series of detention camps. The original conditions at Camp X-Ray were described as "cages, each 8 feet by 8 feet. Constructed on slabs of concrete and covered with sheets of metal and wood, the

WEB SITES CONTAINING GUANTANAMO-RELATED INFORMATION

http://www.guantanamo.com: Web site maintained by World News Network; news and analysis are presented on current events, business, finance, economy, sports, and more. Searchable news is available in 35 languages.

http://web.amnesty.org/pages/guantanamobay-index-eng: Web site maintained by Amnesty International, a Nobel Peace Prize winning antitorture organization that provides information and commentary on the Guantanamo detainees.

http://www.hrw.org/doc/?t=usa_gitmo: Web site maintained by Human Rights Watch on Guantanamo detainees.

collection of cages looked like an oversized dog kennel."[7] It was at these facilities that "The military had strapped muffs over their [the prisoners] ears, surgical masks over their mouths and goggles spray-painted black over their eyes. Authorities described the gear as necessary for security during the long plane trip from Afghanistan," an image that has been repeated several times in the news media.[8]

CONDITIONS OF CONFINEMENT

The conditions of confinement at Guantanamo range from sparse chain-link cages to buildings with dormitory or communal living spaces. At one extreme are small, mesh-sided cells with no privacy; lights are on 24 hours a day. Here, detainees are subjected to a regime not that different from what U.S. prisoners would receive in the various Supermax prisons located within the United States. Prisoners are interrogated at all hours of the day and night, and there have been allegations that prisoners have been abused, tortured, intimidated. Others have reported witnessing the desecration of religious items such as copies of the Koran (the Muslim holy book).[9]

In the first year, the detainees were not allowed access to legal counsel, nor were they permitted visits by friends or family. Moreover, these prisoners were not informed about the formal legal charges against them. Most important, the detainees were denied the right of habeas corpus (the right against illegal imprisonment), albeit and arguably the bedrock of Anglo-American jurisprudence. In fact, "In the case brought forward by the Center for Constitutional Rights, the lower courts ruled that the detainees had no right to file a writ of habeas corpus."[10]

Some detainees have alleged that their U.S. captors were not opposed to torture. Reports have mentioned such tactics as withholding food; depriving prisoners of sleep; forcing them to kneel for hours while being chained to the floor; subjecting them to loud noise, music, or extreme temperatures; or beating them. This kind of treatment usually was relied upon to help break the detainee's will with the hope that he would provide useful intelligence in the war against terror. "The government has admitted that it conducts three hundred interrogations a week. In mid 2004, it had 2,800 soldiers and civilians (including interrogators) among a camp with somewhat more than seven hundred prisoners for two years."[11] Of the prisoners released, some claimed being "interrogated as many as two hundred times, with all kinds of different techniques."[12]

A number of different intelligence agencies have interrogated the detainees at Guantanamo, including members of the Federal Bureau of Investigation (FBI) and the Central Intelligence Agency (CIA). Similarly, members of MI5 (a British intelligence agency) questioned British detainees, and Mossad (an Israeli intelligence agency) interviewed Moroccan detainees.[13]

Although the U.S. military claims that the majority of detainees have provided useful information through the judicious use of rewards, some experts, particularly ex-intelligence agents, question the quality of any information that is the result of coercion.

Faith in the process has led to more resources being pumped into the military base. In support of the plan to expand Gitmo, in mid-2005 the U.S. military awarded a $30 million contract to the Halliburton Corporation—which has close ties to Vice President Dick Cheney—to build a new detention facility.

THE DETAINEES[14]

In the 1980s, Osama bin Laden used his inherited fortune to assist the mujahideen fighters (a military force of Muslims engaged in a jihad, or a holy or religious war against nonbelievers and so-called enemies) in Afghanistan in their guerrilla war against the Soviet Union.

Through the creation of Maktab al-Khadamat (MAK), in 1984, he funneled arms, money, and recruits to the insurgency. In 1988, bin Laden, with the assistance of the more militant members of MAK, began a new organization responsible for committing terrorist actions, popularly known as al Qaeda. Al Qaeda facilitated the rise of the Taliban, the Islamic and Pashtun nationalist movement and former leadership of Afghanistan.

Although countless histories of al Qaeda, the Taliban, and the Soviet invasion and occupation of Afghanistan have been written,[15] the facts can be summarized as followed: In 1979, the Soviet Union invaded Afghanistan. In response, young Muslim fundamentalists from around the world joined forces with mujahideen rebels to fight a guerrilla-type insurgency. This campaign received covert support from the United States, Great Britain, and the Persian Gulf states (Qatar, Bahrain, etc.).[16] In February 1989, the Soviets pulled out of Afghanistan, no longer willing to sustain the cost in terms of both economics and the injuries and deaths incurred over the previous decade. When the Soviets were defeated, the Taliban emerged as the dominant group of Afghanistan and thus established a theocracy, or a government by religious rule.

Meanwhile, many Afghan Arabs were emboldened by their success in fighting the Soviets and sought additional international targets. Simon Reeve notes, "[E]stimates of the total number of Afghan Arabs vary. One source . . . claims the number is close to 17,000, while the highly respected British publication *Jane's Intelligence Review* suggests a figure of more than 14,000 (including some 5,000 Saudis, 3,000 Yemenis, 2,000 Egyptians, 2,800 Algerians, 400 Tunisians, 370 Iraqis, 200 Libyans, and scores of Jordanians)."[17]

According to Reeve, "Some of these men are now responsible for much of the global terrorism threatening the West, while others returned from the Afghan war to start or lead guerrilla movements in their own countries against governments they perceive as being un-Islamic, corrupt or despotic. These veterans of the Afghan jihad have taken the war home to more than 25 countries, including Algeria, Azerbaijan, Bangladesh, Bosnia, Britain, Burma, Chechnya, China, Egypt, France, India, Morocco, Pakistan, the Philippines, Saudi Arabia, Sudan, Tajikistan, Tunisia, the USA, Uzbekistan, and Yemen."[18]

Bin Laden was considered a hero of the insurgency. He eventually took up residence in Sudan, and, along with training new recruits, he invested in several business ventures. Bin Laden's group al Qaeda is estimated to have 5,000 members, "all of whom seem willing to kill and die for the Islamic cause.[19] His soldiers are men . . . young, full of zeal, technically skilled to a high level, and determined to bring terror to the West."[20]

In the meantime, al Qaeda sponsored and committed a number of anti-U.S. terrorist attacks. These incidents included the February 26, 1993, World Trade Center bombing by Ramzi Yousef and his accomplice, Mohammad Salameh, both of whom were members of the al Qaeda terrorist organization.[21] Six people were killed and 1,042 injured. According to Reeve, the incident led to "more hospital casualties than any other event in domestic history apart from the Civil War. Many of those who escaped without apparent physical injury will be scarred mentally for life, and yet it is almost miraculous that in such a huge bomb attack even more were not killed or injured."[22]

Later, on August 7, 1998, bin Laden and al Qaeda were implicated in the bombing attacks on U.S. embassies in Nairobi, Kenya, and Dar es Salaam, Tanzania, which killed 237 and injured 5,000 people, not only Americans but also citizens of these countries. And on October 12, 2000, al Qaeda allegedly bombed a U.S. naval ship docked just off the port of Aden, Yemen; the bombing of the USS *Cole* caused 17 deaths and 30 injuries. Despite international arrest warrants for bin Laden and several members of al Qaeda, the United States and other participating countries were unable to capture them.

Then, on the morning of September 11, 2001, members of al Qaeda managed to commandeer four large jet airplanes shortly after takeoff. Two of the planes crashed into the World Trade Center's twin towers in New York City, another crashed into the Pentagon in Washington, DC, and the last crashed in a field in rural Pennsylvania, thanks to brave passengers who prevented the plane from reaching its intended target (which some say was the White House). Close to 3,000 people died, and U.S. officials initially assumed that al Qaeda was behind the attacks.

Shortly after the attacks of September 11, U.S. national security agencies confirmed that bin Laden and al Qaeda were responsible. Further proof came in the way of a video communiqué from bin Laden celebrating the attack. Not surprisingly, when requested, the Taliban (the regime in power in Afghanistan) was not willing to turn him over.[23] The United States then assembled a coalition of states, including the United Kingdom, Canada, and Pakistan, as well as Afghan political and militia groups (such as the Northern Alliance), to help unseat the Taliban if negotiations failed.

In fall 2001, the Taliban failed to concede, and the United States commenced bombing operations. Shortly thereafter, U.S. Special Forces, with the assistance of the Northern Alliance, began a ground war in Afghanistan. Soon, British, Canadian, German, and Italian military forces joined U.S. fighters. Meanwhile, the Pakistani army was busy securing its country's border against fleeing members of the Taliban and al Qaeda.

As of June 15, 2006, there were approximately 460 so-called enemy combatants, most of whom are members of al Qaeda and the Taliban, detained at the Guantanamo detention facility; some 290 Gitmo prisoners have been released or sent back to their home countries, according to the U.S. Pentagon. In addition, there are numerous individuals in foreign jails and prisons, some of whom are being held at the request of the United States government. Regardless of country, these detainees have been subject to interrogation by FBI officers or other representatives of U.S. national security agencies whenever they have been captured.[24]

In sum, particularly since the U.S. invasion of Afghanistan, numerous individuals have been arrested, detained, tortured, or killed. According to Michael Ratner of the Center for Constitutional Rights, "We don't know everything about what happened to the thousands of people who were eventually turned over to or captured by the United States. Initially, many were sent to detention facilities in Bagram (air base) and Kandahar, Afghanistan, where the first interrogations took place. A number of detainees reported being beaten at these facilities, and there are reliable reports that techniques amounting to torture were employed. . . . Some detainees were apparently sent to third countries in a process called 'rendition'"[25] It is commonly assumed that these detainees are tortured by those countries.

Prisoners are frequently given psychotropic medications for depression, despondency, and psychosis. Meanwhile, in an attempt to deal with the hunger strikers, the military has resorted to force-feeding detainees. There are numerous hunger strikes, and more than 41 suicide attempts have been made by prisoners. In June 2006, three detainees died, and their deaths were ruled suicides. This was the first time since the camp opened that the administration confirmed this method of death by someone in U.S. custody at Gitmo. Whether the detainees committed suicide because of depression or as a political act is unknown.

THE LEGAL STATUS OF DETAINEES

In January 2002, Alberto R. Gonzales, former White House counsel and current U.S. attorney general, advised President George W. Bush that the Geneva Convention should not be used with the detainees. In 1949, in the aftermath of World War II, the countries of the world assembled and produced the Third Geneva Convention. It "requires that any dispute about a prisoner's status be decide by a 'competent tribunal.' American forces provided many such tribunals for prisoners taken in the Persian Gulf War in 1991. But President Bush has refused to comply with the Geneva Convention. He decided that all the Guantanamo prisoners were 'unlawful combatants'—that is, not regular soldiers, but spies, terrorists and the like."[26] In the case of Gitmo, if the Geneva Conventions had been followed, the prisoners would have been considered prisoners of war (POWs), held in POW camps and not subjected to interrogation and torture. "If there is any doubt as to whether they are POWs, there is a special hearing procedure in which a 'competent tribunal' makes individualized determination as whether a detained person is a POW. Until that tribunal meets, a detained person must be treated as a POW."[27]

Most likely, the government "doesn't really want to apply the laws of war across the board. . . . The United States will not call the people held at Guantánamo prisoners of war, or even prisoners, the official designation being 'detained personnel' or simply detainees. The pentagon has made up a new term 'enemy combatant.'"[28] Many jurists argue that the term *enemy combatant* does not have any legal significance.

In July 2004, after several legal challenges, the U.S. Department of Defense allowed Combatant Status Review Tribunals so the detainees could formally contest their enemy combatant status. This would use three neutral officers, including a judge advocate. Despite criticisms from U.S. and foreign jurists that the procedure was a sham, the military finished its reviews by March 2005, and 38 civilians were released.

CONTROVERSIES OVER U.S. POLICIES AND PRACTICES AT GITMO

The decision to house the al Qaeda and Taliban suspects at Guantanamo has been routinely criticized by Americans and foreigners alike. "The violation of the Geneva Convention and that refusal to let the courts consider the issue have cost the United States dearly in the world legal community—the judges and lawyers in societies that, historically, have looked to the United States as the exemplar of a country committed to Law."[29]

Many observers dislike the fact that detainees are held at an offshore prison and that their legal status is unclear. Some argue that if the enemy combatants were held on U.S. soil, then they would be afforded the same civil liberties as

---

INTERVENTIONS ON BEHALF OF DETAINEES

1. Never one to back down from a civil rights fight, the New York City–based Center for Constitutional Rights was contacted by families of individuals who were being held at Guantanamo. The center has initiated proceedings and continues to defend detainees who are held at Guantanamo.

2. In 2002, the International Red Cross (IRC) conducted visits to the camps. Shortly after its initial visits, the IRC issued a report that described the horrendous conditions of the camps as well as the deteriorating mental health of the detainees.

3. In 2003, Human Rights Watch condemned the U.S. treatment of the detainees as enemy combatants and failed to consider them prisoners of war. Who failed to consider them as POWs—Human Rights Watch or the United States?

4. In 2003, United Nations human rights investigators investigated the conditions at Guantanamo. In mid-February 2006, a draft report was released condemning the United States for violating international law and permitting torture.

5. In 2005, Amnesty International released its annual report, which was highly critical of the conditions at Gitmo.

6. In May 2006, the United Nations publicly announced its conclusion: that Guantanamo should be closed.

7. In June 2006, the United States Supreme Court ruled that the tribunals that the U.S. government is using to try the detainees at Gitmo violate both U.S. military law and the Geneva Convention.

those who reside on U.S. soil. Others say that this, in fact, is a moot point because the base is a U.S. possession. Critics object to the effect the detentions will have on public opinion toward the United States.[30] Some suggest it will only foster the impression of the United States as a big, bad bully on the world stage.

A number of individuals and organizations have visited Guantanamo. A handful of congressional delegations have traveled to Guantanamo to inspect the premises and follow up on allegations of abuse. Simultaneously, human rights organizations (e.g., Human Rights Watch and Amnesty International) have inspected Guantanamo and/or have issued reports highly critical of the conditions and reasons for confinement.

Meanwhile, some antiwar activists have secretly hoped that Cuba would remove the Americans from the site. This, in turn, would force the U.S. government to expedite the cases of the suspects. This has not been the case.

It has been argued that many of the detainees had no association with either the Taliban or al Qaeda. When the U.S. military went to Afghanistan, the troops rounded up 10,000 people in the first six months on suspicion of engaging in terrorism or firefights with coalition forces. "Those were not necessarily people found on the battlefield. Many were from Pakistan and the surrounding areas; many were . . . taken in midnight raids that had nothing to do with the Taliban or with al-Qaeda. . . . Villagers and warlords, including members of the Northern Alliance, started turning over their enemies or anyone they didn't like, or finally, anyone they could pick up."[31]

This calls into question whether the detainees were actually involved in any acts of terrorism. According to a *Los Angeles Times* article based on a classified document and cited by Ratner, "as many as 10 percent of the Guantanamo prisoners were 'taxi drivers, farmers, cobblers, and laborers' that some were low-level figures conscripted by the Taliban in the weeks before the collapse of the ruling Afghanistan regime."[32] Ratner goes on to add, "Of the 147 prisoners who had been released two years later, only 13 were then sent to jails. The other 134 were guilty of absolutely nothing. . . . It is certainly conceivable that the majority . . . of the people in Guantanamo had nothing to do with any kind of terrorism."[33] Approximately twenty-three have been released to Afghanistan, five to Great Britain, four to Saudi Arabia, and three to Pakistan. Upon their release, some of the detainees were treated like heroes. Most have said that they were victims of circumstance—simply being in the wrong place at the wrong time.

FUTURE PROSPECTS

Many experts, foreign countries, and respected international nongovernmental organizations believe that the United States is in violation of the Geneva Convention, which specifies the appropriate treatment of prisoners during wartime. The Third Geneva Convention did not specify a difference between prisoners of war and enemy combatants. In short, the Bush administration has refused to bring the detainees to trial, effectively ignoring international legal precedents and standards.

As a compromise, the United States implemented the concept of Combatant Status Review Tribunals. This process, however, has been criticized as simply being a rubber stamp (in other words, the outcome of what to do with the detainee has been decided in advance), and the detainees are relatively powerless to defend themselves regarding the claims made against them.

Some five years after the detainees' capture, the United States advocated military-style tribunals for the 595 detainees being held at Guantanamo. This is amid requests by national and international human rights monitoring organizations for better conditions and for the United States to proceed with processing the individuals using the U.S. criminal justice system rather than military-style tribunals.

On June 30, 2006, however, the Supreme Court ruled in *Hamdam v. Rumsfeld* that the tribunals the U.S. government wished to use to try the detainees violated both U.S. military law and the Geneva Convention, but they did not provide a course of action to be taken other than something to be worked out by the president and Congress.

See Also: Antiterrorism Laws; Cruel and Unusual Punishment; International Criminal Court; International Humanitarian Law Enforcement; Miscarriages of Justice; Prisoner Litigation; Spiritual Care of Inmates; State Crime Control; Supremacy of International Law to National Law; Torture and Enemy Combatants.

Endnotes

1. Diego Garcia would have required agreements with the British, and Asian locations were deemed too vulnerable (Scott Higham, Joe Stephens, and Margo Williams, "Guantanamo—A Holding Cell in the War on Terror," *Washington Post,* May 2, 2004, A01.).
2. Scott Shane, "Seeking an Exit Strategy for Guantanamo," *The New York Times,* June 18, 2006, section 4, 1, 4.
3. *Washington Post,* May 2, 2004.
4. Michael Ratner and Ellen Ray, *Guantanamo: What the World Should Know* (White River Junction, VT: Chelsea Green, 2004), 10.
5. Erik Saar and Viveca Novak, *Inside the Wire* (New York: Penguin, 2005).
6. James Yee and Aimee Molloy, *For God and Country: Faith and Patriotism under Fire* (New York: Public Affairs, 2005).
7. Scott Higham, Joe Stephens, and Margo Williams, "Guantanamo—A Holding Cell in the War on Terror," *Washington Post,* May 2, 2004, A1.
8. Ibid.
9. The Koran controversy originally came to public attention in a *Time* magazine article. Shortly after the publication, it was determined that the story was based on false sources. Later, a U.S. military report confirmed that such incidents had in fact taken place.
10. Ratner and Ray, *Guantanamo,* 4.
11. Ibid., 41.
12. Ibid., 41.
13. Ibid., 42.
14. Portions of this section have appeared in Jeffrey Ian Ross, *Political Terrorism: An Interdisciplinary Approach* (New York: Peter Lang, 2006).
15. M. Griffin, *Reaping the Whirlwind: Afghanistan, Al Qa'ida and the Holy War* (London: Pluto Press, 2003).
16. Simon Reeve, *The New Jackals* (Boston: Northeastern University Press, 1999), 2.

17. Ibid., 3.
18. Ibid.
19. Yossef Bodansky, *Bin Laden: The Man Who Declared War on America* (Roseville, CA: Prima, 2001); A. Rashid, *Taliban* (New Haven, CT: Yale University Press, 2001).
20. Reeve, *The New Jackals,* 4.
21. Ibid., 11–12.
22. Ibid., 15.
23. R. Fawn, "From Ground Zero to the War in Afghanistan," in *Global Responses to Terrorism: 9/11 Afghanistan and Beyond,* ed. M. Buckley and R. Fawn (New York: Routledge, 2003), 11–24.
24. David Cole, *Enemy Aliens* (New York: New Press, 2003).
25. Ratner and Ray, *Guantanamo,* 9–10.
26. Anthony Lewis, "A President beyond the Law," in *Guantanamo: What the World Should Know,* ed. Michael Ratner and Ellen Ray (White River Junction, VT: Chelsea Green, 2004), ix.
27. Ratner and Ray, *Guantanamo,* 11.
28. Ibid., 18.
29. Lewis, "A President beyond the Law," ix
30. Ratner and Ray, *Guantanamo,* 5–6.
31. Ibid., 9.
32. Ibid., 14.
33. Ibid.

Further Reading: Cole, David, *Enemy Aliens* (New York: New Press, 2003); Margulies, Joseph, *Guantanamo and the Abuse of Presidential Power* (New York: Simon and Schuster, 2006); Ratner, Michael, and Ellen Ray, eds., *Guantanamo: What the World Should Know* (White River Junction, VT: Chelsea Green, 2004); Saar, Erik, and Viveca Novak, *Inside the Wire* (New York: Penguin, 2005); Yee, James, and Aimee Molloy, *For God and Country: Faith and Patriotism under Fire* (New York: Public Affairs, 2005).

Jeffrey Ian Ross

GUN CONTROL

INTRODUCTION

Few topics in the realm of U.S. justice and politics elicit a more polarizing response than that of gun control. Issues in gun policy range from the moral to the practical, with implications for law, economics, public health, and a host of other disciplines. At the center of the debate is the fundamental question of whether firearms, specifically those owned and wielded by private citizens, do more harm than good in deterring violent crime. Despite the intense scrutiny from so many fields, however, scholars have reached few solid conclusions to date. The answers to even basic questions (who is victimized, how many are victimized, and at what cost are they victimized) are fiercely disputed, resulting in a nebulous, yet hotly contested, understanding of the interplay between guns and crime.

U.S. gun policy is a complex and difficult issue that is characterized roughly by its two diametrical sides: the progun (or gun rights) camp, which argues that guns are a constitutionally protected, prosocial necessity, and the antigun (or gun control) camp, which asserts that guns are a fundamentally unsafe and extremely costly means to facilitate a variety of social ills. Data exist to support both sides; the difficulty lies in separating partisanship and underlying attitudes from empirical observation and objective analysis. In truth, isolating such objectivity may be a logical impossibility.

BACKGROUND

Outside the United States, guns are sometimes a contentious issue, but rarely at the level witnessed in the United States. Many Westernized nations feature tighter controls on private firearm ownership, particularly for certain types of weapons that could, in the view of their governments, be more readily used to facilitate crime. Australia, for example, experienced a period with relatively little gun regulation prior to the 1980s and 1990s, when a series of high-profile shooting incidents incited progressively harsher reform. Now, guns in Australia are tightly controlled, with restrictions on ownership based on the category of firearm and the evaluation of so-called genuine need on the part of the possessor. Although some low-level debate remains over gun control policies in other countries, the United States is a veritable firestorm of political, academic, and litigious action on all sides of the gun control issue.

The issue of gun control in the United States begins with the interpretation of the U.S. Constitution's Second Amendment. Broadly, the amendment is concerned with security through self-defense; the key difference between the gun rights and gun control perspectives lies with precisely who is entitled to self-defense and how that defense is to be manifested.

THE CONSTITUTIONAL RIGHT TO BEAR ARMS

The Second Amendment, as passed by Congress and later ratified by the states:

A well regulated militia being necessary to the security of a free State, the right of the People to keep and bear arms shall not be infringed.

Supporters of gun rights believe that the Second Amendment applies to individual-level possession of firearms, whereas supporters of gun control argue that the intent was to provide for the formation and readiness of peacekeeping forces such as the Army or state militias.[1] In the former perspective, the right and responsibility to self-defense carries an individualistic connotation. In the latter, self-defense is provided for generally by the state, through publicly governed mechanisms such as police, who are entrusted with powers of arrest and tasked with maintaining order. Additional points concerning the amendment have also been debated and promoted, including the right to rebellion against government tyranny.

At present, the prevailing attitude in the United States asserts the gun rights perspective that the Second Amendment protects and guarantees individual possession. Gun rights supporters, particularly the National Rifle Association (NRA),[2] endorse the interpretation that a "well regulated militia," as quoted in the amendment, refers to an armed populace, and not only to governmental bodies such as the Army or National Guard.[3] This opinion is consistently reflected in public opinion polls on gun ownership. For example, an ABCNews.com poll conducted in 2002 demonstrated that 73 percent of respondents believed that the wording of the Second Amendment indicates a guarantee to private ownership as well as the formation of state militias.[4]

Legal opinion on the gun control issue seems divided, with both sides claiming victory. In some instances, both progun and antigun advocates claim victory in the very same case. The case of *United States v. Miller,*[5] for example, is cited by the Brady Campaign[6] as evidence of the courts' interpretation in favor of gun possession only by militia members, whereas the same case is cited by the NRA[7] as evidence of support for the constitutional guarantee to individual ownership. Dozens of other contradictory instances may be found in federal and circuit court opinions dating back more than a century.

LEGAL DEVELOPMENTS

The use and control of firearms in the United States has traditionally been approached from a fundamentally permissive position, with individual ownership largely unregulated. Notable exceptions to this position exist for the nature and type of firearm, the characteristics of its owner, and the provisions of its transfer—all factors that are monitored by the government. A series of federal laws have provided the framework for this means of gun control in the United States since the Prohibition era. The first and perhaps most influential of these laws was the National Firearms Act of 1934,[8] which placed severe limitations on individuals who wished to own small arms and accessories that were generally assumed to facilitate violent crime. Among the regulated items covered in the act were sound suppressors (or silencers), destructive devices such as hand grenades, short-barreled rifles and shotguns, and fully automatic machine guns. The act makes the unlicensed possession or transfer of such items a criminal offense punishable by up to 10 years in federal prison and/or a substantial monetary fine plus forfeiture of all items that violate the act. The National Firearms Act has remained in effect, largely unaltered, and has enjoyed bipartisan support for more than seventy years—a remarkable feat, given the frequency of legal challenges to legislative gun control.

Specific forms of gun control in the United States have also been enacted through laws intended to supplement the National Firearms Act of 1934. One such provision, the Gun Control Act of 1968,[9] was established following the high-profile assassinations of Martin Luther King Jr. and Robert Kennedy. This act provided tighter regulation of interstate commerce dealing with firearms, established the Federal Firearms License program to prevent individuals from purchasing guns through direct mail order or from out-of-state dealers, and mandated that all firearms produced or imported into the United States bear a serial number for identification purposes.

Certain provisions of the Gun Control Act of 1968 were later clarified and amended in the Gun Owners Protection Act of 1986.[10] This legislation featured several key decisions favoring gun rights supporters. First, it included a formal prohibition of governmental registries linking private guns to individuals. Second, it offered protection for federal firearms licensees from "abusive" inspections on the part of the Bureau of Alcohol, Tobacco, and Firearms. Third, it established a "safe passage" clause for gun owners traveling to and from legal shooting-related sporting events, effectively immunizing them from prosecution for possession or transportation of firearms outside their home jurisdiction. Finally and most critically, the act also clarified the list of persons denied private firearm ownership on public safety grounds, such as individuals who are fugitives from justice or those who have been adjudicated mentally ill. Amendments were added in 1996[11] to prevent ownership for those who have been convicted of domestic violence and those subject to court-issued restraining orders.

Additional restrictions on gun ownership have been imposed since the Gun Owners Protection Act of 1986. In 1993, President Bill Clinton signed the Brady Handgun Violence Protection Act[12] into law. The act was named for former Ronald Reagan Press Secretary James Brady, who was wounded in an assassination attempt by John Hinckley Jr. in 1981. It established a five-day waiting period for handgun purchases involving a federal firearms licensee (dealer) and a private individual (customer). The waiting period was intended to provide an opportunity for criminal background checks on the purchaser, but this system was replaced in 1998 with the establishment of the computerized National Instant Check System (NICS). NICS provides the same functionality but takes only minutes instead of days, preserving the original intent of the Brady Act while greatly streamlining its implementation.

For its part, the United States Supreme Court has never ruled on whether the Second Amendment addresses a fundamental individual right to possess firearms. The closest the Court has come to judgment on this issue is the *Miller* decision,[13] which centered on the extent to which certain firearms, having been restricted under the National Firearms Act of 1934, were, in fact, constitutionally protected under the Second Amendment. In that decision, the Court upheld

---

ASSAULT WEAPONS BAN OF 1994

This wide-ranging federal law affecting semiautomatic handguns, rifles, and shotguns was part of the larger Violent Crime Control and Law Enforcement Act of 1994. The ban made the production of so-called assault weapons that included two or more functional or cosmetic features such as threaded barrels, bayonet mounts, and telescopic stocks illegal in the United States from 1994 to 2004. This law was rendered immaterial, however, due to poorly conceived definitions and a variety of adaptations on the part of domestic gun manufacturers. As for the ban's utility in addressing violent crime, the precise "impact on gun violence has been uncertain," according to an evaluation study by the U.S. Department of Justice.

See Jeffrey A. Roth and Christopher S. Koper, "Impacts of the 1994 Assault Weapons Ban: 1994–96," *National Institute of Justice Research in Brief*, March 1999, 1–12, http://www.ncjrs.org/pdffiles1/173405.pdf.

a lower court ruling stipulating that the item in question (an illegal sawed-off shotgun) was not protected, absent any evidence that indicated that it contributed to the safety and security of the state or was involved in the functioning of a militia. However, the Court did not comment directly on the issue of private ownership of firearms that were not subject to the National Firearms Act, which represent the vast majority of guns in the United States.

IMPORTANT PERSPECTIVES

Groups and individuals who espouse a gun rights outlook are quick to highlight the apparent positive value of gun possession through the use of statistics on defensive gun use. In 1991, criminologist Gary Kleck argued that defensive use is widely successful: Individuals with guns are more likely to prevent the completion of the attempted crime and are less likely to become injured during the event.[14] However, the nature and extent of defensive use is hotly contested. Kleck and colleague Marc Gertz claim that defensive use is underreported, estimating as many as 2.5 million overall defensive gun uses per year,[15] whereas critics claim that the actual number is much smaller, perhaps around 100,000 overall defensive gun uses per year, due to sampling and methodological biases.[16] This disagreement is typical of competing research on gun policy.

Proponents of a strict gun control model point to evidence of the various gun-related costs borne by society. One of those costs may include an increased risk of victimization that accompanies gun possession. Firearms account for the second-highest total of nonnatural deaths in the United States (behind automobiles), and the overall homicide rate in the United States is significantly greater than other industrialized nations;[17] the exact magnitude of the inequity is a matter of which statistics are used. Given the high prevalence of firearm-related homicide, one might presume that gun possession could pose a direct victimization risk if legal guns are used against their owners during the commission of a crime. The number and availability of stolen guns, which are frequently instrumental in the commission of violent crime, may also indirectly influence victimization risk for the rest of the population.

Costs may also be economic in nature. For groups concerned primarily about the costs rather than the benefits of guns, the debate over gun control has spilled over into disciplines such as public health, which has a unique perspective and responsibility as typical first responders to gun violence. The financial burden for emergency response, hospital care, and opportunity costs from lost wages due to gunshot injuries is enormous—around $2 billion by some estimates.[18] Some researchers have begun to regard gun violence as being analogous to a public health epidemic, best visualized with epidemiological models showing patterns of spatial distribution,[19] similar to the spread of pathogens such as influenza, and requiring a similar mobilization of public resources to combat. Self-inflicted injuries carry a cost as well; gun-control advocates note that the prevalence of self-inflicted gunshots in the United States drives the overall trend in gun deaths, with more than 50 percent of gun-related deaths attributable to suicide.[20]

In the 1990s, a well-organized movement, backed financially and philosophically by the National Rifle Association, began to generate grassroots support for so-called shall-issue concealed carry legislation. These laws require government officials to issue a license to carry concealed weapons, absent a compelling reason for denial (e.g., a history of mental illness, substance abuse problems, outstanding warrants, etc.), to anyone who applies and meets minimum state-imposed criteria. Notably missing from the application process is an evaluation of the individual's need to carry a weapon, a controversial part of the shall-issue debate. Proponents of these laws believed that the mechanism for private citizens to obtain licenses to carry concealed firearms would translate into general deterrence against violent crime. In other words, more guns on the street equal more opportunity for self-defense.

An interesting resource for the concealed carry movement was John Lott Jr.'s 1998 book *More Guns, Less Crime: Understanding Crime and Gun-Control Laws*.[21] The book provides complex statistical analyses of the impact of shall-issue permitting laws on violent crime using 15 years of crime rate data for all counties in the United States. Lott reaches the conclusion that the adoption of shall-issue permitting laws result in a decrease for key violent crime rates such as homicide and rape, whereas the laws apparently cause small increases in less serious crime such as larceny and auto theft. He surmises that criminals behave in a manner consistent with rational motives, and increases in general deterrence by way of more legal concealed weapons trigger a change in specialization for career criminals. Lott also concludes that suicide and accident rates related to firearms are unaffected by shall-issue laws.

Despite the complex methodology and expansive data used in the analysis, Lott's conclusions in *More Guns, Less Crime* failed to convince some academics. A series of critical reviews of Lott's book appeared almost immediately in scholarly journals and the popular press. For example, researchers at Carnegie Mellon University reanalyzed Lott's original data in an effort to identify trends that could skew his results.[22] This reanalysis omitted a single state, Florida, which was hypothesized to bias Lott's original conclusions due to a period of high violence from the international drug trade and instability regarding intensive legislative actions to control guns. The effect of removing Florida from the analysis was dramatic: Nearly all effects of shall-issue laws on violent crime rates became nonsignificant.

FUTURE PROSPECTS

Guns are unlikely to become less controversial in the near term. Indeed, the debates about the true benefits and costs of guns may continue for generations. The future of private gun possession in the United States is, to this point, a matter of constitutional entitlement. On a positive note, many key issues dealing with gun control that work on a nonpartisan basis (e.g., possession bans for the mentally ill) seem to enjoy a popular consensus in the United States and elsewhere. This may prove to be a philosophical common ground if comprehensive and balanced gun control reform is ever attempted.

On a more practical level, the issue of whether gun control has an effect on crime is largely unknown. Evidence suggests that there may be a positive benefit of gun ownership in terms of lawful self-defense and deterrent value under certain circumstances and when the analyses are conducted using certain types of data. Contradictory evidence suggests that violent victimization rates increase with gun ownership and that guns carry a heavy societal price tag. Accelerated population growth, the rising cost of health care, and the expansion of certain political agendas suggest that the societal cost of guns may rise in the near future. Although violent crime may be generally in decline, gun crime may rise in certain segments of the population that are most at risk, including minorities and young males. The precise nature of the increase and the appropriate policy response will be fiercely contentious.

See Also: Lethal Force; Militarization of Policing; School Violence; Second Amendment.

Endnotes

1. Since the federal Militia Act of 1903, individual state militias have been organized into the National Guard and have been tasked with supplementing Army units overseas and providing domestic support in relief of natural disasters.
2. The National Rifle Association (NRA), founded in 1871, is the oldest continuously operating civil liberties organization in the United States. It is also, perhaps more significantly, one of the largest and best-funded lobbying organizations in the United States today. Beginning with a more conservative shift in the late 1970s, the NRA has championed laws that promote gun rights and emphasize gun safety for millions of shooting enthusiasts.
3. The NRA posts briefs on Second Amendment interpretation. See National Rifle Association Institute for Legislative Action, "The Constitution, Bill of Rights, and Firearms Ownership in America" (2006), http://www.nraila.org/Issues/Articles/Read.aspx?ID=192.
4. ABC News.com poll, May 8–12, 2002, http://www.pollingreport.com/guns2.htm.
5. *United States v. Miller,* 307 U.S. 174 (1939).
6. The Brady Campaign to Prevent Gun Violence is a nonprofit political organization that lobbies for gun control laws in the United States. The Brady Campaign has been among the chief supporters for laws such as the Brady Handgun Violence Prevention Act (Brady Bill) of 1993 and the Assault Weapons Ban of 1994. See Brady Campaign to Prevent Gun Violence, "The Second Amendment" (2007), http://www.bradycampaign.org/facts/issues/?page=second.
7. See Stefan B. Tahmassebi, "The Second Amendment and the U.S. Supreme Court," *National Rifle Association Institute for Legislative Action* (2000), http://www.nraila.org/Issues/Articles/Read.aspx?ID=7.
8. Internal Revenue Code, 26 U.S.C. § 5801 through 26 U.S.C. § 5872 (1934).
9. Chapter 44 of Title 18, U.S. Code.
10. 18 U.S.C. § 921 et seq.
11. Lautenberg Amendment, 18 U.S.C. § 922(g)(8).
12. 18 U.S.C. § 921 et seq.
13. *United States v. Miller,* 307 U.S. 174 (1939).
14. G. Kleck, *Point Blank: Guns and Violence in America* (New York: Aldine De Gruyter, 1991), 122–24.
15. G. Kleck and M. Gertz, "Armed Resistance to Crime: The Prevalence and Nature of Self-Defense with a Gun," *Journal of Criminal Law and Criminology* 86, no. 1 (1995): 150–82.

16. P. Cook, J. Ludwig, and D. Hemenway, "The Gun Debate's New Mythical Number: How Many Defensive Uses per Year?" *Journal of Policy Analysis and Management* 16, no. 3 (1997): 463–69.

17. A. McClurg, D. Kopel, and B. Denning, eds., *Gun Control and Gun Rights* (New York: New York University Press, 2002), 60–65.

18. P. Cook and J. Ludwig, *Gun Violence: The Real Costs* (New York: Oxford University Press, 2000), 65.

19. J. Fagan, F. Zimring, and J. Kim, "Declining Homicide in New York City: A Tale of Two Trends," *Journal of Criminal Law and Criminology* 88, no. 4 (1998): 1277–1307.

20. Cook and Ludwig, *Gun Violence,* 16–18.

21. J. Lott, *More Guns, Less Crime: Understanding Crime and Gun-Control Laws* (Chicago: University of Chicago Press, 1997).

22. D. Black and D. Nagin, "Do Right-to-Carry Laws Deter Violent Crime?" *Journal of Legal Studies* 27, no. 1 (1998): 209–19.

Further Reading: Cook, P., and J. Ludwig, *Gun Violence: The Real Costs* (New York: Oxford University Press, 2000); Kleck, G., *Point Blank: Guns and Violence in America* (New York: Aldine De Gruyter, 1991); Lott, J., *More Guns, Less Crime: Understanding Crime and Gun-Control Laws* (Chicago: University of Chicago Press, 1997); McClurg, A., D. Kopel, and B. Denning, eds., *Gun Control and Gun Rights* (New York: New York University Press, 2002); Wellford, C., J. Pepper, and C. Petrie, eds., *Firearms and Violence* (Washington, DC: National Academies Press, 2005).

Matt Nobles

H

HAWAIIANS (ETHNIC) AND INCARCERATION

INTRODUCTION

Hawaiians are the most incarcerated ethnic group in Hawaii, a situation causing much controversy because despite claims that Hawaiians are more criminal than other groups, mass Hawaiian incarceration can also be linked to colonialism. In addition, although Hawaii is recognized across the globe as a mecca for racial harmony, the stratification of the carceral landscape along the intersections of race, class, and gender remains ignored. This controversial relationship between the political history of Hawaiians and the disproportionately high rates of imprisonment among them makes this an important case from which to analyze power and dominance. It also provides a vantage point from which to examine the social and political consequences of this mass incarceration and banishment of Hawaiians in both historical and contemporary terms.

BACKGROUND

Since 1974, U.S. continental incarceration rates have more than quadrupled.[1] During the same period, Hawaii's general prison population increased 15-fold, which included a 700 percent increase in the Hawaiian inmate population, far outstripping the general Hawaiian population growth, which increased by roughly only 300 percent over the same period.[2] Officially, Hawaiians represent 20 percent of Hawaii's general population yet make up more than 40 percent of the state's prison population.[3] Yet firsthand accounts of prisoners, families, advocates, and correctional industry professionals reveal Hawaiians actually represent upward of 70 percent of state prison populations. In contrast, whites represent 24 percent of the total populace and 22 percent of the state's prison population, whereas Japanese represent 21 percent of the general population but only 4 percent of the state prison population.[4] Gene Kassebaum explains that although whites and Hawaiians are arrested at comparable rates, the deeper Hawaiians go into the criminal justice system (e.g., sentencing), the more likely they are to be imprisoned.[5] Notably, whites and Japanese are considered dominant ethnic groups in Hawaii, and members of both communities make up the majority of administrative positions in the Department of Public Safety.

The state's current policy of banishment exacerbates the problem, a situation in which 50 percent of Hawaii's prisoners (the majority of whom are Hawaiian) are shipped out of state to private for-profit prison facilities owned by Corrections Corporation of America. State incarceration and especially interstate confinement not only split Hawaiian families and communities but also harm prisoners who eventually return to society often in worse shape than they were before incarceration.[6] Hawaii now ranks in first place in its exportation of prisoners.[7]

HAWAIIANS AND INCARCERATION

- Hawaiians are more likely than whites to be imprisoned despite similar arrest rates.
- Incarceration as a mechanism of colonization has depoliticized Hawaiians in historic and contemporary times. Most studies center the problem in Hawaiian criminal subjectivity, which tends to exaggerate so-called native flaws. This fails to explain mass imprisonment as part of the colonial project.
- As a highly advanced and interdependent society, Hawaiians flourished under their own government, land system, and culture prior to Western contact in 1778. More than 800,000 Hawaiians thrived. Post-Western contact brought with it a series of devastating consequences, including fatal disease, land dispossession, political disenfranchisement, and cultural genocide. Over a short period after Western contact, the Hawaiian population declined 90 percent.
- After many years of conspiring against Queen Lili'uokalani and her people, in 1893 U.S. missionary descendants and businessmen (the Provisional Government) illegally dethroned her and overthrew the Hawaiian government.
- In 1895, 183 loyal citizens of the Hawaiian kingdom attempted to restore Queen Lili'uokalani to the throne. The Provisional Government (now the Republic of Hawai'i) moved swiftly to criminalize the queen and her supporters. Queen Lili'uokalani was arrested, convicted, and imprisoned by the Republic conspirators.
- In 1898, with the assistance of the Republic of Hawai'i and U.S. Minister John L. Stevens, Hawaii was forcefully annexed under U.S. President William McKinley.

THE COLONIAL LEGACY

Scholarly contributions to the study of colonialism in Hawaii are important for understanding the political history of Hawaiians.[8] However, there remains a dearth of studies about the carceral situation and its impact on families and communities.[9] Aside from cursory mention or attempts to explain the problem through Hawaiian criminal subjectivity, the disposal of Hawaiians in mass numbers to penal warehouses remains ignored. Yet a closer examination reveals this condition may very well be linked to the colonial history of Hawaiians.

Hawaii's last ruling sovereign, Queen Lili'uokalani, gave a first-person account of the illegal overthrow of the Hawaiian government and the subsequent acts of resistance by her and her people to the various forms of U.S. colonialist thinking that led to the taking of Hawaii by the United States and the subsequent five-year struggle by Hawaiians to protect the integrity of their country.[10] That struggle included an attempted armed overthrow of the colonial government by Hawaiians to restore their nation, which was the catalyst to the imprisonment of Lili'uokalani and 183 of her most loyal supporters. Lili'uokalani's observation that mass punishment was intended "to terrorize the native people and to humiliate" her is a telling example of how incarceration is linked to the colonial project. It also exemplifies present-day conditions in which Hawaiian imprisonment is neocolonial in its intent and effects.

When theorizing disproportionality through the lens of institutional criminal subjectivity and state violence, the connections become more apparent.[11] As in the case of Lili'uokalani and her supporters' attempt to restore their stolen Hawaiian nation, patterns of criminalization exist in tandem with the birth of the Hawaiian sovereignty movement in the 1970s. In 1972, one woman was imprisoned in Hawaii. In 1982, there were 43—a 4,200 percent increase in just 10 years. From 1992 to 2000, the number of imprisoned women increased from 164 to 500—a 205 percent increase in just eight years in comparison to only a 106 percent increase on the continent during the same period.[12] Hence, between 1982 and 2000, women's imprisonment increased 1,063 percent. Hawaiian women represent more than half of statewide prison populations, and two-thirds report being mothers of at least one minor child.[13] The majority was undereducated and underemployed prior to incarceration.[14] Unsurprisingly, many leaders in the Hawaiian sovereignty movement are Hawaiian women.

In 2002, voters in Hawaii elected its first Republican governor in forty years. Under the new administration, more Hawaiian prisoners have been banished to out-of-state prisons than at any other time in the history of Hawaii. Aside from the fact that Republicanism overshadows past and present trends, another major similarity between the two eras indicates that cultural representations, including narratives of disparagement coming out of the drug war, fuel Hawaiian incarceration. For example, the connection between fabricated drug charges brought against Queen Lili'uokalani by colonial conspirators and the current U.S. War on Drugs both exaggerate and conflate native criminality. Likewise, just as colonialists profiteered from the drug trade while simultaneously justifying revolt against Hawaiians and the armed takeover of their nation, current state maneuvering in drug-scare tactics ensure so-called public safety in today's War on Drugs, galvanizing institutional assault against Hawaiians while simultaneously supplying the demand for criminal bodies in the profitable prison-industrial complex. Systemic vilification[15] through past and present drug crusades has had parallel outcomes whereby Hawaiians are disenfranchised, exploited, and banished from family, community, and politics.

DID YOU KNOW?

- High rates of Hawaiian incarceration can be linked to the Hawaiian sovereignty movement and the War on Drugs.
- Hawaii ranks first place in its exportation of prisoners to out-of-state private prison facilities owned and operated by Corrections Corporation of America.
- Under the current Republican administration, more Hawaiians have been banished to penal warehouses than at any other point in the history of Hawaii.

Cultural representations in both print and media advanced Queen Lili'uokalani's imprisonment and the annexation of Hawaii, whereas twenty-first-century images continue to criminalize Hawaiians. Depictions of native savagery and drug criminality advanced the annexation of Hawaii and the imprisonment of Queen Lili'uokalani. Currently, twenty-first-century images of native criminality continue in the media, such as the hit reality series *Dog the Bounty Hunter*. RaeDeen Karasuda and Katherine Irwin write:

> More than 100 years later, we have a new moral panic, one that is focused on fears of crime. Now criminal justice agents and this reality TV show tell us that the key to public safety is to incarcerate Native Hawaiians—at a rate double that of any other ethnic group in the state. The irony? Public safety equals the criminalization and imprisonment of Native Hawaiians who are severed from their culture. It is important to note that this profit comes at a huge cost to the Native Hawaiian community. The real key to public safety is rehabilitation, including drug treatment, community-based transition programs, and education and employment training—not Dog or punitive crime legislation.[16]

Representation of Hawaiians as poor, drug-addicted, and uncivilized beings remains synonymous with depoliticization and displacement—and prison.

KEY LEGAL DECISIONS

Queen Lili'uokalani never ceased in her efforts to resist the illegal overthrow and annexation of Hawaii. In 1909, she filed a petition against the United States of America, arguing for restitution for stolen Hawaiians lands and restoration of the Hawaiian government.[17] The court described Lili'uokalani's case as one that was unusual even for conquest, pointing out that all of civilization would be outraged if their own property were confiscated and rights annulled.[18] Here, the court recognized the actions of the Republic and the annexation of Hawaii as being clear violations but refused to bring justice to the situation. A closer reading of the ruling on the petition indicates the court's fixation with property, which may be linked to its refusal to reverse institutional wrongdoing. The court acknowledges the existence of motives for material gain and notes the Republic was unable to resist the potential for gain of the crown lands and therefore legally maneuvered the situation so that the courts could not recognize the petitioner's claim.[19]

Denial of Queen Lili'uokalani's legal petition is reflective of the court's handling of Hawaiian cases, and this pattern extends to prisoner litigation and especially prisoner transfers. Two cases in particular reveal the court's hands-off policy. Although the effect is not limited to Hawaiians, both cases involve Hawaiian plaintiffs, with the impact of court decisions on Hawaiians being more prevalent than for any other ethnic group in Hawaii, as Hawaiians make up the majority of the state's prison population and prisoner transfers out of state.

In 1995, the U.S. Supreme Court ruled in favor of Hawaii prison officials in *Sandin v. Conner*.[20] The ruling dramatically changed the way the Court viewed prisoner liberty interests, particularly in regard to prisoner transfers. Demont Conner, a Hawaiian prisoner serving an indeterminate sentence of 30 years to life at the Hālawa Correctional Center, filed suit against prison officials in the U.S. District Court for the District of Hawaii. Several days after Conner resisted a strip search, prison administrators held a disciplinary hearing. In his lawsuit, Conner claimed he was deprived of his procedural due process when the hearing committee refused to allow him to call witnesses. The committee found Conner in violation of one count of high misconduct and two counts of low misconduct, sentencing him to a special disciplinary segregation unit for 30 days and four hours.

In addition to the prison administrator's refusal to allow him to present witnesses, Conner maintained that after his transfer to solitary confinement and subsequent 30-day punishment, prison officials determined he had not committed high misconduct. Before administrators expunged the high misconduct charge, Conner filed the complaint. The U.S. Court of Appeals for the Ninth Circuit determined that Conner indeed had a liberty interest to remain free from being transferred to disciplinary segregation and that there was a disputed question as to whether he received due process under *Wolff v. McDonnell*.[21] However, the U.S. Supreme Court reversed and, in an opinion written by then-Chief Justice William Rehnquist, held that Conner was not entitled to due process under either Hawaii state prison regulations or the due process clause of the U.S. Constitution.

The Court further found that segregated confinement was not significant or out of the ordinary at the maximum-security facility. The majority noted that as Conner's future chances for parole were not affected, the solitary confinement did not warrant special consideration. However, dissenting Justices Ruth Bader Ginsburg, John Paul Stevens, Stephen Breyer, and David Souter wrote that the prisoner had a protected liberty interest under the Fourteenth Amendment's due process clause and that punishment in disciplinary segregation significantly altered the inmate's confinement. Justices Breyer and Souter also questioned the authority of prison officials to impose this punishment.

Although the *Sandin* decision centers on segregation and discipline, it has had far-reaching consequences for prisoners in the context of both intra- and interprison transfers. Since the *Sandin* decision, the Court has generally refused to grapple with the issue of whether certain types of confinement are cruel and unusual under the "a-typicality" clause. Majority opinions since then have focused on confinement (regardless of type or circumstance) as part of the normal course of daily life in prison. In refusing to distinguish between what is cruel and unusual and what is not, the majority has generally ruled that as long as there are no glaring civil rights violations, prisoners should expect cruel or harsh conditions. On the other hand, the minority on the Court has repeatedly worked to define confinement and transfer conditions and due process on a case-by-case basis. In particular, *Sandin* continues to be referenced in regard to prisoner complaints against intra- and interstate prisoner transfers and continues to be part of the seminal literature on prisoner litigation.

One year after the *Sandin* ruling, Congress passed the Prisoner Litigation Reform Act (PLRA) of 1996.[22] In an effort to curtail what was perceived as mounting frivolous inmate litigation and judicial activism, Congress incorporated more restrictive procedural requirements that prisoners must exhaust prior to seeking access to the federal court. Most inmate litigation pre- and post-PLRA has been filed under the Eighth and Fourteenth Amendments.

The PLRA sets forth four major prerequisites before prisoners may gain legal entry into the courts. First, prisoners are required to exhaust all available administrative remedies, regardless of whether remedial action is possible through the process.[23] Critics point to concerns over whether prisoners really enjoy due process, particularly as most complaints are made against the officials who preside over the grievance proceedings. Courts have been split on the meanings of *remedies* and *available*.[24] However, the U.S. Supreme Court put the issue to rest in *Booth v. Churner* in deeming that Congress "mandated exhaustion regardless of the type of relief offered through administrative procedures."[25] The Supreme Court broadly applied the decision a year after *Booth* in *Porter v. Nussle* when it decided that "Congress intended for prisoners to use their grievance systems before going to court, and the PLRA created no exceptions to that rule, even in those situations where a grievance system can not respond to a prisoner's request for relief."[26] Yet despite this ruling, the exhaustion requirement remains controversial.

In an amicus curiae filing to the petition in *Booth v. Churner,* the American Civil Liberties Union (ACLU) et al. pointed out that "Congress did not intend to require prisoners to exhaust administrative remedies that could not provide the requested relief. It certainly did not clearly express such intent. In the absence of a clear expression of congressional intent, this Court should not impose such a requirement."[27] Like their decision in *Sandin,* the majority Court has more broadly restricted the rights of prisoners through the PLRA test.

Second, the PLRA requires plaintiffs to pay all court filing fees in full. Inmates unable to afford to do so must pay at least a "partial initial filing fee" and make "incremental payments each month thereafter until the balance of the filing fee has been paid."[28] Attorney fees are also capped under the PLRA. This is especially problematic given the income limitations of most inmates and the attorneys who represent them.

Third, a three-strikes provision is written into the PLRA, with inmates who have had three or more cases dismissed as frivolous or malicious being required under the law to pay all future filing fees up front. Although an exception is provided for inmates in immediate imminent danger, given the Court's history as seen in *Sandin* and *Booth,* it is likely that impending danger is rarely considered.

Finally, prisoners filing for mental or emotional injury must prove physical injury. Under this clause, compensatory relief may only be sought in cases in which physical injury is present. Although prisons do not provide compensatory remedies, prisoners must still first exhaust administrative grievance processes. Clearly, although Congress passed the PLRA without debate, it remains as one of the most controversial points in prisoner litigation reform.

The decision in *Olim v. Wakinekona* is further cited in regard to prisoner banishment.[29] On August 2, 1976, a committee in a maximum-security prison in Hawaii conducted a study regarding facility programs and determined prisoner Delbert Ka'ahanui Wakinekona was a troublemaker. Three days later, prison officials notified Wakinekona of a classification hearing to be held on August 10, 1976. Prison regulations specifically stated that members of the hearing committee could not be part of the investigative team, yet in this matter, both committees were made up of the same persons. The committee recommended a transfer, which was approved by then-Director Antone Olim. Wakinekona was then moved to California Folsom State Penitentiary to serve the remainder of his sentence.

Wakinekona filed suit in the U.S. District Court for the District of Hawaii based on violation of his due process rights. The suit highlighted procedural violations and bias regarding the committee. The U.S. district court found that prisoners did not have a liberty interest through official regulations in regard to transfers. However, the Ninth Circuit Court of Appeals reversed, holding that the state did indeed create a liberty interest by "promulgating the rule in question and reasoning that the rule gave prisoners a justifiable expectation that they would not be transferred to the mainland absent a hearing, before an impartial committee, concerning the facts alleged in the prehearing notice."[30]

Hawaii prison officials then petitioned the U.S. Supreme Court, who found in their favor, ruling that the prisoner was not deprived of his due process rights and that "prison regulations placed to substantive limitations on official discretion and thus created no liberty interest entitled to protection under the due process."[31] Dissenting Justices Thurgood Marshall, William Brennan, and Stevens wrote that liberty interests were "not limited to whatever a state chooses to bestow" and that "Hawaii's prison regulations created a liberty interest."[32]

Since that ruling, the Court has basically maintained that interstate prison transfers are not cruel or unusual. The Court further asserted that Wakinekona's transfer was not comparable to banishment:

> A transfer of a state prisoner from Hawaii to California, although over an ocean, is not analogous to banishment in the English sense of "beyond the seas" since the prisoner has in no sense been banished as his conviction, not the transfer, deprived him of his right to freely inhabit the state

and the fact that his confinement is placed outside the state of Hawaii is merely a fortuitous consequence of the fact that he must be confined, not an additional element of his punishment, as the prisoner has not been exiled and remains within the United States.[33]

As with the *Sandin* Court, the ruling has been foundational in similar cases in which interstate prison transfers are seen as normal occurrences and part of everyday practices in corrections.[34] This hands-off doctrine approving interstate transfers makes it especially problematic for Hawaiian prisoners and their families, because Hawaiians are the most imprisoned population in Hawaii. Scholars and legal analysts point to a host of concerns, particularly in regard to the integrity of out-of-state private prisons.[35]

The Court's refusal to intervene has meant that contracts between Hawaii and the Corrections Corporation of America (CCA) have remained largely unregulated. Allegations of mismanagement, prisoner abuse, and contract violations abound in regard to CCA. In December 2005, 43-year-old Hawaiian prisoner Sarah Ah Mau died suddenly while in CCA custody after complaining of stomach pains for two months. Although she had been denied medical care, then-Acting Director of Public Safety Frank Lopez insisted there was no connection between Ms. Ah Mau's medical complaints and her death.[36]

The Ah Mau case is a dramatic one, but even routine situations call into question whether accountability exists. For example, in letters written by and on behalf of the Department of Public Safety, prison officials admitted to not knowing the whereabouts of eight inmates under CCA jurisdiction.[37] The correspondence reveals the suspect nature of whether the state handles responsibly its inmates warehoused on the U.S. continent.

Austin Sarat explains that legal texts embody narratives of record, and they "become part of the public record. . . . What seems 'fruitless' today takes on meaning when viewed in the long term. A society now unwilling to see the links between poverty, neglect, and the death penalty, may 'a hundred years from now' be more receptive to that structural narrative."[38] Legal narratives provide historical paper trails and keep a spotlight on the problem. Legal interpretations ensure the prison landscape will not fall behind the iron curtain. Discussion promotes accountability in prison commercialization. Finally, attention to this trend makes certain that the forced diaspora of Hawaiians does not allow them to be relegated to a status of out of sight, out of mind.

FUTURE PROSPECTS

Outsourcing prisoners to carceral complexes on the U.S. continent has had profound social, cultural, and political consequences for Hawaiians that are not limited to the past and present. As one generation wastes away in prison, another is being dispersed throughout the United States. Alongside mass Hawaiian incarceration and banishment, the state's foster care system now burgeons with Hawaiian children. Reports indicate 53 percent of children in foster care are Hawaiian, and the number is climbing.[39] The situation is made more difficult in light of the fact that the current Republican administration recently contracted with CCA to construct a special prison facility in Arizona for holding Hawaii prisoners. The steady flow of prisoner bodies supplied to CCA may get worse, especially as Hawaii lawmakers passed the Three Strikes Law in 2005. In this way, the combination of punitive legislation and outsourcing prisoners is likely to be even more devastating for Hawaiians.

This entry spotlights institutional abuse and contributes to a growing body of literature that seeks to contribute to the decolonization of indigenous groups and communities of color. Deliberate silence in regard to the standardized containment of entire groups of people has not resolved crime problems in modern society. Likewise, continual mulling over why groups are criminal or how they can be saved from themselves has failed to solve issues of public safety while at the same time has allowed purposeful neglect of institutionalized terror against prisoners, families, and marginalized communities. The unique political history and status of Hawaiians lend rare insight into the way in which state violence through institutional punishment rooted in colonialism is interwoven throughout society. By paying serious attention to a problem that has been virtually ignored, the entry contributes new ways of thinking about and dealing with institutional violence against Hawaiians and other disenfranchised communities. It also makes a substantial contribution to the study of mass incarceration and the prison-industrial complex.[40]

Although the main focus of this entry has centered on the collateral consequences and politics of mass Hawaiian imprisonment, it is important to acknowledge the growing movement toward reversing the trend. It is also worthy of mention that there is a growing community of concerned people and a body of literature revealing countless viable and cost-effective alternatives to imprisonment.[41]

See Also: African American Criminal (In) Justice; Convict Criminology; Corrections Education; Dangerous Offenders; Equal Justice and Human Rights; Media Portrayals of Criminal Justice; Prison Violence in the Caribbean; Prisoner Litigation; South Africa and Post-Apartheid Justice.

Endnotes

1. Jeremy Travis and Michelle Waul, *Prisoners Once Removed: The Impact of Incarceration and Reentry on Children, Families, and Communities* (Washington, DC: Urban Institute, 2003).
2. Eleanor C. Nordyke, *The Peopling of Hawai'i* (Honolulu: University of Hawai'i Press, 1989); Mona Bernardino, "Incarceration Trends of Native Hawaiians, Maoris and Aboriginals" (paper presented at University of Hawai'i-Manoa, unpublished, Association of African American Studies (AAAS) Joint Regional Conference on the Pacific Diaspora: Indigenous and Immigrant Communities, Honolulu, April 13–17, 1996); U.S. Census Bureau, *1990 Census of Population, Social and Economic Characteristics, Hawaii*, Report no. 1990 CP-213, Table 110 (Washington, DC:GPO, 1993); National Center for Chronic Disease Prevention and Health Promotion, *Synopses by State: Hawaii—2001* (2001), http://www2.cdc.gov/nccdphp/doh/synopses/; Paige M. Harrison and Allen J. Beck, *Prisoners in 2002* (July 2003), www.ojp.usdoj.gov/bjs/pub/pdf/p02.pdf; Kamehameha Schools, *Aloha Counts: Census 2000 Special Tabulations*

for Native Hawaiians (Honolulu: Kamehameha Schools' Pauahi Publications, 2003); Department of Public Safety, *Distribution of Sentenced Felon Population by Ethnic Group or Race Statewide—End of Fiscal Years 1975, 1982, 1990, and 2001* (unpublished table, Honolulu, 2004); Department of Public Safety, *Distribution of Inmate Population by Ethnicity or Race as of June 30, 2003* (unpublished table, Honolulu, 2003).

3. Department of Public Safety, *Distribution of Inmate Population.*

4. Ibid.

5. Gene Kassebaum, *Report on Criminal Justice and Hawaiians in the 1990's: Ethnic Differences in Imprisonment Rates in the State of Hawai'i* (Honolulu: Alu Like, 1994).

6. I use the term *state* loosely throughout this chapter. The illegal overthrow of the Hawaiian kingdom in 1893 makes this term problematic. Usage of the term is not intended as an agreement. Rather, it is used as a means to highlight the explicit power relation embedded within an institution.

7. Silja J. A. Talvi, "No Room in Prison? Ship 'Em Off: Prisoners Have Become Unwitting Pawns in a Lowest-Bidder-Gets-the-Convict Shuffle Game," *In These Times* (May 10, 2006), http://wwwinthesetimes.com/article/2622/

8. Haunani-Kay Trask, *From a Native Daughter: Colonialism and Sovereignty in Hawai'i* (Monroe, ME: Common Courage, 1999); Haunani-Kay Trask, "Native Social Capital: The Case of Hawaiian Sovereignty and Ka Lāhui Hawaii," *Policy Sciences* 33 (2000): 375–85; Haunani-Kay Trask, "The Birth of the Modern Hawaiian Movement: Kalama Valley, O'ahu," *The Hawaiian Journal of History* 21 (1987): 126–53; Noenoe K. Silva, *Aloha Betrayed: Native Hawaiian Resistance to American Colonialism* (Durham, NC: Duke University Press, 2004); Jon Kamakawiwo'ole Osorio, *Dismembering Lāhui: A History of the Hawaiian Nation to 1887* (Honolulu: University of Hawai'i Press, 2002); Lilikalā Kame'eleihiwa, *Native Land and Foreign Desires: Pehea Lā E Pono Ai?* (Honolulu: Bishop Museum Press, 1992).

9. Graeme Harper, *Colonial and Postcolonial Incarceration* (New York: Continuum, 2001).

10. Lili'uokalani, *Hawaii's Story by Hawaii's Queen* (Honolulu: Mutual, 1990).

11. David Kauzlarich, Christopher W. Mullins, and Rick A. Matthews, "A Complicity Continuum of State Crime," *Contemporary Justice Review* 6, no. 3 (2003): 241–54.

12. Department of Public Safety, *Distribution of Inmate Population.*

13. Ibid.; Janice Joseph, "Introduction to the Special Issue," *The Prison Journal* 81, no. 1 (2001): 3–5.

14. Community Alliance on Prisons, Kat Brady, interview by the author September 2004.

15. Loic Wacquant, "Deadly Symbiosis: When Ghetto and Prison Meet and Mesh," *Punishment and Society* 3, no. 1 (2001): 94–134.

16. RaeDeen Karasuda and Katherine Irwin, "Dog's 'Tough Love' on Crime Isn't Helping," *The Honolulu Advertiser,* A12, September 5, 2005.

17. *Liliuokalani v. United States,* 45 Ct. Cl. 418 (1910).

18. Ibid.

19. Ibid.

20. *Sandin v. Conner,* 515 U.S. 472, 115 S. Ct. 2293, 132 L. Ed. 2d 418 (1995).

21. *Wolff v. McDonnell,* 418 U.S. 539, 94 S. Ct. 2963, 41 L. Ed. 2d 935 (1974); John W. Palmer and Stephen E. Palmer, *Constitutional Rights of Prisoners,* 7th ed. (Cincinnati: Anderson, 2004).

22. Pub. L. No. 104–134 (codified as amended in scattered titles and sections of 18 U.S.C., 28 U.S.C., and 42 U.S.C.); see also H.R. 3019, 104th Congress (1996).

23. Barbara Belbot, "Report on the Prison Litigation Reform Act: What Have the Courts Done So Far?" *The Prison Journal* 84, no. 3 (2004): 290–316.

24. Ibid.

25. *Booth v. Churner,* 532 U.S. 731, 121 S.Ct. 1819, 149 L.Ed. 2d 958 (2001).

26. *Porter v. Nussle,* 534 U.S. 516, 122 S.Ct. 983, 152 L.Ed. 2d 12 (2002).

27. *Booth v. Churner,* "Brief of the American Civil Liberties Union, the Legal Aid Society of the City of New York, and the Prison Reform Advocacy Center as *Amici Curiae* in Support of Petitioner, No. 99–1964" (2001).

28. Palmer and Palmer, *Constitutional Rights of Prisoners,* 358.

29. *Olim v. Wakinekona,* 461 U.S. 238, 103 S. Ct. 1741, 75 L. Ed. 2d 813 (1983).

30. Ibid.

31. Ibid.

32. Ibid.

33. Ibid.

34. David Shichor and Dale K. Sechrest, "Privatization and Flexibility: Legal and Practical Aspects of Interjurisdictional Transfer of Prisoners," *The Prison Journal* 82, no. 3 (2002): 386–407.

35. Mark Finnane and John McGuire, "The Uses of Punishment and Exile: Aborigines in Colonial Australia," *Punishment and Society* 3, no. 2 (2001): 279–98; Malcolm M. Feeley, "Entrepreneurs of Punishment: The Legacy of Privatization," *Punishment and Society* 4, no. 3 (2002): 321–44; Joseph T. Keyes, "Banishing Massachusetts Inmates to Texas: Prisoner Liberty Interests and Interstate Transfers after Sandin v. Conner," *New England Journal on Criminal and Civil Confinement* 23 (Summer, 1997): 603.

36. Kevin Dayton, "Inmate's Death in Ky. to Be Probed," *The Honolulu Advertiser,* January 4, 2006, http://the.honoluluadvertiser.com/article/2006/Jan/04/ln/FP601040347.html/?printon.

37. Bryan C. Yee, Letter to Native Hawaiian Legal Corporation from State of Hawai'i Department of Attorney General, *Bush v. State of Hawai'i,* Civil No. 04–00096 (February 9, 2006); Edwin C. Nacino, Letter to Native Hawaiian Legal Corporation from Roeca, Louie, and Hiraoka, *Bush v. State of Hawai'i,* Civil No. 04–00096 (February 8, 2006).

38. Austin Sarat, *When The State Kills: Capital Punishment and the American Condition* (Princeton, NJ: Princeton University Press, 2001): 176–77.

39. Mary Vorsino, "Foster Program Helps Native Hawaiian Kids," *The Honolulu Star-Bulletin,* July 11, 2005, http://starbulletin.com/2005/07/11/news/story4.html; P.L. 105–89, the Adoption and Safe Families Act of 1997, was signed into effect by the 105th Congress in an effort to promote adoption. Under this federal legislation, children placed in foster care for more than 15 months become legally adoptable. Interviews with incarcerated mothers and fathers reveal that this law is affecting imprisoned Hawaiians and their children.

40. Ruth Wilson Gilmore, *Golden Gulag: Prisons, Surplus, Crisis, and Opposition in Globalizing California* (Berkeley and Los Angeles: University of California Press, 2006); Angela Davis, *Are Prisons Obsolete?* (New York: Seven Stories, 2003).

41. Jeffrey Ian Ross and Stephen C. Richards, *Convict Criminology* (Belmont, CA: Wadsworth, 2003); James Austin and John Irwin, *It's About Time: America's Imprisonment Binge,* 3rd ed. (Belmont, CA: Wadsworth, 2001).

Further Reading: Agozino, Biko, *Counter-Colonial Criminology: A Critique of Imperialist Reason* (London: Pluto, 2003); Gilmore, Ruth Wilson, *Golden Gulag: Prisons, Surplus, Crisis, and Opposition in Globalizing California* (Berkeley and Los Angeles: University of California Press, 2006); Lili'uokalani, *Hawai'i's Story by Hawai'i's Queen* (Honolulu: Mutual, 1990); Marez, Curtis, *Drug Wars: The Political Economy of Narcotics* (Minneapolis: University of Minnesota Press, 2004); Ross, Jeffrey Ian, and Stephen C. Richards, *Convict Criminology* (Belmont, CA: Wadsworth, 2003).

RaeDeen M. Keahiolalo-Karasuda

HOMELAND SECURITY

INTRODUCTION

In today's global environment, with human-caused and natural disasters more ominous, homeland security consists of diverse government agencies, state and local interests, international organizations, and policies and agreements—all of which are engulfed in controversy surrounding, on the one hand, the protection of citizens and the homeland of the United States and, on the other hand, the protection of such fundamental Constitutional principles as the right to privacy or liberty. The importance of developing a homeland-security system came to the attention of the public after the terrorists' attacks of September 11, 2001 (9/11). However, long before 9/11, securing the homeland of the United States was a priority of the United States government, predominately as a directive of criminal justice agencies such as the Federal Bureau of Investigation (FBI), the Department of Alcohol, Tobacco, and Firearms (ATF), and the Border Patrol, as well as state and local police departments.

The protection of the United States homeland involves many international, federal, state, private, tribal, and local law enforcement agencies interacting with one another through broad directions, missions, and goals. The Homeland Security Act of 2002 assigns the Department of Homeland Security the following primary missions:

- To prevent terrorist attacks within the United States.
- To reduce the vulnerability of the United States to terrorism at home.
- To minimize the damage and assist in the recovery from terrorist attacks that occur.
- To act as the focal point regarding natural and human-caused crises and emergency planning.

BACKGROUND

In order to understand the complexity of contemporary homeland security, it is necessary to present a historical overview. Disaster management in the United States began in 1803 when the federal government responded to the devastation of a fire in Portsmouth, New Hampshire.[1] Between the years 1803 and 1950, the federal government responded to more than one hundred incidents, including earthquakes, fires, floods, and tornados. Because local governments were better able to handle their own emergencies, federal government assistance was often carried out in an ad hoc manner, without established methods of coordination.

The first incidents of domestic terrorism in the United States consisted of the brutality shown toward indigenous Native Americans. Such incidents continued after the American Civil War as the Ku Klux Klan used tactics such as lynching, bombing, the burning of homes, violence, and brutality to restore white rule in the South.[2] During this period, posses were formed to assist law enforcement in restoring order. These groups of men consisted of military troops stationed primarily in the South in order to restore order and civility.

The twentieth century brought a more structured role to the federal government in response to natural disasters as they became more prevalent and deadly. The Galveston hurricane of 1900 left more than 8,000 people dead (see table H.1) and spawned a series of federal legislative actions that provided guidance on responding to disasters but without focusing on mitigating circumstances or prevention. An example of this legislation was the 1905 congressional charter of the American Red Cross. Its timely inception was pivotal during the San Francisco earthquake and fire of 1906.

In 1913, the Ohio River flood killed several hundred people and caused millions of dollars of damage. The disaster served as the impetus for the United States House of Representatives to establish the Committee on Flood Control in 1916. Later, $45 million was appropriated for flood-control programs pertaining to the Mississippi and Sacramento Rivers with the passing of the 1917 Flood Control Act. However, in just 10 years, the act had outlived its usefulness, prompting the passing of the Flood Control Act of 1928, which, among other disasters and their consequences, placed devastation caused by the overflowing of the Mississippi River as the responsibility of the federal government.

After the California earthquake of 1933, the federal government provided even more general-relief programs for Americans. During these natural disasters of the early twentieth century, there was little focus on the role of criminal justice agencies in response and recovery. Criminal justice functions were primarily led and conducted by local and state law enforcement personnel.

The attack on Pearl Harbor by the Japanese navy in December 1941 brought to the attention of Americans the need for the government at various levels to focus on human-caused threats to the homeland, as previous disaster management

Table H.1 Selected United States Disasters Causing the Most Death and Damage to Property 1900–2005

Disaster	Year	Property Loss (2005 $)	Deaths
Galveston hurricane	1900	$1 billion	8,000
San Francisco earthquake and fire	1906	$5 billion	5,000
Atlantic-Gulf hurricane	1919	Less than $1 billion	500
Mississippi floods	1927	$3 billion	200
Hurricane San Felipe and Okeechobee flood	1928	Less than $1 billion	2,800
Hurricane Hugo	1989	$11 billion	100
Hurricane Andrew	1992	$33 billion	100
September 11, 2001, terrorists attacks	2001	$19 billion	2,900
Major hurricanes of 2004 (Charley, Frances, Ivan, and Jeanne)	2004	$46 billion	200
Hurricane Katrina	2005	$96 billion	1,300

Source: Frances Townsend, *The Federal Response to Hurricane Katrina: Lessons Learned* (Washington, DC: White House, 2006), http://www.whitehouse.gov/reports/katrina-lessons-learned.pdf.

had focused on natural disasters. Throughout the 1940s and thereafter, threats of foreign attacks stemming from the Cold War stimulated civil defense, emergency-shelters programs, and legislation such as the Disaster Relief Act of 1950, which created the bureaucratic process whereby states would request that the president designate a federal disaster area. During this era, federal guidance made it clear that a homeland-security emergency was the responsibility of local resources, followed by state assets. When those resources were exhausted, the federal government could be requested to assist.

During the 1960s and 1970s, earthquakes, hurricanes, and storms inflicted damage throughout the country, inspiring legislation providing for the refinancing of homes, food assistance, and unemployment assistance. Additionally, civil unrest and disorder in urban areas because of racial tension and social-class frustration demonstrated the inability of local emergency response efforts to prevent and properly respond to disorder and civil unrest. The justice system under emergency conditions broke down because of long-standing structural deficiencies: Well-trained police officers, plans to muster maximum police manpower, and special training for officers were largely unavailable at the local and state levels.[3] Recommendations from the Commission on Civil Disorders in 1968 strongly urged training and preparedness at local levels for domestic emergencies in the future.

A major change in disaster management at the federal level came on March 31, 1979, when President Jimmy Carter signed Executive Order 12127, which created the Federal Emergency Management Agency (FEMA) as the leading federal government agency to prepare for and respond to a disaster on U.S. soil. During the 1980s, FEMA had an all-hazards approach, with a major focus on nuclear-attack scenarios. The 1980s also saw the passage of the Robert T. Stafford Disaster Relief and Emergency Assistance Amendment (otherwise known as the Stafford Act), which brought together all four areas of disaster relief in which the federal government was involved: mitigation, preparedness, response, and recovery. For the first time in the history of the United States, there was a formal process for governors to request federal disaster and emergency assistance from the president when a major disaster or emergency was beyond the capabilities of state and local resources.

These new policies were tested as major disasters such as Hurricane Hugo (1989), Hurricane Andrew (1992), and Hurricane Iniki (1992) exposed the flaws in FEMA. Indeed, critics viewed it as a slow and mismanaged agency. In the 1990s, the vulnerability of the United States to devastating domestic terrorism was also demonstrated by the World Trade Center bombing in 1993 and the Oklahoma City Murrah Federal Building bombing in 1995. Interestingly, it was local law enforcement that brought Timothy McVeigh to custody just 90 minutes after the Oklahoma City explosion; an Oklahoma City highway patrolman pulled over McVeigh for driving without a license.

Improvements in FEMA's operations did come in the 1990s as new technology and leadership, working with state and local governments, increased the preparedness and response of the U.S. emergency agency. Congressional investigation of domestic terrorist activities of the 1990s led to the Nunn-Lungar legislation in 1995, which exposed the inadequacy of the United States to deal effectively with terrorism. The solution was a joint effort of FEMA, the Department of Justice, the Department of Health and Human Resources, and the National Guard to reduce the threat of terrorism in the United States.[4] However, no single organization was given the lead role in or clear directives about the implementation of the joint effort. Perhaps this oversight helped lead to the events of September 11, 2001. The United States had no central government agency prepared to prevent or respond to an event of such magnitude.

In response to 9/11, the Department of Homeland Security (DHS) was created in 2002. Upon its creation, 22 federal entities (several of which were originally criminal justice entities) came together under the DHS to form the second largest agency in the United States government after the Department of Defense. The first secretary was former Pennsylvania Governor Tom Ridge. Since February 15, 2005, former Third Circuit Court of Appeals Judge Michael Chertoff has led the DHS.

Because fear was prevalent throughout the United States, the DHS publicly informed Americans that homeland security was everyone's business. The public was urged to tell criminal justice agencies if they saw suspicious activities that might lead to terrorist activities in the future. Slogans such as "See Something . . . Tell Someone" became common as the DHS prepared Americans for future attacks. To aid public information and preparedness, the Color-Coded Threat Level System was developed. Each level led to certain specified preparedness activities for citizens as well as for government agencies at the federal, state, and local levels. Raising the threat level has had economic, physical, and psychological effects because people respond to fear, not risk.[5] Thus today the color-coded system can be used to address specific regions and industrial sectors based on information about the potential threat.

Table H.2 Color-Coded Threat Level System

Color Code	Threat Condition	Procedures to Occur
Green	Low risk of terrorist attack	Exercises for preparedness, training for emergencies, mitigating vulnerabilities
Blue	Guarded: general risk of terrorist attack	Check procedures, review information, provide information
Yellow	Significant risk of a terrorist attack	Increase surveillance and preparedness
Orange	High risk of a terrorist attack	Coordination at all levels; implement precautions and contingency procedures and restrict access
Red	Severe risk of a terrorist attack (not to be maintained for a substantial amount of time)	Redirect personnel; assign emergency response personnel; preposition equipment and personnel; monitor, redirect, and close facilities

Source: Department of Homeland Security, *National Response Plan: December 2004* (Washington, DC: Department of Homeland Security, 2004).

KEY EVENTS

The events of September 11, 2001, ushered in a new chapter of homeland security in the United States. It is important to note the prophetic findings in September 1999 by the U.S. Commission on National Security/21st Century, cochaired by former Senators Gary Hart and Warren Rudman. The commission reported that within the next 25 years, "[s]tates [nations], terrorists, and other disaffected groups will acquire weapons of mass destruction and mass disruption.... Americans will likely die on American soil, possibly in large numbers."[6] The report goes on to discuss a new world in which U.S. technological, geographic, and military advantages and diplomatic channels will no longer be sufficient to deter destruction. "Deterrence will not work as it once did.... The emerging security environment in the next quarter century will require different military and other national capabilities."[7] The 14 commissioners unanimously agreed in February 2001 that the U.S. federal government should make securing the national homeland its number one priority by making homeland security the primary mission of the National Guard and by establishing a new independent agency called the National Homeland Security Agency.[8]

Yet the tragic events of September 11, 2001, did occur, and four years later, after Hurricane Katrina, came the breakdown of civil society on the Gulf Coast, specifically in New Orleans. These disasters support the conclusion of the United States Commission on National Security/21st Century that the United States homeland-security policies and programs might not be adequate to deter and to respond to threats and disasters facing the country. To assess the validity of the conclusion, it is necessary to review the findings in the *9/11 Report* as well as in the *Katrina Report*.

The *9/11 Report* stressed the shortcomings of U.S. preparedness for and response to the events of September 11, 2001. A total of 41 specific recommendations were made to the federal government. Overall, three major areas were found to be deficient concerning the security of the United States homeland: (1) the lack of communication between agencies; (2) the lack of a central agency to coordinate and take sole responsibility for the protection of the U.S. homeland; and (3) the lack of imagination for deterring, mitigating, preparing for, responding to, and recovering from disasters on U.S. soil.

In December 2005, the 9/11 Commission reconvened to analyze, through a grading system of A through F (with A being the highest), how well the federal government had done in one year to implement the 42 recommendations. Disruption of terrorist funding received the highest grade, an A–. Overall, the evaluation showed that many of the 42 recommendations had not been fully implemented: The 9/11 Commission's evaluation assigned 2 incompletes, 5 Fs, 13 Ds, 9 Cs, 12 Bs, and 1 A–. Fs were assigned to areas such as improvements in airline passenger prescreening and in the allocation of homeland security funds based on risks.[9]

Many of the same shortcomings and mistakes found in the *9/11 Report* are presented in the report on Hurricane Katrina, *The Federal Response to Hurricane Katrina: Lessons Learned*. This report responds to the issues raised in the aftermath of the most destructive natural disaster in U.S. history, because the hurricane and the subsequent breaking of the levees in New Orleans caused more than $96 billion in damage.[10] The report details the events before, during, and after the hurricane and provides 125 recommendations in areas such as national preparedness, communications, logistics and evacuations, public safety, training, professional development and education, and citizen and community preparedness. Specifically in the area of public safety and security, the report states that plans were not in place to replace officers who could not or chose not to report for their duties. Procedures did not exist to streamline the deputizing process of qualified federal law enforcement officers when it became known that 70 percent of the New Orleans police force had been victims of the disaster. Additionally, the continuity of the court system and of prison operations was found to be inadequate.

As a result of the shortcomings and mistakes found in both the *9/11 Report* and the report on Hurricane Katrina, the question arises: What tools are available to the Department of Homeland Security in order to safeguard the United States in the future? The following section offers a discussion of three: the National Response Plan, the Posse Comitatus Act, and the Patriot Act. Along with the new solutions provided by these three tools, however, there has developed a new controversy about their usage and application.

LEGAL DECISIONS AND IMPORTANT DOCUMENTS

Guiding the response to a national emergency is the National Response Plan (NRP).[11] It covers the complex, ever-changing requirements in anticipation of and in response to acts of terrorism, major disasters, and other emergencies. By definition, it establishes a comprehensive, national, all-hazards approach to domestic-incidents management, including prevention, preparedness, response, and recovery. The NRP uses the National Incident Management System (NIMS), which provides the structure of command, communication, coordination, and control of an incident on a field, a regional, and a national level.[12]

The massive document defines terms and lists acronyms, authorities, and references; specific-incident annexes; and emergency support functions (ESFs), all of which detail responsibilities of and coordination with federal, state, local, tribal, private-sector, and nongovernmental entities. The NRP includes 15 ESFs in the areas of transportation; communications; public works and engineering; firefighting; emergency management; mass care, housing, and human services; resource support; public health and medical services; urban search and rescue; oil and hazardous-materials response; agriculture and natural resources; energy; public safety and security; long-term community recovery; and mitigation and final external affairs.

ESF 13, titled "Public Safety and Security Annex," integrates federal public safety and security capabilities and resources to support incidents of national significance. The primary coordinators are the Department of Homeland Security and the Department of Justice. In the event state and local forces (including the National Guard operating under state control) are unable to adequately respond to a civil disturbance, the state legislature or governor (if the legislature cannot convene) may request through the U.S. attorney general the assistance of the federal military under Title 10 of the U.S. Code, Chapter 15. The president may use the military in a state to enforce federal law or to protect constitutional rights. State, local, tribal, and private-sector authorities maintain primary responsibility for public safety and security. When they are overwhelmed, the federal government may aid in responding to a civil disturbance or other incident of significance by providing technical assistance, safety and security assessment, badging and credentialing, access control, site security, traffic control, protection of emergency responders, and surveillance. The use of the military in the United States is extremely controversial, as it is addressed in the United States Constitution as well as in the Posse Comitatus Act.

The Posse Comitatus Act of 1878 (2002) prohibits the use of the U.S Army or the U.S. Air Force for law enforcement purposes, except as otherwise authorized by the United States Constitution; limitations on the use of the U.S. Navy and U.S. Marine Corps exist as a matter of Department of Defense policy. The purpose of the act is to restrict the direct involvement of military personnel in traditional law enforcement activities (including the interdiction of a vehicle, vessel, or aircraft or activities such as apprehension, stop-and-frisk, or similar activity). Originally in 1854, a posse (consisting of able-bodied men older than 15 and including military personnel) could be summoned by marshals to uphold the law. In the South, under the doctrine of posse comitatus, these posses often enforced the Fugitive Slave Act of 1850. Ironically, during Reconstruction in the South after the Civil War, posse comitatus was used to protect the newly freed slaves from the terrorist activities of organizations such as the Ku Klux Klan. An amendment to the Army Appropriations Bill in 1878 became the Posse Comitatus Act, which restricted the ability of U.S. marshals and local sheriffs to conscript military personnel into their posses. The act does not preclude the use of troops if authorized by the president or by Congress.[13]

Interestingly, there is exception to the Posse Comitatus Act under the Insurrection Statutes (Title 10, U.S. Code, sections 331–35). The insurrection statutes authorize the president to direct the armed forces to enforce the law to suppress insurrections and domestic violence. Military forces may be used to restore order and to prevent looting and may engage in other law enforcement activities. The Posse Comitatus Act does not apply to the National Guard, the Coast Guard, state defense forces, or military personnel assigned to military police, shore police, or security duties. In the history of the United States, federal troops have been deployed more than two hundred times to restore order after a homeland-security emergency.[14]

Thus, the use of the military may be an answer to the need of a new strategy to protect the homeland of the United States. The resources, training, and equipment of the United States military can actively support law enforcement in containing homeland-security threats through such methods as border enforcement, investigation, surveillance, apprehension, and protection of potential targets. This answer does not come without limitations, however, because several articles of the U.S. Constitution, as well as the Bill of Rights, offer protection against the use of excessive law enforcement in the United States. Finally, Public Law 107–56 was intended to unite and strengthen Americans by providing appropriate tools required to intercept and obstruct terrorism. President George W. Bush signed this law, more commonly known as the USA Patriot Act, into law on October 26, 2001. According to its official name, the Patriot Act consists of a number of proactive tools to combat terrorist plots. Such tools include electronic surveillance to expand the range of trackable crimes, the wiretapping of suspected terrorists, performing a search with delayed notification (a kind of search also known as "sneak and peak"), searching personal records without probable cause, and easing the ability to obtain search warrants when suspected terrorist-related activities occur. In March 2006, after Congress passed the act, President Bush's signature made 14 of the original provisions permanent and extended 2 others for another four years. Since its origin, the Patriot Act has been controversial as several states and 150 local governments have passed resolutions objecting to the legislation because of its expanded powers and removal of civil liberty protections.[15]

Having contemplated the overzealous potential of law enforcement armed with the reauthorization of the Patriot Act, the American Civil Liberties Union (ACLU) testified to Congress that the provisions can "severely chill constitutionally protected freedoms of speech" and the use of intelligence-gathering probes poses dangers to civil liberties found in the Bill of Rights. Additionally, testimony cited the Supreme Court decision in 1965 that struck down the use of broad warrants that allow the seizure of items such as books on the basis of the ideas they contain.[16]

That the provisions of the Patriot Act are in conflict with the civil liberties of U.S. citizens was demonstrated after the conference Reviving the Islamic Spirit, held in Toronto in December 2004; Muslim American citizens were detained, frisked, photographed, fingerprinted, and threatened with arrest by border agents when they were returning to the United States. ACLU attorneys, citing the incident as a violation of the First and Fourth Amendments of the United States Constitution, claimed that the government could not criminalize U.S. citizens for their religious beliefs.[17]

Thus, homeland security is proactively focused on surveillance, intelligence gathering, and law enforcement. Through these methods, lists of potential targets are made and law officers are trained in ways to prevent terrorism, such as focusing on the following: persons who rent residential or commercial space but do not possess household or commercial furnishings, persons who show interest in renting living or commercial space in direct sight of critical infrastructure or government facilities, persons who make large purchases on a cash basis, persons who purchase one-way tickets, persons who perform Internet or library research on explosives, and persons who are suspected to belong to terrorist groups.

If a person performs one or more of these acts, he or she may be placed under additional surveillance and/or scrutiny while conducting business transactions, boarding public transportation, entering educational facilities, or conducting daily activities. Additionally, because of the international aspect of terrorism, the National Commission on Terrorism warns that law enforcement is designed to put individuals behind bars, not nations.[18] Thus, traditional law enforcement and perhaps the criminal justice system are ineffective for contemporary threats, whether they are human-caused or natural. As a result of possible new law enforcement practices, finding an acceptable balance between infringing on civil rights for security purposes and maintaining civil rights remains a controversial issue for homeland security in the future.

FUTURE PROSPECTS

In light of the devastation by Hurricanes Katrina and Rita in 2005, the possible spread of an influenza pandemic, and constant real or alleged threats of nuclear bombs and other terrorist attacks, homeland security in the United States must be prepared to mitigate, prepare for, respond to, and recover from all potential threats to the country and its citizens at all levels: international, federal, state, tribal, local, and private (including private citizens). Moreover, in response to a new kind of terrorist plot in August 2006, for example, air-travel limitations further restricted the freedoms of Americans. As additional information is made public about the limitations of securing air cargo, mail, and packages, plans of destruction from cyberterrorism, contaminants, and other products clearly demonstrate the new era of securing the homeland and the difficulty these new threats bring. Table H.3 presents projected costs and deaths for just three major disasters planned for by the Department of Homeland Security.

In planning for an influenza pandemic, the implementation plan for the National Strategy for Pandemic Influenza[19] addresses the global threat of the virus H5N1, also known as avian influenza A or bird flu, and its probable arrival in the United States. The plan lists and explains more than two hundred measures critical to containing a pandemic, which has the potential to kill millions of Americans and devastate the nation's economy. The decisions concerning which cities, towns, and perhaps sections of the United States should be quarantined are best left to local and state law enforcement agencies.

The question for the Department of Homeland Security and citizens of the United States is: How many freedoms will be lost in order to maintain the freedoms Americans enjoy today? Homeland security has the task of protecting Americans from natural and human-caused disasters. Even though Hurricane Katrina was the most costly disaster in U.S. history, the potential of human-caused threats, specifically terrorist threats, receives the most attention and financial

Table H.3 Projected Homeland Security Disasters in Death and Property Damage

Disaster	Damage (2005 $)	Deaths
Nuclear device	More than $100 billion	More than 10,000
Pandemic influenza	$87 billion	More than 10,000
Major earthquake	More than $100 billion	1,500

Source: Frances Townsend, *The Federal Response to Hurricane Katrina: Lessons Learned* (Washington, DC: White House, 2006), http://www.whitehouse.gov/reports/katrina-lessons-learned.pdf.

resources because they are linked to international conflicts in the Middle East and to the global war on terror more generally.

Nineteen men carried out the events of September 11, 2001, yet the planning is estimated to have taken more than two years. Perhaps it is this type of patience that will guide Americans to accept the ebbs and flows of homeland-security threats in the midst of color-coded warnings, obscure videos warning of future terrorist acts, and international protests against the United States. Local and state law enforcement agencies have the task of serving and protecting Americans—but at what cost to the freedoms and liberties that most Americans have come to expect?

See Also: Antiterrorism Laws; Foreign Intelligence Surveillance Act; Immigration and Employment Law Enforcement; Patriot Act; State Crime Control.

Endnotes

1. Frances Townsend, *The Federal Response to Hurricane Katrina: Lessons Learned* (Washington, DC: White House, 2006), http://www.whitehouse.gov/reports/katrina-lessons-learned.pdf.
2. J. Fagin, *When Terrorism Strikes Home: Defending the United States* (Boston: Allyn and Bacon, 2006).
3. National Advisory Commission on Civil Disorders, *Report of the National Advisory Commission on Civil Disorders* (Washington, DC: National Advisory Commission on Civil Disorders, 1968).
4. J. Bullock, G. Haddow, D. Coppola, E. Ergin, L. Westerman, and S. Yeletaysi, *Introduction to Homeland Security* (Burlington, MA: Elsevier Butterworth-Heinemann, 2005).
5. G. Becker and Y. Rubinstein, "Fear and the Response to Terrorism: An Economic Analysis" (paper, Cornell University, 2004), http://www.jtac.uchicago.edu/conferences/05/resources/beckerrubinsteinpaper.pdf.
6. United States Commission on National Security/21st Century, *New World Coming: American Security in the 21st Century: Major Themes and Implications* (Washington, DC: United States Commission on National Security/21st Century, 1999), 4, http://govinfo.library.unt.edu/nssg/reports/NWC.pdf.
7. Ibid., 7–8.
8. United States Commission on National Security/21st Century, *Road Map for National Security: Imperative for Change: The Phase III Report of the U.S. Commission on National Security/21st Century* (Washington, DC: United States Commission on National Security/21st Century, 2001), viii, http://govinfo.library.unt.edu/nssg/PhaseIIIFR.pdf.
9. 9/11 Public Discourse Project, *Final Report on 9/11 Commission Recommendations, December 5, 2005* (Washington, DC: 9/11 Public Discourse Project, 2005), http://www.9-11pdp.org.
10. Townsend, *Federal Response to Hurricane Katrina*.
11. Department of Homeland Security, *National Response Plan: December 2004* (Washington, DC: Department of Homeland Security, 2004).
12. Ibid.
13. J. Brinkerhoff, "The Posse Comitatus Act and Homeland Security," *Journal of Homeland Security*, February 2002, http://www.homelandsecurity.org/newjournal/articles/brinkerhoffposseComitatus.htm.
14. Ibid.

15. B. Knowlton, "Ashcroft Pushes Defense of Terror Law," *The New York Times,* August 19, 2003, http://www.nytimes.com/2003/8/19/politics/19cno-patriot.html.

16. American Civil Liberties Union, "Testimony of ACLU National Security Policy Counsel Timothy H. Edgar before the House Judiciary Subcommittee on Crime, Terrorism, and Homeland Security on the USA Patriot Act: Effect of Sections 203(b) and (d) on Information Sharing (4/19/2005)," American Civil Liberties Union, 2006, http://www.aclu.org/safefree/general/17518leg2005419.html.

17. American Civil Liberties Union, "Homeland Security Violates Civil Rights of Muslim American Citizens," *American Civil Liberties Union,* (2006), http://www.aclu.org/safefree/general/17512prs20050420.html (accessed August 20, 2006).

18. National Commission on Terrorism: Countering, *Report of the National Commission on Terrorism, Countering the Threat of International Terrorism* (Washington, DC: National Commission on Terrorism: Countering, 1999), http://www.fas.org/irp/threat/commission.html.

19. Homeland Security Council, *National Strategy for Pandemic Influenza: Implementation Plan* (Washington, DC: Homeland Security Council, 2006).

Further Reading: Department of Homeland Security, *National Response Plan: December 2004* (Washington, DC: Department of Homeland Security, 2004); Fagin, J., *When Terrorism Strikes Home: Defending the United States* (Boston: Allyn and Bacon, 2006); Homeland Security Council, *National Strategy for Pandemic Influenza: Implementation Plan* (Washington, DC: Homeland Security Council, 2006); 9/11 Commission, *The 9/11 Commission Report: Final Report of the National Commission on Terrorist Attacks upon the United States* (New York: Norton, 2004); Patriot Act, Public Law 107–56 (2001); Townsend, Frances, *The Federal Response to Hurricane Katrina: Lessons Learned* (Washington, DC: White House, 2006), http://www.whitehouse.gov/reports/katrina-lessons-learned.pdf.

Everette B. Penn

I

IMMIGRATION AND EMPLOYMENT LAW ENFORCEMENT

INTRODUCTION

Although most people understand the contributions immigrants make to U.S. culture(s) and economy, a much-contended issue is that of illegal immigration and what to do about it. Associated with legal and illegal immigration are the issues of employment, as this is the preferred way for most people to make a living. The controversies come from the lack of consensus on what immigration policies should look like, and these revolve around questions such as: Who should be allowed to immigrate to the United States? How many people should be allowed to immigrate? How can people be prevented from entering the United States illegally, meaning without having obtained legal permission to enter? What should be done when illegal immigrants are found by law enforcement? Are immigrants not responsible for a large number of crimes? Do immigrants not take work away from Americans? Does immigration not increase the likelihood of terrorist attacks on U.S. soil by foreign extremists?

In the past few years, anywhere from close to three-quarters of a million to around 1 million people enter the United States as legal immigrants annually.[1] The numbers went down after the September 11, 2001, attacks, as the responsible terrorists had entered the United States legally, which led to significant changes to the immigration system. According to the U.S. Census Bureau's 2005 American Community Survey,[2] 35.7 million of the close to 289 million people currently living in the United States are immigrants, which represents 12.4 percent of the population, up from 11.2 percent in 2000. Further, from 1990 to 2000, the total population showed a 57 percent increase in the foreign-born population, to 31.1 million, from 19.8 million.[3]

WHERE DO IMMIGRANTS LAND AND SETTLE?

Traditional so-called gateway states for the past immigrants to the United States were California, New York, Texas, Florida, New Jersey, and Illinois.

More recently, newer immigrants have started to settle in states that had customarily seen relatively little of them: Georgia, North Carolina, Massachusetts, Washington, Ohio, South Dakota, Delaware, Missouri, Colorado, New Hampshire, Michigan, Montana, Connecticut, and Nevada.

BACKGROUND

Immigration has always played a very important part in the history of the United States, which is a country of immigrants. It owes its existence to people moving there out of their own free will (early European settlers and more recent immigration) and against their will (enslaved Africans), all of whom contributed greatly to making the United States what it is today.[4] Europeans began settling the area north of the Rio Grande in North America in the 1500s, and the first black people landed (against their will) in English America in 1619.[5] The first U.S. census in 1790 showed close to 4 million people living in the colonies. The largest number of voluntary travelers by far came from England (2 million), followed by Scotland (163,000), Germany (140,000), and Holland (56,000). Almost 700,000 of the total population of the day were slaves from Africa.

Today, estimates of the numerical size of the group of illegal immigrants vary greatly, depending on who generates them. They range from 7 million (Citizenship and Immigration Services, 2003) to 20 million (Bear Stearns Asset Management, 2005) and almost any figure in between: 8.7 million (Census Bureau, 2000), between 11.5 and 12 million (Pew Hispanic Center, March 2006), and between 12 and 15 million (a Tucson, Arizona, Border Patrol union local, 2006).[6] United States immigration officials have said that since 2003, the number of illegal immigrants has grown by as much as 500,000 a year. The annual number of illegal immigrants appears to have exceeded those coming legally for at least the past 10 years (according to Pew Hispanic Center).

A growing problem has been created by the large number of children born in the United States to parents with no legal status. This makes the children automatically U.S. citizens, whereas their parents remain illegal, which makes it very difficult to develop policies for this group of immigrants.[7] Having understood a long time ago the importance of immigration and a system that controls it, the various U.S. administrations have developed and changed policies with the goals of reducing the number of illegal immigrants and regulating the impact legal immigrants have on the domestic labor market. Assessments regarding the success of these policies vary greatly, and late 2006 saw numerous attempts to significantly revamp immigration law.

LEGAL DEVELOPMENTS

The persistent desire of foreigners to start a new life in the United States and the state's need to control exactly who is able to do so made the creation of immigration policy imperative. After a significant period of time without immigration policies, the Immigration Act of 1819, which set standards for vessels bringing immigrants,[8] was the first piece of legislation dealing with immigration. Subsequently, immigration laws have been revamped virtually once a decade.

Following the American Civil War, several states passed immigration laws. The Supreme Court decided in 1875 that the regulation of immigration was a federal responsibility. After immigration increased drastically in 1880, a more general Immigration Act was introduced in 1882, which levied a head tax on immigrants and prevented certain people (e.g., convicts and the mentally ill) from entering the United States. State boards or commissions enforced immigration law with direction from U.S. Treasury Department officials[9] before the Immigration Service was established in 1891.[10] Finally, following a renewed surge in immigration after World War II, a quota system based on the national origin of immigrants was introduced in 1921.[11] This system was revised in 1924, and Congress created the U.S. Border Patrol as an agency within the Immigration Service the same year. Under the modified system, immigration was limited by assigning each nationality a quota based on its representation in the previous U.S. census.

In 1951, a program that had allowed Mexican seasonal labor to work in U.S. agricultural businesses (the Bracero Program, started by California) was turned into a formal agreement between the United States and Mexico. Congress recodified and combined all previous immigration and naturalization law in 1952 into the Immigration and Nationality Act (INA). Along with other immigration laws, treaties, and conventions of the United States, the INA relates to the immigration, temporary admission, naturalization, and removal (deportation) of foreign nationals. The national-origins system remained in place until 1965, when Congress replaced it with a preference system designed to unite immigrant families and attract skilled immigrants to the United States. This was in response to changes in the origins of immigrants that had taken place since the 1920s: The majority of immigrants were no longer from Europe but from Asia and Latin America.

It was also the first time that immigration and employment were linked as the domestic shortage of people with certain skills was attempted to be offset by immigrants who met certain criteria. Although several acts allowed refugees to enter the United States and stay at various times—for example, after World War II, people from communist countries were allowed in, as were other refugees from Europe—a general policy regulating the admission of refugees was only put in place with the Refugee Act of 1980. The act defines a refugee as a person leaving his or her own country because of a "well-founded fear of persecution on account of race, religion, nationality, membership in a particular group, or political opinion."[12]

A significant change to immigration policies was made in 1986, when the Immigration Reform and Control Act was passed; one of the provisions included in the act made it illegal for employers to knowingly hire illegal immigrants. Following this, many modifications to existing laws and introductions of new laws continued to focus on illegal immigration and the employment of undocumented immigrants, as did the reform debate of 2006 and 2007. The Illegal Immigration Reform and Immigrant Responsibility Act of 1996 authorized more border patrol agents along the 2,000-mile United States-Mexico border, created tougher penalties for smuggling people and creating forged documents, and created an expedited removal process for immigrants caught with improper documents.

Throughout history, considerations regarding race have always influenced immigration policies, and legislation ranges from having some racist undertones to being blatantly racist.[13] Examples that stand out include the following: the Chinese Exclusion Act of 1882; the Immigration Act of 1907, which limited the number of Japanese immigrants; the National Origins (First Quota) Act of 1921, which favored immigration from Northern European countries at the expense of Southern and Eastern Europeans; and the National Origins (Second Quota) Act of 1924, which continued the discrimination against Southern and Eastern Europeans and imposed new restrictions on Asian immigration. Arguably, provisions in the 2001 Patriot Act discriminate against certain ethnic and religious groups (Middle Easterners and Muslims) because of their alleged connections with terrorist organizations.

TRENDS IN IMMIGRATION

Whereas people from European countries dominated early stages of immigration, this is no longer the case; for some time now, the majority of immigrants have come from Latin America, South America, and Asia.

The phrase *Mexicanization of U.S. immigration* refers to a more than decade-long trend of Mexicans coming to the United States legally and illegally.

Historically, the peak immigration decade was the years between 1901 and 1910, when 8.8 million legal immigrants were admitted to the United States. The 1990s surpassed this, even without taking into account illegal immigrants.

Because immigrants who came to the United States in the mid-twentieth century (after World War II) are now dying off, the percentage of European-born immigrants has dropped by almost 30 percent since 2001.

Data from 2005 show that foreign-born people and their children now make up 60 percent of the population in the most populous city in the United States: New York City. A similar trend can be seen in many of the suburban counties around the city: In 24 of them, 20 percent of the residents are now born abroad.

The three countries of origin from which the majority of immigrants come today are Mexico (approximately 11 million in 2005), China (almost 1.9 million), and India (1.4 million).

KEY EVENTS AND ISSUES

Within the last 100 years, three events stand out that impacted immigration and corresponding legislation in the United States: World War I (1912–18), World War II (1939–45), and the terrorist attacks of September 11, 2001 (9/11). The most recent event led the George W. Bush administration to introduce the USA PATRIOT Act (Patriot Act) the same year, which established the U.S. Department of Homeland Security and made the U.S. Department of Citizenship and Immigration Services (CIS) a bureau within it (CIS has an Office of Immigration Statistics, which collects data to discern immigration trends and inform policy formulation).

Further, Title 8 of the Code of Federal Regulations (CFR)[14] was amended in 2002 and 2003. The Immigration and Naturalization Service (INS), which was in charge of immigration and enforcement of immigration law for so long as part of the U.S. Department of Justice, does not exist anymore. Aside from the creation of the CIS within the large bureaucratic structure of the Department of Homeland Security, some functions have been streamlined. For example, whereas the U.S. Department of Customs and Immigration and the INS used to be in charge of related tasks, U.S. Immigration and Customs Enforcement (ICE, also a part of Homeland Security) was carved out of the old Customs Department and now focuses exclusively on these issues, such as the arrest and removal of a foreign national who, in governmental language, is called an alien. The formal removal of an alien from the United States was called deportation before the Illegal Immigration Reform and Immigrant Responsibility Act of 1996 and has to be ordered by an immigration judge after it has been determined that immigration laws have been violated. The Department of Immigration and Customs Enforcement can execute a removal without any punishment being imposed or contemplated.[15]

Foreign nationals entering the United States generally fall into one of three categories: lawful permanent residents (LPRs), nonimmigrants, and undocumented migrants (illegal immigrants). Documents have to be issued by U.S. immigration authorities for individuals in the first category, also referred to as a permanent resident alien, resident alien permit holder, and green card holder. A noncitizen of the United States can fall into this category upon arrival by either having obtained the document through the more common and often lengthy application process or by having won it in the "green card lottery," which makes a certain number available every year. These documents are also referred to as immigrant-visas because the holder is allowed to reside and work in the United States without restrictions under legally recognized and lawfully recorded permanent residence as an immigrant. The Immigration Act of 1990 set the flexible numerical limit of individuals falling into this category at 675,000 annually. Exempt from these limits are several categories of people, including immediate relatives of U.S. citizens, refugees, and asylum seekers.

Nonimmigrants may or may not require permission to enter (visa), depending on their purpose for entering the country (work, business, study, travel) and nationality. In general, tourists and business travelers from most Western countries do not have to apply for a visa at a U.S. embassy or consulate general in their country of citizenship, although this is always subject to change (as was done after 9/11). Those who plan to stay in the United States temporarily to study or work need to apply for authorization to do so prior to their arrival. It is not guaranteed that such an application, which often takes six months or more, will be approved or processed in time. For example, improved security measures, increased background checks of applicants, and prolonged processing times after 9/11 significantly lengthened the process.

U.S. employers wanting to employ a foreign national on the basis of his or her job skills in a position for which qualified authorized workers are unavailable in the United States must obtain labor certification. This is one of many instances in which the U.S. Department of Labor is involved with matters pertaining to foreign nationals. Labor certification is issued by the secretary of labor and contains attestations by U.S. employers as to the number of U.S. workers available to undertake the employment sought by an applicant and the effect of the alien's employment on the wages and working conditions of U.S. workers similarly employed. Determination of labor availability in the United States is made at the time of a visa application and at the location where the applicant wishes to work.

There are literally dozens of nonimmigrant visa classifications, including the following, which are among the most common. Students who want to study at U.S. colleges and universities are issued F-1 visas; those participating in cultural exchange programs (including academics and researchers from abroad) get J visas, which generally cannot be renewed; temporary workers with specialized knowledge and skills (including academics and researchers from abroad) get H and other visas. For professionals from Canada or Mexico, there is the TN category under North American Free Trade Agreement (NAFTA) regulations.

Each year, Congress decides how many visas are issued in each category. Although holders of different types of H and other visas play an increasing role in the U.S. economy, significantly fewer have been authorized in recent years despite high demand by U.S. employers. The annual cap is typically reached within the first few months of the fiscal year. For example, for fiscal year 2005, the cap of 65,000 (in fiscal years 2001 to 2003, it was 195,000) was reached on the first day of the fiscal year.

Further, it is standard practice that J visas are associated with a particular educational institution, just as TN and H visas are tied to a particular employer. If the student wants to change universities or the worker his or her employer, a new document must be issued. The length of time that these visas are valid varies, and an application for renewal must be filed with immigration authorities before they expire. Otherwise, he or she loses eligibility to do what the document authorized them to do upon expiration and a new document must be applied for at a U.S. embassy or consulate general in their country of citizenship. Upon expiration of the visa, the immigrant student or worker cannot legally study or work in the United States and generally can remain in the United States no longer than six months.

People falling in the last category, that of undocumented migrants, are commonly referred to as illegal immigrants, which means they entered the country without proper documents and without authorization and knowledge of U.S. immigration authorities. Enforcement of immigration and employment law focuses on this group. They cross the border at unsecured locations, such as forests and rivers, or between inspection points (official border crossings) or pass inspection with forged documents or hidden in vehicles. The majority of illegal immigrants come from Mexico and other Latin, Central, and South American countries in the hopes of finding work and a better economic future.

Although not discussed very often, a large number of undocumented migrants, especially from Mexico, are leaving the United States each year (counterflow). For example, INS data show that, in the 1990s, around half as many people who entered the United States unauthorized every year left it again.[16] In fact, many unauthorized Mexicans do not want to immigrate permanently; they want to get a job, make some money (unemployment and poverty rates are very high in Mexico), and return home to their families. Smaller numbers of illegal immigrants cross the United States-Canada border or the ocean.

Many people who try to enter the United States without authorization (e.g., their applications were rejected because they did not meet certain criteria, they thought they would be rejected, or they never applied for whatever reason) risk their lives. For example, from 1998 through 2002, more than 1,500 illegal immigrants died trying to cross into the United States, mostly of exhaustion and exposure. Another risk when trying to cross the border alone is that of getting caught by the U.S. Border Patrol, whose job is to stop illegal immigration. If that happens, they are generally not detained or charged but sent back across the border. To lower these risks, many pay lots of money for the services of guides, called coyotes, organized in bands that make millions of dollars each year. The guides may accompany them to a location where the border is not secured properly or smuggle them across the border. Being smuggled in the back of a truck or in a container, however, is risky, too, as occupants may suffocate or die from heat exhaustion or lack of water.

Once on U.S. soil, they try to find a job and accommodation and become the responsibility of Department of Immigration and Customs Enforcement, who try to find them and, if successful, take them back across the border; undocumented migrants are generally not charged. With access to the right networks, finding a job can be relatively easy. Further, many employers prefer hiring illegal immigrants because it increases their profit margin. Although the employers can charge the same for their products or services, they can pay the migrants less. Industries that hire a large number of undocumented workers include service industries, natural resources, and construction.[17] The Immigration Reform and Control Act of 1986 included a provision for employer sanctions if employers hired, recruited, or referred for a fee aliens known to be unauthorized to work in the United States. Violators of the law are subject to a series of civil fines for violations or criminal penalties when there is a pattern or practice of violations (historically, the latter was hardly established).

Although the Department of Labor is in charge of enforcing labor-related laws and regulations, such as the Fair Labor Standards Act, which, among other things, provides minimum wage and overtime protections and thus also protects illegal workers,[18] enforcing immigration laws is out of its jurisdiction. For better or worse, historically, the cooperation between the agencies that enforce immigration laws, on the one hand, and employment laws, on the other, has been less than stellar. Despite the provisions of the 1986 law, employers of illegal immigrants were not at the center of enforcement activities for a long time, although increasing attention was paid to the issue in the 1990s.

For example, in 1999, 417 civil fine notices were issued to employers. During the first years of the George W. Bush administration, less attention was paid to employers, and only three civil fine notices were issued in 2003. In 2002, one year before Immigration and Customs Enforcement (ICE) was created within the Department of Homeland Security (DHS), 25 criminal charges were brought against employers. Following bipartisan pressure on the administration in spring 2006, DHS Secretary Michael Chertoff announced a campaign that promised to focus on employers suspected of hiring illegal workers and included more serious sanctions than previously, such as felony charges, huge financial penalties, and the seizing of assets. The more aggressive enforcement of immigration and employment laws by ICE led to 445 criminal arrests of employers within the first seven months of 2006 and to the deportation of the majority of 2,700 illegal immigrants who worked in these operations.[19]

DID YOU KNOW?

Stars or celebrities who are not U.S. citizens but want to get paid for activities they undertake in the United States must get a visa, too. This includes performers and entertainers in every category, such as professional athletes, musicians, actors, magicians, and so on.

A few of the countless famous examples include Wayne Gretzky, Mario Lemieux, Patrick Roy, Michael J. Fox, Donald Sutherland, and Neil Young (from Canada); Siegfried and Roy, Dirk Nowitzki (from Germany); Elton John, the Rolling Stones (from England); and Gérard Depardieu (France; he starred in the movie *Green Card*).

In these cases, the potential for efficiency of the bureaucratic apparatus becomes obvious as many of their applications are processed and proper documents issued within a very short period of time. For example, when a non-U.S. National Hockey League player gets traded from the Toronto Maple Leafs to the New York Rangers, he may be able to play within two days of the trade.

FUTURE PROSPECTS

With anti-immigrant sentiments on the rise between 2000 and 2006, the percentage of people polled who felt that immigrants are a burden because they take jobs and housing grew from 38 percent to 52 percent. Similarly, the percentage of those who felt that immigrants strengthen the United States with their hard work and talents dropped from 50 percent to 41 percent. Into the foreseeable future, at last three controversial debates will continue.

First, several commentators and officials, for example, in Texas, California, and Arizona, have suggested that there is an immigration crisis. Although responsible analyses show that this is not the case, the fact remains that a significant number of immigrants come to and live in the United States illegally. This creates several problems, including an increased likelihood for members in this group to be economically exploited (work for less than minimum wage, do not get paid overtime or do not get paid at all, work in dangerous and labor-law-violating environments, etc.) and to be at higher risk for criminal victimization (particularly violence against women) as perpetrators know that they are not likely to report their victimization to representatives of the state.[20]

The number of undocumented immigrants in the United States alone should be reason enough to undertake a comprehensive reform of U.S. immigration policies, regardless of whether the argument is the policies' lack of effectiveness or a humanitarian one that emphasizes the human, civil, and constitutional rights of unauthorized workers and immigrants in general. The two proposals for reform, one from the Senate and one from the House of Representatives, that were discussed in fall 2006 are far from being passed.

A second important and equally controversial issue relates to legislative changes made after 9/11—the Patriot Act—and their implications for current and prospective immigrants as well as other non-U.S. citizens living in the United States. The Patriot Act of 2001 and the affiliated Enhanced Border Security and Visa Entry Reform Act of 2002 allow for the detention of foreign nationals for up to seven days while law enforcement officials decide whether to file criminal or immigration charges.

In addition, visa screening, border inspections, and the tracking of foreigners has been tightened.[21] For example, it requires non-U.S. citizens, including those residing in the United States temporarily (and legally), to provide border inspectors digital fingerprints and a digital photo, which are taken by the inspector upon entry into the United States. Further, temporary legal residents have to obtain a bar-coded printout when leaving the United States, which they have to turn in when returning to the United States. Prior to this change, immigration authorities had no record of an alien who left the country.

Finally, another controversy ensues over the implementation of the National Security Entry-Exit Registration System (NSEERS), which requires all foreigners from countries with alleged ties to terrorist organizations to register with the government. In December 2002, this led to the detention without bond of thousands of immigrants from Iraq, Iran, and several other countries, although there was no evidence that the individuals had been involved in any terrorist or other criminal activity.[22] Although the situation has improved somewhat in recent years, it is clear that many of the legislative changes are to stay, and critics wonder if immigration restrictions associated with the so-called War on Terror are yet another, and more subtle, way to discriminate against potential immigrants from particular backgrounds.

Little disagreement exists that immigration policies should play an important part in efforts to keep the United States and its residents safe, as is the case with the associated need to know where foreigners are and what they do and to ensure that they engage in legal employment. The problem is, however, to find a way to achieve that which is agreeable to the majority, if not all.

See Also: Antiterrorism Laws; International Humanitarian Law Enforcement; Foreign Intelligence Surveillance Act; Homeland Security; Patriot Act.

Endnotes

1. MPI Staff and Kevin Jernegan, "A New Century: Immigration and the U.S.," *Migration Policy Institute* (Migration Information Source), 2005, http://www.migrationinformation.org/Profiles/display.cfm?ID = 283.
2. The American Community Survey counts only households, not residents in institutions, such as universities or prisons.
3. Rick Lyman, "Census Shows Growth of Immigrants," *The New York Times Online,* August 15, 2006, http://www.nytimes.com/2006/08/15/us/15census.html?ex=1313294400&en=faeaaa9792c67f0c&ei=5088&partner=rssnyt&emc=rss.
4. Howard Zinn, *A People's History of the United States: 1492–Present* (New York: Harper-Collins, 2003).
5. Carlton Martz, Marshall Croddy, and Bill Hayes, *Current Issues of Immigration, 2006* (Washington, DC: Constitutional Rights Foundation, 2006).
6. Brad Knickerbocker, "Illegal Immigrants in the U.S.: How Many Are There?" *Christian Science Monitor Online,* May 16, 2006, http://www.csmonitor.com/2006/0516/p01s02-ussc.html.
7. Ibid.
8. Martz et al., *Current Issues of Immigration.*
9. Marian Smith, "Overview of INS History," *U.S. Citizenship and Immigration Services Online* (1998), http://149.101.23.2/graphics/aboutus/history/articles/oview.htm.
10. Center for Immigration Studies, *History,* (n.d.), http://cis.org/topics/history.html.
11. Martz et al., *Current Issues of Immigration.*
12. Ibid, 18.
13. Howard Zinn, *A People's History of the United States;* and Diana Vellos, "Immigrant Latina Domestic Workers and Sexual Harassment," *American University Journal of Gender and the Law* 407 (1997): 407–32.
14. The U.S. Code and the Code of Federal Regulations codify federal laws, including those that deal with immigration (Title 8 in both documents).
15. U.S. Department of Citizenship and Immigration Services Home Page, http://www.uscis.gov.
16. Martz et al., *Current Issues of Immigration.*
17. National Employment Law Project, "Immigrant Worker Project," (n.d.) http://www.nelp.org/iwp/index.cfm..
18. Ibid. See also the home page of the U.S. Department of Labor, Bureau of Labor Statistics, http://www.bls.gov.
19. Julia Preston, "U.S. Puts Onus on Employers of Immigrants," *The New York Times,* sec A1, July 31, 2006, http://www.nytimes.com.
20. National Employment Law Project, "Immigrant Worker Project," (n.d.) http://www.nelp.org/iwp/index.cfm.
21. MPI Staff and Jernegan, "A New Century."
22. Christine Flowers, "The Difficulties Immigrants Face in the Post-9/11 World: How the War on Terrorism Has Changed Their Legal Status," *FindLaw's Writ: Legal News and Commentary,* May 1, 2003, http://writ.news.findlaw.com/commentary/20030501_flowers.html.

Further Reading: Becker, Cynthia S., *Immigration and Illegal Aliens 2005: Burden or Blessing?* (Florence, KY: Thomson Gale, 2005); Daniels, Roger, *Coming to America: A History of Immigration and Ethnicity in American Life* (New York: Harper Perennial, 2002); Grieco, Elizabeth, *Estimates of the Nonimmigrant Population in the United States: 2004* (Washington, DC: U.S. Department of Homeland Security, Office of Immigration Statistics Policy Directorate, 2006); Larsen, Luke J., *The Foreign-Born Population in the United States: 2003,* Current Population Reports P20–551 (Washington, DC: U.S. Census Bureau, 2004); Zinn, Howard, *A People's History of the United States: 1492–Present* (New York: HarperCollins, 2003).

E. Andreas Tomaszewski

INDIGENT DEFENDANT REPRESENTATION

INTRODUCTION

With the issue of representing indigent defendants now settled, the current controversies revolve around when it is appropriate for this right to be executed. For instance, when does the right attach itself in the state's intervention into a person's life as law enforcement attempts to find culpability for a criminal offense or whether there is an appropriate time when the right to counsel may be waived by an accused indigent? Answers to these questions affect the lives of most persons accused of a criminal offense in the United States. For example, in 1998, two-thirds of federal felony defendants could not afford to retain their own counsel, and in 75 of the most populace counties in the United States the figure was 82 percent.[1] Other arguments have to do with such issues as what is the best way to provide legal services for the indigent or what level of poverty qualifies one for assigned counsel? Finally, are we reaching those indigents who reside outside of the most populous areas in the country?

BACKGROUND

The Sixth Amendment to the United States Constitution provides that "[I]n all criminal prosecutions, the accused shall enjoy the right to … have the Assistance of Counsel for his defense." Even earlier than that, Benjamin Austin argued at the Constitutional Conventions, "As we have an Attorney General who acts in behalf of the State, it is proposed that the Legislature appoint another person (with a fixed salary) as Advocate General for all persons arraigned in criminal prosecutions; whose business should be to appear in behalf of all persons indicted by the State's Attorney."[2] The idea, however, remained dormant for the next one hundred years.

In 1896, however, bills were introduced in 12 state legislatures to establish public defender officers. By 1917, pubic defender bills had been introduced in 20 states. By 1926, there were 12 working pubic defender offices, and by 1933 at least 21 offices were up and running in the United States.[3] This right was pretty much a hollow one until the middle of the twentieth century, however, as most defendants charged with a crime were too poor, as is still the case today, to hire

PUBLIC DEFENDER

The idea of a public defender is actually quite old. Such a system existed in ancient Rome. Later, the ecclesiastical courts of the Middle Ages provided an office of advocate for the poor and an office of the procurator of charity. Both offices were honorable positions, as these courts recognized the needs of accused persons in matters of legal representation. As early as the fifteenth century, Spain has had an officer corresponding to a public defender. And in 1889, Belgium began a policy of public defense. By the turn of the twentieth century, the laws of the following countries provided an office of defenders: Argentina, Belgium, Denmark, England, France, Germany, Hungary, and Mexico. By 1993, in the United States, the following states had adopted public defender systems: California, Connecticut, Illinois, Indiana, Minnesota, Nebraska, Ohio, Tennessee, and Virginia.*

---

*Gregg Barak, *In Defense of Whom? A Critique of Criminal Justice Reform* (Cincinnati, OH: Anderson, 1980).

---

a lawyer on their own. Indeed, the National Legal Aid and Defender Association reports on their Web site that, until the middle of the twentieth century, most criminal defense lawyers worked on a pro bono basis after being appointed by the individual trial judges, even in capital cases, and although there were a few programs to provide representation (i.e. The New York City Legal Aid Society starting in 1896 and the Los Angeles, California, Public Defender in 1914), such services were limited to the largest cities in the country.

LEGAL DEVELOPMENTS

In 1932, the U.S. Supreme Court began a many-year process to change the law to require the appointment of counsel to indigents, first in state capita cases *(Powell v. Alabama)* and then, six years later, to all federal prosecutions *(Johnson v. Zerbst)*. When faced with the question of requiring counsel for indigents in state noncapital cases in 1943, however, it refused to do so *(Betts v. Brady)*. It was not until 1963 in *Gideon v. Wainwright* that the right was extended to state felony cases, and, in 1972 *(Argesinger v Hamlin)*, the Supreme Court held there was a right to assigned counsel for an indigent in any type of criminal proceeding in which there was a possibility of incarceration. In 1961, the right was extended to pretrial situations at the very beginning of the judicial process *(Hamilton v. Alabama)* and even before, in postarrest interrogations *(Miranda v. Arizona,* 1966) and lineups *(United States v. Wade,* 1967) as well as after conviction on appeals *(Douglas v. California,* 1963).

With the issue of an indigent's right to assigned counsel settled, there now is a vast and continually developing body of law, both federal and state, setting forth the parameters of exactly when the right to counsel attaches and whether and when it can be waived.

Counsel can be waived at any stage of the proceedings; however, the right to counsel attaches at the time of arraignment and even before if the police intend to conduct an interrogation or a lineup. The developing body of law primarily focuses on the factual circumstances surrounding whether there was a valid waiver or not. The controversy revolves around the facts. Did what happen amount to a waiver or not? Did the questioning start before the *Miranda* warnings; did they precede the questioning, or did they come afterward? Was the person in custody so as to require warnings?

A prime example would be as follows: In a case, a detective asks a defendant in custody if he wants to tell his side of the story. The defendant says "yes," and before any *Miranda* warnings are given, the defendant starts to incriminate himself, at which point the officer finally gives *Miranda* warnings. The question is whether what took place before the warnings were given was substantive in nature or even whether it was a question to ask at all. There is no such thing as a little bit of questioning; you either are questioned or are not, and this is where controversy lies.

INDIGENT DEFENSE SERVICES

To implement the now-required delivery of indigent criminal defense services, several different programs have developed within most localities. They presumably handle conflicts (i.e., multiple defendants or conflicting loyalties such as prior representation of the victim now accusing the defendant), keep costs down, or provide work for private lawyers.

One method of delivery is with a public defender who is a government official either appointed (i.e., New York) or elected (i.e., Florida) in a particular locality who, along with his or her staff of lawyers, investigators, and so forth, provides representation to the indigent with a government budget line usually much lower than the district attorney. In some localities, such as New York City and its neighboring counties of Nassau and Suffolk, private and separate legal aid societies contract with the local government to provide the major representation in the same manner and structure as a public defender.

Service delivery may also be made with an assigned counsel panel of private lawyers who have agreed to provide representation, as selected, for a previously agreed and usually hourly fee set by a governmental body. The fee usually paid to the assigned counsel is much lower than the normal fee for the service. Indeed, in New York State, the hourly fee was raised to $75.00 in 2003, having been at $40 per hour since 1985. Another option to provide the required legal services is through a contract with one or more lawyers to handle a specific number of cases for a set fee.

Determination of indigence varies by locality and is usually done by the court making the assignment, the agency or lawyer to be assigned, or by some screening agency that is set up for that purpose or is a part of some other branch of the executive department of the locality.

According to the Bureau of Justice Statistics, among the 100 most populous counties in the United States in 1999, public defender programs operated in 90 counties, assigned counsel in 89, and had contract programs in 42, with a total expenditure of $1.2 billion, which is only about 3 percent of all criminal justice monies spent for police, judicial services, and corrections in those counties, with the figure being further broken down to 73 percent to public defenders, 21 percent to assigned counsel, and 6 percent to contract lawyers.[4] This cost, however, is mostly a local one, with county governments in the 100 most populous counties picking up 60 percent of the tab, although in some states such as New York it is a completely local cost.

As for caseload, the same statistics indicate that indigent defense programs with some 6,300 assistant public defenders and more than 30,000 private lawyers handled more than 4 million cases in 1999, with 82 percent going to public defenders, 15 percent to private assigned lawyers, and 3 percent to contract attorneys.[5]

As for outcome, the often-repeated statement that less experienced and lower paid publicly financed lawyers do not provide the same quality of representation as private lawyers is belied by the statistics, which show that the conviction rate in 1999 was about the same regardless of whether the lawyer was retained or assigned. Of those found guilty, however, those represented by assigned lawyers had a higher incarceration rate, although this may be due to the nature of the distribution of types of offenses between retained and public counsel. In terms of length of incarceration, however, those defendants with publicly financed lawyers averaged lesser sentences than those with retained counsel.

FUTURE PROSPECTS

Although it seems clear that the mandate of the Supreme Court to provide counsel to the indigent charged with crime has generally been met, the statistics quoted are really an average for the largest metropolitan areas of the country. They do not take into account the individual case in which the representation fails to meet the standards of a reasonably competent lawyer who has prepared the facts and law of his or her case regardless of whether he or she is assigned or retained and that the quality of representation outside the 100 most populous counties in the country may not be at the same level.

It is also clear that there is no large constituency anywhere in the United States, now or in the past, demanding more and better representation for the indigent charged with crime, and if it were not for the change in law by the Supreme Court starting in 1932, it is doubtful if any but a handful of jurisdictions would have provided representation to those charged with crime who could not afford to hire a lawyer on their own.

See Also: Adversarial Justice; Alternative Responses to Crime by Society; Bail; Prosecutorial Discretion; Trial Consultation.

Endnotes

1. United States Department of Justice, Bureau of Justice Statistics, "Indigent Defense Statistics" (Washington, D.C: GPO, October 1, 2001).
2. Quoted in Reginald H. Smith and John S. Bradway, *Growth of Legal-Aid Work in the United States,* Bulletin No. 607 (Washington, DC: U.S. Government Printing Office, Department of Labor, 1936), 53.

3. Gregg Barak, *In Defense of Whom? A Critique of Criminal Justice Reform* (Cincinnati, OH: Anderson, 1980).

4. United States Department of Justice, Bureau of Justice Statistics, "Indigent Defense Statistics."

5. Ibid.

Further Reading: Braswell, M.C., B.R. McCarthy, and B.J. McCarthy, *Justice, Crime and Ethics* (Cincinnati, OH: Anderson, 1998); Grisham, J., *The Innocent Man: Murder and Injustice in a Small Town* (New York: Doubleday, 2006); Muraskin, R., and M. Muraskin, *Morality and the Law* (Upper Saddle River, NJ: Prentice Hall, 2001); Muraskin, R., and A. Roberts, *Visions for Change: Crime and Justice in the 21st Century* (Upper Saddle River, NJ: Prentice Hall, 2005); Robinson, M.B., *Justice Blind? Ideals and Realities of American Criminal Justice* (Upper Saddle River, NJ: Prentice Hall, 2002).

Roslyn Muraskin and Matthew Muraskin

INTERNATIONAL CRIMINAL COURT

INTRODUCTION

The International Criminal Court (ICC) has been heralded as the most significant development in the international legal order. The Court is the first permanent international tool to address the most heinous international crimes. Critics of the Court maintain that such an institution threatens state sovereignty and advocate further limitations of the Court's jurisdiction. Proponents of the institution view the Court as a potential deterrent and as a tool to empower and provide legal proceedings to victims of the gravest breaches of international law.

On July 1, 2002, the International Criminal Court became a reality with more than one hundred twenty nation-states attending the final convention of the Rome Statute. The Rome Statute required 60 states to become signatories by December 31, 2000 (Article 126), for the statute to enter force. That goal was far exceeded with 139 state signatories at the closing date. The endorsement of the Rome Statute requires states to be signatories and ratified members. The ratification of a state's signature varies with each state's domestic legal system. For example, the United States would need the approval of the Senate for the international signature to be ratified. Support of the ICC stands to become stronger as the 139 states that have endorsed the Rome Statue with their signature become ratified members; as of March 2006, 100 states have become ratified members in accordance with their domestic legal systems. A few states have failed to become signatories due to domestic strife but are willing to participate in the ICC, such as Kazakhstan, Indonesia, and Malaysia. Other states are adamantly opposed to the ICC, such as the Libyan Arab Jamchiriya, India, Pakistan, Saudi Arabia, Turkey, Iraq, and Myanmar.[1]

LEGAL PATHWAYS TO INTERNATIONAL JUSTICE

There are three general approaches to international justice:

1. Enforcement through a state's domestic laws.
2. Enforcement through international criminal courts.
3. Seeking justice through truth commissions.

BACKGROUND

The idea of an international court to adjudicate disputes over international law is not a new idea. Throughout the late nineteenth and twentieth centuries, the idea had been pursued and explored within the international arena. One of the founders and acting president of the International Committee of the Red Cross, Gustave Moynier, was the first to formally propose an international criminal court in 1872. The Franco-Prussian War was plagued by mass atrocities committed by both sides, despite obligations under the First Geneva Convention of 1864. Moynier, distraught at the violations of international treaties, proposed an international criminal court to try persons accused of war crimes. The proposed international court never received any support from international lawyers or state parties. The concept of an international criminal court was not revisited again until after World War I; the framers of the 1919 Treaty of Versailles revived the vision of an international criminal court to try the Kaiser and German war criminals.[2] The call for an international criminal court was compromised, however; punishment for war crimes was to be handled by existing national military tribunals. The failure of the proposed court resulted in trials held in Leipzig, where 888 of the 901 persons accused of war crimes were acquitted, released, or not tried.[3]

In 1937, the League of Nations attempted to establish an international criminal court. Two international conventions were concluded in Geneva, Switzerland, on November 16: the Prevention and Repression of Terrorism and the Creation of an International Criminal Court (League of Nations Document Archived C.547.m.384, 1937). The charter for the creation of an international criminal court required the ratification of the Prevention and Repression of Terrorism Treaty. Neither convention obtained sufficient support for ratification.

World War II postponed any collective interest in an international criminal court. As the war was coming to an end, however, the allied powers directed their attention to the creation of an international institution to try individuals for the most heinous crimes of war. The need for and call to international justice resonated throughout the world. Some had hopes that with the end of the League of Nations and the development of the United Nations (UN), the world was a step closer to instituting a permanent criminal court. The outcome was not an international criminal court, however, but international military tribunals instituted to address crimes against humanity. Nonetheless, this collective drive produced the Nuremberg Principles, which would sit as the foundation of future international law directed at war crime and crimes against humanity. But the hope of a permanent international criminal court was again discouraged.

Although efforts to establish an international criminal court continued over the next several decades by institutional reformers and civil society actors, it was not until 1989 that the international society began to seriously reconsider the establishment of an international criminal court.[4] In 1989, Trinidad and Tobago approached the UN with a proposal for an international criminal court as a device to address drug trafficking and terrorism.[5] Contemporaneously, the International Institute of Higher Studies in Criminal Sciences, in conjunction with the UN, prepared a draft statute that would create an international criminal court with jurisdiction over all international crimes. This draft was submitted to the Eighth United Nations Congress on Crime Prevention and Treatment of Offenders in 1990, recommending that the International Law Commission (ILC) consider the draft.[6] The ILC completed its report, which the UN General Assembly had assigned them in 1989, and submitted it to the 45th session of the General Assembly. The report did not limit the concept of a court to drug trafficking but was expanded to include a more universal criminal court that would cover other forms of international crimes. Although there were tensions and states that would strongly resist this court, an overwhelming number of nation-states appeared ready for the concept and reality of an international criminal court.

The following nine years proved to be challenging as the General Assembly of the UN, preparatory committees, and nongovernmental agencies worked on a proposal for an international criminal court: the Rome Statute. During this time, state representatives, international lawyers, and nongovernmental organizations prepared many drafts stating their preferences for what role the court should play and what crimes would fall within the court's jurisdiction. Ultimately, many compromises had to be made. On July18, 1998, a final vote on the Final Act of the Diplomatic Conference was taken: 120 delegations voted in favor of the Rome Statute, 7 voted against, and 21 abstained. The final vote represented the end of years of efforts to establish a statute for an international criminal court. As a result, the Rome Statute was officially opened for state signatures on July 18, 1998.

KEY EVENTS

During the process of negotiations, significant conflicts occurred over issues of the Court's jurisdiction and its ability to exercise that jurisdiction.[7] States held incompatible views regarding the role of the Court. Many states supported universal jurisdiction of the Court, ensuring a universal justice, whereas other states (mainly the United States) insisted that the acceptance of the ICC's jurisdiction by states was a necessary precondition to jurisdiction. These two positions were heavily debated and resulted in a compromise that was not fully satisfactory to either of the conflicting forces: the like-minded states (LMS), which wanted universal jurisdiction, and the United States (the main challenger), which wanted a system based on compliance at will.

Although there was a general consensus that crimes of genocide, war crimes, and crimes against humanity should be covered by the court's jurisdiction, there were conflicts over the scope of crimes covered under war crimes, crimes against humanity, and the definition for crimes of aggression. Despite the fact that precedence had been set for the definition of aggressive crimes during the International Military Tribunal of the Nuremberg defendants after World War II and in the General Assembly Resolution 3314 of December 1974 (passed with a consensus for the definition of aggression), it remained an irresolvable issue for the committee meeting members.

Crimes of aggression were not the only controversial crime debated during the conference. For example, U.S. delegates insisted that the Court's jurisdiction should only occur if a state was signatory when war crimes were committed on a large scale.[8] This would mean that war crimes would essentially also have to be crimes against humanity before the Court could interject its jurisdiction. The United States was triumphant in this debate, and the condition of jurisdiction over war crimes was included in Article 8 (1) as a part of Part 2 Jurisdiction, Admissibility and Applicable Law. Article 8 (1) states, "the Court shall have jurisdiction in respect of war crimes in particular when committed as part of a plan or policy or as part of a large-scale commission of such crimes." It is this insistence of a large scale of the crime in question that the prosecutor cited as to why the Court will take no case related to the coalition occupation of Iraq, as the verified cases of willful killing and mistreatment number in the double digits, whereas the number of victims, for example in the Democratic Republic of Congo, number in the thousands if not tens of thousands.

In summary, during the process of negotiations of the plenipotentiaries meeting, no one state (including the United States) was a monolithic obstacle. The proceedings were divided rather conspicuously between those like-minded states—more than sixty states, headed by Canada, Australia, and the United Kingdom—who wanted universal jurisdiction, expanded definition of war crimes, an empowered prosecutor, and the exclusion of the Security Council in the court's decision, versus the non-like-minded states, such as the United States, Iraq, Qatar, and China. One of the major concessions made with the insistence of the United States was the inclusion of a complementary court. This ensured that the concept of universality would be diminished by the recognition of the primacy of domestic courts. Another major compromise made at the insistence of the United States was the need for a state to be a signatory. This ensured state willingness to participate in the court versus a court empowered under a universal system of international law governing all of international society.[9]

STRUCTURE

The ICC consists of 100 states forming the Assembly of States Parties (ASP) to the Rome Statue. The Assembly of States Parties is the management oversight and legislative body of the ICC. It is composed of representatives of the states that have ratified and acceded to the Rome Statute. The ASP has a main bureau, consisting of a president, 2 vice presidents, and 18 elected members for a three-year term. The ASP's role is to decide on items such as the adoption of normative texts, the budget, and the election of the judges, the prosecutor, and the deputy prosecutor(s). According to Article 112:7 of the Rome Statute, each state party has one vote, though every effort has to be made to reach decisions by consensus both in the ASP and the bureau. If consensus cannot be reached, decisions are taken by vote.

The Court consists of four chambers: (1) the Presidency; (2) Registry; (3) Judicial Court (made up of the Appeals Chamber, Trial Chamber, and a Pre-Trial Chamber); and (4) Office of the Prosecutor. Each of these plays a significant role in the Court's processes.

The Presidency is an elected office with a term of three years, and it holds responsibility for the administrative duties of the Court, excluding the Office of the Prosecutor. The Presidency coordinates and seeks the concurrence of the Office of the Prosecutor on all matters of mutual concern. The president serves a six-year term on the Appeals Court. The first and second vice presidents serve nine-year terms in the Trial Division. The judges composing the Presidency also serve on a full-time basis. The president and first and second vice presidents are to elected by an absolute majority of the 18 judges of the Court.

The Registry is solely responsible for the administrative and nonjudicial aspects of the Court and for creating a Victims and Witness Unit that provides protective and security measures for witnesses, victims, or others at risk due to testimony given to the court. More specifically, the registrar is responsible for the administration of legal aid matters, court management, victims and witness matters, defense counsel, detention unit, finances, translation, and personnel. In relation to victims, the registrar is responsible for providing notice of the case to victims, assisting them in obtaining legal advice and representation, and, if necessary, providing agreements for relocation and support services (Rule 16 of the Rules of Procedure). The registrar is also responsible for receiving, obtaining, and providing information with states and as the main channel of communication between the Court, states, intergovernmental organizations, and nongovernmental organizations. The ASP by an absolute majority elects the registrar.

The functions of the Judicial Court are divided into chambers, which allow the judges to be on more than one chamber if it serves the functioning of the court in a more efficient manner. The Appellate Chamber is exempt from this, as an appellate judge is prohibited from serving on other chambers (Article 39). The judges constitute a forum of international experts that represents the world's principal legal systems. After the election of the judges, the Court organized itself into Appeals, Pre-Trial, and Trial Chambers.

The Office of the Prosecutor is a separate division of the Court with the responsibility for the investigation of referrals on crimes covered by the ICC. The prosecutor has full authority over the administration of the Prosecutorial Division (Article 42, Rome Statute). Cases brought to the ICC are handled independently by this office, unlike the system used by the UN Security Council, where there must be joint agreement to charges brought forth against individuals for crimes covered under international laws and treatises. A state may refer cases to the Office of the Prosecutor, or the prosecutor may initiate the investigation based on information of a crime being committed within the jurisdiction of the Court (Articles 14 and 15, Rome Statute). The prosecutor may start an investigation upon referral of situations in which there is a reasonable basis to believe that crimes covered by the Rome Statute have been or are being committed. Such referrals must be made by a state party or the UN Security Council. In accordance with the Rome Statute and the Rules of Procedure and Evidence, the chief prosecutor must evaluate the material submitted to him before making the decision to proceed. In addition to state party and Security Council referrals, the chief prosecutor may also receive information on crimes within the jurisdiction of the Court provided by other sources, such as individuals or nongovernmental organizations.

The prosecutor then conducts a preliminary examination of the information in every case. If the prosecutor decides not to pursue a case due to lack of credible information or facts he or she must provide prompt notice informing the state or states that referred the situation under Article 14 or the Security Council under Article 13 (b). If the chief prosecutor decides that there is a reasonable basis to proceed with an investigation, he or she will request the Pre-Trial Chamber to authorize such. The prosecutor evaluates the information and investigates to determine whether there is sufficient basis to prosecute. The prosecutor is solely responsible for the retention, storage, and security of all information and physical evidence obtained during the course of investigation (Rule 10, Rules of Procedure and Evidence). If the prosecutor decides to proceed with the investigation, he or she must first obtain authorization from the Pre-Trial Chamber. Formal prosecution then begins once a Pre-Trial Chamber judge issues an arrest warrant or summons for the accused individual to appear before the Court based on the charges filed by the prosecutor.

Once the accused appears, a hearing is held to determine whether sufficient evidence exists to proceed to the trial stage. It is at this point that the domestic states of those individuals may appear to the Court to challenge its jurisdiction or the admissibility of the case based on state primacy to prosecute.

LEGAL DECISIONS

The Office of the Prosecutor, as of February 2005, has accepted three cases with investigations and two referrals. On June 23, 2004, the first case to be investigated and charged by the ICC was initiated against the Democratic Republic of the Congo (DRC). States, international organizations, and nongovernmental organizations have reported thousands of deaths by mass murder, summary executions, a systemic pattern of rape, torture, forced displacement of populations, and the illegal use of child soldiers. All of these crimes fall under the purview of the Court as these acts constitute crimes against humanity on a large scale. The DRC has been closely analyzed and monitored by the Office of the Prosecutor since July 2003, initially with a focus on crimes committed in the Ituri region.[10] In September 2003, the prosecutor informed the states parties that he was ready to request authorization from the Pre-Trial Chamber to use its powers to start the investigation. This case, once brought forward, will occur in Pre-Trial Chamber I under Presiding Judge Claude Jord. In a letter in November 2003, the government of the DRC welcomed the involvement of the ICC and went one step farther in March 2004 by referring their situation in the country to the Court.

The second case brought to the Court's agenda was against the Lord's Resistance Army of Northern Uganda. The chief prosecutor determined that there was a reasonable basis to open an investigation into the situation in Northern Uganda, following the self-referral by Uganda in December 2003. The alleged crimes being committed in the region include conscription or enlisting of children younger than 15 years old into the army, willful killing, rape, sexual slavery, forced pregnancy, and forced displacement of civilians, which may constitute crimes against humanity under the Rome Statute. This case, once

TWO EXAMPLES OF GENOCIDAL WARFARE IN CONTEMPORARY AFRICA

Democratic Republic of the Congo

The Democratic Republic of the Congo (DRC) has devolved into uncontrolled genocidal warfare between ethnically based factions within an unresolved civil war. Unlike some other examples of this phenomenon within Africa, the DRC's conditions have remained unstable due to international involvement on behalf of its neighbors (e.g., Uganda and Rwanda), transnational corporations (e.g., AngloGold Ashanti), and those corporations' Western trading partners (Metalor technologies and the nation of Switzerland). Central within the conflict (and the war crimes and crimes against humanity perpetrated within the conflict) is the control of rich mineral fields of the nation.

Darfur

There has been large-scale destruction of villages throughout the three states of Darfur in western Sudan. In particular, government forces and militias conducted indiscriminate attacks, including killing of civilians, torture, enforced disappearances, destruction of villages, rape and other forms of sexual violence, pillaging, and forced displacement, throughout the region. Additionally, there are 1.65 million internally displaced persons in Darfur and more than 200,000 refugees from Darfur in neighboring Chad. The United Nations Commission of Inquiry stated that the government of Sudan and the Janjaweed are responsible for serious violations of international human rights and humanitarian law, amounting to crimes under international law. Further, these acts were conducted on a widespread and systematic basis and, therefore, may amount to crimes against humanity.

brought forward, will occur within Pre-Trial Chamber II with Presiding Judge Tuiloma Neroni Slade.

On March 31, 2005, the Office of the Prosecutor received its first referral from the UN Security Council on Darfur (Resolution 1593). A document archive from the International Commission of Inquiry on Darfur was also presented to the prosecutor. The Court identified "particularly grave events, involving high numbers of killings, mass rapes and other forms of extremely serious gender violence for full investigation." The case has been assigned to the Pre-Trial Chamber I, where it will be heard following the investigative stage.

On July 1, 2005, the Office of the Prosecutor received a referral concerning the Central African Republic by the government of the Central African Republic. In February 2006, in accordance with the Rome Statute and the Rules of Procedure and Evidence, the prosecutor began to carry out an analysis to determine whether to initiate an investigation or to drop the case. The case remains in the early investigative stages in which the prosecutor is seeking additional information, "including the gravity of alleged crimes, any relevant national proceedings, and the interests of justice."[11]

By early 2006, two cases have been rejected by the Court: the coalition war on and occupation of Iraq and crimes committed in Venezuela. After the prosecutor's review of documents provided to the Court, the decision in each case was that there were not sufficient grounds according to the requirements of the Rome Statute to proceed with charges. These cases can be brought back to the court, however, if the conditions or evidence needed as outlined by the prosecutor can be provided.

FUTURE PROSPECTS

The cases that have been brought to the Court are an optimistic sign that the Court is being seen and utilized as a legitimate and fully capable institution of social control.

RATIFICATION AND IMPLEMENTATION OF ROME STATUE, APRIL 18, 2006

Rome Statute	Agreement on Privileges and Immunities of the International Court (APIC)
Signatures: 139	Signatures: 62
Ratifications: 100	Ratifications: 37

As currently structured and empowered, however, the ICC cannot fulfill its potential or even its stated mission. Specifically, because nations must voluntarily come under the control of the court, the most powerful and potentially criminogenic states can avoid control simply by refusing participation. To avoid this pitfall, the Court must: (1) attain universal jurisdiction, (2) become fully empowered with its own enforcement agency, and (3) add the much-needed definition of crimes of aggression. These modifications may be necessary for the Court to attain a full level of legitimacy as a full-time institution of social control for all states. Moreover, as the world and global capitalistic interests become more intertwined, a fully empowered universal court is necessary to deter and respond to the most heinous crimes against humanity as a whole.[12]

See Also: State Crime Control; Supremacy of International Law to National Law.

Endnotes

1. See also C. W. Mullins, Dave Kauzlarich, and Dawn Rothe, "The International Criminal Court and the Control of State Crime: Problems and Prospects," *Critical Criminology: An International Journal* 12, no. 3 (2004): 285–308.
2. See also A. Cassesse, *The Rome Statute of the International Criminal Court: A Commentary,* vols. 1–3 (New York: Oxford University Press, 2002).
3. See also M. C. Bassiouni, *A Treatise on International Criminal Law,* vol. 1, *Crimes and Punishment* (Springfield, IL: Charles C. Thomas, Bannerstone House, 1973).

4. See also D. Rothe and Christopher W. Mullins, *The International Criminal Court: Symbolic Gestures and the Generation of Global Social Control* (Landham, CO: Lexington Publishers, 2006).

5. See also L. Sadat, *The International Criminal Court and the Transformation of International Law: Justice for the New Millennium* (Ardsley, NY: Transnational, 2002).

6. See also M. C. Bassiouni, *International Criminal Law,* 2nd ed., vol. 1 (Ardsley, NY: Transnational)

7. Cassesse, *The Rome Statute of the International Criminal Court.*

8. Sadat, *The International Criminal Court and the Transformation of International Law.*

9. Rothe and Mullins, *The International Criminal Court.*

10. For a more detailed discussion, ibid.

11. See also International Criminal Court Documents, "Cases and Situations," 2005, http://www.icc-cpi.int/pressrelease details&id=87&1=en.html.

12. Rothe and Mullins, *The International Criminal Court.*

Further Reading: Bassiouni, M. Cherif, *International Criminal Law,* 2nd ed., vol. 1 (Ardsley, NY: Transnational, 1999); Bassiouni, M. Cherif, *The Statute of the International Criminal Court* (Ardsley, NY: Transnational, 1998); Bassiouni, M., and Veda Nanda, *A Treatise on International Criminal Law,* vol. 1, *Crimes and Punishment* (Springfield, IL: Charles C. Thomas, Bannerstone House, 1973); Cassesse, A., *The Rome Statute of the International Criminal Court: A Commentary,* vols. 1–3 (New York: Oxford University Press, 2002); International Criminal Court (2006), http://www.icc-cpi.int/; Rothe, Dawn, and Christopher W. Mullins, *Symbolic Gestures and the Generation of Social Control: The International Criminal Court* (Landham, CO: Lexington, 2006); Sadat, L., *The International Criminal Court and the Transformation of International Law: Justice for the New Millennium* (Ardsley, NY: Transnational, 2002); Sadat, Leila, and S. Richard Carden, "The New International Criminal Court: An Uneasy Revolution," *Georgetown Law Review* 88 (2000): 381–474.

Dawn L. Rothe and Christopher W. Mullins

INTERNATIONAL HUMANITARIAN LAW ENFORCEMENT

INTRODUCTION

Although observers have debated whether the North Atlantic Treaty Organization's (NATO's) bombing campaign against Serbia on behalf of ethnic Albanians in 1999 violated Article 2 (7) of the United Nations (UN) Charter, which stipulates the duty of noninterference of UN nations in the internal affairs of a sovereign country, it represented a historic precedent in the annals of enforcing international humanitarian law. At the same time, observers have also debated whether the bombing campaign was truly actuated by humanitarian motives; a country's immunity under Article 2 (7) to intervention by other nations can be breached on humanitarian grounds, even in the absence of a UN Security Council resolution authorizing military action. This entry discusses the crystallization and functioning of mechanisms, legal and military, by means of which the world community has sought to enforce international humanitarian law.

THE CASE OF KOSOVO

In the early months of 1999, Western governments learned of the massacres of ethnic Albanians in the southern Yugoslavian province of Kosovo, perpetrated by Serbs under orders from the central government in Belgrade. As time passed, it became clear that the Serbs were seeking to ethnically cleanse the province by terrorizing the Albanian population into fleeing Kosovo. In March 1999, a peace conference under United Nations (UN) auspices resulted in the Rambouillet Accords signed by U.S., Albanian, and British delegations, which provided for the insertion of 30,000 North Atlantic Treaty Organization (NATO) troops into Kosovo to administer it as an independent province. One day after Serbia rejected the accords, NATO unleashed bombing sorties against Serbia that lasted from March 24 until June 11, 1999. A UN Security Council resolution under Chapter VII could have provided the international legal basis for the action; however, no such authorization was forthcoming because China and Russia would have vetoed it. Instead, NATO leaders justified the attack as a legitimate response to an international humanitarian emergency (i.e., the Serbian persecution of Kosovar Albanians).

BACKGROUND

The term *international humanitarian law* (IHL) has achieved broad acceptance by the International Committee of the Red Cross (ICRC) and the UN and appears in numerous international instruments (e.g., the statutes of the international tribunals for Yugoslavia and Rwanda and the preamble to the 1997 Ottawa Mines Convention).[1] It is roughly synonymous with the term *laws of war*—the rules applicable to armed conflict, or *jus in bello,* as opposed to those that govern the legitimate recourse to war, or *jus ad bellum.* The focus of the former *(jus in bello)* is on protecting civilians and military members from unnecessary or disproportionate harm. It includes the laws that regulate armed conflict and military occupation as well as the international prohibition of genocide and crimes against humanity.[2]

Although references to so-called universal laws as superior to actually existing laws are well-documented in world history. The idea that individual nations could prosecute and punish citizens of other countries for violations of international law committed outside their own borders remained undeveloped until the twentieth century. Two nineteenth-century exceptions were pirates and combatant war criminals. Pirates could be tried by any country no matter the site of the depredation, the nationality of the accused, or the nationality of the victim because they were regarded as *hostes humani generes* (enemies of humankind), over whom a Damoclean sword of universal jurisdiction was always poised.[3] Inasmuch as the crimes of pirates plagued all countries, every one had both an interest in punishing and a generally recognized right to punish the scourge of piracy. Offenses against the law of nations by combatant war criminals were, like the misdeeds of pirates, justifiable under a theory of universal jurisdiction that ripened with the enactment of several international treaties in the second half of the nineteenth century.[4] The most important of these treaties were the Geneva Convention of 1864, which tried to protect wounded soldiers in the field, and the Hague Conventions of 1899 and 1907, which sought to protect soldiers and civilians from gratuitous injury.

Despite the genuine concern for combatants and noncombatants reflected in them, the preceding conventions set forth neither an enforcement mechanism nor a quantum of punishment for violations of their norms. Further, the conventions could not penetrate the immunity of government leaders for acts that violated the laws of war. Not until the Paris Peace Conference after World War I did the advocates of international justice finally puncture the carapace of sovereign immunity for a former head of state. The tool that bored a hole in the defense was Article 227 of the Versailles Treaty (the peace treaty concluded between Germany and the Allies), which called for the Kaiser's prosecution for crimes of aggression (*jus ad bellum*). Although the Kaiser evaded indictment, a precedent for enforcing international law against national leaders had been established. Moreover, the postwar settlement created two official channels for resolving disputes that might otherwise erupt into armed confrontation. Both were artifacts of the League of Nations. The first, the League Council, grew out of the Covenant of the League of Nations, which renounced resort to war and instead called for arbitration of disputes by the League Council. The second, the permanent Court of International Justice, adjudicated conflicts between nation-states, but only when the defendant state agreed both to recognize the Court's jurisdiction and to comply with its verdicts.[5]

LEGAL DEVELOPMENTS

The erosion of national leaders' invulnerability to criminal indictment under international law peaked in the aftermath of World War II. The London Charter of 1945, which became the legal basis for the Nuremberg International Military Tribunal, affirmed the criminal liability of heads of state for waging aggressive war and committing war crimes and crimes against humanity.[6] (The affirmation of criminal responsibility for heads of state in Article 7 of the London Charter was reiterated in Article 6 of the Tokyo Charter. This notwithstanding, Emperor Hirohito was never prosecuted on charges of crimes against peace.[7]) The manifold crimes of Germany and Japan begot a wave of postwar initiatives to prevent future outrages against IHL. The very raison d'être of the United Nations was the preservation of peace, and, although Article 2(7) of the UN Charter forbade intervention into a state's domestic affairs, the prohibition could be bypassed through Chapter VII, which empowered the UN Security Council to impose sanctions or intervene militarily against a country if "necessary to maintain or restore international peace and security" (Article 42). Breaches of IHL by sovereign nations, then, could invite a plethora of responses from UN member countries, from economic sanctions, demonstrations, and blockades to military attack.[8]

Because the UN's main purpose was to preserve the peace, the only principle the world's great powers were inclined to accept as a legal (rather than moral) duty was to refrain from military aggression against another country (Article 2 (4)). In other words, the member states of the UN accepted the legal duty to comply with *jus ad bellum,* but not necessarily *jus in bello.* This being said, a tension exists within the UN Charter between its express language and the reticence of member states to be bound legally by IHL. The UN Charter, like the subsequent UN Declaration on Human Rights (1948), states that the central purpose of the UN, the maintenance of peace among the world's nations, can best be served, among other things, by promoting human rights (Article 55). Expanding on this commitment, Article 56 provides for "joint and separate action" by UN member countries "for the achievement of the purposes set forth in Article 55." Arguably, then, violations of IHL might be deemed threats to global stability and, hence, actionable by UN member states under both Article 56 and Chapter VII.

UNITED NATIONS CHARTER, ARTICLE 2 (7)

Nothing contained in the present Charter shall authorize the United Nations to intervene in matters which are essentially within the domestic jurisdiction of any state or shall require the Members to submit such matters to settlement under the present Charter; but this principle shall not prejudice the application of enforcement measures under Chapter VII.

As the international legal scholar Geoffrey Robertson has observed, UN member countries did not exercise this power of humanitarian intervention until the Balkan wars of the 1990s. Until that time, major UN military actions—like the 1950 Korean War and the 1991 Persian Gulf War—were essentially efforts to deter aggressive warfare waged by individual countries (regarded as violations of *jus ad bellum*). Where the UN Charter and UN Declaration of Human Rights lacked an effective mechanism for legally enforcing international humanitarian law, however, this could not be said of subsequent UN conventions. The UN Conventions on Genocide (operative in 1951) and Torture (1984) imposed affirmative legal duties on their signatories. The Genocide Convention required them to prosecute in either a domestic or an international court those individuals accused of committing acts that met the convention's definition of genocide. The "right to life" codified in the Genocide Convention is a part of the *jus cogens,* or compelling law, which justifies armed intervention (either under Chapter VII of the UN Charter or on humanitarian grounds). Similarly, the UN Convention on Torture demands that suspected torturers be arrested and either prosecuted or extradited to a country willing to prosecute them. The fact that the prohibitions of genocide and torture share a common classification as peremptory norms under the *jus cogens* means that each offense is subject to universal jurisdiction.

The wanton criminality of the Nazi regime that nourished such postwar instruments as the UN Charter, the UN Declaration of Human Rights, and the UN Convention on Genocide also produced a new round of Geneva Conventions in 1949. The four provisions, which protect injured combatants, prisoners of war, and civilians, obligated the signatory nations to locate persons suspected of grave breaches of the Geneva Conventions and prosecute them, but only if the alleged violations occurred during an international armed conflict. Geoffrey Robertson speculates that states were loath in 1949 to expose themselves and their agents to mandatory criminal liability for suppressing insurgencies and rebellions within their own territories, a concession that would have unacceptably diminished their sovereignty. This restriction of the Geneva Conventions' protections to conventional wars between nation-states was abolished by the verdict of the International Criminal Tribunal for Yugoslavia in the case of Dusko Tadic (1996), but until that time, signatories were generally not obligated to apply the Geneva Conventions to internal conflicts like armed insurrections or civil wars.[9]

According to the Third and Fourth Geneva Convention, so-called protecting powers nominated by each party to an international conflict would be allowed to monitor the treatment of individuals covered by the Conventions' protections. Robertson points out that in the last half-century the protecting powers clause has been honored in the breach; instead, the ICRC has often served the monitoring function (as it recently did in identifying violations of the Geneva Conventions at Guantanamo Bay detainment camp in Cuba), although its confidentiality restrictions have caused the Red Cross to refuse to provide judicial testimony about offenses against humanitarian law.[10]

The weakness of enforcement mechanisms under the 1949 Geneva Conventions likewise afflicts the 1977 Protocols. Designed to reaffirm and elaborate on their 1949 predecessor, the Protocols impose duties on military commanders to educate their troops on the laws of war and to punish violations. Provision is also made for offending states to pay compensation for breaches of the Geneva Conventions and for establishment of an International Fact-finding Commission to investigate charges of grave breaches. As Robertson observes, although numerous offenses against the Geneva Conventions have occurred since 1977, signatories of the Protocols have never assembled such a commission: It remains a chimera of humane but unenforceable idealism.[11]

IMPORTANT POST-NUREMBERG LEGAL DECISIONS: CIVIL REMEDIES AND CRIMINAL PUNISHMENT

Efforts to enforce international humanitarian law in the post-Nuremberg era have assumed two legal forms: civil and criminal. Each has produced a vein of cases pertinent to contemporary enforcement issues.

The philosophy behind civil enforcement is to impose on offenders against humanitarian law the duty to pay compensation to their victims. One of the earliest cases to address the issue of compensation was the verdict by the New York Court of Appeals in the case of *Filártiga v. Peña-Irala* (1981). The family of a young man tortured to death in Paraguay sued the alleged torturer, a former Paraguayan chief of police who had subsequently become a U.S. resident, for civil damages in a U.S. court on the theory that violations of the law of nations were subject to universal jurisdiction (including civil jurisdiction). The New

York Court of Appeals upheld jurisdiction over the defendant, agreeing that a torturer acting under color of law, as an "enemy of the human race," was liable to a civil action sounding in tort for damages under universal jurisdiction.[12] A similar outcome befell the former Philippine dictator Ferdinand Marcos, sued in Hawaii for acts of torture and disappearances carried out by his regime. The federal appeals court brushed aside his claim of sovereign immunity, and he was found liable to his victims to the amount of $150 million. Although the plaintiffs in the class action suit were able to recover some of the money from a Marcos Swiss bank account, the reality is that victims in such cases are rarely compensated; the defendant often flees the country that has awarded the damages (as did the torturer in *Filártiga*).[13]

FILÁRTIGA V. PEÑA-IRALA

[D]eliberate torture perpetrated under color of official authority violates universally accepted norms of the international law of human rights, regardless of the nationality of the parties.... [A]mong the rights universally proclaimed by all nations is the right to be free of torture. Indeed, for the purposes of civil liability, the torturer has become—like the pirate and slave trader before him—*hostis humanis generis*, an enemy of all mankind.

It is important to grasp that the apportionment of damages in *Filártiga* and the Marcos case did not extend to suits against foreign states for abuses of their police power, which are considered immune to civil action unless proved to be commercially or privately motivated. A leading case is *Saudi Arabia v. Nelson* (1993), in which the plaintiff, a U.S. engineer hired by a U.S. firm to work in Saudi Arabia, sued the Saudi government for wrongful imprisonment and torture inflicted on him for publicizing unsafe work conditions. The U.S. Supreme Court denied the plaintiff's ability to sue the Saudi government under a 1976 federal law, the Foreign Sovereign Immunities Act, which enabled plaintiffs to recover civil damages from national governments for commercial or private acts *(jure gestionis)*. Where such acts were governmental in nature *(jure imperii)*, however, sovereign immunity prevented recovery; the *Nelson* plaintiff's inability to show that the Saudi government's tortious acts were commercial and private, rather than exercises of official power, doomed his lawsuit.[14]

By far the most successful enforcement of international humanitarian law has occurred through criminal trials. These have assumed the form of ad hoc courts, such as the post–World War II tribunals at Nuremberg and Tokyo and the more recent international criminal tribunals for Yugoslavia, Rwanda, and Cambodia; national military trials by individual countries of foreign accused war criminals (e.g., the 12 successor trials by the U.S. National Military Tribunal at Nuremberg and trials by British royal warrant courts, as well as the U.S. Army's prosecution of German defendants for violations of the laws of war at Dachau); and trials by military and civilian courts of their own nationals accused of offenses against humanitarian law, as in the U.S. Army's court-martial of William Calley and the recent conviction and execution of the former dictator Saddam Hussein by an Iraqi court. (At the time of this writing, the work of the International Criminal Court, the first permanent tribunal with jurisdiction over international humanitarian and human rights law, remains inchoate.) Some of the cases tried by the International Criminal Tribunal for Yugoslavia have been assimilated into international customary law. Among the leading cases are the prosecution of Dusko Tadic, which amplified the protections of the 1949 Geneva Conventions to include internal armed conflicts, and the trial of former Serbian president Slobodan Milosevic, which affirmed the criminal liability of former heads of state (the Nuremberg principles) for violations of international law.[15] The 1998 trial by the International Criminal Tribunal for Rwanda of the former Rwandan prime minister, Jean Kambanda, achieved the first conviction of a former head of state for genocide.

A momentous case in the post-Nuremberg efforts to prosecute offenses against international humanitarian law was the 1999 judgment of the British House of Lords regarding the extradition of Augusto Pinochet, former dictator of Chile. Pinochet was arrested in London on a Spanish warrant alleging his responsibility as Chilean president for human rights abuses (including torture). The case stands for the proposition that, for purposes of extradition, English courts have jurisdiction over former heads of state on English soil accused of torture during their tenure in office and could therefore extradite such suspects to countries willing to prosecute them.[16]

FUTURE PROSPECTS

Based on developments since the end of World War II, supporters of enforcing international humanitarian law have grounds for hope tempered by realism. On the one hand, proponents can find reassurance in the creation of institutions to promote regard for basic human rights like the UN, ad hoc criminal tribunals, and the International Criminal Court, as well as international instruments such as the Geneva Conventions, the Conventions on Genocide and Torture, and the Universal Declaration of Human Rights. On the other hand, the process of vindicating international humanitarian law remains subject to the political will of the world's superpowers.

The great powers' inordinate ability to skew enforcement of international law is reflected in the actual text of the UN Charter and the Rome Statute (which established the jurisdictional competencies of the International Criminal Court). Articles 2 (4) ("All members shall refrain in their international relations from the threat or use of force against the territorial integrity or political independence of any state") and 2 (7) (prohibiting the UN from intervening "in matters which are essentially within the domestic jurisdiction of any state") of the UN Charter erect buffers between humanitarian law enforcement and sovereign nations. They are not, however, insuperable barriers, because Chapter VII of the Charter empowers the UN to override Article 2 restrictions by vote of the Security Council if warranted to preserve global peace. In the hands of the

Security Council's permanent members, then, rests enforcement of international humanitarian law; if so inclined, any one of them can veto action to enforce it under Chapter VII. To the geopolitical egoism of the Security Council can be traced the dilatoriness of humanitarian action in the Balkans, Rwanda, and now in Darfur.

Similarly, the International Criminal Court (ICC) is hamstrung by the text of its own founding charter, the Rome Statute of 1998. Although Article 27 of the Rome Statute abolishes immunity for heads of state and government officials who commit crimes under international law, Article 16 enables the UN Security Council to adopt a resolution under Chapter VII of the UN Charter that effectively stops any investigation or prosecution undertaken by the ICC for one year. Thereafter, the Security Council can renew the resolution annually until unfavorable cases have withered away through the death or disappearance of witnesses, the destruction of evidence, or a waning interest in prosecuting or investigating. Furthermore, under Article 17, the ICC must suspend investigation or prosecution of a case if a national legal system is addressing it (the principle of complementarity). Although the ICC prosecutors can reject national whitewashes or sham prosecutions and investigations, they must provide notice to the state that has conducted the inadequate process, thereby enabling state authorities to inform suspects and creating opportunities for the destruction of evidence, tampering with witnesses, and so forth.[17]

Law proceeds incrementally, however, and advocates of a robust enforcement of international humanitarian law would do well to remember that the achievements of due process in national criminal justice systems evolved over centuries of change and conflict. (The examples of the English common law and the Fourth, Fifth, and Sixth Amendment rights of the accused under U.S. law are eloquent on this point.) Oliver Wendell Holmes's lapidary statement that the engine of legal change has been experience rather than logic gives pride of place to the role of history in shaping the substance and form of law.[18] The human experience of tyranny, brutality, and injustice decisively shaped both the contours and contents of international humanitarian law in the twentieth century. In the twenty-first century, advocates have reason to believe that enforcement of international humanitarian law through military intervention, civil remedy, and criminal trial will gradually bring international law into congruence with their deepest longings for justice.

See Also: Guantanamo Detainees; Immigration and Employment Law Enforcement; State Crime Control; Torture and Enemy Combatants.

Endnotes

1. For citations to other treaties, see Adam Roberts and Richard Guelff, *Documents on the Laws of War* (Oxford: Oxford University Press, 2004), 3, n. 3.
2. Ibid., 1–2. The authors note that *jus in bello* and *jus ad bellum,* although distinct, are nonetheless overlapping, particularly in their insistence on the principle of proportionality and the right of self-defense.
3. Universal jurisdiction enables states to prosecute a defendant even if he or she lacks a nexus with the site of the crime, the perpetrator, or the victim. In this respect, universal

jurisdiction (which covers all offenses within the *jus cogens,* or compelling law, such as genocide or torture) differs from that exercised by ordinary courts, which is typically based on the principle of territoriality.

4. Geoffrey Robertson, *Crimes against Humanity: The Struggle for Global Justice* (London: Penguin Press, 1999), 196; Antonio Cassese, *International Criminal Law* (Oxford: Oxford University Press, 2003), 37–38.

5. Robertson, *Crimes against Humanity,* 161–62; M. Cherif Bassiouni, *Crimes against Humanity in International Law* (The Hague, Netherlands: Kluwer Law International, 1999), 505.

6. See Charter of the International Military Tribunal, excerpted in Frank Newman and David Weissbrodt, eds., *International Human Rights: Law, Policy, and Process* (Cincinnati, OH: Anderson, 1996), 198; Bassiouni, *Crimes against Humanity in International Law,* 506.

7. Bassiouni, *Crimes against Humanity in International Law,* 506.

8. See Charter of the United Nations in Newman and Weissbrodt, *International Human Rights,* 4, 10.

9. Robertson, *Crimes against Humanity,* 164–65, 272–74.

10. 1949 Geneva Conventions III and IV, in Roberts and Guelff, *Documents on the Laws of War,* 243–355; Robertson, *Crimes against Humanity,* 166–67.

11. Robertson, *Crimes against Humanity,* 167–71.

12. *Filártiga v. Peña-Irala,* 577 F.Supp. 860 (1980).

13. See the discussion of these cases in Robertson, *Crimes against Humanity,* 216, 236–37.

14. *Saudi Arabia v. Nelson,* 113 S.Ct. 1471 (1993). The British Court of Appeal reached a similar result in the 1996 case of *Al-Adsani v. Government of Kuwait,* 107 ILR 536. Both cases are discussed in Robertson, *Crimes against Humanity,* 354–55.

15. See Cassese, *International Criminal Law;* Robertson, *Crimes against Humanity.*

16. Judgment of the House of Lords (Pinochet No. 3), March 24, 1999, cited in Cassese, *International Criminal Law,* 9.

17. Robertson, *Crimes against Humanity,* 325–26.

18. Oliver Wendell Holmes, *Common Law* (1881), 1. Also available online at http://www.law.harvard.edu/library/collections/special/online-collections/common_law/contents.php.

Further Reading: Cassese, Antonio, *International Criminal Law* (New York: Oxford University Press, 2003); Gutman, Roy, and David Rieff, *Crimes of War: What the Public Should Know* (New York: Norton, 1999); Newman, Frank, and David Weissbrodt, eds., *International Human Rights: Law, Policy, and Process* (Cincinnati, OH: Anderson, 1996); Roberts, Adam, and Richard Guelff, *Documents on the Laws of War* (New York: Oxford University Press, 2003); Robertson, Geoffrey, *Crimes against Humanity: The Struggle for Global Justice* (London: Penguin Press, 1999).

Michael S. Bryant

J

JUVENILE JUSTICE

INTRODUCTION

The history of juvenile justice in the United States contains contradictory and competing ideas about juvenile delinquency and its solutions. Hence, juvenile justice policies have shifted along a continuum of incarceration, on the one end, and rehabilitation, on the other. During times of moral panic over youth delinquency—which are often laced with racial fear and anxiety—the United States has shifted to an incarceration model that relies heavily on punitive policies of discipline. At other times, juvenile justice polices have embodied a model of rehabilitation that stresses support services and counseling for juveniles. Recently, one of the more controversial issues revolving around juvenile is whether juveniles who commit so-called adult crimes should be regarded as adults and subject to the same kinds of punishment or should be cared for as youths in need of treatment and understanding.

BACKGROUND

The first institution in the United States to address juvenile delinquency was the House of Refuge in New York City. Established in 1825, the House of Refuge not only held children convicted of crimes but also held those whose only crime was living in poverty. Soon after the opening of the first House of Refuge, reformers opened houses in Boston and Philadelphia. The public justification for the Houses of Refuge was explicitly religious. Wealthy reformers believed that impoverished children lacked the proper Christian values and morals, including a strong work ethic and respect for authority. As a result, reformers designed the Houses of Refuge to reform youth through disciplined activity, prayer, work, and a heavily regimented day. On the one hand, the Houses of Refuge provided an alternative to the harsh conditions of adult jails and prisons, where children were frequently held. On the other hand, house residents were subjected to harsh training schools where corporal punishment and harsh working conditions were common.

Underneath the religious rhetoric of the conservative reformers was an intense fear of the poor, who, if organized, posed a threat to their class privilege. This gave rise to a widespread moral panic about rising juvenile delinquency rates among poor and working-class youth. At the time, massive economic disparity between the rich and poor profoundly shaped the social landscape. The industrial elite heavily exploited the labor of working-class and immigrant populations in the factories. Riots over working conditions were commonplace. The wealthy elite grew ever weary and saw the Houses of Refuge as necessary reforms to control working-class youth.[1]

Since the construction of first House of Refuge, there has been contentious debate about how best to confront juvenile delinquency. Although the early reformers argued for institutionalization, others questioned the utility of institutions for children. In the 1850s, organizations like the Children's Aid Society argued that the Houses of Refuge were likely to expose children to criminal behavior and lead to more crime. The Children's Aid Society was part of a broader movement called the Child Savers, which argued that the Christian family was the ideal place to combat juvenile delinquency and socialize children. Child Saver organizations established programs to relocate children from the city to families in the west. These families, in theory, would raise the children with so-called proper Christian morals and values and offer better living conditions for impoverished children. In practice, however, the children's new families often treated them as delinquent stepchildren and exploited their labor for profit.[2]

Although the Child Savers argued against institutionalization for white immigrants, they raised few questions about the institutionalization of Native American children in boarding schools and African American children on the plantation. In fact, many Child Savers urged the government to provide more funding for the construction of boarding schools for Native American children. Given prevailing stereotypes, Child Savers argued that the Native American family was immoral, backward, and unfit to raise children. Boarding schools, they believed, were the proper place to socialize Native American children. The boarding schools outlawed children from using their first language, severed family ties, and attempted to replace Native American culture with Protestant values and morals. Boarding school staff forced children to cut their hair upon arrival and adopt European American ways of dress and demeanor. In their attempt to reform Native American children, boarding schools often relied on violent forms of discipline, not unlike those found in the early Houses of Refuge.[3]

Despite resistance to institutionalization, juvenile reform schools continued to grow in the cities, especially in the Northeast. Throughout the late 1800s, the state increasingly participated in the construction and management of reform schools. In 1899, Illinois established the first juvenile court charged with hearing all cases involving juveniles. The court was founded on the idea of *parens patriae,* which asserts that children are developmentally different than adults. Given this, the state has a vested interest in protecting the welfare of children, who cannot protect themselves. Before 1899, there was no formal distinction made between adults and children in the legal system.[4] After the formation of the Illinois juvenile courts, other states soon followed. Juvenile courts sought to control juvenile delinquency through rehabilitation rather than punishment. The courts had the power to remove children from their homes and sentence them to training schools. Although rehabilitation was the goal of training schools, they continued to feel like places of punishment for those confined.

Throughout the early 1900s, reformers continued to experiment with different strategies to control juvenile delinquency. With the rise of the social sciences, researchers explored the causes of delinquency and began to offer social policies based on systematic research. Early criminologists, like Cesare Lombroso, argued that criminality was genetic and traceable by studying the structure and shape of the human body. Biological explanations posited that if people are born criminal, attempts to rehabilitate them would inevitably fail. Other researchers, like William Healy, questioned the more biological explanations and instead argued that juvenile delinquency was a symptom of a child's surroundings—their peers, family, and so on—which all affected their mental health.

The more environmental explanations for juvenile delinquency gathered strength with the creation of the Chicago School of Sociology. Sociologist Clifford Shaw systematically studied juvenile delinquency in Chicago during the 1930s. He argued that delinquency was the product of social disorganization in neighborhoods, which experienced a breakdown of more conventional institutions like the family and church. Informed by theories of social disorganization, the Chicago School helped develop more preventative strategies to combat juvenile delinquency. Social workers were sent out into the community to organize residents and create community institutions that would prevent juvenile delinquency. For Shaw, reform schools were of limited value because they did not address the social causes of delinquency, specifically the structural breakdown of communities. The key to solving problems of juvenile delinquency was the strengthening of community ties and institutions. Despite Shaw's call for more preventative measures, juvenile institutions continued to grow throughout the 1940s and 1950s.

THE MODERN PERIOD: FROM DEINSTITUTIONALIZATION TO GETTING TOUGH

The 1960s gave birth to a new wave of thinking about juvenile delinquency that challenged the continued institutionalization of juveniles. With the rise of the Black Power movement, Chicano Movement, and American Indian Movement, community residents began to argue for more control over the institutions that confined their children. Many questioned the need for more juvenile institutions, which activists argued were not about rehabilitation or reform but rather about controlling and patrolling communities of color. The social uprisings of the 1960s provided the backdrop to the formation of more community-based solutions. Instead of removing children from the community to large-scale institutions, activists argued for more preventative programs, group homes, and transition homes.

Activist calls for deinstitutionalization came to fruition in 1972 when Jerome Miller, director of the Massachusetts Department of Youth Services, closed down all juvenile reform schools and transferred children to smaller residential programs, where they received personalized counseling from trained professionals rather than punishment from prison guards. These new community-based programs were far more successful in reducing recidivism rates that the youth prisons that existed prior to 1972. Following in Miller's footsteps, President Richard Nixon established the 1973 National Advisory Commission on Criminal Justice Standards and Goals. The commission recommended that all large-scale juvenile justice institutions be closed down and replaced by more community-based programs.[5] Juvenile prisons, the commission argued, were more likely to increase crime than prevent it, because children rarely received the necessary rehabilitation in prison-like facilities. In institutions, children learned more about crime and developed distaste for people in positions of authority, all of which increased the chances that a child would reoffend. Nixon, however, disregarded the report, paving the way for increased use of juvenile prisons. Although various states continued to experiment with deinstitutionalization for juveniles, these efforts all but disappeared during the 1980s and 1990s with the rise of the get tough on crime movement.

Although juvenile crime rates during the 1970s and early 1980s remained fairly constant, there was a substantial increase in juvenile crime from 1987 to 1994, especially crimes involving firearms. For example, teenage homicide rates doubled between 1985 and 1994.[6] Conservative criminologists, academics, commentators, and politicians seized the opportunity to push a get tough on crime agenda that argued for less rehabilitation and more punishment. John DiIulio, a political scientist at Princeton, became an academic poster child for the get tough on crime movement when he coined the racially charged word *superpredator.* DiIulio, and a cohort of other conservative academics, used the word *superpredator* to describe the rise of a new kind of juvenile offender that was sociopathic, remorseless, and very dangerous. Fraught with racial stereotypes, DiIulio argued that the new youth offender lacked a moral conscience and values.

This framing of youth crime is reminiscent of how the early reformers framed white immigrant youth during the creation of the Houses of Refuge. DiIulio warned that, by the year 2010, nearly 270,000 superpredators would be roaming the streets, resulting in an unprecedented crime wave. This stoked the already burning flames of racial and class anxiety and provided the justification for new laws and penalties for juvenile offenders. Rehabilitation, conservatives argued, would not work with this new type of juvenile offender. The media ran with the story. Every school shooting, juvenile homicide, and violent crime became a testament to the rise of the superpredator, which became a racially imbued code word for children of color in the inner city. By 1994, nearly 40 percent of all print news that covered children was about crime and violence, mostly involving children of color.[7]

Time, however, did not lend much support to DiIulio's thesis of the superpredator. Crime rates began to drop after 1994, and the new crime wave never hit. In fact, juvenile crime rates have continued to drop. Moreover, DiIulio's description of a new kind of juvenile delinquent did not match well with the data on incarcerated children. Of the 106,000 children in secure facilities in 1997, the overwhelming majority was incarcerated for nonviolent offenses. Thirty-six percent of juveniles were incarcerated for crimes against persons. Only 2 percent of incarcerated children committed homicide, and 6 percent committed sexual assault. Nonviolent offenses were the majority of incarcerated children at 73 percent. Property offenses, like auto theft and shoplifting, accounted for 32 percent. Drug offenses accounted for 9 percent, mostly for drug possession. Public order violations, like being drunk in public, accounted for 10 percent. Technical violations of patrol accounted for 13 percent.[8]

The portrait of incarcerated children is a far cry from the myth of the violent superpredator. Nonetheless, politicians continued to ring the alarm. By capitalizing on the public's racial anxiety and fear of crime, politicians seized their newly found political capital to win elections. This paved the way to making the United States one of the most punitive juvenile justice systems and the largest incarcerator of children in the world.

Moreover, the 1980s and 1990s saw the passing of several punitive laws designed to target youth crime at the federal, state, and local level. At the federal level, the Violent and Repeat Juvenile Offender Act of 1997 encouraged more prosecution of juvenile offenders, increased penalties for gang-related offenses, and increased the use of mandatory minimums for juvenile offenders. At the state level, an increasing number of states passed laws to lower the age at which juveniles could be tried as adults. Some states allowed children as young as 14 to be tried in adult criminal courts. In 2000, California, for example, passed Proposition 21, the Juvenile Crime Initiative. Proposition 21 increased the penalties for gang-related felonies; mandated indeterminate life sentences for carjacking, drive-by shootings, and home invasion robbery; made gang recruitment a felony; and required adult trials for children as young as 14 charged with serious sex offenses and murder. Proposition 21 passed with 62 percent of the vote, even though crime rates among juveniles decreased the previous six years.

At the local level, city prosecutors sought restraining orders against specific gangs in the community. These restraining orders are known as gang injunctions and prohibit actions like walking down the street in groups of four or more, wearing certain clothes, and associating with other gang members. These activities are not crimes in any other neighborhoods except those where injunctions apply. Those who violate these rules can be held with violating a court order, resulting in up to six months in jail for participating in legal activities. Moreover, those convicted of gang-related felonies face additional penalties aside from the actual crime for being in contempt of court for violating the restraining orders.

Los Angeles, for example, has nearly thirty gang injunctions that target more than thirty-five different gangs, nearly all of them comprised of people of color. Although police departments praise gang injunctions as a vital tool in their war on gangs, the use of gang injunctions has raised questions among civil rights advocates, because they overwhelmingly target people of color. The use of gang injunctions is quite similar to how white Southerners used the Black Codes to criminalize and incarcerate large numbers of recently freed African Americans after the abolition of slavery. Black Codes included laws against loitering, socializing in large groups, and vagrancy that applied only to African Americans, much like restraining orders that apply only to specific communities.[9]

A massive increase in the number of children of color in the juvenile justice system has accompanied these get tough on crime federal, state, and local policies. Although African Americans represent roughly 13 percent of the population, they make up nearly 40 percent of all incarcerated children. Latinos represent 13 percent of the general population but 21 percent of incarcerated children in public institutions. Native Americans also have a high rate of incarceration, but because of their numbers in the general population, represent only 1 percent of the incarcerated population. Asian and Pacific Islanders account for 2 percent of the incarcerated population. These low numbers, however, mask the high incarceration rates of Cambodian, Laotian, Hmong, and Samoan children.[10]

These statistics reflect widespread institutional racism within the juvenile justice system. According to the 2007 report *And Justice for Some* by the National Council on Crime and Delinquency, Latino and African American youth are far more likely to be incarcerated in state institutions, even when controlling for the type of offense and prior records. Latino youth are three times more likely to be incarcerated than their white counterparts and spend 112 days longer in secure settings than their white counterparts. African American children are six times more likely to be incarcerated and spend, on average, 61 more days confined than their white counterparts.[11] Moreover, although white children are more likely to use drugs, children of color are three times more likely to be incarcerated for drug crimes.[12]

WHITE AND BLACK JUSTICE

Sara Steen, a professor at Vanderbilt University, and George Bridges, a professor at the University of Washington, provide insight into how race structures the process of juvenile justice. Bridges and Steen systematically studied the written reports submitted by probation officers to the juvenile court system. These reports, based on interviews with accused children, contain the children's life history and the probation officer's sentencing recommendation. After looking at hundreds of reports, Bridges and Steen found that, when explaining the crimes of black children, probation officers point to negative attitudes and personality traits, such as a lack of respect for the law and authority. For white children, however, probation officers highlight more environmental factors, like family and drug abuse. As a result, Steen and Bridges found that probation officers recommended longer sentences for black children, because they were perceived to be dangerous and a threat to society.* Racial stereotypes, they argued, heavily shape the processing of children of color throughout the juvenile justice system.

*George Bridges and Sara Steen, "Racial Disparities in Official Assessments of Juvenile Offenders: Attributional Stereotypes as Mediating Mechanisms of Juvenile Offenders," *American Sociological Review* 63 (August 1998): 554–70.

CONDITIONS OF CONFINEMENT: INCARCERATION VERSUS REHABILITATION

Children awaiting trial are often confined to juvenile detention centers located in their community. Once children are sentenced, they are usually transferred to state institutions located far away from their homes in rural communities. Secure institutions for juveniles, whether detention centers or youth prisons, vary greatly depending on the state. Most states base their juvenile justice policies on the incarceration model and confine youth to large, prisonlike institutions equipped with cells, steel doors, and heavy locks. Services and rehabilitation programs are scarce, because the goal of rehabilitation is replaced with punishment. Other states, however, organize juvenile justice around policies of rehabilitation and run smaller, community-based institutions that offer substantial counseling and rehabilitation programming.

Under the incarceration model, juvenile detention centers and youth prisons treat their captives as human objects to be worked upon, shaped, and molded to meet the institutional demands. Much like the early Houses of Refuge, juvenile detention centers and prisons strictly enforce obedience, passivity, and deference to people in positions of authority. In juvenile detention centers and youth prisons, children are subjected to a series of rules and punishments that, in theory, are supposed to help reform their behavior.

Behavior management programs are often used to achieve these ends. Behavior management programs outline all institutionally acceptable and unacceptable behaviors and impose an artificial hierarchy on the youth, marking those with and those without certain privileges. If a child follows all the rules and obeys the instructions of their guards, they are rewarded with extra time out of their cells, later bedtimes, and more access to the phone.

If a child breaks these institutional rules or defies the orders of their guards, they may be punished with cell confinement, which, in theory, should last anywhere from eight hours to three days but, in reality, may last for several months.

If a child, for example, has a pencil in his or her cell, or if he or she possesses more than five books, the child may be locked in the cell for 16 hours. If a child tucks his or her pants into socks or is found with sagging counting blues (baggy blue jeans), he or she may be locked in the cells for two days. If a child floods the cell, he or she may be locked in the cell for a minimum of three days, with additional punishment depending on behavior while confined.[13]

Grounded in simple operant conditioning, the underlying assumption of the level system is that if compliance is rewarded and noncompliance punished, the youth, like mice in a Skinner box, will eventually learn to adhere to institutional rules and, by extension, those of society. Although the level system is the primary tool of social control inside the secured walls, it is justified on the grounds that if children can be trained to follow rules inside the detention, these newly instilled values will follow them once they leave the institution.

Depending on the institution, children may spend their time housed in large military-barrack-style housing units or in cells similar to those experienced by adults in prison: seven-by-eight-foot cinderblock rooms with a bed, a stainless steal sink and toilet, and a steel door with a narrow window. On average, children spend nearly 14 hours inside their cell. When confined to cells for long periods of time, children often experience feelings of anger, frustration, and boredom, leaving many to feel that they are being warehoused.[14] The stringent rules and punishments exacerbate these feelings among detained and incarcerated youth and set the stage for intense conflict between the confined youth and the guards who must enforce the rules and impose punishments.

Guards and the Incarceration Model

Guards come to work in juvenile facilities for a variety of reasons. Some want to work with children and counsel them. Others, however, work in juvenile institutions because it provides a stable and secure source of income. Guards come from all walks of life. Some are college graduates, others are retired from the military, and others are high school graduates. Increasingly, states require that guards have at least a college education or military experience. Few guards, however, have significant training in how to deal with incarcerated children, especially those in large, prisonlike institutions that operate under the incarceration model.

The training guards receive varies from state to state but usually consists of a training academy and a probationary period of on-the-job training. In Washington, for example, new recruits attend a mandatory two-week training academy sometime during their six-month probationary period of employment. At the academy, guards learn how to observe the children, use disciplinary techniques, and use physical force. During this training, guards learn to always be aware when dealing with detained and incarcerated children. Implicit and sometime explicit in their training is the assumption that the children are, at best, troubled and, at worst, downright dangerous. The *Washington State Juvenile Workers Handbook,* for example, warns new recruits that "the first step in preparing to deal with offenders is to understand the sociopathic personality"[15] The handbook, then, lists characteristics of the so-called sociopathic personality reminiscent of DiIulio's myth of the superpredator: irresponsible, self-centered, feels little or no guilt, sees staff as objects for exploitation, compulsive liar, strong drive for immediate gratification, and adept at manipulation. "You must recognize that a majority of the offender population will be Sociopathic to some degree," the handbook warns.[16]

Although guards are taught to be deeply suspicious of the children, they are offered little training on how larger social forces shape the children's response to the justice system. Guards, for example, are not taught how poverty or racism shape the lives of detained children, nor is there any discussion of how racial and class biases affect how guards interact and perceive the youths. In short, guards leave the academy ill prepared to deal with incarcerated children in any way, except as potential threats. They are taught little that may help them bridge the gap between the two warring worlds found in most juvenile detention centers and youth prisons.

Rather than teaching understanding and building bridges between the guards and children, the academy trains guards to distrust incarcerated youth at every turn, exacerbating the conflict between them.[17]

The Incarceration Model and Abuse

On April 1, 2003, cameras caught two juvenile prison guards physically assaulting two children in a Stockton, California, youth facility. One guard punched a child in his head and face more than 28 times while the child was in a fetal position, arms protecting his head. Aside from the repeated closed-fist punches, guards dropped their knees with heavy force several times on the back of the children's head and neck. Although the incident was caught on tape, the county district attorney dropped all charges against the guards.

This incident, coupled with increasing public scrutiny of the CYA, led to an intensive review of juvenile prisons in the state. The CYA is one of the largest justice systems in the United States, housing more than 4,300 youth, 84 percent of whom are children of color. The CYA relies heavily on the incarceration model to structure institutional polices and practices. Barry Krisberg, director of the National Council on Crime and Delinquency, released his report of the CYA in December 2003. Krisberg found extensive abuse in the six CYA institutions he investigated.

During the first four months of 2003, one state institution documented more than 535 incidents of chemical restraints, such as mace and pepper spray. Mace and pepper spray are used throughout juvenile facilities in the United States and are usually used to break up large disturbances. The 2003 review of the CYA, however, found that chemical restraints were frequently used to remove children from their cells, even when there was no clear reason to do so. Guards refused to allow many children to wash off the chemicals, leaving severe chemical burns on their skin. During the same four-month period, there were 109 incidents involving physical restraints and 236 incidents involving mechanical restraints. Mechanical restrains involve forcing children to rest on their knees for long periods of time with their hands bound behind their back.[18]

Aside from the use of chemical, physical, and mechanical restraints, Krisberg also found that 10 percent to 12 percent of the youth were housed in restrictive houses where they spent 23 hours a day in their cell, with one hour out for recreation. Often during their one hour of recreation, children were chained in five-point restraints, locking ankles together and their wrists to their waist, making it difficult to exercise. Other children were released to small cages called Special Program Areas.

In addition to abuse at the hands of guards, Krisberg also found significant ward-on-ward violence in the CYA. In the six institutions he studied, there were more than 4,000 ward-on-ward physical assaults and 1,000 cases of sexual harassment. This averages to about 10 assaults per day in the six institutions that have a combined total population of 3,800 youths. The 2003 CYA review highlights the rampant violence that youths experience from both guards and other inmates. Although the CYA is one of the larger and more violent youth prison systems in the United States, there is no doubt that violence looms large in the minds of children incarcerated across the United States.[19]

The push toward incarcerating more juveniles in secure facilities has produced some troubling results. If success of incarceration strategies is measured by how many children are arrested after their release, then most states that operate under the incarceration model are failing miserably. In California, for example, nearly 91 percent of those released from the CYA are arrested within three years.[20] In Pennsylvania, nearly 55 percent are rearrested within 18 months, and in Utah, 79 percent are rearrested within a year.[21] These failure rates, coupled with media stories of abuse, have led some organizations to call for a shift from the incarceration model to a rehabilitation model. Organizations like Books Not Bars of Oakland, California, organize formerly incarcerated youth and their parents to protest the continued operation and expansion of large-scale youth prisons. Through protests and political lobbying, Books Not Bars pressures local and state officials to close the large institutions and replace them with smaller facilities that focus on rehabilitation. Their efforts, along with the efforts of other youth justice organizations, have led to a significant drop in the number of youth confined in the CYA.

Alternatives to Incarceration: The Shift to Rehabilitation

Activist demands to close large-scale youth prisons and jails echo the child advocates of the 1930s and 1960s, who challenged the increasing reliance on juvenile institutionalization. Some states, like Missouri, have cast aside the incarceration model in favor of a rehabilitation model that relies heavily on preventative programs, alternatives to incarceration, and community-based solutions. In 1983, Missouri closed its large institutions for juveniles and opened several small community-based rehabilitation centers throughout the state, where residents could be located closer to home. Although most states have facilities that house 100 or more youth, Missouri's institutions house no more than 36 children per facility.[22] Missouri also has a number of different types of facilities, ranging from small, secure institutions to group homes to day treatment centers.

Unlike the large youth prison of other states, Missouri's secure facilities have no cells or barrack-style housing units. Instead, the children are housed in dormitory settings and are allowed to wear their own clothing, rather than institutional uniforms. Guards are replaced with college graduates, who receive specialized training on how best to interact with the children in their keep. As a result, Missouri experiences far less conflict between staff and the youths, paving the way for supportive relationships to develop. Moreover, rather than being closed institutions, community organizations are a vital part of the programming as children are allowed to leave the facilities to work in the community on supervised projects. Missouri also has several group homes where children with less serious offenses are held. In these homes, youths are allowed to attend school and work outside of the facility.

Missouri's rehabilitation model has been far more successful than those in other states. The recidivism rate in Missouri is far less than that of California,

Utah, and Pennsylvania. Only 9 percent of the youth are reincarcerated in juvenile or adult facilities after their release.[23] Moreover, because the facilities in Missouri do not rely heavily on guards, the security costs to run the facility are far cheaper than other states. Whereas California spends nearly $80,000 to house a child in the California Youth Authority, Missouri spends $40,000, with far better results. Missouri continues to be a model for other states and may signal a future shift in national juvenile justice policies.

FUTURE PROSPECTS

The history of juvenile justice in the United States has revolved around several competing approaches to dealing with juvenile delinquency. From the early calls for confinement within Houses of Refuge to the more recent demands for deinstitutionalization in Massachusetts and Missouri, juvenile justice has always shifted and transformed with the times. During periods of moral panics laced with racial anxiety and fear, the United States has moved toward punitive strategies that expose children, especially children of color, to systemic violence and abuse. As youth advocates and activists highlight the failure of more punitive polices, however, states begin to search for more effective strategies that move from incarceration to rehabilitation.

See Also: Boot Camps; Corrections Education; Gang Injunction Laws; Juveniles and Social Justice; Juveniles Treated as Adults; School Violence.

Endnotes

1. Barry Krisberg, *Juvenile Justice: Redeeming Our Children* (Thousand Oaks, CA: Sage, 2005).
2. Ibid.
3. Barbara Finkelstein, "A Crucible of Contradictions: Historical Roots of Violence against Children in the United States," in *The Public Assault on America's Children: Poverty Violence and Juvenile Injustice,* ed. V. Polakow (New York: Teachers College Press, 2000).
4. James Austin and John Irwin, *It's about Time: America's Imprisonment Binge* (Stamford, CT: Wadsworth, 2001).
5. Marc Mauer, *Race to Incarcerate* (New York: New Press, 1999).
6. National Criminal Justice Commission, *The Real War on Crime,* ed. Steven Donziger (New York: HarperPerennial, 1996).
7. LynNell Hancock, "Framing Children in the News: The Face and Color of Youth Crime in America," in *The Public Assault on America's Children: Poverty Violence and Juvenile Injustice,* ed. V. Polakow (New York: Teachers College Press, 2000).
8. Office of Juvenile Justice and Delinquency Prevention, *Juveniles in Correctional Facilities* (Washington, DC: U.S. Department of Justice, 1999).
9. Lerone Bennett, *Before the Mayflower: A History of Black America* (Chicago: Johnson, 1993).
10. Office of Juvenile Justice and Delinquency Prevention, *Juveniles in Correctional Facilities.*
11. National Council on Crime and Delinquency, *And Justice for Some: Differential Treatment of Youth of Color in the Justice System* (San Francisco, CA: NCCD, 2007).

12. Krisberg, *Juvenile Justice.*
13. This information is based on the author's ethnographic research in a juvenile detention center; Christopher Bickel, "Jaded by the System: Authoritarianism and Resistance in a Juvenile Detention Center" (unpublished manuscript, University of California, Santa Barbara, 2004).
14. Ibid.
15. Criminal Justice Training Commission, *Juvenile Workers Academy,* Part 2, "Supervision."
16. Ibid.
17. Bickel, "Jaded by the System."
18. Barry Krisberg, *General Corrections Review of the California Youth Authority* (San Francisco, CA: NCCD, December 2003).
19. Ibid.
20. Center for Juvenile and Criminal Justice, *Reforming the Juvenile Justice System* (Boston, MA: Beacon Press, 2007).
21. Krisberg, *Juvenile Justice.*
22. Missouri Division of Youth Services, "System Change through State Challenge Activities," *Juvenile Justice Bulletin* (Washington, D.C.: Office of Juvenile Justice and Delinquency Prevention, March, 2000).
23. Ibid.

Further Reading: Austin, James, and John Irwin, *It's about Time: America's Imprisonment Binge* (Stamford, CT: Wadsworth, 2001); Books Not Bars, http://www.booksnotbars.org; Krisberg, Barry, *Juvenile Justice: Redeeming Our Children* (Thousand Oaks, CA: Sage, 2005); Mauer, Marc, *Race to Incarcerate* (New York: New Press, 1999); National Council on Crime and Delinquency, http://www.nccd-crc.org; Center on Juvenile and Criminal Justice, http://www.cjcj.org; Polakow, Valarie, *The Public Assault on America's Children: Poverty Violence and Juvenile Injustice* (New York: Teachers College Press, 2000).

Christopher Bickel

JUVENILES AND SOCIAL JUSTICE

INTRODUCTION

Social justice refers to the notion that all individuals and groups in society receive fair treatment: Everyone is entitled to the same basic rights, opportunities, and benefits, and we must share in the obligations, responsibilities, and duties. When we begin to examine the treatment of young people in contemporary U.S. society in relation to social justice, however, several controversial questions are raised: Are children fundamentally different than adults, or are they only smaller or miniature versions with less knowledge? At what age does a child become a competent, capable adult? Once early childhood is over, should young people enjoy the same rights and commensurate responsibilities of adulthood, or should there be a trial period, or training wheels if you will?

A paradox of modern society is that young people are physiologically maturing at an earlier age while, at the same time adults, are extending the duration of childhood. To put it differently, children are growing into adult bodies earlier, and adults are treating them in their adult bodies as children for a longer period of time than was customary just a century ago. This entry examines a few of the more salient issues related to these notions of childhood, their implications for the juvenile justice system, and their relationship to the broader ideals of social justice.

BACKGROUND

Today, at least in the United States, the magic number for adulthood is 18. This is the age when most, but not all, of the rights and responsibilities of adulthood are granted to our young. Persons age 18 and older may enter into legal contracts, are granted the privileges of citizenship, such as voting or running for public office, and must assume the obligations of citizenship, such as jury duty or registering with Selective Service. Some rights, however, are still at least a few years away: for example, the ability to purchase alcoholic beverages or to purchase or possess certain classes of firearms, such as pistols and revolvers. Older citizens believe that some activities are still too risky for persons perceived as having limited experiences and underdeveloped senses of judgment and morality. Furthermore, it is at age 18 is when people become legally responsible for their decisions and behavior. If someone commits a crime, there is no so-called do over or mulligan, he or she must face the adult criminal justice system as opposed to the juvenile justice system.

This was not always the case. It was not until the turn of the twentieth century that social and legal distinctions between children and adults began to be widely recognized and institutionalized. This transformation was the result of more than two centuries of reforms and the construction and reconstruction of childhood and children. Prior to the nineteenth century and the invention of childhood, infancy (those younger than age seven) was the age-marking category differentiating young people from adults. Once a child turned seven, he or she was viewed as generally being old enough to take on rights, duties, and responsibilities with regard to work and family chores— not quite the same as adults, but similar to them. Their treatment was akin in many ways to the treatment of individuals between the ages of 16 and 20 today. Little distinction was made between them and older children, and once the age of 14 was reached, they fully entered adulthood with its corresponding rights and responsibilities. Beginning in the eighteenth century, however, notions of infancy and adulthood started to be reexamined. Young people between the ages of 7 and 14 were not infants, yet they were not considered to be adults. Childhood began to take on a new meaning and was redefined as a separate, discrete phase of development, an age category between infancy and adulthood.[1]

Children in this new phase of development were somehow fundamentally different than older persons who had already passed through it; again, they were not infants but perhaps closer to infants than adults in terms of mental, moral, and emotional maturity. Following this logic, because children are not fully developed, they need adults to care for them and to make decisions they are incapable of making. Moreover, because children do not possess the faculties to make wise life choices, when they make unwise choices, they should not be held to the same standards of accountability to which adults are subject.

It was with the reforms of the Progressive era during the latter part of the nineteenth century and the new conceptions of childhood that the juvenile justice system arose with the first juvenile court being established in Cook County (Chicago) in 1899. In accordance with the new beliefs about the nature of childhood, the juvenile courts rejected the idea that children were rational, capable, responsible beings. Children were incapable of making informed decisions while fully comprehending the consequences of those decisions: They were unable to truly form criminal intent. Because children could not form criminal intent, the notion that the juvenile courts should solely handle criminal cases was also rejected. The courts broadened their jurisdictions to include not only cases in which children had violated criminal law but also those involving behavior adults deemed objectionable. Not surprisingly, in the early years of the juvenile courts, it was misbehavior of the latter variety that occupied the majority of the courts' time: the moral and social transgressions of the new, special age category. In addition, the appropriate way to address these (and more serious) transgressions was treatment, not punishment. Because children were not culpable for their offenses, they should be rehabilitated and nurtured rather than punished the same as adults would be.

Now, more than a century removed from the creation of a special category of young people (different from adults) and the establishment of the first juvenile court (to manage their lapses in judgment), how has the social experiment fared? This question can be answered by examining two separate components: (1) the creation of the special category of young people and beliefs about their limitations and (2) the state and philosophy of the present-day juvenile justice system. A strong statement addressing both of these issues was made in March 2005, when in *Roper v. Simmons*[2] the U.S. Supreme Court ruled persons who committed their crime when younger than age 18 could not receive the death penalty, reversing a 1989 decision in *Stanford v. Kentucky*,[3] in which the Court held that individuals who committed their crimes at age 16 and 17 could be put to death. In part, the ruling in *Roper* was based on the notion that adolescents were too immature, impulsive, and more likely to engage in risky behavior that mature adults would generally avoid.

The Supreme Court said that children, up to and including 16- and 17-year-olds, are not adequately capable of controlling their impulses, nor do they entirely comprehend the consequences of risky or antisocial behavior. The Court's majority argued that an evolving standard of justice since *Stanford* has led state legislatures and broad public opinion to reject the juvenile death penalty. However, no empirical evidence that this change the Court spoke of had actually occurred was produced. At the core of the majority's opinion was their depiction of young people as prone to risk taking and their inability to recognize potential negative outcomes as a consequence of their risky behaviors. Poor decision making and risky behavior were viewed as simply traits of youth; thus, individual youths should not bear the full responsibility for their poor decisions. In other words, youth, or childhood, in and of itself is a mitigating factor. In arguing this point, the Court cited their opinion in *Johnson v. Texas* (1993), in which they declared:

> The relevance of youth as a mitigating factor derives from the fact that the signature qualities of youth are transient; as individuals mature, the impetuousness and recklessness that may dominate in younger years can subside.[4]

The Court thus argued that juveniles are fundamentally different from adults; therefore, they must be held to a different legal standard.

KEY EVENTS: ADOLESCENTS AS INCOMPETENT

The characterization of young people as risk takers is only one of several problematic traits attributed to them: Adolescents are irresponsible, untrustworthy, incorrigible, and emotionally, psychologically, and physically volatile. Many of the traits juveniles presumably possess lead to the belief that they are at best incompetent and sometimes foolish. Some critics have questioned the assumptions made by the Supreme Court and the public in general. For example, William Gardner and his associates argue that legal policy is often based on flawed scientific assumptions or assumptions without empirical evidence at all.[5] Recent work examining the nature of risk taking and similarities and differences between adults and juveniles suggests that perhaps there is not as much difference between the two groups as common knowledge would seem to dictate.[6]

Few would dispute the fact that adolescents engage in risk-taking behavior. What is relevant for the current discussion is whether the risk taking of adolescents is significantly and qualitatively different from risk taking by adults. To gauge the similarities and differences between adults and youth in terms of risk-taking behavior, the term *risk taking* must be defined. There is a wide variety of risk-taking behavior, ranging from socially acceptable and even celebrated activities such as (legal) gambling and extreme sports to various forms of criminal conduct like forcible rape and murder. Eleonora Gullone and her associates suggest four categories of risk-taking behaviors: (1) thrill seeking, (2) rebellion, (3) recklessness, and (4) antisocial behavior.[7] The first category, thrill seeking, can include positive risks that may build character and maturity, whereas the other three are generally detrimental to the person's well-being.

Although Gullone and her colleagues limited their study to adolescents, adults also engage in each of these categories of risk. Activities such as mountaineering and motorcycle racing (thrill seeking), tobacco and illicit drug use (rebellion), unprotected sex and drunken driving (recklessness), and various criminal activities are only a few examples of risky behavior in which adults participate. Are adolescents more prone to engage in these risky behaviors than adults? Comparing the criminal activity of adolescents and adults, the answer is no. In 2004, juveniles accounted for only 16 percent of the people arrested yet make up 26 percent of the population.[8] Although overall disproportionate, juvenile arrests varied considerably by offense. Furthermore, activities such as illicit drug use, driving recklessly, and unsafe sexual practices are not too dissimilar when comparing adults and adolescents.[9]

Gullone and her associates also found that with the three negative forms of risk taking, the higher the perceived risk of the activity, the less likely subjects were to engage in that activity.[10] This is hardly what would be expected from so-called irrational beings. Additionally, in one of the few studies to directly compare adults and adolescents and their risk-taking behavior, Ruth Beyth-Marom and her colleagues found that adults and adolescents had similar outlooks in relation to risk taking, although adults generally recognized more adverse consequences than adolescents.[11] Perhaps this is the principal difference between adults and juveniles with regard to risk-taking behavior. Adults may have a keener or more developed ability to recognize the potential negative consequences of their risky behavior. Once risk is recognized, adults and adolescents behave similarly, but juveniles are not as capable of accurately assessing risk (which supports the argument that their brains are not as fully developed in the region that accounts for reasoning etc., and which is why the Supreme Court ruled as it did in *Roper*). This certainly is consistent with what we believe about the limitations of youth.

According to conventional wisdom, one reason why adolescents engage in risk taking is that they believe they are indestructible and the world revolves around them. They see themselves as being special and different from everyone else and are egocentric. Therefore, they would naturally escape the potential harm that would befall adults when participating in high-risk behaviors. Adolescents simply are not capable of comprehending potential adverse consequences of their behaviors and their own vulnerability to dangers.

Recent research suggests adolescents' presumed inability to accurately perceive risk and then make rational choices based on those perceptions could be physiological in nature. More precisely, adolescents may think differently than adults because their brains have yet to become fully developed.[12] Utilizing magnetic resonance imaging (MRI) technology, neurologists have compared the scans of adults to those of adolescents. Research has consistently shown differences in frontal lobe activity, with less activity and development in this region of adolescent brains. The frontal lobe is the part of the brain responsible for higher thought processes and reasoning. Adolescents' brains are not yet sufficiently developed: They are less able to control their impulses, assess situations, plan courses of action based on their assessments, and implement those courses of action; therefore, adolescents are not entirely responsible for unwise decisions and risky behavior. This explanation for adolescent misbehavior and poor judgment has even entered popular culture, being presented as a defense in a murder trial of a juvenile in the popular television show *Law & Order*.

According to this logic, adults, as opposed to adolescents, have fully developed brains that provide checks and balances on the kinds of behavior associated with higher levels of risk taking: irrational, impulsive, or emotional behavior. As discussed earlier, however, adults also engage in many forms of risky behavior. Moreover, not all adults engage in the same levels of risk taking. For example, men are more likely to be risk takers than women. Risk taking also varies by race, ethnicity, levels of income and education, and even religious affiliation. For example, Zelee Hill and her colleagues reported that unaffiliated and Roman Catholic men were more likely than evangelicals to engage in extramarital sex and to have unprotected extramarital sex.[13] Would neuroscientists suggest that once adults marry and have children their frontal lobes become more developed because single individuals are more likely to engage in risk-taking behavior? It appears as though this is a solution in search of a problem. Similarly, it is possible to argue that the comparatively small stature of juveniles is the cause of their aberrant behavior, a sort of transitory Napoleon complex.

Gardner and his associates note that the handful of studies comparing adults and adolescents show little or no difference in the decision-making skills and risk assessment between the two groups.[14] Perhaps juveniles behave differently because they are expected to behave differently, not because they are actually different. Maybe what we are seeing is nothing more than a self-fulfilling prophesy at work. Perhaps the significant difference is the way adults view adolescent behavior and not the behavior itself, something Frederic Thrasher noted about eighty years ago in his research on play groups and gangs.[15] It is thus curious that society generally is more concerned when adolescents engage in risky behavior, even though adults are more often in as much or even greater danger of serious harm from their own risk-taking behavior.

IMPORTANT THEORY: INFANTILIZING
YOUTH AND SOCIAL CONTROL

Perhaps this is not an issue of behavior but one of power, the power adults exercise over the lives of young people through social and legal policies and practices. The consequences of adults treating children badly has been explored by Robert Regoli and John Hewitt in their theory of differential oppression.[16] They contend that children, in comparison to adults, such as parents, teachers, the clergy, and others, are relatively powerless. Young people are expected, even required, to submit to the power and authority of adults or face severe consequences.[17] This power becomes oppressive when it is exercised to thwart access to valued material and psychological resources. Children are denied the fundamental rights to self-determination and to actively participate in the decisions that directly affect their lives, in part, because of our beliefs about their limited decision-making abilities (see the previous discussion). This, in turn, hinders a child's development of a sense of competence, autonomy, and self-efficacy. This is not to suggest that all exercises of power over children are oppressive. The focus of this theory is that the use of power generally is for the needs and interests of the adult rather than the child. For instance, "Go do your homework" can mean the adult wishes the child to perform well in school and receive a good education, or it can mean "Leave me alone while I'm watching *Springer*." In the latter case, the exercise of power becomes oppression.

In addition, the oppression faced by youths has been exacerbated as childhood has been extended. In other words, the oppression is felt for a longer period of time. In many ways, as children have grown into adult bodies, they are expected to take on many adult responsibilities and behave in accordance to adult standards, yet they are still subject to the whims and demands of the adults around them with little if any recourse for unfair treatment. Ironically, it may be the very concern adults express for the well-being of young people that has increased their level of oppression. Adolescence is a recent construct.[18] Young people formerly transitioned from childhood to adulthood relatively smoothly with clearly defined expectations and demands placed on them. These transitions were marked with the assumption of new privileges and responsibilities. This no longer is the case. Young adults seem to be relegated to a state of limbo, an unending pseudochildhood. Furthermore, the matter of real and substantial differences between adults and young people and how these differences affect decision making and behavior are rarely questioned.

As Regoli and Hewitt have shown, much of the antisocial behavior attributed to young people is accounted for by their reactions to the oppression they experience at the hands of adults. It is precisely the oppression of young people (to protect them) that leads to many forms of antisocial behavior that are associated with the so-called unique condition of youth (see sidebar).[19]

ADAPTIVE RESPONSES TO OPPRESSION

- Passive acceptance is an obedience built upon fear. It is similar to the passive acceptance of the slave role or adaptations of battered women. The child outwardly accepts his or her inferior position but develops a repressed hatred for the oppressor, possibly leading to low self-esteem, drug abuse, or alcoholism.
- Exercise of illegitimate coercive power is the attempt to make something happen. Delinquency provides the youth with an opportunity to establish a sense of autonomy.
- Manipulation of one's peers is an attempt to gain social power. Through manipulation of others within the peer group, a child who has experienced oppression by adults may acquire a sense of strength and control or a degree of empowerment not otherwise felt.
- Retaliation involves striking back at both the people and the institutions the child blames for causing the oppression. School vandalism often occurs because a student is angry at a teacher or principal, and children who assault or kill their parents are generally responding to past experiences of severe maltreatment at the hands of their parents.

Based on differential oppression theory, one of the most common responses to the oppression experienced by young people is the exercise of illegitimate coercive power. Reckless, rebellious, antisocial behavior, or risk taking can be ways of establishing autonomy and control denied to youths by adults. There are tangible and often immediate results from this behavior that can restore the sense of power, potency, and independence of which the youth is deprived. Furthermore, as the risk or rebellious nature of acts utilized to express resistance to adult control increases, the symbolic significance of the acts also increases.

Therefore, risky behaviors such as sexual promiscuity, alcohol and drug use, truancy, and so on are by no means the end result of an unrestrained, illogical, and immature mind; rather, more or less, they are an adaptive, rational, and reasoned response to the oppression they experience from adults.

Is it possible that some of the problems of youth are related to adult definitions of children, adult beliefs about the condition of youth, the subsequent treatment young people receive, and their responses to that treatment? Adults expect young people to behave in illogical and self-destructive ways. They believe they are a special category of risk takers, putting themselves and others in danger, and treat them accordingly. The differences between adults and adolescents in terms of risk taking are not substantial and are not related to a pathological tendency of adolescents to take risks, however, but rather are related to the types of risk people in different age categories are more likely to take. For example, adults engage in risks such as "high stakes gambling, stock market speculation, white collar criminality and extramarital affairs ... [whereas] binge drinking, vandalism, and reckless driving" are typical of the kinds of risks associated with young adults and adolescents.[20]

FUTURE PROSPECTS

To protect children from their own self-destructive tendencies, adults take from them that most precious right of self-determination. In many ways, adults today treat young adults like children, and in many ways adolescents respond by behaving like children, which only reinforces adult beliefs about their limited capabilities and flawed judgment, creating a vicious cycle created by adults in which children find themselves trapped.

It is time to turn back the clock and grant adolescents full membership into society with all the commensurate rights and responsibilities that entail and their consequences. This does not mean that when a child turns age 14, for example, it is time for him or her to "hit the bricks." It means that once children reach the age of actual competence and responsibility, they should be granted the legal authority to determine their own lives. Most certainly, they may consult with other trusted individuals, such as parents, teachers, and the clergy, but ultimately, decisions concerning their lives rest with them.

This means that, as with adults, they must ultimately bear the responsibility for decisions they make. A whole host of new rights would be granted and antisocial behavior would be punished: Privileges and rights could be lost, just as adult felons can lose their liberty (sentenced to prison), voting privileges, and in extreme cases their lives. By rejecting the paternalistic system currently in place, society could actively encourage responsible, adultlike behavior while simultaneously relieving the oppression borne by so many.

Although it is doubtful any adolescent would prefer to face the more severe sanctions of the adult criminal justice system when given the option of the lesser penalties of the juvenile system, it is also true that many would welcome the new rights, privileges, and opportunities they would receive. Furthermore, we believe many young adults would trade the rights of adulthood for a higher standard of accountability. The prospect of gaining full entrance into adult-hood might actively encourage responsible, mature behavior, moving society away from the cycle of infantilizing young adults it now finds itself in, which only perpetuates and encourages reckless, irresponsible, and childish behavior. As an illustration of this point, one of the authors recalled an incident from his high school years. Each spring, as the school year drew to a close, a decades-old tradition started to reappear. This was the time of the annual water wars. Legends of skirmishes past grew as the years wore on, with particularly inge-nious battle tactics becoming part of school lore. Tales of past casualties (both of combatants and innocents) and outwitting administrators began to circulate before the annual rite. Administrators had unsuccessfully attempted to end this tradition because of the damage to student moral and discipline and because of the collateral damage caused by the ever escalating retaliatory strikes, invari-ably culminating with the deployment of the weapons of mass destruction of the water wars—balloons. When these insidious devices made their inevitable appearance late in the year, all semblance of order disappeared. Students ran and ducked for cover between each class or any open period, and janitors were ever present in a futile attempt to mop up after the carnage that occurred every 50 minutes.

All of this, however, came to a dramatic and sudden halt. One spring, just as tales of past exploits began to circulate and plans for revenge were being opera-tionalized, the administration made an announcement: If the water wars ceased, students would be permitted to wear shorts to school! This proposal was such a radical and far-fetched idea (at the time) that the student body was abuzz with the news. Although a sizable minority did not care about the new privilege and planned their strikes as usual, peer pressure mounted. It had been clearly com-municated that any violation of the cease-fire (and resultant loss of shorts privi-leges) would be dealt with quickly and severely. As it turned out, there were no violations, and so the age of wearing short pants in a small, rural community in southwestern Virginia had begun and continues to today.

Yet, although this is a trite and seemingly nonconsequential example, it raises very important questions for criminologists to consider: If the stakes were raised to a higher bar, a bar at which adolescents received full adult status with com-mensurate rights and responsibilities, would they conform to the new expecta-tions of them? Propensity for risk taking varies not only by age but also by other factors. Should adulthood be redefined based upon these other factors, too? Reg-istering to vote, purchasing tobacco or alcohol, and determining who can enter into legal contracts could be a process similar to the risk and rate assessment in-dividuals experience when purchasing auto, home, or life insurance. Because it is likely only a few would advocate this arrangement, in the interests of fairness, perhaps it is time to reexamine cultural definitions of childhood, adolescence, and adulthood. As a society, are we ready to extend the rights and privileges of the Constitution to minors? Or do we continue to rationalize the behavior of treating them as second-class citizens, much like a pit bull, whose owner is responsible for the behavior of the animal? In the interests of social justice and the sake and growth of young people, it is time to hold them responsible for what they do and to simultaneously grant them the rights enjoyed by other U.S. citizens, which begins with the right from which all other rights follow, the right to determine the course of one's life. Without the right to self-determination, all other rights are moot.

See Also: Equal Justice and Human Rights; Gang Injunction Laws; Juvenile Justice; Media Portrayals of Criminal Justice; Restorative Justice; School Violence; Social Justice.

Endnotes

1. John D. Hewitt and Robert M. Regoli, "Holding Serious Juvenile Offenders Responsible: Implications from Differential Oppression Theory," *Free Inquiry in Creative Sociology* 30 (2002): 1–8.
2. *Roper v. Simmons,* 112 S.W. 3d 397 (2005).
3. *Stanford v. Kentucky,* 492 U.S. 361 (1989).
4. *Johnson v. Texas,* 509 U.S. 350 (1993).
5. William Gardner, David Scherer, and Maya Tester, "Asserting Scientific Authority: Cognitive Development and Adolescent Legal Rights," *American Psychologist* 44 (1989): 895–902.
6. John Hewitt, Robert Regoli, and Christopher Kierkus, "Adolescent Risk-Taking as a Justification for Paternalistic Legal Policy," *Justice Policy Journal* 3 (2006): 1–20.
7. Eleonora Gullone, Susan Moore, Simon Moss, and Candice Boyd, "The Adolescent Risk-Taking Questionnaire: Development and Psychometric Evaluation," *Journal of Adolescent Research* 15 (2000): 231–50.
8. Federal Bureau of Investigation, *Crime in the United States, 2004* (Washington, DC: U.S. Department of Justice, 2005).
9. Centers for Disease Control and Prevention, *HIV/AIDS Surveillance Report 2003* (Atlanta: Centers for Disease Control and Prevention, 2004); Xuehao Chu, *The Effects of Age on the Driving Habits of the Elderly: Evidence from the 1990 National Personal Transportation Study: Final Report* (Washington, DC: U.S. Department of Transportation, 1994); National Highway Traffic Safety Administration, *Understanding Youthful Risk Taking and Driving* (Washington, DC: U.S. Department of Transportation, 1995); Office of Applied Statistics, *2004 National Survey on Drug Use and Health* (Washington, DC: U.S. Department of Health and Human Services, 2005).
10. Gullone et al., "The Adolescent Risk-Taking Questionnaire."
11. Ruth Beyth-Marom, Laurel Austin, Baruch Fischhoff, Claire Palmgren, and Marilyn Jacobs-Quandrel, "Perceived Consequences of Risky Behaviors: Adults and Adolescents," *Developmental Psychology* 29 (1993): 549–63.
12. Jay Giedd, Jonathan Blumenthal, Neal Jeffries, F. X. Castellanos, et al., "Brain Development during Childhood and Adolescence: A Longitudinal MRI Study," *Nature Neuroscience* 2 (1999): 861–63; Elkhonon Goldberg, *The Executive Brain: Frontal Lobes and the Civilized Mind* (New York: Oxford University Press, 2001); Elizabeth Sowell, Paul Thompson, Kevin Tessner, and Arthur Toga, "Mapping Continued Brain Growth and Gray Matter Density Reduction in Dorsal Frontal Cortex: Inverse Relationships during Postadolescent Brain Maturation," *Journal of Neuroscience* 21 (2001): 8819–29.
13. Zelee Hill, John Cleland, and Mohamed Ali, "Religious Affiliation and Extramarital Sex among Men in Brazil," *International Family Planning Perspectives* 30 (2004): 20–26.
14. Gardner et al., "Asserting Scientific Authority."
15. Frederic Thrasher, *The Gang* (Chicago: University of Chicago Press, 1927).
16. Robert Regoli and John Hewitt, *Delinquency in Society* (New York: McGraw Hill, 2006).

17. Marian Wright Edelman, *Cradle to Prison Pipeline* (Washington, DC: Children's Defense Fund, 1996).

18. G. Stanley Hall, *Adolescence: Its Psychology and Its Relations to Physiology, Anthropology, Sociology, Sex, Crime, Religion, and Education,* 2 vols. (New York: Appleton, 1904); G. Stanley Hall, *Youth: Its Education, Regiment, and Hygiene* (New York: Appleton, 1906).

19. Regoli and Hewitt, *Delinquency in Society.*

20. Ibid, 27.

Further Reading: Colvin, Mark, *Crime and Coercion* (New York: St. Martin's Press, 2002); Davis, Nanette, *Youth Crisis* (New York: Prager, 1999); Freire, Paulo, *Pedagogy of the Oppressed* (New York, Continuum, 1970); Katz, Jack, *Seductions of Crime: Moral and Sensual Attractions in Doing Evil* (New York: Basic Books, 1988); Lyng, Stephen, *Edgework* (New York: Routledge, 2004); Regoli, Robert, and John Hewitt, *Delinquency in Society,* 6th ed. (New York: McGraw Hill, 2006).

Eric Primm, John D. Hewitt, and Robert M. Regoli

JUVENILES TREATED AS ADULTS

INTRODUCTION

Since the mid-1990s, fear of juvenile crime and criminals has undermined what was considered the norm for many years; that is, most crimes committed by juveniles should be tried in a juvenile court. Using a punitive adult model for adolescents and preteens required the courts to assume that the youthful transgressor was equal to an adult regarding culpability; naturally, there was (is) vast disagreement concerning this issue. Some argue that it is the height of folly to think that an average teenager is incapable of understanding criminal proceedings, whereas others state it is highly unethical for judges and district attorneys to prosecute adolescents in an adult venue.[1] Other controversies question the wisdom, for example, of placing youths in institutional situations in which they are likely to experience physical and/or sexual abuse.

COMPARATIVE VIOLENCE IN ADULT AND JUVENILE INSTITUTIONS

Fifty percent of children incarcerated in adult prisons reported being attacked with a weapon, and 10 percent were sexually attacked. Only 1 percent reported the same in a juvenile institution.

BACKGROUND

In 1899, the first juvenile court system within the United States was established in Cook County, Illinois, and, shortly thereafter, juvenile courts spread to all states in the union.

Within juvenile courts, adolescent offenders are treated differently than their adult counterparts. For instance, what is considered legal for adults may not be legal for juveniles. Violations known as status offenses—such as being truant, running away from home, and using alcohol—are behaviors that are not against the law for adults but are considered infractions if performed by juveniles. The primary aim of juvenile courts is to guide, not punish, adolescents who have violated the law. In addition, although adult law focuses on the offense, juvenile law focuses on the offender, and attempts are made to rehabilitate any transgressors. Other differences include: (1) juveniles are adjudicated rather than pronounced guilty, (2) juvenile records may be sealed at the judge's discretion, and (3) juveniles do not have a right to a jury trial. Moreover, juveniles are usually placed in special facilities, away from hardened, adult criminals. With serious crimes, however, exceptions are made.[2]

Law enforcement has the option of preventative detention, meaning, detaining a youth for his or her protection or the community's protection. Because the juvenile court system is highly individualized, sentences vary from court to court and state to state and may cover a wide range of community-based and residential options. The disposition is based on an adolescent's history and the severity of his or her offenses and includes a significant rehabilitation component. Moreover, the disposition can be for an unspecified period; the court has the authority to send a youth to a specific facility or program until he or she is deemed rehabilitated or until he or she reaches the age of majority. The disposition may also include a restitution component and can be directed at people other than the offender, such his or her parents. Parole combines surveillance with activities to reintegrate the juvenile into the community.

One reason juveniles are transferred to criminal court is the general belief that if adolescents (both violent and nonviolent) are exposed to the adult criminal justice system, any criminal urges would be extinguished. Unfortunately, the literature does not back this supposition. A 1996 study looked at 2,738 juvenile offenders transferred to criminal court in Florida with a matched sample of nontransferred juveniles. Juveniles tried as adults were more likely to be incarcerated, incarcerated for longer periods than those who remained in the juvenile system, and had a higher recidivism rate. Within two years, they were more likely to reoffend, to reoffend earlier, to commit more subsequent offenses, and to commit more serious subsequent offenses than juveniles retained in the juvenile system.[3]

STUDIES ON JUVENILES AND JUSTICE

During 2003, one study, conducted by the John D. and Catherine T. MacArthur Foundation Research Network on Adolescent Development and Juvenile Justice, examined more than 1,400 people between the ages of 11 and 24 in Philadelphia, Los Angeles, northern and eastern Virginia, and northern Florida. Each participant was given an intelligence test and later asked to respond to several hypothetical legal situations, such as whether confessing to a police officer if he or she committed a crime was a smart move. Interestingly, the researcher found that one-third of those aged 11 to 13 and one-fifth of those aged 14 to 15 could not understand the proceedings allayed against them, nor could they supply help to their defense lawyers. The study recommended that states reconsider the minimum age for juveniles to be tried as adults or that a system for evaluating defendants' competency be created.

The report was released on the heels of a 10-year effort by states trying to make it easier to try children as adults.[4]

The question is this: Is it OK to place children with adults in prison, where the older convicts will likely teach them how to be efficacious criminals and where they will probably experience both physical and sexual abuse? For example, one 17-year-old adolescent held with adult convicts in an Idaho jail was sexually tortured and murdered by the adult inmates. In Ohio, a 15-year-old girl was sexually assaulted by a deputy jailer after she was placed in an adult jail for a minor infraction, and in Kentucky, approximately thirty minutes after a 15-year-old was put in a jail cell following an argument with his mother, he hanged himself. In one year, four children held in Kentucky jails committed suicide.[5]

In 1989, a study compared how youths were treated at a number of juvenile training schools with those serving time in adult prisons. Unsurprisingly, five times as many adolescents held in adult prisons answered yes to the question "Has anyone attempted to sexually attack or rape you?" In addition, the statistics regarding youth rape in prisons were coupled with the fact that children placed with adults were twice as likely to report being physically abused by staff. The juveniles in adult prison were also 50 percent more likely to report being attacked with a weapon. Close to 10 percent of the youth interviewed reported a sexual violation.

Little research exists regarding any quantitative data on rape, suicide, and assault rates among the thousands of juveniles sentenced to adult prisons each year or the 65,000 children who pass through the jail system. Several states place suicide as being unspecified in their yearly reports, thus making the problem invisible. Rape in prison is listed under inmate assault; hence, the problem is opaque. Approximately 25,000 children each year have their cases transferred to criminal court instead of being tried in juvenile courts, where the majority of convicted defendants are usually set free by the time they turn 21.[6]

Many judges will not prosecute youths as adults, as if noted in the case of Nathaniel Abraham. At age 11, he was charged with first-degree murder and was to be prosecuted under a 1997 Michigan law that allowed adult prosecutions of children of any age in serious felony cases. Abraham was eventually convicted of second-degree murder, but the presiding judge felt that the new law was flawed and sentenced him to youth detention rather than life imprisonment.[7] In Texas, Lacresha Murray, an 11-year-old girl, was convicted twice for the death of a 2-year-old who spent the day in her home. After extensive questioning, without guardians or an attorney present, she admitted that she might have dropped and then kicked the toddler. The presiding judge dismissed all criminal charges leveled against her.[8]

KEY EVENTS

Between 1992 and 1999, every state except Nebraska passed laws making it easier for juveniles to be tried as adults, according to the National Center for

Juvenile Justice, a private, nonprofit research group. Even though Nebraska passed no new laws on the subject during that seven-year period, it is among the 14 states and the District of Columbia that allow prosecutors to file charges against juveniles in criminal court.[9] Each of the 50 states has specific provisions concerning trying certain juveniles as adults in criminal court (see Table J.1). This procedure is commonly called a *transfer to criminal court* and has three primary mechanisms: judicial waiver, statutory exclusion, and concurrent jurisdiction.

- Forty-five states have judicial waiver provisions, in which the juvenile court judge has the vested authority to waive juvenile court jurisdiction and transfer the case to criminal court, if he or she feels that the crime committed warrants more punishment than is commonly meted out within the juvenile justice system.

  - Threshold criteria that must be met before the court may consider waiver: generally a minimum age, a specified type or level of offense, a sufficiently serious record of previous delinquency, or some combination of the three.
  - In all states in which discretionary waiver is authorized, the juvenile court must conduct a hearing at which the parties are entitled to present evidence bearing on the waiver issue. Generally, state law specifies factors a court must weigh and findings it must make in order to arrive at the determination that a juvenile is no longer amenable to treatment as a juvenile.
  - The prosecution usually bears the burden of proof in a discretionary waiver hearing; however, some states designate special circumstances under which this burden may be shifted to the child. Generally, a prosecutor seeking a waiver to criminal court must make the case for waiver by a preponderance of the evidence.

- Twenty-nine states have statutory exclusion laws excluding youth that commit certain serious offenses and/or repeat offenses from the jurisdiction of the juvenile court. These laws are different from mandatory waiver laws in that with statutory exclusion the adult court has jurisdiction over a case from the beginning, without a juvenile court waiver hearing.
- Seventeen states allow for concurrent jurisdiction of offending youth in both the juvenile and adult court systems. Adolescents aged 14 or older who commit certain felonies are subject to transfer to adult criminal court for prosecution at the discretion of the judge. Transfer proceedings are mandatory in instances of murder or aggravated malicious wounding. Prosecutors in instances of lesser felonies may also directly file for jurisdictional transfers. Once initiated, any transfer to adult court may be petitioned for reverse waiver back to juvenile court.[10]

In addition to state governments, the federal government also has the option of treating children as adults. There are many federal rules regarding juveniles, too many to go into great detail here, including Federal Rule 106, which states the Federal Bureau of Investigation and other federal law enforcement agencies

Table J.1 State-By-State Judicial Waiver Offense and Minimum Age Criteria, 2004

State	Minimum Age for Judicial Waiver	Judicial Waiver Offense and Minimum Age Criteria							
		Any Criminal Offense	Certain Felonies	Capital Crimes	Murder	Certain Person Offenses	Certain Property Offenses	Certain Drug Offenses	Certain Weapon Offenses
Alabama	14	14							
Alaska	NS	NS				NS			
Arizona	NS		NS						
Arkansas	14		14	14	14	14			14
California	14		16		14	14	14	14	
Colorado	12		12		12	12			
Connecticut	14		14	14	14				
Delaware	NS	NS	15		NS	NS	16	15	
District of Columbia	NS	16	15		15	15	15		NS
Florida	14	14							
Georgia	13	15		13	14	13	15		
Hawaii	NS		14		NS				
Idaho	NS	14	NS		NS	NS	NS	NS	
Illinois	13	13	15						
Indiana	NS	14	NS		10			16	
Iowa	14	14							
Kansas	10	10	14			14		14	
Kentucky	14	14	14	14					

416

State									
Louisiana	14				14	14			
Maine	NS		NS		NS	NS			
Maryland	NS	15		NS					
Michigan	14		14						
Minnesota	14		14						
Mississippi	13	13							
Missouri	12		12						
Nevada	14	14	14			14			
New Hampshire	13		15		13	13		15	
New Jersey	14	14	14		14	14	14	14	14
North Carolina	13		13	13					
North Dakota	14	16	14		14	14		14	
Ohio	14		14		14	16	16		
Oklahoma	NS		NS						
Oregon	NS		15		NS	NS	15		
Pennsylvania	14		14			14	14		
Rhode Island	NS	NS	16		17	17			
South Carolina	NS	16	14		NS	NS			
South Dakota	NS		NS						

(continued)

Table J.1 State-By-State Judicial Waiver Offense and Minimum Age Criteria, 2004 (*continued*)

State	Minimum Age for Judicial Waiver	Judicial waiver Offense and Minimum Age Criteria							
		Any Criminal Offense	Certain Felonies	Capital Crimes	Murder	Certain Person Offenses	Certain Property Offenses	Certain Drug Offenses	Certain Weapon Offenses
Tennessee	NS	16			NS	NS			
Texas	14		14	14				14	
Utah	14		14		16	16	16		16
Vermont	10				10	10	10		
Virginia	14		14		14	14			
Washington	NS	NS							
West Virginia	NS		NS		NS	NS	NS	NS	
Wisconsin	14	15	14		14	14	14	14	
Wyoming	13	13							

Note: Ages in the minimum age column may not apply to all offense restrictions but represent the youngest possible age at which a juvenile may be judicially waived to criminal court. NS indicates that no minimum age is specified.

Source: P. Griffin, "Transfer Provisions," in *State Juvenile Justice Profiles* (Pittsburgh: National Center for Juvenile Justice, 2004), http://ojjdp.ncjrs.org/ojstatbb/structure_process/qa04110.asp?qaDate=2004.

should aid local and state authorities in the apprehension of gang members. The rule's language is condescending, stating that local law enforcement has become frustrated with the state criminal systems and that federal assistance is sorely needed. Most defendants serve a bare minimum of time, however, and although the adult criminal system is ineffective in curtailing gang violence, the juvenile system is much worse. Most juvenile delinquents are handled by the state and are usually immediately released or lightly punished; thus, the states need guidance from the federal government.[11]

On the other hand, violent criminals (both adult and adolescent) are gaining a keen respect for the federal criminal system. They are aware of the abolishment of parole as well as the high guidelines and enhanced sentencing for drug- and firearms-related federal crimes. It is imperative for the safety of the citizens of the United States that United States attorneys' offices become more involved in seeking out the most serious juvenile offenders for prosecution as delinquents or transferring them for criminal prosecution as adults[12] (all may be found in the *Criminal Resource Manual*).

Federal Rule 126 states that juveniles charged with serious offenses and who have prior criminal history and have proved unreceptive to treatment in the juvenile justice system may be considered for transfer to adult status. Any decision to transfer should be based upon discussion with the investigating agents, a prosecution policy that targets the most serious juvenile offenders, and a comparison of effective alternatives that may be available in state jurisdiction.[13]

Federal Rule 140 discusses the mandatory transfer of juveniles to adult status. Adult status for juveniles is mandatory if the acts were committed after his or her 16th birthday and would be tried felonies involving the use, attempted use, or threatened use of physical force against another. In addition, if a substantial risk of physical force was used against another in committing the offense, or if a juvenile has previously been found guilty of an act for which an adult would face prison time, then juveniles may be transferred to adult status. Finally, the act would have been one of the offenses set forth in this rule or an offense in violation of a state felony statute.[14]

FUTURE PROSPECTS

Several states have laws stating that it is legal to sentence an adolescent to death, if he or she was convicted of a capital offense. On March 1, 2005, the United States Supreme Court struck down the use of capital punishment for offenders committing crimes before the age of 18 in *Roper v. Simmons*. In 1993, Christopher Simmons (who was 17 at the time) formulated a plan to murder Shirley Crook with two younger friends. In essence, the plan was to commit burglary and murder by breaking and entering, tying up Ms. Crook, and then tossing her from a bridge. At the trial's conclusion, Simmons was sentenced to death. He first moved for the trial court to set aside the conviction and sentence, citing, in part, ineffective assistance of counsel. His young age and impulsivity, along with a troubled background, were brought up as issues that Simmons claimed should have been raised at the sentencing phase. The trial court rejected the motion, and Simmons appealed. Finally, the case was argued in the U.S. Supreme Court. Justice Anthony Kennedy, writing for the majority, cited sociological and scientific articles stating that juveniles are immature and lacking a sense of responsibility when compared to adults.[15]

The Court noted that in recognition of the comparative immaturity and irresponsibility of juveniles, almost every state prohibited those younger than age 18 from voting, serving on juries, or marrying without parental consent. The studies also found that juveniles are also more vulnerable to negative influences and outside pressures, including peer pressure. They have less control, or experience with control, over their own environment. Thus, the Court held that executing someone younger than age 18 at the time of the murder was cruel and unusual punishment.[16]

Little disagreement exists regarding the minute number of teens who should be tried in the adult criminal justice system (with the prominent exception of the death penalty) if they pose a sincere threat to those around them. Likewise, there is little bickering about severely delinquent adolescents (rapists, murderers, arsonists, etc.) receiving commensurate punishment for the scope of their crime. Thousands of young people are being prosecuted daily within the adult system, however, though many are charged with nonviolent crimes. This should give cause for quiet reflection, because the primary reason for youth courts was (is) to adjudicate young people who had broken the law in a nonviolent fashion. If society punishes adolescents as it does adults, even if their transgression does not warrant it, does the get-tough policy benefit the public?

Sadly, the prevailing mindset of many lawmakers is "If you do the crime, do the time—regardless of age." Thus, many adolescents and preteens, whose crime was of a nonviolent nature, will remain incarcerated with adult criminals who will continue their physical and sexual abuse of children, all at taxpayer expense.

See Also: Juvenile Justice; Juveniles and Social Justice; Prison Rape; Prison Sexual Assault.

Endnotes

1. L. Steinberg, *A Prospective Study of Serious Adolescent Offenders in Philadelphia* (Philadelphia: Pennsylvania Council on Crime and Delinquency, 2005).
2. M. Jonson-Reid, "Child Welfare Services and Delinquency: The Need to Know More," *Child Welfare* 83, no. 2 (2004): 157–74.
3. D. M. Bishop, C. E. Frazier, L. Lanza-Kaduce, and L. Winner, "The Transfer of Juveniles to Criminal Court: Does It Make a Difference?" *Crime and Delinquency* 42 (1996): 171–91.
4. Steinberg, *A Prospective Study of Serious Adolescent Offenders.*
5. J. Zeidenberg and V. Schiraldi, *The Risks Juveniles Face When They Are Incarcerated with Adults* (Washington, DC: Justice Policy Institute, 1997), http://www.cjcj.org/pubs/risks/riskspr.html.
6. Senate Committee on the Judiciary: Subcommittee on youth violence, *Fixing a Broken System: A Review of Office of Juvenile Justice and Delinquency Prevention Mandates,* 105th Cong., 1st sess., May 6, 1997 (Washington DC: GPO, 1997), 105–42.
7. Steinberg, *A Prospective Study of Serious Adolescent Offenders.*

8. E. J. Fritsch, T. J. Caeti, and C. Hemmens, "Spare the Needle but Not the Punishment: The Incarceration of Waived Youth in Texas Prisons," *Crime and Delinquency* 42, no. 4 (1996): 593–609.

9. Ibid.

10. Ibid.

11. United States Department of Justice, "Rule 126, Treating Juveniles as Adults for Criminal Prosecution—Generally," *Title 9: Criminal Resource Manual* (Washington, DC: U.S. Government Printing Office, 1997).

12. United States Department of Justice, "Rule 106, Federal Involvement in Prosecuting Gang Activity," *Title 9: Criminal Resource Manual* (Washington, DC: U.S. Government Printing Office, 1997).

13. Ibid.

14. United States Department of Justice, "Rule 140, Mandatory Transfer of Juveniles to Adult Status," *Title 9: Criminal Resource Manual* (Washington, DC: U.S. Government Printing Office, 1997).

15. *Roper v. Simmons,* 543, U.S. 551 (2005).

16. Ibid.

Further Reading: Butts, J., and G. Halemba, *Waiting for Justice: Moving Young Offenders through the Juvenile Court Process* (Pittsburgh: National Center for Juvenile Justice, 1996); Dawson, R. O., "The Future of Juvenile Justice: Is It Time to Abolish the System?" *Journal of Criminal Law and Criminology* 81 (1990): 136–55; Kupchik, A. *Judging Juveniles: Prosecuting Adolescents in Adult and Juvenile Courts* (New York: New York University Press, 2006); Puzzanchera, C. M., "Delinquency Cases Waived to Criminal Court, 1988–1997," *OJJDP Fact Sheet* (Washington, DC: U.S. Government Printing Office, 2000); United States Department of Justice, *Title 9: Criminal Resource Manual* (Washington, DC: U.S. Government Printing Office, 1997).

Cary Stacy Smith and Li-Ching Hung

LETHAL FORCE

INTRODUCTION

Lethal force is the ultimate expression of the right to use aggression granted by the state to its police, and it has been controversial for the same reasons that use of nonlethal force is controversial. Is it an inevitable, albeit unfortunate, by-product of law enforcement in a high crime society, or does it reflect a pernicious form of racial discrimination, or even state-sponsored suppression of the public, the disempowered, in the interest of the elites? This debate is not merely academic—lethal force incidents have been the catalyst for many events of political turmoil. Conflicts over the meaning of lethal force get played out most prominently in efforts by researchers, police, and the public to explain the distribution of and circumstances under which lethal force occurs and can best be controlled.

BACKGROUND

Historically, in the United States, police were charged with using lethal force to protect themselves and others from danger and also to resist escapes. The latter objective, referred to as the fleeing felon rule, originated from common law times, in which most felonies were punishable by death. As use of the death penalty for common law felonies declined, the idea that police should use lethal force to thwart escapes came under increased scrutiny. During the middle to latter portion of the twentieth century, many police departments in the United States became inclined to restrict use of lethal force; a movement that accelerated in the wake of the *Tennessee v. Garner* decision of 1985.

The application of lethal force is a relatively rare occurrence given the number of encounters that police and civilians have daily. The latest FBI figures show that in 2005, 341 individuals died as a result of "justifiable homicide by law enforcement."[1] National figures on fatal police shootings have hovered around the low hundreds for the past 20 years.[2] However, the national data are an imperfect indicator of lethal force uses: they do not cover all police departments, and, most importantly, they do not count nonfatal wounding or all shots fired, which are the most common types of shootings.[3]

FIREARMS AND CHOKE HOLDS

Ninety-nine percent of all lethal force incidents occur with firearms; however, other putatively nonlethal tools of law enforcement can also result in death. The choke hold is a particularly controversial method. This aggressive tactic blocks air to the windpipe or blood flow to the brain, leading to swift unconsciousness. The choke hold was viewed by some departments, most notoriously the Los Angeles Police Department, as a valuable method of overcoming arrest resistance. However, there have been several highly publicized incidents in which suspects died after being given choke holds. As was the case with firearms, deaths occurred disproportionately among minorities. Today, the use of the choke holds by police departments is very limited, restricted to life-saving situations, or proscribed altogether.

There is enormous variation in the use of lethal force across cities. For instance, data from 2001 show a range of 3.27 persons a year in San Diego to 2.15 in Washington, DC, to .71 in New York, to .39 in Boston. The reasons for variation are unclear although departmental size, among other factors, might be important.[4] Young minority males, particularly African Americans, are disproportionately likely to be the targets of lethal force. The most common situations featuring force use are felonies, such as burglary or robbery, and reports of disorder.[5]

THE KEY LEGAL DECISION

Tennessee v. Garner (1985) was pivotal in changing use of lethal force in the United States. Garner, who was an unarmed African American youth, was shot in the back and killed by the Memphis police for leaving the scene of a burglary. This occurred despite the admission of the officer involved that Garner posed no immediate threat. His father sued the city of Memphis, its police department, and the officers involved for wrongful death. The Supreme Court ruled in 1985 that allowing police to shoot an unarmed felon was an impermissible violation of the Fourth Amendment right against seizure without due process "unless it is necessary to prevent escape and the officer has probable cause to believe the suspect poses a significant threat of death or serious physical injury to the officer or others."[6] The ruling established a standard that law enforcement agencies from the federal to the city level all currently follow: Police are allowed to use deadly force to protect life (theirs or others) or if it is necessary to apprehend someone thought to be dangerous.

EXPLAINING THE DISTRIBUTION

Explanations for the distribution of lethal force tend to cluster around two perspectives. In the first, lethal force is viewed as driven largely by "situational contingencies" of policing. Police shootings do tend to reflect exposure to dangerous situations. For example, the paradigmatic study done by James Fyfe found that in most instances, the opponent was armed, thus posing a strong objective threat to the officers involved.[7] Further, police use of lethal force tends to track with homicide rates, although the support for this is stronger in cross-sectional studies than ones examining rates over time.[8] Racial differences in the targets of lethal force have been linked to similar differences in criminal behavior (e.g., percent involved in violent crime) or to differences in the level of threat posed by black suspects (e.g., presence of a weapon).[9]

The second "conflict"[10] perspective views lethal force use as reflecting discrimination and sees racism as partially underlying the source of minority disparities as targets of lethal force. Research in various settings, for instance, in Los Angeles and Memphis, indicates a greater propensity for African Americans to be shot under conditions in which they present an objective lesser threat (for instance, as fleeing felons similar the Garner situation).[11] Also supportive of this point is the fact that the decline in shootings occurring in the wake of *Tennessee v. Garner* occurred largely among black suspects.

The idea that some lethal force incidents reflect overt bigotry on the part of individual officers is an especially huge bone of contention. The idea itself has been challenged by findings that African American officers have, in some areas, been disproportionately involved in such incidents, although this has been attributed to patterns of deployment.[12] Others, pointing to recent cases in which unarmed people or those whose status as threat was questionable (the case of Amadou Diallo being the most notable), argue for the operation of an implicit bias by both black and white officers toward seeing minority suspects as threatening, and thus making the former more likely to use lethal force.[13] Potential support for this view stems from psychological research showing that most whites and blacks hold unconscious biases against blacks; other studies have shown that, with perceptual tests, respondents are more likely to view innocuous objects as weapons when held by black people.[14] While an intriguing possibility, there have been no direct tests of implicit bias among police officers; thus it is difficult to say whether or how it potentially affects their use of lethal force.

A variant of the conflict perspective posits the distribution of lethal force as an expression of the political and economic power of elites over subordinate populations. This perspective is reflected in work by Jacobs and O'Brien (1998), who found that in addition to homicide rates and some measures of social disorganization, measures of black economic/political disadvantage (especially black-white economic inequality) were linked to increased police homicides, both generally and among blacks, while one measure of black political advantage (presence of a black mayor) was linked to lower black fatal homicide rates.[15] Cross-cultural studies on lethal force have shown an intimate connection between the state structures and deaths by the police. Chevigny (1995) found that the amount of transparency in government and the degree to which a country's police operated as entities independent of the military both affected the level of deadly force experienced by various populations.[16]

CONTROLLING THE USE

Another point of controversy concerns how to exercise controls over lethal force. Undeniably, administrative policies can alter patterns of use.[17] Police department rules that restrict the circumstances under which officers can use lethal force, or that demand that lethal force incidents be catalogued, have invariably been followed by reductions in lethal force use. In fact, racial disparities in the use of force were markedly reduced in Memphis following the Garner decision. Interestingly, these restrictions do not result in an increased amount of crime or in increased danger to officers. Improved officer training and understanding of lethal force events have also been suggested as means of reducing their incidence. One potentially valuable heuristic for thinking about lethal force incidents, outlined by Klinger, is Charles Perrow's theory of the normal accident.[18]

Nevertheless, with a few exceptions, efforts by most departments to exercise controls over lethal force are unknown to us. Law enforcement agencies are not normally required to regularly report uses of lethal force. Thus it is difficult for researchers and other outsiders to evaluate police efforts to control force use. Such reviews tend to occur only when there is a push toward reform, usually in the wake of a problem or scandal.

RESPONDING TO CONTROVERSIAL SHOOTING DEATHS

In 1999, an unarmed African immigrant, Amadou Diallo, was shot by four New York City police officers looking for a rape suspect. Under heavy public pressure, the New York Police Department (NYPD) underwent some changes, including discontinuing the controversial "Street Crimes Unit" that was already under investigation for unfairly targeting blacks and Hispanics, and redoubling efforts to establish positive relationships between officers and members of the community. The specific officers involved in the Diallo case (acquitted in the criminal trial) were not disciplined internally; rather, it was suggested that they be "retrained in tactics."* While there were some changes in firearms training (e.g., increased use of low-light simulations), no external reviews of NYPD firearms procedures took place. That would have to wait until 2007, in the wake of another controversial shooting death of an unarmed African American.**

---

*Kevin Flynn, "Panel Urges Retraining, Not Discipline, for Diallo Officers," the *New York Times*, April 26, 2001, http://query.nytimes.com/gst/fullpage.html?res=940CE2D71539F935A15757C0A9679C8B63&sec=&spon=&pagewanted=all (accessed January 23, 2007).

**New York Police Department Press Release 2007-001, January 4, 2007, http://www.nyc.gov/html/nypd/html/dcpi/pr-2007-001.html (accessed January 23, 2007).

Attempts at external control, from the creation of outside force review boards to criminal prosecutions to civil suits, all have been used to push departments to restrict unwarranted use of lethal force, without much success. External review boards can have their findings rendered irrelevant by departmental procedures (as witnessed in a case in Los Angeles).[19] Criminal prosecutions are rare, given close police–prosecutor relations. Those that do occur have a low probability of success, because lethal force cases turn on whether the officer(s) had what is termed a reasonable perception of danger from the target at the time of the application of force, and juries tend to give police officers a wide berth in this judgment.[20]

Civil suits against departments or cities are more likely to meet with success (the cases of Diallo and Patrick Dorismond are two examples). However, they, too, have little success in stimulating change within a given department. Incidents are treated as singular events with no implications for future behavior. As a result, methods of dealing with force issues (lethal and otherwise) do not often get translated into changes in police practice, except in extraordinary circumstances.[21]

FUTURE PROSPECTS

It is clear that better data on lethal force use by the police would help in its control; however, it is equally clear that police are not going to be forthcoming in this regard. This is unfortunate, as lethal force incidents, because of their dramatic nature (literally matters of life and death), affect police and community relations disproportionately to their numbers. Particularly in the case of killings where the victim was found to be objectively harmless, powerful feelings of anger and mistrust are provoked in the community. This in turn provokes a "circle-the-wagons" response by the police, who view the public outcry as an inevitable expression of eternal dissatisfaction that they can do nothing about and as a result forego the potential for changes in force procedures.

One might view the creation of so-called nonlethal weapons as a possible solution. However, these are currently at an embryonic state of development. Further, while the risk of death is diminished with such weapons, it is not nonexistent, as can be seen with controversies over the use of the taser device.[22] Perhaps inevitably, conflicts over lethal force will be with us for the foreseeable future.

See Also: Police and Psychological Screening; Police Brutality; Police Corruption; Police Use of Force.

Endnotes

1. Federal Bureau of Investigation, Expanded Homicide Data Table 13, in *Crime in the United States 2005* (Washington, DC: Federal Bureau of Investigation, 2006), http://www.fbi.gov/ucr/05cius/offenses/expanded_information/data/shrtable_13.html (accessed January 23, 2007).

2. Jodi M. Brown and Patrick Langan, *Policing and Homicide, 1976–98: Justifiable Homicide by Police, Police Officers Murdered by Felons* (Washington, DC: Bureau of Justice Statistics), http://www.ojp.usdoj.gov/bjs/pub/pdf/ph98.pdf (accessed January 23, 2007).

3. James Fyfe, "Too Many Missing Cases: Holes in Our Knowledge about Police Use of Force," *Justice Research and Policy* 4 (2002): 87–102.

4. Ibid, iii.

5. William A. Geller and Michael S. Scott, "Deadly Force: What We Know," in *Thinking about Police: Contemporary Readings,* 2nd ed., ed. Carl B. Klockars and Stephen D. Mastrofski (New York: McGraw Hill, 1991), pp. 446–76 .

6. *Tennessee v. Garner,* 471 U.S. 1.1985, page 1.

7. James J. Fyfe, *Shots Fired: An Analysis of New York City Police Firearms Discharges* (Ph.D. diss., State University of New York–Albany, 1978).

8. See Robert Langworthy, "Police Shooting and Criminal Homicide: The Temporal Relationship," *Journal of Quantitative Criminology,* 2 (1986): 377–88; and John M. MacDonald, Robert J. Kaminski, Geoffrey P. Alpert, and Abraham N. Tennenbaum, "The Temporal Relationship between Police Killings of Civilians and Criminal Homicide: A Refined Version of the Danger-Perception Theory," *Crime and Delinquency* 47 (2001): 155–72.

9. Gellar and Scott, "Deadly Force: What We Know," v. See also James J. Fyfe, "Race and Extreme Police-Citizen Violence," in *Race, Crime and Justice,* ed. R. L. McNeely and Carl E. Pope, pp. 89–108 (Beverly Hills, CA: Sage, 1981).

10. Michael D. White, "Examining the Impact of External Influences on Police Use of Deadly Force over Time," *Evaluation Review* 27 (2003): 53.

11. See James F. Fyfe, "Blind Justice: Police Shootings in Memphis," *Journal of Criminal Law and Criminology,* 73 (1982): 707–22; and Marshall W. Meyer, "Police Shootings at Minorities: The Case of Los Angeles," *Annals of the American Academy of Political and Social Science* 452 (1980): 98–110.

12. Fyfe, "Blind Justice," vii.

13. Cynthia Lee, "'But I Thought He Had a Gun'—Race and Police Use of Deadly Force," *Hastings Race and Poverty Law Journal* (2004), http://ssrn.com/abstract=608781 (accessed November 29, 2006).

14. See B. Keith Payne, Yujiro Shimizu, and Larry L Jacoby, "Mental Control and Visual Illusions: Toward Explaining Race-Biased Weapon Misidentifications," *Journal of Experimental Social Psychology* 41 (2005): 36–47; Shankar Vendantam, "See No Bias," *Washington Post* (January 23, 2005), http://www.washingtonpost.com/ac2/wp-dyn/A27067–2005Jan21?language=printer (accessed January 15, 2007); Malcolm Gladwell, *Blink: The Power of Thinking without Thinking* (New York: Little Brown and Company, 2005), 189–244.

15. David Jacobs and Robert M. O'Brien, "The Determinants of Deadly Force: A Structural Analysis of Police Violence," *American Journal of Sociology* 103 (1980): 837–62.

16. Paul Chevigny, *Edge of the Knife: Police Violence in the Americas* (New York: The New Press, 1995).

17. See Michael D. White, "Assessing the Impact of Administrative Policy on Use of Deadly Force by On- and Off-Duty Police," *Evaluation Review* 24 (2000): 295; Abraham N. Tennenbaum, "The Influence of the Garner Decision on Police Use of Deadly Force," *Journal of Criminal Law and Criminology* 85 (1994): 241–60; and Jerry R. Sparger and David J. Giacopassi, "Memphis Revisited: A Re-Examination of Police Shootings after the Garner Decision," *Justice Quarterly* 9 (1992): 211–25.

18. David Klinger, *Social Theory and the Street Cop: The Case of Deadly Force* (Washington, DC: Police Foundation, 2005).

19. Matt Lait and Scott Glover, "Officer Who Killed Boy, 13, Is Cleared," *New York Times,* January 10, 2007). http://query.nytimes.com/gst/fullpage.html?res=940CE2D71539F935A15757C0A9679C8B63&sec=&spond=all (Accessed January 23, 2007).

20. Darrell L. Ross, "An assessment of *Graham v. Connor,* 10 years later," *Policing: An International Journal of Police Strategies and Management* 25 (2002): 294–318.
21. Chevigny, *Edge of the Knife,* xvi, 101–5.
22. Associated Press, "Chicago Police Investigate Stun Gun Death," MSNBC.com (February 11, 2005), http://www.msnbc.msn.com/id/6955223 (accessed January 24, 2007).

Further Readings: Binder, Arnold, and Peter Scharf, *The Badge and the Bullet: Police Use of Deadly Force* (New York: Praeger, 1983); Chevigny, Paul, *Edge of the Knife: Police Violence in the Americas* (New York: The New Press, 1995); Diallo, Kadiatou, with Craig Wolff, *My Heart Will Cross This Ocean: My Story, My Son, Amadou* (New York: Random House, 2003); Gladwell, Malcolm, *Blink: The Power of Thinking without Thinking* (New York: Little, Brown and Company, 2005); Klinger, David, *Into the Kill Zone: A Cop's Eye View of Deadly Force* (San Francisco: Jossey-Bass, 2005).

Angela Taylor